1995 SUPPLEMENT

CONSTITUTIONAL LAW
Twelfth Edition

INDIVIDUAL RIGHTS IN CONSTITUTIONAL LAW
Fifth Edition

By

GERALD GUNTHER
William Nelson Cromwell Professor of Law,
Stanford University

1995 SUPPLEMENT

By

FREDERICK SCHAUER
Frank Stanton Professor of the First Amendment
John F. Kennedy School of Government
Harvard University

With the assistance of

VIRGINIA WISE
Lecturer on Law
Harvard University

Westbury, New York
THE FOUNDATION PRESS, INC.
1995

TEXT IS PRINTED ON 10% POST
CONSUMER RECYCLED PAPER

PRINTED WITH
SOY INK™

PREFACE

This Supplement covers the major constitutional developments since July 1, 1994, and includes full treatment of the Supreme Court Term that ended on June 29, 1995. Legislative, executive, and administrative developments are included as well, with July 2, 1995, being the cut-off date for such materials.

The Supplement is keyed by specific page numbers for Constitutional Law (Twelfth Edition) and Individual Rights in Constitutional Law (Fifth Edition). As used here, the abbreviation for the former is "12th Ed.", and for the latter "Ind.Rts."

As I have made clear for all of the Supplements since 1983, this one is entirely the work of the undersigned, and any errors or omissions are my responsibility, and not Professor Gunther's.

The Supreme Court's rapidly changing personnel has produced notable changes in constitutional doctrine, changes as dramatic in the 1994 Term as in any Term in recent memory. Yet for all of these changes, and for all their importance, it may be that the most interesting and important developments in constitutional law in 1994–1995 were not developments produced by Supreme Court decisions, and not even developments in American constitutional law conceived more broadly. Rather, the most significant developments in constitutional law may arise from the burgeoning constitutional transformation taking place throughout the world. In Eastern Europe, in the republics of the former Soviet Union, in South Africa, and elsewhere, constitutions are being written and rewritten, courts are be-coming more active in constitutional interpretation, and issues familiar to American constitutionalists are being debated in quite different social and political contexts.

In many of the constitutional discussions taking place outside the United States, the American experience, and the decisions of the Supreme Court of the United States, appear to play a significant role. Newspaper editors and reporters throughout the world make reference to *New York Times Co. v. Sullivan,* for example, as they urge greater protection against liability for defamation, and recent court decisions in Australia, among other countries, indicate that these efforts are not without effect. Similarly, American doctrine with respect to other free speech and free press issues, in criminal procedure, in freedom of religion, and in procedural due process, for example, has played a large role in debates throughout the world both at the level of constitutional drafting and at the level of interpretation of a constitution already in place. And even when the issues are less directly related to particular judicial decisions, as for example with the general questions of federalism and separation of powers, the American experience is often a central player in constitutional debates. Although few of the new constitutions themselves look anything like the Constitution of the United States (the current interim Constitution of the Republic of South Africa, for example, is 113 pages long, in print, in its English version; and the German model of a Constitutional Court distinct from the highest court of general jurisdiction is far more common in new constitutions than the American unified model), there can be little doubt that American constitutional law is now a topic of great international importance and almost as great international influence.

The influence of American constitutionalism, although on balance seemingly a good thing, is not without its pitfalls, and two might be worth mentioning. One is that American constitutionalists, frequently provided an opportunity to spread American constitutional ideas in person or in print to other countries, have on occasion underestimated the social, cultural, and political presuppositions of constitutionalism, presuppositions that vary dramatically throughout the world and limit the possibility and the desirability of transplanting American constitutional ideas to other cultures. When the goal is to provide information about the American approach and its effects in the United States, American constitutionalists can do an enormous amount of good by providing this information to those outside of the United States who are examining various approaches to their own constitutional problems. When the goal is instead to prescribe and to propagate a particular American approach without reference to where it is being used, the risks of assuming arrogantly that the American approach can or should work elsewhere is considerable. The concept of international human rights reminds us that constitutional rights properly have a transnational and non-relative dimension, but it remains a mistake to assume that the contemporary version of American constitutionalism is the key to solving all of the world's problems of constitutional development.

Relatedly, it is too easy to assume because of the pedigree of American constitutionalism that thinking comparatively ought to be largely a matter of export rather than import. Although constitutional courts throughout the world take seriously arguments from American and European law, making an argument in an American court from non-American constitutional law (or, to some extent, from international law) remains highly unusual. The constitutional approaches throughout the world are as diverse as the nations adopting them. Some countries protect positive rights and others do not. Some have explicit limitation clauses in their constitutions, and others resemble the United States in relying on the courts to fashion appropriate limitations on constitutional rights. Some rely on courts of general jurisdiction for constitutional enforcement, some rely on constitutional courts, and some rely in addition on more novel devices, such as the power of the Legal Chancellor in Estonia to require the Parliament to reconsider any legislation the Legal Chancellor believes to be unconstitutional. And on particular issues of substantive constitutional doctrine in areas of freedom of speech, freedom of religion, criminal procedure, and due process, again the variance throughout the world can be instructive. In failing at times to recognize that we can learn from the rest of the world as well as teach it, American constitutionalists run the risk of ignoring a developing source of information and experience, and reinforcing unfortunate stereotypes about American arrogance.

This Supplement remains appropriately devoted to recent developments in American constitutional law, but as we think about those developments it can hardly hurt at least to think of them in light of constitutional developments elsewhere. As I think about them, I have had the advantage of access not only by virtue of travel, but also by virtue of the knowledge that increasingly is dependent on the expertise of those for whom legal information is their primary speciality. For that, and for much else, I remain indescribably grateful to Virginia Wise, my wife and collaborator.

FREDERICK SCHAUER

Pietersburg, South Africa
July, 1995

*

TABLE OF CONTENTS

Numbers on the left indicate where the new materials fit into the casebooks. Cases and legislative material set out at length are in **bold face**.

CHAPTER 9(4). EQUAL PROTECTION

CHAPTER 10(5). THE POST-CIVIL WAR AMENDMENTS AND CIVIL LEGISLATION: CONSTITUTIONAL RESTRAINTS ON PRIVATE CONDUCT; CONGRESSIONAL POWER TO IMPLEMENT THE AMENDMENTS

TABLE OF CONTENTS

CHAPTER 13(8). FREEDOM OF EXPRESSION IN SOME SPECIAL CONTEXTS

CHAPTER 14(9). THE CONSTITUTION AND RELIGION: "ESTABLISHMENT" AND "FREE EXERCISE"

CHAPTER 15(10). PROPER CONDITIONS FOR CONSTITUTIONAL ADJUDICATION: INTERESTED PARTIES; CONCRETE CONTROVERSIES; JUSTICIABLE ISSUES

TABLE OF CONTENTS

TABLE OF CASES

Principal cases are in italic type. Non-principal cases are in roman type. References are to Pages.

1995 SUPPLEMENT

CONSTITUTIONAL LAW
Twelfth Edition

INDIVIDUAL RIGHTS IN CONSTITUTIONAL LAW
Fifth Edition

*

Chapter 1

THE NATURE AND SOURCES OF THE SUPREME COURT'S AUTHORITY

12th ED. and IND. RTS., p. 28
Add at end of footnote 7 (on p. 29):

In the last two Terms, the Court has addressed the issue of retroactivity twice, and each time turned to questions of the relationship between retroactivity and constitutional theory that were far broader than the particular issue before the Court. In JAMES B. BEAM DISTILLING CO. v. GEORGIA, 501 U.S. 529 (1991), the Court addressed the question of the retroactive application of a decision invalidating a state tax as violative of the commerce clause, and Justice SOUTER, in an opinion announcing the judgment of the Court, offered an admirably clear presentation of the central issue. Full retroactive application of the Court's decisions, he explained, is consonant with a "declaratory theory of law," for if the Court is declaring what the law is and has always been, rather than making new law, then retroactive application of the Court's decisions is consistent with the view that the Court's decision has not really changed the law. But although faithful to a declaratory theory of law, he went on, retroactive application is unfaithful to the "fact of life" of changing judicial views on which parties rightfully expect to rely. Thus, he explained, pure prospectivity would better satisfy the requirements of justice and fairness to relying parties, but it would do so at the cost of "relax[ing] the force of precedent [and] minimizing the costs of overruling, [thereby allowing] the courts to act with a freedom comparable to that of legislatures."

The issue was joined more sharply the following Term in HARPER v. VIRGINIA DEPARTMENT OF TAXATION, 510 U.S. ___ (1993). Unlike in James B. Beam, this time there was an opinion of the Court, and it was written by Justice THOMAS. The issue was the potential retroactive application of a recent Court decision (Davis v. Michigan Department of Treasury, 489 U.S. 803 (1989)) dealing with intergovernmental tax immunities, in particular the unconstitutionality of state taxation of federal retirement benefits when commensurate state retirement benefits were not taxed. Although some decisions (e.g., Chevron Oil Co. v. Huson, 404 U.S. 97 (1971)) had indicated that Linkletter's relaxation of the general rule of retroactive application applied to civil as well as criminal cases, Justice Thomas's opinion essentially reinstated the rule that the Court's decisions in civil cases were always to be applied retroactively. "Although [Beam] did not produce a unified opinion for the Court, a majority of Justices agreed that a rule of federal law, once announced and applied to the parties to the controversy, must be given full retroactive effect by all courts adjudicating federal law. In announcing the judgment of the Court, Justice Souter laid down a rule for determining the retroactive effect of a civil decision: After the case announcing any rule of federal law has 'appl[ied]' that rule with respect to the litigants' before the court, no court may 'refuse to apply [that] rule ... retroactively.' Justice Souter's view of retroactivity superseded 'any claim based on the Chevron Oil analysis.' [Beam] controls this case, and we accordingly adopt a rule that fairly reflects the position of a majority of Justices in Beam: When this Court applies a rule of federal law to the parties before it, that rule is the controlling interpretation of federal law and must be given full retroactive effect in all cases still open on direct review and as to all events, regardless of whether such events predate or postdate our announcement of the rule. [This rule prohibits the] selective application of new rules. [We] now prohibit the erection of selective temporal barriers in the application of federal law in noncriminal cases."

The primary dissent came from Justice O'CONNOR, joined by Chief Justice Rehnquist (and joined as to the method of analysis, although not the results of that analysis, in an opinion written by Justice KENNEDY, joined by Justice White). Chiding the majority for failing to adhere to stare decisis and thus confusing an area of law that had previously been thought settled, she urged continuing adherence to the more case-specific and less categori-

1

cal standard in Chevron Oil, a standard that focused on whether or not retroactive application would produce undue hardship, and that would allow "pure prospectivity" in some instances. Finding intimations of a rejection in the majority opinion of any possibility of pure prospectivity, she maintained that that might be the appropriate course in some cases. "When the Court changes its mind, the law changes with it." Moreover, she advocated a more flexible approach to all retroactivity decisions. "The Court offers no justification for disregarding [its previously] settled rule. Nor do I believe it could, for the rule is not a procedural nicety. On the contrary, it is critical to the soundness of our decisional processes. [Any] decision of this Court has wide-ranging applications [far] beyond the particular case in which it issues. The rule we applied in Brecht v. Abrahamson, 507 U.S. ___ (1993), which limits the stare decisis effect of our decisions to questions actually considered and passed on, ensures that this Court does not decide important questions by accident or inadvertence. By adopting a contrary rule in the area of retroactivity, the Court now permanently binds itself to its every unexamined assumption or inattention. Any rule that creates a grave risk that we might resolve important issues of national concern sub silentio, without thought or consideration, cannot be a wise one."

Justice SCALIA's concurring opinion focused directly on Justice O'Connor's dissent, and on its reliance on the principle of stare decisis. Characterizing the issue of retroactivity "as a general problem of jurisprudence," Justice Scalia expressed the view that there was an "irony" in "invoking stare decisis in defense of prospective decisionmaking. Prospective decisionmaking is the handmaid of judicial activism, and the born enemy of stare decisis. It was formulated in the heyday of legal realism and promoted as a 'techniqu[e] of judicial lawmaking' in general, and more specifically as a means of making it easier to overrule prior precedent. Thus, the dissent is saying, in effect, that stare decisis demands the preservation of methods of destroying stare decisis recently invented in violation of stare decisis. [The concept that when the Court changes its mind, the law changes with it] is quite foreign to the American legal and constitutional tradition. It would have struck John Marshall as an extraordinary assertion of raw power. Marbury."

There was also an extended discussion of retroactivity in the statutory context in two cases both involving the question whether the provisions of the Civil Rights Act of 1991 (see below, addition to 12th Ed., p. 708; Ind.Rts., p. 379) applied to cases brought prior to enactment, Landgraf v. USI Film Products, 509 U.S. ___ (1994), and Rivers v. Roadway Express, Inc., 509 U.S. ___ (1994). In deciding that the Act would not be applied retroactively, Justice Stevens, writing for the majority in both cases, noted that the anti-retroactivity principle is not only rooted in deep conceptions of fundamental fairness and the rule of law, but also is embodied in various constitutional provisions, including the Ex Post Facto Clause, the Contracts Clause of Article I, section 10, the Takings Clause of the Fifth Amendment, the prohibition on Bills of Attainder in Article I, sections nine and ten, and aspects of the Due Process Clause. Although these embodiments of the anti-retroactivity principle did not invalidate legislation not covered by any of these provisions, he argued, it did serve to establish a presumption against retroactive legislation that could be overcome only by clear congressional intent that a statute be applied retroactively, an intent Justice Stevens did not find present for any provision of the Civil Rights Act of 1991. In Rivers, Justice Stevens rejected the argument that there was an implied congressional intent of retroactivity because section 102 of the Civil Rights Act of 1991 was intended to be "restorative" of the Court's earlier decisions prior to its decision in Patterson v. McLean Credit Union, 491 U.S. 164 (1989) (see below, 12th Ed., p. 951; Ind.Rts., p. 622, and also accompanying material in this Supplement). "Congress' decision to alter a rule of law established in one of our cases—as petitioners put it, to 'legislatively overrul[e]'—does not, by itself, reveal whether Congress intends the 'overruling' statute to be applied retroactively to events that would otherwise be governed by the judicial decision. A legislative response does not necessarily indicate that Congress viewed the judicial decision as 'wrongly decided' as an interpretive matter. Congress may view the judicial decision as an entirely correct reading of prior law [but] may nevertheless decide that the old law should be amended, but only for the future. Of course, Congress may also decide to announce a new rule that operates retroactively to govern the rights of parties whose rights would otherwise be subject to the rule announced in the judicial decision. Because retroactivity raises special policy concerns, the choice to enact a statute that responds to a judicial decision is quite distinct from the choice to make the responding statute retroactive." Justice Scalia, joined by Justices Kennedy and Thomas, concurred in the judgment in both cases. He agreed with the presumption against retroactivity, but disagreed that it could be overcome by extrinsic evidence of congressional intent, as opposed to a statement in the statute itself. And Justice Scalia also objected to the majority's definition of retroactivity—"whether the new provision attaches legal consequences to events completed before its enactment." Characterizing this as an inappropriate "vested rights" approach, Justice Scalia proposed instead that retroactivity be measured in terms of the time of the particular remedy at issue. Justice Blackmun was the sole dissenter in both cases.

Finally, note Reynoldsville Casket Co. v. Hyde, 518 U.S. ___ (1995), in which the Court held that the Ohio Supreme Court violated the Supremacy Clause in not following the Supreme Court's retroactivity ruling in Harper.

12th ED. and IND. RTS., p. 36

Add at end of footnote 6:

Note in this connection Justice Thomas's concurring opinion in Lockhart v. Fretwell, 507 U.S. ___ (1993), pointing out the error of the Arkansas Court of Appeals in assuming it was bound by the Supremacy Clause to follow the conclusions of the United States Court of Appeals for the Eighth Circuit: "[T]he Court of Appeals appears to have been under the impression that the Arkansas trial court would have been compelled to follow [an Eighth Circuit ruling] by the Supremacy Clause. It was mistaken. The Supremacy Clause demands that state law yield to federal law, but neither federal supremacy nor any other principle of federal law requires that a state court's interpretation of federal law give way to a (lower) federal court's interpretation. In our federal system, a state trial court's interpretation of federal law is no less authoritative than that of the federal court of appeals in whose circuit the trial court is located. An Arkansas trial court is bound by this Court's (and by the Arkansas Supreme Court's and Arkansas Court of Appeals') interpretation of federal law, but if it follows the Eighth Circuit's interpretation of federal law, it does so only because it chooses to and not because it must. I agree with [this] Court's holding that the [Arkansas] Court of Appeals misinterpreted the Sixth Amendment. I wish to make it clear that it misinterpreted the Supremacy Clause as well."

12th ED. and IND. RTS., p. 42

Add as new footnote after "executive autonomy" at end of second full paragraph:

2a. The scope of the President's constitutional power to pardon again became an issue when on December 24, 1992, in the waning days of his Presidency, President Bush pardoned six high-ranking officials for "conduct related to the Iran-Contra affair". (Pres. Proc. 6518, 28 Weekly, Comp. Pres. Doc. 2382). The effect of the pardon was to preclude further investigation of, among others, former Secretary of Defense Caspar Weinberger. President Bush's action prompted proposals such as the one offered in the 104th Congress to amend the Constitution as follows: "The President shall only have the power to grant a reprieve or a pardon for an offense against the United States to an individual who has been convicted of such an offense." H.J. Res. 30.

12th ED. and IND. RTS., p. 43

Add after discussion of Klein:

The question of congressional control over the outcome of specific litigation reappeared in PLAUT v. SPENDTHRIFT FARM, INC., 517 U.S. ___ (1995). At issue was section 27A of the Securities Exchange Act of 1934, added on December 19, 1991, which not only specified the statute of limitations to be applied in certain securities actions, but also provided for the "reinstate[ment]" of causes of action that had been dismissed on statute-of-limitations grounds prior to December 19, 1991, but subsequent to June 19, 1991, the relevance of the latter date being that it was one day after the Supreme Court cases whose ruling on statutes of limitations section 27A sought to change. Writing for the Court, however, Justice SCALIA concluded that the attempt by Congress to reopen litigation that had already been dismissed by an Article III Court violated the constitutional principle of separation of powers.

Justice Scalia's opinion noted the possible relevance of Klein, but held it inapplicable because Klein does not apply to cases in which Congress changes the applicable law. And he noted the possible relevance as well of Hayburn's Case (1792, described below, 12th Ed., p. 1594; Ind.Rts., p. 1265), but concluded that it was inapplicable because here there was no suggestion that officials of non-judicial departments were sitting in direct review of judicial decisions. Nevertheless, however, he concluded for the Court that Article III "gives the Federal Judiciary the power, not merely to rule on cases, but to *decide* them, subject to review only by superior courts in the Article III hierarchy. [By] retroactively commanding the federal courts to reopen final judgments, Congress has violated this fundamental principle." Relying heavily on founding-era documents about "the separation of legislative from judicial power," Justice Scalia concluded that "[W]hen retroactive legislation requires its own application in a case already finally adjudicated, it does no more and no less than 'reverse a determination once made, in a particular case.' Federalist 81. Our decisions [have] uniformly provided fair warning that such an act exceeds the powers of Congress. [To] be sure, section 27A reopens (or directs the reopening of) final judgments in a whole class of cases rather than in any particular suit. We do not see how that makes any difference. The separation-of-powers violation [consists] of depriving judicial judgments of the conclusive effect that they had when they announced, not of acting in a manner—viz., with particular rather than general effect—that is unusual (though, to be sure, not impossible) for a legislature. To be sure, a general statute such as this one may reduce the perception that legislative interference with judicial judgments was prompted by individual favoritism; but it is legislative interference with judicial judgments nonetheless. Not favoritism, nor even corruption, but *power* is the object of the separation of powers prohibition."

Justice BREYER concurred in the judgment, but objected to the majority's categorical rule. To him, the proper principle was that the historical and other evidence supported the conclusion that "at least *sometimes* Congress lacks the power under Article I to reopen an otherwise closed court judgment. [Because] the law before us *both* reopens final judgments *and* lacks the liberty-protecting assurances that prospectivity and greater generality would have provided, we need not, and we should not, go further—to make of the reopening itself, an absolute, always determinative distinction, a 'prophylactic device,' or a foundation for the building of a new 'high wall' between the branches. Indeed, the unnecessary building of such walls is, in itself, dangerous, because the Constitution blends, as well as separates, powers in its effort to create a government that will work for, as well as protect the liberties of, its citizens."

Justice STEVENS, joined by Justice Ginsburg, dissented. He identified several nineteenth century cases in which he argued that the Court had upheld actions similar to that struck down here, and noted that the Court's own setting of a statute of limitations, the action subsequently modified by Congress in the challenged statute, was "a legislative function." "The Court, however, failed to adopt the transition rules that ordinarily attend alterations shortening the time to sue. Congress [has] supplied those rules. The statute reflects the ability of two coequal branches to cooperate in providing for the impartial application of legal rules to particular disputes. The Court's mistrust of such cooperation ill serves the separation of powers."

12th ED. and IND. RTS., p. 47
Add as new footnote after "S2901" at end of second full paragraph:

12. The 104th Congress has before it a variety of proposals to address the jurisdiction of the federal courts in constitutional matters. H.R. 1624 would deny the federal courts power to hear or review any case arising out of any state statute, ordinance, rule or regulation relating to abortion. S. 28 and S. 320 take the opposite tack, mandating Supreme Court review of all lower court decisions declaring state and local anti-abortion measures unconstitutional.

Congress has several measures before it to limit federal courts' ability to grant remedies for constitutional violations. One of the most controversial involves the matter of federal court authority over state referendum issues. When California voters passed Proposition 187, a state referendum proposal limiting illegal alien rights to certain social services, on November 8, 1994, it was immediately challenged in Federal court. Judge Matthew Byrne (C.D.Cal.) issued a temporary restraining order against the implementation and enforcement of Proposition 187 on November 16, 1994. Judge Marilyn Pfaelzer granted a preliminary injunction barring implementation and enforcement of the medical, public education and social services provisions of the measure on December 14, 1994, basing her decision primarily on the federal government's power to control immigration matters (Gregorio T. v. Wilson). On March 13, 1995, Judge Pfaelzer agreed to hear arguments on the merits of the constitutionality of the measure beginning no later than September 5, 1995. On May 4, 1995, the Ninth Circuit agreed to hear an expedited appeal on the merits of the preliminary injunction. Briefs, which will be limited to the injunction issues, are due in mid-June, 1995 ___ F.3d ___ (1995). In Congress, newly-elected Sonny Bono from California introduced H.R. 1170, which would require a three-judge District Court to hear cases challenging the constitutionality of state referendum proposals and would also provide expedited appeal to the Supreme Court for such cases. This measure was reported out of the House Judiciary Committee on June 7, 1995.

Other measures that affect remedies include H.R. 212 and S. 51, which provide that federal judges cannot impose taxation to correct constitutional (or some other) violations, and a constitutional amendment proposal, H.J.Res. 13, which would provide that children have a constitutional right to attend neighborhood schools, thus limiting busing as a remedy. The Prison Litigation Reform Act of 1995 (S. 866), the Prison Litigation Control Act of 1995 (H.R. 695) the habeas corpus reform proposal (S. 623) [discussed below, addition to 12th Ed. and Ind.Rts., p. 64], and the takings legislative proposals (S. 135, S. 145 and H.R. 489) [discussed below, addition to 12th Ed., p. 471; Ind.Rts., p. 142] may also have significant effects on remedies granted by federal courts in constitutional matters.

12th ED. and IND. RTS., p. 51
Add as new footnote after "purpose" at end of second full paragraph:

7b. The 104th Congress has only one anti-busing proposal before it, a constitutional amendment proposal, H.J.Res. 13, which would "prohibit compelling the attendance of a student in a public school other than the public school nearest the residence of such student." This resolution is pending before the House Judiciary Committee.

12th ED. and IND. RTS., p. 58
Add at end of footnote 8:

In ARIZONA v. EVANS, 516 U.S. ___ (1995), Chief Justice REHNQUIST's opinion for a seven-member majority reaffirmed Michigan v. Long. "[We] believe that Michigan v. Long properly serves its purpose and should not be disturbed. Under it, state courts are absolutely free to interpret state constitutional provisions to accord greater protection to individual rights than do similar provisions of the United States Constitution. They are also free to serve as experimental laboratories, in the sense that Justice Brandeis used that term in his dissenting opinion in New State Ice Co. v. Liebmann, 285 U.S. 262, 311 (1932). Under our decision today, [Arizona] remains free to seek whatever solutions it chooses to problems of law enforcement posed by the advent of computerization. Indeed, it is freer to do so because it is disabused of its erroneous view of what the United States Constitution requires." This conclusion was largely in response to a lengthy dissent by Justice GINSBURG, joined by Justice Stevens, who argued that Michigan v. Long should be overruled. "The Long presumption [impedes] the States' ability to serve as laboratories for testing solutions to novel legal problems. I would apply the opposite presumption and assume that Arizona's Supreme Court has ruled for its own State and people, under its own constitutional recognition of individual security against unwarranted state intrusion. [I] would presume, absent a plain statement to the contrary, that a state court's decision of the kind here at issue rests on an independent state-law ground. [Michigan v. Long] is out of sync with the principle that this Court will avoid constitutional questions when an alternative basis of decision fairly presents itself. Most critically, [the] Long presumption interferes prematurely with state-court endeavors to explore different solutions to new problems facing modern society."

12th ED. and IND. RTS., p. 60
Add as footnote after carryover paragraph (after reference to Harris v. Reed):

9. Harris v. Reed, however, was interpreted narrowly by the Court in both Ylst v. Nunnemaker, 501 U.S. 797 (1991), and Coleman v. Thompson, 501 U.S. 722 (1991), with Justice O'Connor's opinion for the Court in Coleman concluding that the presumption in favor of review was to be applied only after the "predicate requirement" has been satisfied, that being a determination that "the relevant state court decision ... fairly appear[s] to rest primarily on federal law or [is] interwoven with federal law." "In the habeas context, the application of the independent and adequate state ground doctrine is grounded in concerns of comity and federalism. [There is little] that the federal courts will gain by applying a presumption of federal review in those cases where the relevant state court decision does not fairly appear to rest primarily on federal law or to be interwoven with such law, and much that the States and state courts will lose. We decline to so expand the Harris presumption." The effect of these decisions seems plainly to immunize a large number of state criminal convictions from federal collateral relief.

For a continuation of the debate about the scope and status of the adequate and independent state ground barrier to review, see the various opinions in Sochor v. Florida, 504 U.S. 527 (1992). And note also Harper v. Virginia Department of Taxation, 510 U.S. ___ (1993), described at length above, addition to 12th Ed. and Ind.Rts., p. 28, holding that the independent and adequate state grounds principle did not extend to state rules regarding the retroactivity of decisions about federal law. "The Supremacy Clause does not allow federal retroactivity doctrine to be supplanted by the invocation of a contrary approach to retroactivity under state law. Whatever freedom state courts may enjoy to limit the retroactive application of their own interpretations of state law cannot extend to their interpretations of federal law."

12th ED. and IND. RTS., p. 61
Add at end of footnote 2:

And on the Court's unwillingness to decide questions that were "not pressed or passed upon below," see, most recently, the controversy in United States v. Williams, 504 U.S. 36 (1992). Court Rule 14.1 provides that only questions set forth in the Petition for Certiorari will be considered by the Court. On the (quite strict) application of this rule, see, most recently, Izumi Seimitsu Kogyo Kabushiki Kaisha v. U.S. Philips Corp., 507 U.S. ___ (1993); Yee v. City of Escondido, 503 U.S. 519 (1992).

12th ED. and IND. RTS., p. 62
Add to text at end of second paragraph:

Although the Court decided an average of 150 cases per year in the 1980's, this number has continued to drop. In the 1994 term the Court issued opinions in only 82 cases, the lowest number since the 1955–56 term. Of these cases, 35 were unanimous and 16 were decided by a 5–4 vote. (New York Times, July 2, 1995, sec. 4, p. 4, col. 1).

12th ED. and IND. RTS., p. 64

Add as new footnote after "workload" at end of first paragraph:

9a. Concerns about the availability of direct and collateral relief for those convicted of crimes occupied a large part of the discussions in connection with several omnibus anti-crime bills recently pending before Congress. The Supreme Court, with a number of Justices frequently voicing objections to the lack of finality in the criminal process generally and in capital cases in particular, weighed in with several sharply worded opinions, most notably in the widely reported case of Robert Alton Harris. A number of federal District Court and Court of Appeals judges in California had issued last-minute stays of execution, many in the last 24 hours, and finally the Supreme Court issued an order concluding with: "No further stays of Robert Alton Harris' execution shall be entered by the federal courts except upon order of this court." Vasquez v. Harris, 503 U.S. 1000 (1992) (per curiam, vacating stay).

Several proposals in the 104th Congress address the issue of federal court caseload, particularly in the context of prisoner litigation. S. 623, introduced by Sen. Hatch, would provide a 1 year statute of limitations for state prisoners to file federal habeas corpus petitions and would also require that Court of Appeals judges grant a certificate of appealability to screen claims. The Senate Judiciary Committee concluded hearings on this bill March 28, 1995. The Prison Litigation Reform Act of 1995, S. 866, sponsored by Senators Dole and Hatch, would also increase burdens on prisoners filing suit in federal courts, particularly in civil litigation. H.R. 695, the Prison Litigation Control Act of 1995, would limit suits brought regarding jail conditions, particularly prison overcrowding, under the Eighth Amendment. H.R. 695 would apply not only to pending and future cases, but also to any outstanding court orders and consent decrees.

Despite the decrease in the number of cases given full consideration by the Court (108 in the 1991 Term, although the number of pages of opinions produced slightly exceeded the 1990 Term, and 82 in the 1994 Term), proposals to deal with the Court's workload continue, including one to implement the recommendations of the Federal Courts Study Committee. H.R. 4357. Although the 102nd Congress on October 29, 1992 (P.L. 102–572, 106 Stat. 4506) adopted many of the proposals of the Federal Courts Study Committee, none of the changes finally adopted were ones significantly affecting the jurisdiction of the Supreme Court. And on the workload question in general, consider the Supreme Court's role in prescribing the rules of practice, procedure, and evidence for the federal courts. Although the Court normally transmits without intervention the recommendations of the Judicial Conference of the United States (see 28 U.S.C. 2073), the degree of Court involvement remains a matter of controversy. On April 22, 1993, Justice Scalia, joined by Justice Thomas and in part by Justice Souter, dissented on substantive grounds from the Court's approval of recommended changes in the sanction (Rule 11) and discovery rules of the Federal Rules of Civil Procedure. Justice White responded with a statement of his own, noting that his expertise in litigation matters was not current enough for him to think he had the expertise necessary to exercise genuine substantive review, and endorsing earlier suggestions of Justices Black and Douglas that Congress ought to eliminate the role of the Court in the rulemaking process.

Chapter 3

THE COMMERCE POWER

12th ED., p. 97

Add at end of footnote 1:

In considering the view that checks on the exercise of the commerce power should come primarily from the political process, consider the relevance of two recent cases holding that infringements on the boundaries between state and federal power are violations of individual rights subject to redress under federal civil rights laws. Although both Golden State Transit Corp. v. Los Angeles, 493 U.S. 103 (1989), and Dennis v. Higgins, 498 U.S. 439 (1991), involved claims that violations of those boundaries by *states* were violations of rights subject to redress under 42 U.S.C. § 1983, both support the proposition that individuals injured by violations of those boundaries have judicially redressable claims. Would the same view apply when the violation of the boundary is by the federal government rather than by the state? If so, is this in tension with Marshall's view in Gibbons and Jackson's in Wickard? In Dennis v. Higgins, Justice White's opinion for the Court rejected the argument that "the Commerce Clause was not designed to benefit individuals, but rather was designed to promote national economic and political union," but Justice Kennedy's dissent, joined by Chief Justice Rehnquist, argued that "[b]enefits to those engaged in commerce [are] incidental to the purpose of the Commerce Clause; they are but evidence of its sound application."

12th ED., p. 142

Add at end of footnote 4:

In Bass the Court interpreted a federal statute narrowly in order to avoid constitutional problems involving the reach of the commerce clause. Conversely, in some areas, such as in its interpretation of the Sherman Antitrust Act, the Court has expanded its interpretation of the jurisdictional predicate of the act (conspiracies "in restraint of trade or commerce among the several states") as the principles of congressional power under the commerce clause have expanded. Thus, in Summit Health, Ltd. v. Pinhas, 500 U.S. 322 (1991), Justice Stevens' majority opinion reaffirmed the Court's willingness (consistent with the legislative history) to interpret the jurisdictional predicate of the Sherman Act to reach all that the Constitution allows, thus allowing jurisdiction where there is no "actual effect on interstate commerce" as long as the conspiracy has a sufficient "nexus" to commerce. Justice Scalia, joined by Justices O'Connor, Kennedy, and Souter, dissented, arguing that what Congress has done should not be interpreted to be equivalent to what Congress could have done, and maintaining that although a broader statute would be constitutional, this statute required a showing of an effect on interstate commerce in the particular case.

12th ED., p. 151

Add to end of footnote 6:

Consider also the Freedom of Choice Act of 1993, H.R. 776, set out below, addition to 12th Ed., p. 553; Ind.Rts., p. 224, introduced to entrench legislatively at the federal level the protections and structure of Roe v. Wade. The Act relies explicitly on the power of Congress to regulate interstate commerce as a basis for asserting federal authority with respect to the regulation of abortion. Note also the Freedom of Access to Clinic Entrances Act (described below, addition to 12th Ed., p. 945; Ind.Rts., p. 616), also using the commerce clause as the predicate for congressional power over access to abortion clinics.

12th ED., p. 156
Add after Katzenbach v. McClung:

UNITED STATES v. LOPEZ

517 U.S. ___, 115 S.Ct. 1624, 131 L.Ed.2d 626 (1995).

Chief Justice REHNQUIST delivered the opinion of the Court.

In the Gun–Free School Zones Act of 1990, Congress made it a federal offense "for any individual knowingly to possess a firearm at a place that the individual knows, or has reasonable cause to believe, is a school zone." The Act neither regulates a commercial activity nor contains a requirement that the possession be connected in any way to interstate commerce. We hold that the Act exceeds the authority of Congress "[t]o regulate Commerce . . . among the several States. . . ."

On March 10, 1992, respondent, who was then a 12th-grade student, arrived at Edison High School in San Antonio, Texas, carrying a concealed .38 caliber handgun and five bullets. Acting upon an anonymous tip, school authorities confronted respondent, who admitted that he was carrying the weapon. He was arrested and charged under Texas law with firearm possession on school premises. The next day, the state charges were dismissed after federal agents charged respondent by complaint with violating the Gun–Free School Zones Act of 1990. A federal grand jury indicted respondent on one count of knowing possession of a firearm at a school zone, in violation of § 922(q). Respondent moved to dismiss his federal indictment on the ground that § 922(q) "is unconstitutional as it is beyond the power of Congress to legislate control over our public schools." The District Court denied the motion, concluding that § 922(q) "is a constitutional exercise of Congress' well-defined power to regulate activities in and affecting commerce, and the 'business' of elementary, middle and high schools . . . affects interstate commerce." Respondent waived his right to a jury trial. The District Court conducted a bench trial, found him guilty of violating § 922(q), and sentenced him to six months' imprisonment and two years' supervised release. On appeal, respondent challenged his conviction based on his claim that § 922(q) exceeded Congress' power to legislate under the Commerce Clause. The Court of Appeals for the Fifth Circuit agreed and reversed respondent's conviction. Because of the importance of the issue, we granted certiorari, and we now affirm.

We start with first principles. The Constitution creates a Federal Government of enumerated powers. As Madison wrote, "[t]he powers delegated by the proposed Constitution to the federal government are few and defined. Those which are to remain in the State governments are numerous and indefinite." Federalist 45. [The] Constitution delegates to Congress the power "[t]o regulate Commerce with foreign Nations, and among the several States, and with the Indian Tribes." The Court, through Chief Justice Marshall, first defined the nature of Congress' commerce power in Gibbons v. Ogden. [The] Gibbons Court, however, acknowledged that limitations on the commerce power are inherent in the very language of the Commerce Clause. "It is not intended to say that these words comprehend that commerce, which is completely internal, which is carried on between man and man in a State, or between different parts of the same State, and which does not extend to or affect other States. Such a power would be inconvenient, and is certainly unnecessary."

[For] nearly a century thereafter, the Court's Commerce Clause decisions dealt but rarely with the extent of Congress' power, and almost entirely with the Commerce Clause as a limit on state legislation that discriminated against interstate commerce. Under this line of precedent, the Court held that certain categories of activity such as "production," "manufacturing," and "mining" were within the province of state governments, and thus were beyond the power of Congress. [In] 1887, Congress enacted the Interstate Commerce Act, and in 1890, Congress enacted the Sherman Antitrust Act. These laws ushered in a new era of federal regulation under the commerce power. When cases involving these laws first reached this Court, we imported from our negative Commerce Clause cases the approach that Congress could not regulate activities such as "production," "manufacturing," and "mining." Simultaneously, however, the Court held that, where the interstate and intrastate aspects of commerce were so mingled together that full regulation of interstate commerce required incidental regulation of intrastate commerce, the Commerce Clause authorized such regulation.

In Schecter Poultry, the Court struck down regulations that fixed the hours and wages of individuals employed by an intrastate business because the activity being regulated related to interstate commerce only indirectly. In doing so, the Court characterized the distinction between direct and indirect effects of intrastate transactions upon interstate commerce as "a fundamental one, essential to the maintenance of our constitutional system." Activities that affected interstate commerce directly were within Congress' power; activities that affected interstate commerce indirectly were beyond Congress' reach. The justification for this formal distinction was rooted in the fear that otherwise "there would be virtually no limit to the federal power and for all practical purposes we should have a completely centralized government."

Two years later, in the watershed case of NLRB v. Jones & Laughlin Steel Corp., the Court [departed] from the distinction between "direct" and "indirect" effects on interstate commerce. Jones & Laughlin[, as well as Darby and Wickard,] ushered in an era of Commerce Clause jurisprudence that greatly expanded the previously defined authority of Congress under that Clause. In part, this was a recognition of the great changes that had occurred in the way business was carried on in this country. Enterprises that had once been local or at most regional in nature had become national in scope. But the doctrinal change also reflected a view that earlier Commerce Clause cases artificially had constrained the authority of Congress to regulate interstate commerce.

But even these modern-era precedents which have expanded congressional power under the Commerce Clause confirm that this power is subject to outer limits. In Jones & Laughlin, the Court warned that the scope of the interstate commerce power "must be considered in the light of our dual system of government and may not be extended so as to embrace effects upon interstate commerce so indirect and remote that to embrace them, in view of our complex society, would effectually obliterate the distinction between what is national and what is local and create a completely centralized government." Since that time, the Court has heeded that warning and undertaken to decide whether a rational basis existed for concluding that a regulated activity sufficiently affected interstate commerce.

[Consistent] with this structure, we have identified three broad categories of activity that Congress may regulate under its commerce power. First, Congress may regulate the use of the channels of interstate commerce. Second, Congress is empowered to regulate and protect the instrumentalities of interstate commerce, or persons or things in interstate commerce, even though the threat may come only from intrastate activities. Finally, Congress' commerce authority includes the power to regulate those activities having a substantial relation to interstate commerce, Jones & Laughlin Steel, those activities that substantially affect interstate commerce.[1]

Within this final category, admittedly, our case law has not been clear whether an activity must "affect" or "substantially affect" interstate commerce in order to be within Congress' power to regulate it. [We] conclude, consistent with the great weight of our case law, that the proper test requires an analysis of whether the regulated activity "substantially affects" interstate commerce.

We now turn to consider the power of Congress, in the light of this framework, to enact § 922(q). The first two categories of authority may be quickly disposed of: § 922(q) is not a regulation of the use of the channels of interstate commerce, nor is it an attempt to prohibit the interstate transportation of a commodity through the channels of commerce; nor can § 922(q) be justified as a regulation by which Congress has sought to protect an instrumentality of interstate commerce or a thing in interstate commerce. Thus, if § 922(q) is to be sustained, it must be under the third category as a regulation of an activity that substantially affects interstate commerce.

First, we have upheld a wide variety of congressional Acts regulating intrastate economic activity where we have concluded that the activity substantially affected interstate commerce. Where economic activity substantially affects interstate commerce, legislation regulating that activity will be sustained. Even Wickard, [perhaps] the most far reaching example of Commerce Clause authority over intrastate activity, involved economic activity in a way that the possession of a gun in a school zone does not. [Section] 922(q) is a criminal statute that by its terms has nothing to do with "commerce" or any sort of economic enterprise, however broadly one might define those terms. Section 922(q) is not an essential part of a larger regulation of economic activity,

---

1. On the distinction between congressional power over activities *in* interstate commerce, as to which there is no requirement of substantiality, and activities in intrastate commerce that have substantial effects on interstate commerce, see also United States v. Robertson, 518 U.S. ___ (1995). [Ed.]

in which the regulatory scheme could be undercut unless the intrastate activity were regulated. It cannot, therefore, be sustained under our cases upholding regulations of activities that arise out of or are connected with a commercial transaction, which viewed in the aggregate, substantially affects interstate commerce.

Second, § 922(q) contains no jurisdictional element which would ensure, through case-by-case inquiry, that the firearm possession in question affects interstate commerce. For example, in United States v. Bass, the Court interpreted former 18 U.S.C. § 1202(a), which made it a crime for a felon to "receiv[e], posses[s], or transpor[t] in commerce or affecting commerce . . . any firearm." The Court interpreted the possession component [to] require an additional nexus to interstate commerce both because the statute was ambiguous and because "unless Congress conveys its purpose clearly, it will not be deemed to have significantly changed the federal-state balance." [The] Court thus interpreted the statute to reserve the constitutional question whether Congress could regulate, without more, the "mere possession" of firearms. Unlike the statute in Bass, § 922(q) has no express jurisdictional element which might limit its reach to a discrete set of firearm possessions that additionally have an explicit connection with or effect on interstate commerce.

Although as part of our independent evaluation of constitutionality under the Commerce Clause we of course consider legislative findings, and indeed even congressional committee findings, regarding effect on interstate commerce, the Government [in its brief] concedes that "[n]either the statute nor its legislative history contain[s] express congressional findings regarding the effects upon interstate commerce of gun possession in a school zone." We agree [that] Congress normally is not required to make formal findings as to the substantial burdens that an activity has on interstate commerce. But to the extent that congressional findings would enable us to evaluate the legislative judgment that the activity in question substantially affected interstate commerce, even though no such substantial effect was visible to the naked eye, they are lacking here.

The Government argues that Congress has accumulated institutional expertise regarding the regulation of firearms through previous enactments. We agree, however, with the Fifth Circuit that importation of previous findings to justify § 922(q) is especially inappropriate here because the "prior federal enactments or Congressional findings [do not] speak to the subject matter of section 922(q) or its relationship to interstate commerce. Indeed, section 922(q) plows thoroughly new ground and represents a sharp break with the long-standing pattern of federal firearms legislation."

The Government's essential contention, in fine, is that we may determine here that § 922(q) is valid because possession of a firearm in a local school zone does indeed substantially affect interstate commerce. The Government argues that possession of a firearm in a school zone may result in violent crime and that violent crime can be expected to affect the functioning of the national economy in two ways. First, the costs of violent crime are substantial, and, through the mechanism of insurance, those costs are spread throughout the population. Second, violent crime reduces the willingness of individuals to travel to areas within the country that are perceived to be unsafe. The Government also argues that the presence of guns in schools poses a substantial threat to the educational process by threatening the learning environment. A handicapped educational process, in turn, will result in a less productive citizenry. That, in turn, would have an adverse effect on the Nation's economic well-being. As a result, the Government argues that Congress could rationally have concluded that § 922(q) substantially affects interstate commerce.

We pause to consider the implications of the Government's arguments. The Government admits, under its "costs of crime" reasoning, that Congress could regulate not only all violent crime, but all activities that might lead to violent crime, regardless of how tenuously they relate to interstate commerce. Similarly, under the Government's "national productivity" reasoning, Congress could regulate any activity that it found was related to the economic productivity of individual citizens: family law (including marriage, divorce, and child custody), for example. Under the theories that the Government presents in support of § 922(q), it is difficult to perceive any limitation on federal power, even in areas such as criminal law enforcement or education where States historically have been sovereign. Thus, if we were to accept the Government's arguments, we are hard-pressed to posit any activity by an individual that Congress is without power to regulate.

Although Justice Breyer argues that acceptance of the Government's rationales would not authorize a general federal police power, he is unable to identify any activity that the States may regulate but Congress may not. [Justice] Breyer focuses, for the most part, on the threat that firearm possession in and near schools poses to the educational process and the potential economic consequences flowing from that threat. Specifically, the dissent reasons that (1) gun-related violence is a serious problem; (2) that problem, in turn, has an adverse effect on classroom learning; and (3) that adverse effect on classroom learning, in turn, represents a substantial threat to trade and commerce. This analysis would be equally applicable, if not more so, to subjects such as family law and direct regulation of education.

For instance, if Congress can, pursuant to its Commerce Clause power, regulate activities that adversely affect the learning environment, then, a fortiori, it also can regulate the educational process directly. Congress could determine that a school's curriculum has a "significant" effect on the extent of classroom learning. As a result, Congress could mandate a federal curriculum for local elementary and secondary schools because what is taught in local schools has a significant "effect on classroom learning," and that, in turn, has a substantial effect on interstate commerce. [Justice] Breyer's rationale lacks any real limits because, depending on the level of generality, any activity can be looked upon as commercial. Under the dissent's rationale, Congress could just as easily look at child rearing as "fall[ing] on the commercial side of the line" because it provides a "valuable service—namely, to equip [children] with the skills they need to survive in life and, more specifically, in the workplace." Ibid. We do not doubt that Congress has authority under the Commerce Clause to regulate numerous commercial activities that substantially affect interstate commerce and also affect the educational process. That authority, though broad, does not include the authority to regulate each and every aspect of local schools.

Admittedly, a determination whether an intrastate activity is commercial or noncommercial may in some cases result in legal uncertainty. But, so long as Congress' authority is limited to those powers enumerated in the Constitution, and so long as those enumerated powers are interpreted as having judicially enforceable outer limits, congressional legislation under the Commerce Clause always will engender "legal uncertainty." [The] Constitution mandates this uncertainty by withholding from Congress a plenary police power that would authorize enactment of every type of legislation. Congress has operated within this framework of legal uncertainty ever since this Court determined that it was the judiciary's duty "to say what the law is." Marbury v. Madison. Any possible benefit from eliminating this "legal uncertainty" would be at the expense of the Constitution's system of enumerated powers.

In Jones & Laughlin, we held that the question of congressional power under the Commerce Clause "is necessarily one of degree." To the same effect is the concurring opinion of Justice Cardozo in Schecter Poultry: "There is a view of causation that would obliterate the distinction of what is national and what is local in the activities of commerce. Motion at the outer rim is communicated perceptibly, though minutely, to recording instruments at the center. A society such as ours 'is an elastic medium which transmits all tremors throughout its territory; the only question is of their size.' " These are not precise formulations, and in the nature of things they cannot be. But we think they point the way to a correct decision of this case. The possession of a gun in a local school zone is in no sense an economic activity that might, through repetition elsewhere, substantially affect any sort of interstate commerce. Respondent was a local student at a local school; there is no indication that he had recently moved in interstate commerce, and there is no requirement that his possession of the firearm have any concrete tie to interstate commerce.

To uphold the Government's contentions here, we would have to pile inference upon inference in a manner that would bid fair to convert congressional authority under the Commerce Clause to a general police power of the sort retained by the States. Admittedly, some of our prior cases have taken long steps down that road, giving great deference to congressional action. The broad language in these opinions has suggested the possibility of additional expansion, but we decline here to proceed any further. To do so would require us to conclude that the Constitution's enumeration of powers does not presuppose something not enumerated, and that there never will be a distinction between what is truly national and what is truly local. This we are unwilling to do.

[Affirmed.]

Justice KENNEDY, with whom Justice O'CONNOR joins, concurring.

The history of the judicial struggle to interpret the Commerce Clause during the transition from the economic system the Founders knew to the single, national market still emergent in our own era counsels great restraint before the Court determines that the Clause is insufficient to support an exercise of the national power. That history gives me some pause about today's decision, but I join the Court's.

[Chief] Justice Marshall announced that the national authority reaches "that commerce which concerns more States than óne" and that the commerce power "is complete in itself, may be exercised to its utmost extent, and acknowledges no limitations, other than are prescribed in the constitution." Gibbons. His statements can be understood now as an early and authoritative recognition that the Commerce Clause grants Congress extensive power and ample discretion to determine its appropriate exercise. The progression of our Commerce Clause cases from Gibbons to the present was not marked, however, by a coherent or consistent course of interpretation; for neither the course of technological advance nor the foundational principles for the jurisprudence itself were self-evident to the courts that sought to resolve contemporary disputes by enduring principles.

[At] the midpoint of the 19th century, the Court embraced the principle that the States and the National Government both have authority to regulate certain matters absent the congressional determination to displace local law or the necessity for the Court to invalidate local law because of the dormant national power. Cooley v. Board of Wardens. But the utility of that solution was not at once apparent, and difficulties of application persisted. One approach the Court used to inquire into the lawfulness of state authority was to draw content-based or subject-matter distinctions, thus defining by semantic or formalistic categories those activities that were commerce and those that were not. For instance, in deciding that a State could prohibit the in-state manufacture of liquor intended for out-of-state shipment, it distinguished between manufacture and commerce. Though that approach likely would not have survived even if confined to the question of a State's authority to enact legislation, it was not at all propitious when applied to the quite different question of what subjects were within the reach of the national power when Congress chose to exercise it.

This became evident when the Court began to confront federal economic regulation enacted in response to the rapid industrial development in the late 19th century. Thus, it relied upon the manufacture-commerce dichotomy in E.C. Knight. [Conspiracies] to control manufacture, agriculture, mining, production, wages, or prices, the Court explained, had too "indirect" an effect on interstate commerce. [Even] before the Court committed itself to sustaining federal legislation on broad principles of economic practicality, it found it necessary to depart from these decisions. The Court disavowed E.C. Knight's reliance on the manufacturing-commerce distinction in Standard Oil Co. of New Jersey v. United States, 221 U.S. 1 (1911), declaring that approach "unsound." [In] another line of cases, the Court addressed Congress' efforts to impede local activities it considered undesirable by prohibiting the interstate movement of some essential element. In the Lottery Case, the Court rejected the argument that Congress lacked power to prohibit the interstate movement of lottery tickets because it had power only to regulate, not to prohibit. In Hammer v. Dagenhart, however, the Court insisted that the power to regulate commerce "is directly the contrary of the assumed right to forbid commerce from moving," and struck down a prohibition on the interstate transportation of goods manufactured in violation of child labor laws.

Even while it was experiencing difficulties in finding satisfactory principles in these cases, the Court was pursuing a more sustainable and practical approach in other lines of decisions, particularly those involving the regulation of railroad rates. [Even] the most confined interpretation of "commerce" would embrace transportation between the States, so the rate cases posed much less difficulty for the Court than cases involving manufacture or production. Nevertheless, the Court's recognition of the importance of a practical conception of the commerce power was not altogether confined to the rate cases. In Swift, the Court [explained] that "commerce among the States is not a technical legal conception, but a practical one, drawn from the course of business." [Reluctance] of the Court to adopt that approach in all of its cases caused inconsistencies in doctrine to persist, however. In addressing New Deal legislation the Court resuscitated the abandoned abstract distinction between direct and indirect effects on interstate commerce.

The case that seems to mark the Court's definitive commitment to the practical conception of the commerce power is Jones & Laughlin, where the Court sustained labor laws that applied to manufacturing facilities, making no real attempt to distinguish Carter and Schechter. The deference given to Congress has since been confirmed. Darby overruled Hammer v. Dagenhart. And in Wickard, the Court disapproved E.C. Knight and the entire line of direct-indirect and manufacture-production cases. [Later] examples of the exercise of federal power where commercial transactions were the subject of regulation include Heart of Atlanta Motel, Katzenbach v. McClung, and Perez v. United States. These and like authorities are within the fair ambit of the Court's practical conception of commercial regulation and are not called in question by our decision today.

The history of our Commerce Clause decisions contains at least two lessons of relevance to this case. The first [is] the imprecision of content-based boundaries used without more to define the limits of the Commerce Clause. The second, [of] even greater consequence, is that the Court as an institution and the legal system as a whole have an immense stake in the stability of our Commerce Clause jurisprudence as it has evolved to this point. Stare decisis operates with great force in counseling us not to call in question the essential principles now in place respecting the congressional power to regulate transactions of a commercial nature. That fundamental restraint on our power forecloses us from reverting to an understanding of commerce that would serve only an 18th–century economy, dependent then upon production and trading practices that had changed but little over the preceding centuries; it also mandates against returning to the time when congressional authority to regulate undoubted commercial activities was limited by a judicial determination that those matters had an insufficient connection to an interstate system. Congress can regulate in the commercial sphere on the assumption that we have a single market and a unified purpose to build a stable national economy. [It] does not follow, however, that in every instance the Court lacks the authority and responsibility to review congressional attempts to alter the federal balance. This case requires us to consider our place in the design of the Government and to appreciate the significance of federalism in the whole structure of the Constitution.

Of the various structural elements in the Constitution, separation of powers, checks and balances, judicial review, and federalism, only concerning the last does there seem to be much uncertainty respecting the existence, and the content, of standards that allow the judiciary to play a significant role in maintaining the design contemplated by the Framers. Although the resolution of specific cases has proved difficult, we have derived from the Constitution workable standards to assist in preserving separation of powers and checks and balances. These standards are by now well accepted. Judicial review is also established beyond question, and though we may differ when applying its principles, its legitimacy is undoubted. Our role in preserving the federal balance seems more tenuous.

There is irony in this, because of the four structural elements in the Constitution just mentioned, federalism was the unique contribution of the Framers to political science and political theory. Though on the surface the idea may seem counterintuitive, it was the insight of the Framers that freedom was enhanced by the creation of two governments, not one. The theory that two governments accord more liberty than one requires for its realization two distinct and discernable lines of political accountability: one between the citizens and the Federal Government; the second between the citizens and the States. If, as Madison expected, the federal and state governments are to control each other and hold each other in check by competing for the affections of the people, those citizens must have some means of knowing which of the two governments to hold accountable for the failure to perform a given function. Were the Federal Government to take over the regulation of entire areas of traditional state concern, areas having nothing to do with the regulation of commercial activities, the boundaries between the spheres of federal and state authority would blur and political responsibility would become illusory. The resultant inability to hold either branch of the government answerable to the citizens is more dangerous even than devolving too much authority to the remote central power.

To be sure, one conclusion that could be drawn from The Federalist Papers is that the balance between national and state power is entrusted in its entirety to the political process. [Whatever] the judicial role, it is axiomatic that Congress does have substantial discretion and control over the federal balance. For these reasons, it would be mistaken and mischievous for the political branches to forget that the sworn obligation to preserve and protect the Constitution in maintaining the federal balance is their own in the first and primary instance. In the Webster–Hayne Debates and the debates over the Civil Rights Acts, some Congresses have accepted responsibility to confront the great questions of the proper federal balance in terms of lasting consequences for the constitutional design. The political branches of the Government must fulfill this grave constitutional obligation if democratic liberty and the federalism that secures it are to endure.

At the same time, the absence of structural mechanisms to require those officials to undertake this principled task, and the momentary political convenience often attendant upon their failure to do so, argue against a complete renunciation of the judicial role. Although it is the obligation of all officers of the Government to respect the constitutional design, the federal balance is too essential a part of our constitutional structure and plays too vital a role in securing freedom for us to admit inability to intervene when one or the other level of Government has tipped the scales too far.

In the past this Court has participated in maintaining the federal balance through judicial exposition of doctrines such as abstention, the rules for determining the primacy of state law, the doctrine of adequate and independent state grounds, the whole jurisprudence of preemption, and many of the rules governing our habeas jurisprudence. Our ability to preserve this principle under the Commerce Clause has presented a much greater challenge. [But] as the branch whose distinctive duty it is to declare "what the law is," we are often called upon to resolve questions of constitutional law not susceptible to the mechanical application of bright and clear lines. The substantial element of political judgment in Commerce Clause matters leaves our institutional capacity to intervene more in doubt than when we decide cases, for instance, under the Bill of Rights even though clear and bright lines are often absent in the latter class of disputes. But our cases do not teach that we have no role at all in determining the meaning of the Commerce Clause.

[The] statute before us upsets the federal balance to a degree that renders it an unconstitutional assertion of the commerce power, and our intervention is required. [Unlike] the earlier cases to come before the Court here neither the actors nor their conduct have a commercial character, and neither the purposes nor the design of the statute have an evident commercial nexus. The statute makes the simple possession of a gun within 1,000 feet of the grounds of the school a criminal offense. In a sense any conduct in this interdependent world of ours has an ultimate commercial origin or consequence, but we have not yet said the commerce power may reach so far. If Congress attempts that extension, then at the least we must inquire whether the exercise of national power seeks to intrude upon an area of traditional state concern.

An interference of these dimensions occurs here, for it is well established that education is a traditional concern of the States. The proximity to schools, including of course schools owned and operated by the States or their subdivisions, is the very premise for making the conduct criminal. In these circumstances, we have a particular duty to insure that the federal-state balance is not destroyed.

While it is doubtful that any State, or indeed any reasonable person, would argue that it is wise policy to allow students to carry guns on school premises, considerable disagreement exists about how best to accomplish that goal. In this circumstance, the theory and utility of our federalism are revealed, for the States may perform their role as laboratories for experimentation to devise various solutions where the best solution is far from clear. If a State or municipality determines that harsh criminal sanctions are necessary and wise to deter students from carrying guns on school premises, the reserved powers of the States are sufficient to enact those measures. Indeed, over 40 States already have criminal laws outlawing the possession of firearms on or near school grounds. Other, more practicable means to rid the schools of guns may be thought by the citizens of some States to be preferable for the safety and welfare of the schools those States are charged with maintaining. These might include inducements to inform on violators where the information leads to arrests or confiscation of the guns; programs to encourage the voluntary surrender of guns with some provision for amnesty; penalties imposed on parents or guardians for failure to supervise the child; laws providing for suspension or expulsion of gun-toting students, or programs for expulsion with assignment to special facilities.

The statute now before us forecloses the States from experimenting and exercising their own judgment in an area to which States lay claim by right of history and expertise, and it does so by regulating an activity beyond the realm of commerce in the ordinary and usual sense of that term. The tendency of this statute to displace state regulation in areas of traditional state concern is evident from its territorial operation. There are over 100,000 elementary and secondary schools in the United States. Each of these now has an invisible federal zone extending 1,000 feet beyond the (often irregular) boundaries of the school property. In some communities no doubt it would be difficult to navigate without infringing on those zones. Yet throughout these areas, school officials would find their own programs for the prohibition of guns in danger of displacement by the federal authority unless the State chooses to enact a parallel rule. [Absent] a stronger connection or identification with commercial concerns that are central to the Commerce Clause, [this] interference contradicts the federal balance the Framers designed and that this Court is obliged to enforce....

Justice THOMAS, concurring.

The Court today properly concludes that the Commerce Clause does not grant Congress the authority to prohibit gun possession within 1,000 feet of a school, as it attempted to do in the Gun–Free School Zones Act of 1990. Although I join the majority, I write separately to observe that our case law has drifted far from the original understanding of the Commerce Clause. In a future case, we ought to temper our Commerce Clause jurisprudence in a manner that both makes sense of our more recent case law and is more faithful to the original understanding of that Clause.

We have said that Congress may regulate not only "Commerce ... among the several states," but also anything that has a "substantial effect" on such commerce. This test, if taken to its logical extreme, would give Congress a "police power" over all aspects of American life. Unfortunately, we have never come to grips with this implication of our substantial effects formula. Although we have supposedly applied the substantial effects test for the past 60 years, we always have rejected readings of the Commerce Clause and the scope of federal power that would permit Congress to exercise a police power; our cases are quite clear that there are real limits to federal power. Indeed, on this crucial point, the majority and Justice Breyer agree in principle: the Federal Government has nothing approaching a police power.

While the principal dissent concedes that there are limits to federal power, the sweeping nature of our current test enables the dissent to argue that Congress can regulate gun possession. But it seems to me that the power to regulate "commerce" can by no means encompass authority over mere gun possession, any more than it empowers the Federal Government to regulate marriage, littering, or cruelty to animals, throughout the 50 States. Our Constitution quite properly leaves such matters to the individual States, notwithstanding these activities' effects on interstate commerce. Any interpretation of the Commerce Clause that even suggests that Congress could regulate such matters is in need of reexamination.

In an appropriate case, I believe that we must further reconsider our "substantial effects" test with an eye toward constructing a standard that reflects the text and history of the Commerce Clause without totally rejecting our more recent Commerce Clause jurisprudence. Today, however, I merely support the Court's conclusion with a discussion of the text, structure, and history of the Commerce Clause and an analysis of our early case law. My goal is simply to show how far we have departed from the original understanding and to demonstrate that the result we reach today is by no means "radical." I also want to point out the necessity of refashioning a coherent test that does not tend to "obliterate the distinction between what is national and what is local and create a completely centralized government." Jones & Laughlin.

I. At the time the original Constitution was ratified, "commerce" consisted of selling, buying, and bartering, as well as transporting for these purposes. See 1 S. Johnson, A Dictionary of the English Language (4th ed. 1773) (defining commerce as "Intercour[s]e; exchange of one thing for another; interchange of any thing; trade; traffick"). This understanding finds support in the etymology of the word, which literally means "with merchandise." See 3 Oxford English Dictionary 552 (2d ed. 1989) (com—"with"; merci—"merchandise"). In fact, when Federalists and Anti–Federalists discussed the Commerce Clause during the ratification period, they often used trade (in its selling/bartering sense) and commerce interchangeably.

As one would expect, the term "commerce" was used in contradistinction to productive activities such as manufacturing and agriculture. Alexander Hamilton, for example, repeatedly treated commerce, agriculture, and manufacturing as three separate endeavors. The same distinctions were made in the state ratification conventions.

Moreover, interjecting a modern sense of commerce into the Constitution generates significant textual and structural problems. For example, one cannot replace "commerce" with a different type of enterprise, such as manufacturing. When a manufacturer produces a car, assembly cannot take place "with a foreign nation" or "with the Indian Tribes." Parts may come from different States or other nations and hence may have been in the flow of commerce at one time, but manufacturing takes place at a discrete site. Agriculture and manufacturing involve the production of goods; commerce encompasses traffic in such articles.

[The] Constitution not only uses the word "commerce" in a narrower sense than our case law might suggest, it also does not support the proposition that Congress has authority over all activities that "substantially affect" interstate commerce. The Commerce Clause does not state that Congress may "regulate matters that substantially affect commerce with foreign Nations, and among the several States, and with the Indian Tribes." In contrast, the Constitution itself temporarily prohibited amendments that would "affect" Congress' lack of authority to prohibit or restrict the slave trade or to enact unproportioned direct taxation. Clearly, the Framers could have drafted a Constitution that contained a "substantially affects interstate commerce" clause had that been their objective.

In addition to its powers under the Commerce Clause, Congress has the authority to enact such laws as are "necessary and proper" to carry into execution its power to regulate commerce among the several States. But on this Court's understanding of congressional power under these two Clauses, many of Congress' other enumerated powers under Art. I, § 8 are wholly superfluous. After all, if Congress may regulate all matters that substantially affect commerce, there is no need for the Constitution to specify that Congress may enact bankruptcy laws, or coin money and fix the standard of weights and measures, or punish counterfeiters of United States coin and securities. Likewise, Congress would not need the separate authority to establish post offices and post roads, or to grant patents and copyrights, or to "punish Piracies and Felonies committed on the high Seas," It might not even need the power to raise and support an Army and Navy, for fewer people would engage in commercial shipping if they thought that a foreign power could expropriate their property with ease. Indeed, if Congress could regulate matters that substantially affect interstate commerce, there would have been no need to specify that Congress can regulate international trade and commerce with the Indians. As the Framers surely understood, these other branches of trade substantially affect interstate commerce.

Put simply, much if not all of Art. I, § 8 (including portions of the Commerce Clause itself) would be surplusage if Congress had been given authority over matters that substantially affect interstate commerce.

An interpretation of cl. 3 that makes the rest of § 8 superfluous simply cannot be correct. Yet this Court's Commerce Clause jurisprudence has endorsed just such an interpretation: the power we have accorded Congress has swallowed Art. I, § 8. Indeed, if a "substantial effects" test can be appended to the Commerce Clause, why not to every other power of the Federal Government? There is no reason for singling out the Commerce Clause for special treatment. Accordingly, Congress could regulate all matters that "substantially affect" the Army and Navy, bankruptcies, tax collection, expenditures, and so on. In that case, the clauses of § 8 all mutually overlap, something we can assume the Founding Fathers never intended.

Our construction of the scope of congressional authority has the additional problem of coming close to turning the Tenth Amendment on its head. Our case law could be read to reserve to the United States all powers not expressly prohibited by the Constitution. Taken together, these fundamental textual problems should, at the very least, convince us that the "substantial effects" test should be reexamined.

II. The exchanges during the ratification campaign reveal the relatively limited reach of the Commerce Clause and of federal power generally. The Founding Fathers confirmed that most areas of life (even many matters that would have substantial effects on commerce) would remain outside the reach of the Federal Government. Such affairs would continue to be under the exclusive control of the States.

Early Americans understood that commerce, manufacturing, and agriculture, while distinct activities, were intimately related and dependent on each other—that each "substantially affected" the others. After all, items produced by farmers and manufacturers were the primary articles of commerce at the time. If commerce was more robust as a result of federal superintendence, farmers and manufacturers could benefit. Thus, Oliver Ellsworth of Connecticut attempted to convince farmers of the benefits of regulating commerce. "Your property and riches depend on a ready demand and generous price for the produce you can annually spare," he wrote, and these conditions exist "where trade flourishes and when the merchant can freely export the produce of the country" to nations that will pay the highest price. Yet, despite being well aware that agriculture, manufacturing, and other matters substantially affected commerce, the founding generation did not cede authority over all these activities to Congress. [It was a] well-known truth that the new Government would have only the limited and enumerated powers found in the Constitution. Agriculture and manufacture, since they were not surrendered to the Federal Government, were state concerns. Even before the passage of the Tenth Amendment, it was apparent that Congress would possess only those powers "herein granted" by the rest of the Constitution.

Where the Constitution was meant to grant federal authority over an activity substantially affecting interstate commerce, the Constitution contains an enumerated power over that particular activity. Indeed, the Framers knew that many of the other enumerated powers in § 8 dealt with matters that substantially affected interstate commerce. Madison, for instance, spoke of the bankruptcy power as being "intimately connected with the regulation of commerce." Federalist 42. Likewise, Hamilton urged that "[i]f we mean to be a commercial people or even to be secure on our Atlantic side, we must endeavour as soon as possible to have a navy." Federalist 24.

In short, the Founding Fathers were well aware of what the principal dissent calls " 'economic . . . realities.' " Even though the boundary between commerce and other matters may ignore "economic reality" and thus seem arbitrary or artificial to some, we must nevertheless respect a constitutional line that does not grant Congress power over all that substantially affects interstate commerce.

III. If the principal dissent's understanding of our early case law were correct, there might be some reason to doubt this view of the original understanding of the Constitution. According to that dissent, Chief Justice Marshall's opinion in Gibbons established that Congress may control all local activities that "significantly affect interstate commerce." And, "with the exception of one wrong turn subsequently corrected," this has been the "traditiona[l]" method of interpreting the Commerce Clause. In my view, the dissent is wrong about the holding and reasoning of Gibbons. Because this error leads the dissent to characterize the first 150 years of this Court's case law as a "wrong turn," I feel compelled to put the last 50 years in proper perspective.

A. In Gibbons, the Court examined whether a federal law that licensed ships to engage in the "coasting trade" preempted a New York law granting a 30–year monopoly to Robert Livingston and Robert Fulton to navigate the State's waterways by steamship. In concluding that it did, the Court noted that Congress could regulate "navigation" because "[a]ll America . . . has uniformly understood, the word 'commerce,' to comprehend navigation. It was so understood, and must have been so understood, when the constitution was framed." The Court also observed that federal power over commerce "among the several States" meant that Congress could regulate commerce conducted partly within a State. Because a portion of interstate commerce and foreign commerce would almost always take place within one or more States, federal power over interstate and foreign commerce necessarily would extend into the States.

At the same time, the Court took great pains to make clear that Congress could not regulate commerce "which is completely internal, which is carried on between man and man in a State, or between different parts of the same State, and which does not extend to or affect other States." Moreover, while suggesting that the Constitution might not permit States to regulate interstate or foreign commerce, the Court observed that "[i]nspection laws, quarantine laws, health laws of every description, as well as laws for regulating the internal commerce of a State" were but a small part "of that immense mass of legislation . . . not surrendered to a general government." From an early moment, the Court rejected the notion that Congress can regulate everything that affects interstate commerce. That the internal commerce of the States and the numerous state inspection, quarantine, and health laws had substantial effects on interstate commerce cannot be doubted. Nevertheless, they were not "surrendered to the general government."

Of course, the principal dissent is not the first to misconstrue Gibbons. For instance, the Court has stated that Gibbons "described the federal commerce power with a breadth never yet exceeded." Wickard. I believe that this misreading stems from two statements in Gibbons.

First, the Court made the uncontroversial claim that federal power does not encompass "commerce" that "does not extend to or affect other States." From this statement, the principal dissent infers that whenever an activity affects interstate commerce, it necessarily follows that Congress can regulate such activities. Of course, Chief Justice Marshall said no such thing and the inference the dissent makes cannot be drawn. There is a much better interpretation of the "affect[s]" language: because the Court had earlier noted that the commerce power did not extend to wholly intrastate commerce, the Court was acknowledging that although the line between intrastate and interstate/foreign commerce would be difficult to draw, federal authority could not be construed to cover purely intrastate commerce. Commerce that did not affect another State could never be said to be commerce "among the several States."

But even if one were to adopt the dissent's reading, the "affect[s]" language, at most, permits Congress to regulate only intrastate commerce that substantially affects interstate and foreign commerce. There is no reason to believe that Chief Justice Marshall was asserting that Congress could regulate all activities that affect interstate commerce.

The second source of confusion stems from the Court's praise for the Constitution's division of power between the States and the Federal Government: "The genius and character of the whole government seem to be, that its action is to be applied to all the external concerns of the nation, and to those internal concerns which affect the States generally; but not to those which are completely within a particular State, which do not affect other States, and with which it is not necessary to interfere, for the purpose of executing some of the general powers of the government."

In this passage, the Court merely was making the well understood point that the Constitution commits matters of "national" concern to Congress and leaves "local" matters to the States. The Court was not saying that whatever Congress believes is a national matter becomes an object of federal control. The matters of national concern are enumerated in the Constitution: war, taxes, patents, and copyrights, uniform rules of naturalization and bankruptcy, types of commerce, and so on. Gibbons' emphatic statements that Congress could not regulate many matters that affect commerce confirm that the Court did not read the Commerce Clause as granting Congress control over matters that "affect the States generally." Gibbons simply cannot be construed as the principal dissent would have it.

B. I am aware of no cases prior to the New Deal that characterized the power flowing from the Commerce Clause as sweepingly as does our substantial effects test. My review of the case law indicates that the substantial effects test is but an innovation of the 20th century.

Even before Gibbons, Chief Justice Marshall, [in] Cohens v. Virginia, noted that Congress had "no general right to punish murder committed within any of the States," and that it was "clear that congress cannot punish felonies generally.". The Court's only qualification was that Congress could enact such laws for places where it enjoyed plenary powers—for instance, over the District of Columbia. Thus, whatever effect ordinary murders, or robbery, or gun possession might have on interstate commerce (or on any other subject of federal concern) was irrelevant to the question of congressional power.

United States v. Dewitt, 9 Wall. 41 (1870), marked the first time the Court struck down a federal law as exceeding the power conveyed by the Commerce Clause. In a two-page opinion, the Court invalidated a nationwide law prohibiting all sales of naphtha and illuminating oils. In so doing, the Court remarked that the Commerce Clause "has always been understood as limited by its terms; and as a virtual denial of any power to interfere with the internal trade and business of the separate States." The law in question was "plainly a regulation of police," which could have constitutional application only where Congress had exclusive authority, such as the territories.

In E.C. Knight, this Court held that mere attempts to monopolize the manufacture of sugar could not be regulated pursuant to the Commerce Clause. Raising echoes of the discussions of the Framers regarding the intimate relationship between commerce and manufacturing, the Court declared that "[c]ommerce succeeds to manufacture, and is not a part of it." [Whether] or not manufacturing, agriculture, or other matters substantially affected interstate commerce was irrelevant. As recently as 1936, the Court continued to insist that the Commerce Clause did not reach the wholly internal business of the States. Carter v. Carter Coal Co. The Federal Government simply could not reach such subjects regardless of their effects on interstate commerce.

These cases all establish a simple point: from the time of the ratification of the Constitution to the mid–1930's, it was widely understood that the Constitution granted Congress only limited powers, notwithstanding the Commerce Clause. Moreover, there was no question that activities wholly separated from business, such as gun possession, were beyond the reach of the commerce power. If anything, the "wrong turn" was the Court's dramatic departure in the 1930's from a century and a half of precedent.

IV. Apart from its recent vintage and its corresponding lack of any grounding in the original understanding of the Constitution, the substantial effects test suffers from the further flaw that it appears to grant Congress a police power over the Nation. When asked at oral argument if there were any limits to the Commerce Clause, the Government was at a loss for words. Likewise, the principal dissent insists that there are limits, but it cannot muster even one example. Indeed, the dissent implicitly concedes that its reading has no limits when it criticizes the Court for "threaten[ing] legal uncertainty in an area of law that ...

seemed reasonably well settled." The one advantage of the dissent's standard is certainty: it is certain that under its analysis everything may be regulated under the guise of the Commerce Clause.

The substantial effects test suffers from this flaw, in part, because of its "aggregation principle." Under so-called "class of activities" statutes, Congress can regulate whole categories of activities that are not themselves either "interstate" or "commerce." In applying the effects test, we ask whether the class of activities as a whole substantially affects interstate commerce, not whether any specific activity within the class has such effects when considered in isolation.

The aggregation principle is clever, but has no stopping point. Suppose all would agree that gun possession within 1,000 feet of a school does not substantially affect commerce, but that possession of weapons generally (knives, brass knuckles, nunchakus, etc.) does. Under our substantial effects doctrine, even though Congress cannot single out gun possession, it can prohibit weapon possession generally. But one always can draw the circle broadly enough to cover an activity that, when taken in isolation, would not have substantial effects on commerce. Under our jurisprudence, if Congress passed an omnibus "substantially affects interstate commerce" statute, purporting to regulate every aspect of human existence, the Act apparently would be constitutional. Even though particular sections may govern only trivial activities, the statute in the aggregate regulates matters that substantially affect commerce.

V. This extended discussion of the original understanding and our first century and a half of case law does not necessarily require a wholesale abandonment of our more recent opinions.[2] It simply reveals that our substantial effects test is far removed from both the Constitution and from our early case law and that the Court's opinion should not be viewed as "radical" or another "wrong turn" that must be corrected in the future. The analysis also suggests that we ought to temper our Commerce Clause jurisprudence.

Unless the dissenting Justices are willing to repudiate our long-held understanding of the limited nature of federal power, I would think that they too must be willing to reconsider the substantial effects test in a future case. If we wish to be true to a Constitution that does not cede a police power to the Federal Government, our Commerce Clause's boundaries simply cannot be "defined" as being " 'commensurate with the national needs' " or self-consciously intended to let the Federal Government " 'defend itself against economic forces that Congress decrees inimical or destructive of the national economy.' " Such a formulation of federal power is no test at all: it is a blank check.

At an appropriate juncture, I think we must modify our Commerce Clause jurisprudence. Today, it is easy enough to say that the Clause certainly does not empower Congress to ban gun possession within 1,000 feet of a school.

---

2. Although I might be willing to return to the original understanding, I recognize that many believe that it is too late in the day to undertake a fundamental reexamination of the past 60 years. Consideration of stare decisis and reliance interests may convince us that we cannot wipe the slate clean. [Footnote by Justice Thomas.]

Justice STEVENS, dissenting.

The welfare of our future "Commerce with foreign Nations, and among the several States" is vitally dependent on the character of the education of our children. I therefore agree entirely with Justice Breyer's explanation of why Congress has ample power to prohibit the possession of firearms in or near schools—just as it may protect the school environment from harms posed by controlled substances such as asbestos or alcohol. I also agree with Justice Souter's exposition of the radical character of the Court's holding and its kinship with the discredited, pre-Depression version of substantive due process. I believe, however, that the Court's extraordinary decision merits this additional comment.

Guns are both articles of commerce and articles that can be used to restrain commerce. Their possession is the consequence, either directly or indirectly, of commercial activity. In my judgment, Congress' power to regulate commerce in firearms includes the power to prohibit possession of guns at any location because of their potentially harmful use; it necessarily follows that Congress may also prohibit their possession in particular markets. The market for the possession of handguns by school-age children is, distressingly, substantial. Whether or not the national interest in eliminating that market would have justified federal legislation in 1789, it surely does today.

Justice SOUTER, dissenting.

In reviewing congressional legislation under the Commerce Clause, we defer to what is often a merely implicit congressional judgment that its regulation addresses a subject substantially affecting interstate commerce "if there is any rational basis for such a finding." Hodel v. Virginia Surface Mining & Reclamation Assn., Inc., 452 U.S. 264 (1981). If that congressional determination is within the realm of reason, "the only remaining question for judicial inquiry is whether 'the means chosen by Congress [are] reasonably adapted to the end permitted by the Constitution.'" Hodel, quoting Heart of Atlanta Motel.

The practice of deferring to rationally based legislative judgments "is a paradigm of judicial restraint." FCC v. Beach Communications, Inc., 508 U.S. ___ (1993). In judicial review under the Commerce Clause, it reflects our respect for the institutional competence of the Congress on a subject expressly assigned to it by the Constitution and our appreciation of the legitimacy that comes from Congress's political accountability in dealing with matters open to a wide range of possible choices.

It was not ever thus, however, as even a brief overview of Commerce Clause history during the past century reminds us. The modern respect for the competence and primacy of Congress in matters affecting commerce developed only after one of this Court's most chastening experiences, when it perforce repudiated an earlier and untenably expansive conception of judicial review in derogation of congressional commerce power. A look at history's sequence will serve to show how today's decision tugs the Court off course, leading it to suggest opportunities for further developments that would be at odds with the rule of restraint to which the Court still wisely states adherence.

I. Notwithstanding the Court's recognition of a broad commerce power in Gibbons, Congress saw few occasions to exercise that power prior to Reconstruction, and it was really the passage of the Interstate Commerce Act of 1887 that opened a new age of congressional reliance on the Commerce Clause for authority to exercise general police powers at the national level. Although the Court upheld a fair amount of the ensuing legislation as being within the commerce power, the period from the turn of the century to 1937 is better noted for a series of cases applying highly formalistic notions of "commerce" to invalidate federal social and economic legislation.

These restrictive views of commerce subject to congressional power complemented the Court's activism in limiting the enforceable scope of state economic regulation. It is most familiar history that during this same period the Court routinely invalidated state social and economic legislation under an expansive conception of Fourteenth Amendment substantive due process. The fulcrums of judicial review in these cases were the notions of liberty and property characteristic of laissez-faire economics, whereas the Commerce Clause cases turned on what was ostensibly a structural limit of federal power, but under each conception of judicial review the Court's character for the first third of the century showed itself in exacting judicial scrutiny of a legislature's choice of economic ends and of the legislative means selected to reach them.

It was not merely coincidental, then, that sea changes in the Court's conceptions of its authority under the Due Process and Commerce Clauses occurred virtually together, in 1937, with West Coast Hotel v. Parrish [12 Ed., p. 455] and NLRB v. Jones & Laughlin Steel. In West Coast Hotel, the Court's rejection of a due process challenge to a state law fixing minimum wages for women and children marked the abandonment of its expansive protection of contractual freedom. Two weeks later, Jones & Laughlin affirmed congressional commerce power to authorize NLRB injunctions against unfair labor practices. The Court's finding that the regulated activity had a direct enough effect on commerce has since been seen as beginning the abandonment, for practical purposes, of the formalistic distinction between direct and indirect effects.

In the years following these decisions, deference to legislative policy judgments on commercial regulation became the powerful theme under both the Due Process and Commerce Clauses, and in due course that deference became articulate in the standard of rationality review. In due process litigation, the Court's statement of a rational basis test came quickly. The parallel formulation of the Commerce Clause test came later, only because complete elimination of the direct/indirect effects dichotomy and acceptance of the cumulative effects doctrine, Wickard, so far settled the pressing issues of congressional power over commerce as to leave the Court for years without any need to phrase a test explicitly deferring to rational legislative judgments. The moment came, however, with the challenge to congressional Commerce Clause authority to prohibit racial discrimination in places of public accommodation, when the Court simply made explicit what the earlier cases had implied: "where we find that the legislators, in light of the facts and testimony before them, have a rational basis for finding a chosen regulatory scheme necessary to the protection of commerce, our investigation is at an end." Katzenbach v. McClung. Thus, under commerce, as under due process, adoption of rational basis review expressed the recognition that the Court had no sustainable basis for subjecting economic regulation as such to judicial policy judgments, and for the past half-century the Court has no more turned back in the direction of formalistic Commerce Clause review (as in deciding whether regulation of commerce was sufficiently direct) than it has inclined toward reasserting the substantive authority of Lochner due process (as in the inflated protection of contractual autonomy).

II. There is today, however, a backward glance at both the old pitfalls, as the Court treats deference under the rationality rule as subject to gradation according to the commercial or noncommercial nature of the immediate subject of the challenged regulation. The distinction between what is patently commercial and what is not looks much like the old distinction between what directly affects commerce and what touches it only indirectly. And the act of calibrating the level of deference by drawing a line between what is patently commercial and what is less purely so will probably resemble the process of deciding how much interference with contractual freedom was fatal. Thus, it seems fair to ask whether the step taken by the Court today does anything but portend a return to the untenable jurisprudence from which the Court extricated itself almost 60 years ago. The answer is not reassuring. To be sure, the occasion for today's decision reflects the century's end, not its beginning. But if it seems anomalous that the Congress of the United States has taken to regulating school yards, the act in question is still probably no more remarkable than state regulation of bake shops 90 years ago. In any event, there is no reason to hope that the Court's qualification of rational basis review will be any more successful than the efforts at substantive economic review made by our predecessors as the century began. Taking the Court's opinion on its own terms, Justice BREYER has explained both the hopeless porosity of "commercial" character as a ground of Commerce Clause distinction in America's highly connected economy, and the inconsistency of this categorization with our rational basis precedents from the last 50 years.

Further glosses on rationality review, moreover, may be in the offing. Although this case turns on commercial character, the Court gestures toward two other considerations that it might sometime entertain in applying rational basis scrutiny (apart from a statutory obligation to supply independent proof of a jurisdictional element): does the congressional statute deal with subjects of traditional state regulation, and does the statute contain explicit factual findings supporting the otherwise implicit determination that the regulated activity substantially affects interstate commerce? Once again, any appeal these considerations may have depends on ignoring the painful lesson learned in 1937, for neither of the Court's suggestions would square with rational basis scrutiny.

A. The Court observes that the Gun–Free School Zones Act operates in two areas traditionally subject to legislation by the States, education and enforcement of criminal law. The suggestion is either that a connection between commerce and these subjects is remote, or that the commerce power is simply weaker when it touches subjects on which the States have historically been the primary legislators. Neither suggestion is tenable. As for remoteness, it may or may not be wise for the National Government to deal with education, but Justice Breyer has surely demonstrated that the commercial prospects of an illiterate State or Nation are not rosy, and no argument should be needed to show that hijacking interstate shipments of cigarettes can affect commerce substantially, even though the States have traditionally prosecuted robbery. And as for the notion that the commerce power diminishes the closer it gets to customary state concerns, that idea has been flatly rejected, and not long ago. The commerce power, we have often observed, is plenary. Justice Harlan put it this way in speaking for the Court in Maryland v. Wirtz: "There is no general doctrine implied in the Federal Constitution that the two governments, national and state, are each to exercise its powers so as not to interfere with the free and full exercise of the powers of the other ... [I]t is clear that the Federal Government, when acting within a delegated power, may override countervailing state interests...."

[Nor] is there any contrary authority in the reasoning of our cases imposing clear statement rules in some instances of legislation that would significantly alter the state-national balance. In the absence of a clear statement of congressional design, for example, we have refused to interpret ambiguous federal statutes to limit fundamental state legislative prerogatives, Gregory v. Ashcroft, our understanding being that such prerogatives, through which "a State defines itself as a sovereign," are "powers with which Congress does not readily interfere". Likewise, when faced with two plausible interpretations of a federal criminal statute, we generally will take the alternative that does not force us to impute an intention to Congress to use its full commerce power to regulate conduct traditionally and ably regulated by the States.

These clear statement rules, however, are merely rules of statutory interpretation, to be relied upon only when the terms of a statute allow, and in cases implicating Congress's historical reluctance to trench on state legislative prerogatives or to enter into spheres already occupied by the States. They are rules for determining intent when legislation leaves intent subject to question. But our hesitance to presume that Congress has acted to alter the state-federal status quo (when presented with a plausible alternative) has no relevance whatever to the enquiry whether it has the commerce power to do so or to the standard of judicial review when Congress has definitely meant to exercise that power. Indeed, to allow our hesitance to affect the standard of review would inevitably degenerate into the sort of substantive policy review that the Court found indefensible 60 years ago. The Court does not assert (and could not plausibly maintain) that the commerce power is wholly devoid of congressional authority to speak on any subject of traditional state concern; but if congressional action is not forbidden absolutely when it touches such a subject, it will stand or fall depending on the Court's view of the strength of the legislation's commercial justification. And here once again history raises its objections that the Court's previous essays in overriding congressional policy choices under the Commerce Clause were ultimately seen to suffer two fatal weaknesses: when dealing with Acts of Congress (as distinct from state legislation subject to review under the theory of dormant commerce power) nothing in the Clause compelled the judicial activism, and nothing about the judiciary as an institution made it a superior source of policy on the subject Congress dealt with. There is no reason to expect the lesson would be different another time.

B. There remain questions about legislative findings. The Court of Appeals expressed the view that the result in this case might well have been different if Congress had made explicit findings that guns in schools have a substantial effect on interstate commerce, and the Court today does not repudiate that position. Might a court aided by such findings have subjected this legislation to less exacting scrutiny (or, put another way, should a court have deferred to such findings if Congress had made them)? The answer to either question must be no, although as a general matter findings are important and to be hoped for in the difficult cases.

It is only natural to look for help with a hard job, and reviewing a claim that Congress has exceeded the commerce power is much harder in some cases than in others. A challenge to congressional regulation of interstate garbage hauling would be easy to resolve; review of congressional regulation of gun possession in school yards is more difficult, both because the link to interstate commerce is less obvious and because of our initial ignorance of the relevant facts. In a case comparable to this one, we may have to dig hard to make a responsible judgment about what Congress could reasonably find, because the case may be close, and because judges tend not to be familiar with the facts that may or may not make it close. But while the ease of review may vary from case to case, it does not follow that the standard of review should vary, much less that explicit findings of fact would even directly address the standard.

The question for the courts, as all agree, is not whether as a predicate to legislation Congress in fact found that a particular activity substantially affects interstate commerce. The legislation implies such a finding, and there is no reason to entertain claims that Congress acted ultra vires intentionally. Nor is the question whether Congress was correct in so finding. The only question is whether the legislative judgment is within the realm of reason. Congressional findings do not, however, directly address the question of reasonableness; they tell us what Congress actually has found, not what it could rationally find. If, indeed, the Court were to make the existence of explicit congressional findings dispositive in some close or difficult cases something other than rationality review would be afoot. The resulting congressional obligation to justify its policy choices on the merits would imply either a judicial authority to review the justification (and, hence, the wisdom) of those choices, or authority to require Congress to act with some high degree of deliberateness, of which express findings would be evidence. But review for congressional wisdom would just be the old judicial pretension discredited and abandoned in 1937, and review for deliberateness would be as patently unconstitutional as an Act of Congress mandating long opinions from this Court. Such a legislative process requirement would function merely as an excuse for covert review of the merits of legislation under standards never expressed and more or less arbitrarily applied. Under such a regime, in any case, the rationality standard of review would be a thing of the past.

On the other hand, to say that courts applying the rationality standard may not defer to findings is not, of course, to say that findings are pointless. They may, in fact, have great value in telling courts what to look for, in establishing at least one frame of reference for review, and in citing to factual authority. The research underlying Justice Breyer's dissent was necessarily a major undertaking; help is welcome, and it not incidentally shrinks the risk that judicial research will miss material scattered across the public domain or buried under pounds of legislative record. Congressional findings on a more particular plane than this record illustrates would accordingly have earned judicial thanks. But thanks do not carry the day as long as rational possibility is the touchstone, and I would not allow for the possibility, as the Court's opinion may, that the addition of congressional findings could in principle have affected the fate of the statute here.

III. Because Justice Breyer's opinion demonstrates beyond any doubt that the Act in question passes the rationality review that the Court continues to espouse, today's decision may be seen as only a misstep, its reasoning and its suggestions not quite in gear with the prevailing standard, but hardly an epochal case. I would not argue otherwise, but I would raise a caveat. Not every epochal case has come in epochal trappings. Jones & Laughlin did not reject the direct-indirect standard in so many words; it just said the relation of the regulated subject matter to commerce was direct enough. But we know what happened.

I respectfully dissent.

Justice BREYER, with whom Justice STEVENS, Justice SOUTER, and Justice GINSBURG join, dissenting.

The issue in this case is whether the Commerce Clause authorizes Congress to enact a statute that makes it a crime to possess a gun in, or near, a school. In my view, the statute falls well within the scope of the commerce power as this Court has understood that power over the last half-century.

I. In reaching this conclusion, I apply three basic principles of Commerce Clause interpretation. First, the power to "regulate Commerce ... among the several States," encompasses the power to regulate local activities insofar as they significantly affect interstate commerce. As the majority points out, the Court, in describing how much of an effect the Clause requires, sometimes has used the word "substantial" and sometimes has not. And, as the majority also recognizes in quoting Justice Cardozo, the question of degree (how much effect) requires an estimate of the "size" of the effect that no verbal formulation can capture with precision. I use the word "significant" because the word "substantial" implies a somewhat narrower power than recent precedent suggests. But, to speak of "substantial effect" rather than "significant effect" would make no difference in this case.

Second, in determining whether a local activity will likely have a significant effect upon interstate commerce, a court must consider, not the effect of an individual act (a single instance of gun possession), but rather the cumulative effect of all similar instances (i.e., the effect of all guns possessed in or near schools). Wickard.

Third, the Constitution requires us to judge the connection between a regulated activity and interstate commerce, not directly, but at one remove. Courts must give Congress a degree of leeway in determining the existence of a significant factual connection between the regulated activity and interstate commerce—both because the Constitution delegates the commerce power directly to Congress and because the determination requires an empirical judgment of a kind that a legislature is more likely than a court to make with accuracy. The traditional words "rational basis" capture this leeway. Thus, the specific question before us, as the Court recognizes, is not whether the "regulated activity sufficiently affected interstate commerce," but, rather, whether Congress could have had "a rational basis" for so concluding.

I recognize that we must judge this matter independently. "[S]imply because Congress may conclude that a particular activity substantially affects interstate commerce does not necessarily make it so." Hodel. And, I also recognize that Congress did not write specific "interstate commerce" findings into the law under which Lopez was convicted. Nonetheless, as I have already noted, the matter that we review independently (i.e., whether there is a "rational basis") already has considerable leeway built into it. And, the absence of findings, at most, deprives a statute of the benefit of some extra leeway. This extra deference, in principle, might change the result in a close case, though, in practice, it has not made a critical legal difference. And, it would seem particularly unfortunate to make the validity of the statute at hand turn on the presence or absence of findings. Because Congress did make findings (though not until after Lopez was prosecuted), doing so would appear to elevate form over substance.

In addition, [there] is no special need here for a clear indication of Congress' rationale. The statute does not interfere with the exercise of state or local authority. Moreover, any clear statement rule would apply only to determine Congress' intended result, not to clarify the source of its authority or measure the level of consideration that went into its decision, and here there is no doubt as to which activities Congress intended to regulate.

II. Applying these principles to the case at hand, we must ask whether Congress could have had a rational basis for finding a significant (or substantial) connection between gun-related school violence and interstate commerce. Or, to put the question in the language of the explicit finding that Congress made when it amended this law in 1994: Could Congress rationally have found that "violent crime in school zones," through its effect on the "quality of education," significantly (or substantially) affects "interstate" or "foreign commerce"? As long as one views the commerce connection, not as a "technical legal conception," but as "a practical one," Swift, the answer to this question must be yes. Numerous reports and studies—generated both inside and outside government—make clear that Congress could reasonably have found the empirical connection that its law, implicitly or explicitly, asserts. (See Appendix [omitted here, as are the references to the documentation within the body of the opinion. Ed.] for a sample of the documentation ...)

For one thing, reports, hearings, and other readily available literature make clear that the problem of guns in and around schools is widespread and extremely serious. These materials report, for example, that four percent of American high school students (and six percent of inner-city high school students) carry a gun to school at least occasionally; that 12 percent of urban high school students have had guns fired at them; that 20 percent of those students have been threatened with guns; and that, in any 6-month period, several hundred thousand schoolchildren are victims of violent crimes in or near their schools. And, they report that this widespread violence in schools throughout the Nation significantly interferes with the quality of education in those schools. Based on reports such as these, Congress obviously could have thought that guns and learning are mutually exclusive. And, Congress could therefore have found a substantial educational problem—teachers unable to teach, students unable to learn—and concluded that guns near schools contribute substantially to the size and scope of that problem.

Having found that guns in schools significantly undermine the quality of education in our Nation's classrooms, Congress could also have found, given the effect of education upon interstate and foreign commerce, that gun-related violence in and around schools is a commercial, as well as a human, problem. Education, although far more than a matter of economics, has long been inextricably intertwined with the Nation's economy. When this Nation began, most workers received their education in the workplace, typically (like Benjamin Franklin) as apprentices. As late as the 1920's, many workers still received general education directly from their employers—from large corporations, such as General Electric, Ford, and Goodyear, which created schools within their firms to help both the worker and the firm. As public school enrollment grew in the early 20th century, the need for industry to teach basic educational skills diminished. But, the direct economic link between basic education and industrial productivity remained. Scholars estimate that nearly a quarter of America's economic growth in the early years of this century is traceable directly to increased schooling; that investment in "human capital" (through spending on education) exceeded investment in "physical capital" by a ratio of almost two to one; and that the economic returns to this investment in education exceeded the returns to conventional capital investment.

In recent years the link between secondary education and business has strengthened, becoming both more direct and more important. Scholars on the subject report that technological changes and innovations in management techniques have altered the nature of the workplace so that more jobs now demand greater educational skills. There is evidence that "service, manufacturing or construction jobs are being displaced by technology that requires a better-educated worker or, more likely, are being exported overseas"; that "workers with truly few skills by the year 2000 will find that only one job out of ten will remain"; and that "[o]ver the long haul the best way to encourage the growth of high-wage jobs is to upgrade the skills of the work force."

Increasing global competition also has made primary and secondary education economically more important. The portion of the American economy attributable to international trade nearly tripled between 1950 and 1980, and more than 70 percent of American-made goods now compete with imports. Yet, lagging worker productivity has contributed to negative trade balances and to real hourly compensation that has fallen below wages in 10 other industrialized nations. At least some significant part of this serious productivity problem is attributable to students who emerge from classrooms without the reading or mathematical skills necessary to compete with their European or Asian counterparts, and, presumably, to high school dropout rates of 20 to 25 percent (up to 50 percent in inner cities).

[Finally,] there is evidence that, today more than ever, many firms base their location decisions upon the presence, or absence, of a work force with a basic education. Scholars on the subject report, for example, that today, "[h]igh speed communication and transportation make it possible to produce most products and services anywhere in the world"; that "[m]odern machinery and production methods can therefore be combined with low wage workers to drive costs down"; that managers can perform "back office functions anywhere in the world now," and say that if they " 'can't get enough skilled workers here' " they will " 'move the skilled jobs out of the country;' " with the consequence that "rich countries need better education and retraining, to reduce the supply of unskilled workers and to equip them with the skills they require for tomorrow's jobs." In light of this increased importance of education to individual firms, it is no surprise that half of the Nation's manufacturers have become involved with setting standards and shaping curricula for local schools, that 88 percent think this kind of involvement is important, that more than 20 States have recently passed educational reforms to attract new business, and that business magazines have begun to rank cities according to the quality of their schools.

The economic links I have just sketched seem fairly obvious. Why then is it not equally obvious, in light of those links, that a widespread, serious, and substantial physical threat to teaching and learning also substantially threatens the commerce to which that teaching and learning is inextricably tied? That is to say, guns in the hands of six percent of inner-city high school students and gun-related violence throughout a city's schools must threaten the trade and commerce that those schools support. The only question, then, is whether the latter threat is (to use the majority's terminology) "substantial." And, the evidence of (1) the extent of the gun-related violence problem, (2) the extent of the resulting negative effect on classroom learning, and (3) the extent of the consequent negative commercial effects, when taken together, indicate a threat to trade and commerce that is "substantial." At the very least, Congress could rationally have concluded that the links are "substantial."

Specifically, Congress could have found that gun-related violence near the classroom poses a serious economic threat (1) to consequently inadequately educated workers who must endure low paying jobs, and (2) to communities and businesses that might (in today's "information society") otherwise gain, from a well-educated work force, an important commercial advantage, of a kind that location near a railhead or harbor provided in the past. Congress might also have found these threats to be no different in kind from other threats that this Court has found within the commerce power, such as the threat that loan sharking poses to the "funds" of "numerous localities," Perez, and that unfair labor practices pose to instrumentalities of commerce. As I have pointed out, Congress has written that "the occurrence of violent crime in school zones" has brought about a "decline in the quality of education" that "has an adverse impact on interstate commerce and the foreign commerce of the United States." The violence-related facts, the educational facts, and the economic facts, taken together, make this conclusion rational. And, because under our case law the sufficiency of the constitutionally necessary Commerce Clause link between a crime of violence and interstate commerce turns simply upon size or degree, those same facts make the statute constitutional.

To hold this statute constitutional is not to "obliterate" the "distinction of what is national and what is local,"; nor is it to hold that the Commerce Clause permits the Federal Government to "regulate any activity that it found was related to the economic productivity of individual citizens," to regulate "marriage, divorce, and child custody," or to regulate any and all aspects of education. For one thing, this statute is aimed at curbing a particularly acute threat to the educational process— the possession (and use) of life-threatening firearms in, or near, the classroom. The empirical evidence that I have discussed above unmistakably documents the special way in which guns and education are incompatible. This Court has previously recognized the singularly disruptive potential on interstate commerce that acts of violence may have. Perez. For another thing, the immediacy of the connection between education and the national economic well-being is documented by scholars and accepted by society at large in a way and to a degree that may not hold true for other social institutions. It must surely be the rare case, then, that a statute strikes at conduct that (when considered in the abstract) seems so removed from commerce, but which (practically speaking) has so significant an impact upon commerce.

In sum, a holding that the particular statute before us falls within the commerce power would not expand the scope of that Clause. Rather, it simply would apply preexisting law to changing economic circumstances. It would recognize that, in today's economic world, gun-related violence near the classroom makes a significant difference to our economic, as well as our social, well-being.

III. [The] majority's holding [creates] three serious legal problems. First, the majority's holding runs contrary to modern Supreme Court cases that have upheld congressional actions despite connections to interstate or foreign commerce that are less significant than the effect of school violence. In Perez, the Court held that the Commerce Clause authorized a federal statute that makes it a crime to engage in loan sharking ("[e]xtortionate credit transactions") at a local level. The Court said that Congress may judge that such transactions, "though purely intrastate, ... affect interstate commerce." Presumably, Congress reasoned that threatening or using force, say with a gun on a street corner, to collect a debt occurs sufficiently often so that the activity (by helping organized crime) affects commerce among the States. But, why then cannot Congress also reason that the threat or use of force—the frequent consequence of possessing a gun—in or near a school occurs sufficiently often so that such activity (by inhibiting basic education) affects commerce among the States? The negative impact upon the national economy of an inability to teach basic skills seems no smaller (nor less significant) [than] that of organized crime.

[In Katzenbach v. McClung and Daniel v. Paul], the Court understood that the specific instance of discrimination (at a local place of accommodation) was part of a general practice that, considered as a whole, caused not only the most serious human and social harm, but had nationally significant economic dimensions as well. It is difficult to distinguish the case before us, for the same critical elements are present. Businesses are less likely to locate in communities where violence plagues the classroom. Families will hesitate to move to neighborhoods where students carry guns instead of books. (Congress expressly found in 1994 that "parents may decline to send their children to school" in certain areas "due to concern about violent crime and gun violence." And (to look at the matter in the most narrowly commercial manner), interstate publishers therefore will sell fewer books and other firms will sell fewer school supplies where the threat of violence disrupts learning. Most importantly, like the local racial discrimination at issue in McClung and Daniel, the local instances here, taken together and considered as a whole, create a problem that causes serious human and social harm, but also has nationally significant economic dimensions. In Wickard, [in order] to find [the] effects on commerce significant in amount, the Court had to give Congress the benefit of the doubt. Why would the Court, to find a significant (or "substantial") effect here, have to give Congress any greater leeway?

The second legal problem the Court creates comes from its apparent belief that it can reconcile its holding with earlier cases by making a critical distinction between "commercial" and noncommercial "transaction[s]." That is to say, the Court believes the Constitution would distinguish between two local activities, each of which has an identical effect upon interstate commerce, if one, but not the other, is "commercial" in nature. As a general matter, this approach fails to heed this

Court's earlier warning not to turn "questions of the power of Congress" upon "formula[s]" that would give "controlling force to nomenclature such as 'production' and 'indirect' and foreclose consideration of the actual effects of the activity in question upon interstate commerce." Wickard. Moreover, the majority's test is not consistent with what the Court saw as the point of the cases that the majority now characterizes. Although the majority today attempts to categorize Perez, McClung, and Wickard as involving intrastate "economic activity," the Courts that decided each of those cases did not focus upon the economic nature of the activity regulated. Rather, they focused upon whether that activity affected interstate or foreign commerce.

[More] importantly, if a distinction between commercial and non-commercial activities is to be made, this is not the case in which to make it. The majority clearly cannot intend such a distinction to focus narrowly on an act of gun possession standing by itself, for such a reading could not be reconciled with either the civil rights cases (McClung and Daniel) or Perez—in each of those cases the specific transaction (the race-based exclusion, the use of force) was not itself "commercial." And, if the majority instead means to distinguish generally among broad categories of activities, differentiating what is educational from what is commercial, then, as a practical matter, the line becomes almost impossible to draw. Schools that teach reading, writing, mathematics, and related basic skills serve both social and commercial purposes, and one cannot easily separate the one from the other. American industry itself has been, and is again, involved in teaching. When, and to what extent, does its involvement make education commercial? Does the number of vocational classes that train students directly for jobs make a difference? Does it matter if the school is public or private, nonprofit or profit-seeking? Does it matter if a city or State adopts a voucher plan that pays private firms to run a school? Even if one were to ignore these practical questions, why should there be a theoretical distinction between education, when it significantly benefits commerce, and environmental pollution, when it causes economic harm?

Regardless, if there is a principled distinction that could work both here and in future cases, Congress (even in the absence of vocational classes, industry involvement, and private management) could rationally conclude that schools fall on the commercial side of the line. In 1990, the year Congress enacted the statute before us, primary and secondary schools spent $230 billion—that is, nearly a quarter of a trillion dollars—which accounts for a significant portion of our $5.5 trillion Gross Domestic Product for that year. The business of schooling requires expenditure of these funds on student transportation, food and custodial services, books, and teachers' salaries. And, these expenditures enable schools to provide a valuable service—namely, to equip students with the skills they need to survive in life and, more specifically, in the workplace. Certainly, Congress has often analyzed school expenditure as if it were a commercial investment, closely analyzing whether schools are efficient, whether they justify the significant resources they spend, and whether they can be restructured to achieve greater returns. Why could Congress, for Commerce Clause purposes, not consider schools as roughly analogous to commercial investments from which the Nation derives the benefit of an educated work force?

The third legal problem created by the Court's holding is that it threatens legal uncertainty in an area of law that, until this case, seemed reasonably well settled. Congress has enacted many statutes (more than 100 sections of the United States Code), including criminal statutes (at least 25 sections), that use the words "affecting commerce" to define their scope, see, e.g., 18 U.S.C. § 844(i) (destruction of buildings used in activity affecting interstate commerce), and other statutes that contain no jurisdictional language at all, see, e.g., 18 U.S.C. § 922(*o*)(1) (possession of machine guns). Do these, or similar, statutes regulate noncommercial activities? If so, would that alter the meaning of "affecting commerce" in a jurisdictional element? More importantly, in the absence of a jurisdictional element, are the courts nevertheless to take Wickard (and later similar cases) as inapplicable, and to judge the effect of a single noncommercial activity on interstate commerce without considering similar instances of the forbidden conduct? However these questions are eventually resolved, the legal uncertainty now created will restrict Congress' ability to enact criminal laws aimed at criminal behavior that, considered problem by problem rather than instance by instance, seriously threatens the economic, as well as social, well-being of Americans.

IV. In sum, to find this legislation within the scope of the Commerce Clause would [interpret] the [Commerce] Clause as this Court has traditionally interpreted it. [Upholding] this legislation would do no more than simply recognize that Congress had a "rational basis" for finding a significant connection between guns in or near schools and (through their effect on education) the interstate and foreign commerce they threaten. [I] would reverse the judgment of the Court of Appeals . . . .[3]

12th ED., p. 174

Add at end of first paragraph of footnote 4:

The issue of precedent in constitutional cases was sharply aired on the last day of the 1991 Term when the Court in Payne v. Tennessee, 501 U.S. 808 (1991), overruled a 1987 case and a 1989 case in holding that victim impact statements were admissible during the penalty phase of a capital trial. Chief Justice Rehnquist's opinion of the Court acknowledged the benefits of adhering to the principle of stare decisis, but noted as well that the practical impossibility of legislative correction in constitutional cases made the principle least applicable in that context. Moreover, he argued that "considerations in favor of stare

---

3. Is there a relationship between a view about the reach of the commerce power and a view about the interpretation of federal statutes relying on that power? In Allied–Bruce Terminix Companies, Inc. v. Dobson, 515 U.S. ___ (1995), the Court faced the question whether the words "evidencing" and "involving" in the jurisdictional portion of the Federal Arbitration Act—"a contract evidencing a transaction involving commerce"—were to be taken as limiting, or whether instead that provision should be interpreted as extending to the full reach of Congress' power under the commerce clause. Justice Breyer's majority opinion, joined by Chief Justice Rehnquist and Justices Stevens, O'Connor, Kennedy, Souter, and Ginsburg, upheld the broader reading, with Justice Thomas, joined by Justice Scalia, dissenting and arguing that the relevant words limited what would otherwise have been a jurisdiction reaching to the constitutional maximum.

decisis are at their acme in cases involving property or contract rights, where reliance interests are involved, [but] the opposite is true in cases such as the present one involving procedural and evidentiary rules. [The] Court has during the past 20 Terms overruled in whole or in part 33 of its previous decisions. [The cases overruled here] were decided by the narrowest of margins, over spirited dissents challenging the basic underpinnings of those decisions. They have been questioned by members of the Court in later decisions, and have defied consistent application by the lower courts. [Reconsidering] these decisions now, we conclude [that] they were wrongly decided and should be, and now are, overruled."

Justice Scalia's concurring opinion rejected the dissent's argument that overruling a precedent requires a "special justification," and urged rejection of any view that would leave "in place [an] important constitutional decision with plainly inadequate rational support [for] the sole reason that it once attracted five votes." Justice Souter's concurrence, however, joined by Justice Kennedy, acknowledged that a "special justification" was necessary for overruling one of the Court's own precedents, but found it in the unworkability of the existing rule. Justice Marshall, however, joined by Justice Blackmun, dissented, opening with the observation that "[p]ower, not reason, is the new currency of this Court's decisionmaking," arguing that nothing had changed in five years except "the personnel of this Court." He urged departure from precedent only where there was a "special justification," Arizona v. Rumsey, 467 U.S. 203 (1984), and did not find it here. He further objected to the majority's decision to "limit full protection" of the principles of stare decisis to cases involving property and contract rights, as well as to the language in the majority opinion that seemed to "invite[ ] state actors to renew the very policies deemed unconstitutional in the hope that this Court may now reverse course."

In Hilton v. South Carolina Public Railways Commission, 502 U.S. 197 (1991), the Court, with Justice Kennedy writing the opinion, reiterated its belief both in the importance of stare decisis in promoting "stability, predictability, and respect for judicial authority," and in the considerably greater importance of stare decisis in statutory than in constitutional cases. Other cases decided in the 1991 Term discussed issues of stare decisis more explicitly than had been the case in the past, and this trend culminated in the opinions in PLANNED PARENTHOOD OF SOUTHEASTERN PENNSYLVANIA v. CASEY, 505 U.S. ___ (1992), set out below, addition to 12th Ed., p. 553; Ind.Rts., p. 224, where a heated debate about stare decisis was one of the centerpieces of the controversy over whether to overrule or reaffirm Roe v. Wade.

Questions about the weight of precedent presuppose the existence of a precedent rule in some earlier case that a subsequent court will then follow or overrule. But some rules may have more weight than others, even within a regime of stare decisis. Consider the following from Chief Justice Rehnquist's majority opinion in Brecht v. Abrahamson, 507 U.S. ___ (1993): "Petitioner contends that we are bound by these [earlier] cases, by way of stare decisis. [But] since we have never squarely addressed the issue, and have at most assumed the applicability of [the rule now at issue,] we are free to address the issue on the merits."

12th ED., p. 175
Add after discussion of Bowen v. American Hospital:

The possibility that Tenth Amendment federalism concerns would surface in principles of statutory construction became a firm reality in GREGORY v. ASHCROFT, 501 U.S. 452 (1991), in which the Court refused to interpret the Age Discrimination in Employment Act of 1967 as supplanting a provision of the Missouri Constitution mandating that judges retire at age 70.

The Age Discrimination in Employment Act makes it unlawful for an employer to discharge any employee over the age of 40 for reason of age. A 1974 amendment included states and their political subdivisions as employers subject to the requirements of the Act, but excluded from the definition of "employee" any "person elected to public office" and any "appointee on the policymaking level." Judges in Missouri are first appointed by the governor and then subject to a retention election, and

Missouri argued that that made judges either elected officials or policy-making employees, in either case being exempt from the prohibition on mandatory retirement by reason of age contained in the federal law.

Writing for the majority, Justice O'CONNOR agreed with Missouri's interpretation of the Act, and expressly announced a principle of statutory construction incorporating the kinds of federalism concerns raised in cases from National League of Cities to Garcia. She began with a lengthy statement outlining the general arguments for federalism and for state autonomy in the face of federal power. "As every schoolchild learns, our Constitution establishes a system of dual sovereignty between the States and the Federal Government. [The] States thus retain substantial sovereign authority under our constitutional system. [Perhaps] the principal benefit of the federalist system is a check on abuses of government power. [One] fairly can dispute whether our federalist system has been quite as successful in checking government abuse as Hamilton promised, but there is no doubt about the design." Justice O'Connor quoted Madison's statement in Federalist 51 that there is a "double security" pursuant to which the different governments control both themselves and each other, and argued that "[t]hese twin powers will act as mutual restraints only if they are credible. [The] Federal Government holds a decided advantage in this delicate balance: the Supremacy Clause. As long as it is acting within the powers granted it in the Constitution, Congress may impose its will on the States. Congress may legislate in areas traditionally regulated by the States. This is an extraordinary power in a federalist system. It is a power that we must assume Congress does not exercise lightly."

Noting that the provision of the Missouri Constitution establishing qualifications for judges and mandating retirement at age 70 "is a decision of the most fundamental sort for a sovereign entity," Justice O'Connor maintained that "interference with this decision [would] upset the usual constitutional balance of federal and state powers." As a result she adopted the principle, already found in other contexts (see Atascadero State Hospital v. Scanlon, 473 U.S. 234 (1985) (Eleventh Amendment)), that Congress would be taken to have encroached on state power in this context only if there was a "plain statement" to that effect. Relying on a series of cases involving discrimination on the basis of alienage (below, 12th Ed., pp. 680–84), she seemed to indicate that the plain statement rule would be applied when and only when congressional action would infringe on the essential "political functions" of state governments, of which establishing the qualifications of the most important government officials was clearly one.

Justice O'Connor acknowledged that Garcia "constrained [our] ability to consider the limits that the state-federal balance places on Congress' powers under the Commerce Clause. But there is no need to do so if we hold that the ADEA does not apply to state judges. Application of the plain statement rule thus may avoid a potential constitutional problem. Indeed, inasmuch as this Court in Garcia has left primarily to the political process the protection of the States against intrusive exercises of Congress' Commerce Clause powers, we must be absolutely certain that Congress intended such an exercise. [In] light of the

ADEA's clear exclusion of most important public officials, it is at least ambiguous whether Congress intended that appointed judges nonetheless be included. In the face of such ambiguity, we will not attribute to Congress an intent to intrude on state governmental functions regardless of whether Congress acted pursuant to its Commerce Clause powers or Section 5 of the Fourteenth Amendment." (On the Fourteenth Amendment aspect of the decision, see further below, addition to 12th Ed., p. 992). Finding that there was "at least" sufficient ambiguity in the policymaking-level exception such that it would be held to exempt state judges absent a clearer statement of Congress to the contrary, the Court did not resolve whether the retention election was also sufficient to exempt these judges as elected officials.[1]

Justice WHITE, joined by Justice Stevens, concurred in the judgment, but dissented from the majority's new plain statement rule, finding it "unwise," "infeasible," and in any event "unnecessary to the proper resolution of this case." He started by arguing that the majority's reliance on the Eleventh Amendment and alienage discrimination cases was misplaced, and then went on to maintain that the "majority's plain statement rule [directly] contravenes our decisions in [Garcia and South Carolina v. Baker.] [The] majority disregards those decisions in its attempt to carve out areas of state activity that will receive special protection from federal legislation. [The] majority asserts that its plain statement rule is helpful in avoiding a 'potential constitutional problem.' It is far from clear, however, why there would be a constitutional problem [in] light of our decisions in Garcia and Baker." Justice White also objected to the majority's failure to explain clearly the scope of the new plain statement rule, and wondered whether it applied only to cases involving qualifications of state officials, or more broadly to all state governmental functions. And he wondered as well whether the plain statement rule would put aside otherwise applicable approaches to interpreting legislation that would allow or mandate an inquiry into the purpose or history of a federal statute. Moreover, "[t]he majority's departures from established precedent are even more disturbing when it is realized [that] this case can be affirmed based on simple statutory construction. [It] is clear that the decisionmaking engaged in by common-law judges [demonstrates] the policymaking nature of the judicial function. [Moreover, the] statutory exception refers to appointees 'on the policymaking level,' not 'policymaking employees,' Thus, whether or not judges actually *make* policy, they certainly are on the same *level* as policymaking officials in other branches of government and therefore are covered by the exception."

Justice BLACKMUN, joined by Justice Marshall, dissented, agreeing "entirely" with Justice White's argument against the new plain statement rule, but arguing that judges were not within any of the relevant

1. The Court also held, relying on seemingly well-settled precedents, that the Missouri provision mandating judicial retirement at age 70 did not violate the equal protection clause of the Fourteenth Amendment. See Massachusetts v. Murgia, 1985, described below, 12th Ed., p. 701; Ind.Rts., p. 372. Note also the now-pending H.R. 1571 and S. 849, which seek to include elected judges under the provisions of the Age Discrimination in Employment Act.

exceptions and were thus within the scope of the ADEA. In addition, "the EEOC, which is charged with the enforcement of the ADEA, has determined that an appointed state judge is covered by the ADEA. This Court's precedent dictates that we defer to the EEOC's permissible interpretation of the ADEA."

NEW YORK v. UNITED STATES

505 U.S. 144, 112 S.Ct. 2408, 120 L.Ed.2d 120 (1992).

Justice O'CONNOR delivered the opinion of the Court.

This case implicates one of our Nation's newest problems of public policy and perhaps our oldest question of constitutional law. The public policy issue involves the disposal of radioactive waste: In this case, we address the constitutionality of three provisions of the Low–Level Radio-active Waste Policy Amendments Act of 1985, 42 U.S.C. 2021b et seq.

The constitutional question is as old as the Constitution: It consists of discerning the proper division of authority between the Federal Government and the States. We conclude that while Congress has substantial power under the Constitution to encourage the States to provide for the disposal of the radioactive waste generated within their borders, the Constitution does not confer upon Congress the ability simply to compel the States to do so. We therefore find that only two of the Act's three provisions at issue are consistent with the Constitution's allocation of power....

I. We live in a world full of low level radioactive waste. Radioac-tive material is present in luminous watch dials, smoke alarms, measure-ment devices, medical fluids, research materials, and the protective gear and construction materials used by workers at nuclear power plants. Low level radioactive waste is generated by the Government, by hospi-tals, by research institutions, and by various industries. The waste must be isolated from humans for long periods of time, often for hundreds of years. Millions of cubic feet of low level radioactive waste must be disposed of each year. Our Nation's first site for the land disposal of commercial low level radioactive waste opened in 1962 in Beatty, Nevada. Five more sites opened in the following decade: Maxey Flats, Kentucky (1963), West Valley, New York (1963), Hanford, Wash-ington (1965), Sheffield, Illinois (1967), and Barnwell, South Carolina (1971). Between 1975 and 1978, the Illinois site closed because it was full, and water management problems caused the closure of the sites in Kentucky and New York. As a result, since 1979 only three disposal sites—those in Nevada, Washington, and South Carolina—have been in operation. Waste generated in the rest of the country must be shipped to one of these three sites for disposal.

In 1979, the Washington and Nevada sites [shut] down temporarily, leaving South Carolina to shoulder the responsibility of storing low level radioactive waste produced in every part of the country. [Faced] with the possibility that the Nation would be left with no disposal sites for low level radioactive waste, Congress responded by enacting the Low–Level Radioactive Waste Policy Act. [The] Act authorized States to enter into regional compacts that, once ratified by Congress, would have the authority [to] restrict the use of their disposal facilities to waste generated within member States. The Act included no penalties for States that failed to participate in this plan.

By 1985, only three approved regional compacts had operational disposal facilities, [the] compacts formed around South Carolina, Nevada, and Washington. [The] 1980 Act would have given these three compacts the ability to exclude waste from nonmembers, and the remaining 31 States would have had no assured outlet for their [waste.] With this prospect looming, Congress once again took up the issue. [The] result was the legislation challenged here, the Low–Level Radioactive Waste Policy Amendments Act of 1985.

The 1985 Act was again based largely on a proposal submitted by the National Governors' Association. [The] Act embodies a compromise among the sited and unsited States. The sited States agreed to extend for seven years the period in which they would accept [waste] from other States. In exchange, the unsited States agreed to end their reliance on the sited States by 1992. The mechanics of this compromise are intricate. [The] Act authorizes States to "enter into such [interstate] compacts as may be necessary to provide for the establishment and operation of regional disposal facilities for low-level radioactive waste." For an additional seven years beyond the period contemplated by the 1980 Act, from the beginning of 1986 through the end of 1992, the three existing disposal sites "shall make disposal capacity available for low-level radioactive waste generated by any source," with certain exceptions not relevant here. But the three States in which the disposal sites are located are permitted to exact a graduated surcharge for waste arriving from outside the regional compact—in 1986–1987, $10 per cubic foot; in 1988–1989, $20 per cubic foot; and in 1990–1992, $40 per cubic foot. After the seven-year transition period expires, approved regional compacts may exclude [waste] generated outside the region.

The Act provides three types of incentives to encourage the States to comply with their statutory obligation to provide for the disposal of waste generated within their borders.

1. Monetary incentives. One quarter of the surcharges collected by the sited States must be transferred to an escrow account held by the Secretary of Energy. The Secretary then makes payments from this account to each State that has complied with a series of deadlines. By July 1, 1986, each State was to have ratified legislation either joining a regional compact or indicating an intent to develop a disposal facility within the State. By January 1, 1988, each unsited compact was to have identified the State in which its facility would be located, and each compact or stand-alone State was to have developed a siting plan and taken other identified steps. By January 1, 1990, each State or compact was to have filed a complete application for a license to operate a disposal facility, or the Governor of any State that had not filed an application was to have certified that the State would be capable of

disposing of all waste generated in the State after 1992. The rest of the account is to be paid out to those States or compacts able to dispose of all low level radioactive waste generated within their borders by January 1, 1993. Each State that has not met the 1993 deadline must either take title to the waste generated within its borders or forfeit to the waste generators the incentive payments it has received.

2. *Access incentives.* The second type of incentive involves the denial of access to disposal sites. States that fail to meet the July 1986 deadline may be charged twice the ordinary surcharge for the remainder of 1986 and may be denied access to disposal facilities thereafter. States that fail to meet the 1988 deadline may be charged double surcharges for the first half of 1988 and quadruple surcharges for the second half of 1988, and may be denied access thereafter. States that fail to meet the 1990 deadline may be denied access. Finally, States that have not filed complete applications by January 1, 1992, for a license to operate a disposal facility, or States belonging to compacts that have not filed such applications, may be charged triple surcharges.

3. *The take title provision.* The third type of incentive is the most severe: ["If] a State (or, where applicable, a compact region) in which low-level radioactive waste is generated is unable to provide for the disposal of all such waste generated within such State or compact region by January 1, 1996, each State in which such waste is generated, upon the request of the generator or owner of the waste, shall take title to the waste, be obligated to take possession of the waste, and shall be liable for all damages directly or indirectly incurred by such generator or owner as a consequence of the failure of the State to take possession of the waste as soon after January 1, 1996, as the generator or owner notifies the State that the waste is available for shipment."

These three incentives are the focus of petitioners' constitutional challenge. In the seven years since the Act took effect, Congress has approved nine regional compacts, encompassing 42 of the States. All six unsited compacts and four of the unaffiliated States have met the first three statutory milestones. New York, a State whose residents generate a relatively large share of the Nation's low level radioactive waste, did not join a regional compact. Instead, the State complied with the Act's requirements by enacting legislation providing for the siting and financing of a disposal facility in New York. The State has identified five potential sites, three in Allegany County and two in Cortland County. Residents of the two counties oppose the State's choice of location.

Petitioners—the State of New York and the two counties—filed this suit against the United States in 1990. They sought a declaratory judgment that the Act is inconsistent with the Tenth Amendment [and] the Guarantee Clause of Article IV.

II. A. [Federalism] questions can be viewed in either of two ways. In some cases the Court has inquired whether an Act of Congress is authorized by one of the powers delegated to Congress in Article I. In other cases the Court has sought to determine whether an Act of Congress invades the province of state sovereignty reserved by the Tenth Amendment. *Garcia.* In a case like this one, [the] two inquiries are mirror images of each other. If a power is delegated to Congress, [the] Tenth Amendment expressly disclaims any reservation of that power to the States; if a power is an attribute of state sovereignty reserved by the Tenth Amendment, it is necessarily a power the Constitution has not conferred on Congress. It is in this sense that the Tenth Amendment "states but a truism that all is retained which has not been surrendered." Darby.

[Congress] exercises its conferred powers subject to the limitations contained in the Constitution. Thus [under] the Commerce Clause Congress may regulate publishers engaged in interstate commerce, but Congress is constrained in the exercise of that power by the First Amendment. The Tenth Amendment likewise restrains the power of Congress, but this limit is not derived from the text of the Tenth Amendment itself, which [is] essentially a tautology. Instead, the Tenth Amendment confirms that the power of the Federal Government is subject to limits that may, in a given instance, reserve power to the States. The Tenth Amendment thus directs us to determine [whether] an incident of state sovereignty is protected by a limitation on an Article I power.

[The] Federal Government undertakes activities today that would have been unimaginable to the Framers in two senses; first, because the Framers would not have conceived that any government would conduct such activities; and second, because the Framers would not have believed that the Federal Government, rather than the States, would assume such responsibilities. Yet the powers conferred upon the Federal Government by the Constitution were phrased in language broad enough to allow for the expansion of the Federal Government's role. Among the provisions of the Constitution that have been particularly important in this regard, three concern us here.

First, the Constitution allocates to Congress the power "to regulate Commerce ... among the several States." [As] interstate commerce has become ubiquitous, activities once considered purely local have come to have effects on the national economy, and have accordingly come within the scope of Congress' commerce power.

Second, the Constitution authorizes Congress "to pay the Debts and provide for the ... general Welfare of the United States." Art. I, sec. 8, cl. 1. [While] the spending power is [subject to restrictions,] these [have] not been so severe as to prevent the regulatory authority of Congress from generally keeping up with the growth of the federal budget.

[Finally,] the Constitution provides that "the Laws of the United States ... shall be the supreme Law of the Land ... any Thing in the Constitution or Laws of any State to the Contrary notwithstanding." U.S. Const., Art. VI, cl. 2. As the Federal Government's willingness to exercise power within the confines of the Constitution has grown, the authority of the States has correspondingly diminished to the extent that federal and state policies have conflicted. We have observed that the Supremacy Clause gives the Federal Government "a decided advantage in the delicate balance" the Constitution strikes between State and Federal power. Gregory.

The actual scope of Federal [authority] with respect to the States has changed over the years, [but] the constitutional structure underlying and limiting that authority has not. In the end, just as a cup may be half empty or half full, it makes no difference whether one views the question at issue in this case as one of ascertaining the limits of the power delegated to the Federal Government under the affirmative provisions of the Constitution or one of discerning the core of sovereignty retained by the States under the Tenth Amendment. Either way, we must determine whether any of the three challenged provisions of the Act oversteps the boundary between federal and state authority.

B. Petitioners do not contend that Congress lacks the power to regulate the disposal of low level radioactive waste. Space in radioactive waste disposal sites is frequently sold by residents of one State to residents of another. Regulation of the resulting interstate market in waste disposal is therefore well within Congress' authority under the Commerce Clause. Petitioners likewise do not dispute that under the Supremacy Clause Congress could, if it wished, pre-empt state radioactive waste regulation. Petitioners contend only that the Tenth Amendment limits the power of Congress to regulate in the way it has chosen. Rather than addressing the problem of waste disposal by directly regulating the generators and disposers of waste, petitioners argue, Congress has impermissibly directed the States to regulate in this field.

Most of our recent cases interpreting the Tenth Amendment have concerned the authority of Congress to subject state governments to generally applicable laws. The Court's jurisprudence in this area has traveled an unsteady path. This case presents no occasion to apply or revisit [these] cases, as this is not a case in which Congress has subjected a State to the same legislation applicable to private parties. This case instead concerns the circumstances under which Congress may use the States as implements of regulation; [whether] Congress may direct or otherwise motivate the States to regulate in a particular field or a particular way. [A] few principles guide our resolution of the issue.

1. As an initial matter, Congress may not simply "commandeer the legislative processes of the States by directly compelling them to enact and enforce a federal regulatory program." Hodel v. Virginia Surface Mining. [The] Court reached the same conclusion the following year in FERC v. Mississippi. These [were] not innovations. While Congress has substantial powers to govern the Nation directly, including in areas of intimate concern to the States, the Constitution has never been understood to confer upon Congress the ability to require the States to govern according to Congress' instructions. [Indeed,] the question whether the Constitution should permit Congress to employ state governments as regulatory agencies was a topic of lively debate among the Framers. Under the Articles of Confederation, Congress lacked the authority in most respects to govern the people directly. [The] inadequacy of this governmental structure was responsible in part for the Constitutional Convention. [As] Hamilton saw it, "we must resolve to

incorporate into our plan those ingredients which may be considered as forming the characteristic difference between a league and a government; we must extend the authority of the Union to the persons of the citizens—the only proper objects of government." The new National Government "must carry its agency to the persons of the citizens. It must stand in need of no intermediate legislations ... The government of the Union, like that of each State, must be able to address itself immediately to the hopes and fears of individuals." Federalist 16.

The Convention generated a great number of proposals for the structure of the new Government, but two quickly took center stage. Under the Virginia Plan, [Congress] would exercise legislative authority directly upon individuals, without employing the States as intermediaries. Under the New Jersey Plan, [Congress] would continue to require the approval of the States before legislating, as [under] the Articles of Confederation. [One] frequently expressed objection to the New Jersey Plan was that it might require the Federal Government to coerce the States into implementing legislation. [Under] one preliminary draft of what would become the New Jersey Plan, state governments would occupy a position relative to Congress similar to that contemplated by the Act at issue in this case: "The laws of the United States ought, as far as may be consistent with the common interests of the Union, to be carried into execution by the judiciary and executive officers of the respective states, wherein the execution thereof is required." This idea apparently never even progressed so far as to be debated by the delegates. [In] the end, the Convention opted for a Constitution in which Congress would exercise its legislative authority directly over individuals rather than over States; [it] rejected the New Jersey Plan in favor of the Virginia Plan. This choice was made clear to the subsequent state ratifying conventions. Oliver Ellsworth, a member of the Connecticut delegation in Philadelphia, explained the distinction to his State's convention: "This Constitution does not attempt to coerce sovereign bodies, states, in their political capacity.... But this legal coercion singles out the ... individual." Charles Pinckney, another delegate at the Constitutional Convention, emphasized to the South Carolina House of Representatives that in Philadelphia "the necessity of having a government which should at once operate upon the people, and not upon the states, was conceived to be indispensable by every delegation present." Rufus King, one of Massachusetts' delegates, returned home to support ratification by recalling the Commonwealth's unhappy experience under the Articles of Confederation and arguing: "Laws, to be effective, therefore, must not be laid on states, but upon individuals."

[In] providing for a stronger central government, therefore, the Framers explicitly chose a Constitution that confers upon Congress the power to regulate individuals, not States. [This] Court has consistently respected this choice. We have always understood that even where Congress has the authority under the Constitution to pass laws requiring or prohibiting certain acts, it lacks the power directly to compel the States to require or prohibit those acts....

2. This is not to say that Congress lacks the ability to encourage a State to regulate in a particular way, or that Congress may not hold out

incentives to the States as a method of influencing a State's policy choices. Our cases have identified a variety of methods, short of outright coercion, by which Congress may urge a State to adopt a legislative program consistent with federal interests. Two of these methods are of particular relevance here. First, under Congress' spending power, "Congress may attach conditions on the receipt of federal funds." South Dakota v. Dole [1987; below, 12th Ed., p. 196.] [Second,] where Congress has the authority to regulate private activity under the Commerce Clause, we have recognized Congress' power to offer States the choice of regulating that activity according to federal standards or having state law pre-empted by federal regulation. This arrangement, which has been termed "a program of cooperative federalism," Hodel, is replicated in numerous federal statutory schemes. These include the Clean Water Act, the Occupational Safety and Health Act of 1970, the Resource Conservation and Recovery Act of 1976, and the Alaska National Interest Lands Conservation Act.

By either of these two methods, [the] residents of the State retain the ultimate decision as to whether or not the State will comply. If a State's citizens view federal policy as sufficiently contrary to local interests, they may elect to decline a federal grant. If state residents would prefer their government to devote its attention and resources to problems other than those deemed important by Congress, they may choose to have the Federal Government rather than the State bear the expense of a federally mandated regulatory program, and they may continue to supplement that program to the extent state law is not preempted. Where Congress encourages state regulation rather than compelling it, state governments remain responsive to the local electorate's preferences; state officials remain accountable to the people.

By contrast, where the Federal Government compels States to regulate, the accountability of both state and federal officials is diminished. If the citizens of New York, for example, do not consider that making provision for the disposal of radioactive waste is in their best interest, they may elect state officials who share their view. That view can always be pre-empted under the Supremacy Clause if is contrary to the national view, but in such a case it is the Federal Government that makes the decision in full view of the public, and federal officials [will] suffer the consequences if the decision turns out to be detrimental or unpopular. But where the Federal Government directs the States to regulate, state officials [may] bear the brunt of public disapproval, while the federal officials who devised the regulatory program may remain insulated from the electoral ramifications of their decision. Accountability is thus diminished when, due to federal coercion, elected state officials cannot regulate in accordance with the views of the local electorate in matters not pre-empted by federal regulation....

III. The Act could plausibly be understood either as a mandate to regulate or as a series of incentives. Under petitioners' view, however, [the] Act would clearly "commandeer the legislative processes of the States by directly compelling them to enact and enforce a federal regulatory program. We must reject this interpretation. ["Where] an otherwise acceptable construction of a statute would raise serious constitutional problems, the Court will construe the statute to avoid such problems unless such construction is plainly contrary to the intent of Congress." Edward J. DeBartolo Corp. v. Fla. Gulf Coast Bldg. & Const. Trades Council, 485 U.S. 568 (1988). We therefore decline petitioners' invitation to construe [the above language], alone and in isolation, as a command to the States independent of the remainder of the Act. Construed as a whole, the Act comprises three sets of "incentives" for the States to provide for the disposal of low level radioactive waste generated within their borders. We consider each in turn.

A. The first set of incentives works in three steps. First, Congress has authorized States with disposal sites to impose a surcharge on waste received from other States. Second, the Secretary of Energy collects a portion of this surcharge and places the money in an escrow account. Third, States achieving a series of milestones receive portions of this fund.

The first of these steps is an unexceptionable exercise of Congress' power to authorize the States to burden interstate commerce. While the Commerce Clause has long been understood to limit the States' ability to discriminate against interstate commerce, that limit may be lifted, as it has been here, by an expression of the "unambiguous intent" of Congress. [The] second step [is] no more than a federal tax on interstate commerce, which petitioners do not claim to be an invalid exercise of either Congress' commerce or taxing power. The third step is a conditional exercise of Congress' authority under the Spending Clause: Congress has placed conditions—the achievement of the milestones—on the receipt of federal funds.

[Petitioners] contend nevertheless that the form of these expenditures removes them from the scope of Congress' spending power. Petitioners [argue] that because the money collected and redisbursed to the States is kept in an account separate from the general treasury, because the Secretary holds the funds only as a trustee, and because the States themselves are largely able to control whether they will pay into the escrow account or receive a share, the Act "in no manner calls for the spending of federal funds." [The] authority to "pay the Debts and provide for the ... general Welfare" has never, however, been thought to mandate a particular form of accounting. A great deal of federal spending comes from segregated trust funds collected and spent for a particular purpose. The Spending Clause [does not] deprive Congress of the power to structure federal spending in this manner. [The] Act's first set of incentives [is] thus well within the authority of Congress under the Commerce and Spending Clauses. Because the first set of incentives is supported by affirmative constitutional grants of power to Congress, it is not inconsistent with the Tenth Amendment.

B. In the second set of incentives, Congress has authorized States and regional compacts with disposal sites gradually to increase the cost of access to the sites, and then to deny access altogether, to waste generated in States that do not meet federal deadlines. As a simple regulation, this provision would be within the power of Congress to authorize the States to discriminate against interstate commerce.

Where federal regulation of private activity is within the scope of the Commerce Clause, we have recognized the ability of Congress to offer States the choice of regulating that activity according to federal standards or having state law pre-empted by federal regulation.

[The] Act's second set of incentives thus represents a conditional exercise of Congress' commerce power, along the lines of those we have held to be within Congress' authority. As a result, the second set of incentives does not intrude on the sovereignty reserved to the States by the Tenth Amendment.

C. The take title provision is of a different character. This third so-called "incentive" offers States, as an alternative to regulating pursuant to Congress' direction, the option of taking title to and possession of the waste generated within their borders and becoming liable for all damages waste generators suffer as a result of the States' failure to do so promptly. In this provision, Congress has crossed the line distinguishing encouragement from coercion. [The] take title provision offers state governments a "choice" of either accepting ownership of waste or regulating according to the instructions of Congress. Respondents do not claim that the Constitution would authorize Congress to impose either option as a freestanding requirement. On one hand, the Constitution would not permit Congress simply to transfer radioactive waste from generators to state governments. Such a forced transfer [would be] no different than a congressionally compelled subsidy from state governments to radioactive waste producers. The same is true of the provision requiring the States to become liable for the generators' damages. Standing alone, this provision would be indistinguishable from an Act of Congress directing the States to assume the liabilities of certain state residents. Either type of federal action would "commandeer" state governments into the service of federal regulatory purposes, and would for this reason be inconsistent with the Constitution's division of authority between federal and state governments. On the other hand, the second alternative held out to state governments—regulating pursuant to Congress' direction—would, standing alone, present a simple command to state governments to implement legislation enacted by Congress. As we have seen, the Constitution does not empower Congress to subject state governments to this type of instruction.

Because an instruction to state governments to take title to waste, standing alone, would be beyond the authority of Congress, and because a direct order to regulate, standing alone, would also be beyond the authority of Congress, it follows that Congress lacks the power to offer the States a choice between the two. Unlike the first two sets of incentives, the take title incentive does not represent the conditional exercise of any congressional power enumerated in the Constitution. In this provision, Congress has not held out the threat of exercising its spending power or its commerce power; it has instead held out the threat, should the States not regulate according to one federal instruction, of simply forcing the States to submit to another federal instruction. A choice between two unconstitutionally coercive regulatory techniques is no choice at all. Either way, "the Act commandeers the legislative processes of the States by directly compelling them to enact and enforce a federal regulatory program," an outcome that has never been understood to lie within the authority conferred upon Congress by the Constitution.

[The] take title provision appears to be unique. No other federal statute has been cited which offers a state government no option other than that of implementing legislation enacted by Congress. Whether one views the take title provision as lying outside Congress' enumerated powers, or as infringing upon the core of state sovereignty reserved by the Tenth Amendment, the provision is inconsistent with the federal structure of our Government ...

IV.   Respondents raise a number of objections to this understanding of the limits of Congress' power.

A.   The United States proposes three alternative views of the constitutional line separating state and federal authority. While each view concedes that Congress generally may not compel state governments to regulate pursuant to federal direction, each purports to find a limited domain in which such coercion is permitted. [First,] the United States argues that the Constitution's prohibition of congressional directives to state governments can be overcome where the federal interest is sufficiently important to justify state submission. This argument contains a kernel of truth: In determining whether the Tenth Amendment limits the ability of Congress to subject state governments to generally applicable laws, the Court has in some cases stated that it will evaluate the strength of federal interests in light of the degree to which such laws would prevent the State from functioning as a sovereign; that is, the extent to which such generally applicable laws would impede a state government's responsibility to represent and be accountable to the citizens of the State. EEOC v. Wyoming; Transportation Union v. Long Island Ry; National League of Cities v. Usery. The Court has more recently departed from this approach. But whether or not a particularly strong federal interest enables Congress to bring state governments within the orbit of generally applicable federal regulation, no Member of the Court has ever suggested that such a federal interest would enable Congress to command a state government to enact state regulation. No matter how powerful the federal interest involved, the Constitution simply does not give Congress the authority to require the States to regulate. [Where] a federal interest is sufficiently strong to cause Congress to legislate, it must do so directly; it may not conscript state governments as its agents.

Second, the United States argues that the Constitution does, in some circumstances, permit federal directives to state governments. Various cases are cited for this proposition, but none support it. Some of these cases discuss the well established power of Congress to pass laws enforceable in state courts. These cases involve no more than an application of the Supremacy Clause's provision that federal law "shall be the supreme Law of the Land," enforceable in every State. More to the point, all involve congressional regulation of individuals, not congressional requirements that States regulate. Federal statutes enforceable in state courts do, in a sense, direct state judges to enforce them, but this sort of federal "direction" of state judges is mandated by the text of the Supremacy Clause. No comparable constitutional provision authorizes Congress to command state legislatures to legislate. Additional cases [discuss] the power of federal courts to order state officials to comply with federal law. Again, however, the text of the Constitution plainly confers this authority on the federal courts [in] Article III. The Constitution contains no analogous grant of authority to Congress.

[Third,] the United States [argues] that the Constitution envisions a role for Congress as an arbiter of interstate disputes. [While] the Framers no doubt endowed Congress with the power to regulate interstate commerce in order to avoid further instances of the interstate trade disputes that were common under the Articles of Confederation, the Framers did not intend that Congress should exercise that power through the mechanism of mandating state regulation. The Constitution established Congress as "a superintending authority over the reciprocal trade" among the States, Federalist 42, by empowering Congress to regulate that trade directly, not by authorizing Congress to issue trade-related orders to state governments....

B. Respondents focus their attention on the process by which the Act was formulated. They correctly observe that public officials representing the State of New York lent their support to the Act's enactment. [Respondents] note that the Act embodies a bargain among the sited and unsited States, a compromise to which New York was a willing participant and from which New York has reaped much benefit. Respondents then pose what appears at first to be a troubling question: How can a federal statute be found an unconstitutional infringement of State sovereignty when state officials consented to the statute's enactment?

The answer follows from an understanding of the fundamental purpose served by our Government's federal structure. The Constitution does not protect the sovereignty of States for the benefit of the States or state governments as abstract political entities, or even for the benefit of the public officials governing the States. To the contrary, the Constitution divides authority between federal and state governments for the protection of individuals. State sovereignty is not just an end in itself. [Where] Congress exceeds its authority relative to the States, therefore, the departure from the constitutional plan cannot be ratified by the "consent" of state officials.

[State] officials thus cannot consent to the enlargement of the powers of Congress beyond those enumerated in the Constitution. Indeed, the facts of this case raise the possibility that powerful incentives might lead both federal and state officials to view departures from the federal structure to be in their personal interests. Most citizens recognize the need for radioactive waste disposal sites, but few want sites near their homes. As a result, while it would be well within the authority of either federal or state officials to choose where the disposal sites will be, it is likely to be in the political interest of each individual official to avoid being held accountable to the voters for the choice of location. If a federal official is faced with the alternatives of choosing a location or directing the States to do it, the official may well prefer the latter, as a means of shifting responsibility for the eventual decision. If a state official is faced with the same set of alternatives—choosing a location or having Congress direct the choice of a location—the state official may also prefer the latter, as it may permit the avoidance of personal responsibility. The interests of public officials thus may not coincide with the Constitution's intergovernmental allocation of authority. Where state officials purport to submit to the direction of Congress in this manner, federalism is hardly being advanced....

V. Petitioners also contend that the Act is inconsistent with the Constitution's Guarantee Clause, which directs the United States to "guarantee to every State in this Union a Republican Form of Government." U.S. Const., Art. IV, sec. 4. Because we have found the take title provision of the Act irreconcilable with the powers delegated to Congress by the Constitution and hence with the Tenth Amendment[, we] need only address the applicability of the Guarantee Clause to the Act's other two challenged provisions.

We approach the issue with some trepidation, because the Guarantee Clause has been an infrequent basis for litigation throughout our history. In most of the cases in which the Court has been asked to apply the Clause, the Court has found the claims presented to be nonjusticiable under the "political question" doctrine. [below, 12th Ed., pp. 1651ff.; Ind.Rts., pp. 1322ff.] The view that the Guarantee Clause implicates only nonjusticiable political questions has its origin in Luther v. Borden [1849; below, 12th Ed., p. 1657; Ind.Rts., p. 1228], in which the Court was asked to decide, in the wake of Dorr's Rebellion, which of two rival governments was the legitimate government of Rhode Island. The Court held that "it rests with Congress," not the judiciary, "to decide what government is the established one in a State." Over the following century, this limited holding metamorphosed into the sweeping assertion that "violation of the great guaranty of a republican form of government in States cannot be challenged in the courts." Colegrove v. Green, 328 U.S. 549 (1946). This view has not always been accepted[, but we] need not resolve this difficult question today. Even if we assume that petitioners' claim is justiciable, neither the monetary incentives provided by the Act nor the possibility that a State's waste producers may find themselves excluded from the disposal sites of another State can reasonably be said to deny any State a republican form of government. As we have seen, these two incentives represent permissible conditional exercises of Congress' authority [in] forms that have now grown commonplace. Under each, Congress offers the States a legitimate choice rather than issuing an unavoidable command. The States thereby retain the ability to set their legislative agendas; state government officials remain accountable to the local electorate. The twin threats imposed by the first two challenged provisions of the Act—that New York may miss out on a share of federal spending or that those generating radioactive waste within New York may lose out-of-state disposal outlets—do not pose any realistic risk of altering the form or the method of functioning of New York's government....

VI. Having determined that the take title provision exceeds the powers of Congress, we must consider whether it is severable from the rest of the Act. "The standard for determining the severability of an unconstitutional provision is well established: Unless it is evident that the Legislature would not have enacted those provisions which are within its power, independently of that which is not, the invalid part may be dropped if what is left is fully operative as a law." Alaska Airlines v. Brock, 480 U.S. 678 (1987). [It] is apparent [that] the take title provision may be severed without doing violence to the rest of the Act. The Act [still] serves Congress' objective of encouraging the States to attain local or regional self-sufficiency in the disposal of low level radioactive waste. It still includes two incentives that coax the States along this road. [The] purpose of the Act is not defeated by the invalidation of the take title provision, so we may leave the remainder of the Act in force.

VII. [The] shortage of disposal sites for radioactive waste is a pressing national problem, but a judiciary that licensed extra-constitutional government with each issue of comparable gravity would, in the long run, be far worse. States are not mere political subdivisions of the United States. State governments are neither regional offices nor administrative agencies of the Federal Government. The positions occupied by state officials appear nowhere on the Federal Government's most detailed organizational chart. Whatever the outer limits of [State] sovereignty may be, one thing is clear: The Federal Government may not compel the States to enact or administer a federal regulatory program. The Constitution [does] not [authorize] Congress simply to direct the States to provide for the disposal of the radioactive waste generated within their borders. While there may be many constitutional methods of achieving regional self-sufficiency in radioactive waste disposal, the method Congress has chosen is not one of them.

[Affirmed] in part and reversed in part.

Justice WHITE, with whom Justice BLACKMUN and Justice STEVENS join, concurring in part and dissenting in part.

I. [My] disagreement with the Court's analysis begins at the basic descriptive level of how the legislation [came] to be enacted. The Court goes some way toward setting out the bare facts, but its omissions cast the statutory context of the take title provision in the wrong light. To read the Court's version of events, one would think that Congress was the sole proponent of a solution to the Nation's low-level radioactive waste problem. Not so. The 1980 Act and its amendatory Act of 1985 resulted from the efforts of state leaders to achieve a state-based set of remedies to the problem. They sought not federal pre-emption or intervention, but rather congressional sanction of interstate compromises they had reached.

The [events] in 1979 that precipitated movement toward legislation were the temporary closing of the Nevada disposal site in July [and] the temporary shutting of the Washington disposal site [in] October. At that time the facility in South Carolina received approximately three-quarters of the Nation's low-level radioactive waste, and the Governor ordered a 50 percent reduction in the amount his State's plant would accept for disposal. The imminence of a crisis [cannot] be overstated.

In December the National Governors' Association convened an eight-member task force to coordinate policy proposals on behalf of the States. In May 1980, the State Planning Council on Radioactive Waste Management submitted the following unanimous recommendation to President Carter: "The national policy of the United States on low-level radioactive waste shall be that every State is responsible for the disposal of the low-level radioactive waste generated by nondefense related activities within its boundaries and that States are authorized to enter into interstate compacts, as necessary, for the purpose of carrying out this responsibility." This recommendation was adopted by the National Governors' Association a few months later. The Governors recognized that the Federal Government could assert its preeminence, [but] requested instead that Congress oversee state-developed regional solutions. [The] Governors went further [in] recommending that "Congress should authorize the states to enter into interstate compacts to establish regional disposal sites" and that "such authorization should include the power to exclude waste generated outside the region from the regional disposal site." [The] 1980 Act announced the "policy of the Federal Government that ... each State is responsible for providing for the availability of capacity either within or outside the State for the disposal of low-level radioactive waste generated within its borders." This Act further authorized States to "enter into such compacts as may be necessary to provide for the establishment and operation of regional disposal facilities for low-level radioactive waste," compacts to which Congress would have to give its consent.

[The] attempts by States to enter into compacts and to gain congressional approval sparked a new round of political squabbling between elected officials from unsited States, who generally opposed ratification of the compacts that were being formed, and their counterparts from the sited States, who insisted that the promises made in the 1980 Act be honored. In its effort to keep the States at the forefront of the policy amendment process, the National Governors' Association organized more than a dozen meetings to achieve a state consensus. These discussions were not merely academic. The sited States grew increasingly and justifiably frustrated by the seeming inaction of unsited States in meeting the projected actions called for in the 1980 Act. Thus, as the end of 1985 approached, the sited States viewed the January 1, 1986 deadline established in the 1980 Act as a "drop-dead" date, on which the regional compacts could begin excluding the entry of out-of-region waste. Since by this time the three disposal facilities operating in 1980 were still the only such plants accepting waste, the unsited States perceived a very serious danger if the three existing facilities actually carried out their threat to restrict access to the waste generated solely within their respective compact regions.

A movement thus arose to achieve a compromise between the sited and the unsited States, in which the sited States agreed to continue accepting waste in exchange for the imposition of stronger measures to guarantee compliance with the unsited States' assurances that they would develop alternate disposal facilities. [The] bill that [became] the 1985 Act "represented the diligent negotiating undertaken by" the

National Governors' Association and "embodied" the "fundamentals of their settlement." In sum, the 1985 Act was very much the product of cooperative federalism, in which the States bargained among themselves to achieve compromises for Congress to sanction....

II. [Curiously] absent from the Court's analysis is any effort to place the take title provision within the overall context of the legislation. [The] 1980 and 1985 statutes were enacted against a backdrop of national concern over the availability of additional waste disposal facilities. Congress could have pre-empted the field by directly regulating the disposal of this waste pursuant to its powers, [but] instead unanimously assented to the States' request for congressional ratification of agreements to which they had acceded. [I] am unmoved by the Court's vehemence in taking away Congress' authority to sanction a recalcitrant unsited State now that New York has reaped the benefits of the sited States' concessions.

A. In my view, New York's actions subsequent to enactment of the 1980 and 1985 Acts fairly indicate its approval of the interstate agreement process embodied in those laws within the meaning of Art. I, sec. 10, cl. 3, of the Constitution, which provides that "no State shall, without the Consent of Congress, ... enter into any Agreement or Compact with another State." First, the States—including New York—worked through their Governors to petition Congress for the 1980 and 1985 Acts. [Second,] New York acted in compliance with the requisites of both statutes in key respects, thus signifying its assent to the agreement achieved among the States as codified in these laws. [The] State should be estopped from asserting the unconstitutionality of a provision that seeks merely to ensure that, after deriving substantial advantages from the 1985 Act, New York [must] live up to its bargain by establishing an in-state [facility] or assuming liability for its failure to act.

B. [Seen] as a term of an agreement entered into between the several States, this measure proves to be less constitutionally odious than the Court opines. First, the practical effect of New York's position is that because it is unwilling to honor its obligations to provide in-state storage facilities, [other] States with such plants must accept New York's waste, whether they wish to or not. Otherwise, the many economically and socially-beneficial producers of such waste in the State would have to cease their operations. The Court's refusal to force New York to accept responsibility for its own problem inevitably means that some other State's sovereignty will be impinged by it being forced, for public health reasons, to accept New York's waste. I do not understand [federalism] to impede the National Government from acting as referee among the States to prohibit one from bullying another.

Moreover, it is utterly reasonable that, in crafting a delicate compromise, [Congress] would have to ratify some punitive measure as the ultimate sanction for noncompliance. The take title provision, though surely onerous, does not take effect [if] the State lives up to its bargain of providing a waste disposal facility either within the State or in another State pursuant to a regional compact arrangement or a separate contract.

Hard public policy choices sometimes require strong measures, and the Court's holding, while not irremediable, essentially misunderstands that the 1985 take title provision was part of a complex interstate agreement about which New York should not now be permitted to complain.

III.   The Court announces that it has no occasion to revisit such decisions as Gregory, South Carolina v. Baker, Garcia, EEOC v. Wyoming, and National League of Cities, because "this is not a case in which Congress has subjected a State to the same legislation applicable to private parties."   Although this statement sends the welcome signal that the Court does not intend to cut a wide swath through our recent Tenth Amendment precedents, it nevertheless is unpersuasive. [The] Court's distinction between a federal statute's regulation of States and private parties for general purposes, as opposed to a regulation solely on the activities of States, is unsupported by our recent Tenth Amendment cases.   [Moreover,] the Court makes no effort to explain why this purported distinction should affect the analysis of Congress' power. [The] distinction, facilely thrown out, is not based on any defensible theory.   [An] incursion on state sovereignty hardly seems more constitutionally acceptable if the federal statute that "commands" specific action also applies to private parties.   The alleged diminution in state authority over its own affairs is not any less because the federal mandate restricts the activities of private parties.

I would also submit, in this connection, that the Court's attempt to carve out a doctrinal distinction for statutes that purport solely to regulate State activities is especially unpersuasive after Garcia.   [In] Garcia, we stated the proper inquiry: "We are convinced that the fundamental limitation that the constitutional scheme imposes on the Commerce Clause to protect the States as States is one of process rather than one of result.   Any substantive restraint on the exercise of Commerce Clause powers must find its justification in the procedural nature of this basic limitation, and it must be tailored to compensate for possible failings in the national political process rather than to dictate a sacred province of state autonomy."   Where it addresses this aspect of respondents' argument, the Court tacitly concedes that a failing of the political process cannot be shown in this case because it refuses to rebut the unassailable arguments that the States were well able to look after themselves in the legislative process that culminated in the 1985 Act's passage.   [The] Court rejects this process-based argument by resorting to generalities and platitudes about the purpose of federalism being to protect individual rights.   Ultimately, I suppose, the entire structure of our federal constitutional government can be traced to an interest in establishing checks and balances to prevent the exercise of tyranny against individuals.   But these fears seem extremely far distant to me in a situation such as this.   We face a crisis of national proportions in the disposal of low-level radioactive waste, and Congress has acceded to the wishes of the States by permitting local decisionmaking rather than imposing a solution from Washington.   [For] me, the Court's civics lecture has a decidedly hollow ring at a time when action, rather than rhetoric, is needed to solve a national problem.[1]

IV.   Though I disagree with the Court's conclusion that the take title provision is unconstitutional, I do not read its opinion to preclude Congress from adopting a similar measure through its powers under the Spending or Commerce Clauses.   The Court makes clear that its objection is [only] to the alleged "commandeering" quality of the take title provision.   . . .

V.   The ultimate irony of the decision today is that in its formalistically rigid obeisance to "federalism," the Court gives Congress fewer incentives to defer to the wishes of state officials in achieving local solutions to local problems.   This legislation was a classic example of Congress acting as arbiter among the States in their attempts to accept responsibility for managing a problem of grave import.   The States urged the National Legislature not to impose from Washington a solution to the country's low-level radioactive waste management problems. Instead, they sought a reasonable level of local and regional autonomy consistent with [the] Constitution.   By invalidating the measure designed to ensure compliance for recalcitrant States, such as New York, the Court upsets the delicate compromise achieved among the States and forces Congress to erect several additional formalistic hurdles to clear before achieving exactly the same objective.   Because the Court's justifications for undertaking this step are unpersuasive to me, I respectfully dissent.

Justice STEVENS, concurring in part and dissenting in part.

Under the Articles of Confederation, the Federal Government had the power to issue commands to the States.   Because that indirect exercise of federal power proved ineffective, the Framers of the Constitution empowered the Federal Government to exercise legislative authority directly over individuals within the States, even though that direct

---

1.   With selective quotations from the era in which the Constitution was adopted, the majority attempts to bolster its holding that the take title provision is tantamount to federal "commandeering" of the States. In view of the many Tenth Amendment cases decided over the past two decades in which resort to the kind of historical analysis generated in the majority opinion was not deemed necessary, I do not read the majority's many invocations of history to be anything other than elaborate window-dressing.   Certainly nowhere does the majority announce that its rule is compelled by an understanding of what the Framers may have thought about statutes of the type at issue here.   Moreover, I would observe that, while its quotations add a certain flavor to the opinion, the majority's historical analysis has a distinctly wooden quality.   One would not know from reading the majority's account, for instance, that the nature of federal-state relations changed fundamentally after the Civil War.   That conflict produced in its wake a tremendous expansion in the scope of the Federal Government's law-making authority, so much so that the persons who helped to found the Republic would scarcely have recognized the many added roles the National Government assumed for itself.   Moreover, the majority fails to mention the New Deal era, in which the Court recognized the enormous growth in Congress' power under the Commerce Clause.   While I believe we should not be blind to history, neither should we read it so selectively as to restrict the proper scope of Congress' powers under Article I, especially when the history not mentioned by the majority fully supports a more expansive understanding of the legislature's authority than may have existed in the late 18th-century. . . .   [Footnote by Justice White.]

authority constituted a greater intrusion on State sovereignty. Nothing in that history suggests that the Federal Government may not also impose its will upon the several States as it did under the Articles. The Constitution enhanced, rather than diminished, the power of the Federal Government.

The notion that Congress does not have the power to issue "a simple command to state governments to implement legislation enacted by Congress" is incorrect and unsound. There is no such limitation in the Constitution. The Tenth Amendment surely does not impose any limit on Congress' exercise of the powers delegated to it by Article I. Nor does the structure of the constitutional order or the values of federalism mandate such a formal rule.

[For] these reasons, as well as those set forth by Justice White, I respectfully dissent.

12th ED., p. 175
Add at end of Note 5:

In light of the fact that National League of Cities applied only to cases involving "integral government functions," what is the difference between National League of Cities and the rule announced by the majority in Gregory? If there is a difference in theory, is it likely to be a difference in practice? How often does Congress legislate in terms clear enough to satisfy Gregory's "plain statement" standard?

Chapter 4

OTHER NATIONAL POWERS IN
THE 1787 CONSTITUTION

12th ED., p. 184

Add at end of footnote 5:

Even if a tax designed to punish is within legislative power, it may still be deemed a criminal statute for other purposes, such as the determination that successive criminal and tax proceedings may under some circumstances violate the Double Jeopardy Clause of the Fifth Amendment. Montana Department of Revenue v. Kurth Ranch, 510 U.S. ___ (1994).

12th ED., p. 200

Add as new footnote at end of South Dakota v. Dole:

* For a more recent discussion of conditional spending, and one in which Justice O'Connor's majority opinion (primarily focused on the Tenth Amendment) follows the largely deferential approach of South Dakota v. Dole, see New York v. United States, 505 U.S. 144 (1992), set out above, addition to 12th Ed., p. 175.

12th ED., p. 201

Add at end of footnote 1 (on p. 202):

Although the 102nd Congress had before it (but did not pass) the Constitutional Convention Implementation Act, which would have limited the scope of the agenda of a constitutional convention, no such proposals have as yet been introduced in the 103rd Congress. The only measure regarding a constitutional convention pending in the 104th Congress is S.Res. 102, which would petition the states to call a convention to consider a balanced budget amendment.

Chapter 5

STATE REGULATION AND THE NATIONAL ECONOMY: CONSTITUTIONAL LIMITS AND CONGRESSIONAL ORDERING

12th ED., p. 247

Add as new footnote at end of Philadelphia v. New Jersey:

4. Philadelphia v. New Jersey was followed in Fort Gratiot Sanitary Landfill, Inc. v. Michigan Department of Natural Resources, 504 U.S. 353 (1992). There the Court struck down a Michigan law that prohibited private landfill operators from accepting solid waste originating outside the county in which the facilities were located. In response to Michigan's argument that this case was unlike Philadelphia v. New Jersey because the discrimination was largely intrastate among counties, Justice Stevens' majority opinion relied heavily on Dean Milk Co. v. Madison, which follows immediately below. Chief Justice Rehnquist, joined by Justice Blackmun, dissented, arguing that the restriction was based on legitimate environmental and health reasons rather than economic protectionism. "[T]he laws of economics suggest that landfills will sprout in places where land is cheapest and population densities least. [I] see no reason in the Commerce Clause, however, that requires cheap-land States to become the waste repositories for their brethren, ...".

In Chemical Waste Management, Inc. v. Hunt, 504 U.S. 334 (1992), the Court followed both Philadelphia v. New Jersey and Fort Gratiot in striking down an Alabama law imposing a hazardous waste disposal fee on hazardous wastes generated outside of Alabama and deposited at Alabama facilities, but not imposing an equivalent fee on Alabama-generated wastes. Justice White's majority opinion found no difference between the discriminatory tax here and the discriminatory prohibition in Philadelphia v. New Jersey, and Chief Justice Rehnquist was the only dissenter.

The Court in Chemical Waste Management left open the possibility that a differential charge for in-state and out-of-state waste might survive dormant commerce clause scrutiny if the differential could be justified in terms of a differential cost for disposing of in-state and out-of-state wastes. The Court confronted this question in OREGON WASTE SYSTEMS, INC. v. OREGON DEPARTMENT OF ENVIRONMENTAL QUALITY, 508 U.S. ___ (1994), but again struck down the charge. Here Oregon charged a fee of $0.85 per ton for the disposal of in-state waste and $2.25 for the disposal of out-of-state waste, but argued that the different charges merely served to equalize the total charges rather than penalizing the disposal of out-of-state waste. Writing for a 7–2 majority, however, Justice THOMAS, with the benefit of a heavy presumption, rejected Oregon's argument and disallowed the differential fee. " '[D]iscrimination' simply means differential treatment of in-state and out-of-state economic interests that benefits the former and burdens the latter. If a restriction on commerce is discriminatory, it is virtually per se invalid. [Because] the Oregon surcharge is discriminatory, the virtually per se rule of invalidity provides the proper legal standard here, not the [Pike v. Bruce Church] balancing test. [Our] cases require that justifications for discriminatory restrictions on commerce pass the 'strictest scrutiny.' The State's burden of justification is so heavy that 'facial discrimination by itself may be a fatal defect.' "

Applying this heavy presumption of invalidity, Justice Thomas found insufficient Oregon's argument that the difference between $0.85 and $2.25 was designed simply to make the out-of-state waste "pay" for costs charged in other and less direct ways (such as by general taxation) with respect to in-state waste. Because the alleged other taxes pertaining to in-state waste were not levied on "substantially equivalent events" as those imposed with respect to out-of-state waste, there was no way to determine equivalence in amount, and thus no way for Oregon to justify such a wide differential. Chief Justice REHNQUIST, joined by Justice Blackmun, dissented, arguing that Oregon had sufficiently documented and justified the cost-based nature of its surcharge, relying heavily on the importance of encouraging responsible solutions to the solid waste disposal problem, and concluding that the Court's decision "turns the Commerce Clause on its head. Oregon's neighbors will operate under a competitive advantage [as] they can now produce solid waste with reckless abandon and avoid paying concomitant state taxes to develop new landfills and clean up retired landfill sites. [The] Court today leaves states with only two options; become a dumper and ship as much waste as possible to a less populated State, or become a dumpee, and stoically accept waste from more densely populated States."

Note also C & A Carbone, Inc. v. Town of Clarkstown, 509 U.S. ___ (1994), discussed at greater length below, addition to 12th Ed., p. 252, in which the Court again invalidated a restriction on solid waste disposal on dormant commerce grounds. In Carbone the Court again found the law to be discriminatory, but only after concluding that a regulation imposing a restriction (to use a particular waste processing plant) was discriminatory even though it discriminated against some in-state interests as well as all out-of-state ones. (The 104th Congress has several proposals before it to modify the decision in C&A Carbone. S. 534 would allow governors to ban some garbage imports, limit the imports to 1993 levels, and impose a fee on out-of-state trash, but would continue to allow states to ship their waste across state lines at reduced levels and would allow the "flow-control" ordinances invalidated in Carbone. S. 534 was passed by a 94–6 vote in the Senate on May 16, 1995. The House Commerce Subcommittee on Commerce, Trade and Hazardous Materials approved a different version of the legislation on May 18, 1995. The full House Committee on Commerce is expected to discuss the issue in June, 1995. The other proposals, all pending in committee, designed to deal with the interstate transportation of hazardous waste issue are H.R. 342, 603, 1080, 1085, 1180, 1249, 1288 and S. 373, 398, 465, 485, 542, 589.)

Philadelphia v. New Jersey's presumptive prohibition on explicit state discrimination against interstate commerce applies as well to explicit state discrimination against *foreign* commerce. Kraft General Foods, Inc. v. Iowa Dept. of Revenue and Finance, 505 U.S. 71 (1992). On restrictions on state taxation of foreign commerce, see e.g., Barclays Bank PLC v. Franchise Tax Board of California, 513 U.S. ___ (1994).

12th Ed., p. 252
Add at end of Note 2 on "Discriminatory Effect.":

Dean Milk's analysis of what constituted discrimination was followed in C & A CARBONE, INC. v. TOWN OF CLARKSTOWN, 509 U.S. ___ (1994). In order to provide for the disposal of local solid waste, Clarkstown constructed a new solid waste transfer station. But in order to make that new facility economically viable, the town enacted a "flow control ordinance," which mandated that all solid waste be processed at a designated transfer station before leaving the municipality. The Carbone company objected to the requirement, which it argued imposed an additional cost on its operations, especially its transportation of local waste to out-of-state facilities. Among its other arguments, the town maintained that the requirement could not be discriminatory, because it applied to in-state as well as out-of-state facilities and processors. Writing for the Court, however, Justice KENNEDY relied on Dean Milk to reject this claim, concluding that the town's restriction discriminated between in-town (and therefore in-state) and out-of-state processors, a discrimination not lessened by the existence of discrimination between in-town (and therefore in-state) and out-of-town (some of it in-state) discrimination. Justice O'CONNOR, concurring only in the judgment, disagreed with the majority's discrimination analysis. She concluded that the ordinance " 'discriminate[d]' evenhandedly against all 'potential participants in the waste processing business, while benefiting only the chosen operator of the transfer facility." This, to her, was sufficient for there to be no discrimination against interstate commerce. She went on, however, to conclude, relying in part on a Pike v. Bruce Church balancing analysis, that even though there was no discrimination against interstate commerce, there was in fact "an excessive burden on interstate trade when considered in relation to the local benefits conferred. [The ordinance] is intended to ensure the financial viability of the transfer facility. [This] purpose can be achieved by other means that would have a less dramatic impact on the flow of goods. For example, the town could finance the project by imposing taxes, by issuing municipal bonds, or even by lowering its price. [Over] 20 states have enacted statutes authorizing local governments to adopt flow control laws. If the localities in these states impose the type of restriction on the movement of waste that Clarkstown has adopted, the free movement of solid waste in the stream of commerce will be severely impaired. Indeed, pervasive flow control would result in the type of balkanization the [Commerce] Clause is primarily intended to prevent." Justice SOUTER, joined by Chief Justice Rehnquist and Justice Blackmun, dissented. In refusing to find this a case of discrimination, Justice Souter relied in part on the fact that the ordinance favored a single processor and not a class of local processors, and that the single processor favored "is essentially an agent of the municipal government. [Any] discrimination [thus] fails to produce the sort of entrepreneurial favoritism we have previously defined and condemned as protectionist. [Thus, other] Clarkstown investors face the same prohibition, which is to say that [the ordinance's] exclusion of private capital is part of a broader exclusion of private capital, not a discrimination against out-of-state investors as such. [Subjecting] out-of-town investors and facilities to the same constraints as local ones is not economic protectionism. [Moreover,] the burden falls entirely on Clarkstown residents. [Here] we can confidently say that the only business lost as a result of this ordinance is business lost in Clarkstown, as customers who had used Carbone's facility drift away in response to any higher fees Carbone may have to institute to afford its share of city services; but business lost in Clarkstown as a result of a Clarkstown ordinance is not a burden that offends the Constitution."

12th ED., p. 261
Add after Note 3 (Minnesota v. Clover Leaf):

WEST LYNN CREAMERY, INC. v. HEALY, 513 U.S. ___ (1994): In yet another milk case, Massachusetts, in an effort to support the Massachusetts milk production industry, imposed an assessment on all milk dealers selling milk to Massachusetts retailers. The funds received from the assessment were then distributed, based on an allocation formula, to the Massachusetts milk producers whose economic vitality was the purpose of the plan. The dealers who paid the assessment, however, turned out to have purchased approximately two thirds of their milk from non-Massachusetts producers. The dealers challenged the plan as a form of economic protectionism violative of the dormant commerce clause, and the Court, with Justice STEVENS writing for the majority, agreed.

Justice Stevens said the plan was essentially indistinguishable from Bacchus Imports, Ltd. v. Dias, described above in Note 1 of this section. As in Bacchus, this plan "involve[d] a broad-based tax on a single kind of good and special provisions for in-state producers. [It] is obvious that the result in Bacchus would have been the same if instead of exempting certain Hawaiian liquors from tax, Hawaii had rebated the amount of tax collected from the sale of those liquors. And if a discriminatory tax rebate is unconstitutional, Massachusetts' [plan] is surely invalid; for Massachusetts not only rebates to domestic milk producers the tax paid on the sale of Massachusetts milk, but also the tax paid on the sale of milk produced elsewhere." Justice Stevens went on to reject the state's various justifications for the plan, especially its argument that non-discriminatory taxes on all milk dealers are valid, and subsidies are valid (although in an important footnote Justice Stevens hinted that some dimensions of the constitutionality of subsidies to help local industries might remain open), and so the combination of the two is valid as well. This does not follow, Justice Stevens concluded, for "our cases have eschewed formalism for a sensitive, case-by-case analysis of purposes and effects. [When] a nondiscriminatory tax is coupled with a subsidy to one of the groups hurt by the tax, a state's political processes can no longer be relied upon to prevent legislative abuse, because one of the in-state interests which would otherwise lobby against the tax has been mollified by the subsidy."

Justice SCALIA, joined by Justice Thomas, concurred in the judgment only. He reiterated his objection to any "negative Commerce Clause" power in the courts at all, but reiterated as well his willingness on stare decisis grounds to invalidate laws that were facially discriminatory against interstate commerce and laws that were indistinguishable from laws previously held unconstitutional by the Court. Because he would put in the latter category subsidies to the in-state portion of an industry financed from non-discriminatory taxes on the same industry, Justice Scalia said he would have invalidated this plan on those grounds alone. But he objected to what he claimed was the majority's willingness to strike down or at least examine closely "every state law which obstructs a national market. [The Court] seems to have canvassed the entire corpus of negative-Commerce-Clause opinions, culled out every free-market snippet of reasoning, and melded them into the sweeping principle that the Constitution is violated by any state law or regulation that 'artificially encourage[s] in-state production even when the same goods could be produced at lower costs in other states.'" Chief Justice REHNQUIST, joined by Justice Blackmun, dissented. For him this plan was little more than the kind of subsidy to in-state industry that the Court had long permitted. "No decided case supports the Court's conclusion that the negative Commerce Clause prohibits the State from using money that it has lawfully obtained through a neutral tax on milk dealers and distributing it as a subsidy to dairy farmers. [The] wisdom of a messianic insistence on a grim sink-or-swim policy of laissez-faire economics would be debatable had Congress chosen to enact it; but Congress has done nothing of the kind. It is the Court which has imposed [a] policy which bodes ill for the values of federalism."

12th ED., p. 261
Add at end of Note 4:

In Wyoming v. Oklahoma, 502 U.S. 437 (1992), however, the Court relied solely on discrimination language, mentioning neither balancing nor Pike, in striking down an Oklahoma statute requiring that 10% of the coal used in Oklahoma generating plants had to be Oklahoma-mined. Although Chief Justice Rehnquist and Justices Scalia and Thomas did not reach the merits (see below, addition to 12th Ed., p. 1621; Ind.Rts., p. 1292), Justice White's opinion for the remaining six relied heavily on Philadelphia v. New Jersey, Baldwin v. Seelig, and Hunt v. Washington Apple in finding Oklahoma's requirement invalid without the necessity of a balancing analysis. In a footnote, Justice White followed Brown–Forman Distillers Corp. v. New York State Liquor Auth., 476 U.S. 573 (1986) (noted briefly above, 12th Ed., p. 224), in indicating that Pike-influenced balancing is appropriate only when a statute has "only indirect effects on interstate commerce and regulates even-handedly."

12th ED., p. 274
Add to end of footnote 1:

More recently, Justice Scalia has indicated that the constraints of stare decisis have led him to conclusions less at odds with existing approaches than he would otherwise prefer. In Itel Containers International Corp. v. Huddleston, 507 U.S. ___ (1993), a case involving a tax alleged to constitute an impermissible tax on foreign commerce in violation of both the Foreign Commerce and Import–Export Clauses, the Court upheld the tax. Justice Scalia concurred in part and concurred in the judgment: "I have previously recorded my view that the Commerce Clause contains no 'negative' component, no self-operative prohibition upon the States' regulation of commerce. [Tyler.] On *stare decisis* grounds, however, I will enforce a self-executing, 'negative' Commerce Clause in two circumstances: (1) against a state law that facially discriminates against interstate commerce, and (2) against a state law that is indistinguishable from a type of law previously held unconstitutional by this Court. These acknowledgments of precedent serve the principal purposes of *stare decisis,* which are to protect reliance interests and to foster stability in the law. I do not believe, however, that either of those purposes is significantly furthered by continuing to apply the vague and open-ended tests that are the current content of our negative-Commerce Clause jurisprudence, such as the four-factor test set forth in Complete Auto Transit, Inc. v. Brady, 430 U.S. 274 (1977) [a taxation case], or the 'balancing' approach of Pike v. Bruce Church."

12th ED., p. 300
Add at end of footnote 3:

The Court's most recent recapitulation, slightly different from earlier ones, is in Wisconsin Public Intervenor v. Mortier, 501 U.S. 597 (1991), holding that the Federal Insecticide, Fungicide, and Rodenticide Act did not pre-empt the regulation of pesticides by local governments. The 1991 Term also brought a number of widely reported preemption cases. In Morales v. Trans World Airlines, Inc., 504 U.S. 374 (1992), Justice Scalia's majority opinion held that state regulation of deceptive airline fare advertising under state consumer protection laws was preempted by the Airline Deregulation Act of 1978. But in American Airlines, Inc. v. Wolens, 515 U.S. ___ (1995), the Court held that the preclusion of state regulation in Morales did not preclude state court enforcement of private contractual agreements (here the terms of a frequent-flyer program). In Cipollone v. Liggett Group, Inc., 505 U.S. 504 (1992), a majority of the Court held that state common law damage actions based on the hazards of cigarette smoking were partially preempted and partially permitted by the 1965 Federal Cigarette Labeling and Advertising Act and its 1965 amendments. In reaching that conclusion, Justice Stevens, speaking for a majority on some issues and a plurality on others, relied on a presumption against the preemption of "state police power regulations," and thus construed the relevant provisions of the federal law narrowly. Justice Scalia, joined by Justice Thomas, objected to what he called an "extraordinary and unprecedented principle of federal statutory construction: that express preemption provisions must be construed narrowly" where they conflicted with traditional state police power regulations and remedies. And in Gade v. National Solid Wastes Management Association, 505 U.S. 88 (1992), the Court's division about the relevant presumptions became sharper, here in the context of an implied preemption claim. Writing partly for the Court and partly for a plurality, Justice O'Connor's opinion found an Illinois hazardous waste licensing scheme impliedly pre-empted by certain Occupational Safety and Health Administration regulations, even though the Illinois scheme was designed to serve environmental as well as worker safety goals. Justice Souter's dissent, joined by Justices Blackmun, Stevens, and Thomas, and Justice Kennedy's concurrence, both objected to the majority's expansion of the role of implied pre-emption in this case. "In light of our rule that federal pre-emption of state law is only to be found in a clear congressional purpose to supplant exercises of the States' traditional police powers, the text of the Act fails to support the Court's conclusion. In CSX Transportation, Inc. v. Easterwood, 508 U.S. ___ (1993), however, there was no disagreement with the statement in Justice White's majority opinion that "In the interest of avoiding unintended encroachment on the authority of the States, [a] court interpreting a federal statute pertaining to a subject traditionally governed by state law will be reluctant to find pre-emption." In its most recent efforts to delineate broad standards that would guide pre-emption inquiries, the Court, in Freightliner Corp. v. Myrick, 517 U.S. ___ (1995), held, interpreting Cipollone, that an express pre-emption clause does not preclude a finding of implied pre-emption, although it may support an inference to that effect.

An interesting twist on the preemption issue emerged after extensive Congressional debate on the funding of abortions. Henry Hyde, sponsor of the original Hyde Amendment prohibiting federal funding for abortions in any circumstances, see Harris v. McRae, 12th Ed., p. 534, Ind.Rts., p. 205, proposed an amendment to an appropriations bill on June 30, 1993, which would allow abortions to be federally funded in the case of rape or incest. The appropriations bill with the rape and incest amendment was eventually passed and signed into law (P.L. 103–112). The Center for Reproductive Law and Policy then filed suit in Arkansas and Colorado on November 8, 1993, claiming that the federal law preempted state constitutional provisions prohibiting Medicaid funding for abortions except to save the life of the mother. In the Colorado suit, Hern v. Beye, an order enjoining the state of Colorado from enforcing provisions contrary to federal law was granted May 12, 1994, primarily on pre-emption grounds. The order was affirmed by the 10th Circuit on June 8, 1995. In Little Rock Family Planning Services v. Dalton, 860 F.Supp. 609 (E.D.Ark.1994), plaintiffs also prevailed in a summary judgment motion based on pre-emption grounds.

12th ED., p. 300
Add at end of footnote 1:

In Wyoming v. Oklahoma, 502 U.S. 437 (1992), however, described above, addition to 12th Ed., p. 261, the Court reiterated and relied on the "plain statement" rule of South–Central Timber and Maine v. Taylor, and made no mention either of implicit permission or of the Northwest Central case.

12th ED., p. 302
Add as footnote at end of Note 3 (on McCarran Act):

2a. Thus, a state statute regulating the "business of insurance" effectively "pre-empts" inconsistent federal laws that do not "specifically relate[ ] to the business of insurance." See, most recently, United States Department of Treasury v. Fabe, 509 U.S. ___ (1993).

12th ED., p. 306
Add at end of footnote 3:

The most recent case, and one that attracted considerable attention, is Quill Corp. v. North Dakota, 504 U.S. 298 (1992), holding it permissible under the due process clause but impermissible under the dormant commerce clause for a state to attempt to tax out-of-state mail order businesses with neither outlets nor representatives in the state, and whose only contacts with the state were by common carrier or the mails. In continuing to adhere to the bright-line rule of National Bellas Hess, Inc. v. Illinois Department of Revenue, 386 U.S. 753 (1967), Justice Stevens' opinion for the Court relied not only on virtues of stare decisis, but on the greater abilities of Congress than the courts to resolve issues about the "burdens that use taxes impose on interstate commerce." By making clear that such taxes burden commerce but do not violate the due process clause, Justice Stevens emphasized, the way was now clear for Congress to decide what it wished to do in this area. Relatedly, in Oklahoma Tax Commission v. Jefferson Lines, Inc., 517 U.S. ___ (1995), the Court upheld against a commerce clause objection Oklahoma's imposition of a sales tax on the full price of transportation (here, bus tickets) originating in the state, even if the travel ended in another state. Note also Associated Industries of Missouri v. Lohman, 507 U.S. ___ (1994), a unanimous decision, with Justice Thomas writing for the Court, striking down a supposedly compensating use tax that in some localities exceeded the sales tax that the use tax was intended to compensate for.

12th ED., p. 307
Add at end of footnote 3:

The most recent case is Trinova Corp. v. Michigan Department of Treasury, 498 U.S. 358 (1991), upholding the Michigan Single Business Tax, a form of value added tax, against commerce clause and due process objections. Concurring in the judgment, Justice Scalia reiterated his view that commerce clause analysis, whether for taxes or for other forms of regulation, should be limited to determining whether the tax or regulation is "facially discriminatory."

12th ED., p. 308
Add to footnote 3:

And for a decision applying Davis, see Barker v. Kansas, 503 U.S. 594 (1992).

12th ED., p. 310
Add at beginning of footnote 2:

For a detailed example of the interstate compact process at work, see New York v. United States, 505 U.S. 144 (1992), set out above, addition to 12th Ed., p. 175. In Hess v. Port Authority Trans-Hudson Corp., 515 U.S. ___ (1994), a 5–4 Supreme Court held that entities created pursuant to interstate compacts were not entitled to Eleventh Amendment immunity from suit in the same way that states were.

Chapter 6

SEPARATION OF POWERS: THE PRESIDENT, CONGRESS, AND THE COURT

12th ED., p. 322
Add at end of note 2a:

In Youngstown, the Government expressly acknowledged that there was no statutory authority for the seizure. Had there been a statutory authorization, and had the President exceeded it, his actions would have been unconstitutional, just as in Youngstown itself, because of the lack of inherent presidential authority under either the Executive or Commander-in-Chief powers. Suppose, however, that a President acts beyond a statutory authorization, but within what could have been, but was not, authorized. Does the President's "ultra vires" act constitute a constitutional violation just because the President may not, in general, act without congressional authorization? That was the argument in Dalton v. Specter, 509 U.S. ___ (1994), where there was an attempt to enjoin the closure of the Philadelphia Naval Shipyard, allegedly in violation of the Defense Base Closure and Realignment Act of 1990. Because neither that Act nor any other appeared to allow judicial review as a statutory matter, the claimants argued that the allegedly ultra vires action of the President was for that reason unconstitutional, and thus reviewable as any other unconstitutional presidential action. But the Supreme Court, with Chief Justice REHNQUIST writing for the majority (and for a unanimous Court on this issue), rejected that claim. "Because no statutory authority was claimed [in Youngstown,] the case necessarily turned on whether the Constitution authorized the President's actions. Youngstown thus involved the conceded absence of any statutory authority, not a claim that the President acted in excess of such authority. The case cannot be read for the proposition that an action taken by the President in excess of his statutory authority necessarily violates the Constitution."

12th ED., p. 339
Add at end of footnote 1:

Both balanced budget constitutional amendment proposals (S.J.Res. 41, H.J.Res. 103) were defeated in the 103rd Congress. The new Republican majority of the 104th Congress, however, made the balanced budget amendment a centerpiece of their Contract with America and promised to consider the legislation within the first 100 days. H.J.Res. 1 and S.J.Res. 1 required that the Federal budget be balanced, unless three-fifths of both houses voted to suspend the requirement, and that this be accomplished by 2002 or two years after enactment of the constitutional amendment, whichever was later. H.J.Res. 1 was reported out of the House Judiciary Committee on January 11, 1995 by a vote of 20–13, split along party lines. The full House easily passed the resolution on January 26, 1995 by a vote of 300–132. The measure then went to the Senate. One of Senator Nunn's concerns about the amendment was his fear that Federal courts might be given too much power under the amendment to control taxation. He cited Missouri v. Jenkins (1990, 12th Ed., p. 749;

68

Ind.Rts., p. 420) as the source of his concern, and Senate sponsors of the amendment finally agreed (92–8) to an amendment which would have prohibited any federal court, including the Supreme Court, from deciding whether the budget was actually balanced. After much negotiation and delay, on March 2, 1995, H.J.Res. 1 failed passage in the Senate by a vote of 65–35, two votes short of the required two-thirds majority needed. Senator Dole, a Presidential candidate, vowed to call for a revote on the measure shortly before the 1996 elections.

In a related development, the power of the President to veto line items in the budget has broad support in the 104th Congress. H.R. 2, granting such power, was passed by the House on February 6, 1995, by a vote of 294–134. Two Senate versions of the bill were proposed, S. 4 and S. 14. S. 4 passed the Senate on March 23, 1995 by a vote of 69–29. The House refused to concur in the Senate version, and on June 20, 1995, a conference committee was appointed to work out the differences between the bills. Constitutional amendment proposals to give the President line-item veto authority include S.J.Res. 2, 15, 16 and H.J.Res. 4, 6, 17, 43, 47.

Meanwhile, in the states, where a proposal to call a constitutional convention for the purpose of offering a balanced budget amendment has been making the rounds of the legislatures for 20 years, the initiative seemed to have stalled before the congressional vote. Missouri, the 32nd of the 34 states needed to call a convention, approved a resolution in 1983, but since that date three states, Florida, Alabama, and Louisiana, have rescinded their resolutions calling for a convention. It is possible that organizers of the balanced budget convention movement, such as the National Taxpayers Union, may renew their efforts in the states now that the congressional drive has fallen short. In that event, questions about the validity of the rescissions, as well as questions about who determines questions about the validity of the rescissions, may come to the fore. On the question of justiciability, see below, 12th Ed., pp. 1653–54; Ind.Rts., pp. 1324–25. See also above, 12th Ed., p. 201 n. 1.

12th ED., p. 339
Add as new Note immediately after Bowsher v. Synar:

THE CONTINUING STRINGENCY OF SEPARATION OF POWERS REVIEW

The Court continues to take seriously both separation of powers themes generally and its holdings in Chadha and Bowsher particularly. In METROPOLITAN WASHINGTON AIRPORTS AUTHORITY v. CITIZENS FOR THE ABATEMENT OF AIRCRAFT NOISE, INC., 501 U.S. 252 (1991), the Court confronted a challenge to an Act of Congress that conditioned the transfer of Dulles and National airports from the federal government to the Metropolitan Washington Airports Authority on the creation by the Authority of a Board of Review composed of nine Members of Congress and having veto power over Authority decisions. The challengers to this condition argued that it in effect put members of Congress in a position of executing and administering the airports after transfer, thus violating the principle of separation of executive and legislative powers.

By a 6–3 decision, with Justice STEVENS writing for the majority, the Court agreed and held that the Board of Review violated separation of powers principles. The majority first rejected claims that the Board of Review was something other than an arm of Congress. "We thus confront an entity created at the initiative of Congress, the powers of which Congress has delineated, the purpose of which is to protect an acknowledged federal interest, and membership in which is restricted to congressional officials. Such an entity necessarily exercises sufficient federal power as an agent of Congress to mandate separation-of-powers scrutiny." At this point, however, Justice Stevens found it unnecessary to choose between two alternative grounds for the decision. If the actions of the Board were characterized as executive or administrative, then the Board served as an arm of Congress performing executive functions in violation of the principles set forth in Bowsher v. Synar. But if the Board's functions were instead seen to be legislative, then its decisions would be legislative decisions taken without compliance with the requirements of bicameralism and presentment, and thus in violation of constitutional principles set out in INS v. Chadha. Although Justice Stevens saw no need to decide among these alternative routes to the same conclusion, he did note the implications of a contrary ruling. "Given the scope of the federal power to dispense benefits to the States in a variety of forms and subject to a host of statutory conditions, Congress could, if this Board of Review were valid, use similar expedients to enable its Members or its agents to retain control, outside the ordinary legislative process, of the activities of state grant recipients charged with executing virtually every aspect of national policy."

Justice WHITE, joined by Chief Justice Rehnquist and Justice Marshall, dissented, again objecting that "the Court strikes down yet another innovative and otherwise lawful governmental experiment in the name of separation of powers. [For] the first time in its history, the Court employs separation-of-powers doctrine to invalidate a body created under state law." Justice White felt this case plainly distinguishable from Bowsher, for here the power of removal could be exercised only indirectly by removing members from those Committees membership on which was a prerequisite to Board of Review membership. And he saw the power to be exercised by the Board as so plainly not legislative that reliance on Chadha was misplaced. He thought that by protecting the power of the Executive Branch where that Branch had at no time objected, the Court "utterly ignores the Executive's ability to protect itself through, among other things, the veto. Should Congress ever undertake such improbable projects as transferring national parklands to the States on the condition that its agents control their oversight, there is little doubt that the President would be equal to the task of safeguarding his or her interests."

12th Ed., p. 351
Add at end of footnote 1:

For a more recent Appointments Clause case, see Weiss v. United States, 507 U.S. ___ (1994). At issue was the claim that judges in military courts martial, all of whom were appointed to their military rank in conformity with the Appointments Clause, were required to be separately appointed, again in accordance with the provisions of the Appointments Clause, before they could serve as court martial judges. Rejecting the claim, Chief Justice Rehnquist, writing for a unanimous Court, acknowledged that the Appointments Clause applied to military officers and to judges in military courts martial. But because the duties of judges in military courts martial were not totally distinct from the duties of military officers in general, he concluded, and because it was the intent of Congress that the office of military judge not be a distinct one at this level, no separate appointment to the office of military judge was necessary. In a lengthy and careful concurring opinion, Justice Souter focused on the distinction in the Appointments Clause between principal and inferior officers. If military judges were principal officers, a separate appointment would be necessary, he argued. But he concluded that, although the case was a close one, some deference to the congressional intent that these officers be treated as inferior officers was appropriate. In light of that, he was willing to conclude that these were inferior and not principal officers, and thus in no need of a separate appointment according to the Appointments Clause.

12th ED., p. 359

Add at end of footnote 5:

In Touby v. United States, 500 U.S. 160 (1991), the Court once again rejected a non-delegation argument, relying on language in J.W. Hampton, Jr. & Co. v. United States, 276 U.S. 394 (1928), indicating that Congress does not engage in forbidden delegation so long as it "lay[s] down by legislative act an intelligible principle to which the person or body authorized to [act] is directed to conform." Justice O'Connor's opinion for a unanimous Court also made clear that neither the non-delegation doctrine nor any other aspect of separation of powers jurisprudence had any applicability to distribution of authority within a branch, but only to "the distribution of powers *among* the three coequal Branches."

On the related separation of powers issue of legislative interference with the powers of Article III courts, see, most recently, Plaut v. Spendthrift Farm, Inc., 517 U.S. ___ (1995), described at length above, 12th Ed., p. 43.

12th ED., p. 370

Insert as footnote following last full paragraph, "the operation of those political processes":

6. Ongoing tensions in Bosnia and the continuing controversy between President Clinton and Congress about the role of American troops, both in the context of the United Nations and NATO operations, have once again brought debate about the War Powers Resolution to the fore. Several proposals are before the 104th Congress. S. 564, the Use of Force Act, introduced by Senator Biden, and H.J.Res. 95, the War Powers Amendments of 1995, introduced by Rep. DeFazio, articulate in some detail the circumstances in which the President is authorized to commit United States forces short of war. S. 5, the Peace Powers Act of 1995, introduced by Senator Dole, and H.R. 1111, introduced by Rep. Dornan, would repeal the War Powers Resolution. These bills attempt to address the role of war powers in the post-Cold War period, require that the President consult with Congress in every possible instance before committing U.S. forces into hostilities, and also require that certain reports be submitted by the President if there is no declaration of war. H.R. 277 would require that cost-benefit statements be prepared before a declaration of war by Congress or the President.

12th ED., p. 372

Add at end of footnote 2:

Impeachment continues to be a pressing topic. United States District Judges Alcee Hastings (since elected to Congress from Florida) and Walter Nixon mounted challenges to the procedures employed by the Senate in their trials. With the Hastings case pending, Nixon's challenge reached the Supreme Court in the 1992 Term, where the Court held that determining the procedures to be employed in the Senate constituted a nonjusticiable "political question," largely because of the import of the word "sole" in Article 1, section 2, clause 5, giving the Senate the "sole power to try all Impeachments." The case, Nixon v. United States, is set out below, addition to 12th Ed., p. 393. In a District Court opinion issued after the Nixon case was decided by the Supreme Court, Judge Sporkin distinguished the facts of the Hastings and Nixon cases by noting that Hastings had been acquitted of criminal charges. "As strongly as this Court believes that Judge Hastings' fundamental rights were violated, the Court recognizes that the Nixon decision compels that Judge Hastings' case be dismissed. This Court believes that the events surrounding plaintiff's impeachment and conviction are an unfortunate chapter in the history of this country." (Hastings v. New York, 837 F.Supp. 3, 5 (D.D.C.1993)).

In the 1994 term, the Justice Department appealed the en banc decision of the Ninth Circuit Court of Appeals, overturning charges against District Court Judge Robert Aguilar of disclosing an FBI wiretap to an ex-mobster and obstructing justice, 21 F.3d 1475 (1994). Judge Aguilar had been under threat of impeachment by the 103rd Congress. On June 21,

1995, the Supreme Court affirmed the wiretap conviction 8–1. In a separate 6–3 vote, the Justices reversed an obstruction of justice charge against Aguilar (United States v. Aguilar, 519 U.S. ___ (1995)). Judge Aguilar was still receiving a salary and holding settlement conferences up to the date of the Supreme Court decision. Another federal judge, Robert Collins, chose to resign while in prison rather than face impeachment proceedings.

Congress is also facing misconduct charges against some of its own members, several of whom are attempting novel constitutional defenses. Rep. Joseph McDade (R–Pa.) was indicted in May 1992 for accepting bribes to steer federal contracts to companies in his congressional district. McDade challenged the indictment on the basis of the Speech and Debate clause (Art. I, sec. 6, paragraph 1), contending that the activities in question were part of his legislative duties and thus insulated from interference by other branches of government. His arguments were supported by a brief filed by the leaders of both parties in the House of Representatives. The Third Circuit upheld the indictment, 28 F.3d 283 (1994), and the Supreme Court denied certiorari on March 6, 1995. (McDade v. United States). Rep. Rostenkowski (D.–Ill) has also advanced similar arguments in his embezzlement case pending before the D.C. Circuit.

Congressional proposals to deal with the problem of federal judges' felony convictions include H.R. 350 (which would stop salary payments to convicted Federal judges) and S. 52 (which would suspend convicted judges without pay), and constitutional amendment proposal S.J.Res. 5 which would require forfeiture of office by any federal official appointed by the President (including but not limited to federal judges) automatically upon a felony conviction and exhaustion of direct appeals.

12th ED., p. 377

Add to end of footnote 1 (on p. 378):

Although subordinate executive officials possess only qualified immunity, the plaintiff alleging the malice that would defeat the immunity must meet a heightened pleading standard, the purpose of which, first stated in Harlow itself, is to spare federal officials the burden of discovery or defense for actions that do not appear to be well-grounded. See Siegert v. Gilley, 500 U.S. 226 (1991), described below, addition to 12th Ed., p. 597; Ind.Rts., p. 268.

In Wyatt v. Cole, 504 U.S. 158 (1992), the Court, with Justice O'Connor writing for the majority, held that the qualified immunity of Harlow and Mitchell was not available to non-governmental parties charged under 42 U.S.C. § 1983 or analogous laws with violating the constitutional rights of others. Chief Justice Rehnquist, joined by Justices Souter and Thomas, dissented.

In connection with Nixon v. Fitzgerald, consider the current controversy regarding the sexual harassment suit filed in the United States District Court for the District of Arkansas against President Clinton by Paula Corbin Jones. The suit, based on events allegedly occurring prior to the President's taking office as President, alleges federal civil rights violations and raises claims under Arkansas law for defamation and intentional infliction of emotional distress. On June 27, 1994, the President's personal attorney for this matter, Robert S. Bennett, filed a motion to delay proceedings until the issue of presidential immunity had been resolved. Mr. Bennett said that a separate motion on the immunity issue, relying heavily on Nixon v. Fitzgerald, would be filed on August 5, 1994.

12th ED., p. 392

Add as new paragraphs at end of footnote 3:

In the wake of charges of sexual harassment against Senator Bob Packwood of Oregon, the Senate Rules Committee received a citizen petition asking it to recommend that the Senate refuse to seat Packwood as the result of what the petitioners claimed was election fraud in not disclosing during his 1992 re-election campaign that such charges had been made against him. Amid considerable discussion of whether such action was barred by the Powell case, the Committee on May 20, 1993, voted 16–0 not to consider the petition, although the substantive charges remain pending before the Senate Ethics Committee.

12th ED., p. 393
Add in place of Note 2:

NIXON v. UNITED STATES

506 U.S. ___, 113 S.Ct. 732, 122 L.Ed.2d 1 (1993).

Chief Justice REHNQUIST delivered the opinion of the Court.

Petitioner Walter L. Nixon, Jr., asks this court to decide whether Senate Rule XI, which allows a committee of Senators to hear evidence against an individual who has been impeached and to report that evidence to the full Senate, violates the Impeachment Trial Clause, Art. I, § 3, cl. 6. That Clause provides that the "Senate shall have the sole Power to try all Impeachments." But before we reach the merits of such a claim, we must decide whether it is "justiciable." [We] conclude that it is not.

Nixon, a former Chief Judge of the United States District Court for the Southern District of Mississippi, was convicted by a jury [of] making false statements before a federal grand jury and sentenced to prison. The grand jury investigation stemmed from reports that Nixon had accepted a gratuity from a Mississippi businessman in exchange for asking a local district attorney to halt the prosecution of the businessman's son.

[On] May 10, 1989, the House of Representatives adopted three articles of impeachment for high crimes and misdemeanors. The first two articles charged Nixon with giving false testimony before the grand jury and the third article charged him with bringing disrepute on the Federal Judiciary. After the House presented the articles to the Senate, the Senate voted to invoke its own Impeachment Rule XI, under which the presiding officer appoints a committee of Senators to "receive evidence and take testimony." The Senate committee held four days of hearings, during which 10 witnesses, including Nixon, testified. Pursuant to Rule XI, the committee presented the full Senate with a complete transcript of the proceeding and a report stating the uncontested facts and summarizing the evidence on the contested facts. Nixon and the House impeachment managers submitted extensive final briefs to the full Senate and delivered arguments from the Senate floor during the three hours set aside for oral argument in front of that body. Nixon himself gave a personal appeal, and several Senators posed questions directly to both parties. The Senate voted by more than the constitutionally required two-thirds majority to convict Nixon on the first two articles. The presiding officer then entered judgment removing Nixon [as District] Judge. Nixon thereafter commenced the present suit, arguing that Senate Rule XI violates the constitutional grant of authority to the Senate to "try" all impeachments because it prohibits the whole Senate from taking part in the evidentiary hearings. [The] District Court held that his claim was nonjusticiable, and the Court of Appeals for the District of Columbia Circuit agreed.

A controversy is nonjusticiable—i.e., involves a political question— where there is "a textually demonstrable constitutional commitment of the issue to a coordinate political department; or a lack of judicially discoverable and manageable standards for resolving it . . ." Baker. But the courts must, in the first instance, interpret the text in question and determine whether and to what extent the issue is textually committed. As the discussion that follows makes clear, the concept of a textual commitment to a coordinate political department is not completely separate from the concept of a lack of judicially discoverable and manageable standards for resolving it; the lack of judicially manageable standards may strengthen the conclusion that there is a textually demonstrable commitment to a coordinate branch.

[Art. I, § 3, cl. 6 provides]: "The Senate shall have the sole Power to try all Impeachments. When sitting for that Purpose, they shall be on Oath or Affirmation. When the President of the United States is tried, the Chief Justice shall preside: And no Person shall be convicted without the Concurrence of two thirds of the Members present." [Petitioner] argues that the word "try" in the first sentence imposes by implication [the] requirement [that] the proceedings must be in the nature of a judicial trial. From there petitioner goes on to argue that this limitation precludes the Senate from delegating to a select committee the task of hearing the testimony of witnesses. " '[T]ry' means more than simply 'vote on' or 'review' or 'judge.' In 1787 and today, trying a case means hearing the evidence, not scanning a cold record." Petitioner concludes from this that courts may review whether or not the Senate "tried" him before convicting him.

There are several difficulties with this position. [The] word "try," both in 1787 and later, has considerably broader meanings than those to which petitioner would limit it. Older dictionaries define try as "[t]o examine" or "[t]o examine as a judge." S. Johnson, A Dictionary of the English Language (1785). In more modern usage the term has various meanings. For example, try can mean "to examine or investigate judicially," "to conduct the trial of," or "to put to the test by experiment, investigation, or trial." Webster's Third New International Dictionary (1971). Petitioner submits that "try," as contained in T. Sheridan, Dictionary of the English Language (1796), means "to examine as a judge; to bring before a judicial tribunal." Based on the variety of definitions, however, we cannot say that the Framers used the word "try" as an implied limitation on the method by which the Senate might proceed in trying impeachments.

[The] conclusion that the use of the word "try" in the first sentence [lacks] sufficient precision to afford any judicially manageable standard of review [is] fortified by the existence of the three very specific requirements that the Constitution does impose on the Senate when trying impeachments: the members must be under oath, a two-thirds vote is required to convict, and the Chief Justice presides when the President is tried. These limitations are quite precise, and their nature suggests that the Framers did not intend to impose additional limitations [by] the use of the word "try" in the first sentence.

Petitioner devotes only two pages in his brief to negating the significance of the word "sole," [but we] think [it] is of considerable significance. Indeed, the word "sole" appears only one other time in the Constitution—with respect to the House of Representatives' "sole Power of Impeachment." Art. I, § 2, cl. 5. The common sense meaning of the word "sole" is that the Senate alone shall have authority to determine whether an individual should be acquitted or convicted. The dictionary definition bears this out. "Sole" is defined as "having no companion," "solitary," "being the only one," and "functioning ... independently and without assistance or interference." Webster's (1971). If the courts may review the actions of the Senate [to] determine whether that body "tried" an impeached official, it is difficult to see how the Senate would be "functioning ... independently and without assistance or interference."

Nixon asserts that the word "sole" has no substantive meaning. [He] argues that the word is nothing more than a mere "cosmetic edit" added by the Committee of Style after the delegates had approved the substance of the Impeachment Trial Clause. There are two difficulties with this argument. First, accepting [the] proposition that the Committee of Style had no authority [to] alter the meaning of the Clause, Records of the Federal Convention of 1787 (M. Farrand ed. 1966), we must presume that the Committee's reorganization or rephrasing accurately captured what the Framers meant in their unadorned language. That is, we must presume that the Committee did its job. [We] agree with the Government that "the word 'sole' is entitled to no less weight than any other word of the text." [Second,] carrying Nixon's argument to its logical conclusion would constrain us to say that the second to last draft would govern in every instance where the Committee of Style added an arguably substantive word. Such a result is at odds with the fact that the Convention passed the Committee's version, and with the well established rule that the plain language of the enacted text is the best indicator of intent.

[Petitioner] finally argues that even if significance be attributed to the word "sole" in the first sentence of the clause, the authority granted is to the Senate, and this means that "the Senate—not the courts, not a lay jury, not a Senate Committee—shall try impeachments." It would be possible to read [the] Clause this way, but it is not a natural reading. Petitioner's interpretation would bring into judicial purview not merely the sort of claim made by petitioner, but other similar claims based on the conclusion that the word "Senate" has imposed by implication limitations on procedures which the Senate might adopt. Such limitations would be inconsistent with the construction of the Clause as a whole, which [sets] out three express limitations in separate sentences.

The history [of] the impeachment provisions support[s] our reading of the constitutional language. The parties do not offer evidence of a single word in the history of the Constitutional Convention or in contemporary commentary that even alludes to the possibility of judicial review in the context of the impeachment powers. This silence is quite meaningful in light of the several explicit references to the availability of judicial review as a check on the Legislature's power with respect to bills of attainder, ex post facto laws, and statutes. Federalist 78. The Framers labored over the question of where the impeachment power should lie. Significantly, in at least two considered scenarios the power was placed with the Federal Judiciary. Indeed, Madison and the Committee of Detail proposed that the Supreme Court should have the power to determine impeachments. Despite these proposals, the Convention ultimately decided that the Senate would have "the sole Power to Try all Impeachments." According to Hamilton, the Senate was the "most fit depositary of this important trust" because its members are representatives of the people. Federalist 65.

[There] are two additional reasons why the Judiciary, and the Supreme Court in particular, were not chosen to have any role in impeachments. First, the Framers recognized that most likely there would be two sets of proceedings for individuals who commit impeachable offenses—the impeachment trial and a separate criminal trial. In fact, the Constitution explicitly provides for two separate proceedings. Art. I, § 3, cl. 7. The Framers deliberately separated the two forums to avoid raising the specter of bias and to ensure independent judgments. [Certainly] judicial review of the Senate's "trial" would introduce the same risk of bias as would participation in the trial itself.

Second, judicial review would be inconsistent with the Framers' insistence that our system be one of checks and balances. In our constitutional system, impeachment was designed to be the only check on the Judicial Branch by the Legislature. [Judicial] involvement in impeachment proceedings, even if only for purposes of judicial review, [would] eviscerate the "important constitutional check" placed on the Judiciary by the Framers. Federalist 81. Nixon's argument would place final reviewing authority with respect to impeachments in the hands of the same body that the impeachment process is meant to regulate. Nevertheless, Nixon argues that judicial review is necessary in order to place a check on the Legislature. Nixon fears that if the Senate is given unreviewable authority to interpret the Impeachment Trial Clause, there is a grave risk that the Senate will usurp judicial power. The Framers anticipated this objection and created two constitutional safeguards to keep the Senate in check. The first safeguard is that the whole of the impeachment power is divided between the two legislative bodies, with the House given the right to accuse and the Senate given the right to judge. [The] second safeguard is the two-thirds supermajority vote requirement. Hamilton explained that "[a]s the concurrence of two-thirds of the senate will be requisite to a condemnation, the security to innocence, from this additional circumstance, will be as complete as itself can desire."

In addition to the textual commitment argument, we are persuaded that the lack of finality and the difficulty of fashioning relief counsel against justiciability. We agree with the Court of Appeals that opening the door of judicial review to the procedures used by the Senate in trying impeachments would "expose the political life of the country to months, or perhaps years, of chaos." This lack of finality would manifest itself most dramatically if the President were impeached. The legitimacy of any successor, and hence his effectiveness, would be impaired severely, not merely while the judicial process was running its course, but during any retrial that a differently constituted Senate might conduct if its first judgment of conviction were invalidated. Equally uncertain is the question of what relief a court may give other than simply setting aside the judgment of conviction. Could it order the reinstatement of a convicted federal judge, or order Congress to create an additional judgeship if the seat had been filled in the interim?

Petitioner finally contends that a holding of nonjusticiability cannot be reconciled with [Powell.] [Our] conclusion in Powell was based on the fixed meaning of "[q]ualifications" set forth in Art. I, § 2. The claim by the House that its power to "be the Judge of the Elections, Returns and Qualifications of its own Members" was a textual commitment of unreviewable authority was defeated by the existence of this separate provision specifying the only qualifications which might be imposed for House membership. The decision as to whether a member satisfied these qualifications was placed with the House, but the decision as to what these qualifications consisted of was not. In the case before us, there is no separate provision of the Constitution which could be defeated by allowing the Senate final authority to determine the meaning of the word "try" in the Impeachment Trial Clause. We agree with Nixon that courts possess power to review either legislative or executive action that transgresses identifiable textual limits. [But] we conclude [that] the word "try" in the Impeachment Clause does not provide an identifiable textual limit on the authority which is committed to the Senate.

[Affirmed.]

Justice STEVENS, concurring.

For me, the debate about the strength of the inferences to be drawn from the use of the words "sole" and "try" is far less significant than the central fact that the Framers decided to assign the impeachment power to the Legislative Branch. The disposition of the impeachment of Samuel Chase in 1805 demonstrated that the Senate is fully conscious of the profound importance of that assignment, and nothing in the subsequent history of the Senate's exercise of this extraordinary power suggests otherwise. See A. Beveridge, The Life of John Marshall (1919); W. Rehnquist, Grand Inquests (1992). Respect for a coordinate Branch of the Government forecloses any assumption that improbable hypotheticals like those mentioned by Justice White and Justice Souter will ever occur. Accordingly, the wise policy of judicial restraint, coupled with the potential anomalies associated with a contrary view, provide a sufficient justification for my agreement with the views of the Chief Justice.

Justice WHITE, with whom Justice BLACKMUN joins, concurring in the judgment.

Petitioner contends that the method by which the Senate convicted him [violates] the Constitution. [The] Court is of the view that the Constitution forbids us even to consider his contention. I find no such prohibition and would therefore reach the merits of the claim. I concur in the judgment because the Senate fulfilled its constitutional obligation to "try" petitioner.

I. [As] a practical matter, it will likely make little difference whether the Court's or my view controls this case. This is so because the Senate has very wide discretion in specifying impeachment trial procedures and because it is extremely unlikely that the Senate would abuse its discretion and insist on a procedure that could not be deemed a trial by reasonable judges. Even taking a wholly practical approach, I would prefer not to announce an unreviewable discretion in the Senate to ignore completely the constitutional direction to "try" impeachment cases. When asked at oral argument whether that direction would be satisfied if, after a House vote to impeach, the Senate, without any procedure whatsoever, unanimously found the accused guilty of being "a bad guy," counsel for the United States answered that the Government's theory "leads me to answer that question yes." Especially in light of this advice from the Solicitor General, I would not issue an invitation to the Senate to find an excuse, in the name of other pressing business, to be dismissive of its critical role in the impeachment process.

Practicalities aside, however, [the] meaning of a constitutional provision is at issue, [and] my disagreement with the Court should be stated.

II. [Of] course the issue in the political question doctrine is not whether the Constitutional text commits exclusive responsibility for a particular governmental function to one of the political branches. There are numerous instances of this sort of textual commitment, e.g., Art. I, § 8, and disputes implicating these provisions are [not] nonjusticiable. Rather, the issue is whether the Constitution has given one of the political branches final responsibility for interpreting the scope [of] such a power.

Although Baker directs the Court to search for "a textually demonstrable constitutional commitment" of such responsibility, there are few, if any, explicit and unequivocal instances in the Constitution of this sort of textual commitment. [The] courts therefore are usually left to infer the presence of a political question from the text and structure of the Constitution. In drawing the inference that the Constitution has committed final interpretive authority to one of the political branches, courts are sometimes aided by textual evidence that the judiciary was not meant to exercise judicial review—a coordinate inquiry expressed in Baker's "lack of judicially discoverable and manageable standards" criterion. See Coleman v. Miller, 307 U.S. 433 (1939), where the Court refused to determine the life span of a proposed constitutional amendment given Art. V's placement of the amendment process with Congress and the lack of any judicial standard for resolving the question.

A. The majority finds a clear textual commitment in the Constitution's use of the word "sole." [In] disagreeing with the Court, I note that the Solicitor General stated at oral argument that "[w]e don't rest our submission on sole power to try." The Government was well advised in this respect. The significance of the Constitution's use of the term "sole" lies not in the infrequency with which the term appears, but in the fact that it appears exactly twice, in parallel provisions concerning impeachment. That the word "sole" is found only in the House and Senate Impeachment Clauses demonstrates that its purpose is to emphasize the distinct role of each in the impeachment process. As the majority notes, the Framers, following English practice, were very much concerned to separate the prosecutorial from the adjudicative aspects of impeachment. Giving each House "sole" power with respect to its role in impeachments effected this division of labor. While the majority is thus right to interpret the term "sole" to indicate that the Senate ought to "functio[n] independently and without assistance or interference," it wrongly identifies the judiciary, rather than the House, as the source of potential interference with which the Framers were concerned when they employed the term "sole."

Even if the [Clause] is read without regard to its companion clause, the Court's willingness to abandon its obligation to review the constitutionality of legislative acts merely on the strength of the word "sole" is perplexing. Consider, by comparison, the treatment of Art. I, § 1, which grants "All legislative powers" to the House and Senate. As used in that context "all" is nearly synonymous with "sole"—both connote entire and exclusive authority. Yet the Court has never thought it would unduly interfere with the operation of the Legislative Branch to entertain difficult and important questions as to the extent of the legislative power.

[The] majority also claims support in the history and early interpretations of the Impeachment Clauses, noting the various arguments in support of the current system made at the Constitutional Convention and expressed powerfully by Hamilton in Federalist 65 and 66. [The] majority's review of the historical record thus explains why the power to try impeachments properly resides with the Senate. It does not explain, however, the sweeping statement that the judiciary was "not chosen to have any role in impeachments." Not a single word in the historical materials cited by the majority addresses judicial review of the Impeachment Trial Clause. [What] the relevant history mainly reveals is deep ambivalence among many of the Framers over the very institution of impeachment, which [is] not easily reconciled with our system of checks and balances. [The] branch of the Federal Government which is possessed of the authority to try impeachments, by having final say over the membership of each branch, holds a potentially unanswerable power over the others. In addition, that branch, insofar as it is called upon to try not only members of other branches, but also its own, will have the advantage of being the judge of its own members' causes.

It is no surprise, then, that the question of impeachment greatly vexed the Framers. The pages of the Convention debates reveal diverse plans for resolving this exceedingly difficult issue. Both before and during the convention, Madison maintained that the judiciary ought to try impeachments. Shortly thereafter, however, he devised a quite complicated scheme that involved the participation of each branch. Jefferson likewise had attempted to develop an interbranch system for impeachment trials in Virginia. Even Hamilton's eloquent defense of the scheme adopted by the Constitution was based on a pragmatic decision to further the cause of ratification rather than a strong belief in the superiority of a scheme vesting the Senate with the sole power to try impeachments. While at the Convention, Hamilton advocated that impeachment trials be conducted by a court made up of state court judges. Four months after publishing Federalist 65 and 66, however, he urged the New York Ratifying Convention to amend the Clause he had so ably defended to have the Senate, the Supreme Court, and judges from each state jointly try impeachments.

The historical evidence reveals above all else that the Framers were deeply concerned about placing in any branch the "awful discretion, which a court of impeachments must necessarily have." Federalist 65. Viewed against this history, the discord between the majority's position and the basic principles of checks and balances underlying the Constitution's separation of powers is clear. In essence, the majority suggests that the Framers' conferred upon Congress a potential tool of legislative dominance yet at the same time rendered Congress' exercise of that power one of the very few areas of legislative authority immune from any judicial review. [In] a truly balanced system, impeachments tried by the Senate would serve as a means of controlling the largely unaccountable judiciary, even as judicial review would ensure that the Senate adhered to a minimal set of procedural standards in conducting impeachment trials.

B. The majority also contends that the term "try" does not present a judicially manageable standard. [It] is apparently on this basis that the majority distinguishes Powell. [The] majority finds this case different from Powell only on the grounds that, whereas the qualifications of Art. I, § 2 are readily susceptible to judicial interpretation, the term "try" does not provide an "identifiable textual limit on the authority which is committed to the Senate."

This argument comes in two variants. The first, which asserts that one simply cannot ascertain the sense of "try" which the Framers employed and hence cannot undertake judicial review, is clearly untenable. To begin with, one would intuitively expect that, in defining the power of a political body to conduct an inquiry into official wrongdoing, the Framers used "try" in its legal sense. That intuition is borne out by reflection on the alternatives. The third clause of Art. I, § 3 cannot seriously be read to mean that the Senate shall "attempt" or "experiment with" impeachments. It is equally implausible to say that the Senate is charged with "investigating" impeachments given that this description would substantially overlap with the House of Representatives' "sole" power to draw up articles of impeachment.

[The] other variant of the majority position focuses not on which sense of "try" is employed in the Impeachment Trial Clause, but on whether the legal sense of that term creates a judicially manageable standard. [Yet,] as the Government itself conceded at oral argument, the term "try" is hardly so elusive as the majority would have it. Were the Senate, for example, to adopt the practice of automatically entering a judgment of conviction whenever articles of impeachment were delivered from the House, it is quite clear that the Senate will have failed to "try" impeachments. Indeed in this respect, "try" presents no greater, and perhaps fewer, interpretive difficulties than some other constitutional standards that have been found amenable to familiar techniques of judicial construction, including, for example, "Commerce ... among the several States," and "due process of law."[1]

III. The majority's conclusion that "try" is incapable of meaningful judicial construction is not without irony. One might think that if any class of concepts would fall within the definitional abilities of the judiciary, it would be that class having to do with procedural justice. Examination of the remaining question—whether proceedings in accordance with Senate Rule XI are compatible with the Impeachment Trial Clause—confirms this intuition.

Petitioner bears the rather substantial burden of demonstrating that, simply by employing the word "try," the Constitution prohibits the Senate from relying on a fact-finding committee. It is clear that the Framers were familiar with English impeachment practice and with that of the States employing a variant of the English model at the time of the Constitutional Convention. Hence there is little doubt that the term "try" as used in Art. I, § 3, cl. 6 meant that the Senate should conduct its proceedings in a manner somewhat resembling a judicial proceeding. Indeed, it is safe to assume that Senate trials were to follow the practice in England and the States, which contemplated a formal hearing on the charges, at which the accused would be represented by counsel, evidence would be presented, and the accused would have the opportunity to be heard.

Petitioner argues, however, that because committees were not used in state impeachment trials prior to the Convention, the word "try" cannot be interpreted to permit their use. It is, however, a substantial leap to infer from the absence of a particular device of parliamentary procedure that its use has been forever barred by the Constitution. And there is textual and historical evidence that undermines the inference sought to be drawn in this case.

The fact that Art. III, § 2, cl. 3 specifically exempts impeachment trials from the jury requirement provides some evidence that the Framers were anxious not to have additional specific procedural requirements read into the term "try." [It] is also noteworthy that the delegation of fact-finding by judicial and quasi-judicial bodies was hardly unknown to the Framers. Jefferson, at least, was aware that the House of Lords sometimes delegated fact-finding in impeachment trials to committees and recommended use of the same to the Senate. The States also had on occasion employed legislative committees to investigate whether to draw up articles of impeachment. More generally, in colonial govern-

---

1. The majority's in terrorem argument against justiciability—that judicial review of impeachments might cause national disruption and that the courts would be unable to fashion effective relief—merits only brief attention. In the typical instance, court review of impeachments would no more render the political system dysfunctional than has this litigation. [Even] as applied to the special case of the President, the majority's argument merely points out that, were the Senate to convict the President without any kind of a trial, a constitutional crisis might well result. It hardly follows that the Court ought to refrain from upholding the Constitution in all impeachment cases. Nor does it follow that, in cases of Presidential impeachment, the Justices ought to abandon their Constitutional responsibilities because the Senate has precipitated a crisis. [Footnote by Justice White.]

ments and state legislatures, contemnors appeared before committees to answer the charges against them. [Particularly] in light of the Constitution's grant to each House of the power to "determine the Rules of its Proceedings," see Art. I, § 5, cl. 2, the existence of legislative and judicial delegation strongly suggests that the Impeachment Trial Clause was not designed to prevent employment of a factfinding committee.

In short, textual and historical evidence reveals that the Impeachment Trial Clause was not meant to bind the hands of the Senate beyond establishing a set of minimal procedures. Without identifying the exact contours of these procedures, it is sufficient to say that the Senate's use of a factfinding committee under Rule XI is entirely compatible with the Constitution's command that the Senate "try all impeachments." . . .

Justice SOUTER, concurring in the judgment.

I agree with the Court that this case presents a nonjusticiable political question. Because my analysis differs somewhat from the Court's, however, I concur in its judgment by this separate opinion.

As we cautioned in Baker, "the 'political question' label" tends "to obscure the need for case-by-case inquiry." The need for such close examination is nevertheless clear from our precedents, which demonstrate [the] functional nature of the political question doctrine, [deriving] in large part from prudential concerns about the respect we owe the political departments. Not all interference is inappropriate or disrespectful, however, and application of the doctrine ultimately turns, as Learned Hand put it, on "how importunately the occasion demands an answer." L. Hand, The Bill of Rights 15 (1958).

This occasion does not demand an answer. The Impeachment Trial Clause commits to the Senate "the sole Power to try all Impeachments," subject to three procedural requirements. [It] seems fair to conclude that the Clause contemplates that the Senate may determine, within broad boundaries, such subsidiary issues as the procedures for receipt and consideration of evidence necessary to satisfy its duty to "try" impeachments. Other significant considerations confirm a conclusion that this case presents a nonjusticiable political question. [As] the Court observes, judicial review of an impeachment trial would under the best of circumstances entail significant disruption of government.

One can, nevertheless, envision different and unusual circumstances that might justify a more searching review of impeachment proceedings. If the Senate were to act in a manner seriously threatening the integrity of its results, convicting, say, upon a coin-toss, or upon a summary determination that an officer of the United States was simply "a bad guy," judicial interference might well be appropriate. In such circumstances, the Senate's action might be so far beyond the scope of its constitutional authority, and the consequent impact on the Republic so great, as to merit a judicial response despite the prudential concerns that would ordinarily counsel silence. . . .

U.S. TERM LIMITS, INC. v. THORNTON

517 U.S. ___, 115 S.Ct. 1842, 131 L.Ed.2d 881 (1995).

Justice STEVENS delivered the opinion of the Court.

The Constitution sets forth qualifications for membership in the Congress of the United States. Article I, § 2, cl. 2 [provides]: "No Person shall be a Representative who shall not have attained to the Age of twenty five Years, and been seven Years a Citizen of the United States, and who shall not, when elected, be an Inhabitant of that State in which he shall be chosen." Article I, § 3, cl. 3 [similarly] provides: "No Person shall be a Senator who shall not have attained to the Age of thirty Years, and been nine Years a Citizen of the United States, and who shall not, when elected, be an Inhabitant of that State for which he shall be chosen."

Today's cases present a challenge to an amendment to the Arkansas State Constitution that prohibits the name of an otherwise-eligible candidate for Congress from appearing on the general election ballot if that candidate has already served three terms in the House of Representatives or two terms in the Senate. The Arkansas Supreme Court held that the amendment violates the Federal Constitution. We agree. [If] the qualifications set forth in the text of the Constitution are to be changed, that text must be amended.

I. At the general election on November 3, 1992, the voters of Arkansas adopted Amendment 73 to their State Constitution. Proposed as a "Term Limitation Amendment," its preamble stated: "The people of Arkansas find and declare that elected officials who remain in office too long become preoccupied with reelection and ignore their duties as representatives of the people. Entrenched incumbency has reduced voter participation and has led to an electoral system that is less free, less competitive, and less representative than the system established by the Founding Fathers. Therefore, the people of Arkansas, exercising their reserved powers, herein limit the terms of the elected officials." The limitations in Amendment 73 apply to three categories of elected officials. Section 1 provides that no elected official in the executive branch of the state government may serve more than two 4–year terms. Section 2 applies to the legislative branch of the state government; it provides that no member of the Arkansas House of Representatives may serve more than three 2–year terms and no member of the Arkansas Senate may serve more than two 4–year terms. Section 3, the provision at issue in these cases, applies to the Arkansas Congressional Delegation. It provides: "(a) Any person having been elected to three or more terms as a member of the United States House of Representatives from Arkansas shall not be certified as a candidate and shall not be eligible to have his/her name placed on the ballot for election to the United States House of Representatives from Arkansas. "(b) Any person having been elected to two or more terms as a member of the United States Senate from Arkansas shall not be certified as a candidate and shall not be eligible to have his/her name placed on the ballot for election to the United States Senate from Arkansas."

[On] November 13, 1992, respondent Bobbie Hill [and] the League of Women Voters of Arkansas filed a complaint in the Circuit Court for Pulaski County, Arkansas, seeking a declaratory judgment that § 3 of Amendment 73 is "unconstitutional and void." [The] State of Arkansas [intervened] as a party defendant in support of the amendment. Several proponents of the amendment also intervened, including petitioner U.S. Term Limits, Inc. On cross-motions for summary judgment, the Circuit Court held that § 3 of Amendment 73 violated Article I of the Federal Constitution. [The] Arkansas Supreme Court affirmed. [The] State of Arkansas [and] the intervenors petitioned for writs of certiorari. Because of the importance of the issues, we granted both petitions and consolidated the cases for argument. We now affirm.

II. [The] constitutionality of Amendment 73 depends critically on the resolution of two distinct issues. The first is whether the Constitution forbids States from adding to or altering the qualifications specifically enumerated in the Constitution. The second is [whether] the fact that Amendment 73 is formulated as a ballot access restriction rather than as an outright disqualification is of constitutional significance. Our resolution of these issues draws upon our prior resolution of a related but distinct issue: whether Congress has the power to add to or alter the qualifications of its Members.

[In] Powell [the] principal issue was whether the power granted to each House in Art. I, § 5, to judge the "Qualifications of its own Members" includes the power to impose qualifications other than those set forth in the text of the Constitution. [We] held that it does not. Because of the obvious importance of the issue, the Court's review of the history and meaning of the relevant constitutional text was especially thorough....

THE ISSUE IN POWELL

In November 1966, Adam Clayton Powell, Jr., was elected from [New] York to serve in the House of Representatives for the 90th Congress. Allegations that he had engaged in serious misconduct while serving as a committee chairman during the 89th Congress led to the appointment of a Select Committee to determine his eligibility to take his seat. That Committee found that Powell met the age, citizenship, and residency requirements set forth in Art. I, § 2, cl. 2. The Committee also found, however, that Powell had wrongfully diverted House funds for the use of others and himself and had made false reports on expenditures of foreign currency. Based on those findings, the House [adopted] House Resolution 278, excluding Powell from membership in the House. [Powell filed] suit seeking a declaratory judgment that the House Resolution was invalid because Art. I, § 2, cl. 2, sets forth the exclusive qualifications for House membership. We [accepted] that contention, concluding that the House of Representatives has no "authority to exclude any person, duly elected by his constituents, who meets all the requirements for membership expressly prescribed in the Constitution." ...

POWELL'S RELIANCE ON HISTORY

We started our analysis in Powell by examining the British experience with qualifications for membership in Parliament, focusing in particular on the experience of John Wilkes. While serving as a member of Parliament, Wilkes had published an attack on a peace treaty with France. This literary endeavor earned Wilkes a conviction for seditious libel and a 22–month prison sentence. In addition, Parliament declared Wilkes ineligible for membership and ordered him expelled. Despite (or perhaps because of) these difficulties, Wilkes was reelected several times. Parliament, however, persisted in its refusal to seat him. After several years of Wilkes' efforts, the House of Commons voted to expunge the resolutions that had expelled Wilkes and had declared him ineligible, labeling those prior actions " 'subversive of the rights of the whole body of electors of this kingdom.' " After reviewing Wilkes' "long and bitter struggle for the right of the British electorate to be represented by men of their own choice," we concluded [that] "on the eve of the Constitutional Convention, English precedent stood for the proposition that 'the law of the land had regulated the qualifications of members to serve in parliament' and those qualifications were 'not occasional but fixed.' " Against this historical background, we viewed the Convention debates as manifesting the Framers' intent that the qualifications in the Constitution be fixed and exclusive. We found particularly revealing the debate concerning a proposal made by the Committee of Detail that would have given Congress the power to add property qualifications. James Madison argued that such a power would vest " 'an improper & dangerous power in the Legislature.' " " 'A Republic may be converted into an aristocracy or oligarchy as well by limiting the number capable of being elected, as the number authorised to elect.' "

[We] also recognized [that] the post-Convention ratification debates confirmed that the Framers understood the qualifications in the Constitution to be fixed and unalterable by Congress. [In] response to the antifederalist charge that the new Constitution favored the wealthy and well-born, Alexander Hamilton wrote: " 'The truth is that there is no method of securing to the rich the preference apprehended but by prescribing qualifications of property either for those who may elect or be elected. But this forms no part of the power to be conferred upon the national government. The qualifications of the persons who may choose or be chosen, as has been remarked upon other occasions, are defined and fixed in the Constitution, and are unalterable by the legislature.' "

[Our] historical analysis in Powell was both detailed and persuasive. We thus conclude now, as we did in Powell, that history shows that, with respect to Congress, the Framers intended the Constitution to establish fixed qualifications.[1]

---

1. The text of the Qualifications Clauses also supports the result we reached in Powell. John Dickinson of Delaware observed that the enumeration of a few qualifications "would by implication tie up the hands of the Legislature from supplying omissions." Justice Story made the same point: "It would seem but fair reasoning upon the plainest principles of interpretation, that when the constitution established certain qualifications, as necessary for office, it meant to exclude all others, as prerequisites. From the very nature of such a provision, the affirmation of these qualifica-

POWELL'S RELIANCE ON DEMOCRATIC PRINCIPLES

In Powell, [we] noted that allowing Congress to impose additional qualifications would violate that "fundamental principle of our representative democracy ... 'that the people should choose whom they please to govern them.'" [This] broad principle incorporated at least two fundamental ideas. First, [the] egalitarian concept that the opportunity to be elected was open to all. We noted in particular Madison's statement in The Federalist that "'[u]nder these reasonable limitations [enumerated in the Constitution], the door of this part of the federal government is open to merit of every description, whether native or adoptive, whether young or old, and without regard to poverty or wealth, or to any particular profession of religious faith.'"

[Second,] we recognized the critical postulate that sovereignty is vested in the people, and [confers] on the people the right to choose freely their representatives to the National Government. [We] noted that "Robert Livingston ... endorsed this same fundamental principle: 'The people are the best judges who ought to represent them. To dictate and control them, to tell them whom they shall not elect, is to abridge their natural rights.'" [Thus we] agreed with the sentiment expressed on behalf of Wilkes' admission to Parliament: "'That the right of the electors to be represented by men of their own choice, was so essential for the preservation of all their other rights, that it ought to be considered as one of the most sacred parts of our constitution.'"

Powell thus establishes two important propositions: first, that the "relevant historical materials" compel the conclusion that, at least with respect to qualifications imposed by Congress, the Framers intended the qualifications listed in the Constitution to be exclusive; and second, that that conclusion is equally compelled by an understanding of the "fundamental principle of our representative democracy ... 'that the people should choose whom they please to govern them.'"

POWELL'S HOLDING

Petitioners argue somewhat half-heartedly that the narrow holding in Powell, which involved the power of the House to exclude a member, [does] not control the more general question whether Congress has the power to add qualifications. [But] our conclusion that Congress may not alter or add to the qualifications in the Constitution was integral to our analysis and outcome. [We] confirmed this [in] Nixon v. United States. ["Our] conclusion in Powell was based on the fixed meaning of '[q]ualifications' set forth in Art. I, § 2. The claim by the House that its power to 'be the Judge of the Elections, Returns and Qualifications of its own Members' was a textual commitment of unreviewable authority was

tions would seem to imply a negative of all others." [As] Dickinson's comment demonstrates, the Framers' were well aware of the expressio unius argument that would result from their wording of the Qualifications Clauses; they adopted that wording nonetheless. There thus is no merit either to the dissent's suggestion that Story was the first to articulate the expressio unius argument, or to the dissent's assertion that that argument is completely without merit. [Footnote by Justice Stevens.]

defeated by the existence of this separate provision specifying the only qualifications which might be imposed for House membership." [2]

[We thus] reaffirm that the qualifications for service in Congress set forth in the text of the Constitution are "fixed," at least in the sense that they may not be supplemented by Congress.

III. Our reaffirmation of Powell does not necessarily resolve the specific questions presented in these cases. For petitioners argue that whatever the constitutionality of additional qualifications for membership imposed by Congress, [Powell does] not support the conclusion that the Constitution prohibits additional qualifications imposed by States. In the absence of such a constitutional prohibition, petitioners argue, the Tenth Amendment and the principle of reserved powers require that States be allowed to add such qualifications. [We] disagree for two independent reasons. First, [the] power to add qualifications is not within the "original powers" of the States, and thus is not reserved to the States by the Tenth Amendment. Second, even if States possessed some original power in this area, [the] Framers intended the Constitution to be the exclusive source of qualifications for members of Congress, and that the Framers thereby "divested" States of any power to add qualifications.

The "plan of the convention" [draws] a basic distinction between the powers of the newly created Federal Government and the powers retained by the pre-existing sovereign States. As Chief Justice Marshall explained, "it was neither necessary nor proper to define the powers retained by the States. These powers proceed, not from the people of America, but from the people of the several States; and remain, after the adoption of the constitution, what they were before, except so far as they may be abridged by that instrument." Sturges v. Crowninshield, 4 Wheat. 122 (1819). This classic statement by the Chief Justice endorsed Hamilton's reasoning in Federalist 32 that the plan of the Constitutional Convention did not contemplate "[a]n entire consolidation of the States into one complete national sovereignty," but only a partial consolidation in which "the State governments would clearly retain all the rights of

---

2. Justice Thomas's dissent purports to agree with the outcome of Powell, but rejects the reasoning in the opinion. The dissent treats Powell as simply an application of the "default rule" that if "the Constitution is silent about the exercise of a particular power—that is, where the Constitution does not speak either expressly or by necessary implication—the Federal Government lacks that power and the States enjoy it." However, there is not a word in [Powell] suggesting that the decision rested on the "default rule" that undergirds the dissent's entire analysis. On the contrary, [our] conclusion in Powell was based on our understanding of the "fixed meaning of '[q]ualifications' set forth in Art. I, § 2." We concluded that the Framers affirmatively intended the qualifications set forth in the text of the Constitution to be exclusive in order to effectuate the principle that in a representative democracy the people should choose whom they please to govern them. Moreover, the Court has never treated the dissent's "default rule" as absolute. In McCulloch, for example, Chief Justice Marshall rejected the argument that the Constitution's silence on state power to tax federal instrumentalities requires that States have the power to do so. Under the dissent's unyielding approach, it would seem that McCulloch was wrongly decided. Similarly, the dissent's approach would invalidate our dormant Commerce Clause jurisprudence, because the Constitution is clearly silent on the subject of state legislation that discriminates against interstate commerce.... [Footnote by Justice Stevens.]

sovereignty which they before had, and which were not, by that act, exclusively delegated to the United States." ...

SOURCE OF THE POWER

[Petitioners'] Tenth Amendment argument misconceives the nature of the right at issue because that Amendment could only "reserve" that which existed before. As Justice Story recognized, "the states can exercise no powers whatsoever, which exclusively spring out of the existence of the national government, which the constitution does not delegate to them. No state can say, that it has reserved, what it never possessed." Justice Story's position thus echoes that of Chief Justice Marshall in McCulloch[, where] the Court rejected the argument that the Constitution's silence on the subject of state power to tax corporations chartered by Congress implies that the States have "reserved" power to tax such federal instrumentalities. As Chief Justice Marshall pointed out, an "original right to tax" such federal entities "never existed, and the question whether it has been surrendered, cannot arise."

[With] respect to setting qualifications for service in Congress, no such right existed before the Constitution was ratified. [When] the Constitutional Convention convened, the Framers were presented with, and eventually adopted a variation of, "a plan not merely to amend the Articles of Confederation but to create an entirely new National Government with a National Executive, National Judiciary, and a National Legislature." In adopting that plan, the Framers envisioned a uniform national system, rejecting the notion that the Nation was a collection of States, and instead creating a direct link between the National Government and the people of the United States. In that National Government, representatives owe primary allegiance not to the people of a State, but to the people of the Nation. As Justice Story observed, each Member of Congress is "an officer of the union, deriving his powers and qualifications from the constitution, and neither created by, dependent upon, nor controllable by, the states.... Those officers owe their existence and functions to the united voice of the whole, not of a portion, of the people." Representatives and Senators are as much officers of the entire union as is the President. States thus "have just as much right, and no more, to prescribe new qualifications for a representative, as they have for a president[ ]."

[The] Constitution reflects the Framers' general agreement with the approach later articulated by Justice Story. [Art.] I, § 5, cl. 1 provides: "Each House shall be the Judge of the Elections, Returns and Qualifications of its own Members." The text [thus] gives the representatives of all the people the final say in judging the qualifications of the representatives of any one State. For this reason, the dissent falters when it states that "the people of Georgia have no say over whom the people of Massachusetts select to represent them in Congress."

Two other sections [further] support our view of the Framers' vision. First, [the] Constitution provides that the salaries of representatives should "be ascertained by Law, and paid out of the Treasury of the

United States," Art. I, § 6, rather than by individual States. The salary provisions reflect the view that representatives owe their allegiance to the people, and not to States. Second, the provisions governing elections reveal [that] powers over the election of federal officers had to be delegated to, rather than reserved by, the States. It is surely no coincidence that the context of federal elections provides one of the few areas in which the Constitution expressly requires action by the States, namely that "[t]he Times, Places and Manner of holding Elections for Senators and Representatives, shall be prescribed in each State by the legislature thereof." This duty parallels the duty under Article II that "Each State shall appoint, in such Manner as the Legislature thereof may direct, a Number of Electors." Art II., § 1, cl. 2. These Clauses are express delegations of power to the States to act with respect to federal elections.

[In] short, as the Framers recognized, electing representatives to the National Legislature was a new right, arising from the Constitution itself. The Tenth Amendment thus provides no basis for concluding that the States possess reserved power to add qualifications to those that are fixed in the Constitution. Instead, any state power to set the qualifications for membership in Congress must derive not from the reserved powers of state sovereignty, but rather from the delegated powers of national sovereignty. In the absence of any constitutional delegation to the States of power to add qualifications to those enumerated in the Constitution, such a power does not exist.

THE PRECLUSION OF STATE POWER

Even if [States] possessed as part of their original powers some control over congressional qualifications, the text and structure of the Constitution, the relevant historical materials, and, most importantly, the "basic principles of our democratic system" all demonstrate that the Qualifications Clauses were intended to preclude the States from exercising any such power. . . .

The Convention and Ratification Debates

The [evidence] indicates the Framers' intent that States have no role in the setting of qualifications. In Federalist 52 [Madison explicitly] contrasted the state control over the qualifications of electors with the lack of state control over the qualifications of the elected: "The qualifications of the elected, being less carefully and properly defined by the State constitutions, and being at the same time more susceptible of uniformity, have been very properly considered and regulated by the convention. A representative of the United States must be of the age of twenty-five years; must have been seven years a citizen of the United States; must, at the time of his election be an inhabitant of the State he is to represent; and, during the time of his service must be in no office under the United States. Under these reasonable limitations, the door of this part of the federal government is open to merit of every description, whether native or adoptive, whether young or old, and without regard to poverty or wealth, or to any particular profession of religious faith." [3]

[The] provisions in the Constitution governing federal elections confirm the Framers' intent that States lack power to add qualifications. The Framers feared that the diverse interests of the States would undermine the National Legislature, and thus they adopted provisions intended to minimize the possibility of state interference with federal elections. For example, [the] Framers required in Art. I, § 2, cl. 1, that the qualifications for federal electors be the same as those for state electors. [Similarly,] in Art. I, § 4, cl. 1, though giving the States the freedom to regulate the "Times, Places and Manner of holding Elections," the Framers created a safeguard against state abuse by giving Congress the power to "by Law make or alter such Regulations." The Convention debates make clear that the Framers' overriding concern was the potential for States' abuse of the power to set the "Times, Places and Manner" of elections. [As] Hamilton later noted: "Nothing can be more evident than that an exclusive power of regulating elections for the national government, in the hands of the State legislatures, would leave the existence of the Union entirely at their mercy."

[The] Framers' discussion of the salary of representatives reveals similar concerns. When the issue was first raised, Madison argued that congressional compensation should be fixed in the Constitution, rather than left to state legislatures, because otherwise "it would create an improper dependence." [Edmund] Randolph agreed that "[i]f the States were to pay the members of the Nat[ional] Legislature, a dependence would be created that would vitiate the whole System." [The] Convention ultimately agreed to vest in Congress the power to set its own compensation.

In light of the Framers' evident concern that States would try to undermine the National Government, they could not have intended

---

3. The dissent places a novel and implausible interpretation on this paragraph. Consistent with its entire analysis, the dissent reads Madison as saying that the sole purpose of the Qualifications Clause was to set minimum qualifications that would prevent the States from sending incompetent representatives to Congress. [The] text of Federalist 52 belies the dissent's reading. First, Madison emphasized that "[t]he qualifications of the elected ... [were] more susceptible of uniformity." His emphasis on uniformity would be quite anomalous if he envisioned that States would create for their representatives a patchwork of qualifications. Second, the idea that Madison was in fact concerned that States would open the doors to national service too widely is entirely inconsistent with Madison's emphasizing that the Constitution kept "the door ... open to merit of every description, whether native or adoptive, whether young or old, and without regard to poverty or wealth, or to any particular profession of religious faith." [Though] the dissent attempts to minimize the extensiveness of state-imposed qualifications by focusing on the qualifications that States imposed on delegates to Congress and the age restrictions that they imposed on state legislators, the dissent neglects to give appropriate attention to the abundance of property, religious, and other qualifications that States imposed on state elected officials. As we describe in some detail, nearly every State had property qualifications, and many States had religious qualifications, term limits, or other qualifications. As Madison surely recognized, without a constitutional prohibition, these qualifications could be applied to federal representatives. We cannot read Madison's comments on the "open door" of the Federal Government as anything but a rejection of the "unduly high" barriers imposed by States. [Footnote by Justice Stevens.]

States to have the power to set qualifications. Indeed, one of the more anomalous consequences of petitioners' argument is that it accepts federal supremacy over the procedural aspects of determining the times, places, and manner of elections while allowing the states carte blanche with respect to the substantive qualifications for membership in Congress. The dissent nevertheless contends that the Framers' distrust of the States with respect to elections does not preclude the people of the States from adopting eligibility requirements to help narrow their own choices. As the dissent concedes, however, the Framers were unquestionably concerned that the States would simply not hold elections for federal officers, and therefore the Framers gave Congress the power to "make or alter" state election regulations. Yet under the dissent's approach, the States could achieve exactly the same result by simply setting qualifications for federal office sufficiently high that no one could meet those qualifications. [It] is inconceivable that the Framers would provide a specific constitutional provision to ensure that federal elections would be held while at the same time allowing States to render those elections meaningless by simply ensuring that no candidate could be qualified for office.

[We] find further evidence of the Framers' intent in Art. 1, § 5, cl. 1, which provides: "Each House shall be the Judge of the Elections, Returns and Qualifications of its own Members." That Art. I vests a federal tribunal with ultimate authority to judge a Member's qualifications is fully consistent with the understanding that those qualifications are fixed in the Federal Constitution, but not with the understanding that they can be altered by the States. If the States had the right to prescribe additional qualifications [for] their own representatives, state law would provide the standard for judging a Member's eligibility. [The] judging of questions concerning rights which depend on state law is not, however, normally assigned to federal tribunals. [We] also find compelling the complete absence in the ratification debates of any assertion that States had the power to add qualifications. In those debates, the question whether to require term limits, or "rotation," was a major source of controversy. The draft of the Constitution that was submitted for ratification contained no provision for rotation. In arguments that echo in the preamble to Amendment 73, opponents of ratification condemned the absence of a rotation requirement. [At] several ratification conventions, participants proposed amendments that would have required rotation. The Federalists' responses to those criticisms and proposals addressed the merits of the issue, arguing that rotation was incompatible with the people's right to choose. [Regardless] of which side has the better of the debate over rotation, it is most striking that nowhere in the extensive ratification debates have we found any statement by either a proponent or an opponent of rotation that the draft constitution would permit States to require rotation for the representatives of their own citizens. If the participants in the debate had believed that the States retained the authority to impose term limits, it is inconceivable that the Federalists would not have made this obvious response to the arguments of the pro-rotation forces. . . .

Congressional Experience

Congress' subsequent experience with state-imposed qualifications provides further evidence of the general consensus on the lack of state power in this area. In Powell, we [noted] that during the first 100 years of its existence, "Congress strictly limited its power to judge the qualifications of its members to those enumerated in the Constitution." Congress first confronted the issue in 1807 when it faced a challenge to the qualifications of William McCreery, a Representative from Maryland who allegedly did not satisfy a residency requirement imposed by that State. In recommending that McCreery be seated, the Report of the House Committee on Elections noted: " 'The committee proceeded to examine the Constitution, with relation to the case submitted to them, and find that qualifications of members are therein determined, without reserving any authority to the State Legislatures to change, add to, or diminish those qualifications; and that, by that instrument, Congress is constituted the sole judge of the qualifications prescribed by it, and are obliged to decide agreeably to the Constitutional rules.' " [Commentators] at the time apparently viewed the seating of McCreery as confirmation of the States' lack of power to add qualifications. [In] a letter to Joseph Cabell, Thomas Jefferson noted the argument that "to add new qualifications to those of the Constitution would be as much as alteration as to detract from them"; he then added: "And so I think the House of Representatives of Congress decided in some case; I believe that of a member from Baltimore." ["By] the decision in this case, [and that in another contested election], it seems to have been settled that the States have not a right to require qualifications from members, different from, or in addition to, those prescribed by the constitution."

[The] Senate experience with state-imposed qualifications further supports our conclusions. In 1887, for example, the Senate seated Charles Faulkner of West Virginia, despite the fact that a provision of the West Virginia Constitution purported to render him ineligible to serve. The Senate Committee on Privileges and Elections unanimously concluded that "no State can prescribe any qualification to the office of United States Senator in addition to those declared in the Constitution of the United States." The Senate Committee on Rules and Administration reached the same conclusion in 1964 when faced with a challenge to Pierre Salinger, who had been appointed to serve as Senator from California. ("It is well settled that the qualifications established by the U.S. Constitution for the office of U.S. Senator are exclusive, and a State cannot, by constitutional or statutory provisions, add to or enlarge upon those qualifications"). We recognize that "congressional practice has been erratic" [Powell] and that the precedential value of congressional exclusion cases is "quite limited." Nevertheless, those incidents [support the] result we reach today.

Democratic Principles

Our conclusion that States lack the power to impose qualifications vindicates the same "fundamental principle of our representative democracy" [we] recognized in Powell, namely that "the people should choose whom they please to govern them." [The] Powell Court recognized that an egalitarian ideal—that election to the National Legislature should be open to all people of merit—provided a critical foundation for the Constitutional structure. This egalitarian theme echoes throughout the constitutional debates. In Federalist 57 [Madison] wrote: "Who are to be the objects of popular choice? Every citizen whose merit may recommend him to the esteem and confidence of his country. No qualification of wealth, of birth, of religious faith, or of civil profession is permitted to fetter the judgment or disappoint the inclination of the people." [The] egalitarian ideal, so valued by the Framers, is thus compromised to the same degree by additional qualifications imposed by States as by those imposed by Congress.

Similarly, we believe that state-imposed qualifications [would] undermine the second critical idea recognized in Powell: that an aspect of sovereignty is the right of the people to vote for whom they wish. Again, the source of the qualification is of little moment in assessing the qualification's restrictive impact.

Finally, state-imposed restrictions, unlike the congressionally imposed restrictions, [violate] a third idea central to this basic principle: that the right to choose representatives belongs not to the States, but to the people. [The] Framers, in perhaps their most important contribution, conceived of a Federal Government directly responsible to the people, possessed of direct power over the people, and chosen directly, not by States, but by the people. [They] implemented this ideal most clearly in the provision, extant from the beginning of the Republic, that calls for the Members of the House of Representatives to be "chosen every second Year by the People of the several States." Art. I, § 2, cl. 1. Following the adoption of the 17th Amendment in 1913, this ideal was extended to elections for the Senate. The Congress of the United States, therefore, is not a confederation of nations in which separate sovereigns are represented by appointed delegates, but is instead a body composed of representatives of the people. [Ours] is a "government of the people, by the people, for the people." A. Lincoln, Gettysburg Address (1863). [The] Constitution [creates] a uniform national body representing the interests of a single people. Permitting individual States to formulate diverse qualifications for their representatives would result in a patchwork of state qualifications, undermining the uniformity and the national character that the Framers envisioned and sought to ensure....

State Practice

Petitioners attempt to overcome this formidable array of evidence against the States' power to impose qualifications by arguing that the practice of the States immediately after the adoption of the Constitution demonstrates their understanding that they possessed such power. One may properly question the extent to which the States' own practice is a reliable indicator of the contours of restrictions that the Constitution imposed on States, especially when no court has ever upheld a state-imposed qualification of any sort. But petitioners' argument is unpersuasive even on its own terms. At the time of the Convention, "[a]lmost all the State Constitutions required members of their Legislatures to possess considerable property." Despite this near uniformity, only [Virginia] placed similar restrictions on members of Congress. [Just] 15 years after imposing a property qualification, Virginia replaced that requirement with a provision requiring that representatives be only "qualified according to the constitution of the United States." Moreover, several States [revised] their Constitutions at around the time of the Federal Constitution. In the revised Constitutions, each State retained property qualifications for its own state elected officials yet placed no property qualification on its congressional representatives.

The contemporaneous state practice with respect to term limits is similar. At the time of the Convention, States widely supported term limits in at least some circumstances. The Articles of Confederation contained a provision for term limits. [In] addition, many States imposed term limits on state officers, four placed limits on delegates to the Continental Congress, and several States voiced support for term limits for Members of Congress. Despite this widespread support, no State sought to impose any term limits on its own federal representatives. Thus, a proper assessment of contemporaneous state practice provides further persuasive evidence of a general understanding that the qualifications in the Constitution were unalterable by the States.

[In] sum, the available historical and textual evidence, read in light of the basic principles of democracy underlying the Constitution and recognized by this Court in Powell, reveal the Framers' intent that neither Congress nor the States should possess the power to supplement the exclusive qualifications set forth in the text of the Constitution.

IV. Petitioners argue that, even if States may not add qualifications, Amendment 73 is constitutional because it is not such a qualification, and [is] a permissible exercise of state power to regulate the "Times, Places and Manner of Holding Elections." We reject these contentions.

Unlike §§ 1 and 2 of Amendment 73, which create absolute bars to service for long-term incumbents running for state office, § 3 merely provides that certain Senators and Representatives shall not be certified as candidates and shall not have their names appear on the ballot. They may run as write-in candidates and, if elected, they may serve. Petitioners contend that only a legal bar to service creates an impermissible qualification, and that Amendment 73 is therefore consistent with the Constitution.

[We] need not decide whether petitioners' narrow understanding of qualifications is correct because, even if it is, Amendment 73 may not stand. [Amendment] 73 is an indirect attempt to accomplish what the Constitution prohibits Arkansas from accomplishing directly. As the [Arkansas] Supreme Court recognized, [the] "intent and the effect of Amendment 73 are to disqualify congressional incumbents from further service." We must [accept] the State Court's view of the purpose of its own law: we are thus authoritatively informed that the sole purpose of § 3 of Amendment 73 was to attempt to achieve a result [forbidden] by the Federal Constitution. [The] preamble of Amendment 73 states explicitly: "[T]he people of Arkansas ... herein limit the terms of elected officials." Sections 1 and 2 create absolute limits on the number of terms that may be served. There is no hint that § 3 was intended to have any other purpose.

Petitioners [contest] the Arkansas Supreme Court's conclusion that the Amendment has the same practical effect as an absolute bar. They argue that the possibility of a write-in campaign creates a real possibility for victory, especially for an entrenched incumbent. One may reasonably question the merits of that contention. Indeed, we are advised by the state court that there is nothing more than a faint glimmer of possibility that the excluded candidate will win. [But] even if petitioners are correct that incumbents may occasionally win reelection as write-in candidates, there is no denying that the ballot restrictions will make it significantly more difficult for the barred candidate to win the election. In our view, an amendment with the avowed purpose and obvious effect of evading the requirements of the Qualifications Clauses by handicapping a class of candidates cannot stand.

[Petitioners] make the related argument that Amendment 73 merely regulates the "Manner" of elections, and that the Amendment is therefore a permissible exercise of state power under Article I, § 4, cl. 1 (the Elections Clause) to regulate the "Times, Places and Manner" of elections. We cannot agree. A necessary consequence of petitioners' argument is that Congress itself would have the power to "make or alter" a measure such as Amendment 73. That the Framers would have approved of such a result is unfathomable. [Moreover,] petitioners' broad construction of the Elections Clause is fundamentally inconsistent with the Framers' view of that Clause. The Framers intended the Elections Clause to grant States authority to create procedural regulations, not to provide States with license to exclude classes of candidates from federal office. [Hamilton] made [the] point in Federalist 60, in which he [expressly] distinguished the broad power to set qualifications from the limited authority under the Elections Clause, noting that "there is no method of securing to the rich the preference apprehended but by prescribing qualifications of property either for those who may elect or be elected. But this forms no part of the power to be conferred upon the national government. Its authority would be expressly restricted to the regulation of the times, the places, and the manner of elections."

Our cases interpreting state power under the Elections Clause reflect the same understanding. [For] example, in Storer v. Brown, 415 U.S. 724 (1974), the case on which petitioners place principal reliance, we upheld the validity of certain provisions of the California Election Code. In so doing, we emphasized [the] "States' strong interest in maintaining the integrity of the political process by preventing interparty raiding," and explained that the specific requirements applicable to independents were "expressive of a general state policy aimed at maintaining the integrity of the various routes to the ballot." [The] provisions at issue in Storer and [were] thus constitutional because they regulated election procedures and did not even arguably impose any substantive qualification rendering a class of potential candidates ineligible for ballot position. They served the state interest in protecting the integrity and regularity of the election process, an interest independent of any attempt to evade the constitutional prohibition against the imposition of additional qualifications for service in Congress. And they did not involve measures that exclude candidates from the ballot without reference to the candidates' support in the electoral process.

[We] do not understand the dissent to contest [that] if the qualifications for Congress are fixed in the Constitution, then a State-passed measure with the avowed purpose of imposing indirectly such an additional qualification violates the Constitution. The dissent, instead, raises two objections, challenging the assertion that the Arkansas amendment has the likely effect of creating a qualification, and suggesting that the true intent of Amendment 73 was not to evade the Qualifications Clause but rather to simply "level the playing field." Neither of these objections has merit. As to the first, it is simply irrelevant to our holding today. [Our] prior cases strongly suggest that write-in candidates will have only a slim chance of success, and the Arkansas plurality agreed. However, we expressly do not rest on this Court's prior observations regarding write-in candidates. Instead, we hold that a state amendment is unconstitutional when it has the likely effect of handicapping a class of candidates and has the sole purpose of creating additional qualifications indirectly. As to the second argument, we find wholly unpersuasive the dissent's suggestion that Amendment 73 was designed merely to "level the playing field." [It] is obvious that the sole purpose of Amendment 73 was to limit the terms of elected officials [and,] therefore, may not stand.

V. The merits of term limits, or "rotation," have been the subject of debate since the formation of our Constitution, when the Framers unanimously rejected a proposal to add such limits to the Constitution. The cogent arguments on both sides of the question that were articulated during the process of ratification largely retain their force today. Over half the States have adopted measures that impose such limits on some offices either directly or indirectly, and the Nation as a whole, notably by constitutional amendment, has imposed a limit on the number of terms that the President may serve. Term limits, like any other qualification for office, unquestionably restrict the ability of voters to vote for whom they wish. On the other hand, such limits may provide for the infusion of fresh ideas and new perspectives, and may decrease the likelihood that representatives will lose touch with their constituents. It is not our province to resolve this longstanding debate.

We are, however, firmly convinced that allowing the several States to adopt term limits for congressional service would effect a fundamental change in the constitutional framework. Any such change must come not by legislation adopted either by Congress or by an individual State, but rather—as have other important changes in the electoral process— through the Amendment procedures set forth in Article V. [Members] of Congress are chosen by separate constituencies, but [they] become, when elected, servants of the people of the United States. They are not merely delegates appointed by separate, sovereign States; they occupy offices that are integral and essential components of a single National Government. In the absence of a properly passed constitutional amendment, allowing individual States to craft their own qualifications for Congress would thus erode the structure envisioned by the Framers, a structure that was designed, in the words of the Preamble to our Constitution, to form a "more perfect Union."

[Affirmed.]

Justice KENNEDY, concurring.

I join the opinion of the Court.

[Federalism] was our Nation's own discovery. The Framers split the atom of sovereignty. It was the genius of their idea that our citizens would have two political capacities, one state and one federal, each protected from incursion by the other. The resulting Constitution created a legal system unprecedented in form and design, establishing two orders of government, each with its own direct relationship, its own privity, its own set of mutual rights and obligations to the people who sustain it and are governed by it. It is appropriate to recall these origins, which instruct us as to the nature of the two different governments created and confirmed by the Constitution.

A distinctive character of the National Government, the mark of its legitimacy, is that it owes its existence to the act of the whole people who created it. It must be remembered that the National Government too is republican in essence and in theory. [Once] the National Government was formed under our Constitution, the same republican principles continued to guide its operation and practice. [The] Court confirmed this principle in McCulloch, when it said, "The government of the Union, then . . . is, emphatically, and truly, a government of the people. In form and in substance it emanates from them. Its powers are granted by them, and are to be exercised directly on them, and for their benefit." [It] is true that "the people of each State retained their separate political identities," for the Constitution takes care both to preserve the States and to make use of their identities and structures at various points in organizing the federal union. It does not at all follow from this that the sole political identity of an American is with the State of his or her residence. It denies the dual character of the Federal Government which is its very foundation to assert that the people of the United States do not have a political identity as well, one independent of, though consistent with, their identity as citizens of the State of their residence.

[It] might be objected that because the States ratified the Constitution, the people can delegate power only through the States or by acting in their capacities as citizens of particular States. But in McCulloch, the Court set forth its authoritative rejection of this idea: "The Convention which framed the constitution was indeed elected by the State legislatures. But the instrument . . . was submitted to the people." [Of] course, because the Framers recognized that state power and identity were essential parts of the federal balance, the Constitution is solicitous of the prerogatives of the States, even in an otherwise sovereign federal province. The Constitution uses state boundaries to fix the size of congressional delegations, ensures that each State shall have at least one representative, grants States certain powers over the times, places, and manner of federal elections (subject to congressional revision), requires that when the President is elected by the House of Representatives, the delegations from each State have one vote, and allows States to appoint electors for the President. Nothing in the Constitution or The Federalist Papers, however, supports the idea of state interference with the most basic relation between the National Government and its citizens, the selection of legislative representatives. [The] federal character of congressional elections flows from the political reality that our National Government is republican in form and that national citizenship has privileges and immunities protected from state abridgement by the force of the Constitution itself.

[Not] the least of the incongruities in the position advanced by Arkansas is the proposition, necessary to its case, that it can burden the rights of resident voters in federal elections by reason of the manner in which they earlier had exercised it. If the majority of the voters had been successful in selecting a candidate, they would be penalized from exercising that same right in the future. [This] observation serves to illustrate the extent of the State's attempted interference with the federal right to vote (and the derivative right to serve if elected by majority vote) in a congressional election, rights that do not derive from the state power in the first instance but that belong to the voter in his or her capacity as a citizen of the United States.

It is maintained by our dissenting colleagues that the State of Arkansas seeks nothing more than to grant its people surer control over the National Government, a control, it is said, that will be enhanced by the law at issue here. The arguments for term limitations [are] not lacking in force; but the issue [is] not the efficacy of those measures but whether they have a legitimate source, given their origin in the enactments of a single State. There can be no doubt, if we are to respect the republican origins of the Nation and preserve its federal character, that there exists a federal right of citizenship, a relationship between the people of the Nation and their National Government, with which the States may not interfere. Because the Arkansas enactment intrudes upon this federal domain, it exceeds the boundaries of the Constitution.

Justice THOMAS, with whom The Chief Justice [REHNQUIST], Justice O'CONNOR, and Justice SCALIA join, dissenting.

It is ironic that the Court bases today's decision on the right of the people to "choose whom they please to govern them." Under our Constitution, there is only one State whose people have the right to "choose whom they please" to represent Arkansas in Congress. The Court holds, however, that neither the elected legislature of that State nor the people themselves (acting by ballot initiative) may prescribe any qualifications for those representatives. The majority therefore defends the right of the people of Arkansas to "choose whom they please to govern them" by invalidating a provision that won nearly 60% of the votes cast in a direct election and that carried every congressional district in the State.

I dissent. Nothing in the Constitution deprives the people of each State of the power to prescribe eligibility requirements for the candidates who seek to represent them in Congress. The Constitution is simply silent on this question. And where the Constitution is silent, it raises no bar to action by the States or the people.

I. Because the majority fundamentally misunderstands the notion of "reserved" powers, I start with some first principles. Contrary to the majority's suggestion, the people of the States need not point to any affirmative grant of power in the Constitution in order to prescribe qualifications for their representatives in Congress, or to authorize their elected state legislators to do so.

A. Our system of government rests on one overriding principle: all power stems from the consent of the people. To phrase the principle in this way, however, is to be imprecise about something important to the notion of "reserved" powers. The ultimate source of the Constitution's authority is the consent of the people of each individual State, not the consent of the undifferentiated people of the Nation as a whole. The ratification procedure erected by Article VII makes this point clear. The Constitution took effect once it had been ratified by the people gathered in convention in nine different States. But the Constitution went into effect only "between the States so ratifying the same." [In] Madison's words, the popular consent upon which the Constitution's authority rests was "given by the people, not as individuals composing one entire nation, but as composing the distinct and independent States to which they respectively belong." Federalist 39.

When they adopted the Constitution, of course, the people of each State surrendered some of their authority to the United States (and hence to entities accountable to the people of other States as well as to themselves). [Because] the people of the several States are the only true source of power, however, the Federal Government enjoys no authority beyond what the Constitution confers. [In] each State, the remainder of the people's powers—"[t]he powers not delegated to the United States by the Constitution, nor prohibited by it to the States"—are either delegated to the state government or retained by the people. The Federal Constitution does not specify which of these two possibilities obtains; it is up to the various state constitutions to declare which powers the people of each State have delegated to their state government. As far as the Constitution is concerned, then, the States can exercise all powers that the Constitution does not withhold from them. The Federal Government and the States thus face different default rules: where the Constitution is silent about the exercise of a particular power—that is, where the Constitution does not speak either expressly or by necessary implication—the Federal Government lacks that power and the States enjoy it.

These basic principles are enshrined in the Tenth Amendment, which [avoids] taking any position on the division of power between the state governments and the people of the States: it is up to the people of each State to determine which "reserved" powers their state government may exercise. [To] be sure, when the Tenth Amendment uses the phrase "the people," it does not specify whether it is referring to the people of each State or the people of the Nation as a whole. But the latter interpretation would make the Amendment pointless: there would have been no reason to provide that where the Constitution is silent about whether a particular power resides at the state level, it might or might not do so. In addition, it would make no sense to speak of powers as being reserved to the undifferentiated people of the Nation as a whole, because the Constitution does not contemplate that those people will either exercise power or delegate it. The Constitution simply does not recognize any mechanism for action by the undifferentiated people of the Nation. Thus, the amendment provision of Article V calls for amendments to be ratified not by a convention of the national people, but by conventions of the people in each State or by the state legislatures elected by those people. Likewise, the Constitution calls for Members of Congress to be chosen State by State, rather than in nationwide elections. Even the selection of the President—surely the most national of national figures—is accomplished by an electoral college made up of delegates chosen by the various States, and candidates can lose a Presidential election despite winning a majority of the votes cast in the Nation as a whole.

In short, the notion of popular sovereignty that undergirds the Constitution does not erase state boundaries, but rather tracks them. The people of each State obviously did trust their fate to the people of the several States when they consented to the Constitution; not only did they empower the governmental institutions of the United States, but they also agreed to be bound by constitutional amendments that they themselves refused to ratify. At the same time, however, the people of each State retained their separate political identities.

B. [According] to the majority, the States possess only those powers that the Constitution affirmatively grants to them or that they enjoyed before the Constitution was adopted; the Tenth Amendment "could only 'reserve' that which existed before." From the fact that the States had not previously enjoyed any powers over the particular institutions of the Federal Government established by the Constitution, the majority derives a rule precisely opposite to the one that the Amendment actually prescribes: " '[T]he states can exercise no powers whatsoever, which exclusively spring out of the existence of the national government, which the constitution does not delegate to them.' " 1 J. Story, Commentaries on the Constitution of the United States § 627.

The majority's essential logic is that the state governments could not "reserve" any powers that they did not control at the time the Constitution was drafted. But it was not the state governments that were doing the reserving. [Given] the fundamental principle that all governmental powers stem from the people of the States, it would simply be incoherent to assert that the people of the States could not reserve any powers that they had not previously controlled.

The Tenth Amendment's use of the word "reserved" does not help the majority's position. If someone says that the power to use a particular facility is reserved to some group, he is not saying anything about whether that group has previously used the facility. He is merely saying that the people who control the facility have designated that group as the entity with authority to use it. The Tenth Amendment is similar: the people of the States, from whom all governmental powers stem, have specified that all powers not prohibited to the States by the Federal Constitution are reserved "to the States respectively, or to the people."

The majority is therefore quite wrong to conclude that the people of the States cannot authorize their state governments to exercise any powers that were unknown to the States when the Federal Constitution was drafted. [The] only true support for [the majority's] view of the Tenth Amendment comes from Joseph Story's 1833 treatise on constitutional law. Justice Story was a brilliant and accomplished man, and one cannot casually dismiss his views. On the other hand, he was not a member of the Founding generation, and his Commentaries on the Constitution were written a half century after the framing. Rather than representing the original understanding of the Constitution, they represent only his own understanding. In a range of cases concerning the federal/state relation, moreover, this Court has deemed positions taken in Story's commentaries to be more nationalist than the Constitution warrants. In this case too, Story's position that the only powers reserved to the States are those that the States enjoyed before the framing conflicts with both the plain language of the Tenth Amendment and the underlying theory of the Constitution.

2. The majority also sketches out [an] alternative (and narrower) argument. Again citing Story, the majority suggests that it would be inconsistent with the notion of "national sovereignty" for the States or the people of the States to have any reserved powers over the selection of Members of Congress. The majority apparently reaches this conclusion in two steps. First, it asserts that because Congress as a whole is an institution of the National Government, the individual Members of Congress "owe primary allegiance not to the people of a State, but to the people of the Nation." Second, it concludes that because each Member of Congress has a nationwide constituency once he takes office, it would be inconsistent with the Framers' scheme to let a single State prescribe qualifications for him.

Political scientists can debate about who commands the "primary allegiance" of Members of Congress once they reach Washington. From the framing to the present, however, the selection of the Representatives and Senators from each State has been left entirely to the people of that State or to their state legislature. [The] selection of representatives in Congress is indisputably an act of the people of each State, not some abstract people of the Nation as a whole. [Although] the United States obviously is a Nation, and although it obviously has citizens, the Constitution does not call for Members of Congress to be elected by the undifferentiated national citizenry; indeed, it does not recognize any mechanism at all (such as a national referendum) for action by the undifferentiated people of the Nation as a whole. Even at the level of national politics, then, there always remains a meaningful distinction between someone who is a citizen of the United States and of Georgia and someone who is a citizen of the United States and of Massachusetts. The Georgia citizen who is unaware of this distinction will have it pointed out to him as soon as he tries to vote in a Massachusetts congressional election.

In short, while the majority is correct that the Framers expected the selection process to create a "direct link" between members of the House of Representatives and the people, the link was between the Representatives from each State and the people of that State; the people of Georgia have no say over whom the people of Massachusetts select to represent them in Congress. This arrangement must baffle the majority, whose understanding of Congress would surely fit more comfortably within a system of nationwide elections. But the fact remains that when it comes to the selection of Members of Congress, the people of each State have retained their independent political identity.

[The] majority seeks support from the Constitution's specification that Members of Congress "shall receive a Compensation for their Services, to be ascertained by Law, and paid out of the Treasury of the United States." But the fact that Members of Congress draw a federal salary once they have assembled hardly means that the people of the States lack reserved powers over the selection of their representatives. [As] for the fact that a State has no reserved power to establish qualifications for the office of President, it surely need not follow that a State has no reserved power to establish qualifications for the Members of Congress who represent the people of that State. Because powers are reserved to the States "respectively," it is clear that no State may legislate for another State: even though the Arkansas legislature enjoys the reserved power to pass a minimum-wage law for Arkansas, it has no power to pass a minimum-wage law for Vermont. For the same reason, Arkansas may not decree that only Arkansas citizens are eligible to be President of the United States; the selection of the President is not up to Arkansas alone, and Arkansas can no more prescribe the qualifications for that office than it can set the qualifications for Members of Congress from Florida. But none of this suggests that Arkansas cannot set qualifications for Members of Congress from Arkansas. . . .

3. In a final effort to deny that the people of the States enjoy "reserved" powers over the selection of their representatives in Congress, the majority suggests that the Constitution expressly delegates to the States certain powers over congressional elections. Such delegations of power, the majority argues, would be superfluous if the people of the States enjoyed reserved powers in this area.

Only one constitutional provision—the Times, Places and Manner Clause of Article I—even arguably supports the majority's suggestion. [Contrary] to the majority's assumption, however, this Clause does not delegate any authority to the States. Instead, it simply imposes a duty upon them. The majority gets it exactly right: by specifying that the state legislatures "shall" prescribe the details necessary to hold congressional elections, the Clause "expressly requires action by the States." This command meshes with one of the principal purposes of Congress' "make or alter" power: to ensure that the States hold congressional elections in the first place, so that Congress continues to exist. [Constitutional] provisions that impose affirmative duties on the States are hardly inconsistent with the notion of reserved powers. Of course, the second part of the Times, Places and Manner Clause does grant a power rather than impose a duty. As its contrasting uses of the words "shall" and "may" confirm, however, the Clause grants power exclusively to Congress, not to the States. If the Clause did not exist at all, the States would still be able to prescribe the times, places, and manner of holding congressional elections; the deletion of the provision would simply deprive Congress of the power to override these state regulations....

II. I take it to be established, then, that the people of Arkansas do enjoy "reserved" powers over the selection of their representatives in Congress. Purporting to exercise those reserved powers, they have agreed among themselves that [those] whom they have already elected to three or more terms in the House of Representatives or to two or more terms in the Senate should not be eligible to appear on the ballot for reelection, but should nonetheless be returned to Congress if enough voters are sufficiently enthusiastic about their candidacy to write in their names. Whatever one might think of the wisdom of this arrangement, we may not override the decision of the people of Arkansas unless something in the Federal Constitution deprives them of the power to enact such measures.

The majority settles on "the Qualifications Clauses" as the constitutional provisions that Amendment 73 violates. Because I do not read those provisions to impose any unstated prohibitions on the States, it is unnecessary for me to decide whether the majority is correct to identify Arkansas' ballot-access restriction with laws fixing true term limits or otherwise prescribing "qualifications" for congressional office. As I discuss in Part A below, the Qualifications Clauses are merely straightforward recitations of the minimum eligibility requirements that the Framers thought it essential for every Member of Congress to meet. [Because] the text of the Qualifications Clauses does not support its position, the majority turns instead to its vision of the democratic principles that animated the Framers. But the majority's analysis goes to a question that is not before us: whether Congress has the power to prescribe qualifications for its own members. As I discuss in Part B, the democratic principles that contributed to the Framers' decision to withhold this power from Congress do not prove that the Framers also deprived the people of the States of their reserved authority to set eligibility requirements for their own representatives. In Part C, I review the majority's more specific historical evidence. To the extent that they bear on this case, the records of the Philadelphia Convention affirmatively support my unwillingness to find hidden meaning in the Qualifications Clauses, while the surviving records from the ratification debates help neither side. As for the postratification period, five States supplemented the constitutional disqualifications in their very first election laws. The historical evidence thus refutes any notion that the Qualifications Clauses were generally understood to be exclusive. Yet the majority must establish just such an understanding in order to justify its position that the Clauses impose unstated prohibitions on the States and the people. In my view, the historical evidence is simply inadequate to warrant the majority's conclusion that the Qualifications Clauses mean anything more than what they say.

A.   [The] majority is quite correct that the "negative phrasing" of [the Qualification] Clauses has little relevance.   [They] would mean the same thing had they been enacted in the form that the Philadelphia Convention referred them to the Committee of Style: "Every Member of the House of Representatives shall be of the age of twenty-five years at least; shall have been a citizen of the United States for at least seven years before his election; and shall be, at the time of his election, an inhabitant of the State in which he shall be chosen."   But these different formulations [merely] establish minimum qualifications.   They are quite different from an exclusive formulation, such as the following: "Every Person who shall have attained to the age of twenty five Years, and been seven Years a Citizen of the United States, and who shall, when elected, be an Inhabitant of that State in which he shall be chosen, shall be eligible to be a Representative."   At least on their face, then, the Qualifications Clauses do nothing to prohibit the people of a State from establishing additional eligibility requirements for their own representatives.

Joseph Story thought that such a prohibition was nonetheless implicit in the constitutional list of qualifications, because "[f]rom the very nature of such a provision, the affirmation of these qualifications would seem to imply a negative of all others."   This argument rests on the maxim expressio unius est exclusio alterius.   When the Framers decided which qualifications to include in the Constitution, they also decided not to include any other qualifications in the Constitution.   In Story's view, it would conflict with this latter decision for the people of the individual States to decide, as a matter of state law, that they would like their own representatives in Congress to meet additional eligibility requirements.

To spell out the logic underlying this argument is to expose its weakness.   Even if one were willing to ignore the distinction between requirements enshrined in the Constitution and other requirements that the Framers were content to leave within the reach of ordinary law, Story's application of the expressio unius maxim takes no account of federalism.   At most, the specification of certain nationwide disqualifications in the Constitution implies the negation of other nationwide disqualifications; it does not imply that individual States or their people are barred from adopting their own disqualifications on a state-by-state basis.

[The] Qualifications Clauses do prevent the individual States from abolishing all eligibility requirements for Congress.   This restriction on state power reflects the fact that when the people of one State send immature, disloyal, or unknowledgeable representatives to Congress, they jeopardize not only their own interests but also the interests of the people of other States.   [The] Qualifications Clauses [list] the requirements that the Framers considered essential to protect the competence of the National Legislature.   If the people of a State decide that they would like their representatives to possess additional qualifications, however, they have done nothing to frustrate the policy behind the

Qualifications Clauses. Anyone who possesses all of the constitutional qualifications, plus some qualifications required by state law, still has all of the federal qualifications. Accordingly, the fact that the Constitution specifies certain qualifications that the Framers deemed necessary to protect the competence of the National Legislature does not imply that it strips the people of the individual States of the power to protect their own interests by adding other requirements for their own representatives. The people of other States could legitimately complain if the people of Arkansas decide, in a particular election, to send a 6–year–old to Congress. But the Constitution gives the people of other States no basis to complain if the people of Arkansas elect a freshman representative in preference to a long-term incumbent. That being the case, it is hard to see why the rights of the people of other States have been violated when the people of Arkansas decide to enact a more general disqualification of long-term incumbents.

The majority responds that "a patchwork of state qualifications" would "undermin[e] the uniformity and the national character that the Framers envisioned and sought to ensure." Yet the Framers thought it perfectly consistent with the "national character" of Congress for the Senators and Representatives from each State to be chosen by the legislature or the people of that State. The majority never explains why Congress' fundamental character permits this state-centered system, but nonetheless prohibits the people of the States and their state legislatures from setting any eligibility requirements for the candidates who seek to represent them....

B. Although the Qualifications Clauses neither state nor imply the prohibition that it finds in them, the majority infers from the Framers' "democratic principles" that the Clauses must have been generally understood to preclude the people of the States and their state legislatures from prescribing any additional qualifications for their representatives in Congress. But the majority's evidence on this point establishes only two more modest propositions: (1) the Framers did not want the Federal Constitution itself to impose a broad set of disqualifications for congressional office, and (2) the Framers did not want the Federal Congress to be able to supplement the few disqualifications that the Constitution does set forth. The logical conclusion is simply that the Framers did not want the people of the States and their state legislatures to be constrained by too many qualifications imposed at the national level. The evidence does not support the majority's more sweeping conclusion that the Framers intended to bar the people of the States and their state legislatures from adopting additional eligibility requirements to help narrow their own choices.

I agree with the majority that Congress has no power to prescribe qualifications for its own Members. This fact, however, does not show that the Qualifications Clauses contain a hidden exclusivity provision. The reason for Congress' incapacity is not that the Qualifications Clauses deprive Congress of the authority to set qualifications, but rather that nothing in the Constitution grants Congress this power. In the absence of such a grant, Congress may not act. But deciding whether the

Constitution denies the qualification-setting power to the States and the people of the States requires a fundamentally different legal analysis.

[The] fact that the Framers did not grant a qualification-setting power to Congress does not imply that they wanted to bar its exercise at the state level. One reason why the Framers decided not to let Congress prescribe the qualifications of its own members was that incumbents could have used this power to perpetuate themselves or their ilk in office. As Madison pointed out, [Members] of Congress would have an obvious conflict of interest if they could determine who may run against them. But neither the people of the States nor the state legislatures would labor under the same conflict of interest when prescribing qualifications for Members of Congress, and so the Framers would have had to use a different calculus in determining whether to deprive them of this power. As the majority argues, democratic principles contributed to the Framers' decision to withhold the qualification-setting power from Congress. But [it] is wrong to suggest that the same principles [led] the Framers to deny this power to the people of the States and the state legislatures. There is a world of difference between a self-imposed constraint and a constraint imposed from above.

Congressional power over qualifications would have enabled the representatives from some States, acting collectively in the National Legislature, to prevent the people of another State from electing their preferred candidates. The John Wilkes episode in 18th–century England illustrates the problems that might result. [Americans] who remembered these events might well have wanted to prevent the National Legislature from fettering the choices of the people of any individual State (for the House of Representatives) or their state legislators (for the Senate). Yet this is simply to say that qualifications should not be set at the national level for offices whose occupants are selected at the state level. The majority never identifies the democratic principles that would have been violated if a state legislature, in the days before the Constitution was amended to provide for the direct election of Senators, had imposed some limits of its own on the field of candidates that it would consider for appointment. Likewise, the majority does not explain why democratic principles forbid the people of a State from adopting additional eligibility requirements to help narrow their choices among candidates seeking to represent them in the House of Representatives. Indeed, the invocation of democratic principles to invalidate Amendment 73 seems particularly difficult in the present case, because Amendment 73 remains fully within the control of the people of Arkansas. If they wanted to repeal it (despite the 20–point margin by which they enacted it less than three years ago), they could do so by a simple majority vote.

The majority appears to believe that restrictions on eligibility for office are inherently undemocratic. [Yet when] the people of a State themselves decide to restrict the field of candidates whom they are willing to send to Washington as their representatives, they simply have not violated the principle that "the people should choose whom they please to govern them." (remarks of Alexander Hamilton at the New York convention). At one point, the majority suggests that the principle identified by Hamilton encompasses not only the electorate's right to choose, but also "the egalitarian concept that the opportunity to be elected [is] open to all." To the extent that the second idea has any content independent of the first, the majority apparently would read the Qualifications Clauses to create a personal right to be a candidate for Congress, and then to set that right above the authority of the people of the States to prescribe eligibility requirements for public office. But we have never suggested that "the opportunity to be elected" is open even to those whom the voters have decided not to elect. [The] majority ultimately concedes that its "egalitarian concept" derives entirely from the electorate's right to choose. If the latter is not violated, then neither is the former. In seeking ratification of the Constitution, James Madison did assert that "[u]nder these reasonable limitations [set out in the House Qualifications Clause], the door of this part of the federal government is open to merit of every description ..." The majority stresses this [in] support of its "egalitarian concept." But there is no reason to interpret these statements as anything more than claims that the Constitution [imposes] relatively few disqualifications for congressional office.

[Moreover,] the right to choose may include the right to winnow. To appreciate this point, it is useful to consider the Constitution as it existed before the Seventeenth Amendment was adopted in 1913. The Framers' scheme called for the legislature of each State to choose the Senators from that State. The majority offers no reason to believe that state legislatures could not adopt prospective rules to guide themselves in carrying out this responsibility; not only is there no express language in the Constitution barring legislatures from passing laws to narrow their choices, but there also is absolutely no basis for inferring such a prohibition. Imagine the worst-case scenario: a state legislature, wishing to punish one of the Senators from its State for his vote on some bill, enacts a qualifications law that the Senator does not satisfy. The Senator would still be able to serve out his term; the Constitution provides for senators to be chosen for 6–year terms, and a person who has been seated in Congress can be removed only if two-thirds of the Members of his House vote to expel him. While the Senator would be disqualified from seeking reappointment, under the Framers' Constitution the state legislature already enjoyed unfettered discretion to deny him reappointment anyway. Instead of passing a qualifications law, the legislature could simply have passed a resolution declaring its intention to appoint someone else the next time around. Thus, the legislature's power to adopt laws to narrow its own choices added nothing to its general appointment power.

While it is easier to coordinate a majority of state legislators than to coordinate a majority of qualified voters, the basic principle should be the same in both contexts. Just as the state legislature enjoyed virtually unfettered discretion over whom to appoint to the Senate, so the qualified voters of the State enjoyed virtually unfettered discretion over whom to elect to the House of Representatives. If there is no reason to believe that the Framers' Constitution barred state legislatures from adopting prospective rules to narrow their choices for Senator, then there is also no reason to believe that it barred the people of the States from adopting prospective rules to narrow their choices for Representative.

I would go further, for I see nothing in the Constitution that precludes the people of each State (if they so desire) from authorizing their elected state legislators to prescribe qualifications on their behalf. If the people of a State decide that they do not trust their state legislature with this power, they are free to amend their state constitution to withdraw it.   This arrangement seems perfectly consistent with the Framers' scheme. [But] one need not agree with me that the people of each State may delegate their qualification-setting power in order to uphold Arkansas' Amendment 73[, which] is not the act of a state legislature; it is the act of the people of Arkansas, adopted at a direct election and inserted into the state constitution.   The majority never explains why giving effect to the people's decision would violate the "democratic principles" that undergird the Constitution.

C.   In addition to its arguments about democratic principles, the majority asserts that more specific historical evidence supports its view that the Framers did not intend to permit supplementation of the Qualifications Clauses.   But when one focuses on the distinction between congressional power to add qualifications for congressional office and the power of the people or their state legislatures to add such qualifications, one realizes that this assertion has little basis.   In particular, the detail with which the majority recites the historical evidence set forth in Powell should not obscure the fact that this evidence has no bearing on the question now before the Court. [If] anything, the solidity of the evidence supporting Powell's view that Congress lacks the power to supplement the constitutional disqualifications merely highlights the weakness of the majority's evidence that the States and the people of the States also lack this power.

[Unable] to glean from the Philadelphia Convention any direct evidence that helps its position, the majority seeks signs of the Framers' unstated intent in the Framers' comments about [other] constitutional provisions.   The majority infers from these provisions that the Framers wanted "to minimize the possibility of state interference with federal elections."   But even if the majority's reading of its evidence were correct, the most that one could infer is that the Framers did not want state legislatures to be able to prescribe qualifications that would narrow the people's choices.   However wary the Framers might have been of permitting state legislatures to exercise such power, there is absolutely no reason to believe that the Framers feared letting the people themselves exercise this power.   In any event, none of the provisions cited by the majority is inconsistent with state power to add qualifications for congressional office.

[The] majority cites the constitutional requirement that congressional salaries be "ascertained by Law, and paid out of the Treasury of the United States."   Like the Qualifications Clauses themselves, however, the salary provision can be seen as simply another means of protecting the competence of the National Legislature.   As reflected in the majority's own evidence, one of the recurring themes of the debate over this provision was that if congressional compensation were left up to the States, parsimonious States might reduce salaries so low that only incapable people would be willing to serve in Congress. As the majority stresses, some delegates to the Philadelphia Convention did argue that leaving congressional compensation up to the various States would give Members of Congress "an improper dependence" upon the States. These delegates presumably did not want state legislatures to be able to tell the members of Congress from their State, "Vote against Bill A or we will slash your salary"; such a power would approximate a power of recall, which the Framers denied to the States when they specified the terms of Members of Congress. The Framers may well have thought that state power over salary, like state power to recall, would be inconsistent with the notion that Congress was a national legislature once it assembled. But state power over initial eligibility requirements does not raise the same concerns: it was perfectly coherent for the Framers to leave selection matters to the state level while providing for Members of Congress to draw a federal salary once they took office. Thus, the Compensation Clause seems wholly irrelevant; contrary to the majority's suggestion, it does not address elections at all.

[The] majority emphasizes "[e]ach House [of Congress] shall be the Judge of the Elections, Returns and Qualifications of its own Members." [According] to the majority, however, [this] implies that the Framers could not have intended state law ever to "provide the standard for judging a Member's eligibility." My conclusion that States may prescribe eligibility requirements for their Members of Congress does not necessarily mean that the term "Qualifications" includes such state-imposed requirements. One surely could read the term simply to refer back to the requirements that the Framers had just listed in the Qualifications Clauses, and not to encompass whatever requirements States might add on their own. The Framers had deemed the constitutional qualifications essential to protect the competence of Congress, and hence the national interest. It is quite plausible that the Framers would have wanted each House to make sure that its Members possessed these qualifications, but would have left it to the States to enforce whatever qualifications were imposed at the state level to protect state interests.

But even if this [is] incorrect, I see nothing odd in the notion that a House of Congress might have to consider state law in judging the "Qualifications" of its Members. [Because] it generally is state law that determines what is necessary to win an election and whether any particular ballot is valid, each House of Congress clearly must look to state law in judging the "Elections" and "Returns" of its Members. It would hardly be strange if each House had to do precisely the same thing in judging "Qualifications." [More] generally, there is no basis for the majority's assertion that the Framers would not have charged "federal tribunals" with the task of "judging ... questions concerning rights which depend on state law." Cases involving questions of federal law hardly exhaust the categories of cases that the Framers authorized the federal courts to decide.

[The] structure of the Constitution also undermines the majority's suggestion that it would have been bizarre for the Framers to give

Congress supervisory authority over state time, place, and manner regulations but not over state qualifications laws. Although the Constitution does set forth a few nationwide disqualifications for the office of Presidential elector, no one contends that these disqualifications implicitly prohibit the States from adding any other eligibility requirements; instead, Article II leaves the States free to establish qualifications for their delegates to the electoral college. Nothing in the Constitution, moreover, gives Congress any say over the additional eligibility requirements that the people of the States or their state legislatures may choose to set. Yet under Article II, "[t]he Congress may determine the Time of chusing the Electors ..." The majority thus creates an unwarranted divergence between Article I's provisions for the selection of Members of Congress and Article II's provisions for the selection of members of the electoral college. Properly understood, the treatment of congressional elections in Article I parallels the treatment of Presidential elections in Article II. Under Article I as under Article II, the States and the people of the States do enjoy the reserved power to establish substantive eligibility requirements for candidates, and Congress has no power to override these requirements. But just as Article II authorizes Congress to prescribe when the States must select their Presidential electors, so Article I gives Congress the ultimate authority over the times, places, and manner of holding congressional elections.

The majority's only response is that my reading of the Constitution would permit States to use their qualification-setting power to achieve the very result that Congress' "make or alter" power was designed to avoid. According to the majority, States could set qualifications so high that no candidate could meet them, and Congress would be powerless to do anything about it. Even if the majority were correct that Congress could not nullify impossible qualifications, however, the Constitution itself proscribes such state laws. The majority surely would concede that under the Framers' Constitution, each state legislature had an affirmative duty to appoint two people to the Senate. In exactly the same way that § 3 requires the States to send people to the Senate, § 2 also requires the States to send people to the House. The majority apparently is concerned that [Congress] would not be able to enforce the constitutional proscription on impossible qualifications; enforcement would instead be relegated to the courts, the Executive Branch, or the political process. But this concern is equally applicable whether one adopts my view of the Qualifications Clauses or the majority's view. Both the majority and I agree that it is unconstitutional for States to establish impossible qualifications for congressional office. Both the majority and I also agree that it is theoretically conceivable that a State might defy this proscription by erecting an impossible qualification. Whether Congress may use its "make or alter" power to override such laws turns entirely on how one reads the "make or alter" power; it has nothing to do with whether one believes that the Qualifications Clauses are exclusive.

It would not necessarily be unusual if the Framers had decided against using Congress' "make or alter" power to guard against state laws that disqualify everyone from service in the House. After all, although this power extended to the times and manner of selecting Senators as well as Representatives, it did not authorize Congress to pick the Senators from a State whose legislature defied its constitutional obligations and refused to appoint anyone. This does not mean that the States had no duty to appoint Senators, or that the States retained the power to destroy the Federal Government by the simple expedient of refusing to meet this duty. It merely means that the Framers did not place the remedy with Congress.

But the flaws in the majority's argument go deeper. Contrary to the majority's basic premise, Congress can nullify state laws that establish impossible qualifications. If a State actually holds an election and only afterwards purports to disqualify the winner for failure to meet an impossible condition, Congress certainly would not be bound by the purported disqualification. It is up to each House of Congress to judge the "[q]ualifications" of its Members for itself. Even if this task includes the responsibility of judging qualifications imposed by state law, Congress obviously would have not only the power but the duty to treat the unconstitutional state law as a nullity. Thus, Congress could provide the appropriate remedy for the State's defiance, simply by seating the winner of the election.

It follows that the situation feared by the majority would arise only if the State refused to hold an election in the first place, on the ground that no candidate could meet the impossible qualification. But Congress unquestionably has the power to override such a refusal. [Congress] can make a regulation providing for the State to hold a congressional election at a particular time and place, and in a particular manner.[1]

[In] discussing the ratification period, the majority stresses two principal data. One of these pieces of evidence is no evidence at all—literally. The majority devotes considerable space to the fact that the recorded ratification debates do not contain any affirmative statement that the States can supplement the constitutional qualifications. For the majority, this void is "compelling" evidence that "unquestionably reflects the Framers' common understanding that States lacked that power." The majority reasons that delegates at several of the ratifying conventions attacked the Constitution for failing to require Members of Congress to rotate out of office. If supporters of ratification had believed that the individual States could supplement the constitutional qualifications, the majority argues, they would have blunted these attacks by pointing out that rotation requirements could still be added State by State.

But the majority's argument cuts both ways. The recorded ratification debates also contain no affirmative statement that the States cannot supplement the constitutional qualifications. While ratification was

---

1. Even if there is anything left of the majority's argument on this point, it would still have no bearing on whether the Framers intended to preclude the people of each State from supplementing the constitutional qualifications. Just as the Framers had no fear that the people of a State would destroy congressional elections by entirely disenfranchising themselves, so the Framers surely had no fear that the people of the States would destroy congressional elections by entirely disqualifying all candidates. [Footnote by Justice Thomas.]

being debated, the existing rule in America was that the States could prescribe eligibility requirements for their delegates to Congress, even though the Articles of Confederation gave Congress itself no power to impose such qualifications. If the Federal Constitution had been understood to deprive the States of this significant power, one might well have expected its opponents to seize on this point in arguing against ratification.

The fact is that arguments based on the absence of recorded debate at the ratification conventions are suspect, because the surviving records of those debates are fragmentary. We have no records at all of the debates in several of the conventions, and only spotty records from most of the others. If one concedes that the absence of relevant records from the ratification debates is not strong evidence for either side, then the majority's only significant piece of evidence from the ratification period is Federalist 52. [It] is true that Federalist 52 contrasts the Constitution's treatment of the qualifications of voters in elections for the House of Representatives with its treatment of the qualifications of the Representatives themselves. [But] while Madison did say that the qualifications of the elected were "more susceptible of uniformity" than the qualifications of electors, he did not say that the Constitution prescribes anything but uniform minimum qualifications for congressmen. That, after all, is more than it does for congressional electors.

[State] practice immediately after the ratification of the Constitution refutes the majority's suggestion that the Qualifications Clauses were commonly understood as being exclusive. Five States supplemented the constitutional disqualifications in their very first election laws, and the surviving records suggest that the legislatures of these States considered and rejected the interpretation of the Constitution that the majority adopts today. As the majority concedes, the first Virginia election law erected a property qualification for Virginia's contingent in the Federal House of Representatives. What is more, while the Constitution merely requires representatives to be inhabitants of their State, the legislatures of five of the seven States that divided themselves into districts for House elections added that representatives also had to be inhabitants of the district that elected them. Three of these States adopted durational residency requirements too, insisting that representatives have resided within their districts for at least a year (or, in one case, three years) before being elected. [Although] we have no record of the legislative debates over Virginia's election law, a letter written by one of the members of the House of Delegates during the relevant period indicates that [the] legislature considered the possible constitutional objection to additional disqualifications. In that letter, Edward Carrington (an opponent of the district residency requirement) expressed his view that the requirement "may exceed the powers of the Assembly," but acknowledged that there was "no prospect of its being struck out" because Federalists as well as Anti–Federalists at least professed to "think it right." Carrington was correct about the views of his colleagues: by a vote of 80 to 32, the House of Delegates rejected a motion to delete the added qualifications, while a similar motion in the State Senate lost by a vote of 12 to 3.

[The] majority also points out that no State required its own federal representatives to rotate out of office after serving one or more terms. At the time of the framing, however, such requirements were increasingly disfavored on policy grounds. The advantages of incumbency were substantially fewer then than now, and turnover in office was naturally quite high. The perceived advantages of term limits were therefore smaller than they are today. But the perceived disadvantages were just as great: term limits prevented the States or the people of the States from keeping good legislators in office, even if they wanted to do so. It is true that under the Articles of Confederation, four States had imposed term limits on their delegates to Congress. But three of these provisions added nothing to the limits in the Articles themselves, and the other one contained only a minor variation on the provision in the Articles. Indeed, though the majority says that "many States imposed term limits on state officers," it appears that at the time of the framing only Pennsylvania imposed any restriction on the reelection of members of the state legislature, and Pennsylvania deleted this restriction when it adopted a new Constitution in 1790.

[We] are left [with] state treatment of property qualifications. It is true that nine of the state constitutions in effect at the time of the framing required members of the lower house of the state legislature to possess some property, and that four of these constitutions were revised shortly after the framing but continued to impose such requirements. Only one State, by contrast, established a property qualification for the Federal House of Representatives. But the fact that more States did not adopt congressional property qualifications does not mean that the Qualifications Clauses were commonly understood to be exclusive; there are a host of other explanations for the relative liberality of state election laws. And whatever the explanation, the fact remains that five of the election laws enacted immediately after ratification of the Constitution imposed additional qualifications that would clearly be unconstitutional under today's holding. This history of state practice [refutes] the majority's position that the Qualifications Clauses were generally understood to include an unstated exclusivity provision.

The same is true of the final category of historical evidence discussed by the majority: controversies in the House and the Senate over seating candidates who were duly elected but who arguably failed to satisfy qualifications imposed by state law. As the majority concedes, "congressional practice has been erratic" and is of limited relevance anyway. Actions taken by a single House of Congress in 1887 or in 1964 shed little light on the original understanding of the Constitution. Presumably for that reason, the majority puts its chief emphasis on the 1807 debate in the House of Representatives about whether to seat Maryland's William McCreery. I agree with the majority that this debate might lend some support to the majority's position if it had transpired as reported in Powell. But the Court's discussion—both in Powell and today—is misleading. A Maryland statute dating from 1802 had created a district entitled to send two representatives to the House, one of whom had to be a resident of Baltimore County and the other of whom had to be a resident of Baltimore City. McCreery was elected to the Ninth Congress as a resident of Baltimore City. After his reelection to the Tenth Congress, however, his qualifications were challenged on the ground that because he divided his time between his summer estate in Baltimore County and his residence in Washington, D.C., he was no longer a resident of Baltimore City at all. As the majority notes, a report of the House Committee of Elections recommended that McCreery be seated on the ground that state legislatures have no authority to add to the qualifications set forth in the Constitution. But the Committee's submission of this initial report sparked a heated debate that spanned four days, with many speeches on both sides of the issue. Finally, a large majority of the House voted to recommit the report to the Committee of Elections. The Committee thereupon deleted all references to the constitutional issue and issued a revised report that focused entirely on the factual question whether McCreery satisfied the state residency requirement. After receiving the new report, the House seated McCreery with a resolution simply saying: "Resolved, That William McCreery is entitled to his seat in this House." By overwhelming majorities, the House rejected both a proposal to specify that McCreery possessed "the qualifications required by the law of Maryland," and a proposal to declare only that he was "duly qualified, agreeably to the constitution of the United States." Far from supporting the majority's position, the McCreery episode merely demonstrates that the 10th House of Representatives was deeply divided over whether state legislatures may add to the qualifications set forth in the Constitution.

The majority needs more than that. The prohibition that today's majority enforces is found nowhere in the text of the Qualifications Clauses. In the absence of evidence that the Clauses nonetheless were generally understood at the time of the framing to imply such a prohibition, we may not use the Clauses to invalidate the decisions of a State or its people.

III. It is radical enough for the majority to hold that the Constitution implicitly precludes the people of the States from prescribing any eligibility requirements for the congressional candidates who seek their votes. This holding, after all, does not stop with negating the term limits that many States have seen fit to impose on their Senators and Representatives. Today's decision also means that no State may disqualify congressional candidates whom a court has found to be mentally incompetent, who are currently in prison, or who have past vote-fraud convictions. Likewise, after today's decision, the people of each State must leave open the possibility that they will trust someone with their vote in Congress even though they do not trust him with a vote in the election for Congress. See, e.g., R.I.Gen.Laws § 17–14–1.2 (1988) (restricting candidacy to people "qualified to vote").

In order to invalidate § 3 of Amendment 73, however, the majority must go farther. The bulk of the majority's analysis—like Part II of my dissent—addresses the issues that would be raised if Arkansas had prescribed "genuine, unadulterated, undiluted term limits." But as the parties have agreed, Amendment 73 does not actually create this kind of disqualification. It does not say that covered candidates may not serve any more terms in Congress if reelected, and it does not indirectly achieve the same result by barring those candidates from seeking reelection. It says only that if they are to win reelection, they must do so by write-in votes.

One might think that this is a distinction without a difference. As the majority notes, "[t]he uncontested data submitted to the Arkansas Supreme Court" show that write-in candidates have won only six congressional elections in this century. But while the data's accuracy is indeed "uncontested," petitioners filed an equally uncontested affidavit challenging the data's relevance. As political science professor James S. Fay swore to the Arkansas Supreme Court, "[m]ost write-in candidacies in the past have been waged by fringe candidates, with little public support and extremely low name identification." To the best of Professor Fay's knowledge, in modern times only two incumbent Congressmen have ever sought reelection as write-in candidates. One of them was Dale Alford of Arkansas, who had first entered the House of Representatives by winning 51% of the vote as a write-in candidate in 1958; Alford then waged a write-in campaign for reelection in 1960, winning a landslide 83% of the vote against an opponent who enjoyed a place on the ballot. The other incumbent write-in candidate was Philip J. Philbin of Massachusetts, who—despite losing his party primary and thus his spot on the ballot—won 27% of the vote in his unsuccessful write-in candidacy. According to Professor Fay, "when a write-in candidate is well-known and well-funded, it is quite possible for him or her to win an election."

The majority responds that whether "the Arkansas amendment has the likely effect of creating a qualification" is "simply irrelevant to our holding today." [According] to the majority, "[w]e must, of course, accept the State Court's view of the purpose of its own law: we are thus authoritatively informed that the sole purpose of Amendment 73 was to attempt to achieve a result that is forbidden by the Federal Constitution." I am not sure why the intent behind a law should affect our analysis under the Qualifications Clauses. If a law does not in fact add to the constitutional qualifications, the mistaken expectations of the people who enacted it would not seem to affect whether it violates the alleged exclusivity of those Clauses. But in any event, the majority is wrong about what "the State Court" has told us. Even the plurality below did not flatly assert that the desire to "disqualify" congressional incumbents was the sole purpose behind § 3 of Amendment 73. [In] any event, inquiries into legislative intent are even more difficult than usual when the legislative body whose unified intent must be determined consists of 825,162 Arkansas voters.

The majority nonetheless thinks it clear that the goal of § 3 is "to prevent the election of incumbents." In reaching this conclusion at the summary-judgment stage, however, the majority has given short shrift to petitioners' contrary claim. Petitioners do not deny that § 3 of Amendment 73 intentionally handicaps a class of candidates, in the sense that it decreases their pre-existing electoral chances. But petitioners do deny that § 3 is intended to (or will in fact) "prevent" the covered candidates from winning reelection, or "disqualify" them from further service. One of petitioners' central arguments is that congressionally conferred advantages have artificially inflated the pre-existing electoral chances of the covered candidates, and that Amendment 73 is merely designed to level the playing field on which challengers compete with them.

To understand this argument requires some background. Current federal law (enacted, of course, by congressional incumbents) confers numerous advantages on incumbents, and these advantages are widely thought to make it "significantly more difficult" for challengers to defeat them. For instance, federal law gives incumbents enormous advantages in building name recognition and good will in their home districts. See, e.g., 39 U.S.C. § 3210 (permitting Members of Congress to send "franked" mail free of charge); 2 U.S.C. §§ 61–1, 72a, 332 (permitting Members to have sizable taxpayer-funded staffs); 2 U.S.C. § 123b (establishing the House Recording Studio and the Senate Recording and Photographic Studios). At the same time that incumbent Members of Congress enjoy these in-kind benefits, Congress imposes spending and contribution limits in congressional campaigns that "can prevent challengers from spending more . . . to overcome their disadvantage in name recognition." Brief for State of Washington as Amicus Curiae (statement of former 10–term Representative William E. Frenzel). Many observers believe that the campaign-finance laws also give incumbents an "enormous fund-raising edge" over their challengers by giving a large financing role to entities with incentives to curry favor with incumbents. In addition, the internal rules of Congress put a substantial premium on seniority, with the result that each Member's already plentiful opportunities to distribute benefits to his constituents increase with the length of his tenure. In this manner, Congress effectively "fines" the electorate for voting against incumbents. Cynics see no accident in any of this. As former Representative Frenzel puts it: "The practice . . . is for incumbents to devise institutional structures and systems that favor incumbents." In fact, despite his service from 1971 to 1989 on the House Administration Committee (which has jurisdiction over election laws), Representative Frenzel can identify no instance in which Congress "changed election laws in such a way as to lessen the chances of re-election for incumbents or to improve the election opportunities for challengers."

At the same time that incumbents enjoy the electoral advantages that they have conferred upon themselves, they also enjoy astonishingly high reelection rates. As Lloyd Cutler reported in 1989, "over the past thirty years a weighted average of ninety percent of all House and Senate incumbents of both parties who ran for reelection were reelected, even at times when their own party lost control of the Presidency itself." Cutler, Now is the Time for All Good Men . . ., 30 Wm. & Mary L.Rev. 387 (1989). Even in the November 1994 elections, which are widely considered to have effected the most sweeping change in Congress in recent memory, 90 percent of the incumbents who sought reelection to the House were successful, and nearly half of the losers were completing only their first terms. [The] voters of Arkansas evidently believe that incumbents would not enjoy such overwhelming success if electoral contests were truly fair—that is, if the government did not put its thumb on either side of the scale. [Given] this context, petitioners portray § 3 of Amendment 73 as an effort at the state level to offset the electoral advantages that congressional incumbents have conferred upon themselves at the federal level.

[I] do not [suggest] that States have unbridled power to handicap particular classes of candidates, even when those candidates enjoy federally conferred advantages that may threaten to skew the electoral process. But laws that allegedly have the purpose and effect of handicapping a particular class of candidates traditionally are reviewed under the First and Fourteenth Amendments rather than the Qualifications Clauses. [I] would read the Qualifications Clauses to do no more than what they say....

Chapter 8(3)

SUBSTANTIVE DUE PROCESS: RISE, DECLINE, REVIVAL

12th ED., p. 473; IND. RTS., p. 144

Add at end of footnote 4:

As in Connolly, the Court continues to be unsympathetic to takings claims based on the allegedly retroactive application of laws modifying pension plans. See Concrete Pipe and Products of California, Inc. v. Construction Laborers Pension Trust for Southern California, 510 U.S. ___ (1993).

12th ED., p. 475: IND. RTS., p. 146

Add at end of footnote 7:

In YEE v. ESCONDIDO, CALIFORNIA, 503 U.S. 519 (1992), the Court faced at least part of the takings issue with respect to rent control, here in the context of California's Mobilehome Residence Law, which authorizes local rent control for the spaces on which mobile homes are located. The plaintiffs did not argue that rent control in general constituted a taking, but only that rent control in the unique economic circumstances of mobile home residency had the effect of granting mobile home residents rights of permanent occupancy on land owned by others. As a result, the plaintiffs argued that this constituted a physical occupation governed by the Loretto per se rule. In an opinion written by Justice O'CONNOR, however, and joined on this issue by all members of the Court, the physical occupation claim was rejected. Justice O'Connor noted that although the wealth transfer in the mobile home case may be especially apparent because the value of such a home on rent-controlled property goes up immediately, this is not sufficient to identify a physical occupation. "Because the Escondido rent control ordinance does not compel a landowner to suffer the physical occupation of his property, it does not effect a per se taking under Loretto."

The Court refused to address the question whether the mobile home rent control constituted a regulatory taking. Although suggesting that the degree of wealth transfer and limitation on choosing tenants might be relevant to that issue (and Justices Blackmun and Souter concurred in the judgment only because they did not wish to join this part of the majority opinion), and although acknowledging that the regulatory takings issue was ripe for decision, Justice O'Connor concluded that this aspect of the case had not been set forth as a question for decision in the Petition for Certiorari. As a result, the Court refused to indicate whether this or similar ordinances might, even though not physical occupation takings, still be regulatory takings (under Penn Central) requiring compensation.

12th ED., p. 476; IND. RTS., p. 147

Add before Note on Public Use:

LUCAS v. SOUTH CAROLINA COASTAL COUNCIL

505 U.S. ___, 112 S.Ct. 2886, 120 L.Ed.2d 798 (1992).

Justice SCALIA delivered the opinion of the Court.

In 1986, petitioner David H. Lucas paid $975,000 for two residential lots on the Isle of Palms in Charleston County, South Carolina, on which he intended to build single family homes. In 1988, however, the South Carolina Legislature enacted the Beachfront Management Act, which had the direct effect of barring petitioner from erecting any permanent habitable structures on his two parcels. A state trial court found that this prohibition rendered Lucas's parcels "valueless." This case requires us to decide whether the Act's dramatic effect on the economic value of Lucas's lots accomplished a taking of private property under the Fifth and Fourteenth Amendments requiring the payment of "just compensation."

I. A. South Carolina's expressed interest in intensively managing development activities in the so-called "coastal zone" dates from 1977 when, in the aftermath of Congress's passage of the federal Coastal Zone Management Act of 1972, the legislature enacted a Coastal Zone Management Act of its own. In its original form, the South Carolina Act required owners of coastal zone land that qualified as a "critical area" (defined in the legislation to include beaches and immediately adjacent sand dunes) to obtain a permit from the newly created South Carolina Coastal Council (respondent here) prior to committing the land to a "use other than the use the critical area was devoted to on [September 28, 1977]."

In the late 1970's, Lucas and others began extensive residential development of the Isle of Palms, a barrier island situated eastward of the City of Charleston. Toward the close of the development cycle for one residential subdivision known as "Beachwood East," Lucas in 1986 purchased the two lots at issue in this litigation for his own account. No portion of the lots, which were located approximately 300 feet from the beach, qualified as a "critical area" under the 1977 Act; accordingly, at the time Lucas acquired these parcels, he was not legally obliged to obtain a permit from the Council in advance of any development activity. His intention with respect to the lots was to do what the owners of the immediately adjacent parcels had already done: erect single-family residences. He commissioned architectural drawings for this purpose.

The Beachfront Management Act brought Lucas's plans to an abrupt end. Under that 1988 legislation, the Council was directed to establish a "baseline" connecting the landward-most "point[s] of erosion ... during the past forty years." [The] Council fixed this baseline landward of Lucas's parcels. That was significant, for under the Act construction of occupable improvements was flatly prohibited seaward of a line drawn 20 feet landward of [the] baseline. The Act provided no exceptions.

B. Lucas promptly filed suit in the South Carolina Court of Common Pleas, contending that the Act's [complete] extinguishment of his property's value entitled him to compensation regardless of whether the legislature had acted in furtherance of legitimate police power objectives. Following a bench trial, the court agreed. Among its factual determinations was the finding that "at the time Lucas purchased the two lots, both were zoned for single-family residential construction and ... there were no restrictions imposed upon such use of the property by either the State of South Carolina, the County of Charleston, or the Town of the

Isle of Palms." The trial court further found that the Act decreed a permanent ban on construction insofar as Lucas's lots were concerned, and that this prohibition "deprive[d] Lucas of any reasonable economic use of the lots, ... eliminated the unrestricted right of use, and render[ed] them valueless." The court thus concluded that Lucas's properties had been "taken" by operation of the Act, and [ordered] "just compensation" in the amount of $1,232,387.50.

The Supreme Court of South Carolina reversed. It found dispositive what it described as Lucas's concession "that the Beachfront Management Act [was] properly and validly designed to preserve ... South Carolina's beaches." [The] court believed itself bound to accept the "uncontested ... findings" of the South Carolina legislature that new construction in the coastal zone [threatened] this public resource. The Court ruled that when a regulation respecting the use of property is designed "to prevent serious public harm," no compensation is owing [regardless] of the regulation's effect on the property's value.

II. As a threshold matter, we [address] the Council's suggestion that this case is inappropriate for plenary review. After briefing and argument before the South Carolina Supreme Court, but prior to issuance of that court's opinion, the Act was amended to authorize the Council [to] issue "special permits" for the construction or reconstruction of habitable structures seaward of the baseline. According to the Council, this amendment renders Lucas's claim of a permanent deprivation unripe, as Lucas may yet be able to secure permission to build. [These] considerations would preclude review had the South Carolina Supreme Court rested its judgment on ripeness grounds. [That court] shrugged off the possibility of further [proceedings,] however, preferring to dispose of Lucas's takings claim on the merits. This unusual disposition does not preclude Lucas from applying for a permit under the 1990 amendment for future construction, and challenging [any] denial. But it does preclude, both practically and legally, any takings claim with respect to Lucas's past deprivation, i.e., for his having been denied construction rights during the period before the 1990 amendment. [Lucas] has properly alleged Article III injury-in-fact in this case, with respect to both the pre–1990 and post–1990 constraints placed on the use of his parcels by the Beachfront Management Act. That there is a discretionary "special permit" procedure by which he may regain—for the future, at least—beneficial use of his land goes only to the prudential "ripeness" of Lucas's challenge, and [we] do not think it prudent to apply that prudential requirement here.

III. A. Prior to Justice Holmes' exposition in Pennsylvania Coal v. Mahon, it was generally thought that the Takings Clause reached only [the] functional equivalent of a "practical ouster of [the owner's] possession." Northern Trans. Co. v. Chicago, 99 U.S. 635 (1879). Justice Holmes recognized in Mahon, however, that if the protection against physical appropriations of private property was to be meaningfully enforced, the government's power to redefine the range of interests included in the ownership of property was necessarily constrained by constitutional limits. [These] considerations gave birth in that case to the oft-cited maxim that, "while property may be regulated to a certain extent, if regulation goes too far it will be recognized as a taking." Nevertheless, Mahon offered little insight into when, and under what circumstances, a given regulation would be seen as going "too far" for purposes of the Fifth Amendment. In 70–odd years of succeeding "regulatory takings" jurisprudence, we have generally eschewed any "set formula" for determining how far is too far, preferring to "engag[e] in ... essentially ad hoc, factual inquiries." Penn Central. We have, however, described at least two discrete categories of regulatory action as compensable without case-specific inquiry into the public interest advanced in support of the restraint. The first encompasses regulations that compel the property owner to suffer a physical "invasion" of his property. In general (at least with regard to permanent invasions), no matter how minute the intrusion, and no matter how weighty the public purpose behind it, we have required compensation.

[The] second situation in which we have found categorical treatment appropriate is where regulation denies all economically beneficial or productive use of land. As we have said on numerous occasions, the Fifth Amendment is violated when land-use regulation "does not substantially advance legitimate state interests or denies an owner economically viable use of his land." [1]

We have never set forth the justification for this rule. Perhaps it is simply [that] total deprivation of beneficial use is, from the landowner's point of view, the equivalent of a physical appropriation. "[F]or what is the land but the profits thereof [?]" 1 E. Coke, Institutes ch. 1. Surely, at least, in the extraordinary circumstance when no productive or economically beneficial use of land is permitted, it is less realistic to indulge our usual assumption that the legislature is simply "adjusting the benefits and burdens of economic life," Penn Central, in a manner that secures an "average reciprocity of advantage" to everyone concerned. And the functional basis for permitting the government, by regulation, to affect property values without compensation—that "Government hardly could go on if to some extent values incident to property could not be diminished without paying for every such change in the

---

1. Regrettably, the rhetorical force of our "deprivation of all economically feasible use" rule is greater than its precision, since the rule does not make clear the "property interest" against which the loss of value is to be measured. When, for example, a regulation requires a developer to leave 90% of a rural tract in its natural state, it is unclear whether [the] situation is one in which the owner has been deprived of all economically beneficial use of the burdened portion of the tract, or [one] in which the owner has suffered a mere diminution in value of the tract as a whole. (For an extreme—and, we think, unsupportable—view of the relevant calculus, see Penn Central, where the state court examined the diminution in a particular parcel's value [in] light of the total value of the taking claimant's other holdings in the vicinity.) [The] answer to this difficult question may lie in how the owner's reasonable expectations have been shaped by the State's law of property—i.e., whether and to what degree the State's law has accorded legal recognition and protection to the particular interest in land with respect to which the takings claimant alleges a diminution in (or elimination of) value. [We] avoid this difficulty in the present case, since the "interest in land" that Lucas has pleaded (a fee simple interest) is an estate with a rich tradition of protection at common law, and the Court of Common Pleas found that the Act left each of Lucas's [lots] without economic value. [Footnote by Justice Scalia.]

general law"—does not apply to the relatively rare situations where the government has deprived a landowner of all economically beneficial uses.

On the other side of the balance, affirmatively supporting a compensation requirement, is the fact that regulations that leave the owner of land without economically beneficial or productive options for its use— typically, as here, by requiring land to be left substantially in its natural state—carry with them a heightened risk that private property is being pressed into some form of public service under the guise of mitigating serious public harm. [The] many statutes on the books, both state and federal, that provide for the use of eminent domain to impose servitudes on private scenic lands preventing developmental uses, or to acquire such lands altogether, suggest the practical equivalence in this setting of negative regulation and appropriation. We think, in short, that there are good reasons for our frequently expressed belief that when the owner of real property has been called upon to sacrifice all economically beneficial uses in the name of the common good, that is, to leave his property economically idle, he has suffered a taking.[2]

B. The trial court found Lucas's two beachfront lots to have been rendered valueless by respondent's enforcement of the coastal-zone construction ban. Under Lucas's theory of the case, which rested upon our "no economically viable use" statements, that finding entitled him to compensation. [The] South Carolina Supreme Court, however, thought otherwise. In its view, the Act was no ordinary enactment, but involved an exercise of "police powers" to mitigate the harm to the public interest that petitioner's use of his land might occasion. [It] is correct that many of our prior opinions have suggested that "harmful or noxious uses" of property may be proscribed by government regulation without the requirement of compensation. Mugler v. Kansas [1887; above, 12th Ed., p. 438; Ind.Rts., p. 109.] For a number of reasons, however, we think the South Carolina Supreme Court was too quick to

---

2. Justice Stevens criticizes the "deprivation of all economically beneficial use" rule as "wholly arbitrary", in that "[the] landowner whose property is diminished in value 95% recovers nothing," while the landowner who suffers a complete elimination of value "recovers the land's full value." This analysis errs in its assumption that the landowner whose deprivation is one step short of complete is not entitled to compensation. Such an owner might not be able to claim the benefit of our categorical formulation, but "[the] economic impact of the regulation on the claimant and ... the extent to which the regulation has interfered with distinct investment-backed expectations" are keenly relevant to takings analysis generally. Penn Central. It is true that in at least some cases the landowner with 95% loss will get nothing, while the landowner with total loss will recover in full. But that occasional result is no more strange than the gross disparity between the landowner whose premises are taken for a highway (who recovers in full) and the landowner whose property is reduced to 5% of its former value by the highway (who recovers nothing). Takings law is full of these "all-or-nothing" situations.

Justice Stevens similarly misinterprets our focus on "developmental" uses of property (the uses proscribed by the Act) as betraying an "assumption that the only uses of property cognizable under the Constitution are developmental uses." We make no such assumption. Though our prior takings cases evince an abiding concern for the productive use of, and economic investment in, land, there are plainly a number of noneconomic interests in land whose impairment will invite exceedingly close scrutiny under the Takings Clause. Loretto (interest in excluding strangers from one's land). [Footnote by Justice Scalia.]

conclude that that principle decides the present case. The "harmful or noxious uses" principle was the Court's early attempt to describe in theoretical terms why government may, consistent with the Takings Clause, affect property values by regulation without incurring an obligation to compensate—a reality we nowadays acknowledge explicitly with respect to the full scope of the State's police power. [These] cases are better understood as resting not on any supposed "noxious" quality of the prohibited uses but rather on the ground that the restrictions were reasonably related to the implementation of a policy—not unlike historic preservation—expected to produce a widespread public benefit and applicable to all similarly situated property. "Harmful or noxious use" analysis was [simply] the progenitor of our more contemporary statements that "land-use regulation does not effect a taking if it substantially advance[s] legitimate state interests." Nollan. The transition from our early focus on control of "noxious" uses to our contemporary understanding of the broad realm within which government may regulate without compensation was an easy one, since the distinction between "harm-preventing" and "benefit-conferring" regulation is often in the eye of the beholder. It is quite possible, for example, to describe in either fashion the ecological, economic, and aesthetic concerns that inspired the South Carolina legislature in the present case. One could say that imposing a servitude on Lucas's land is necessary in order to prevent his use of it from "harming" South Carolina's ecological resources; or, instead, in order to achieve the "benefits" of an ecological preserve.[3] Whether one or the other of the competing characterizations will come to one's lips in a particular case depends primarily upon one's evaluation of the worth of competing uses of real estate. A given restraint will be seen as mitigating "harm" to the adjacent parcels or securing a "benefit" for them, depending upon the observer's evaluation of the relative importance of the use that the restraint favors. Whether Lucas's construction of single-family residences on his parcels should be described as bringing "harm" to South Carolina's adjacent ecological resources thus depends principally upon whether the describer believes that the State's use interest in nurturing those resources is so important that any competing adjacent use must yield.[4]

---

3. In the present case, in fact, some of the "[South Carolina] legislature's 'findings'" to which the South Carolina Supreme Court purported to defer in characterizing the purpose of the Act as "harm-preventing," seem to us phrased in "benefit-conferring" language instead. For example, they describe the importance of a construction ban in enhancing "South Carolina's annual tourism industry revenue," in "provid[ing] habitat for numerous species of plants and animals, several of which are threatened or endangered," and in "provid[ing] a natural healthy environment for the citizens of South Carolina to spend leisure time which serves their physical and mental well-being." It would be pointless to make the outcome of this case hang upon this terminology, since the same interests could readily be described in "harm-preventing" fashion.... [Footnote by Justice Scalia.]

4. In Justice Blackmun's view, even with respect to regulations that deprive an owner of all developmental or economically beneficial land uses, the test for required compensation is whether the legislature has recited a harm-preventing justification for its action. Since such a justification can be formulated in practically every case, this amounts to a test of whether the legislature has a stupid staff.... [Footnote by Justice Scalia.]

When it is understood that "prevention of harmful use" was merely our early formulation of the police power justification necessary to sustain (without compensation) any regulatory diminution in value; and that the distinction between regulation that "prevents harmful use" and that which "confers benefits" is difficult, if not impossible, to discern on an objective, value-free basis; it becomes self-evident that noxious-use logic cannot serve as a touchstone to distinguish regulatory "takings"— which require compensation—from regulatory deprivations that do not require compensation. A fortiori the legislature's recitation of a noxious-use justification cannot be the basis for departing from our categorical rule that total regulatory takings must be compensated. If it were, departure would virtually always be allowed.

[Where] the State seeks to sustain regulation that deprives land of all economically beneficial use, we think it may resist compensation only if the logically antecedent inquiry into the nature of the owner's estate shows that the proscribed use interests were not part of his title to begin with. [A] property owner necessarily expects the uses of his property to be restricted, from time to time, by various measures newly enacted by the State in legitimate exercise of its police powers. [And] in the case of personal property, by reason of the State's traditionally high degree of control over commercial dealings, he ought to be aware of the possibility that new regulation might even render his property economically worthless (at least if the property's only economically productive use is sale or manufacture for sale), Andrus v. Allard, 444 U.S. 51 (1979) (prohibition on sale of eagle feathers). In the case of land, however, [the] notion pressed by the Council that title is somehow held subject to the "implied limitation" that the State may subsequently eliminate all economically valuable use is inconsistent with the historical compact recorded in the Takings Clause that has become part of our constitutional culture.[5]

Where "permanent physical occupation" of land is concerned, we have refused to allow the government to decree it anew (without compensation), no matter how weighty the asserted "public interests" involved—though we assuredly would permit the government to assert a permanent easement that was a pre-existing limitation upon the landowner's title. We believe similar treatment must be accorded confiscatory regulations, i.e., regulations that prohibit all economically beneficial use of land: Any limitation so severe cannot be newly legislated or decreed (without compensation), but must inhere in the title itself, in the

---

5. After accusing us of "launch[ing] a missile to kill a mouse," Justice Blackmun expends a good deal of throw-weight of his own upon a noncombatant, arguing that our description of the "understanding" of land ownership that informs the Takings Clause is not supported by early American experience. That is largely true, but entirely irrelevant. The practices of the States prior to incorporation of the Takings and Just Compensation Clauses—which, as Justice Blackmun acknowledges, occasionally included outright physical appropriation of land without compensation—were out of accord with any plausible interpretation of those provisions. Justice Blackmun is correct that early constitutional theorists did not believe the Takings Clause embraced regulations of property at all, but even he does not suggest (explicitly, at least) that we renounce the Court's contrary conclusion in Mahon. Since the text of the Clause can be read to encompass regulatory as well as physical deprivations, [we] decline to do so as well. [Footnote by Justice Scalia.]

restrictions that background principles of the State's law of property and nuisance already place upon land ownership. A law or decree with such an effect must, in other words, do no more than duplicate the result that could have been achieved in the courts—by adjacent landowners (or other uniquely affected persons) under the State's law of private nuisance, or by the State under its complementary power to abate nuisances that affect the public generally, or otherwise.[6]

On this analysis, the owner of a lake bed, for example, would not be entitled to compensation when he is denied the requisite permit to engage in a landfilling operation that would have the effect of flooding others' land. Nor the corporate owner of a nuclear generating plant, when it is directed to remove all improvements from its land upon discovery that the plant sits astride an earthquake fault. Such regulatory action may well have the effect of eliminating the land's only economically productive use, but it does not proscribe a productive use that was previously permissible under relevant property and nuisance principles. The use of these properties for what are now expressly prohibited purposes was always unlawful, and [it] was open to the State at any point to make the implication of those background principles of nuisance and property law explicit. In light of our traditional resort to "existing rules or understandings that stem from an independent source such as state law" to define the range of interests that qualify for protection as "property" under the Fifth (and Fourteenth) amendments, this recognition that the Takings Clause does not require compensation when an owner is barred from putting land to a use that is proscribed by those "existing rules or understandings" is surely unexceptional. When, however, a regulation that declares "off-limits" all economically productive or beneficial uses of land goes beyond what the relevant background principles would dictate, compensation must be paid to sustain it.

[It] seems unlikely that common-law principles would have prevented the erection of any habitable or productive improvements on petitioner's land; they rarely support prohibition of the "essential use" of land. The question, however, is one of state law to be dealt with on remand. [To] win its case South Carolina must do more than proffer the legislature's declaration that the uses Lucas desires are inconsistent with the public interest. [Instead,] as it would be required to do if it sought to restrain Lucas in a common-law action for public nuisance, South Carolina must identify background principles of nuisance and property law that prohibit the uses he now intends in the circumstances in which the property is presently found. Only on this showing can the State fairly claim that, in proscribing all such beneficial uses, the Beachfront Management Act is taking nothing.

[Reversed and remanded.]

Justice KENNEDY, concurring in the judgment.

---

6. The principal "otherwise" that we have in mind is litigation absolving the State (or private parties) of liability for the destruction of "real and personal property, in cases of actual necessity, to prevent the spreading of a fire" or to forestall other grave threats to the lives and property of others. [Footnote by Justice Scalia.]

The case comes to the Court in an unusual posture. [After] the suit was initiated but before it reached us, South Carolina amended its Beachfront Management Act to authorize the issuance of special permits at variance with the Act's general limitations. Petitioner has not applied for a special permit but may still do so. The availability of this alternative, if it can be invoked, may dispose of petitioner's claim of a permanent taking. [The] potential for future relief does not control our disposition, [however,] because whatever may occur in the future cannot undo what has occurred in the past. The Act was enacted in 1988. It may have deprived petitioner of the use of his land in an interim period. [It] is well established that temporary takings are as protected by the Constitution as are permanent ones.

[Although] we establish a framework for remand, moreover, we do not decide the ultimate question of whether a temporary taking has occurred in this case. [The] finding of no value must be considered under the Takings Clause by reference to the owner's reasonable, investment-backed expectations. The Takings Clause, while conferring substantial protection on property owners, does not eliminate the police power of the State to enact limitations on the use of their property. The rights conferred by the Takings Clause and the police power of the State may coexist without conflict. Property is bought and sold, investments are made, subject to the State's power to regulate. Where a taking is alleged from regulations which deprive the property of all value, the test must be whether the deprivation is contrary to reasonable, investment-backed expectations.

There is an inherent tendency towards circularity in this synthesis, of course; for if the owner's reasonable expectations are shaped by what courts allow as a proper exercise of governmental authority, property tends to become what courts say it is. Some circularity must be tolerated in these matters, however, as it is in other spheres. The definition, moreover, is not circular in its entirety. The expectations protected by the Constitution are based on objective rules and customs that can be understood as reasonable by all parties involved.

In my view, reasonable expectations must be understood in light of the whole of our legal tradition. The common law of nuisance is too narrow a confine for the exercise of regulatory power in a complex and interdependent society. The State should not be prevented from enacting new regulatory initiatives in response to changing conditions, and courts must consider all reasonable expectations whatever their source. The Takings Clause does not require a static body of state property law; it protects private expectations to ensure private investment. I agree with the Court that nuisance prevention accords with the most common expectations of property owners who face regulation, but I do not believe this can be the sole source of state authority to impose severe restrictions. Coastal property may present such unique concerns for a fragile land system that the State can go further in regulating its development and use than the common law of nuisance might otherwise permit....

Justice BLACKMUN, dissenting.

Today the Court launches a missile to kill a mouse.

[South] Carolina prohibited [Lucas] from building a permanent structure on his property from 1988 to 1990. Relying on an unreviewed (and implausible) state trial court finding that this restriction left Lucas' property valueless, this Court granted review to determine whether compensation must be paid in cases where the State prohibits all economic use of real estate. According to the Court, such an occasion never has arisen in any of our prior cases, and the Court imagines that it will arise "relatively rarely" or only in "extraordinary circumstances." Almost certainly it did not happen in this case. Nonetheless, the Court presses on to decide the issue, and as it does, it ignores its jurisdictional limits, remakes its traditional rules of review, and creates simultaneously a new categorical rule and an exception (neither of which is rooted in our prior case law, common law, or common sense). I protest not only the Court's decision, but each step taken to reach it. [My] fear is that the Court's new policies will spread beyond the narrow confines of the present case. For that reason, I, like the Court, will give far greater attention to this case than its narrow scope suggests—not because I can intercept the Court's missile, or save the targeted mouse, but because I hope perhaps to limit the collateral damage.

I. A. [Here Justice Blackmun reviewed the history of South Carolina coastal protection legislation.]

B. [Lucas] is a contractor, manager, and part owner of the Wild Dune development on the Isle of Palms. He has lived there since 1978. In 1986, he purchased two of the last four pieces of vacant property in the development. The area is notoriously unstable. In roughly half of the last 40 years, all or part of petitioner's property was part of the beach or flooded twice daily by the ebb and flow of the tide. Between 1957 and 1963, petitioner's property was under water. Between 1963 and 1973 the shoreline was 100 to 150 feet onto petitioner's property. In 1973 the first line of stable vegetation was about halfway through the property. Between 1981 and 1983, the Isle of Palms issued 12 emergency orders for sandbagging to protect property in the Wild Dune development. Determining that local habitable structures were in imminent danger of collapse, the Council issued permits for two rock revetments to protect condominium developments near petitioner's property from erosion; one of the revetments extends more than halfway onto one of his lots.

C. The South Carolina Supreme Court's [decision] rested on two premises that until today were unassailable—that the State has the power to prevent any use of property it finds to be harmful to its citizens, and that a state statute is entitled to a presumption of constitutionality. [Nothing] in the record undermines the General Assembly's assessment that prohibitions on building in front of the setback line are necessary to protect people and property from storms, high tides, and beach erosion. Because that legislative determination cannot be disregarded in the absence of such evidence, and because its determination of harm to life and property from building is sufficient to prohibit that use under this Court's cases, the South Carolina Supreme Court correctly found no taking.

II. My disagreement with the Court begins with its decision to review this case. This Court has held consistently that a land-use challenge is not ripe for review until there is a final decision about what uses of the property will be permitted. [Even] if I agreed with the Court that there were no jurisdictional barriers to deciding this case, I still would not try to decide it. The Court creates its new taking jurisprudence based on the trial court's finding that the property had lost all economic value. This finding is almost certainly erroneous. Petitioner still can enjoy other attributes of ownership, such as the right to exclude others, "one of the most essential sticks in the bundle of rights that are commonly characterized as property." Kaiser Aetna v. United States, 444 U.S. 164 (1979). Petitioner can picnic, swim, camp in a tent, or live on the property in a movable trailer. [Petitioner] also retains the right to alienate the land, which would have value for neighbors and for those prepared to enjoy proximity to the ocean without a house.

Yet the trial court, apparently believing that "less value" and "valueless" could be used interchangeably, found the property "valueless." [The] trial court appeared to believe that the property could be considered "valueless" if it was not available for its most profitable use. Absent that erroneous assumption, I find no evidence in the record supporting the trial court's conclusion that the damage to the lots by virtue of the restrictions was "total." [Clearly,] the Court was eager to decide this case. But eagerness, in the absence of proper jurisdiction, must be—and in this case should have been—met with restraint.

III. The Court's willingness to dispense with precedent in its haste to reach a result is not limited to its initial jurisdictional decision. The Court also alters the long-settled rules of review. The South Carolina Supreme Court's decision to defer to legislative judgments in the absence of a challenge from petitioner comports with one of this Court's oldest maxims: "the existence of facts supporting the legislative judgment is to be presumed." United States v. Carolene Products Co., 304 U.S. 144 (1938). [Rather] than invoking these traditional rules, the Court decides the State has the burden to convince the courts that its legislative judgments are correct. . . .

IV. The Court does not reject the South Carolina Supreme Court's decision simply on the basis of its disbelief and distrust of the legislature's findings. It also takes the opportunity to create a new scheme for regulations that eliminate all economic value. From now on, there is a categorical rule finding these regulations to be a taking unless the use they prohibit is a background common-law nuisance or property principle.

A. I first question the Court's rationale in creating a category that obviates a "case-specific inquiry into the public interest advanced," if all economic value has been lost. [This] Court repeatedly has recognized the ability of government, in certain circumstances, to regulate property without compensation no matter how adverse the financial effect on the owner may be. [Our] cases rest on the principle that the State has full power to prohibit an owner's use of property if it is harmful to the public. [It] would make no sense under this theory to suggest that an owner has a constitutionally protected right to harm others, if only he makes the proper showing of economic loss.

B. Ultimately even the Court cannot embrace the full implications of its per se rule: it eventually agrees that there cannot be a categorical rule for a taking based on economic value that wholly disregards the public need asserted. Instead, the Court decides that it will permit a State to regulate all economic value only if the State prohibits uses that would not be permitted under "background principles of nuisance and property law."

[The] Court rejects the notion that the State always can prohibit uses it deems a harm to the public without granting compensation because "the distinction between 'harm-preventing' and 'benefit-conferring' regulation is often in the eye of the beholder." [The] Court, however, fails to explain how its proposed common law alternative escapes the same trap. The threshold inquiry for imposition of the Court's new rule, "deprivation of all economically valuable use," itself cannot be determined objectively. As the Court admits, whether the owner has been deprived of all economic value of his property will depend on how "property" is defined. The "composition of the denominator in our 'deprivation' fraction," is the dispositive inquiry. Yet there is no "objective" way to define what that denominator should be. [The] Court's decision in Keystone illustrates this principle perfectly. In Keystone, the Court determined that the "support estate" was "merely a part of the entire bundle of rights possessed by the owner." Thus, the Court concluded that the support estate's destruction merely eliminated one segment of the total property. The dissent, however, characterized the support estate as a distinct property interest that was wholly destroyed. The Court could agree on no "value-free basis" to resolve this dispute.

Even more perplexing, however, is the Court's reliance on common-law principles of nuisance in its quest for a value-free taking jurisprudence. In determining what is a nuisance at common law, state courts make exactly the decision that the Court finds so troubling when made by the General Assembly today: they determine whether the use is harmful. Common-law public and private nuisance law is simply a determination whether a particular use causes harm. There is nothing magical in the reasoning of judges long dead. They determined a harm in the same way as state judges and legislatures do today. If judges in the 18th and 19th centuries can distinguish a harm from a benefit, why not judges in the 20th century, and if judges can, why not legislators?
. . .

C. Finally, the Court justifies its new rule that the legislature may not deprive a property owner of the only economically valuable use of his land, even if the legislature finds it to be a harmful use, because such action is not part of the "long recognized" "understandings of our citizens." [Any] other course is "inconsistent with the historical compact recorded in the Takings Clause." It is not clear from the Court's opinion where our "historical compact" or "citizens' understanding" comes from, but it does not appear to be history.

The principle that the State should compensate individuals for property taken for public use was not widely established in America at the time of the Revolution. [Even] into the 19th century, state governments often felt free to take property for roads and other public projects without paying compensation to the owners. [Although,] prior to the adoption of the Bill of Rights, America was replete with land use regulations describing which activities were considered noxious and forbidden, the Taking Clause originally did not extend to regulations of property, whatever the effect.

[Nor] does history indicate any common-law limit on the State's power to regulate harmful uses even to the point of destroying all economic value. Nothing in the discussions in Congress concerning the Taking Clause indicates that the Clause was limited by the common-law nuisance doctrine. Common law courts themselves rejected such an understanding. [In] short, I find no clear and accepted "historical compact" or "understanding of our citizens" justifying the Court's new taking doctrine. Instead, the Court seems to treat history as a grab-bag of principles, to be adopted where they support the Court's theory, and ignored where they do not. [What] makes the Court's analysis unworkable is its attempt to package the law of two incompatible eras and peddle it as historical fact.

V. The Court makes sweeping[, misguided] and unsupported changes in our taking doctrine. While it limits these changes to the most narrow subset of government regulation—those that eliminate all economic value from land—these changes go far beyond what is necessary to secure petitioner Lucas' private benefit. One hopes they do not go beyond the narrow confines the Court assigns them to today.

I dissent.

Justice STEVENS, dissenting.

Today the Court restricts one judge-made rule and expands another. In my opinion it errs on both counts. Proper application of the doctrine of judicial restraint would avoid the premature adjudication of an important constitutional question. Proper respect for our precedents would avoid an illogical expansion of the concept of "regulatory takings."

I. As the Court notes, South Carolina's Act has been amended to permit some construction of residences seaward of the line that frustrated petitioner's proposed use of his property. Until he exhausts his right to apply for a special permit under that amendment, petitioner is not entitled to an adjudication by this Court of the merits of his permanent takings claim. It is also not clear that he has a viable "temporary takings" claim. [It] is not the habit of the Court to decide questions of a constitutional nature unless absolutely necessary to a decision of the case." Cavalierly dismissing the doctrine of judicial restraint, the Court today tersely announces that "we do not think it prudent to apply that prudential requirement here." I respectfully disagree and would save consideration of the merits for another day. Since, however, the Court has reached the merits, I shall do so as well.

II. In its analysis of the merits, the Court starts from the premise that this Court has adopted a "categorical rule that total regulatory takings must be compensated," and then sets itself to the task of identifying the exceptional cases in which a State may be relieved of this categorical obligation. [In] my opinion, the Court is doubly in error. The categorical rule the Court establishes is an unsound and unwise addition to the law and the Court's formulation of the exception to that rule is too rigid and too narrow.

The Categorical Rule

As the Court recognizes, Mahon provides no support for its—or, indeed, any—categorical rule. To the contrary, Justice Holmes recognized that such absolute rules ill fit the inquiry into "regulatory takings." Thus, in the paragraph that contains his famous observation that a regulation may go "too far" and thereby constitute a taking, the Justice wrote: "As we already have said, this is a question of degree—and therefore cannot be disposed of by general propositions." [In] addition to lacking support in past decisions, the Court's new rule is wholly arbitrary. A landowner whose property is diminished in value 95% recovers nothing, while an owner whose property is diminished 100% recovers the land's full value. The case at hand illustrates this arbitrariness well. The Act not only prohibited the building of new dwellings in certain areas, it also prohibited the rebuilding of houses that were "destroyed beyond repair by natural causes or by fire." Thus, if the homes adjacent to Lucas' lot were destroyed by a hurricane one day after the Act took effect, the owners would not be able to rebuild, nor would they be assured recovery. Under the Court's categorical approach, Lucas (who has lost the opportunity to build) recovers, while his neighbors (who have lost both the opportunity to build and their homes) do not recover.

[Moreover,] because of the elastic nature of property rights, the Court's new rule will also prove unsound in practice. In response to the rule, courts may define "property" broadly and only rarely find regulations to effect total takings. [On] the other hand, developers and investors may market specialized estates to take advantage of the Court's new rule. The smaller the estate, the more likely that a regulatory change will effect a total taking. Thus, an investor may, for example, purchase the right to build a multi-family home on a specific lot, with the result that a zoning regulation that allows only single-family homes would render the investor's property interest "valueless." In short, the categorical rule will likely have one of two effects: Either courts will alter the definition of the "denominator" in the takings "fraction," rendering the Court's categorical rule meaningless, or investors will manipulate the relevant property interests, giving the Court's rule sweeping effect. To my mind, neither of these results is desirable or appropriate, and both are distortions of our takings jurisprudence. . . .

The Nuisance Exception

Like many bright-line rules, the categorical rule established in this case is only "categorical" for a page or two in the U.S. Reports. No sooner does the Court state that "total regulatory takings must be compensated," than it quickly establishes an exception to that rule. The exception provides that a regulation that renders property valueless is not a taking if it prohibits uses of property that were not "previously permissible under relevant property and nuisance principles." The Court thus rejects the basic holding in Mugler. There we held that a state-wide statute that prohibited the owner of a brewery from making alcoholic beverages did not effect a taking, even though the use of the property had been perfectly lawful and caused no public harm before the statute was enacted. [Under] the Court's opinion today, if a state should decide to prohibit the manufacture of asbestos, cigarettes, or concealable firearms, for example, it must be prepared to pay for the adverse economic consequences of its decision. One must wonder if Government will be able to "go on" effectively if it must risk compensation "for every such change in the general law." Mahon. The Court's holding today effectively freezes the State's common law, denying the legislature much of its traditional power to revise the law governing the rights and uses of property. Until today, I had thought that we had long abandoned this approach to constitutional law.

[Arresting] the development of the common law is not only a departure from our prior decisions; it is also profoundly unwise. The human condition is one of constant learning and evolution—both moral and practical. Legislatures implement that new learning; in doing so they must often revise the definition of property and the rights of property owners. Thus, when the Nation came to understand that slavery was morally wrong and mandated the emancipation of all slaves, it, in effect, redefined "property." On a lesser scale, our ongoing self-education produces similar changes in the rights of property owners: New appreciation of the significance of endangered species, the importance of wetlands, and the vulnerability of coastal lands shapes our evolving understandings of property rights.

Of course, some legislative redefinitions of property will effect a taking and must be compensated—but it certainly cannot be the case that every movement away from common law does so. There is no reason, and less sense, in such an absolute rule. We live in a world in which changes in the economy and the environment occur with increasing frequency and importance. [The] rule that should govern a decision in a case of this kind should focus on the future, not the past.[1]

The Court's categorical approach rule will, I fear, greatly hamper the efforts of local officials and planners who must deal with increasingly complex problems in land-use and environmental regulation. [The] rigid rules fixed by the Court today clash with this enterprise: "fairness and justice" are often disserved by categorical rules.

---

1. Even measured in terms of efficiency, the Court's rule is unsound. The Court today effectively establishes a form of insurance against certain changes in land-use regulations. Like other forms of insurance, the Court's rule creates a "moral hazard" and inefficiencies: In the face of uncertainty about changes in the law, developers will overinvest, safe in the knowledge that if the law changes adversely, they will be entitled to compensation. [Footnote by Justice Stevens.]

III. [Neglected] by the Court today is the first, and in some ways, the most important factor in takings analysis: the character of the regulatory action. [One] of the central concerns of our takings jurisprudence is "prevent[ing] the public from loading upon one individual more than his just share of the burdens of government." Monongahela Nav. Co. v. United States, 148 U.S. 312 (1893). We have, therefore, in our takings law frequently looked to the generality of a regulation of property.[2] [In] analyzing takings claims, courts have long recognized the difference between a regulation that targets one or two parcels of land and a regulation that enforces a state-wide policy. [In] considering Lucas' claim, the generality of the Beachfront Management Act is significant. The Act does not target particular landowners, but rather regulates the use of the coastline of the entire State. [This] generality indicates that the Act is not an effort to expropriate owners of undeveloped land. . . .

[I] respectfully dissent.

Statement of Justice SOUTER.

I would dismiss the writ of certiorari in this case as having been granted improvidently. After briefing and argument it is abundantly clear that an unreviewable assumption on which this case comes to us is both questionable as a conclusion of Fifth Amendment law and sufficient to frustrate the Court's ability to render certain the legal premises on which its holding rests.

The petition for review was granted on the assumption that the state by regulation had deprived the owner of his entire economic interest in the subject property. Such was the state trial court's conclusion, which the state supreme court did not review. It is apparent now that [the] trial court's conclusion is highly questionable. While the respondent now wishes to contest the point, the Court is certainly right to refuse to take up the issue, which is not fairly included within the question presented, and has received only the most superficial and one-sided treatment before us. Because the questionable conclusion of total deprivation cannot be reviewed, the Court is precluded from attempting to clarify the concept of total (and, in the Court's view, categorically compensable) taking on which it rests. [Under] these circumstances, I believe it proper for me to vote to dismiss the writ, despite the Court's contrary preference.

DOLAN v. CITY OF TIGARD
513 U.S. ___, 114 S.Ct. 2309, 129 L.Ed.2d 304 (1994).

Chief Justice REHNQUIST delivered the opinion of the Court.

Petitioner challenges the decision of the Oregon Supreme Court [that] the city of Tigard could condition the approval of her building permit on the dedication of a portion of her property for flood control

---

2. This principle of generality is well-rooted in our broader understandings of the Constitution as designed in part to control the "mischiefs of faction." Federalist No. 10. . . . [Footnote by Justice Stevens.]

and traffic improvements. We granted certiorari to resolve a question left open by our decision in Nollan v. California Coastal Comm'n of what is the required degree of connection between the exactions imposed by the city and the projected impacts of the proposed development.

I.   Oregon enacted a comprehensive land use management program in 1973. The program required all Oregon cities and counties to adopt new comprehensive land use plans that were consistent with the state-wide planning goals [implemented] by land use regulations. [Pursuant] to the State's requirements, the city of Tigard, a community of some 30,000 residents on the southwest edge of Portland, developed a comprehensive plan and codified it in its Community Development Code (CDC). The CDC requires property owners in the area zoned Central Business District to comply with a 15% open space and landscaping requirement, which limits total site coverage, including all structures and paved parking, to 85% of the parcel. After the completion of a transportation study that identified congestion in the Central Business District as a particular problem, the city adopted a plan for a pedestrian/bicycle pathway intended to encourage alternatives to automobile transportation for short trips. The CDC requires that new development facilitate this plan by dedicating land for pedestrian pathways where provided for in the pedestrian/bicycle pathway plan.

The city also adopted a Master Drainage Plan. The Drainage Plan noted that flooding occurred in several areas along Fanno Creek, including areas near petitioner's property. The Drainage Plan also established that the increase in impervious surfaces associated with continued urbanization would exacerbate these flooding problems. To combat these risks, the Drainage Plan suggested a series of improvements to the Fanno Creek Basin, including channel excavation in the area next to petitioner's property. Other recommendations included ensuring that the floodplain remains free of structures and that it be preserved as greenways to minimize flood damage to structures. The Drainage Plan concluded that the cost of these improvements should be shared based on both direct and indirect benefits, with property owners along the waterways paying more due to the direct benefit that they would receive. [The] CDC and the Tigard Park Plan carry out these recommendations.

Petitioner Florence Dolan owns a plumbing and electric supply store located on Main Street in the Central Business District. [The] store covers approximately 9,700 square feet on the eastern side of a 1.67–acre parcel, which includes a gravel parking lot. Fanno Creek flows through the southwestern corner of the lot and along its western boundary. [Petitioner] applied to the city for a permit to redevelop the site. Her proposed plans called for nearly doubling the size of the store to 17,600 square feet, and paving a 39–space parking lot. The existing store, located on the opposite side of the parcel, would be razed in sections as construction progressed on the new building. In the second phase of the project, petitioner proposed to build an additional structure on the northeast side of the site for complementary businesses, and to provide more parking. The proposed expansion and intensified use are consistent with the city's zoning scheme in the Central Business District.

The Planning Commission granted petitioner's permit application subject to conditions imposed by the CDC. The CDC establishes the following standard for site development review approval: "Where land-fill and/or development is allowed within and adjacent to the 100–year floodplain, the city shall require the dedication of sufficient open land area for greenway adjoining and within the floodplain. This area shall include portions at a suitable elevation for the construction of a pedestri-an/bicycle pathway within the floodplain in accordance with the adopted pedestrian/bicycle plan." Thus, the Commission required that petitioner dedicate the portion of her property lying within the [floodplain] for improvement of a storm drainage system along Fanno Creek and that she dedicate an additional 15–foot strip of land adjacent to the floodplain as a pedestrian/bicycle pathway. The dedication required by that condi-tion encompasses approximately 7,000 square feet, or roughly 10% of the property. In accordance with city practice, petitioner could rely on the dedicated property to meet the 15% open space and landscaping require-ment mandated by the city's zoning scheme.

[Petitioner] requested variances from the CDC standards. [The] Commission denied the request [and] made a series of findings concern-ing the relationship between the dedicated conditions and the projected impacts of petitioner's project. First, the Commission noted that "[i]t is reasonable to assume that customers and employees of the future uses of this site could utilize a pedestrian/bicycle pathway adjacent to this development for their transportation and recreational needs." The Commission noted that the site plan has provided for bicycle parking [and] "[i]t is reasonable to expect that some of the users of the bicycle parking provided for by the site plan will use the pathway adjacent to Fanno Creek if it is constructed." In addition, the Commission found that creation of a convenient, safe pedestrian/bicycle pathway system as an alternative means of transportation "could offset some of the traffic demand on [nearby] streets and lessen the increase in traffic conges-tion." The Commission went on to note that the required floodplain dedication would be reasonably related to petitioner's request to intensi-fy the use of the site given the increase in the impervious surface. [The] "anticipated increased storm water flow from the subject property to an already strained creek and drainage basin can only add to the public need to manage the stream channel and floodplain for drainage pur-poses." Based on this anticipated increased storm water flow, the Commission concluded that "the requirement of dedication of the flood-plain area on the site is related to the applicant's plan to intensify development on the site." The City Council approved the Commission's final order.

[Petitioner] appealed to the Land Use Board of Appeals (LUBA) on the ground that the city's dedication requirements were not related to the proposed development, and, therefore, those requirements constitut-ed an uncompensated taking of their property under the Fifth Amend-ment. In evaluating the federal taking claim, LUBA assumed that the city's findings about the impacts of the proposed development were supported by substantial evidence. Given the undisputed fact that the proposed larger building and paved parking area would increase the amount of impervious surfaces and the runoff into Fanno Creek, LUBA concluded that "there is a 'reasonable relationship' between the proposed development and the requirement to dedicate land along Fanno Creek for a greenway." With respect to the pedestrian/bicycle pathway, LUBA noted the Commission's finding that a significantly larger retail sales building and parking lot would attract larger numbers of customers and employees and their vehicles. It again found a "reasonable relationship" between alleviating the impacts of increased traffic from the development and facilitating the provision of a pedestrian/bicycle pathway as an alternative means of transportation. The Oregon Court of Appeals [and] the Oregon Supreme Court affirmed....

II.   [One] of the principal purposes of the Takings Clause is "to bar Government from forcing some people alone to bear public burdens which, in all fairness and justice, should be borne by the public as a whole." Armstrong v. United States, 364 U.S. 40 (1960). Without question, had the city simply required petitioner to dedicate a strip of land along Fanno Creek for public use, rather than conditioning the grant of her permit to redevelop her property on such a dedication, a taking would have occurred. Nollan. Such public access would deprive petitioner of the right to exclude others, "one of the most essential sticks in the bundle of rights that are commonly characterized as property." Kaiser Aetna v. United States, 444 U.S. 164 (1979).

On the other side of the ledger, the authority of state and local governments to engage in land use planning has been sustained against constitutional challenge as long ago as our decision in Euclid. "Government hardly could go on if to some extent values incident to property could not be diminished without paying for every such change in the general law." Pennsylvania Coal. A land use regulation does not effect a taking if it "substantially advance[s] legitimate state interests" and does not "den[y] an owner economically viable use of his land." Agins v. Tiburon, 447 U.S. 255 (1980).

The sort of land use regulations discussed in the cases just cited, however, differ in two relevant particulars from the present case. First, they involved essentially legislative determinations classifying entire areas of the city, whereas here the city made an adjudicative decision to condition petitioner's application for a building permit on an individual parcel. Second, the conditions imposed were not simply a limitation on the use petitioner might make of her own parcel, but a requirement that she deed portions of the property to the city. In Nollan we held that governmental authority to exact such a condition was circumscribed by the Fifth and Fourteenth Amendments. Under the well-settled doctrine of "unconstitutional conditions," the government may not require a person to give up a constitutional right—here the right to receive just compensation when property is taken for a public use—in exchange for a discretionary benefit conferred by the government where the property sought has little or no relationship to the benefit. Perry v. Sindermann [1972; below, 12th Ed., p. 587; Ind.Rts., p. 258]; Pickering v. Board of Ed. [1968; below, 12th Ed., p. 1434; Ind.Rts., p. 1105].

Petitioner contends that the city has forced her to choose between the building permit and her right under the Fifth Amendment to just compensation for the public easements. Petitioner does not quarrel with the city's authority to exact some forms of dedication as a condition for the grant of a building permit, but challenges the showing made by the city to justify these exactions. She argues that the city has identified "no special benefits" conferred on her, and has not identified any "special quantifiable burdens" created by her new store that would justify the particular dedications required from her which are not required from the public at large.

III. [We] must first determine whether the "essential nexus" exists between the "legitimate state interest" and the permit condition exacted by the city. Nollan. If we find that a nexus exists, we must then decide the required degree of connection between the exactions and the projected impact of the proposed development. We were not required to reach this question in Nollan, because we [the] connection did not meet even the loosest standard. Here, however, we must decide this question.

A. We addressed the essential nexus question in Nollan. [There] the Coastal Commission's regulatory authority was set completely adrift from its constitutional moorings when it claimed that a nexus existed between visual access to the ocean and a permit condition requiring lateral public access along the Nollan's beachfront lot. How enhancing the public's ability to "traverse to and along the shorefront" served the same governmental purpose of "visual access to the ocean" from the roadway was beyond our ability to countenance. The absence of a nexus left the Coastal Commission in the position of simply trying to obtain an easement through gimmickry, which converted a valid regulation of land use into "an out-and-out plan of extortion."

No such gimmicks are associated with the permit conditions [in] this case. Undoubtedly, the prevention of flooding along Fanno Creek and the reduction of traffic congestion in the Central Business District qualify as the type of legitimate public purposes we have upheld. It seems equally obvious that a nexus exists between preventing flooding along Fanno Creek and limiting development within the [floodplain]. Petitioner proposes to double the size of her retail store and to pave her now-gravel parking lot, thereby expanding the impervious surface on the property and increasing the amount of stormwater run-off into Fanno Creek. The same may be said for the city's attempt to reduce traffic congestion by providing for alternative means of transportation. In theory, a pedestrian/bicycle pathway provides a useful alternative means of transportation for workers and shoppers....

B. The second part of our analysis requires us to determine whether the degree of the exactions demanded by the city's permit conditions bear the required relationship to the projected impact of petitioner's proposed development. Here the Oregon Supreme Court deferred to what it termed the "city's unchallenged factual findings" supporting the dedication conditions and found them to be reasonably related to the impact of the expansion of petitioner's business. [The] city relies on the Commission's rather tentative findings that increased stormwater flow from petitioner's property "can only add to the public need to manage the [floodplain] for drainage purposes" to support its conclusion that the "requirement of dedication of the floodplain area on the site is related to the applicant's plan to intensify development on the site." The city made the following specific findings relevant to the pedestrian/bicycle pathway: "In addition, the proposed expanded use of this site is anticipated to generate additional vehicular traffic thereby increasing congestion on nearby collector and arterial streets. Creation of a convenient, safe pedestrian/bicycle pathway system as an alternative means of transportation could offset some of the traffic demand on these nearby streets and lessen the increase in traffic congestion."

The question [is] whether these findings are constitutionally sufficient to justify the conditions imposed by the city on petitioner's building permit. Since state courts have been dealing with this question a good deal longer than we have, we turn to representative decisions made by them. In some States, very generalized statements as to the necessary connection between the required dedication and the proposed development seem to suffice. We think this standard is too lax to adequately protect petitioner's right to just compensation if her property is taken for a public purpose. Other state courts require a very exacting correspondence, described as the "specifi[c] and uniquely attributable" test. We do not think the Federal Constitution requires such exacting scrutiny, given the nature of the interests involved. A number of state courts have taken an intermediate position, requiring the municipality to show a "reasonable relationship" between the required dedication and the impact of the proposed development. Typical is the Supreme Court of Nebraska's opinion in Simpson v. North Platte, 292 N.W.2d 297 (1980), where that court stated: "The distinction, therefore, which must be made between an appropriate exercise of the police power and an improper exercise of eminent domain is whether the requirement has some reasonable relationship or nexus to the use to which the property is being made or is merely being used as an excuse for taking property simply because at that particular moment the landowner is asking the city for some license or permit." [Some] form of the reasonable relationship test has been adopted in many other jurisdictions. Despite any semantical differences, general agreement exists among the courts "that the dedication should have some reasonable relationship to the needs created by the [development]." We think the "reasonable relationship" test adopted by a majority of the state courts is closer to the federal constitutional norm than either of those previously discussed. But we do not adopt it as such, partly because the term "reasonable relationship" seems confusingly similar to the term "rational basis" which describes the minimal level of scrutiny under the Equal Protection Clause of the Fourteenth Amendment. We think a term such as "rough proportionality" best encapsulates what we hold to be the requirement of the Fifth Amendment. No precise mathematical calculation is required, but the city must make some sort of individualized determination that the required dedication is related both in nature and extent to the impact of the proposed development.[1]

1. Justice Stevens dissent takes us to task for placing the burden on the city to justify the required dedication. He is correct in arguing that in evaluating most gen-

Justice Stevens dissent relies upon a law review article for the proposition that the city's conditional demands for part of petitioner's property are "a species of business regulation that heretofore warranted a strong presumption of constitutional validity." But simply denominating a governmental measure as a "business regulation" does not immunize it from constitutional challenge on the grounds that it violates a provision of the Bill of Rights. In Marshall v. Barlow's, Inc., 436 U.S. 307 (1978), we held that a statute authorizing a warrantless search of business premises in order to detect OSHA violations violated the Fourth Amendment. And in Central Hudson Gas & Electric Corp. v. Public Service Comm'n of N.Y., 447 U.S. 557 (1980), we held that an order of the New York Public Service Commission, designed to cut down the use of electricity because of a fuel shortage, violated the First Amendment insofar as it prohibited advertising by a utility company to promote the use of electricity. We see no reason why the Takings Clause of the Fifth Amendment, as much a part of the Bill of Rights as the First Amendment or Fourth Amendment, should be relegated to the status of a poor relation in these comparable circumstances. We turn now to analysis of whether the findings relied upon by the city here [satisfied] these requirements.

It is axiomatic that increasing the amount of impervious surface will increase the quantity and rate of storm-water flow from petitioner's property. Therefore, keeping the floodplain open and free from development would likely confine the pressures on Fanno Creek created by petitioner's development. In fact, because petitioner's property lies within the Central Business District, the Community Development Code already required that petitioner leave 15% of it as open space. [But] the city demanded more—it not only wanted petitioner not to build in the floodplain, but it also wanted petitioner's property along Fanno Creek for its Greenway system. The city has never said why a public greenway, as opposed to a private one, was required in the interest of flood control.

The difference to petitioner, of course, is the loss of her ability to exclude others. [This] right to exclude others is "one of the most essential sticks in the bundle of rights that are commonly characterized as property." Kaiser Aetna. [The] city contends that the recreational easement along the Greenway is only ancillary to the city's chief purpose in controlling flood hazards. It further asserts that unlike the residential property at issue in Nollan, petitioner's property is commercial in character and therefore, her right to exclude others is compromised. [Admittedly,] petitioner wants to build a bigger store to attract members of the public to her property. She also wants, however, to be able to control the time and manner in which they enter. [Yet under the city's

erally applicable zoning regulations, the burden properly rests on the party challenging the regulation to prove that it constitutes an arbitrary regulation of property rights. Here, by contrast, the city made an adjudicative decision to condition petition-er's application for a building permit on an individual parcel. In this situation, the burden properly rests on the city. Nollan.... [Footnote by Chief Justice Rehnquist.]

plan petitioner] would lose all rights to regulate the time in which the public entered onto the Greenway, regardless of any interference it might pose with her retail store. Her right to exclude would not be regulated, it would be eviscerated. If petitioner's proposed development had somehow encroached on existing greenway space in the city, it would have been reasonable to require petitioner to provide some alternative greenway space for the public either on her property or elsewhere. But that is not the case here. We conclude that the findings [do] not show the required reasonable relationship between the floodplain easement and the petitioner's proposed new building.

With respect to the pedestrian/bicycle pathway, we have no doubt that the city was correct in finding that the larger retail sales facility proposed by petitioner will increase traffic on the streets of the Central Business District. [Dedications] for streets, sidewalks, and other public ways are generally reasonable exactions to avoid excessive congestion from a proposed property use. But [here] the city has not met its burden of demonstrating that the additional number of vehicle and bicycle trips generated by the petitioner's development reasonably relate to the city's requirement for a dedication of the pedestrian/bicycle pathway easement. The city simply found that the creation of the pathway "could offset some of the traffic demand ... and lessen the increase in traffic congestion." No precise mathematical calculation is required, but the city must make some effort to quantify its findings in support of the dedication for the pedestrian/bicycle pathway beyond the conclusory statement that it could offset some of the traffic demand generated.

IV. Cities have long engaged in the commendable task of land use planning, made necessary by increasing urbanization particularly in metropolitan areas such as Portland. The city's goals of reducing flooding hazards and traffic congestion, and providing for public greenways, are laudable, but there are outer limits to how this may be done. "A strong public desire to improve the public condition [will not] warrant achieving the desire by a shorter cut than the constitutional way of paying for the change." Pennsylvania Coal.

[Reversed.]

Justice STEVENS, with whom Justices BLACKMUN and GINS-BURG join, dissenting.

The record does not tell us the dollar value of petitioner Florence Dolan's interest in excluding the public from the greenway adjacent to her hardware business. The mountain of briefs that the case has generated nevertheless makes it obvious that the pecuniary value of her victory is far less important than the rule of law that this case has been used to establish. It is unquestionably an important case.

Certain propositions are not in dispute. The enlargement of the Tigard unit in Dolan's chain of hardware stores will have an adverse impact on the city's legitimate and substantial interests in controlling drainage in Fanno Creek and minimizing traffic congestion in Tigard's business district. That impact is sufficient to justify an outright denial of her application for approval of the expansion. The city has nevertheless agreed to grant Dolan's application if she will comply with two conditions, each of which admittedly will mitigate the adverse effects of her proposed development. The disputed question is whether the city has violated the Fourteenth Amendment by refusing to allow Dolan's planned construction to proceed unless those conditions are met. The Court is correct in concluding that the city may not attach arbitrary conditions to a building permit or to a variance even when it can rightfully deny the application outright. I also agree that state court decisions dealing with ordinances that govern municipal development plans provide useful guidance in a case of this kind. Yet the Court's description of the doctrinal underpinnings of its decision, the phrasing of its fledgling test of "rough proportionality," and the application of that test to this case run contrary to the traditional treatment of these cases and break considerable and unpropitious new ground.

I. Candidly acknowledging the lack of federal precedent for its exercise in rulemaking, the Court purports to find guidance in 12 "representative" state court decisions. To do so is certainly appropriate. The state cases the Court consults, however, either fail to support or decidedly undermine the Court's conclusions in key respects. First, although discussion of the state cases permeates the Court's analysis of the appropriate test to apply in this case, the test on which the Court settles is not naturally derived from those courts' decisions. [The] Court also decides for the first time that the city has the burden of establishing the constitutionality of its conditions by making an "individualized determination" that the condition in question satisfies the proportionality requirement. Not one of the state cases cited by the Court announces anything akin to a "rough proportionality" requirement. For the most part, moreover, those cases that invalidated municipal ordinances did so on state law or unspecified grounds roughly equivalent to Nollan's "essential nexus" requirement. [In] only one of the seven cases upholding a land use regulation did the losing property owner petition this Court for certiorari. Although 4 of the 12 opinions mention the Federal Constitution—two of those only in passing—it is quite obvious that neither the courts nor the litigants imagined they might be participating in the development of a new rule of federal law. Thus, although these state cases do lend support to the Court's reaffirmation of Nollan's reasonable nexus requirement, the role the Court accords them in the announcement of its newly minted second phase of the constitutional inquiry is remarkably inventive.

In addition, the Court ignores the state courts' willingness to consider what the property owner gains from the exchange in question. [In] this case, [Dolan's] acceptance of the permit, with its attached conditions, would provide her with benefits that may well go beyond any advantage she gets from expanding her business. [The] state court decisions also are enlightening in the extent to which they required that the entire parcel be given controlling importance. All but one of the cases involve challenges to provisions in municipal ordinances requiring developers to dedicate either a percentage of the entire parcel (usually 7 or 10 percent of the platted subdivision) or an equivalent value in cash (usually a certain dollar amount per lot) to help finance the construction of roads, utilities, schools, parks and playgrounds. In assessing the legality of the conditions, the courts gave no indication that the transfer of an interest in realty was any more objectionable than a cash payment. None of the decisions identified the surrender of the fee owner's "power to exclude" as having any special significance. Instead, the courts uniformly examined the character of the entire economic transaction.

II. [Our] own cases [also] require the analysis to focus on the impact of the city's action on the entire parcel of private property. In Penn Central, we stated that takings jurisprudence "does not divide a single parcel into discrete segments and attempt to determine whether rights in a particular segment have been entirely abrogated." Instead, this Court focuses "both on the character of the action and on the nature and extent of the interference with rights in the parcel as a whole." Andrus v. Allard, 444 U.S. 51 (1979), reaffirmed the nondivisibility principle, [stating] that "[a]t least where an owner possesses a full 'bundle' of property rights, the destruction of one 'strand' of the bundle is not a taking, because the aggregate must be viewed in its entirety."

[The] Court's narrow focus on one strand in the property owner's bundle of rights is particularly misguided in a case involving the development of commercial property. As Professor Johnston has noted: "The subdivider is a manufacturer, processer, and marketer of a product; land is but one of his raw materials. In subdivision control disputes, the developer is not defending hearth and home against the king's intrusion, but simply attempting to maximize his profits from the sale of a finished product. As applied to him, subdivision control exactions are actually business regulations." Johnston, Constitutionality of Subdivision Control Exactions: The Quest for A Rationale, 52 Cornell L.Q. 871 (1967). The exactions associated with the development of a retail business are likewise a species of business regulation that heretofore warranted a strong presumption of constitutional validity. In Johnston's view, "if the municipality can demonstrate that its assessment of financial burdens against subdividers is rational, impartial, and conducive to fulfillment of authorized planning objectives, its action need be invalidated only in those extreme and presumably rare cases where the burden of compliance is sufficiently great to deter the owner from proceeding with his planned development." The city of Tigard has demonstrated that its plan is rational and impartial and that the conditions at issue are "conducive to fulfillment of authorized planning objectives." Dolan, on the other hand, has offered no evidence that her burden of compliance has any impact at all on the value or profitability of her planned development.

[The] Court's assurances that its "rough proportionality" test leaves ample room for cities to pursue the "commendable task of land use planning,"—even twice avowing that "[n]o precise mathematical calculation is required,"—are wanting given the result that test compels here. Under the Court's approach, a city must not only "quantify its findings," and make "individualized determination[s]" with respect to the nature and the extent of the relationship between the conditions and the impact, but also demonstrate "proportionality." The correct inquiry should instead concentrate on whether the required nexus is present and venture beyond considerations of a condition's nature or germaneness only if the developer establishes that a concededly germane condition is so grossly disproportionate to the proposed development's adverse effects that it manifests motives other than land use regulation on the part of the city ...

III. Applying its new standard, the Court finds two defects in the city's case. First, while the record would adequately support a requirement that Dolan maintain the portion of the floodplain on her property as undeveloped open space, it does not support the additional requirement that the floodplain be dedicated to the city. Second, while the city adequately established the traffic increase that the proposed development would generate, it failed to quantify the offsetting decrease in automobile traffic that the bike path will produce. Even under the Court's new rule, both defects are, at most, nothing more than harmless error. [If] the Court proposes to have the federal judiciary micromanage state decisions of this kind, it is indeed extending its welcome mat to a significant new class of litigants. Although there is no reason to believe that state courts have failed to rise to the task, property owners have surely found a new friend today.

IV. The Court has made a serious error by abandoning the traditional presumption of constitutionality and imposing a novel burden of proof on a city implementing an admittedly valid comprehensive land use plan. Even more consequential than its incorrect disposition of this case, however, is the Court's resurrection of a species of substantive due process analysis [frequently] identified with a [case] that accorded similar substantive protection to a baker's liberty interest in working 60 hours a week and 10 hours a day. Lochner. The so-called "regulatory takings" doctrine that the Holmes dictum [in Pennsylvania Coal] kindled has an obvious kinship with the line of substantive due process cases that Lochner exemplified. Besides having similar ancestry, both doctrines are potentially open-ended sources of judicial power to invalidate state economic regulations that Members of this Court view as unwise or unfair.

This case inaugurates an even more recent judicial innovation than the regulatory takings doctrine: the application of the "unconstitutional conditions" label to a mutually beneficial transaction between a property owner and a city. The Court tells us that the city's refusal to grant Dolan a discretionary benefit infringes her right to receive just compensation for the property interests that she has refused to dedicate to the city "where the property sought has little or no relationship to the benefit." Although it is well settled that a government cannot deny a benefit on a basis that infringes constitutionally protected interests— "especially [one's] interest in freedom of speech," Perry v. Sindermann—the "unconstitutional conditions" doctrine provides an inadequate framework in which to analyze this case. Dolan has no right to be compensated for a taking unless the city acquires the property interests that she has refused to surrender. Since no taking has yet occurred, there has not been any infringement of her constitutional right to compensation. Even if Dolan should accept the city's conditions in exchange for the benefit that she seeks, it would not necessarily follow that she had been denied "just compensation" since it would be appropriate to consider the receipt of that benefit in any calculation of "just compensation." Particularly in the absence of any evidence on the point, we should not presume that the discretionary benefit the city has offered is less valuable than the property interests that Dolan can retain or surrender at her option. But even if that discretionary benefit were so trifling that it could not be considered just compensation when it has "little or no relationship" to the property, the Court fails to explain why the same value would suffice when the required nexus is present. In this respect, the Court's reliance on the "unconstitutional conditions" doctrine is assuredly novel, and arguably incoherent. The city's conditions are by no means immune from constitutional scrutiny. The level of scrutiny, however, does not approximate the kind of review that would apply if the city had insisted on a surrender of Dolan's First Amendment rights in exchange for a building permit. One can only hope that the Court's reliance today on First Amendment cases, and its candid disavowal of the term "rational basis" to describe its new standard of review, do not signify a reassertion of the kind of superlegislative power the Court exercised during the Lochner era.

The Court has decided to apply its heightened scrutiny to a single strand—the power to exclude—in the bundle of rights that enables a commercial enterprise to flourish in an urban environment. That intangible interest is undoubtedly worthy of constitutional protection—much like the grandmother's interest in deciding which of her relatives may share her home in Moore v. East Cleveland [1977; below, 12th Ed., p. 555; Ind.Rts., p. 226.] Both interests are protected from arbitrary state action by the Due Process Clause. It is, however, a curious irony that Members of the majority in this case would impose an almost insurmountable burden of proof on the property owner in the Moore case while saddling the city with a heightened burden in this case. In its application of what is essentially the doctrine of substantive due process, the Court confuses the past with the present. On November 13, 1922, the village of Euclid, Ohio, adopted a zoning ordinance that effectively confiscated 75 percent of the value of property owned by the Ambler Realty Company. Despite its recognition that such an ordinance "would have been rejected as arbitrary and oppressive" at an earlier date, the Court (over the dissent of Justices Van Devanter, McReynolds and Butler) upheld the ordinance. Today's majority should heed the words of Justice Sutherland: "Such regulations are sustained, under the complex conditions of our day, for reasons analogous to those which justify traffic regulations, which, before the advent of automobiles and rapid transit street railways, would have been condemned as fatally arbitrary and unreasonable. And in this there is no inconsistency, for while the meaning of constitutional guaranties never varies, the scope of their application must expand or contract to meet the new and different conditions which are constantly coming within the field of their operation. In a changing world, it is impossible that it should be otherwise."

In our changing world one thing is certain: uncertainty will characterize predictions about the impact of new urban developments on the risks of floods, earthquakes, traffic congestion, or environmental harms.

When there is doubt concerning the magnitude of those impacts, the public interest in averting them must outweigh the private interest of the commercial entrepreneur. If the government can demonstrate that the conditions it has imposed in a land-use permit are rational, impartial and conducive to fulfilling the aims of a valid land-use plan, a strong presumption of validity should attach to those conditions. The burden of demonstrating that those conditions have unreasonably impaired the economic value of the proposed improvement belongs squarely on the shoulders of the party challenging the state action's constitutionality. That allocation of burdens has served us well in the past. The Court has stumbled badly today by reversing it.

I respectfully dissent.

Justice SOUTER, dissenting.

This case, like Nollan, invites the Court to examine the relationship between conditions imposed by development permits, requiring landowners to dedicate portions of their land for use by the public, and governmental interests in mitigating the adverse effects of such development. Nollan declared the need for a nexus between the nature of an exaction of an interest in land (a beach easement) and the nature of governmental interests. The Court treats this case as raising a further question, not about the nature, but about the degree, of connection required between such an exaction and the adverse effects of development. The Court's opinion announces a test to address this question, but as I read the opinion, the Court does not apply that test to these facts, which do not raise the question the Court addresses.

First, as to the floodplain and Greenway, the Court acknowledges that an easement of this land for open space [is] reasonably related to flood control, but argues that the "permanent recreational easement" for the public on the Greenway is not so related. If that is so, it is not because of any lack of proportionality between permit condition and adverse effect, but because of a lack of any rational connection at all between exaction of a public recreational area and the governmental interest in providing for the effect of increased water runoff. That is merely an application of Nollan's nexus analysis. [But the city] never sought to justify the public access portion of the dedication as related to flood control. It merely argued that whatever recreational uses were made of the bicycle path and the one foot edge on either side, were incidental to the permit condition requiring dedication of the 15-foot easement for an 8-foot-wide bicycle path and for flood control, including open space requirements and relocation of the bank of the river by some five feet. It seems to me such incidental recreational use can stand or fall with the bicycle path, which the city justified by reference to traffic congestion. [As] to the bicycle path, the Court again acknowledges the "theor[etically]" reasonable relationship between "the city's attempt to reduce traffic congestion by providing [a bicycle path] for alternative means of transportation," and the "correct" finding of the city that "the larger retail sales facility proposed by petitioner will increase traffic on the streets of the Central Business District." The Court only faults the city for saying that the bicycle path "could" rather than "would" offset the increased traffic from the store. That again, as far as I can tell, is an application of Nollan, for the Court holds that the stated connection ("could offset") between traffic congestion and bicycle paths is too tenuous; only if the bicycle path "would" offset the increased traffic by some amount, could the bicycle path be said to be related to the city's legitimate interest in reducing traffic congestion.

I cannot agree that the application of Nollan is a sound one here, since it appears that the Court has placed the burden of producing evidence of relationship on the city, despite the usual rule in cases involving the police power that the government is presumed to have acted constitutionally. Having thus assigned the burden, the Court concludes that the City loses based on one word ("could" instead of "would"), and despite the fact that this record shows the connection the Court looks for. Dolan has put forward no evidence that the burden of granting a dedication for the bicycle path is unrelated in kind to the anticipated increase in traffic congestion, nor, if there exists a requirement that the relationship be related in degree, has Dolan shown that the exaction fails any such test. The city, by contrast, calculated the increased traffic flow that would result from Dolan's proposed development to be 435 trips per day, and its Comprehensive Plan, applied here, relied on studies showing the link between alternative modes of transportation, including bicycle paths, and reduced street traffic congestion. Nollan, therefore, is satisfied, and on that assumption the city's conditions should not be held to fail a further rough proportionality test or any other that might be devised to give meaning to the constitutional limits. [In] any event, on my reading, the Court's conclusions about the city's vulnerability carry the Court no further than Nollan has gone already, and I do not view this case as a suitable vehicle for taking the law beyond that point. . . . *

* The 104th Congress has before it several proposals to codify various dimension of takings jurisprudence. The proposal under most active consideration began as H.R. 925, which would allow landowners to demand compensation for federal regulatory actions under environmental laws if those actions would diminish the fair market value of the property by 20%. H.R. 925 passed by a vote of 277–148, and was then incorporated into H.R. 9, an omnibus regulatory reform bill. H.R. 9 was passed in the House on March 3, 1995 by a vote of 277–141, and sent on to the Senate Governmental Affairs Committee, where it is pending. Other proposals include the Private Property Rights Restoration Act (S. 145) proposed by Presidential contender Senator Gramm, the Omnibus Property Rights Act of 1995 (S. 605), the Property Rights Litigation Relief Act of 1995 (S. 135), and its House counterpart (H.R. 489). All of these bills require that any taking exceeding a certain dollar amount or percentage of the property value will constitute a taking requiring compensation. S. 22 would require Federal agencies to prepare private property "takings impact" analyses before the agency could proceed.

12th ED., p. 490; IND. RTS., p. 161
Add at end of footnote 12:

And in General Motors Corp. v. Romein, 503 U.S. 181 (1992), a unanimous Court, with Justice O'Connor writing the opinion, held that it need not reach the issue of contractual impairment because "there was no contractual agreement regarding the specific workers' compensation terms allegedly at issue. [Contrary] to petitioners' suggestion, we have not held that all state regulations are implied terms of every contract entered into while they are effective, especially when the regulations themselves cannot be fairly interpreted to require such incorporation. For the most part, state laws are implied into private contracts regardless of the assent of the parties only when those laws affect the validity, construction, and enforcement of contracts. [Changes] in the laws that make a contract legally enforceable may trigger Contract Clause scrutiny if they impair the obligation of pre-existing contracts, even if they do not alter any of the contracts' bargained-for terms[, but the] 1987 statute did not change the legal enforceability of the employment contracts here."

12th ED., p. 490; IND. RTS., p. 161

Add at end of footnote 1:

In General Motors Corp. v. Romein, 503 U.S. 181 (1992), a unanimous Court characterized due process scrutiny of retroactive regulatory legislation in traditionally minimal terms as requiring "a legitimate legislative purpose furthered by rational means."

12th ED., p. 491; IND. RTS., p. 162

Add to footnote 3:

And see also Concrete Pipe and Products of California, Inc. v. Construction Laborers Pension Trust for Southern California, 510 U.S. ___ (1993), upholding one aspect of the Multiemployer Pension Plan Amendments Act of 1980 against substantive due process, procedural due process, and takings challenges based on the Act's alleged retroactive application. Justice Souter's majority opinion quoted Gray to the effect that "it is now well established that legislative Acts adjusting the burdens and benefits of economic life come to the Court with a presumption of constitutionality," and can only be overturned on a showing "that the legislature has acted in an arbitrary and irrational way." Still more recently, the Court in United States v. Carlton, 513 U.S. ___ (1994), once again upheld a retroactive change in tax laws against a substantive due process challenge. Justice Blackmun's majority opinion noted that the existing standard, pursuant to which retroactive tax laws were constitutionally permissible unless "harsh and oppressive," was equivalent to the prohibition only on "arbitrary and irrational" action imposed "generally to enactments in the sphere of economic policy." Justice O'Connor concurred in the judgment, expressing some willingness to take more seriously in other cases the possibility that retroactive changes in tax laws could violate the constraints of substantive due process. Justice Scalia, joined by Justice Thomas, also concurred in the judgment, continuing to insist that "substantive due process" was "an oxymoron," and that "the Due Process Clause guarantees *no* substantive rights, but only (as it says) process." He also chided the majority for applying its substantive due process analysis in a way that treated economic and property rights differently from and worse than other rights. The "categorical and inexplicable exclusion of so-called 'economic rights' (even though the Due Process Clause explicitly applies to 'property') unquestionably involves policymaking rather than neutral legal analysis."

12th ED., p. 519; IND. RTS., p. 190

Add to footnote 12:

In the earlier parts of the hearings and debates preceding the confirmation of Justice Thomas, considerable attention was devoted to questions of constitutional interpretation. The focal point of these debates turned out to be the question of "natural law," for Justice Thomas had earlier articulated what appeared to be a sympathy for such a position, and had done so in the context of praising an article opposing abortion.

As ordinarily understood within legal theory, "natural law" is commonly contrasted with "positivism," with the latter maintaining that it is possible to identify legal norms by use of some test not necessarily incorporating moral factors. By contrast, classical natural law theory holds that it is necessarily the case that the identification of a legal norm requires reference to moral norms antecedent to what appears to be the positive law. There is little indication, however, that this theoretical debate animated the concerns about Justice Thomas, for the connections between either of these positions and any particular interpretive stance about law in general or constitutional law in particular are at best highly circuitous. Instead, Justice Thomas' seeming sympathy for "natural law" was taken instead to mark a sympathy for "natural rights" and the view that there are rights antecedent to the Constitution, with the role of the judiciary including the enforcement of those antecedent rights regardless of whether they were embodied in the constitutional text.

As so understood, the position attributed to Justice Thomas was similar to the position sometimes described as "noninterpretivist." The concern of some of Thomas' opponents, therefore, seemed not so much a concern about the theoretical validity of non-interpretivism, but rather a concern about what for Thomas would be the sources of these antecedent rights, and in what way they figured in constitutional adjudication. Here the reference to "natural law" may have triggered the suspicion that, because one branch of natural law theory traces its roots to Aquinas and has been a central part of Catholic theology, and because Justice Thomas had received a Catholic education, that his reference to "natural law" indicated a preference for finding his antecedent rights within the Catholic tradition, although nothing in the idea of natural law itself speaks to the source, rather than the status, of the antecedent rights.

When questioned about these issues at the Senate Judiciary Committee hearings, Justice Thomas indicated that his interest in natural law was philosophical and political, and did not relate to his views about adjudication or the role of the judge. "I don't think that an appeal, a direct appeal, to natural law is a part of adjudicating cases ... In constitutional analysis and methodology, there isn't any direct reference to natural law ... At no time did I feel nor do I feel now that natural law is anything more than the background to our Constitution ... But when it is in the Constitution, it is not a natural right; it is a constitutional right ... [Natural law] is not a method of interpreting or a method of adjudicating in the constitutional law area."

12th ED., p. 521; IND. RTS., p. 192
Add as new footnote after last sentence on page:

17a. The 104th Congress continues to wrestle with the abortion issue in a variety of contexts, from the failure of Dr. Henry Foster's nomination as Surgeon General to resolutions condemning a spate of anti-abortion violence, notably the widely-reported cases of Paul Hill and John Salvi, both accused of gunning down abortion clinic workers, to funding decisions about abortions in appropriation bills. There are more "right to life" constitutional amendment proposals in the 104th Congress than in the 103rd, including H.J.Res. 18, 23, 26, 72 and 90, but all are pending in committee as of the closing date of this supplement and seem unlikely to pass. S. 28 and S. 320, the Unborn Children's Civil Rights Act, would prohibit abortions. S. 24 and S. 316, the Civil Rights of Infants Act, would prohibit abortions based on the gender of a fetus. H.R. 231 would deny tax deductions for medical expenses relating to abortion. The Freedom of Choice Act, H.R. 776, see below addition to 12th Ed., p. 553; Ind.Rts. p. 224, which would codify Roe v. Wade, is also pending and also seems unlikely to pass.

12th ED., p. 530; IND. RTS., p. 201
Add at end of footnote 7:

Note that the Freedom of Choice Act of 1995, H.R. 776 (see below, addition to 12th Ed., p. 553; Ind.Rts., p. 224, immediately following Planned Parenthood of Southeastern Pennsylvania v. Casey), would allow states to impose the requirement that a parent, a guardian or "other responsible adult" be involved in the decision by a minor to have an abortion.

12th ED., p. 553; IND. RTS., p. 224
Add at end of abortion materials:

RUST v. SULLIVAN
500 U.S. 173, 111 S.Ct. 1759, 114 L.Ed.2d 233 (1991).

Chief Justice REHNQUIST delivered the opinion of the Court.

These cases concern a facial challenge to Department of Health and Human Services (HHS) regulations which limit the ability of Title X fund recipients to engage in abortion related activities. The [Court] of Appeals for the Second Circuit upheld the regulations, finding them to be a permissible construction of the statute as well as consistent with the First and Fifth Amendments of the Constitution. [We] affirm.

I. A. In 1970, Congress enacted Title X of the Public Health Service Act (Act), 42 U.S.C. 300–300a–41, which provides federal funding for family planning services. The Act authorizes the Secretary to "make grants to and enter into contracts with public or nonprofit private entities to assist in the establishment and operation of voluntary family planning projects which shall offer a broad range of acceptable and effective family planning methods and services." Grants and contracts under Title X must "be made in accordance with such regulations as the Secretary may promulgate." Section 1008 of the Act, however, provides that "[n]one of the funds appropriated under this subchapter shall be used in programs where abortion is a method of family planning." That restriction was intended to ensure that Title X funds would "be used only to support preventive family planning services, population research, infertility services, and other related medical, informational, and educational activities." H.R.Conf.Rep.

In 1988, the Secretary promulgated new regulations designed to provide " 'clear and operational guidance' to grantees about how to preserve the distinction between Title X programs and abortion as a method of family planning." 53 Fed.Reg. 2923. The regulations clarify, through the definition of the term "family planning," that Congress intended Title X funds "to be used only to support preventive family planning services." Accordingly, Title X services are limited to "preconceptual counseling, education, and general reproductive health care," and expressly exclude "pregnancy care (including obstetric or prenatal care)." 42 CFR 59.2 (1989). The regulations "focus the emphasis of the Title X program on its traditional mission: The provision of preventive family planning services specifically designed to enable individuals to determine the number and spacing of their children, while clarifying that pregnant women must be referred to appropriate prenatal care services."

The regulations attach three principal conditions on the grant of federal funds for Title X projects. First, [they] specify that a "Title X project may not provide counseling concerning the use of abortion as a method of family planning or provide referral for abortion as a method of family planning." Because Title X is limited to preconceptional services, the program does not furnish services related to childbirth. Only in the context of a referral out of the Title X program is a pregnant woman given transitional information. Title X projects must refer every pregnant client "for appropriate prenatal and/or social services by furnishing a list of available providers that promote the welfare of the mother and the unborn child." The list may not be used indirectly to encourage or promote abortion, "such as by weighing the list of referrals in favor of health care providers which perform abortions, by including on the list of referral providers health care providers whose principal business is the provision of abortions, by excluding available providers who do not provide abortions, or by 'steering' clients to providers who offer abortion as a method of family planning." The Title X project is expressly prohibited from referring a pregnant woman to an abortion provider, even upon specific request. One permissible response to such an inquiry is that "the project does not consider abortion an appropriate method of family planning and therefore does not counsel or refer for abortion."

Second, the regulations broadly prohibit a Title X project from [activities] that "encourage, promote or advocate abortion as a method of family planning." Forbidden activities include lobbying for legislation that would increase the availability of abortion as a method of family planning, developing or disseminating materials advocating abortion as a method of family planning, providing speakers to promote abortion as a method of family planning, using legal action to make abortion available in any way as a method of family planning, and paying dues to any group that advocates abortion as a method of family planning as a substantial part of its activities.

Third, the regulations require that Title X projects be organized so that they are "physically and financially separate" from prohibited abortion activities. To be deemed physically and financially separate, "a Title X project must have an objective integrity and independence from prohibited activities. Mere bookkeeping separation of Title X funds from other monies is not sufficient." The regulations provide [factors] for the Secretary to consider in [determining] integrity and independence, such as the existence of separate [records and personnel], and the degree of physical separation of the project from facilities for prohibited activities.

B. Petitioners are Title X grantees and doctors [suing] on behalf of themselves and their patients. Respondent is the Secretary of the Department of Health and Human Services. After the regulations had been promulgated, [petitioners] filed [actions challenging] the facial validity of the regulations [on] the grounds that they were not authorized by Title X and that they violate the First and Fifth Amendment rights of Title X clients and the First Amendment rights of Title X health providers. [The] District Court rejected petitioners' [challenges] to the regulations and granted summary judgment in favor of the Secretary. A panel of the Court of Appeals for the Second Circuit affirmed. Applying [Chevron] U.S.A. Inc. v. Natural Resources Defense Council, Inc., 467 U.S. 837 (1984), the Court of Appeals determined that the regulations were a permissible construction of the statute that legitimately effectuated Congressional intent. [Turning] to petitioners' constitutional challenges to the regulations, the Court of Appeals rejected petitioners' Fifth Amendment challenge. It held that the regulations do not impermissibly burden a woman's right to an abortion because the "government may validly choose to favor childbirth over abortion and to implement that choice by funding medical services relating to childbirth but not those relating to abortion." [The] court likewise found that the "Secretary's implementation of Congress's decision not to fund abortion counseling, referral or advocacy also does not [violate] the First Amendment rights of health care providers or of women."

II. [Petitioners] are challenging the facial validity of the regulations. Thus, we are concerned only with the question whether, on their face, the regulations are both authorized by the Act, and can be construed in such a manner that they can be applied to a set of individuals without infringing upon constitutionally protected rights. Petitioners face a heavy burden in seeking to have the regulations invalidated as facially unconstitutional. "A facial challenge to a legislative Act is, of course, the most difficult challenge to mount successfully, since the challenger must establish that no set of circumstances exists under which the Act would be valid. The fact that [the regulations] might operate unconstitutionally under some conceivable set of circumstances is insufficient to render [them] wholly invalid." United States v. Salerno, 481 U.S. 739 (1987).

We turn first to petitioners' contention that the regulations exceed the Secretary's authority under Title X. . . .

A. We need not dwell on the plain language of the statute because we agree with every court to have addressed the issue that the language is ambiguous. The language of section 1008—that "[n]one of the funds appropriated under this subchapter shall be used in programs where abortion is a method of family planning"—does not speak directly to the issues of counseling, referral, advocacy, or program integrity. If a statute is "silent or ambiguous with respect to the specific issue, the question for the court is whether the agency's answer is based on a permissible construction of the statute." Chevron.

The Secretary's construction of Title X may not be disturbed as an abuse of discretion if it reflects a plausible construction of the plain language of the statute and does not otherwise conflict with Congress' expressed intent. In determining whether a construction is permissible, "[t]he court need not conclude that the agency construction was the only one it could permissibly have adopted . . . or even the reading the court would have reached if the question initially had arisen in a judicial proceeding." Id. Rather, substantial deference is accorded to the interpretation of the authorizing statute by the agency authorized with administering it.

The broad language of Title X plainly allows the Secretary's construction of the statute. By its own terms, section 1008 prohibits the use of Title X funds "in programs where abortion is a method of family planning." Title X does not define the term "method of family planning," nor [enumerate] what [services] are entitled to Title X funding. Based on the broad directives provided [in section 1008], we are unable to say that the Secretary's construction [to] require a ban on counseling, referral, and advocacy within the Title X project is impermissible.

The [courts] that have examined the legislative history have all found [that] the legislative history is ambiguous with respect to Congress' intent. [We] join these courts in holding that the legislative history [fails] to shed light on relevant congressional intent. At no time did Congress directly address the issues of abortion counseling, referral, or advocacy. [When] we find [that] the legislative history is ambiguous and unenlightening on the matters with respect to which the regulations deal, we customarily defer to the expertise of the agency. Petitioners argue, however, that the regulations are entitled to little or no deference because they "reverse a longstanding agency policy that permitted nondirective counseling and referral for abortion," and thus represent a sharp break from the Secretary's prior construction of the statute [to] permit nondirective counseling and to encourage coordination with local and state family planning services. [But] in Chevron, we held that a revised interpretation deserves deference because "[a]n initial agency interpretation is not instantly carved in stone" and "the agency, to engage in informed rulemaking, must consider varying interpretations and the wisdom of its policy on a continuing basis." [We] find that the Secretary amply justified his change of interpretation with a "reasoned analysis." The Secretary explained that the regulations are a result of his determination, in the wake of the critical reports of the General Accounting Office (GAO) and the Office of the Inspector General (OIG), that prior policy failed [to] provide "clear and operational guidance to grantees to preserve the distinction between Title X programs and abortion as a method of family planning." He also determined that the new regulations are more in keeping with the original intent of the statute, are justified by client experience under the prior policy, and are supported by a shift in attitude against the "elimination of unborn children by abortion." We believe that these justifications are sufficient to support the Secretary's revised approach. Having concluded that the plain language and legislative history are ambiguous, [we] must defer to the Secretary's permissible construction of the statute.

B. We turn next to the "program integrity" requirements embodied at section 59.9 of the regulations, mandating separate facilities, personnel, and records. [The] Secretary defends the separation requirements [on] the grounds that they are necessary to assure that [grantees] apply federal funds only to federally authorized purposes and [avoid] creating the appearance that the government is supporting abortion-related activities. The program integrity regulations were promulgated in direct response to the observations in the GAO and OIG reports that "[b]ecause the distinction between the recipient's title X and other activities may not be easily recognized, the public can get the impression that Federal funds are being improperly used for abortion activities."

[We] agree that the program integrity requirements are based on a permissible construction of the statute and are not inconsistent with Congressional intent. [The] legislative history is clear about very little, and program integrity is no exception. [There is, however,] the statement that it is the "intent of both Houses that the funds authorized under this legislation be used only to support preventive family planning services ... The conferees have adopted the language contained in section 1008, which prohibits the use of such funds for abortion, in order to make this intent clear." When placed in context, [the legislative history does not] render the Secretary's interpretation of the statute impermissible. [Indeed,] if one thing is clear from the legislative history, it is that Congress intended that Title X funds be kept separate and distinct from abortion-related activities. [Certainly] the Secretary's interpretation of the statute that separate facilities are necessary, especially in light of the express prohibition of section 1008, cannot be judged unreasonable. Accordingly, we defer to the Secretary's reasoned determination that the program integrity requirements are necessary to implement the prohibition.

Petitioners also contend that the regulations must be invalidated because they raise serious questions of constitutional law. [Under] this canon of statutory construction, "[t]he elementary rule is that every reasonable construction must be resorted to in order to save a statute from unconstitutionality." Edward J. Debartolo Corp. v. Florida Gulf Coast Building and Construction Trades Council, 485 U.S. 568 (1988), quoting Hooper v. California, 155 U.S. 648 (1895). [The] principle [is] a categorical one: "as between two possible interpretations of a statute, by one of which it would be unconstitutional and by the other valid, our plain duty is to adopt that which will save the Act." Blodgett v. Holden, 275 U.S. 142 (1927) (opinion of Holmes, J.). This principle is based at least in part on the fact that a decision to declare an act of Congress unconstitutional "is the gravest and most delicate duty that this Court is called on to perform." Id. Following Hooper, cases [developed] the corollary doctrine that "[a] statute must be construed, if fairly possible, so as to avoid not only the conclusion that it is unconstitutional but also grave doubts upon that score." This canon is followed out of respect for Congress, which we assume legislates in the light of constitutional limitations. It is qualified by the proposition that "avoidance of a difficulty will not be pressed to the point of disingenuous evasion." Moore Ice Cream Co. v. Rose, 289 U.S. 373 (1933).

Here Congress forbade the use of appropriated funds in programs where abortion is a method of family planning. It authorized the Secretary to promulgate regulations implementing this provision. The extensive litigation regarding governmental restrictions on abortion since [Roe] v. Wade suggests that it was likely that any set of regulations promulgated by the Secretary—other than the ones in force prior to 1988 and found by him to be [ineffectual]—would be challenged on constitutional grounds. While we do not think that the constitutional arguments made by petitioners [are] without some force, [we] hold [below] that they do not carry the day. Applying the canon of construction under discussion as best we can, we hold that the regulations promulgated by the Secretary do not raise the sort of "grave and doubtful constitutional questions" that would lead us to assume Congress did not intend to authorize their issuance. Therefore, we need not invalidate the regulations in order to save the statute from unconstitutionality.

III. Petitioners contend that the regulations violate the First Amendment by impermissibly discriminating based on viewpoint because they prohibit "all discussion about abortion as a lawful option—including counseling, referral, and the provision of neutral and accurate information about ending a pregnancy—while compelling the clinic or counselor to provide information that promotes continuing a pregnancy to term." They assert that the regulations violate the "free speech rights of private health care organizations that receive Title X funds, of their staff, and of their patients" by impermissibly imposing "viewpoint-discriminatory conditions on government subsidies" and "thus penaliz[e] speech funded with non-Title X monies." [Relying] on Regan v. Taxation With Representation of Washington [1983; below, 12th Ed., p. 1446; Ind.Rts., p. 1117] and Arkansas Writers Project, Inc. v. Ragland [1987; below, 12th Ed., p. 1499; Ind.Rts., p. 1170], petitioners also assert that while the Government may place certain conditions on the receipt of federal subsidies, it may not "discriminate invidiously in its subsidies in such a way as to 'ai[m] at the suppression of dangerous ideas.'" Regan, quoting Cammarano v. United States, 358 U.S. 498 (1959).

There is no question but that the [prohibition is] constitutional. In Maher v. Roe, we upheld a state welfare regulation under which Medicaid recipients received payments for services related to childbirth, but not for nontherapeutic abortions. [We] held that the government may "make a value judgment favoring childbirth over abortion, and ... implement that judgment by the allocation of public funds." Here the Government is exercising the authority it possesses under Maher and McRae to subsidize family planning services which will lead to conception and child birth, and declining to "promote or encourage abortion." The Government can [selectively] fund a program to encourage certain activities it believes to be in the public interest, without at the same time funding an alternate program which seeks to deal with the problem in another way. In so doing, the Government has not discriminated on the basis of viewpoint; it has merely chosen to fund one activity to the exclusion of the other. "[A] legislature's decision not to subsidize the exercise of a fundamental right does not infringe the right." Regan. "A refusal to fund protected activity, without more, cannot be equated with the imposition of a 'penalty' on that activity." McRae. "There is a basic difference between direct state interference with a protected activity and state encouragement of an alternative activity consonant with legislative policy." Maher.

The challenged regulations implement the statutory prohibition by prohibiting counseling, referral, and the provision of information regarding abortion as a method of family planning. [The] Title X program is designed not for prenatal care, but to encourage family planning. A doctor who wished to offer prenatal care [could] properly be prohibited from doing so because such service is outside the scope of the federally funded program. The regulations prohibiting abortion counseling and referral are of the same ilk; "no funds appropriated for the project may be used in programs where abortion is a method of family planning," and a doctor [may] be prohibited in the course of his project duties from counseling abortion or referring for abortion. This is not a case of the Government "suppressing a dangerous idea," but of a prohibition on a project grantee or its employees from engaging in activities outside of its scope.

To hold that the Government unconstitutionally discriminates on the basis of viewpoint when it chooses to fund a program dedicated to advance certain permissible goals, because the program in advancing those goals necessarily discourages alternate goals, would render numerous government programs constitutionally suspect. When Congress established a National Endowment for Democracy to encourage other countries to adopt democratic principles, it was not constitutionally required to fund a program to encourage competing lines of political philosophy such as Communism and Fascism. Petitioners' assertions [boil] down to the position that if the government chooses to subsidize one protected right, it must subsidize analogous counterpart rights. But [within] far broader limits than petitioners are willing to concede, when the government appropriates public funds to establish a program it is entitled to define the limits of that program.

[Reliance] upon [Arkansas] Writers Project is misplaced. That case involved a state sales tax which discriminated between magazines on the basis of their content. Relying on this fact, and on the fact that the tax "targets a small group within the press," [the] Court held the tax invalid. But we have here not [a] general law singling out a disfavored group on the basis of speech content, but a case of the Government refusing to fund activities, including speech, which are specifically excluded from the scope of the project funded.

Petitioners [claim] that the regulations would not, in [a] medical emergency, permit a Title X project to refer a woman whose pregnancy places her life in imminent peril to a provider of abortions or abortion-related services. This case, of course, involves only a facial challenge to the regulations, and we do not have before us any [specific] fact situation. On their face, we do not read the regulations to bar abortion referral or counseling in such circumstances. Abortion counseling as a "method of family planning" is prohibited, and it does not seem that a medically necessitated abortion in such circumstances would be the equivalent of its uses as a "method of family planning." [Moreover,] the regulations themselves contemplate that a Title X project would be permitted to engage in otherwise prohibited abortion-related activity in such circumstances. Section 59.8(a)(2) provides a specific exemption for emergency care and requires Title X recipients "to refer the client immediately to an appropriate provider of emergency medical services."

[Petitioners] also contend that the restrictions [are] impermissible because they condition the receipt of a benefit, in this case Title X funding, on the relinquishment of a constitutional right, the right to engage in abortion advocacy and counseling. [Petitioners] argue that "even though the government may deny [a] ... benefit for any number of reasons, there are some reasons upon which the government may not rely. It may not deny a benefit to a person on a basis that infringes his constitutionally protected interests—especially, his interest in freedom of speech." Petitioners' [argument] is unavailing, however, because here the government is not denying a benefit to anyone, but is instead simply insisting that public funds be spent for the purposes for which they were authorized. The Secretary's regulations do not force the Title X grantee to give up abortion-related speech; they merely require that the grantee keep such activities separate and distinct from Title X activities. Title X expressly distinguishes between a Title X grantee and a Title X project. The grantee, which normally is a health care organization, may receive funds from a variety of sources for a variety of purposes. The grantee receives Title X funds, however, for the specific and limited purpose of establishing and operating a Title X project. The regulations govern the scope of the Title X project's activities, and leave the grantee unfettered in its other activities. The Title X grantee can continue to perform abortions, provide abortion-related services, and engage in abortion advocacy; it simply is required to conduct those activities through programs that are separate [from] the project that receives Title X funds.

In contrast, our "unconstitutional conditions" cases involve situations in which the government has placed a condition on the recipient of the subsidy rather than on a particular program or service, thus effectively prohibiting the recipient from engaging in the protected conduct outside the scope of the federally funded program. In FCC v. League of Women Voters of California [1984; below, 12th Ed., p. 1500; Ind.Rts., p. 1171] we invalidated a federal law providing that noncommercial television and radio stations that receive federal grants may not "engage in editorializing." Under that law, a recipient of federal funds was "barred absolutely from all editorializing" because it "is not able to segregate its activities according to the source of its funding" and thus "has no way of limiting the use of its federal funds to all noneditorializing activities." [We] expressly recognized, however, that were Congress to permit the recipient stations to "establish 'affiliate' organizations which could then use the station's facilities to editorialize with nonfederal funds, such a statutory mechanism would plainly be valid."

[Similarly,] in Regan we held that Congress could [reasonably] refuse to subsidize the lobbying activities of tax-exempt charitable organizations by prohibiting such organizations from using tax-deductible contributions to support their lobbying efforts. [We] explained that such organizations remained free "to receive deductible contributions to support ... nonlobbying activit[ies]." Thus, a charitable organization could create, under section 501(c)(3) of the Internal Revenue Code of 1954, an affiliate to conduct its nonlobbying activities using tax-deductible contributions, and at the same time establish, under section 501(c)(4), a separate affiliate to pursue its lobbying efforts without such contributions. Given that alternative, the Court concluded that "Congress has not infringed any First Amendment rights or regulated any First Amendment activity[; it] has simply chosen not to pay for [appellee's] lobbying." We also noted that appellee "would, of course, have to ensure that the section 501(c)(3) organization did not subsidize the section 501(c)(4) organization; otherwise, public funds might be spent on an activity Congress chose not to subsidize." The condition that federal funds will be used only to further the purposes of a grant does not violate constitutional rights.

[By] requiring that the Title X grantee engage in abortion related activity separately from activity receiving federal funding, Congress has [not] denied it the right to engage in abortion-related activities. Congress has merely refused to fund such activities out of the public fisc, and the Secretary has simply required a certain degree of separation from the Title X project in order to ensure the integrity of the federally funded program.

The same principles apply to petitioners' claim that the regulations abridge the free speech rights of the grantee's staff. Individuals who are voluntarily employed for a Title X project must perform their duties in accordance with the regulation's restrictions on abortion counseling and referral. The employees remain free, however, to pursue abortion-related activities when [not] acting under the auspices of the Title X project. The regulations [do] not in any way restrict the activities of those persons acting as private individuals. The employees' freedom of expression is limited during the time that they actually work for the project; but this limitation is a consequence of their decision to accept employment in a project, the scope of which is permissibly restricted by the funding authority.[1]

This is not to suggest that funding by the Government, even when coupled with the freedom of the fund recipients to speak outside the scope of the Government-funded project, is invariably sufficient to justify government control over the content of expression. For example, this Court has recognized that the existence of a Government "subsidy," in the form of Government-owned property, does not justify the restriction of speech in areas that have "been traditionally open to the public for expressive activity." United States v. Kokinda [1990; below, 12th Ed., p. 1441; Ind.Rts., p. 1112]. [Similarly,] we have recognized that the university is a traditional sphere of free expression so fundamental to the functioning of our society that the Government's ability to control speech within that sphere by means of conditions attached to the expenditure of Government funds is restricted by the vagueness and overbreadth doctrines of the First Amendment. Keyishian v. Board of Regents [1967; below, 12th Ed., p. 1422; Ind. Rts., p. 1093]. It could be argued by analogy that traditional relationships such as that between doctor and patient should enjoy [First Amendment] protection [even] when subsidized by the Government. We need not resolve that question here, however, because the [regulations] do not significantly impinge upon the doctor-patient relationship. Nothing in them requires a doctor to represent as his own any opinion that he does not in fact hold. Nor is the doctor-patient relationship established by the Title X program suffi-ciently all-encompassing so as to justify an expectation on the part of the patient of comprehensive medical advice. The program does not provide postconception medical care, and therefore a doctor's silence with regard to abortion cannot reasonably be thought to mislead a client into thinking that the doctor does not consider abortion an appropriate option for her. The doctor is always free to make clear that advice regarding abortion is simply beyond the scope of the program. ...

---

1. Petitioners also contend that the reg-ulations violate the First Amendment by penalizing speech funded with non-Title X monies. They argue that since Title X re-quires that grant recipients contribute to the financing of Title X projects through the use of matching funds and grant-related income, the regulation's restrictions on abortion counseling and advocacy penalize privately funded speech. We find this argu-ment flawed. [The] recipient is in no way compelled to operate a Title X project; to avoid the force of the regulations, it can simply decline the subsidy. By accepting Title X funds, a recipient voluntarily con-sents to any restrictions placed on any matching funds or grant-related income. Potential grant recipients can choose be-tween accepting Title X funds—subject to the Government's conditions that they pro-vide matching funds and forgo abortion counseling and referral in the Title X pro-ject—or declining the subsidy and financing their own unsubsidized program. We have never held that the Government violates the First Amendment simply by offering that choice. [Footnote by Chief Justice Rehnquist.]

IV. We turn now to petitioners' argument that the regulations violate a woman's Fifth Amendment right to choose whether to terminate her pregnancy. We recently reaffirmed [that] " 'the Due Process Clauses generally confer no affirmative right to governmental aid, even where such aid may be necessary to secure life, liberty, or property interests of which the government itself may not deprive the individual.' " Webster, quoting DeShaney v. Winnebago County Dept. of Social Services [1989; below, 12th Ed., p. 924; Ind. Rts., p. 595]. The Government has no constitutional duty to subsidize an activity merely because the activity is constitutionally protected and may validly choose to fund childbirth over abortion and " 'implement that judgment by the allocation of public funds' " for medical services relating to childbirth but not to those relating to abortion. Webster. The Government has no affirmative duty to "commit any resources to facilitating abortions," and its decision to fund childbirth but not abortion "places no governmental obstacle in the path of a woman who chooses to terminate her pregnancy, but rather, by means of unequal subsidization of abortion and other medical services, encourages alternative activity deemed in the public interest." McRae.

[The] regulations do not impermissibly burden a woman's Fifth Amendment rights. [Just] as Congress' refusal to fund abortions in McRae left "an indigent woman with at least the same range of choice in deciding whether to obtain a medically necessary abortion as she would have had if Congress had chosen to subsidize no health care costs at all," and "Missouri's refusal to allow public employees to perform abortions in public hospitals leaves a pregnant woman with the same choices as if the State had chosen not to operate any public hospitals," Webster, Congress' refusal to fund abortion counseling and advocacy leaves a pregnant woman with the same choices as if the government had chosen not to fund family-planning services at all. The difficulty that a woman encounters when a Title X project does not provide abortion counseling or referral leaves her in no different position than she would have been if the government had not enacted Title X.

In Webster we stated that "[h]aving held that the State's refusal [in Maher] to fund abortions does not violate Roe v. Wade, it strains logic to reach a contrary result for the use of public facilities and employees." It similarly would strain logic, in light of the more extreme restrictions in those cases, to find that the mere decision to exclude abortion-related services from a federally funded pre-conceptual family planning program, is unconstitutional.

Petitioners also argue that by impermissibly infringing on the doctor/patient relationship and depriving a Title X client of information concerning abortion as a method of family planning, the regulations violate a woman's Fifth Amendment right to medical self-determination. [They] argue that under our decisions [the] government cannot interfere with a woman's right to make an informed and voluntary choice by placing restrictions on the patient/doctor dialogue.

In Akron, we invalidated a city ordinance requiring all physicians to make specified statements to the patient prior to performing an abortion in order to ensure that the woman's consent was "truly informed." Similarly, in Thornburgh, we struck down a state statute mandating that a list of agencies offering alternatives to abortion and a description of fetal development be provided to every woman considering terminating her pregnancy through an abortion. Critical to our decisions [to] invalidate a governmental intrusion into the patient/doctor dialogue was the fact that the laws in both cases required all doctors within their respective jurisdictions to provide all pregnant patients contemplating an abortion a litany of information, regardless of whether the patient sought the information or whether the doctor thought the information necessary to the patient's decision. Under the Secretary's regulations, however, a doctor's ability to provide, and a woman's right to receive, information concerning abortion and abortion-related services outside the context of the Title X project remains unfettered. It would undoubtedly be easier for a woman seeking an abortion if she could receive information about abortion from a Title X project, but the Constitution does not require that the Government distort the scope of its mandated program in order to provide that information.

Petitioners contend, however, that most Title X clients are effectively precluded by indigency and poverty from seeing a health care provider who will provide abortion-related services. But once again, even these [clients] are in no worse position than if Congress had never enacted Title X. "The financial constraints that restrict an indigent woman's ability to enjoy the full range of constitutionally protected freedom of choice are the product not of governmental restrictions on access to abortion, but rather of her indigency." McRae....

[Affirmed].

Justice BLACKMUN, with whom Justice MARSHALL joins, and with whom Justice STEVENS joins as to Parts II and III, and with whom Justice O'CONNOR joins as to Part I, dissenting.

Casting aside established principles of statutory construction and administrative jurisprudence, the majority [unnecessarily] passes upon important questions of constitutional law. In so doing, the Court, for the first time, upholds viewpoint-based suppression of speech solely because it is imposed on those dependent upon the Government for economic support. Under essentially the same rationale, the majority upholds direct regulation of dialogue between a pregnant woman and her physician when that regulation has both the purpose and the effect of manipulating her decision as to the continuance of her pregnancy....

I. The majority does not dispute that "[f]ederal statutes are to be so construed as to avoid serious doubt of their constitutionality." Machinists v. Street, 367 U.S. 740 (1961). Nor does the majority deny that this principle is fully applicable to cases [in] which a plausible but constitutionally suspect statutory interpretation is embodied in an administrative regulation. Rather, in its zeal to address the constitutional issues, the majority sidesteps this established canon of construction with the feeble excuse that the challenged Regulations "do not raise the sort of 'grave and doubtful constitutional questions,' ... that would lead us to assume Congress did not intend to authorize their issuance."

This facile response [is] disingenuous at best. Whether or not one believes that these Regulations are valid, it avoids reality to contend that they do not give rise to serious constitutional questions. The canon is applicable [not] because "it was likely that [the Regulations] ... would be challenged on constitutional grounds," but because the question squarely presented by the Regulations—the extent to which the Government may attach an otherwise unconstitutional condition to the receipt of a public benefit—implicates a troubled area of our jurisprudence in which a court ought not entangle itself unnecessarily. [This] verity is evidenced by the fact that two of the three Courts of Appeals that have entertained challenges to the Regulations have invalidated them on constitutional grounds. That a bare majority of this Court today reaches a different result does not change the fact that the constitutional questions raised by the Regulations are both grave and doubtful.

Nor is this a case in which the statutory language itself requires us to address a constitutional question. Section 1008 provides simply: "None of the funds appropriated under this title shall be used in programs where abortion is a method of family planning." The majority concedes that this language "does not speak directly to the issues of counseling, referral, advocacy, or program integrity," and that "the legislative history is ambiguous" in this respect. Consequently, the language [easily] sustains a constitutionally trouble-free interpretation. [Indeed,] it would appear that our duty to avoid passing unnecessarily upon important constitutional questions is strongest where, as here, the language of the statute is decidedly ambiguous. It is both logical and eminently prudent to assume that when Congress intends to press the limits of constitutionality in its enactments, it will express that intent in explicit and unambiguous terms. Because I conclude that a plainly constitutional construction of section 1008 [is entirely reasonable,] I would reverse the judgment of the Court of Appeals on this ground without deciding the constitutionality of the [Regulations.]

II. I also strongly disagree with the majority's disposition of petitioners' constitutional claims. . . .

A. Until today, the Court never has upheld viewpoint-based suppression of speech simply because that suppression was a condition upon the acceptance of public funds. Whatever [the] Government's power to condition the receipt of its largess upon the relinquishment of constitutional rights, it surely does not extend to a condition that suppresses [freedom] of speech based solely upon the content or viewpoint of that speech. Nothing [in] Regan can be said to challenge this long-settled understanding. In Regan, the Court upheld a content-neutral provision of the Internal Revenue Code [that] disallowed a particular tax-exempt status to organizations that "attempt[ed] to influence legislation," while affording such status to veterans' organizations irrespective of their lobbying activities. [The] Court explained: "The case would be different if Congress were to discriminate invidiously in its subsidies in such a way as to "ai[m] at the suppression of dangerous ideas." ". . . We find no indication that the statute was intended to suppress any ideas or any demonstration that it has had that effect." The separate concurrence in Regan joined the Court's opinion precisely "[b]ecause 26 U.S.C. section

501's discrimination between veterans' organizations and charitable organizations is not based on the content of their speech."

It cannot seriously be disputed that the [provisions] at issue [constitute] content-based regulation of speech. Title X grantees may provide counseling and referral regarding any of a wide range of family planning and other topics, save abortion. The Regulations are also clearly viewpoint-based. While suppressing speech favorable to abortion with one hand, the Secretary compels anti-abortion speech with the other. For example, the Department of Health and Human Services' own description of the Regulations makes plain that "Title X projects are required to facilitate access to prenatal care and social services, including adoption services, that might be needed by the pregnant client to promote her well-being and that of her child, while making it abundantly clear that the project is not permitted to promote abortion by facilitating access to abortion through the referral process." Moreover, [if] a client asks directly about abortion, a Title X physician or counselor is required to say, in essence, that the project does not consider abortion to be an appropriate method of family planning.

[The] Regulations pertaining to "advocacy" are even more explicitly viewpoint-based. These provide: "A Title X project may not encourage, promote or advocate abortion as a method of family planning." They explain: "This requirement prohibits actions to assist women to obtain abortions or increase the availability or accessibility of abortion for family planning purposes." The Regulations do not, however, proscribe or even regulate anti-abortion advocacy. These are clearly restrictions aimed at the suppression of "dangerous ideas."

Remarkably, the majority concludes that "the Government has not discriminated on the basis of viewpoint; it has merely chosen to fund one activity to the exclusion of another." But the [claim] that the Regulations merely limit a Title X project's speech to preventive or preconceptional services rings hollow in light of the broad range of non-preventive services that the Regulations authorize. [By] refusing to fund those family-planning projects that advocate abortion because they advocate abortion, the Government plainly has targeted a particular viewpoint. The majority's reliance on the fact that the Regulations pertain solely to funding decisions simply begs the question. Clearly, there are some bases upon which government may not rest its decision to fund or not to fund. For example, the Members of the majority surely would agree that government may not base its decision to support an activity upon considerations of race. As demonstrated above, our cases make clear that ideological viewpoint is a similarly repugnant ground upon which to base funding decisions.

[Unlike Regan,] the Regulations [are] not limited to lobbying but extend to all speech having the effect of encouraging, promoting, or advocating abortion as a method of family planning. Thus, in addition to their impermissible focus upon the viewpoint of regulated speech, the provisions intrude upon [the] very words spoken to a woman by her physician. By manipulating the content of the doctor/patient dialogue, the Regulations upheld today force each of the petitioners "to be an instrument for fostering public adherence to an ideological point of view [he or she] finds unacceptable." Wooley v. Maynard [1977; below, 12th Ed., p. 1558; Ind. Rts., p. 1229.] ...[1]

B. The Court concludes that the challenged Regulations do not violate the First Amendment rights of [staff] members because any limitation of the employees' freedom of expression is simply a consequence of their decision to accept employment at a federally funded project. But it has never been sufficient to justify an otherwise unconstitutional condition upon public employment that the employee may escape the condition by relinquishing his or her job. [The] majority attempts to circumvent this principle by emphasizing that Title X physicians and counselors "remain free ... to pursue abortion-related activities when [acting] as private individuals." Under the majority's reasoning, the First Amendment could be read to tolerate any governmental restriction upon an employee's speech so long as that restriction is limited to the funded workplace. This is a dangerous proposition, and one the Court has rightly rejected in the past. [E.g., Rankin v. McPherson, 1987; below, 12th Ed., p. 1445; Ind. Rts., p. 1116]. [At] the least, such conditions require courts to balance the speaker's interest in the message against those of government in preventing its dissemination.

[Here] the speaker's interest in the communication is both clear and vital. In addressing the family planning needs of their clients, the physicians and counselors who staff Title X projects seek to provide [the] full range of information and options regarding [health] and reproductive freedom. Indeed, the legitimate expectations of the patient and the ethical responsibilities of the medical profession demand no less. "The patient's right of self decision can be effectively exercised only if the patient possesses enough information to enable an intelligent choice.... The physician has an ethical obligation to help the patient make choices from among the therapeutic alternatives consistent with good medical practice." Current Opinions, the Council on Ethical and Judicial Affairs of the American Medical Association P 8.08 (1989). [When] a client becomes pregnant, the full range of therapeutic alternatives includes the abortion option, and Title X counselors' interest in providing this information is compelling. The Government's articulated interest in distorting the doctor/patient dialogue—ensuring that federal funds are not

---

1. The majority attempts to obscure the breadth of its decision through its curious contention that "the Title X program regulations do not significantly impinge upon the doctor-patient relationship." That the doctor-patient relationship is substantially burdened by a rule prohibiting the dissemination by the physician of pertinent medical information is beyond serious dispute. This burden is undiminished by the fact that the relationship at issue here is not an "all-encompassing" one. A woman seeking the services of a Title X clinic has every reason to expect, as do we all, that her physician will not withhold relevant information regarding the very purpose of her visit. To suggest otherwise is to engage in uninformed fantasy. Further, to hold that the doctor-patient relationship is somehow incomplete where a patient lacks the resources to seek comprehensive healthcare from a single provider is to ignore the situation of a vast number of Americans. As Justice Marshall has noted in a different context: "It is perfectly proper for judges to disagree about what the Constitution requires. But it is disgraceful for an interpretation of the Constitution to be premised upon unfounded assumptions about how people live." United States v. Kras, 409 U.S. 434 (1973) (dissenting opinion). [Footnote by Justice Blackmun.]

spent for a purpose outside the scope of the program—falls far short of that necessary to justify the suppression of truthful information and professional medical opinion regarding constitutionally protected conduct. . . .

III.   By far the most disturbing aspect of today's ruling is the effect it will have on the Fifth Amendment rights of the women who, supposedly, are beneficiaries of Title X programs.   The majority [relies] primarily upon the decisions in McRae and Webster.   There were dissents in those cases, and we continue to believe that they were wrongly and unfortunately decided.   Be that as it may, even if one accepts [the] Court's theorizing in those cases, the majority's reasoning in the present cases is flawed.

Until today, the Court has allowed to stand only those restrictions upon reproductive freedom that, while limiting the availability of abortion, have left intact a woman's ability to decide without coercion whether she will continue her pregnancy to term.   [Today's] decision abandons that principle, and with disastrous results.   Contrary to the majority's characterization, this is not a case in which individuals seek government aid in exercising their fundamental rights.   The Fifth Amendment right asserted by petitioners is the right of a pregnant woman to be free from affirmative governmental interference in her decision.   Roe and its progeny are not so much about a medical procedure as they are about a woman's fundamental right to self-determination.   Those cases serve to vindicate the idea that "liberty," if it means anything, must entail freedom from governmental domination in making the most intimate and personal of decisions.   By suppressing medically pertinent information and injecting a restrictive ideological message unrelated to considerations of maternal health, the Government places formidable obstacles in the path of Title X clients' freedom of choice and thereby violates their Fifth Amendment rights.

It is crystal-clear that the aim of the challenged provisions—an aim the majority cannot escape noticing—is not simply to ensure that federal funds are not used to perform abortions, but to "reduce the incidence of abortion."   42 CFR 59.2.   [The] Regulations require Title X physicians and counselors to provide information pertaining only to childbirth, to refer a pregnant woman for prenatal care irrespective of her medical situation, and, upon direct inquiry, to respond that abortion is not an "appropriate method" of family planning.

The undeniable message conveyed by this forced speech [is] that abortion nearly always is an improper medical option.   Although her physician's words [are] strictly controlled by the Government and wholly unrelated to her particular medical situation, the Title X client will reasonably construe them as professional advice to forgo her right to obtain an abortion.   As would most rational patients, many of these women will follow that perceived advice and carry their pregnancy to term, despite their needs to the contrary and despite the safety of the abortion procedure for the vast majority of them.   Others, delayed by the Regulations' mandatory prenatal referral, will be prevented from acquiring abortions during the period in which the process is medically sound and constitutionally protected.

In view of the inevitable effect of the Regulations, the majority's conclusion that "[t]he difficulty that a woman encounters when a Title X project does not provide abortion counseling or referral leaves her in no different position than she would have been if the government had not enacted Title X," is insensitive and contrary to common human experience. Both the purpose and result of the challenged Regulations is to deny women the ability voluntarily to decide their procreative destiny. For these women, the Government will have obliterated the freedom to choose as surely as if it had banned abortions outright. The denial of this freedom is not a consequence of poverty but of the Government's ill-intentioned distortion of information it has chosen to provide.

The substantial obstacles to bodily self-determination [are] doubly offensive because they are effected by manipulating the very words spoken by physicians and counselors to their patients. In our society, the doctor/patient dialogue embodies a unique relationship of trust. The specialized nature of medical science and the emotional distress often attendant to health-related decisions requires that patients place their complete confidence [in] the hands of medical professionals. One seeks a physician's aid not only for medication or diagnosis, but also for guidance, professional judgment, and vital emotional support. Accordingly, each of us attaches profound importance and authority to the words of advice spoken by the physician.

It is for this reason that we have guarded so jealously the doctor/patient dialogue from governmental intrusion. The majority's approval of the [Regulations] flies in the face of our repeated warnings that regulations tending to "confine the attending physician in an undesired and uncomfortable straitjacket in the practice of his profession," cannot endure. Planned Parenthood of Central Mo. v. Danforth.

The majority attempts to distinguish our holdings in Akron and Thornburgh [because] those cases applied to all physicians within a jurisdiction while the Regulations now before the Court pertain to the narrow class of healthcare professionals employed at Title X projects. But [the] deprivation of liberty by the Government is no less substantial because it affects few rather than many. It cannot be that an otherwise unconstitutional infringement of choice is made lawful because it touches only some of the Nation's pregnant women and not all of them....

IV. In its haste further to restrict the right of every woman to control her reproductive freedom and bodily integrity, the majority [contorts] this Court's decided cases to arrive at its preordained result. [While] technically leaving intact the fundamental right protected by Roe v. Wade, the Court, "through a relentlessly formalistic catechism," McRae (Marshall, J., dissenting), once again has rendered the right's substance nugatory. This is a course nearly as noxious as overruling Roe directly, for if a right is found to be unenforceable, even against flagrant attempts by government to circumvent it, then it ceases to be a right at all....

Justice STEVENS, dissenting.

In my opinion, the Court has not paid sufficient attention to the language of the controlling statute or to the consistent interpretation [by] the responsible cabinet officers [over] 18 years.

The relevant text of the "Family Planning Services and Population Research Act of 1970" has remained unchanged since its enactment. The preamble to the Act states that it was passed:

"To promote public health and welfare by expanding, improving, and better coordinating the family planning services and population research activities of the Federal Government, and for other purposes."

The declaration of congressional purposes emphasizes the importance of educating the public about family planning services. Thus, section 2 of the Act states, in part, that the purpose of the Act is ["(5)] to develop and make readily available information (including educational materials) on family planning and population growth to all persons desiring such information."

In contrast to the statutory emphasis on making relevant information readily available to the public, the statute contains no suggestion that Congress intended to authorize the suppression or censorship of any information. [Not] a word in the statute [authorizes] the Secretary to impose any restrictions on the dissemination of truthful information or professional advice by grant recipients. [The] original regulations promulgated in 1971 by the Secretary of Health, Education and Welfare so interpreted the statute. [Like] the statute itself, the regulations prohibited conduct, not speech. The same is true of the regulations promulgated in 1986. [They] also prohibited grant recipients from performing abortions but did not purport to censor or mandate any kind of speech. The entirely new approach adopted by [in] 1988 was not, in my view, authorized by the statute. [In] a society that abhors censorship and in which policymakers have traditionally placed the highest value on the freedom to communicate, it is unrealistic to conclude that statutory authority to regulate conduct implicitly authorized the Executive to regulate speech.

Because [the] 1970 Act did not authorize the Secretary to censor the speech of grant recipients or their employees, I would hold the challenged regulations invalid. [Even] if I thought the statute were ambiguous, however, I would reach the same result for the reasons stated in Justice O'Connor's dissenting opinion. As she also explains, if a majority of the Court had reached this result, it would be improper to comment on the constitutional issues that the parties have debated. Because the majority has reached out to decide the constitutional questions, however, I am persuaded that Justice Blackmun is correct in concluding that the majority's arguments merit a response. I am also persuaded that Justice Blackmun has correctly analyzed these issues. I have therefore joined Parts II and III of his opinion.

Justice O'CONNOR, dissenting.

"[W]here an otherwise acceptable construction of a statute would raise serious constitutional problems, the Court will construe the statute to avoid such problems unless such construction is plainly contrary to the intent of Congress." DeBartolo. Justice Blackmun has explained well why this long-standing canon of statutory construction applies in this case, and I join Part I of his dissent. Part II demonstrates why the challenged regulations ["raise] serious constitutional problems": the regulations place content-based restrictions on the speech of Title X fund recipients, restrictions directed precisely at speech concerning one of "the most divisive and contentious issues that our Nation has faced in recent years."

One may well conclude [that] the regulations are unconstitutional for this reason. I do not join Part II of the dissent, however, for the same reason that I do not join Part III, in which Justice Blackmun concludes that the regulations are unconstitutional under the Fifth Amendment. The canon of construction that Justice Blackmun correctly applies here is grounded in large part upon our time-honored practice of not reaching constitutional questions unnecessarily. This Court acts at the limits of its power when it invalidates a law on constitutional grounds. [In] this case, we need only tell the Secretary that his regulations are not a reasonable interpretation of the statute; we need not tell Congress that it cannot pass such legislation. If we rule solely on statutory grounds, Congress retains the power to force the constitutional question by legislating more explicitly. It may instead choose to do nothing. That decision should be left to Congress; we should not tell Congress what it cannot do before it has chosen to do it. It is enough in this case to conclude that neither the language nor the history of section 1008 compels the Secretary's interpretation, and that the interpretation raises serious First Amendment concerns. On this basis alone, I would [invalidate] the challenged regulations.

The regulations upheld in Rust v. Sullivan remained in limbo for much of 1991 and early 1992. A provision to suspend enforcement of the rules was included in the fiscal 1992 Labor and Health and Human Services appropriations bill (H.R. 2707), which was passed by both houses of Congress. President Bush vetoed that bill on November 18, 1991, however, and Congress failed to override that veto. H.R. 3090, and its companion S. 323, reauthorizations of the Family Planning Act Amendments, also sought to rescind the regulations at issue in Rust. On March 20, 1992, however, a directive was sent to all regional administrators of the family planning program by William R. Archer III, Deputy Assistant Secretary of Health and Human Services, stating, "Nothing in these regulations is to prevent a woman from receiving complete medical information about her condition from a physician." This directive did not impede the progress of the proposed legislation, however, which again was passed by both houses of Congress, and again was vetoed by President Bush. Two days after his inauguration, however, President Clinton issued a Memorandum for the Secretary of the Health and Human Services ordering the suspension of the regulations at issue in *Rust*. Entitled "Memorandum on the Title X 'Gag Rule,' " the Memorandum said that "The Gag Rule endangers women's lives and health by preventing them from receiving complete and accurate medical information and interferes with the doctor-patient relationship by prohibiting information that medical professionals are otherwise ethically and legally required to give to their patients. [You] have informed me that you will suspend the Gag Rule pending the promulgation of new regulations [, and] I hereby direct you to take that action as soon as possible." 29 Weekly Comp. Pres. Doc. 87. Health and Human Services is in the process of complying with the President's order. Proposed new rules to replace the Gag Rule were published at 58 Fed.Reg. 7464 (February 1, 1993), but had still not yet been finally adopted at the closing date of the 1995 Supplement. Note also Rep. Schroeder's proposal, H.R. 641, pending in the 104th Congress, the Women's Right to Know Act, which would overturn the result in Rust v. Sullivan.

PLANNED PARENTHOOD OF SOUTHEASTERN PENNSYLVANIA v. CASEY

505 U.S. ___, 112 S.Ct. 2791, 120 L.Ed.2d 674 (1992).

Justice O'CONNOR, Justice KENNEDY, and Justice SOUTER announced the judgment of the Court and delivered the opinion of the Court with respect to Parts I, II, III, V–A, V–C, and VI, an opinion with respect to Part V–E, in which Justice STEVENS joins, and an opinion with respect to Parts IV, V–B, and V–D.

I. Liberty finds no refuge in a jurisprudence of doubt. Yet 19 years after our holding that the Constitution protects a woman's right to terminate her pregnancy in its early stages, [Roe's] definition of liberty is still questioned. Joining the respondents as amicus curiae, the United States, as it has done in five other cases in the last decade, again asks us to overrule Roe.

At issue in these cases are five provisions of the Pennsylvania Abortion Control Act of 1982 as amended in 1988 and 1989. The Act requires that a woman seeking an abortion give her informed consent prior to the abortion procedure, and specifies that she be provided with certain information at least 24 hours before the abortion is performed. For a minor to obtain an abortion, the Act requires the informed consent of one of her parents, but provides for a judicial bypass option. [Another] provision [requires] that, unless certain exceptions apply, a married woman seeking an abortion must sign a statement indicating that she has notified her husband of her intended abortion. The Act exempts compliance with these requirements in the event of a "medical emergency." [In] addition, [the] Act imposes [reporting] requirements on facilities that provide abortion services.

Before [these] provisions took effect, petitioners [brought] this suit seeking declaratory and injunctive relief. Each provision was challenged as unconstitutional on its face. The District Court [held] all the provisions at issue here unconstitutional, entering a permanent injunction against [enforcement.] The Court of Appeals affirmed in part and reversed in part, upholding all of the regulations except for the husband notification requirement.

[After] considering the fundamental constitutional questions resolved by Roe, principles of institutional integrity, and the rule of stare decisis, we are led to conclude this: the essential holding of Roe should be retained and once again reaffirmed. It must be stated at the outset and with clarity that Roe's essential holding, the holding we reaffirm, has three parts. First is a recognition of the right of the woman to choose to have an abortion before viability and to obtain it without undue interference from the State. Before viability, the State's interests are not strong enough to support a prohibition of abortion or the imposition of a substantial obstacle to the woman's effective right to elect the procedure. Second is a confirmation of the State's power to restrict abortions after fetal viability, if the law contains exceptions for pregnancies which endanger a woman's life or health.. And third is the principle that the State has legitimate interests from the outset of the pregnancy in protecting the health of the woman and the life of the fetus that may become a child. These principles do not contradict one another; and we adhere to each.

II. Constitutional protection of the woman's decision to terminate her pregnancy derives from the Due Process Clause of the Fourteenth Amendment. [The] controlling word [is] "liberty." Although a literal reading might suggest that [the Clause] governs only the procedures by which a State may deprive persons of liberty, for at least 105 years [Mugler v. Kansas, 123 U.S. 623 (1887)] the Clause has been understood to contain a substantive component as well, one "barring certain government actions regardless of the fairness of the procedures used to implement them." Daniels v. Williams, 474 U.S. 327 (1986). [It] is tempting, as a means of curbing the discretion of federal judges, to suppose that liberty encompasses no more than those rights already guaranteed to the individual against federal interference by the express provisions of the first eight amendments to the Constitution. But of course this Court has never accepted that view. It is also tempting, for the same reason, to suppose that the Due Process Clause protects only those practices, defined at the most specific level, that were protected against government interference by other rules of law when the Fourteenth Amendment was ratified. But such a view would be inconsistent with our law. It is a promise of the Constitution that there is a realm of personal liberty which the government may not enter. [Neither] the Bill of Rights nor the specific practices of States at the time of the adoption of the Fourteenth Amendment marks the outer limits of the substantive sphere of liberty which the Fourteenth Amendment protects. See U.S. Const.Amend. 9. [It] is settled now, as it was when the Court heard arguments in Roe, that the Constitution places limits on a State's right to interfere with a person's most basic decisions about family and parenthood, as well as bodily integrity. The inescapable fact is that adjudication of substantive due process claims may call upon the Court [to] exercise that same capacity which by tradition courts always have exercised: reasoned judgment. Its boundaries are not susceptible of expression as a simple rule. That does not mean we are free to invalidate state policy choices with which we disagree; yet neither does it permit us to shrink from the duties of our office. [Men] and women of good conscience can disagree, and we suppose some always shall disagree, about the profound moral and spiritual implications of terminating a pregnancy, even in its earliest stage. Some of us as individuals find abortion offensive to our most basic principles of morality, but that cannot control our decision. Our obligation is to define the liberty of all, not to mandate our own moral code. The underlying constitutional issue is whether the State can resolve these philosophic questions in such a definitive way that a woman lacks all choice in the matter, except perhaps in those rare circumstances in which the pregnancy is itself a danger to her own life or health, or is the result of rape or incest.

It is conventional constitutional doctrine that where reasonable people disagree the government can adopt one position or the other. Ferguson v. Skrupa; Williamson v. Lee Optical. That theorem, however, assumes a state of affairs in which the choice does not intrude upon a protected liberty. Thus, while some people might disagree about whether or not the flag should be saluted, or disagree about the proposition that it may not be defiled, [a] State may not compel or enforce one view or the other. Our law affords constitutional protection to personal decisions relating to marriage, procreation, contraception, family relationships, child rearing, and education. [These] matters, involving the most intimate and personal choices a person may make in a lifetime, choices central to personal dignity and autonomy, are central to the liberty protected by the Fourteenth Amendment. At the heart of liberty is the right to define one's own concept of existence, of meaning, of the universe, and of the mystery of human life. Beliefs about these matters could not define the attributes of personhood were they formed under compulsion of the State.

These considerations begin our analysis of the woman's interest in terminating her pregnancy but cannot end it, for this reason: though the abortion decision may originate within the zone of conscience and belief, it is more than a philosophic exercise. Abortion is a unique act. It is an act fraught with consequences for others: for the woman who must live with the implications of her decision; for the persons who perform and assist in the procedure; for the spouse, family, and society which must confront the knowledge that these procedures exist, procedures some deem nothing short of an act of violence against innocent human life; and, depending on one's beliefs, for the life or potential life that is aborted.

Though abortion is conduct, it does not follow that the State is entitled to proscribe it in all instances. That is because the liberty of the woman is at stake in a sense unique to the human condition and so unique to the law. The mother who carries a child to full term is subject to anxieties, to physical constraints, to pain that only she must bear. That these sacrifices have from the beginning of the human race been endured by woman with a pride that ennobles her in the eyes of others and gives to the infant a bond of love cannot alone be grounds for the State to insist she make the sacrifice. Her suffering is too intimate and personal for the State to insist, without more, upon its own vision of the woman's role, however dominant that vision has been in the course of our history and our culture.   The destiny of the woman must be shaped to a large extent on her own conception of her spiritual imperatives and her place in society.

[In] some critical respects the abortion decision is of the same character as the decision to use contraception, to which Griswold, Eisenstadt, and Carey afford constitutional protection.   We have no doubt as to the correctness of those decisions.   They support the reasoning in Roe relating to the woman's liberty because they involve personal decisions concerning not only the meaning of procreation but also human responsibility and respect for it.   As with abortion, reasonable people will have differences of opinion about these matters.   One view is based on such reverence for the wonder of creation that any pregnancy ought to be welcomed and carried to full term no matter how difficult it will be to provide for the child and ensure its well-being. Another is that the inability to provide for the nurture and care of the infant is a cruelty to the child and an anguish to the parent.   These are intimate views with infinite variations, and their deep, personal character underlay our [contraception] decisions.   The same concerns are present when the woman confronts the reality that, perhaps despite her attempts to avoid it, she has become pregnant.   It was this dimension of personal liberty that Roe sought to protect, and its holding invoked the reasoning and the tradition of the precedents we have discussed, granting protection to substantive liberties of the person.   Roe was, of course, an extension of those cases and, as the decision itself indicated, the separate States could act in some degree to further their own legitimate interests in protecting pre-natal life.

[While] we appreciate the weight of the arguments made on behalf of the State in the case before us, arguments which in their ultimate formulation conclude that Roe should be overruled, the reservations any of us may have in reaffirming the central holding of Roe are outweighed by the explication of individual liberty we have given combined with the force of stare decisis.   We turn now to that doctrine.

III.   A.   The obligation to follow precedent begins with necessity, and a contrary necessity marks its outer limit.   With Cardozo, we recognize that no judicial system could do society's work if it eyed each issue afresh in every case that raised it.   The Nature of the Judicial Process 149 (1921).   Indeed, the very concept of the rule of law [requires] such continuity over time that a respect for precedent is, by definition, indispensable.   At the other extreme, a different necessity would make itself felt if a prior judicial ruling should come to be seen so clearly as error that its enforcement was for that very reason doomed.

Even when the decision to overrule a prior case is not [virtually] foreordained, [the] rule of stare decisis is not an "inexorable command," and certainly it is not such in every constitutional case, Burnet v. Coronado Oil Gas Co., 285 U.S. 393 (1932) (Brandeis, dissenting). Rather, when this Court reexamines a prior holding, its judgment is customarily informed by a series of prudential and pragmatic considerations designed to test the consistency of overruling a prior decision with the ideal of the rule of law, and to gauge the respective costs of reaffirming and overruling a prior case. Thus, for example, we may ask whether the rule has proved to be intolerable simply in defying practical workability; whether the rule is subject to a kind of reliance that would lend a special hardship to the consequences of overruling and add inequity to the cost of repudiation; whether related principles of law have so far developed as to have left the old rule no more than a remnant of abandoned doctrine; or whether facts have so changed or come to be seen so differently, as to have robbed the old rule of significant application or justification.

So in this case we may inquire whether Roe's central rule has been found unworkable; whether the rule's limitation on state power could be removed without serious inequity to those who have relied upon it or significant damage to the stability of the society governed by the rule in question; whether the law's growth in the intervening years has left Roe's central rule a doctrinal anachronism discounted by society; and whether Roe's premises of fact have so far changed in the ensuing two decades as to render its central holding somehow irrelevant or unjustifiable in dealing with the issue it addressed.

1. Although Roe has engendered opposition, it has in no sense proven "unworkable," representing as it does a simple limitation beyond which a state law is unenforceable. While Roe has [required] judicial assessment of [laws] affecting the exercise of the choice guaranteed against government infringement, and although the need for such review will remain as a consequence of today's decision, [these] determinations fall within judicial competence.

2. The inquiry into reliance counts the cost of a rule's repudiation as it would fall on those who have relied reasonably on the rule's continued application. Since the classic case for weighing reliance heavily in favor of following the earlier rule occurs in the commercial context, where advance planning of great precision is most obviously a necessity, it is no cause for surprise that some would find no reliance worthy of consideration in support of Roe. [Abortion] is customarily chosen as an unplanned response to the consequence of unplanned activity or to the failure of conventional birth control, and except on the assumption that no intercourse would have occurred but for Roe's holding, such behavior may appear to justify no reliance claim. [This] argument would be premised on the hypothesis that reproductive planning could take virtually immediate account of any sudden restoration of state authority to ban abortions. To eliminate the issue of reliance that easily, however, one would need to limit cognizable reliance to specific instances of sexual activity. But to do this would be simply to refuse to face the fact that for two decades of economic and social developments, people have organized intimate relationships and made choices that define their views of themselves and their places in society, in reliance on the availability of abortion in the event that contraception should fail. The ability of women to participate equally in the economic and social life of the Nation has been facilitated by their ability to control their reproductive lives. [While] the effect of reliance on Roe cannot be

exactly measured, neither can the certain cost of overruling Roe for people who have ordered their thinking and living around that case be dismissed.

3. No evolution of legal principle has left Roe's doctrinal footings weaker than they were in 1973. No development of constitutional law since the case was decided has [left] Roe behind as a mere survivor of obsolete constitutional thinking. [The] Roe Court itself placed its holding in the succession of cases most prominently exemplified by Griswold. When it is so seen, Roe is clearly in no jeopardy, since subsequent [developments] have neither disturbed, nor do they threaten to diminish, the scope of recognized protection accorded to the liberty relating to intimate relationships, the family, and decisions about whether or not to beget or bear a child. Roe, however, may be seen not only as an exemplar of Griswold liberty but as a rule (whether or not mistaken) of personal autonomy and bodily integrity, with doctrinal affinity to cases recognizing limits on governmental power to mandate medical treatment or to bar its rejection. If so, our cases since Roe accord with Roe's view that a State's interest in the protection of life falls short of justifying any plenary override of individual liberty claims. Cruzan v. Missouri Dept. of Health [1990; below, 12th Ed., p. 575; Ind.Rts., p. 246.]

[Nor] will courts building upon Roe be likely to hand down erroneous decisions as a consequence. Even on the assumption that the central holding of Roe was in error, that error would go only to the strength of the state interest in fetal protection, not to the recognition afforded [the] woman's liberty. [The] soundness of this prong of [Roe] is apparent from a consideration of the alternative. If indeed the woman's interest in deciding whether to bear and beget a child had not been recognized as in Roe, the State might as readily restrict a woman's right to choose to carry a pregnancy to term as to terminate it, to further asserted state interests in population control, or eugenics, for example. Yet Roe has been sensibly relied upon to counter any such suggestions. Arnold v. Bd. of Educ., 880 F.2d 305 (11th Cir.1989) ([concluding] that government officials violate the Constitution by coercing a minor to have an abortion); Avery v. Cty. of Burke, 660 F.2d 111 (4th Cir.1981) (county agency inducing teenage girl to undergo unwanted sterilization on the basis of misrepresentation that she had sickle cell trait).

4. [Time] has overtaken some of Roe's factual assumptions: advances in maternal health care allow for abortions safe to the mother later in pregnancy than was true in 1973, and advances in neonatal care have advanced viability to a point somewhat earlier. But these facts go only to the scheme of time limits on the realization of competing interests, and [have] no bearing on the [central] holding that viability marks the earliest point at which the State's interest in fetal life is constitutionally adequate to justify a legislative ban on nontherapeutic abortions. The soundness or unsoundness of that constitutional judgment in no sense turns on whether viability occurs at approximately 28 weeks, as was usual at the time of Roe, at 23 to 24 weeks, as it sometimes does today, or at some moment even slightly earlier in pregnancy, as it may if fetal respiratory capacity can somehow be enhanced in the future. Whenever it may occur, the attainment of

viability may continue to serve as the critical fact, just as it has done since Roe; [no] change in Roe's factual underpinning has left its central holding obsolete, and none supports an argument for overruling it.

5. The sum of the precedential inquiry to this point shows Roe's underpinnings unweakened in any way affecting its central holding. While it has engendered disapproval, it has not been unworkable. An entire generation has come of age free to assume Roe's concept of liberty in defining the capacity of women to act in society, and to make reproductive decisions; no erosion of principle going to liberty or personal autonomy has left Roe's central holding a doctrinal remnant; Roe portends no developments at odds with other precedent for the analysis of personal liberty; and no changes of fact have rendered viability more or less appropriate as the point at which the balance of interests tips. Within the bounds of normal stare decisis analysis, [the] stronger argument is for affirming Roe's central holding, with whatever degree of personal reluctance any of us may have, not for overruling it.

B. In a less significant case, stare decisis analysis [would] stop at the point we have reached. But the sustained and widespread debate Roe has provoked calls for some comparison between that case and others of comparable dimension that have responded to national controversies and taken on the impress of the controversies addressed. Only two such decisional lines from the past century present themselves for examination, and in each instance the result reached by the Court accorded with the principles we apply today.

The first example is that line of cases identified with Lochner v. New York. [The] Lochner decisions were exemplified by Adkins v. Children's Hospital, in which this Court held it to be an infringement of constitutionally protected liberty of contract to require the employers of adult women to satisfy minimum wage standards. Fourteen years later, West Coast Hotel v. Parrish signalled the demise of Lochner by overruling Adkins. In the meantime, the Depression had come and, with it, the lesson that seemed unmistakable to most people by 1937, that the interpretation of contractual freedom protected in Adkins rested on fundamentally false factual assumptions about the capacity of a relatively unregulated market to satisfy minimal levels of human welfare. [The] facts upon which the earlier case had premised a constitutional resolution of social controversy had proved to be untrue, and history's demonstration of their untruth not only justified but required the new choice of constitutional principle that West Coast Hotel announced.

[The] second comparison that 20th century history invites is with the cases employing the separate-but-equal rule. [They] began with Plessy v. Ferguson [1896; below, 12th Ed., p. 646; Ind.Rts., p. 317], holding that legislatively mandated racial segregation in public transportation works no denial of equal protection. [The] Plessy Court considered "the underlying fallacy of the plaintiff's argument to consist in the assumption that the enforced separation of the two races stamps the colored race with a badge of inferiority. If this be so, it is not by reason of anything found in the act, but solely because the colored race chooses to put that construction upon it." Whether, as a matter of historical fact, the Justices in the Plessy majority believed this or not, this understanding of the implication of segregation was the stated justification for the Court's opinion. But this understanding of the facts and the rule it was stated to justify were repudiated in Brown v. Bd. of Educ. [1954; below, 12th Ed., p. 648; Ind.Rts., p. 319.] The Court in Brown [observed] that whatever may have been the understanding in Plessy's time of the power of segregation to stigmatize those who were segregated with a "badge of inferiority," it was clear by 1954 that legally sanctioned segregation had just such an effect, to the point that racially separate [facilities] were deemed inherently unequal. Society's understanding of the facts upon which a constitutional ruling was sought in 1954 was thus fundamentally different from the basis claimed for the decision in 1896. While we think Plessy was wrong the day it was decided, we must also recognize that the Plessy Court's explanation for its decision was so clearly at odds with the facts apparent to the Court in 1954 that the decision to reexamine Plessy was on this ground alone not only justified but required.

West Coast Hotel and Brown each rested on facts, or an understanding of facts, changed from those which furnished the claimed justifications for the earlier constitutional resolutions. [In] constitutional adjudication as elsewhere in life, changed circumstances may impose new obligations, and the thoughtful part of the Nation could accept each decision to overrule a prior case as a response to the Court's constitutional duty. Because the case before us presents no such occasion it could be seen as no such response. Because neither the factual underpinnings of Roe's central holding nor our understanding of it has changed (and because no other indication of weakened precedent has been shown), the Court could not pretend to be reexamining the prior law with any justification beyond a present doctrinal disposition to come out differently from the Court of 1973. To overrule prior law for no other reason than that would run counter to the view [that] a decision to overrule should rest on some special reason over and above the belief that a prior case was wrongly decided. Mitchell v. W.T. Grant, 416 U.S. 600 (1974) (Stewart, dissenting) ("A basic change in the law upon a ground no firmer than a change in our membership invites the popular misconception that this institution is little different from the two political branches of the Government. No misconception could do more lasting injury to this Court and to the system of law which it is our abiding mission to serve").

C. [As] Americans of each succeeding generation are rightly told, the Court cannot buy support for its decisions by spending money and, except to a minor degree, it cannot independently coerce obedience to its decrees. The Court's power lies, rather, in its legitimacy, a product of substance and perception that shows itself in the people's acceptance of the Judiciary as fit to determine what the Nation's law means and to declare what it demands. The underlying substance of this legitimacy is of course the warrant for the Court's decisions in the Constitution and the lesser sources of legal principle on which the Court draws. But even when justification is furnished by apposite legal principle, something more is required. Because not every conscientious claim of principled justification will be accepted as such, the justification claimed must be beyond dispute. The Court must take care to speak and act in ways that allow people to accept its decisions on the terms the Court claims for them, as grounded truly in principle, not as compromises with social and political pressures having, as such, no bearing on the principled choices that the Court is obliged to make. Thus, the Court's legitimacy depends on making legally principled decisions under circumstances in which their principled character is sufficiently plausible to be accepted by the Nation.

The need for principled action to be perceived as such is implicated to some degree whenever [any appellate court] overrules a prior case. [In] two circumstances, however, the Court would almost certainly fail to receive the benefit of the doubt in overruling prior cases. There is, first, a point beyond which frequent overruling would overtax the country's belief in the Court's good faith. Despite the variety of reasons that may inform and justify a decision to overrule, we cannot forget that such a decision is usually perceived (and perceived correctly) as [a] statement that a prior decision was wrong. There is a limit to the amount of error that can plausibly be imputed to prior courts. If that limit should be exceeded, disturbance of prior rulings would be taken as evidence that justifiable reexamination of principle had given way to drives for particular results in the short term. The legitimacy of the Court would fade with the frequency of its vacillation.

That first circumstance can be described as hypothetical; the second is to the point here and now. Where, in the performance of its judicial duties, the Court decides a case in such a way as to resolve the sort of intensely divisive controversy reflected in Roe and those rare, comparable cases, its decision has a dimension that the resolution of the normal case does not carry. It is the dimension present whenever the Court's interpretation of the Constitution calls the contending sides of a national controversy to end their national division by accepting a common mandate rooted in the Constitution. The Court is not asked to do this very often, having thus addressed the Nation only twice in our lifetime, in [Brown] and Roe. But when the Court does act in this way, its decision requires an equally rare precedential force to counter the inevitable efforts to overturn it and to thwart its implementation. Some of those efforts may be mere unprincipled emotional reactions; others may proceed from principles worthy of profound respect. But whatever the premises of opposition may be, only the most convincing justification under accepted standards of precedent could suffice to demonstrate that a later decision overruling the first was anything but a surrender to political pressure, and an unjustified repudiation of the principle on which the Court staked its authority in the first instance. So to overrule under fire in the absence of the most compelling reason to reexamine a watershed decision would subvert the Court's legitimacy beyond any serious question. The country's loss of confidence in the judiciary would be underscored by an equally certain and equally reasonable condemnation for another failing in overruling unnecessarily and under pressure. Some cost will be paid by anyone who approves or implements a constitutional decision where it is unpopular, or who refuses to work to undermine the decision or to force its reversal. The price may be criticism or ostracism, or it may be violence. An extra price will be paid by those who themselves disapprove of the decision's results when viewed outside of constitutional terms, but who nevertheless struggle to accept it, because they respect the rule of law. To all those who will be so tested by following, the Court implicitly undertakes to remain steadfast, lest in the end a price be paid for nothing. The promise of constancy, once given, binds its maker for as long as the power to stand by the decision survives and the understanding of the issue has not changed so fundamentally as to render the commitment obsolete.

[Like] the character of an individual, the legitimacy of the Court must be earned over time. So, indeed, must be the character of a Nation of people who aspire to live according to the rule of law. Their belief in themselves as such a people is not readily separable from their understanding of the Court invested with the authority to decide their constitutional cases and speak before all others for their constitutional ideals. If the Court's legitimacy should be undermined, then, so would the country be in its very ability to see itself through its constitutional ideals. The Court's concern with legitimacy is not for the sake of the Court but for the sake of the Nation.

[The] Court's duty in the present case is clear. In 1973, it confronted the already-divisive issue of governmental power to limit personal choice to undergo abortion, for which it provided a new resolution based on the [Fourteenth] Amendment. Whether or not a new social consensus is developing on that issue, its divisiveness is no less today than in 1973, and pressure to overrule the decision, like pressure to retain it, has grown only more intense. A decision to overrule Roe's essential holding under the existing circumstances would address error, if error there was, at the cost of [profound] and unnecessary damage to the Court's legitimacy, and to the Nation's commitment to the rule of law. It is therefore imperative to adhere to the essence of Roe's original decision, and we do so today.

IV. [We] conclude that the basic decision in Roe was based on a constitutional analysis which we cannot now repudiate. The woman's liberty is not so unlimited, however, that from the outset the State cannot show its concern for the life of the unborn, and at a later point in fetal development the State's interest in life has sufficient force so that the right of the woman to terminate the pregnancy can be restricted.

That brings us [to] the point where much criticism has been directed at Roe, a criticism that always inheres when the Court draws a specific rule from what in the Constitution is but a general standard. We conclude, however, that the urgent claims of the woman to retain the ultimate control over her destiny and her body [require] us to perform that function. Liberty must not be extinguished for want of a line that is clear. And it falls to us to give some real substance to the woman's liberty to determine whether to carry her pregnancy to full term.

We conclude the line should be drawn at viability, so that before that time the woman has a right to choose to terminate her pregnancy. We adhere to this principle for two reasons. First [is] stare decisis.

[Although] we must overrule those parts of Thornburgh and Akron I which [are] inconsistent with Roe's statement that the State has a legitimate interest in promoting the life or potential life of the unborn, the central premise of those cases represents an unbroken commitment [to] the essential holding of Roe.

[The] second reason is that the concept of viability [is] the time at which there is a realistic possibility of maintaining and nourishing a life outside the womb, so that the independent existence of the second life can [be] the object of state protection that now overrides the rights of the woman. [Legislatures] may draw lines which appear arbitrary without the necessity of offering a justification. But courts may not. We must justify the lines we draw. And there is no line other than viability which is more workable. [The] woman's right to terminate her pregnancy before viability is the most central principle of Roe.

[On] the other side of the equation is the interest of the State in the protection of potential life. [The] weight to be given this state interest, not the strength of the woman's interest, was the difficult question faced in Roe. We do not need to say whether each of us, had we been Members of the Court when the valuation of the State interest came before it as an original matter, would have concluded [that] its weight is insufficient to justify a ban on abortions prior to viability even when it is subject to certain exceptions. The [immediate] question is not the soundness of Roe's resolution of the issue, but the precedential force that must be accorded to its holding.

[Yet] it must be remembered that Roe speaks with clarity in establishing not only the woman's liberty but also the State's "important and legitimate interest in potential life." That portion of [Roe] has been given too little acknowledgement [in] subsequent cases [holding] that any regulation touching upon the abortion decision must survive strict scrutiny, to be sustained only if drawn in narrow terms to further a compelling state interest. [In] resolving this tension, we choose to rely upon Roe, as against the later cases. [The] trimester framework no doubt was erected to ensure that the woman's right to choose not become so subordinate to the State's interest in promoting fetal life that her choice exists in theory but not in fact. We do not agree, however, that the trimester approach is necessary to accomplish this objective.

[Though] the woman has a right to choose to terminate or continue her pregnancy before viability, it does not [follow] that the State is prohibited from taking steps to ensure that this choice is thoughtful and informed. Even in the earliest stages of pregnancy, the State may enact rules and regulations designed to encourage her to know that there are philosophic and social arguments of great weight that can be brought to bear in favor of continuing the pregnancy to full term and that there are procedures and institutions to allow adoption of unwanted children as well as a certain degree of state assistance if the mother chooses to raise the child herself.

[We] reject the trimester framework, which we do not consider to be part of the essential holding of Roe. Measures aimed at ensuring that a woman's choice contemplates the consequences for the fetus do not necessarily interfere with the right recognized in Roe, although those measures have been found to be inconsistent with the rigid trimester framework announced. [The] trimester framework suffers from these basic flaws: in its formulation it misconceives the nature of the pregnant woman's interest; and in practice it undervalues the State's interest in potential life.

[As] our jurisprudence relating to all liberties save perhaps abortion has recognized, not every law which makes a right more difficult to exercise is, ipso facto, an infringement of that right. Numerous forms of state regulation might have the incidental effect of increasing the cost or decreasing the availability of medical care, whether for abortion or any other medical procedure. The fact that a law which serves a valid purpose, one not designed to strike at the right itself, has the incidental effect of making it more difficult or more expensive to procure an abortion cannot be enough to invalidate it. Only where state regulation imposes an undue burden on a woman's ability to make this decision does the power of the State reach into the heart of the [protected] liberty.

[Roe] was express in its recognition of the State's "important and legitimate interest[s] in preserving and protecting the health of the pregnant woman [and] in protecting the potentiality of human life." The trimester framework, however, does not fulfill Roe's own promise that the State has an interest in protecting fetal life or potential life. Roe began the contradiction by using the trimester framework to forbid any regulation of abortion designed to advance that interest before viability. This [is incompatible] with the recognition that there is a substantial state interest in potential life throughout pregnancy. [Not] all burdens on the right to decide whether to terminate a pregnancy will be undue. In our view, the undue burden standard is the appropriate means of reconciling the State's interest with the woman's constitutionally protected liberty.

[Because] we set forth a standard of general application to which we intend to adhere, it is important to clarify what is meant by an undue burden. A finding of an undue burden is a shorthand for the conclusion that a state regulation has the purpose or effect of placing a substantial obstacle in the path of a woman seeking an abortion of a nonviable fetus. A statute with this purpose is invalid because the means chosen by the State to further the interest in potential life must be calculated to inform the woman's free choice, not hinder it. And a statute which [has] the effect of placing a substantial obstacle in the path of a woman's choice cannot be considered a permissible means of serving its legitimate ends. [In] our considered judgment, an undue burden is an unconstitutional burden. Understood another way, we answer the question, left open in previous opinions, [whether] a law designed to further the State's interest in fetal life which imposes an undue burden on the woman's decision before fetal viability could be constitutional. The answer is no.

Some guiding principles should emerge. What is at stake is the woman's right to make the ultimate decision, not a right to be insulated from all others in doing so. Regulations which do no more than create a structural mechanism by which the State, or the parent or guardian of a minor, may express profound respect for the life of the unborn are permitted, if they are not a substantial obstacle to the woman's exercise of the right to choose. Unless it has that effect on her right of choice, a state measure designed to persuade her to choose childbirth over abortion will be upheld if reasonably related to that goal. Regulations designed to foster the health of a woman seeking an abortion are valid if they do not constitute an undue burden.

Even when jurists reason from shared premises, some disagreement is inevitable. That is to be expected in the application of any legal standard which must accommodate life's complexity. We do not expect it to be otherwise with respect to the undue burden standard. We give this summary:

(a) To protect the central right recognized by Roe while at the same time accommodating the State's profound interest in potential life, we will employ the undue burden analysis as explained in this opinion. An undue burden exists, and therefore a provision of law is invalid, if its purpose or effect is to place a substantial obstacle in the path of a woman seeking an abortion before the fetus attains viability.

(b) We reject the rigid trimester framework of Roe. To promote the State's profound interest in potential life, throughout pregnancy the State may take measures to ensure that the woman's choice is informed, and measures designed to advance this interest will not be invalidated as long as their purpose is to persuade the woman to choose childbirth over abortion. These measures must not be an undue burden on the right.

(c) As with any medical procedure, the State may enact regulations to further the health or safety of a woman seeking an abortion. Unnecessary health regulations that have the purpose or effect of presenting a substantial obstacle to a woman seeking an abortion impose an undue burden on the right.

(d) Our adoption of the undue burden analysis does not disturb the central holding of Roe, and we reaffirm that holding. [A] State may not prohibit any woman from making the ultimate decision to terminate her pregnancy before viability.

(e) We also reaffirm Roe's holding that "subsequent to viability, the State in promoting its interest in the potentiality of human life may, if it chooses, regulate, and even proscribe, abortion except where it is necessary, in appropriate medical judgment, for the preservation of the life or health of the mother." ...

V. The Court of Appeals applied what it believed to be the undue burden standard and upheld each of the provisions except for the husband notification requirement. We agree generally with this conclusion, but refine the undue burden analysis in accordance with the principles articulated above....

A. Because it is central to the operation of various other requirements, we begin with the statute's definition of medical emergency, "[that] condition which, on the basis of the physician's good faith clinical judgment, so complicates the medical condition of a pregnant woman as to necessitate the immediate abortion of her pregnancy to avert her death or for which a delay will create serious risk of substantial and irreversible impairment of a major bodily function." [The] District Court found that there were three serious conditions [not] covered by the statute: preeclampsia, inevitable abortion, and premature ruptured membrane. Yet [it] is undisputed that under some circumstances each of these conditions could lead to an illness with substantial and irreversible consequences. While the definition could be interpreted in an unconstitutional manner, the Court of Appeals construed the phrase "serious risk" to include those circumstances: "[We] read the medical emergency exception as intended by the legislature to assure that compliance with its abortion regulations would not in any way pose a significant threat to the life or health of a woman." As we said in Brockett v. Spokane Arcades, 472 U.S. 491 (1985): "Normally ... we defer to the construction of a state statute given it by the lower federal courts." Indeed, we have said that we will defer to lower court interpretations of state law unless they amount to "plain" error. Palmer v. Hoffman, 318 U.S. 109 (1943). This "reflects our belief that district courts and courts of appeals are better schooled in and more able to interpret the laws of their respective States." Frisby v. Schultz, 487 U.S. 474 (1988). We [conclude] that the [definition] imposes no undue burden on a woman's abortion right.

B. We next consider the informed consent requirement. Except in a medical emergency, the statute requires that at least 24 hours before performing an abortion a physician inform the woman of the nature of the procedure, the health risks of the abortion and of childbirth, and the "probable gestational age of the unborn child." The physician or a qualified nonphysician must inform the woman of the availability of printed materials published by the State describing the fetus and providing information about medical assistance for childbirth, information about child support from the father, and a list of agencies which provide adoption and other services as alternatives to abortion. An abortion may not be performed unless the woman certifies in writing that she has been informed of the availability of these printed materials and has been provided them if she chooses to view them.

[As] with any medical procedure, the State may require a woman to give her written informed consent to an abortion. [To] the extent Akron I and Thornburgh find a constitutional violation when the government requires [the] giving of truthful, nonmisleading information about the nature of the procedure, the attendant health risks and those of childbirth, and the "probable gestational age" of the fetus, those cases go too far [and] are overruled. [It] cannot be questioned that psychological well-being is a facet of health. Nor can it be doubted that most women considering an abortion would deem the impact on the fetus relevant, if not dispositive, to the decision. In attempting to ensure that a woman apprehend the full consequences of her decision, the State furthers the legitimate purpose of reducing the risk that a woman may elect an abortion, only to discover later, with devastating psychological consequences, that her decision was not fully informed. [We] also see no reason why the State may not require doctors to inform a woman seeking an abortion of the availability of materials relating to the consequences to the fetus, even when those consequences have no direct relation to her health. An example illustrates the point. We would think it constitutional for the State to require that in order for there to be informed consent to a kidney transplant operation the recipient must be supplied with information about risks to the donor as well as risks to himself or herself. [Similarly, we] conclude [that] informed choice need not be defined in such narrow terms that all considerations of the effect on the fetus are made irrelevant. [We] depart from [Akron] and Thornburgh to the extent that we permit a State to further its legitimate goal of protecting the life of the unborn by enacting legislation aimed at ensuring a decision that is mature and informed, even when in so doing the State expresses a preference for childbirth over abortion.

[The] statute does not prevent the physician from exercising his or her medical judgment. Whatever constitutional status the doctor-patient relation may have as a general matter, in the present context it is derivative of the woman's position. [The] doctor-patient relation here is entitled to the same solicitude it receives in other contexts. [A] requirement that a doctor give a woman certain information as part of obtaining her consent to an abortion is, for constitutional purposes, no different from a requirement that a doctor give certain specific information about any medical procedure. All that is left of petitioners' argument is an asserted First Amendment right of a physician not to provide information about the risks of abortion, and childbirth, in a manner mandated by the State. To be sure, the physician's First Amendment rights not to speak are implicated, but only as part of the practice of medicine, subject to reasonable licensing and regulation by the State.

The statute also requires us to reconsider the holding in Akron I that the State may not require that a physician, as opposed to a qualified assistant, provide information relevant to a woman's informed consent. Since there is no evidence [that] requiring a doctor to give the information as provided by the statute would amount in practical terms to a substantial obstacle to a woman seeking an abortion, we conclude that it is not an undue burden. [The] States [have] broad latitude to decide that particular functions may be performed only by licensed professionals, even if an objective assessment might suggest that those same tasks could be performed by others.

[Our] analysis of Pennsylvania's 24–hour waiting period between the provision of the information deemed necessary to informed consent and the performance of an abortion under the undue burden standard requires us to reconsider the premise behind the decision in Akron I invalidating a parallel requirement. [We] consider that conclusion to be wrong. The idea that important decisions will be more informed and deliberate if they follow some period of reflection does not strike us as unreasonable, particularly where the statute directs that important information become part of the background of the decision. [In] theory, at least, the waiting period is a reasonable measure to implement the State's interest in protecting the life of the unborn, a measure that does not amount to an undue burden.

Whether the mandatory 24–hour waiting period is nonetheless invalid because in practice it is a substantial obstacle to a woman's choice to terminate her pregnancy is a closer question. The findings of fact [indicate] that because of the distances many women must travel to reach an abortion provider, the practical effect will often be a delay of much more than a day because the waiting period requires that a woman seeking an abortion make at least two visits to the doctor. The District Court also found that in many instances this will increase the exposure of women seeking abortions to "the harassment and hostility of anti-abortion protestors demonstrating outside a clinic." As a result, [for] those women who have the fewest financial resources, those who must travel long distances, and those who have difficulty explaining their whereabouts to husbands, employers, or others, the 24–hour waiting period will be "particularly burdensome." These findings are troubling, [but] they do not demonstrate that the waiting period constitutes an undue burden. [A] particular burden is not of necessity a substantial obstacle. Whether a burden falls on a particular group is a distinct inquiry from whether it is a substantial obstacle even as to the women in that group. . . .

C. [Pennsylvania's] abortion law provides, except in cases of medical emergency, that no physician shall perform an abortion on a married woman without receiving a signed statement from the woman that she has notified her spouse that she is about to undergo an abortion. The woman has the option of providing an alternative signed statement certifying that her husband is not the man who impregnated her; that her husband could not be located; that the pregnancy is the result of spousal sexual assault which she has reported; or that the woman believes that notifying her husband will cause him or someone else to inflict bodily injury upon her.

[The] District Court [made] detailed findings of fact regarding the effect of this statute: "273. The vast majority of women consult their husbands prior to deciding to terminate their pregnancy . . . 279. The 'bodily injury' exception could not be invoked by a married woman whose husband, if notified, would, in her reasonable belief, threaten to (a) publicize her intent to have an abortion to family, friends or acquaintances; (b) retaliate against her in future child custody or divorce proceedings; (c) inflict psychological intimidation or emotional harm upon her, her children or other persons; (d) inflict bodily harm on other persons such as children, family members or other loved ones; or (e) use his control over finances to deprive of necessary monies for herself or her children . . . 281. Studies reveal that family violence occurs in two million families in the United States. This figure [substantially] understates (because battering is usually not reported until it reaches life-threatening proportions) the actual number of families affected by domestic violence. In fact, researchers estimate that one of every two women will be battered at some time in their life . . . [284.] Women of all class levels, educational backgrounds, and racial, ethnic and religious groups are battered . . . 285. Wife-battering or abuse can take on many physical and psychological forms . . . 286. Married women, victims of battering, have been killed in Pennsylvania and throughout the United

States ... 287. Battering can often involve a substantial amount of sexual abuse, including marital rape and sexual mutilation ... 288. In a domestic abuse situation, it is common for the battering husband to also abuse the children in an attempt to coerce the wife ... 289. Mere notification of pregnancy is frequently a flashpoint for battering and violence within the family. . . . The battering husband may deny parentage and use the pregnancy as an excuse for abuse ... 290. Secrecy typically shrouds abusive families. [Battering] husbands often threaten their wives or her children with further abuse if she tells an outsider of the violence and tells her that nobody will believe her ... 291. Even when confronted directly by medical personnel or other helping professionals, battered women often will not admit to the battering because they have not admitted to themselves that they are battered ... 294. A woman in a shelter or a safe house unknown to her husband is not 'reasonably likely' to have bodily harm inflicted upon her by her batterer, however her attempt to notify her husband pursuant to section 3209 could accidentally disclose her whereabouts to her husband ... 295. Marital rape is rarely discussed with others or reported to law enforcement authorities, and of those reported only few are prosecuted ... 296. It is common for battered women to have sexual intercourse with their husbands to avoid being battered. While this type of coercive sexual activity would be spousal sexual assault as defined by the Act, many women may not consider it to be so and others would fear disbelief ... 297. The marital rape exception to section 3209 cannot be claimed by women who are victims of coercive sexual behavior other than penetration. The 90–day reporting requirement of the spousal sexual assault statute further narrows the class of sexually abused wives who can claim the exception, since many of these women may be psychologically unable to discuss or report the rape for several years after the incident ...' ".

These findings are supported by studies of domestic violence. The American Medical Association [indicates] that in an average 12–month period in this country, approximately two million women are the victims of severe assaults by their male partners. In a 1985 survey, women reported that nearly one of every eight husbands had assaulted their wives during the past year. [Other] studies fill in the rest of this troubling picture. Physical violence is only the most visible form of abuse. Psychological abuse, particularly forced social and economic isolation of women, is also common. Many victims of domestic violence remain with their abusers, perhaps because they perceive no superior alternative. Many abused women who find temporary refuge in shelters return to their husbands, in large part because they have no other source of income. Returning to one's abuser can be dangerous. [Thirty] percent of female homicide victims are killed by their male partners.

The limited research that has been conducted with respect to notifying one's husband about an abortion, although involving samples too small to be representative, also supports the [findings] of fact. The vast majority of women notify their male partners of their decision to obtain an abortion. In many cases in which married women do not notify their husbands, the pregnancy is the result of an extramarital affair. Where the husband is the father, the primary reason women do not notify their husbands is that the husband and wife are experiencing marital difficulties, often accompanied by incidents of violence. Ryan & Plutzer, When Married Women Have Abortions: Spousal Notification and Marital Interaction, 51 J. Marriage & Family 41 (1989). This information and the District Court's findings reinforce what common sense would suggest. In well-functioning marriages, spouses discuss important intimate decisions such as whether to bear a child. But there are millions of women in this country who are the victims of regular physical and psychological abuse at the hands of their husbands. Should these women become pregnant, they may have very good reasons for not wishing to inform their husbands of their decision to obtain an abortion. [The] spousal notification requirement is thus likely to prevent a significant number of women from obtaining an abortion. It does not merely make abortions a little more difficult or expensive to obtain; for many women, it will impose a substantial obstacle. [The] significant number of women who fear for their safety and the safety of their children are likely to be deterred from procuring an abortion as surely as if the Commonwealth had outlawed abortion in all cases.

Respondents [point] out that [the spousal notification requirement] imposes almost no burden at all for the vast majority of women seeking abortions. They begin by noting that only about 20 percent of the women who obtain abortions are married. They then note that of these women about 95 percent notify their husbands of their own volition. Thus, respondents argue, the effects of [the requirement] are felt by only one percent of the women who obtain abortions. [And] since some of these women will be able to notify their husbands without adverse consequences or will qualify for one of the exceptions, the statute affects fewer than one percent of women seeking abortions. For this reason, it is asserted, the statute cannot be invalid on its face.

We disagree. [The] analysis does not end with the one percent of women upon whom the statute operates; it begins there. Legislation is measured [by] its impact on those whose conduct it affects. [The] proper focus of [inquiry] is the group for whom the law is a restriction, not the group for whom the law is irrelevant.

[The conclusion that the spousal notification requirement is invalid] is in no way inconsistent with our decisions upholding parental notification or consent requirements. Those enactments, and our judgment that they are constitutional, are based on the quite reasonable assumption that minors will benefit from consultation with their parents and that children will often not realize that their parents have their best interests at heart. We cannot adopt a parallel assumption about adult women. We recognize that a husband has a "deep and proper concern and interest in his wife's pregnancy and in the [fetus] she is carrying." Danforth. [And] if this case concerned a State's ability to require the mother to notify the father before taking some action with respect to a living child raised by both, [it] would be reasonable to conclude [that] the father's interest in the welfare of the child and the mother's interest are equal. Before birth, however, the issue takes on a very different cast. It is an inescapable biological fact that state regulation with respect to the child a woman is carrying will have a far greater impact on the mother's liberty than on the father's.

[There] was a time, not so long ago, when a different understanding of the family and of the Constitution prevailed. In Bradwell v. Illinois, 16 Wall. 130 (1873), three Members of this Court reaffirmed the common-law principle that "a woman had no legal existence separate from her husband, who was regarded as her head and representative in the social state; and, notwithstanding some recent modifications of this civil status, many of the special rules of law flowing from and dependent upon this cardinal principle still exist in full force in most States." [These] views, of course, are no longer consistent with our understanding of the family, the individual, or the Constitution. [For] the great many women who are victims of abuse inflicted by their husbands, or whose children are the victims of such abuse, a spousal notice requirement enables the husband to wield an effective veto over his wife's decision. [The] husband's interest in the life of the child [does] not permit the State to empower him with this troubling degree of authority over his wife. The contrary view leads to consequences reminiscent of the common law. A husband has no enforceable right to require a wife to advise him before she exercises her personal choices. If a husband's interest in the potential life of the child outweighs a wife's liberty, the State could require a married woman to notify her husband before she uses a postfertilization contraceptive. Perhaps next in line would be a statute requiring pregnant married women to notify their husbands before engaging in conduct causing risks to the fetus. After all, if the husband's interest in the fetus' safety is a sufficient predicate for state regulation, the State could reasonably conclude that pregnant wives should notify their husbands before drinking alcohol or smoking. Perhaps married women should notify their husbands before using contraceptives or before undergoing any type of surgery that may have complications affecting the husband's interest in his wife's reproductive organs. And if a husband's interest justifies notice in any of these cases, one might reasonably argue that it justifies exactly what Danforth held it did not justify—a requirement of the husband's consent as well. A State may not give to a man the kind of dominion over his wife that parents exercise over their children. [Women] do not lose their constitutionally protected liberty when they marry. The Constitution protects all individuals, male or female, married or unmarried, from the abuse of governmental power, even where that power is employed for the supposed benefit of a member of the individual's family ...

D. We next consider the parental consent provision. Except in a medical emergency, an unemancipated young woman under 18 may not obtain an abortion unless she and one of her parents (or guardian) provides informed consent as defined above. If neither a parent nor a guardian provides consent, a court may authorize the performance of an abortion upon a determination that the young woman is mature and capable of giving informed consent and has in fact given her informed consent, or that an abortion would be in her best interests.

We have been over most of this ground before. [We] reaffirm today that a State may require a minor seeking an abortion to obtain the consent of a parent or guardian, provided there is an adequate judicial bypass procedure. . . .

E. Under the recordkeeping and reporting requirements of the statute, every facility which performs abortions is required to file a report stating its name and address as well as the name and address of any related entity, such as a controlling or subsidiary organization. In the case of state-funded institutions, the information becomes public. For each abortion performed, a report must be filed identifying: the physician; the facility; the referring physician or agency; the woman's age; the number of prior pregnancies and prior abortions she has had; gestational age; the type of abortion procedure; the date of the abortion; whether there were any pre-existing medical conditions which would complicate pregnancy; medical complications with the abortion; where applicable, the basis for the determination that the abortion was medically necessary; the weight of the aborted fetus; and whether the woman was married, and if so, whether notice was provided or the basis for the failure to give notice. Every abortion facility must also file quarterly reports showing the number of abortions performed broken down by trimester. In all events, the identity of each woman who has had an abortion remains confidential.

[We] think [all these] provisions except that relating to spousal notice are constitutional. Although they do not relate to the State's interest in informing the woman's choice, they do relate to health. The collection of information with respect to actual patients is a vital element of medical research, and so it cannot be said that the requirements serve no purpose other than to make abortions more difficult. Nor do we find that the requirements impose a substantial obstacle to a woman's choice. At most they might increase the cost of some abortions by a slight amount. While at some point increased cost could become a substantial obstacle, there is no such showing [here.] . . .

VI. Our Constitution is a covenant running from the first generation of Americans to us and then to future generations. It is a coherent succession. Each generation must learn anew that the Constitution's written terms embody ideas and aspirations that must survive more ages than one. We accept our responsibility not to retreat from interpreting the full meaning of the covenant in light of all of our precedents. We invoke it once again to define the freedom guaranteed by the Constitution's own promise, the promise of liberty.

Justice STEVENS, concurring in part and dissenting in part.

The portions of the Court's opinion that I have joined are more important than those with which I disagree. . . .

I. The Court is unquestionably correct in concluding that the doctrine of stare decisis has controlling significance in a case of this kind, notwithstanding an individual justice's concerns about the merits. The central holding of Roe has been "part of our law" for almost two decades. It was a natural sequel to the protection of individual liberty established in Griswold. The societal costs of overruling Roe at this late date would be enormous. Roe is an integral part of a correct understanding of both the concept of liberty and the basic equality of men and women.

Stare decisis also provides a sufficient basis for my agreement with the joint opinion's reaffirmation of Roe's post-viability analysis. [I] also accept [that] the State's obligation to protect the life or health of the mother must take precedence over any duty to the unborn. [Roe rejected] the argument "that the fetus is a 'person' within the language and meaning of the Fourteenth Amendment." [As] a matter of federal constitutional law, a developing organism that is not yet a "person" does not have what is sometimes described as a "right to life." [1] . . .

II. My disagreement with the joint opinion begins with its understanding of the trimester framework. Contrary to the suggestion of the joint opinion, it is not a "contradiction" to recognize that the State may have a legitimate interest in potential human life and, at the same time, to conclude that that interest does not justify the regulation of abortion before viability (although other interests, such as maternal health, may). The fact that the State's interest is legitimate does not tell us when, if ever, that interest outweighs the [interest] in personal liberty. It is appropriate, therefore, to consider more carefully the nature of the interests at stake.

First, [the] State's interest must be secular; consistent with the First Amendment the State may not promote a theological or sectarian interest. Moreover, [the] state interest in potential human life is not an interest in loco parentis, for the fetus is not a person. Identifying the State's interests—which the States rarely articulate with any precision— makes clear that the interest in protecting potential life is not grounded in the Constitution. It is, instead, an indirect interest supported by both humanitarian and pragmatic concerns. Many of our citizens believe that any abortion reflects an unacceptable disrespect for potential human life and that the performance of more than a million abortions each year is intolerable; many find third-trimester abortions performed when the fetus is approaching personhood particularly offensive. The State has a legitimate interest in minimizing such offense. The State may also have a broader interest in expanding the population, believing society would benefit from the services of additional productive citizens—or that the potential human lives might include the occasional Mozart or Curie.

---

1. ["The] suggestion that states are free to declare a fetus a person [assumes] that a state can curtail some persons' constitutional rights by adding new persons to the constitutional population. The constitutional rights of one citizen are of course very much affected by who or what else also has constitutional rights, because the rights of others may compete or conflict with his. So any power to increase the constitutional population by unilateral decision would be, in effect, a power to decrease rights the national Constitution grants to others. If a state could declare trees to be persons with a constitutional right to life, it could prohibit publishing newspapers or books in spite of the First Amendment's guarantee of free speech, which could not be understood as a license to kill. [Once] we understand that the suggestion we are considering has that implication, we must reject it. If a fetus is not part of the constitutional population, under the national constitutional arrangement, then states have no power to overrule that national arrangement by themselves declaring that fetuses have rights competitive with the constitutional rights of pregnant women." Dworkin, Unenumerated Rights: Whether and How Roe Should be Overruled, 59 U.Chi.L.Rev. 381 (1992). [Footnote by Justice Stevens.]

These [kinds] of concerns [comprise] the State's interest in potential human life.

In counterpoise is the woman's constitutional interest in liberty. One aspect of this liberty is a right to bodily integrity, a right to control one's person. This right is neutral on the question of abortion: The Constitution would be equally offended by an absolute requirement that all women undergo abortions as by an absolute prohibition on abortions. "Our whole constitutional heritage rebels at the thought of giving government the power to control men's minds." Stanley v. Georgia [1969; below, 12th Ed., p. 1105; Ind.Rts., p. 776.] The same holds true for the power to control women's bodies.

[Weighing] the State's interest in potential life and the woman's liberty interest, I agree [that] the State may "express a preference for normal childbirth," that the State may take steps to ensure that a woman's choice "is thoughtful and informed," and that "States are free to enact laws to provide a reasonable framework for a woman to make a decision that has such profound and lasting meaning." Serious questions arise, however, when a State attempts to "persuade the woman to choose childbirth over abortion." Decisional autonomy must limit the State's power to inject into a woman's most personal deliberations its own views of what is best. The State may promote its preferences by funding childbirth, by [maintaining] alternatives to abortion, and by espousing the virtues of family; but it must respect the individual's freedom to make such judgments.

[The] principles established in [our previous] cases [should] govern our decision today. [Those] sections requir[ing] a physician or counselor to provide the woman with a range of materials clearly designed to persuade her to choose not to undergo the abortion [are unconstitutional.] While the State is free [to] produce and disseminate such material, the State may not inject such information into the woman's deliberations just as she is weighing such an important choice....

III. The 24–hour waiting period [raises] even more serious concerns. Such a requirement arguably furthers the State's interests in two ways, neither of which is permissible. First, it may be argued that the 24–hour delay is justified by the mere fact that it is likely to reduce the number of abortions, thus furthering the State's interest in potential life. But [the] State cannot further its interests by simply wearing down the ability of the pregnant woman to exercise her constitutional right.

Second, it can more reasonably be argued that the 24–hour delay furthers the State's interest in ensuring that the woman's decision is informed and thoughtful. But there is no evidence that the mandated delay benefits women or that it is necessary to enable the physician to convey any relevant information to the patient. The mandatory delay thus appears to rest on outmoded and unacceptable assumptions about the decisionmaking capacity of women. While there are [reasons] for the State to view with skepticism the ability of minors to make decisions, none [applies] to an adult woman's decisionmaking ability. Just as we have left behind the belief that a woman must consult her husband before undertaking serious matters, so we must reject the notion that a woman is less capable of deciding matters of gravity....

IV. [A] correct application of the "undue burden" standard leads to the same conclusion. [A] state-imposed burden on the exercise of a constitutional right is measured both by its effects and by its character: A burden may be "undue" either because [it] is too severe or because it lacks a legitimate, rational justification.[2] The 24–hour delay requirement fails both parts of this test. [The] counseling provisions are similarly infirm. Whenever government commands private citizens to speak or to listen, careful review [is] particularly appropriate. [Here] the statute requires that [the prescribed] information be given to all women seeking abortions, including those for whom such information is [of] little decisional value. [I] conclude that the information requirements do not serve a useful purpose and thus constitute an unnecessary—and therefore undue—burden on the woman's constitutional liberty to decide to terminate her pregnancy.

Accordingly, while I disagree with Parts IV, V–B, and V–D of the joint opinion, I join the remainder of the Court's opinion.

Justice BLACKMUN, concurring in part, concurring in the judgment in part, and dissenting in part.

I join parts I, II, III, V–A, V–C, and VI of the joint opinion of Justices O'Connor, Souter, and Kennedy.

Three years ago, four Members of this Court appeared poised to "cas[t] into darkness the hopes and visions of every woman in this country" who had come to believe that the Constitution guaranteed her the right to reproductive choice. All that remained between the promise of Roe and the darkness of the plurality was a single, flickering flame. Decisions since Webster gave little reason to hope that this flame would cast much light. But now, just when so many expected the darkness to fall, the flame has grown bright.

I do not underestimate the significance of today's joint opinion. Yet I remain steadfast [that] the right to reproductive choice is entitled to the full protection afforded [before] Webster. And I fear for the darkness as four Justices anxiously await the single vote necessary to extinguish the light.

I. Make no mistake, the joint opinion [is] an act of personal courage and constitutional principle. [The] authors of the joint opinion today join Justice Stevens and me in concluding that "the essential holding of Roe should be retained and once again reaffirmed." [Five]

2. The meaning of any legal standard can only be understood by reviewing the actual cases in which it is applied. For that reason, I discount both Justice Scalia's comments on past descriptions of the standard, and the attempt to give it crystal clarity in the joint opinion. The several opinions supporting the judgment in Griswold are less illuminating than the central holding of the case, which appears to have passed the test of time. The future may also demonstrate that a standard that analyzes both the severity of a regulatory burden and the legitimacy of its justification will provide a fully adequate framework for the review of abortion legislation even if the contours of the standard are not authoritatively articulated in any single opinion. [Footnote by Justice Stevens.]

Members of this Court today recognize that "the Constitution protects a woman's right to terminate her pregnancy in its early stages."

A fervent view of individual liberty and the force of stare decisis have led the Court to this conclusion. Today a majority reaffirms that the Due Process Clause establishes a realm [of personal liberty] whose outer limits cannot be determined by interpretations [that] focus only on the specific practices of States at the time the Fourteenth Amendment was adopted. [The] reaffirmation of Roe's central holding is also based on the force of stare decisis. [What] has happened today should serve as a model for future Justices and a warning to all who have tried to turn this Court into yet another political branch.[1]

In striking down the spousal notification requirement, the Court has established a framework for evaluating abortion regulations that responds to the social context of women facing issues of reproductive choice. [The] Court inquires, based on expert testimony, empirical studies, and common sense, whether "in a large fraction of the cases in which [the restriction] is relevant, it will operate as a substantial obstacle to a woman's choice to undergo an abortion." [And] in applying its test, the Court remains sensitive to the unique role of women in the decision-making process ...

II.   Today, no less than yesterday, the Constitution [requires] that abortion restrictions be subjected to the strictest of judicial scrutiny.

A.   [State] restrictions on abortion violate a woman's right of privacy in two ways. First, compelled continuation of a pregnancy infringes upon a woman's right to bodily integrity by imposing substantial physical intrusions and significant risks of physical harm. [Further,] when the State restricts a woman's right to terminate her pregnancy, it deprives a woman of the right to make her own decision about reproduction and family planning—critical life choices that this Court long has deemed central to the right to privacy. The decision to terminate or continue a pregnancy has no less an impact on a woman's life than decisions about contraception or marriage. Because motherhood has a dramatic impact on a woman's educational prospects, employment opportunities, and self-determination, restrictive abortion laws deprive her of basic control over her life.

---

1.   Justice Scalia urges the Court to "get out of this area" and leave questions regarding abortion entirely to the States. Putting aside the fact that what he advocates is nothing short of an abdication by the Court of its constitutional responsibilities, Justice Scalia is uncharacteristically naive if he thinks that overruling Roe and holding that restrictions on a woman's right to an abortion are subject only to rational-basis review will enable the Court henceforth to avoid reviewing abortion-related issues. State efforts to regulate and prohibit abortion in a post-Roe world undoubtedly would raise a host of distinct and important constitutional questions meriting review by this Court. For example, does the Eighth Amendment impose any limits on the degree or kind of punishment a State can inflict upon physicians who perform, or women who undergo, abortions? What effect would differences among States in their approaches to abortion have on a woman's right to engage in interstate travel? Does the First Amendment permit States that choose not to criminalize abortion to ban all advertising providing information about where and how to obtain abortions? [Footnote by Justice Blackmun.]

[A] State's restrictions on a woman's right to terminate her pregnancy also implicate constitutional guarantees of gender equality. [By] restricting the right to terminate pregnancies, the State conscripts women's bodies into its service, forcing women to continue their pregnancies, suffer the pains of childbirth, and in most instances, provide years of maternal care. The State does not compensate women for their services; instead, it assumes that they owe this duty as a matter of course. This assumption—that women can simply be forced to accept the "natural" status and incidents of motherhood—appears to rest upon a conception of women's role that has triggered the protection of the Equal Protection Clause. Craig v. Boren [12th Ed., p. 661; Ind.Rts., p. 332] . . .

B. [Limitations] on the right of privacy are permissible only if they survive "strict" constitutional scrutiny—only if the governmental entity imposing the restriction can demonstrate that the limitation is both necessary and narrowly tailored to serve a compelling governmental interest. [Roe] implemented these principles through a framework designed "to insure that the woman's right to choose not become so subordinate to the State's interest in promoting fetal life that her choice exists in theory but not in fact." [No] majority of this Court has ever agreed upon an alternative approach. The factual premises of the trimester framework have not been undermined, and the Roe framework is far more administrable, and far less manipulable, than the "undue burden" standard.

[Nonetheless,] three criticisms of the trimester framework continue to be uttered. First, the trimester framework is attacked because its key elements do not appear in the text of the Constitution. My response to this attack remains the same as it was in Webster: "Were this a true concern, we would have to abandon most of our constitutional jurisprudence. [The] critical elements of countless constitutional doctrines nowhere appear in the Constitution's text." [The] second criticism is that the framework more closely resembles a regulatory code than a body of constitutional doctrine. Again, my answer remains the same as in Webster. "[I]f this were a true and genuine concern, we would have to abandon vast areas of our constitutional jurisprudence. [That] numerous constitutional doctrines result in narrow differentiations between similar circumstances does not mean that this Court has abandoned adjudication in favor of regulation."

The [more genuine] criticism is that [the trimester framework] fails to find the State's interest in potential human life compelling throughout pregnancy. No member of this Court—nor for that matter, the Solicitor General—has ever questioned our holding in Roe that an abortion is not "the termination of life entitled to Fourteenth Amendment protection." Accordingly, a State interest in protecting fetal life is not grounded in the Constitution. Nor, consistent with our Establishment Clause, can it be a theological or sectarian interest. It is, instead, a legitimate interest grounded in humanitarian or pragmatic concerns. But [legitimate] interests are not enough. To overcome the burden of strict scrutiny, the interests must be compelling. . . .

C. Application of [strict scrutiny] results in the invalidation of all the challenged provisions. Indeed, as this Court has invalidated virtually identical provisions in prior cases, stare decisis requires that we again strike them down.

This Court has upheld [consent] requirements only where [they] genuinely further important health-related state concerns. [Measured] against these principles, some aspects of the Pennsylvania [scheme] are unconstitutional. While it is unobjectionable to require that the patient be informed of the nature of the procedure, the health risks, and the probable gestational age of the unborn child, I remain unconvinced that there is a vital state need for insisting that the information be provided by a physician rather than a counselor.

[The] 24–hour waiting period [is] also clearly unconstitutional. [As] Justice Stevens insightfully concludes, the mandatory delay rests either on outmoded or unacceptable assumptions about the decisionmaking capacity of women or the belief that the decision to terminate the pregnancy is presumptively wrong. The requirement that women consider this [slanted] information for an additional 24 hours [will] only influence the woman's decision in improper ways.

[The statute] requires a physician to obtain the informed consent of a parent or guardian before performing an abortion on an unemancipated minor or an incompetent woman. [While] the State has an interest in encouraging parental involvement in the minor's abortion decision, [this statute] is not narrowly drawn to serve that interest.

Finally, the statute requires every facility performing abortions to report its activities to the Commonwealth. [The] Commonwealth attempts to justify its required reports on the ground that the public has a right to know how its tax dollars are spent. A regulation designed to inform the public about public expenditures does not further the Commonwealth's interest in protecting maternal health. . . .

III. At long last, the Chief Justice admits it. Gone are the contentions that the issue need not be (or has not been) considered. There [for] all to see is what was expected: "We believe that Roe was wrongly decided, and that it can and should be overruled consistently with our traditional approach to stare decisis in constitutional cases." If there is much reason to applaud the advances made by the joint opinion today, there is far more to fear from the Chief Justice's opinion.

The Chief Justice's criticism of Roe follows from his stunted conception of individual liberty. While recognizing that Due Process protects more than simple physical liberty, he then goes on to construe [our] personal-liberty cases as establishing only a laundry list of particular rights, rather than a principled account of how these particular rights are grounded in a more general right of privacy. This constricted view is reinforced by the Chief Justice's exclusive reliance on tradition as a source of fundamental rights. He argues that the record in favor of a right to abortion is no stronger than the record in Michael H. v. Gerald D. [below, 12th Ed., p. 562; Ind.Rts., p. 233], where the plurality found no fundamental right to visitation privileges by an adulterous father, or in Bowers v. Hardwick [below, 12th Ed., p. 565; Ind.Rts., p. 236], where the Court found no fundamental right to engage in homosexual sodomy, or in a case involving the "firing of a gun [into] another person's body." In the Chief Justice's world, a woman considering whether to terminate a pregnancy is entitled to no more protection than adulterers, murderers, and so-called "sexual deviates." Given the Chief Justice's exclusive reliance on tradition, people using contraceptives seem the next likely candidate for his list of outcasts.

Even more shocking than the Chief Justice's cramped notion of individual liberty is his complete omission of any discussion of the effects that compelled childbirth and motherhood have on women's lives. The only expression of concern with women's health is purely instrumental—for the Chief Justice only women's psychological health is a concern, and only to the extent that he assumes that every woman who decides to have an abortion does so without serious consideration of the moral implications of their decision. In short, the Chief Justice's view of the State's compelling interest in maternal health has less to do with health than it does with compelling women to be maternal.

Nor does the Chief Justice give any serious consideration to [stare] decisis. For the Chief Justice, the facts that gave rise to Roe are surprisingly simple: "women become pregnant, there is a point somewhere, depending on medical technology, where a fetus becomes viable, and women give birth to children." This characterization [allows] the Chief Justice quickly to discard the joint opinion's reliance argument by asserting that "reproductive planning could take [virtually] immediate account of a decision overruling Roe."

The Chief Justice's narrow conception of individual liberty and stare decisis leads him to propose the same standard of review proposed by the plurality in Webster. [Under] his standard, States can ban abortion if that ban is rationally related to a legitimate state interest—a standard which the United States calls "deferential, but not toothless." Yet when pressed at oral argument to describe the teeth, the best protection that the Solicitor General could offer to women was that a prohibition, enforced by criminal penalties, with no exception for the life of the mother, "could raise very serious questions." Perhaps, the Solicitor General offered, the failure to include an exemption for the life of the mother would be "arbitrary and capricious." If, as the Chief Justice contends, the undue burden test is made out of whole cloth, the so-called "arbitrary and capricious" limit is the Solicitor General's "new clothes."

Even if it is somehow "irrational" for a State to require a woman to risk her life for her child, what protection is offered for women who become pregnant through rape or incest? Is there anything arbitrary or capricious about a State's prohibiting the sins of the father from being visited upon his offspring? But, we are reassured, there is always the protection of the democratic process. While there is much to be praised about our democracy, our country since its founding has recognized that there are certain fundamental liberties that are not to be left to the whims of an election. A woman's right to reproductive choice is one of those fundamental liberties. Accordingly, that liberty need not seek refuge at the ballot box.

IV. In one sense, the Court's approach is worlds apart from that of the Chief Justice and Justice Scalia. And yet, in another sense, the distance between the two approaches is short—the distance is but a single vote. I am 83 years old. I cannot remain on this Court forever, and when I do step down, the confirmation process for my successor well may focus on the issue before us today. That, I regret, may be exactly where the choice between the two worlds will be made.

Chief Justice REHNQUIST, with whom Justice WHITE, Justice SCALIA, and Justice THOMAS join, concurring in the judgment in part and dissenting in part.

The joint opinion, following its newly-minted variation on stare decisis, retains the outer shell of Roe, but beats a wholesale retreat from the substance of that case. We believe that Roe was wrongly decided, and that it can and should be overruled consistently with our traditional approach to stare decisis in constitutional cases. We would adopt the approach of the plurality in Webster, and uphold the challenged provisions in their entirety.

I. [The] state of our post-Roe decisional law dealing with the regulation of abortion is confusing and uncertain, indicating that a reexamination of that line of cases is in order. Unfortunately for those who must apply this Court's decisions, the reexamination undertaken today leaves the Court no less divided than beforehand. Although they reject the trimester framework that formed the underpinning of Roe, Justices O'Connor, Kennedy, and Souter adopt a revised undue burden standard to analyze the challenged regulations. We conclude, however, that such an outcome is an unjustified constitutional compromise, one which leaves the Court in a position to closely scrutinize all types of abortion regulations despite the fact that it lacks the power to do so.

In construing ["liberty,"] we have recognized that its meaning extends beyond freedom from physical restraint. [But our opinions do] not endorse any all-encompassing "right of privacy." In Roe, the Court recognized a "guarantee of personal privacy" which "is broad enough to encompass a woman's decision whether or not to terminate her pregnancy." We are now of the view that, in terming this right fundamental, the Court in Roe read the earlier opinions upon which it based its decision much too broadly. Unlike marriage, procreation and contraception, abortion "involves the purposeful termination of potential life." Harris v. McRae. The abortion decision must therefore "be recognized as sui generis, different in kind from the others that the Court has protected under the rubric of personal or family privacy and autonomy." Thornburgh (White, dissenting). One cannot ignore the fact that a woman is not isolated in her pregnancy, and that the decision to abort necessarily involves the destruction of a fetus.

Nor do the historical traditions of the American people support the view that the right to terminate one's pregnancy is "fundamental." The common law which we inherited from England made abortion after "quickening" an offense. At the time of the adoption of the Fourteenth Amendment, statutory prohibitions or restrictions on abortion were commonplace; in 1868, at least 28 of the then-37 States and 8 Territories had statutes banning or limiting abortion. By the turn of the century virtually every State had a law prohibiting or restricting abortion on its books. By the middle of the present century, a liberalization trend had set in. But 21 of the restrictive abortion laws in effect in 1868 were still in effect in 1973 when Roe was decided, and an overwhelming majority of the States prohibited abortion unless necessary to preserve the life or health of the mother. On this record, it can scarcely be said that any deeply rooted tradition of relatively unrestricted abortion in our history supported the classification of the right to abortion as "fundamental." ...

II. The joint opinion cannot bring itself to say that Roe was correct as an original matter, but the authors are of the view that "the immediate question is not the soundness of Roe's resolution of the issue, but the precedential force that must be accorded to its holding." Instead of claiming that Roe was correct as a matter of original constitutional interpretation, the opinion therefore contains an elaborate discussion of stare decisis. This discussion of the principle of stare decisis appears to be almost entirely dicta, because the joint opinion does not apply that principle in dealing with Roe. Roe decided that a woman had a fundamental right to an abortion. The joint opinion rejects that view. Roe decided that abortion regulations were to be subjected to "strict scrutiny." [The] joint opinion rejects that view. Roe analyzed abortion regulation under a rigid trimester framework. [The] joint opinion rejects that framework.

Stare decisis is defined in Black's Law Dictionary as meaning "to abide by, or adhere to, decided cases." Whatever the "central holding" of Roe that is left after the joint opinion finishes dissecting it is surely not the result of that principle. While purporting to adhere to precedent, the joint opinion instead revises it. Roe continues to exist, but only in the way a storefront on a western movie set exists: a mere facade to give the illusion of reality. Decisions following Roe [are] frankly overruled in part under the "undue burden" standard.

[Authentic] principles of stare decisis do not require that any portion of [Roe] be kept intact. [Erroneous] decisions in [constitutional] cases are uniquely durable, because correction through legislative action, save for constitutional amendment, is impossible. [Our] constitutional watch does not cease merely because we have spoken before on an issue; when it becomes clear that a prior constitutional interpretation is unsound we are obliged to reexamine the question. The joint opinion discusses several stare decisis factors which, it asserts, point toward retaining a portion of Roe. Two of these factors are that the main "factual underpinning" of Roe has remained the same, and that its doctrinal foundation is no weaker now than it was in 1973. Of course, what might be called the basic facts which gave rise to Roe have remained the same—women become pregnant, there is a point somewhere, depending on medical technology, where a fetus becomes viable, and women give birth to children. But this is only to say that the same facts which gave rise to Roe will continue to give rise to similar cases. It is not a reason, in and of itself, why those cases must be decided in the same incorrect manner as was the first case to deal with the question.

The joint opinion also points to reliance interests [to] explain why precedent must be followed for precedent's sake. Certainly where reliance is truly at issue, as in the case of judicial decisions that have formed the basis for private decisions, "[c]onsiderations in favor of stare decisis are at their acme." Payne v. Tennessee, 501 U.S. ___ (1991). But [any] traditional notion of reliance is not applicable here. [The] joint opinion thus turns to what can only be described as an unconventional—and unconvincing—notion of reliance, a view based on the surmise that the availability of abortion since Roe has led to "two decades of economic and social developments" that would be undercut if the error of Roe were recognized. The joint opinion's assertion [is] undeveloped and totally conclusory. In fact, one can not be sure to what economic and social developments the opinion is referring. Surely it is dubious to suggest that women have reached their "places in society" in reliance upon Roe, rather than as a result of their determination to obtain higher education and compete with men in the job market, and of society's increasing recognition of their ability to fill positions that were previously thought to be reserved only for men. In the end, having failed to put forth any evidence to prove any true reliance, the joint opinion's argument is based solely on generalized assertions about the national psyche, on a belief that the people of this country have grown accustomed to the Roe decision over the last 19 years and have "ordered their thinking and living around" it. As an initial matter, one might inquire how the joint opinion can view the "central holding" of Roe as so deeply rooted in our constitutional culture, when it so casually uproots and disposes of that same decision's trimester framework. Furthermore, at various points in the past, the same could have been said about this Court's erroneous decisions that the Constitution allowed "separate but equal" treatment of minorities, or that "liberty" under the Due Process Clause protected "freedom of contract." The "separate but equal" doctrine lasted 58 years after Plessy, and Lochner's protection of contractual freedom lasted 32 years. However, the simple fact that a generation or more had grown used to these major decisions did not prevent the Court from correcting its errors in those cases, nor should it prevent us [here.]

Apparently realizing that conventional stare decisis principles do not support its position, the joint opinion advances a belief that retaining a portion of Roe is necessary to protect the "legitimacy" of this Court. Because the Court must take care to render decisions "grounded truly in principle," and not simply as political and social compromises, the joint opinion properly declares it to be this Court's duty to ignore the public criticism and protest that may arise as a result of a decision. Few would quarrel with this statement, although it may be doubted that Members of this Court, holding their tenure as they do during constitutional "good behavior," are at all likely to be intimidated by such public protests.

But the joint opinion goes on to state that when the Court "resolve[s] the sort of intensely divisive controversy reflected in Roe and those rare, comparable cases," its decision is exempt from reconsideration under established principles of stare decisis in constitutional cases. [This] is a truly novel principle, one which is contrary to both the

Court's historical practice and to the Court's traditional willingness to tolerate criticism of its opinions. Under this principle, when the Court has ruled on a divisive issue, it is apparently prevented from overruling that decision for the sole reason that it was incorrect, unless opposition to the original decision has died away.

[The] joint opinion picks out and discusses two prior rulings it believes are of the "intensely divisive" variety, and concludes that they are of comparable divisiveness. It appears very odd indeed that the joint opinion chooses as benchmarks two cases in which the Court chose not to adhere to erroneous constitutional precedent, but instead enhanced its stature by acknowledging and correcting its error, apparently in violation of the joint opinion's "legitimacy" principle. One might also wonder how it is that the joint opinion puts these, and not others, in the "intensely divisive" category, and how it assumes that these are the only two lines of cases of comparable dimension to Roe. There is no reason to think that either Plessy or Lochner produced the sort of public protest when they were decided that Roe did. There were undoubtedly large segments of the bench and bar who agreed with the dissenting views in those cases, but surely that cannot be what the Court means when it uses the term "intensely divisive," or many other cases would have to be added to the list. In terms of public protest, however, Roe, so far as we know, was unique. But just as the Court should not respond to that sort of protest by retreating from the decision simply to allay the concerns of the protesters, it should likewise not respond by determining to adhere to the decision at all costs lest it seem to be retreating under fire. Public protests should not alter the normal application of stare decisis, lest perfectly lawful protest activity be penalized by the Court itself.

Taking the joint opinion on its own terms, we doubt that its distinction between Roe, on the one hand, and Plessy and Lochner, on the other, withstands analysis. The joint opinion acknowledges that the Court improved its stature by overruling Plessy on a deeply divisive issue. And our decision in West Coast Hotel [was] rendered at a time when Congress was considering President Roosevelt's proposal to "reorganize" this Court and enable him to name six additional Justices in the event that any member of the Court over the age of 70 did not elect to retire. It is difficult to imagine a situation in which the Court would face more intense opposition to a prior ruling than it did at that time, and, under the general principle proclaimed in the joint opinion, the Court seemingly should have responded to this opposition by stubbornly refusing to reexamine the Lochner rationale, lest it lose legitimacy by appearing to "overrule under fire." The joint opinion agrees that the Court's stature would have been seriously damaged if in Brown and West Coast Hotel it had dug in its heels and refused to apply normal principles of stare decisis to the earlier decisions. But the opinion contends that the Court was entitled to overrule Plessy and Lochner in those cases, despite the existence of opposition to the original decisions, only because both the Nation and the Court had learned new lessons in the interim. This is at best a feebly supported, post hoc rationalization. [For] example, the opinion asserts that the Court could justifiably overrule its decision in Lochner only because the Depression had convinced "most people" that constitutional protection of contractual freedom contributed to an economy that failed to protect the welfare of all. Surely the joint opinion does not mean to suggest that people saw this Court's failure to uphold minimum wage statutes as the cause of the Great Depression! In any event, the Lochner Court did not base its rule upon the policy judgment that an unregulated market was fundamental to a stable economy; it simply believed, erroneously, that "liberty" under the Due Process Clause protected the "right to make a contract." Nor is it the case that the people of this Nation only discovered the dangers of extreme laissez faire economics because of the Depression. State laws regulating maximum hours and minimum wages were in existence well before that time. [These] statutes were indeed enacted because of a belief on the part of their sponsors that "freedom of contract" did not protect the welfare of workers, demonstrating that that belief manifested itself more than a generation before the Great Depression. Whether "most people" had come to share it in the hard times of the 1930's is [entirely] speculative. The crucial failing at that time was not that workers were not paid a fair wage, but that there was no work available at any wage.

When the Court finally recognized its error in West Coast Hotel, it did not engage in the post hoc rationalization that the joint opinion attributes to it; it did not state that Lochner had been based on an economic view that had fallen into disfavor, and that it therefore should be overruled. [The] theme of the opinion is that the Court had been mistaken as a matter of constitutional law when it embraced "freedom of contract" 32 years previously.

The joint opinion also agrees that the Court acted properly in rejecting the doctrine of "separate but equal" in Brown. In fact, the opinion lauds Brown in comparing it to Roe. This is strange, in that under the opinion's "legitimacy" principle the Court would seemingly have been forced to adhere to its erroneous decision in Plessy because of its "intensely divisive" character. To us, adherence to Roe today under the guise of "legitimacy" would seem to resemble more closely adherence to Plessy on the same ground. Fortunately, the Court did not choose that option in Brown, and instead frankly repudiated Plessy. The joint opinion concludes that such repudiation was justified only because of newly discovered evidence that segregation had the effect of treating one race as inferior to another. But it can hardly be argued that this was not urged upon those who decided Plessy, as Justice Harlan observed in his dissent that the law "puts the brand of servitude and degradation upon a large class of our fellow-citizens, our equals before the law." [The] same arguments made before the Court in Brown were made in Plessy as well. The Court in Brown simply recognized, as Justice Harlan had recognized beforehand, that the Fourteenth Amendment does not permit racial segregation. The rule of Brown is not tied to popular opinion about the evils of segregation; it is a judgment that the Equal Protection Clause does not permit racial segregation, no matter whether the public might come to believe that it is beneficial.

[There] is also a suggestion in the joint opinion that the propriety of overruling a "divisive" decision depends in part on whether "most people" would now agree that it should be overruled. Either the demise of opposition or its progression to substantial popular agreement apparently is required to allow the Court to reconsider a divisive decision. How such agreement would be ascertained, short of a public opinion poll, the joint opinion does not say. But surely even the suggestion is totally at war with the idea of "legitimacy" in whose name it is invoked. The Judicial Branch derives its legitimacy, not from following public opinion, but from deciding by its best lights whether legislative enactments [comport] with the Constitution.

[There] are other reasons why the joint opinion's discussion of legitimacy is unconvincing as well. In assuming that the Court is perceived as "surrender[ing] to political pressure" when it overrules a controversial decision, the joint opinion forgets that there are two sides to any controversy. The joint opinion asserts that [the] Court must refrain from overruling a controversial decision lest it be viewed as favoring those who oppose the decision. But a decision to adhere to prior precedent is subject to the same criticism, for in such a case one can easily argue that the Court is responding to those who have demonstrated in favor of the original decision. The decision in Roe has engendered large demonstrations, including repeated marches on this Court and on Congress, both in opposition to and in support of that opinion. A decision either way can therefore be perceived as favoring one group or the other. But this perceived dilemma arises only if one assumes [that] the Court should make its decisions with a view toward speculative public perceptions. If one assumes instead [that] the Court's legitimacy is enhanced by faithful interpretation of the Constitution irrespective of public opposition, such self-engendered difficulties may be put to one side.

Roe is not this Court's only decision to generate conflict. Our decisions in some recent capital cases, and in Bowers v. Hardwick, have also engendered demonstrations in opposition. The joint opinion's message to such protesters appears to be that they must cease their activities in order to serve their cause, because their protests will only cement in place a decision which by normal standards of stare decisis should be reconsidered. [Strong] and often misguided criticism of a decision should not render the decision immune from reconsideration, lest a fetish for legitimacy penalize freedom of expression.

The end result of the joint opinion's paeans of praise for legitimacy is the enunciation of a brand new standard for evaluating state regulation of a woman's right to abortion—the "undue burden" standard. [Roe] adopted a "fundamental right" standard under which state regulations could survive only if they met the requirement of "strict scrutiny." While we disagree with that standard, it at least had a recognized basis [at] the time Roe was decided. The same cannot be said for the "undue burden" standard, created largely out of whole cloth by the authors of the joint opinion. [Despite] the efforts of the joint opinion, the undue burden standard presents nothing more workable than the trimester framework. [Under] the guise of the Constitution, this Court will still impart its own preferences on the States in the form of a complex abortion code.

The sum of the joint opinion's labors in the name of stare decisis and "legitimacy" is this: Roe stands as a sort of judicial Potemkin Village, which may be pointed out to passers by as a monument to the importance of adhering to precedent. But behind the facade, an entirely new method of analysis, without any roots in constitutional law, is imported to decide the constitutionality of state laws regulating abortion. Neither stare decisis nor "legitimacy" are truly served by such an effort.

We have stated above our belief that the Constitution does not subject state abortion regulations to heightened scrutiny. [A] woman's interest in having an abortion is a form of liberty protected by the Due Process Clause, but States may regulate abortion procedures in ways rationally related to a legitimate state interest. . . .

III. A. [The] Act imposes certain requirements related to informed consent [and] imposes a 24–hour waiting period. [We] conclude that this provision [is] rationally related to the State's interest in assuring that a woman's consent to an abortion be a fully informed decision. [An] accurate description of the gestational age of the fetus and of the risks involved in carrying a child to term helps to further [the foregoing] interests and the State's legitimate interest in unborn human life. Although petitioners contend that it is unreasonable for the State to require that a physician, as opposed to a nonphysician counselor, disclose this information, we agree with the Court of Appeals that a State "may rationally decide that physicians are better qualified than counselors to impart this information and answer questions about the medical aspects of the available alternatives."

[We also] do not [believe] that a [waiting] period is unconstitutional. Petitioners are correct that such a provision will result in delays for some women that might not otherwise exist, therefore placing a burden on their liberty. But the provision [helps] ensure that a woman's decision [is] a well-considered one, and reasonably furthers the State's legitimate interest in maternal health and in the unborn life of the fetus.

B. [Before] an unemancipated woman under the age of 18 may obtain an abortion she must either furnish the consent of one of her parents [or] opt for the judicial procedure that allows her to bypass the consent requirement. [A] requirement of parental consent to abortion, like myriad other restrictions placed upon minors in other contexts, is reasonably designed to further [an] important and legitimate state interest. In our view, it is entirely "rational for the State to conclude that, in most instances, the family will strive to give a lonely or even terrified minor advice that is both compassionate and mature." Akron II. . . .

C. [The] spousal notification provision [requires] that [the] woman must sign a statement indicating that she has notified her husband of her planned abortion. [We] first emphasize that Pennsylvania has not imposed a spousal consent requirement of the type the Court struck down in Danforth. [This] case involves a much less intrusive requirement of spousal notification, not consent. [It] is not enough for petitioners to show that, in some "worst-case" circumstances, the notice provision will operate as a grant of veto power to husbands. Because they are making a facial challenge to the provision, they must "show that no set of circumstances exists under which the [provision] would be valid." Akron II. This they have failed to do.

The question before us is therefore whether the spousal notification requirement rationally furthers any legitimate state interests. We conclude that it does. First, a husband's interests in procreation within marriage and in the potential life of his unborn child are certainly substantial ones. [By] providing that a husband will usually know of his spouse's intent to have an abortion, the provision makes it more likely that the husband will participate in deciding the fate of his unborn child, a possibility that might otherwise have been denied him. [In] our view, the spousal notice requirement is a rational attempt by the State to improve truthful communication between spouses and encourage collaborative decisionmaking, and thereby fosters marital integrity. [It] is unrealistic to assume that every husband-wife relationship is either (1) so perfect that this type of truthful and important communication will take place as a matter of course, or (2) so imperfect that, upon notice, the husband will react selfishly, violently, or contrary to the best interests of his wife. [The] Legislature was in a position to weigh the likely benefits of the provision against its likely adverse effects, and presumably concluded, on balance, that the provision would be beneficial. Whether this was a wise decision or not, we cannot say that it was irrational ...

D. The Act also imposes various reporting requirements. [These] reporting requirements rationally further the State's legitimate interests in advancing the state of medical knowledge concerning maternal health and prenatal life, in gathering statistical information with respect to patients, and in ensuring compliance with other provisions of the Act. [Petitioners] contend, however, that the forced public disclosure of the information given by facilities receiving public funds serves no legitimate state interest. We disagree. [As] the Court of Appeals observed, "[w]hen a state provides money to a private commercial enterprise, there is a legitimate public interest in informing taxpayers who the funds are benefiting and what services the funds are supporting." ...

IV. [We] therefore would hold that each of the challenged provisions [is] consistent with the Constitution. It bears emphasis that our conclusion in this regard does not carry with it any necessary approval of these regulations. Our task is, as always, to decide only whether the challenged provisions of a law comport with the Constitution. If, as we believe, these do, their wisdom as a matter of public policy is for the people of Pennsylvania to decide.

Justice SCALIA, with whom the Chief Justice (REHNQUIST), Justice WHITE, and Justice THOMAS join, concurring in the judgment in part and dissenting in part.

My views on this matter are unchanged from those I set forth [in] Webster and Akron II. The States may, if they wish, permit abortion-on-demand, but the Constitution does not require them to do so. The permissibility of abortion, and the limitations upon it, are to be resolved like most important questions in our democracy: by citizens trying to persuade one another and then voting. [The] Court is correct in adding the qualification that this "assumes a state of affairs in which the choice does not intrude upon a protected liberty,"—but the crucial part of that qualification is the penultimate word. A State's choice between two positions on which reasonable people can disagree is constitutional even when (as is often the case) it intrudes upon a "liberty" in the absolute sense. Laws against bigamy, for example—which entire societies of reasonable people disagree with—intrude upon men and women's liberty to marry and live with one another. But bigamy happens not to be a liberty specially "protected" by the Constitution.

That is, quite simply, the issue in this case: not whether the power of a woman to abort her unborn child is a "liberty" in the absolute sense; or even whether it is a liberty of great importance to many women. Of course it is both. The issue is whether it is a liberty protected by the Constitution. I am sure it is not. I reach that conclusion not because of anything so exalted as my views concerning the "concept of existence, of meaning, of the universe, and of the mystery of human life." Rather, I reach it for the same reason I reach the conclusion that bigamy is not constitutionally protected—because of two simple facts: (1) the Constitution says absolutely nothing about it, and (2) the longstanding traditions of American society have permitted it to be legally proscribed.[1]

[But] the Court does not wish to be fettered by any such limitations on its preferences. The Court's statement that it is "tempting" to acknowledge the authoritativeness of tradition in order to "cur[b] the discretion of federal judges" is of course rhetoric rather than reality; no government official is "tempted" to place restraints upon his own freedom of action, which is why Lord Acton did not say "Power tends to purify." The Court's temptation is in the quite opposite and more natural direction—towards systematically eliminating checks upon its own power; and it succumbs.

Beyond that brief summary of the essence of my position, I will not swell the United States Reports with repetition of what I have said before; and applying the rational basis test, I would uphold the Pennsylvania statute in its entirety. I must, however, respond to a few of the more outrageous arguments in today's opinion, which it is beyond human nature to leave unanswered. I shall discuss each of them under a quotation from the Court's opinion to which they pertain.

> "The inescapable fact is that adjudication of substantive due process claims may call upon the Court in interpreting the Constitution to exercise that same capacity which by tradition courts always have exercised: reasoned judgment."

1. [It] does not follow that the Constitution does not protect childbirth simply because it does not protect abortion. The Court's contention that the only way to protect childbirth is to protect abortion shows the utter bankruptcy of constitutional analysis deprived of tradition as a validating factor. It drives one to say that the only way to protect the right to eat is to acknowledge the constitutional right to starve oneself to death. [Footnote by Justice Scalia.]

Assuming that the question before us is to be resolved at such a level of philosophical abstraction, in such isolation from the traditions of American society, as by simply applying "reasoned judgment," I do not see how that could possibly have produced the answer the Court arrived at in Roe. Today's opinion describes the methodology of Roe, quite accurately, as weighing against the woman's interest the State's "important and legitimate interest in protecting the potentiality of human life." But "reasoned judgment" does not begin by begging the question, as Roe unquestionably did by assuming that what the State is protecting is the mere "potentiality of human life." The whole argument of abortion opponents is that what the Court calls the fetus and what others call the unborn child is a human life. Thus, whatever answer Roe came up with after conducting its "balancing" is bound to be wrong, unless it is correct that the human fetus is in some critical sense merely potentially human. There is of course no way to determine that as a legal matter; it is in fact a value judgment. Some societies have considered newborn children not yet human, or the incompetent elderly no longer so.

The authors of the joint opinion [do] not squarely contend that Roe was a correct application of "reasoned judgment"; merely that it must be followed, because of stare decisis. But in their exhaustive discussion of all the factors that go into the determination of when stare decisis should be observed and when disregarded, they never mention "how wrong was the decision on its face?" Surely, if "[t]he Court's power lies ... in its legitimacy, a product of substance and perception," the "substance" part of the equation demands that plain error be acknowledged and eliminated. Roe was plainly wrong—even on the Court's methodology of "reasoned judgment," and even more so (of course) if the proper criteria of text and tradition are applied. The emptiness of the "reasoned judgment" that produced Roe is displayed in plain view by the fact that, after more than 19 years of effort by some of the brightest (and most determined) legal minds in the country, after more than 10 cases upholding abortion rights in this Court, and after dozens upon dozens of amicus briefs submitted in this and other cases, the best the Court can do to explain how it is that the word "liberty" must be thought to include the right to destroy human fetuses is to rattle off a collection of adjectives that simply decorate a value judgment and conceal a political choice. The right to abort, we are told, inheres in "liberty" because it is among "a person's most basic decisions"; it involves a "most intimate and personal choic[e]; " it is "central to personal dignity and autonomy" ; it "originate[s] within the zone of conscience and belief" ; it is "too intimate and personal" for state interference; it reflects "intimate views" of a "deep, personal character" ; it involves "intimate relationships," and notions of "personal autonomy and bodily integrity" ; and it concerns a particularly "important decisio[n]." But it is obvious to anyone applying "reasoned judgment" that the same adjectives can be applied to many forms of conduct that this Court [has] held are not entitled to constitutional protection—because, like abortion, they are forms of conduct that have long been criminalized in American society. Those adjectives might be applied, for example, to homosexual sodomy, polygamy, adult incest, and suicide, all of which are equally "intimate" and "deep[ly] personal" decisions involving "personal autonomy and bodily integrity," and all of which can constitutionally be proscribed because it is our unquestionable constitutional tradition that they are proscribable. It is not reasoned judgment that supports the Court's decision; only personal predilection. Justice Curtis's warning is as timely today as it was 135 years ago: "[W]hen a strict interpretation of the Constitution, according to the fixed rules which govern the interpretation of laws, is abandoned, and the theoretical opinions of individuals are allowed to control its meaning, we have no longer a Constitution; we are under the government of individual men, who for the time being have power to declare what the Constitution is, according to their own views of what it ought to mean." Dred Scott v. Sandford, 19 How. 393 (1857) (Curtis, J., dissenting).

"Liberty finds no refuge in a jurisprudence of doubt."

One might have feared to encounter this august and sonorous phrase in an opinion defending the real Roe, rather than the revised version fabricated by the authors of the joint opinion. The shortcomings of Roe did not include lack of clarity: Virtually all regulation of abortion before the third trimester was invalid. But to come across this phrase in the joint opinion—which calls upon federal district judges to apply an "undue burden" standard as doubtful in application as it is unprincipled in origin—is really more than one should have to bear. [Because] the three Justices now wish to "set forth a standard of general application," the joint opinion announces that "it is important to clarify what is meant by an undue burden." I certainly agree with that, but I do not agree that the joint opinion succeeds in the announced endeavor. To the contrary, its efforts at clarification make clear only that the standard is inherently manipulable. [The] joint opinion explains that a state regulation imposes an "undue burden" if it "has the purpose or effect of placing a substantial obstacle in the path of a woman seeking an abortion of a nonviable fetus." An obstacle is "substantial," we are told, if it is "calculated [,] [not] to inform the woman's free choice, [but to] hinder it." This latter statement cannot possibly mean what it says. Any regulation of abortion that is intended to advance what the joint opinion concedes is the State's "substantial" interest in protecting unborn life will be "calculated [to] hinder" a decision to have an abortion. It thus seems more accurate to say that the joint opinion would uphold abortion regulations only if they do not unduly hinder the woman's decision. That, of course, brings us right back to square one: Defining an "undue burden" as an "undue hindrance" (or a "substantial obstacle") hardly "clarifies" the test. Consciously or not, the joint opinion's verbal shell game will conceal raw judicial policy choices concerning what is "appropriate" abortion legislation.

[I] do not [have] any objection to the notion that, in applying legal principles, one should rely only upon the facts contained in the record properly subject to judicial notice. But what is remarkable about the joint opinion's fact-intensive analysis is that it does not result in any measurable clarification of the "undue burden" standard. Rather, the approach of the joint opinion is, for the most part, simply to highlight certain facts in the record that apparently strike the three Justices as particularly significant in establishing (or refuting) the existence of an undue burden; after describing these facts, the opinion then simply announces that the provision either does or does not impose a "substantial obstacle" or an "undue burden." We do not know whether the same conclusions could have been reached on a different record, or in what respects the record would have had to differ before an opposite conclusion would have been appropriate. The inherently standardless nature of this inquiry invites the district judge to give effect to his personal preferences about abortion. By finding and relying upon the right facts, he can invalidate [almost] any abortion restriction that strikes him as "undue"—subject, of course, to the possibility of being reversed by a Circuit Court or Supreme Court that is as unconstrained in reviewing his decision as he was in making it.

To the extent I can discern any meaningful content in the "undue burden" standard as applied in the joint opinion, it appears to be that a State may not regulate abortion in such a way as to reduce significantly its incidence. [As] Justice Blackmun recognizes (with evident hope), the "undue burden" standard may ultimately require the invalidation of each provision upheld today if it can be shown [that] the State is too effectively "express[ing] a preference for childbirth over abortion." Reason finds no refuge in this jurisprudence of confusion.

> "While we appreciate the weight of the arguments ... that Roe should be overruled, the reservations any of us may have in reaffirming the central holding of Roe are outweighed by the explication of individual liberty we have given combined with the force of stare decisis."

The Court's reliance upon stare decisis can best be described as contrived. It insists upon the necessity of adhering not to all of Roe, but only to what it calls the "central holding." It seems to me that stare decisis ought to be applied even to the doctrine of stare decisis, and I confess never to have heard of this new, keep-what-you-want-and-throw-away-the-rest version. I wonder whether, as applied to Marbury v. Madison, [the] new version of stare decisis would be satisfied if we allowed courts to review the constitutionality of only those statutes that (like the one in Marbury) pertain to the jurisdiction of the courts. I am certainly not in a good position to dispute that the Court has saved the "central holding" of Roe, since to do that effectively I would have to know what the Court has saved, which in turn would require me to understand (as I do not) what the "undue burden" test means. I must confess, however, that I have always thought, and I think a lot of other people have always thought, that the arbitrary trimester framework [was] quite as central to Roe as the arbitrary viability test which the Court today retains. It seems particularly ungrateful to carve the trimester framework out of the core of Roe, since its very rigidity (in sharp contrast to the utter indeterminability of the "undue burden" test) is probably the only reason the Court is able to say [that] Roe "has in no sense proven unworkable." I suppose the Court is entitled to call a "central holding" whatever it wants to call a "central holding"—which is, come to think of it, perhaps one of the difficulties with this modified version of stare decisis....

"Where, in the performance of its judicial duties, the Court decides a case in such a way as to resolve the sort of intensely divisive controversy reflected in Roe ..., its decision has a dimension that the resolution of the normal case does not carry. It is the dimension present whenever the Court's interpretation of the Constitution calls the contending sides of a national controversy to end their national division by accepting a common mandate rooted in the Constitution."

The Court's description of the place of Roe in the social history of the United States is unrecognizable. Not only did Roe not [resolve] the deeply divisive issue of abortion; it did more than anything else to nourish it, by elevating it to the national level where it is infinitely more difficult to resolve. National politics were not plagued by abortion protests, national abortion lobbying, or abortion marches on Congress, before Roe was decided. Profound disagreement existed among our citizens over the issue—as it does over other issues, such as the death penalty—but that disagreement was being worked out at the state level. As with many other issues, the division of sentiment within each State was not as closely balanced as it was among the population of the Nation as a whole, meaning not only that more people would be satisfied with the results of state-by-state resolution, but also that those results would be more stable. Pre–Roe, moreover, political compromise was possible. Roe's mandate for abortion-on-demand destroyed the compromises of the past, rendered compromise impossible for the future, and required the entire issue to be resolved uniformly, at the national level. At the same time, Roe created a vast new class of abortion consumers and abortion proponents by eliminating the moral opprobrium that had attached to the act. ("If the Constitution guarantees abortion, how can it be bad?"—not an accurate line of thought, but a natural one.) Many favor all of those developments, and it is not for me to say that they are wrong. But to portray Roe as the statesmanlike "settlement" of a divisive issue, a jurisprudential Peace of Westphalia that is worth preserving, is nothing less than Orwellian. Roe fanned into life an issue that has inflamed our national politics in general, and has obscured with its smoke the selection of Justices to this Court in particular, ever since. And by keeping us in the abortion-umpiring business, it is the perpetuation of that disruption, rather than of any pax Roeana, that the Court's new majority decrees.

"[T]o overrule under fire ... would subvert the Court's legitimacy ... "To all those who will be ... tested by following, the Court implicitly undertakes to remain steadfast.... The promise of constancy, once given, binds its maker for as long as the power to stand by the decision survives and ... the commitment [is not] obsolete ... "[The American people's] belief in themselves as ... a people [who aspire to live according to the rule of law] is not readily separable from their understanding of the Court invested with the authority to decide their constitutional cases and speak before all others for their constitutional ideals. If the Court's legitimacy should be undermined, then, so would the country be in its very ability to see itself through its constitutional ideals."

The Imperial Judiciary lives. It is instructive to compare this Nietzschean vision of us unelected, life-tenured judges—leading a Volk who will be "tested by following," and whose very "belief in themselves" is mystically bound up in their "understanding" of a Court that "speak[s] before all others for their constitutional ideals"—with the somewhat more modest role envisioned for these lawyers by the Founders. "The judiciary ... has ... no direction either of the strength or of the wealth of the society, and can take no active resolution whatever. It may truly be said to have neither FORCE nor WILL but merely judgment." Federalist 78. Or [compare] this ecstasy of a Supreme Court in which there is, especially on controversial matters, no shadow of change or hint of alteration ("There is a limit to the amount of error that can plausibly be imputed to prior courts"), with the more democratic views of a more humble man: "[T]he candid citizen must confess that if the policy of the Government upon vital questions affecting the whole people is to be irrevocably fixed by decisions of the Supreme Court, [the] people will have ceased to be their own rulers, having to that extent practically resigned their Government into the hands of that eminent tribunal." A. Lincoln, First Inaugural Address.

It is particularly difficult, in the circumstances of the present decision, to sit still for the Court's lengthy lecture upon the virtues of "constancy," of "remain[ing] steadfast," of adhering to "principle." Among the five Justices who purportedly adhere to Roe, at most three agree upon the principle that constitutes adherence (the joint opinion's "undue burden" standard)—and that principle is inconsistent with Roe. To make matters worse, two of the three, in order thus to remain steadfast, had to abandon previously stated positions. It is beyond me how the Court expects these accommodations to be accepted "as grounded truly in principle, not as compromises with social and political pressures having, as such, no bearing on the principled choices that the Court is obliged to make." The only principle the Court "adheres" to, it seems to me, is the principle that the Court must be seen as standing by Roe. That is not a principle of law (which is what I thought the Court was talking about), but a principle of Realpolitik—and a wrong one at that.

I cannot agree with, indeed I am appalled by, the Court's suggestion that the decision whether to stand by an erroneous constitutional decision must be strongly influenced—against overruling, no less—by the substantial and continuing public opposition the decision has generated. The Court's judgment that any other course would "subvert the Court's legitimacy" must be another consequence of reading the error-filled history book that described the deeply divided country brought together by Roe. In my history-book, the Court was covered with dishonor and deprived of legitimacy by Dred Scott v. Sandford, an erroneous (and widely opposed) opinion that it did not abandon, rather than by West Coast Hotel, which produced the famous "switch in time" from the Court's erroneous (and widely opposed) constitutional opposition to the social measures of the New Deal.

But whether it would "subvert the Court's legitimacy" or not, the notion that we would decide a case differently from the way we otherwise would have in order to show that we can stand firm against public disapproval is frightening. It is a bad enough idea, even in the head of someone like me, who believes that the text of the Constitution, and our traditions, say what they say and there is no fiddling with them. But when it is in the mind of a Court that believes the Constitution has an evolving meaning; that the Ninth Amendment's reference to "othe[r]" rights is not a disclaimer, but a charter for action; and that the function of this Court is to "speak before all others for [the people's] constitutional ideals" unrestrained by meaningful text or tradition—then the notion that the Court must adhere to a decision for as long as the decision faces "great opposition" and the Court is "under fire" acquires a character of almost czarist arrogance. We are offended by these marchers who descend upon us, every year on the anniversary of Roe, to protest our saying that the Constitution requires what our society has never thought the Constitution requires. These people who refuse to be "tested by following" must be taught a lesson. We have no Cossacks, but at least we can stubbornly refuse to abandon an erroneous opinion that we might otherwise change—to show how little they intimidate us. Of course, as the Chief Justice points out, we have been subjected to what the Court calls "political pressure" by both sides of this issue. Maybe today's decision not to overrule Roe will be seen as buckling to pressure from that direction. Instead of engaging in the hopeless task of predicting public perception—a job not for lawyers but for political campaign managers—the Justices should do what is legally right by asking two questions: (1) Was Roe correctly decided? (2) Has Roe succeeded in producing a settled body of law? If the answer to both questions is no, Roe should undoubtedly be overruled.

In truth, I am as distressed as the Court is—and expressed my distress several years ago, see Webster—about the "political pressure" directed to the Court: the marches, the mail, the protests aimed at inducing us to change our opinions. How upsetting it is, that so many of our citizens (good people, not lawless ones, on both sides of this abortion issue, and on various sides of other issues as well) think that we Justices should properly take into account their views, as though we were engaged not in ascertaining an objective law but in determining some kind of social consensus. The Court would profit, I think, from giving less attention to the fact of this distressing phenomenon, and more attention to the cause of it. That cause permeates today's opinion: a new mode of constitutional adjudication that relies not upon text and traditional practice to determine the law, but upon what the Court calls "reasoned judgment," which turns out to be nothing but philosophical predilection and moral intuition. All manner of "liberties," the Court tells us, inhere in the Constitution and are enforceable by this Court— not just those mentioned in the text or established in the traditions of our society. Why even the Ninth Amendment [is,] despite our contrary understanding for almost 200 years, a literally boundless source of additional, unnamed, unhinted-at "rights," definable and enforceable by us, through "reasoned judgment."

What makes all this relevant to the bothersome application of "political pressure" against the Court are the twin facts that the

American people love democracy and the American people are not fools. As long as this Court thought (and the people thought) that we Justices were doing essentially lawyers' work up here—reading text and discerning our society's traditional understanding of that text—the public pretty much left us alone. Texts and traditions are facts to study, not convictions to demonstrate about. But if in reality our process of constitutional adjudication consists primarily of making value judgments; if we can ignore a long and clear tradition clarifying an ambiguous text, [if our] pronouncement of constitutional law rests primarily on value judgments, then a free and intelligent people's attitude towards us can be expected to be (ought to be) quite different. The people know that their value judgments are quite as good as those taught in any law school—maybe better. If [the] "liberties" protected by the Constitution are [undefined] and unbounded, then the people should demonstrate, to protest that we do not implement their values instead of ours. Not only that, but confirmation hearings for new Justices should deteriorate into question-and-answer sessions in which Senators go through a list of their constituents' most favored and most disfavored alleged constitutional rights, and seek the nominee's commitment to support or oppose them. Value judgments, after all, should be voted on, not dictated; and if our Constitution has somehow accidently committed them to the Supreme Court, at least we can have a sort of plebiscite each time a new nominee to that body is put forward. Justice Blackmun not only regards this prospect with equanimity, he solicits it.

. . .

There is a poignant aspect to today's opinion. Its length, and what might be called its epic tone, suggest that its authors believe they are bringing to an end a troublesome era in the history of our Nation and of our Court. [There] comes vividly to mind a portrait by Emanuel Leutze that hangs in the Harvard Law School: Roger Brooke Taney, painted in 1859, the 82d year of his life, the 24th of his Chief Justiceship, the second after his opinion in Dred Scott. He is all in black, sitting in a shadowed red armchair, left hand resting upon a pad of paper in his lap, right hand hanging limply, almost lifelessly, beside the inner arm of the chair. He sits facing the viewer, and staring straight out. There seems to be on his face, and in his deep-set eyes, an expression of profound sadness and disillusionment. Perhaps he always looked that way, even when dwelling upon the happiest of thoughts. But those of us who know how the lustre of his great Chief Justiceship came to be eclipsed by Dred Scott cannot help believing that he had that case—its already apparent consequences for the Court, and its soon-to-be-played-out consequences for the Nation—burning on his mind. I expect that two years earlier he, too, had thought himself "call[ing] the contending sides of national controversy to end their national division by accepting a common mandate rooted in the Constitution."

It is no more realistic for us in this case, than it was for him in that, to think that an issue of the sort they both involved—an issue involving life and death, freedom and subjugation—can be "speedily and finally settled" by the Supreme Court, as President James Buchanan in his inaugural address said the issue of slavery in the territories would be. Quite to the contrary, by foreclosing all democratic outlet for the deep passions this issue arouses, by banishing the issue from the political forum that gives all participants, even the losers, the satisfaction of a fair hearing and an honest fight, by continuing the imposition of a rigid national rule instead of allowing for regional differences, the Court merely prolongs and intensifies the anguish.

We should get out of this area, where we have no right to be, and where we do neither ourselves nor the country any good by remaining.*

Consider the proposed Freedom of Choice Act, introduced in the 104th Congress by Rep. Torkildsen.

Section 1.   Short Title.

This Act may be cited as the "Freedom of Choice Act of 1995".

Section 2.   Congressional Statement of Findings and Purpose.

(a) Findings.—Congress finds the following:

(1) The 1973 Supreme Court decision in Roe v. Wade established constitutionally based limits on the power of States to restrict the right of a woman to choose to terminate a pregnancy.   Under the strict scrutiny standard enunciated in Roe v. Wade, States were required to demonstrate that laws restricting the right of a woman to choose to terminate a pregnancy were the least restrictive means available to achieve a compelling State interest.   Since 1989, the Supreme Court has no longer applied the strict scrutiny standard in reviewing challenges to the constitutionality of State laws restricting such rights.

(2) As a result of the Supreme Court's recent modification of the strict scrutiny standard enunciated in Roe v. Wade, certain States have restricted the right of women to choose to terminate a pregnancy or to utilize some forms of contraception, and these restrictions operate cumulatively to—

(A)(i) increase the number of illegal or medically less safe abortions, often resulting in physical impairment, loss of reproductive capacity or death to the women involved;

(ii) burden interstate commerce by forcing women to travel from States in which legal barriers render contraception or abortion unavailable or unsafe to other States or foreign nations;

* The Justices' most recent statements on abortion are found in their opinions in Bray v. Alexandria Women's Health Clinic, 1993, described at length below, addition to 12th Ed., p. 945; Ind.Rts., p. 616, dealing with the power of the federal civil rights laws to be used against those who blockaded or otherwise unlawfully obstructed abortion clinics.

(iii) interfere with freedom of travel between and among the various States;

(iv) burden the medical and economic resources of States that continue to provide women with access to safe and legal abortion; and

(v) interfere with the ability of medical professionals to provide health services;

(B) obstruct access to and use of contraceptive and other medical techniques that are part of interstate and international commerce;

(C) discriminate between women who are able to afford interstate and international travel and women who are not, a disproportionate number of whom belong to racial or ethnic minorities; and

(D) infringe upon women's ability to exercise full enjoyment of rights secured to them by Federal and State law, both statutory and constitutional.

(3) Although Congress may not by legislation create constitutional rights, it may, where authorized by its enumerated powers and not prohibited by a constitutional provision, enact legislation to create and secure statutory rights in areas of legitimate national concern.

(4) Congress has the affirmative power both under section 8 of Article I of the Constitution of the United States and under section 5 of the Fourteenth Amendment of the Constitution to enact legislation to prohibit State interference with interstate commerce, liberty or equal protection of the laws.

(b) Purpose.—It is the purpose of this Act to establish, as a statutory matter, limitations upon the power of States to restrict the freedom of a woman to terminate a pregnancy in order to achieve the same limitations as provided, as a constitutional matter, under the strict scrutiny standard of review enunciated in Roe v. Wade and applied in subsequent cases from 1973 to 1988.

Section 3.   Freedom to Choose.

(a) In General.—A State—

(1) may not restrict the freedom of a woman to choose whether or not to terminate a pregnancy before fetal viability;

(2) may restrict the freedom of a woman to choose whether or not to terminate a pregnancy after fetal viability unless such a termination is necessary to preserve the life or health of the woman; and

(3) may impose requirements on the performance of abortion procedures if such requirements are medically necessary to protect the health of women undergoing such procedures.

(b) Rules of Construction.—Nothing in this Act shall be construed to—

(1) prevent a State from protecting unwilling individuals from having to participate in the performance of abortions to which they are conscientiously opposed;

(2) prevent a State from declining to pay for the performance of abortions; or

(3) prevent a State from requiring a minor to involve a parent, guardian, or other responsible adult before terminating a pregnancy.

Section 4.   Definition of State.

As used in this Act, the term "State" includes the District of Columbia, the Commonwealth of Puerto Rico, and each other territory or possession of the United States.

12th ED., p. 564; IND. RTS., p. 235
Add at end of footnote 20:

Justice Scalia expanded further on his views in PACIFIC MUTUAL LIFE INSURANCE CO. v. HASLIP, 499 U.S. 1 (1991), a case in which Justice Blackmun for the majority upheld the award of punitive damages in civil cases against a due process challenge urging that the size and arbitrariness of punitive damage awards violated the due process requirement of fundamental fairness. Although not holding that all awards of punitive damages were immune from due process challenge, the majority concluded that there were sufficient safeguards in the Alabama procedure before the Court to guard against potentially unconstitutional arbitrariness in the application of punitive damages. Concurring in the judgment, Justice Scalia made clear that his views about the dispositiveness of historical practice did not apply to the specific provisions of the Bill of Rights. "In principle, what is important enough to have been included within the Bill of Rights has good claim to being an element of 'fundamental fairness,' whatever history might say." But to "say that unbroken historical usage cannot save a procedure that violates one of the explicit procedural guarantees of the Bill of Rights (applicable through the Fourteenth Amendment) is not necessarily to say that such usage cannot demonstrate the procedure's compliance with the more general guarantee of 'due process.'" Emphasizing that his principle of the conclusive effect of historical practice applied neither to the equal protection clause nor to the provisions of the Bill of Rights, Justice Scalia claimed to be following Justice Cardozo in Snyder in "affirm[ing] that no procedure firmly rooted in the practices of our people can be so 'fundamentally unfair' as to deny due process of law."

Justice Kennedy's separate concurrence acknowledged that Justice Scalia's "historical approach to questions of procedural due process has much to commend it. I cannot say with the confidence maintained by Justice Scalia, however, that widespread adherence to a historical practice always forecloses further inquiry when a party challenges an ancient institution or procedure as violative of due process. But I agree that the judgment of history should govern the outcome of the case before us."

Justice O'Connor, however, dissented, arguing that due process requires clear standards for the imposition of punitive damages, standards not found in the Alabama procedure at issue. Applying the Mathews v. Eldridge (1976; described below, 12th Ed., p. 599; Ind. Rts., p. 270) standard and its view that due process was not a "technical conception with a fixed content unrelated to time, place, and circumstances," Justice O'Connor agreed that the majority had "properly rejected" Justice Scalia's historical approach. "Due process is not a fixed notion. Although history creates a strong presumption of continued validity, [circumstances] today are different than they were 200 years ago, and nothing in the Fourteenth Amendment requires us to blind ourselves to this fact. Just the opposite is true. The Due Process Clause demands that we possess some degree of confidence that the procedures employed to deprive persons of life, liberty, and property are capable of producing fair and reasonable results. When we lose that confidence, a change must be made."

The question of due process limitations on punitive damages awards surfaced again in TXO PRODUCTION CORP. v. ALLIANCE RESOURCES CORP., 510 U.S. ___ (1993). In a common law tort action for slander of title, arising out of a dispute between two corporations about the ownership and use of drilling rights, a West Virginia jury had awarded actual damages of $19,000 and punitive damages of $10,000,000. The defendant argued that the amount of punitive damages, especially when compared both to actual damages and to punitive damage awards in other jurisdictions and in other trials in West Virginia, was so much larger than the norm and than the actual damages as to constitute a substantive due process violation. In announcing the judgment of the Court, however, Justice STEVENS, joined by Chief Justice Rehnquist and Justice Blackmun, articulated a "reasonableness" standard for the evaluation of punitive damages awards, a standard he suggested was related to but not identical to the "rational basis" test used elsewhere within the domain of substantive due process. Under this standard there was a "strong presumption" of validity, a presumption that could not be overcome by recourse to the kinds of comparative judgments urged by the petitioner. And since in this case the award had been based on a pattern of unlawful predatory conduct by the defendant, and was not disproportionate to the defendant's resources or the size of the full matter in controversy, Justice Stevens found the reasonableness standard satisfied. Concurring in the judgment, Justice KENNEDY urged a more rigorous scrutiny, focusing not only on the size of the award but on the reasons available in the record to explain it. In this case, however, he found even his more rigorous standard satisfied. And Justice SCALIA, joined by Justice Thomas, also concurred only in the judgment, since for them there was no justification for any scrutiny at all in this area, and no warrant in the constitution for applying the idea of substantive due process to the size of jury verdicts. Justice O'CONNOR, however, joined by Justice White and in part by Justice Souter, reiterated from Haslip her view that substantive and procedural due process required more searching review of punitive damage awards, a review that in this case, given what seemed to her to be strong evidence of a jury desire to punish the defendant just because of its size and out-of-state status, would have led her to strike down the punitive damages award. (In connection with the punitive damages cases, note also Austin v. United States, 511 U.S. ___ (1993), and Alexander v. United States, 511 U.S. ___ (1993), holding that forfeitures implicate the "excessive fines" clause of the Eight Amendment, and are therefore subject to judicial constitutional evaluation to ensure that they are not disproportionate to the underlying offense producing the forfeiture.)

Most recently, in HONDA MOTOR CO., LTD. v. OBERG, 513 U.S. ___ (1994), the Court held that an amendment to the Oregon Constitution, drastically limiting judicial review of punitive damages awards, violated the due process clause of the Fourteenth Amendment. Writing for the Court, Justice STEVENS characterized the earlier decisions in Haslip and TXO as having been based on the procedural component of the due process clause, and thus proceeded to conclude that "our analysis [should] focus on Oregon's departure from traditional procedures. [Judicial] review of the size of punitive damages awards has been a safeguard against excessive verdicts for as long as punitive damages have been awarded. [Yet there] is a dramatic difference between the judicial review of punitive damages awards under the common law and the scope of review available in Oregon. [Oregon's] abrogation of a well-established common law protection against arbitrary deprivations of property raises a presumption that its procedures violate the Due Process Clause. [Punitive] damages pose an acute danger of arbitrary deprivation of property. Jury instructions typically leave the jury with wide discretion in choosing amounts, and the presentation of a defendant's net worth creates the potential that juries will use their verdicts to express biases against big businesses, particularly those without strong local presences. Judicial review of the amount awarded was one of the few procedural safeguards which the common law provided against that danger. Oregon has removed that safeguard without providing any substitute procedure." Justice SCALIA wrote a brief concurring opinion reiterating the importance of the existence of the traditional procedure in evaluating the procedural due process claim. Justice GINSBURG, joined by Chief Justice Rehnquist, dissented. She questioned the majority's reliance on the procedures that happened traditionally to exist at common law, and argued that the procedures Oregon had in place to limit arbitrary punitive damages awards were sufficient to satisfy the requirements set out in Haslip and TXO.

12th ED., p. 573; IND. RTS., p. 244

Add at beginning of footnote 2:

On other substantive and procedural due process aspects of commitment of the mentally ill, see Foucha v. Louisiana, 504 U.S. 71 (1992), described at length below, addition to 12th Ed., p. 598; Ind. Rts., p. 269. And note also Heller v. Doe, 510 U.S. ___ (1993), described at length below, addition to 12th Ed., p. 635; Ind.Rts., p. 306.

12th ED., p. 573; IND. RTS., p. 244

Add at end of footnote 2:

In Collins v. Harker Heights, Texas, 503 U.S. 115 (1992), a unanimous Supreme Court, with Justice Stevens writing the opinion, held that Youngberg and other cases on the due process requirement of minimum standards for treatment were restricted to cases involving what would otherwise be a deprivation of liberty, as with pretrial detainees, persons in mental institutions, and convicted felons. Where, as in Collins, the substantive due process claim was based on an argument about minimal safety conditions for a government *employee*, the absence of a deprivation of liberty made the Youngberg-based argument inapplicable.

In the context of physical confinement, note also RENO v. FLORES, 507 U.S. __ (1993), a challenge to an Immigration and Naturalization Service regulation mandating custody (pending a deportation hearing) for potentially deportable juveniles who could not be released to parents, close relatives, or legal guardians. The alien juveniles argued that they had a substantive due process right to be free from physical confinement, and that the INS could not show a compelling interest in requiring them to remain in child care institutions where non-institutional alternatives were available. Justice SCALIA's opinion for the court, while recognizing the substantive due process right to freedom from physical confinement, denied its applicability here, and refused to recognize a fundamental right for juveniles to be released from custody in these circumstances. Justice O'CONNOR's concurring opinion, joined by Justice Souter, emphasized that for her the custody did trigger due process scrutiny, but that the requirements of both substantive and procedural due process had been met. Justice STEVENS, joined by Justice Blackmun, dissented, arguing that the right to freedom from physical restraint mandated individualized consideration of whether less custodial alternatives were available for individual children.

12th ED., p. 597; IND. RTS., p. 268

Add as new paragraph at end of Note 2:

Paul v. Davis was reaffirmed and applied in a related context in SIEGERT v. GILLEY, 500 U.S. 226 (1991), in which Chief Justice REHNQUIST's opinion for the Court relied heavily on Paul v. Davis to hold that a federal damages action based on Bivens v. Six Unknown Federal Narcotics Agents (1971, described below, 12th Ed., p. 1624; Ind. Rts., p. 1295) could not be maintained where the cause of action was based on action by a federal official that had allegedly injured the plaintiff's reputation. The Chief Justice, moreover, held that the "lack of any constitutional protection for the interest in reputation" was not a function of the *consequences* of the loss of reputation, and that as a result the Paul v. Davis principle was fully applicable even when the plaintiff alleged tangible loss (here the loss of future employment) as a result of the reputational injury. Justice KENNEDY concurred in the judgment only, believing that the case could have been decided solely on the basis of principles about the pleading requirements in the face of a defendant's claim of immunity. Justice MARSHALL, joined by Justices Blackmun and Stevens, dissented, arguing that dismissing the loss of future governmental employment prospects caused by the reputational injury represented an unwarranted extension of Paul v. Davis. Where, as here, it was difficult for the plaintiff to practice his profession outside of the context of government employment, a reputational injury that precluded future governmental employment, Justice Marshall argued, must be treated as the equivalent to dismissal from present governmental employment.

12th ED., p. 598; IND. RTS., p. 269

Add after first sentence of footnote 7:

In Sandin v. Conner, 518 U.S. ___ (1995), the Court explicitly rejected the approach of Hewitt v. Helms, holding that the procedural protections of the due process clause were triggered not merely by the fact of punitive action, but only for those restrictions that "impose[ ] atypical and significant hardship on [an] inmate in relation to the ordinary incidents of prison life."

12th ED., p. 598: IND. RTS., p. 269

Add before parenthetical at end of footnote 7:

Harper was followed in Riggins v. Nevada, 504 U.S. 127 (1992), with Justice O'Connor's majority opinion reaffirming that the due process clause protected the "interest in avoiding the involuntary administration of antipsychotic drugs."

12th ED., p. 598; IND. RTS., p. 269

Add as new paragraphs at end of footnote 7:

A combination of substantive and procedural due process issues have arisen in a number of other cases involving commitment of the mentally ill. In O'Connor v. Donaldson, 422 U.S. 563 (1975), the Court held it an unconstitutional deprivation of due process to continue to confine a mentally ill person who was no longer harmful to self or others. In Addington v. Texas, 441 U.S. 418 (1979), the Court's focus was more procedural, holding that civil commitment of the mentally ill required not only notice and a hearing, but also that the conditions justifying commitment be proved by clear and convincing evidence. And in Jones v. United States, 463 U.S. 354 (1983), the Court held that although the procedural requirements of Addington need not be followed in order to confine a person acquitted of a crime by reason of insanity, due process still required that such person be released when no longer dangerous.

The issue arose most recently in Foucha v. Louisiana, 504 U.S. 71 (1992), in which the majority, with the opinion written by Justice White, struck down as violative of due process a Louisiana scheme pursuant to which a person acquitted by reason of insanity who no longer suffers from any mental illness must still affirmatively prove he is no longer dangerous in order to secure his release. Relying on Vitek v. Jones and the cases noted just above, the Court held that the nature of continuing commitment must "bear some reasonable relation to the purpose for which the individual is committed." Where, as here, the reasons for the initial commitment were found no longer to exist, continued confinement, violated the substantive due process interest in not being deprived of one's liberty on general grounds of dangerousness. Justice O'Connor, although refusing to join the majority's conclusion that there was also an equal protection violation by virtue of discrimination between the mentally ill and others, joined the Court's due process conclusions. Justice Kennedy, however, joined by Chief Justice Rehnquist, dissented, relying largely on the distinction between a simple acquittal and a judgment of not guilty by reason of insanity. The latter verdict, he argued, is not the equivalent of a simple acquittal, and thus a continuing confinement on grounds of dangerousness for a not guilty by reason of insanity acquittee is part of an essentially criminal proceeding in which the defendant has been found by a jury to have committed a criminal act. Justice Thomas, joined by Chief Justice Rehnquist and Justice Scalia, also dissented. Like Justice Kennedy he relied heavily on the existence of a proceeding that had adjudged the defendant to have harmed society by virtue of a criminal act. This proceeding, he argued, satisfied the demands of procedural due process. As to the demands of substantive due process, he chastised the majority for departing for existing substantive due process jurisprudence by neither specifying clearly the nature of the fundamental right involved nor the standard of review applicable to its abridgment. "To the extent the Court invalidates the Louisiana scheme on the ground that it violates some general substantive due process right to 'freedom from bodily restraint' that triggers strict scrutiny, it is wrong—and dangerously so. To the extent the Court suggests that Louisiana has violated some more limited right to freedom from indefinite commitment in a mental facility [that] triggers some unknown standard of review, it is also wrong. [Whatever] the exact scope of the fundamental right to 'freedom from bodily restraint' recognized by our cases, it certainly cannot be defined at the exceedingly great level of generality the Court suggests today.   There is simply no basis in our society's history or in the precedents of this Court to support the existence of a sweeping, general fundamental right to 'freedom from bodily restraint' applicable to *all* persons in *all* contexts."   Finding this legislative scheme to be "at the very least, substantively reasonable," Justice Thomas concluded that it did not violate Snyder's (above, 12th Ed., p. 414; Ind. Rts., p. 85) standard of "offend[ing] some principle of justice so rooted in the traditions and conscience of our people as to be ranked as fundamental," and thus presented no basis for judicial invalidation.

12th ED., p. 599; IND. RTS., p. 270

Add at end of first paragraph of footnote 2:

The most recent of these cases is Connecticut v. Doehr, 501 U.S. 1 (1991), holding that prejudgment real estate attachment violated due process requirements unless preceded either by a hearing or by a showing and finding of particular exigency.

12th ED., p. 600; IND. RTS., p. 271

Add at end of second paragraph of footnote 1:

For a lengthy survey of the contexts in which the Mathews v. Eldridge approach has been employed, see the opinion of Justice Souter in Burns v. United States, 501 U.S. 129 (1991), dissenting from Justice Marshall's opinion for the Court holding that a sentence greater than that set out in the Federal Sentencing Guidelines may be imposed only after notice to the parties stating that the court is considering such an action.

Chapter 9(4)

EQUAL PROTECTION

12th ED., p. 624; IND. RTS., p. 295
Insert new footnote following "by the mere rationality test."

After Massachusetts Bd. of Retirement v. Murgia, age discrimination continues to be an active area of legislative concern, as legislatures continue to struggle with determining which classes are to be protected against age discrimination. The 104th Congress has before it H.R. 849, a bill which would continue to exempt state and local firefighters and law enforcement officers from the Age Discrimination in Employment Act. This measure was passed by the House on March 28, 1995, and awaits action by the Senate. Two bills, however, S. 849 and H.R. 1571, have been introduced which would explicitly bring elected and appointed judges under the coverage of the Age Discrimination in Employment Act.

12th ED., p. 625; IND. RTS., p. 296
Add at end of footnote 8:

For a more recent example of extremely deferential rationality review, see Justice Souter's opinion for a unanimous Court in Burlington Northern Railroad Co. v. Ford, 504 U.S. 648 (1992), upholding a Montana venue provision that allowed out-of-state corporate defendants to be sued in any county, but that required that in-state corporate defendants be sued only where they had their principal place of business.

12th ED., p. 635; IND. RTS., p. 306
Add at end of footnote 1:

In NORDLINGER v. HAHN, 505 U.S. 1 (1992), the Court proceeded to distinguish Allegheny Pittsburgh and uphold California's Proposition 13, imposing an acquisition-value taxation system and consequently benefiting longer-term property owners at the expense of newer property owners. Justice BLACKMUN's majority opinion distinguished Allegheny Pittsburgh, but explicitly not on the grounds that the action in Allegheny Pittsburgh was taken administratively rather than legislatively (or by referendum). Rather, the distinction was based on the presence in California of facts justifying the inference that the benefits of an acquisition-value taxation scheme were actually desired. Commencing with the observation that the rational-basis standard "is especially deferential in the context of classifications made by complex tax laws," Justice Blackmun went on to conclude that "the Equal Protection Clause does not demand for purposes of rational-basis review that a legislature or governing decisionmaker actually articulate at any time the purpose or rationale supporting its classification. Fritz. Nevertheless, this Court's review does require that a purpose may conceivably or may reasonably have been the purpose and policy of the relevant governmental decisionmaker. Allegheny Pittsburgh was the rare case where the facts precluded any plausible inference that the reason for the unequal assessment practice was to achieve the benefits of an acquisition-value tax scheme. By contrast, [Proposition 13] was enacted precisely to achieve the benefits of an acquisition-value system. Allegheny Pittsburgh is not controlling here." Justice THOMAS concurred in part and in the result, but was unpersuaded by the majority's distinction of Allegheny Pittsburgh, and would have upheld the classification in both cases: "I understand that the Court prefers to distinguish Allegheny Pittsburgh, but in doing so [has] left our equal protection jurisprudence in disarray. The analysis appropriate to this case is straightforward. Unless a classification involves suspect classes or fundamental rights, judicial scrutiny under the Equal Protection Clause demands only a conceivable rational basis for the challenged state distinction. This basis need not be one identified by the State itself; in fact, States need not articulate any reasons at all for their actions. Proposition 13 [satisfies] this standard—but so, for the same reasons, did the scheme employed in Webster

217

County." Justice STEVENS dissented, and was the only Justice who proposed that the rational basis standard be applied with more bite and less deference. "[T]he selective provision benefits based on the timing of one's membership in a class (whether that class be the class of residents or the class of property owners) is rarely a 'legitimate state interest.' Similarly situated neighbors have an equal right to share in the benefits of local government. It would obviously be unconstitutional to provide one with more or better fire or police protection than the other; it is just as plainly unconstitutional to require one to pay five times as much in property taxes as the other for the same government services. [The] severe inequalities created by Proposition 13 are arbitrary and unreasonable and do not rationally further a legitimate state interest."

Writing for a majority a year later in FEDERAL COMMUNICATIONS COMMISSION v. BEACH COMMUNICATIONS, INC., 508 U.S. ___ (1993), Justice THOMAS relied heavily on Fritz in emphasizing an extremely deferential stance. In upholding a distinction between cable facilities in the Cable Communications Policy Act of 1984, he cited Fritz repeatedly, and provided the following recapitulation: "Whether embodied in the Fourteenth Amendment or inferred from the Fifth, equal protection is not a license for courts to judge the wisdom, fairness, or logic of legislative choices. In areas of social and economic policy, a statutory classification that neither proceeds along suspect lines nor infringes fundamental constitutional rights must be upheld against equal protection challenge if there is any reasonably conceivable set of facts that could provide a rational basis for the classification. Where there are 'plausible reasons' for Congress' action, 'our inquiry is at an end.' Fritz. This standard of review is a paradigm of judicial restraint. On rational-basis review, a classification [comes] to us bearing a strong presumption of validity, and those attacking the rationality of the legislative classification have the burden 'to negative every conceivable basis which might support it.' Lehnhausen v. Lake Shore Auto Parts Co., 410 U.S. 356 (1973). Moreover, because we never require a legislature to articulate its reasons for enacting a statute, it is entirely irrelevant for constitutional purposes whether the conceived reason for the challenged distinction actually motivated the legislature. Thus the absence of 'legislative facts' explaining the distinction 'on the record' has no significance in rational-basis analysis. In other words, a legislative choice is not subject to courtroom fact-finding and may be based on rational speculation unsupported by evidence or empirical data." Relying again on Fritz, Justice Thomas said that these limitations on review have "added force" when the legislature is engaged in line-drawing. "In establishing the franchise requirement, Congress had to draw the line somewhere; it had to choose which facilities to franchise. This necessity renders the precise coordinates of the resulting legislative judgment virtually unreviewable, since the legislature must be allowed to approach a perceived problem incrementally. Williamson." Justice STEVENS concurred in the judgment, reaffirming from his opinion in Fritz his desire for somewhat less deferential review "when the actual rationale for the legislation is unclear" and "when Congress imposes a burden on one group, but leaves unaffected another that is similarly, though not identically, situated. [Judicial] review under the 'conceivable set of facts' test is tantamount to no review at all."

Several weeks later, in HELLER v. DOE, 510 U.S. ___ (1993), the Court followed the formulations in FCC v. Beach Communications in upholding a Kentucky scheme that treated the involuntary commitment of the mentally retarded differently from the involuntary commitment of the mentally ill. Because of the procedural posture of the case, the argument for heightened scrutiny was not considered, and thus the only question was whether a lower standard of proof (clear and convincing evidence, as opposed to proof beyond a reasonable doubt) for cases involving commitment of the mentally retarded, along with granting greater rights of intervention for relatives and guardians of the mentally retarded, could satisfy rational basis scrutiny. Writing for the majority, Justice KENNEDY quoted extensively from Beach Communications in concluding that differences in the ease of diagnosis and in the invasiveness of the treatments justified the different standards. In dissent, Justice SOUTER, joined in part by Justices Stevens, Blackmun, and O'Connor, argued that although the disparate rights of participation satisfied rational basis standards, the difference in the burden of proof did not. Relying extensively on numerous professional publications from the mental health field, Justice Souter concluded that no plausible argument, including the majority's arguments about diagnostic ease and invasiveness, could justify the distinction even under the lowest possible scrutiny. (Consider in this regard the possibility that for Justice Souter the category of mental health justified applying more "bite" to rational basis scrutiny than would have been the case for other legislative distinctions.)

Equal protection questions in general, and questions about the standard of review in particular, have been at the center of recent lower court litigation regarding sexual orientation. Much of this litigation has involved the military, whose traditional policy of excluding gays and lesbians has been changed only slightly by recent regulations limiting the extent to which military officials may actively investigate the sexual orientation of members of the service. Most of this litigation seeks to challenge the basic military policy of deeming homosexuality incompatible with military service. A prominent and recent example is Cammermeyer v. Aspin, 850 F.Supp. 910 (W.D.Wash.1994), in which Judge Zilly ordered the United States Army and the Washington National Guard to reinstate Colonel Margarethe Cammermeyer after having discharged her against her will because she had admitted, upon questioning in connection with a security clearance, that she was a lesbian. Two issues emerged as central. The first was the distinction between conduct and orientation. Recognizing that Bowers v. Hardwick (1986; above, 12th Ed., p. 565; Ind.Rts., p. 236) forclosed a challenge to the Army's power to dismiss Colonel Cammermeyer on the basis of homosexual conduct, Judge Zilly distinguished conduct from orientation, and concluded that there was no evidence that Colonel Cammermeyer had done anything but disclose her orientation, an orientation that Judge Zilly said could not necessarily be equated with having engaged in the kind of conduct that would justify dismissal. "The Court concludes that plaintiff's acknowledgement of her lesbian orientation itself is not reliable evidence of her desire or propensity to engage in homosexual conduct. The Court therefore concludes that there is no rational basis for the Government's underlying contention that homosexual orientation equals 'desire or propensity to engage' in homosexual conduct."

Judge Zilly's selection of a rational basis standard was the other central issue. Because the Court of Appeals for the Ninth Circuit had, in High Tech Gays v. Defense Industrial Security Clearance Office, 895 F.2d 563 (9th Cir.1990), rejected arguments for heightened standards of review in cases of sexual orientation, Judge Zilly applied the rational basis standard dictated in that case. He relied heavily on Heller v. Doe, however, for his definition of the rational basis standard, concluding that under that version of rationality review the military's policy could not be rationally defended, but was only the embodiment of a "prejudice" that could not withstand even Heller-variety rationality review.

Courts continue to try to define the parameters of equal protection in a variety of military contexts. In Dahl v. Secretary of the Navy, 830 F.Supp. 1319 (E.D.Cal.1993), Judge Schwartz found that the Navy's policy of excluding homosexuals violated an enlistee's right to equal protection. The case of Keith Meinhold involved a servicemember discharged from the Navy for admitting that he was gay. The Ninth Circuit, relying heavily on a court's duty to interpret regulations to preserve their constitutionality, and also on general deference to the military's judgment, found that an inference of homosexual conduct or intent to engage in such conduct could not be inferred in Meinhold's particular case from his statements. Meinhold was allowed to resume his position in the Navy. A nationwide injunction against the Department of Defense regulations could not be supported in Meinhold, however, because other statements by servicemembers might support a "desire" to engage in prohibited conduct strong enough to support an inference of future homosexual conduct. Meinhold v. U.S. Dept. of Defense, 34 F.3d 1469 (9th Cir.1994). On March 30, 1995, six active-duty and reserve servicemembers won a victory when Judge Nickerson declared the so-called "don't ask, don't tell" policy, codified at 10 U.S.C. § 654(b)(2), and the directives implementing the policy, invalid under both the First Amendment and the equal protection dimension of the due process clause of the Fifth Amendment. Able v. United States, 880 F.Supp. 968 (E.D.N.Y.1995).

Some cases, however, have upheld military restrictions on homosexuality. The case of Steffan v. Perry, 41 F.3d 677 (D.C.Cir.1994) involved the forced resignation of a midshipman from the Naval Academy. The majority opinion of Judge Silberman, in an en banc review, relied heavily on a rational basis standard, but found that admission of homosexuality itself was so related to conduct that both Naval Academy regulations and Department of Defense policy easily met the rational basis threshold. There were several dissenting opinions. In Philips v. Perry, 883 F.Supp. 1319 (W.D.Wash.1995), statements made to a senior officer regarding homosexual conduct with non-servicemembers was sufficient to establish an intent to engage in future homosexual conduct, and were held by the court not protected by the First Amendment as political speech. The discharge of the servicemember was upheld.

12th ED., p. 653: IND. RTS., p. 324

Add at end of footnote 2:

Debates about the propriety of judicial reliance on contestable or changeable social science findings, particular with reference to psychology, continue to take place. See especially the clash between the majority and the dissent in Lee v. Weisman (1992; below, addition to 12th Ed., p. 1529; Ind.Rts., p. 1200), regarding the appropriateness of reliance on psychological studies to reach conclusions about the issue of the voluntariness of prayers in school ceremonies, and the dispute in Planned Parenthood of Southeastern Pennsylvania v. Casey (1992; below, addition to 12th Ed., p. 553; Ind.Rts., p. 224), about various issues relating to the conditions under which states can require that parents or spouses be notified prior to a woman's abortion.

12th ED., p. 675; IND. RTS., p. 346

Add as new Note 4 after Note 3 (Mississippi University for Women):

4. J.E.B. v. ALABAMA ex rel. T.B., 508 U.S. ___ (1994): Here the Court struck down gender-based peremptory challenges to jurors, thus following its similar action eight years earlier in Batson v. Kentucky, 476 U.S. 79 (1986) in the case of race-based peremptory challenges (see below, 12th Ed., p. 705; Ind.Rts., p. 376). In J.E.B., the underlying case was a proceeding brought by the state to establish paternity and award child support. The state used its peremptory challenges to strike male jurors, the consequence of which was the empaneling of an all-woman jury. Writing for the Court, Justice BLACKMUN found that action by the state unconstitutional. The state had argued that " 'gender discrimination in this country ... has never reached the level of discrimination' against African–Americans, and therefore gender discrimination, unlike racial discrimination, is tolerable in the courtroom." Justice Blackmun rejected the argument, however, and went on to find Alabama's justifications insufficient:

"We need not determine [whether] women or racial minorities have suffered more at the hands of discriminatory state actors during the decades of our Nation's history. It is necessary only to acknowledge that 'our Nation has had a long and unfortunate history of sex discrimination,' Frontiero, a history which warrants the heightened scrutiny we afford all gender-based classifications today. Under our equal protection jurisprudence, gender-based classifications require 'an exceedingly persuasive justification' in order to survive constitutional scrutiny. [In] making this assessment, we do not weigh the value of peremptory challenges as an institution against our asserted commitment to eradicate invidious discrimination from the courtroom. Instead, we consider whether peremptory challenges based on gender stereotypes provide substantial aid to a litigant's effort to secure a fair and impartial jury. Far from proffering an exceptionally persuasive justification for its gender-based peremptory challenges, respondent maintains that its decision to strike virtually all the males from the jury '[may] reasonably have been based upon the perception, supported by history, that men otherwise totally qualified to serve on a jury might be more sympathetic and receptive to the arguments of a man alleged in a paternity action to be the father of an out-of-wedlock child, while women equally qualified to serve on an jury might be more sympathetic and receptive to the arguments of the complaining witness who bore the child.' We shall not accept as a defense to gender-based peremptory challenges 'the very stereotype the law condemns.' Powers v. Ohio, 499 U.S. 400 (1991). Respondent's rationale [is] reminiscent of the arguments [previously] advanced to justify the total exclusion of women from juries. Respondent offers virtually no support for the conclusion that gender alone is an accurate predictor of juror's attitudes; yet it urges this Court to condone the same stereotypes that justified the wholesale exclusion of women from juries and the ballot box. [The state] seems to assume that gross generalizations that would be deemed impermissible if made on the basis of race are somehow permissible when made on the basis of gender. [When] state actors exercise peremptory challenges in reliance on gender stereotypes, they ratify and reinforce prejudicial views of the relative abilities of men and women. [The] potential for [public cynicism about jury neutrality] is particularly acute in cases where gender-related issues are prominent, such as cases involving rape, sexual harassment, or paternity. [In] view of these concerns, the Equal Protection Clause prohibits discrimination in jury selection on the basis of gender, or on the assumption that an individual will be biased in a particular case for no reason other than the fact that the person happens to be a woman or happens to be a man."

In an important concurring opinion, Justice O'CONNOR expressed concern about the continued erosion of the necessarily discretionary and intuitive aspect of peremptory strikes, even though she agreed with the majority, at least with respect to peremptory strikes by the government. The importance of her opinion, however, lies in its contrast with Justice Blackmun's on the issue of the relevance of gender to juror attitudes. "Nor is the value of the peremptory challenge to the litigant diminished when the peremptory is exercised in a gender-based manner. We know that like race, gender matters. A plethora of studies make clear that in rape cases, for example, female jurors are somewhat more likely to vote to convict than male jurors. Moreover, although there have been no similarly definitive studies regarding, for example, sexual harassment, child custody, or spousal or child abuse, one need not be a sexist to share the intuition that in certain cases a person's gender and resulting life experience will be relevant to his or her view of the case. [Individuals] are not expected to ignore as jurors what they know as men—or women. Today's decision severely limits a litigant's ability to act on this intuition, for the import of our holding is that any correlation between a juror's gender and attitudes is irrelevant as a matter of constitutional law. But to say that gender makes no difference as a matter of law is not to say that gender makes no difference as a matter of fact. [Today's] decision is a statement that, in an effort to eliminate the potential discriminatory use of the peremptory, gender is now governed by the special rule of relevance formerly reserved for race. Though we gain much from this statement, we cannot ignore what we lose. In extending Batson to gender we have [diminished] the ability of litigants to act on sometimes accurate gender-based assumptions about juror attitudes.

These concerns reinforce my conviction that today's decision should be limited to a prohibition on the government's use of gender-based peremptory challenges [because the] Equal Protection Clause prohibits only discrimination by state actors."

Justice KENNEDY also issues a concurring opinion, emphasizing that "it is important to recognize that a juror sits not as a representative of a racial or sexual group but as an individual citizen. Nothing would be more pernicious to the jury system than for society to presume that persons of different backgrounds go to the jury room to voice prejudice. [Once] seated, a juror should not give free rein to some racial or gender bias of his or her own. [A juror] who allows racial or gender bias to influence assessment of the case breaches the compact and renounces his or her oath. [The] jury pool must be representative of the community, but that is a structural mechanism for preventing bias, not enfranchising it."

Chief Justice REHNQUIST wrote a brief dissenting opinion, concluding that "the two sexes differ, both biologically and, to a diminishing extent, in experience. It is not merely 'stereotyping' to say that these differences may produce a difference in outlook which is brought into the jury room. Accordingly, use of peremptory challenges on the basis of sex is generally not the sort of derogatory and invidious act which peremptory challenges directed at black jurors may be." Justice SCALIA, joined by Chief Justice Rehnquist and Justice Thomas, also dissented, and at much greater length. He opened by chastising the majority for what he perceived to be an excess willingness to follow contemporary political trends. "Today's opinion is an inspiring demonstration of how thoroughly up-to-date and right-thinking we Justices are in matters pertaining to the sexes (or as the Court would have it, genders), and how sternly we disapprove the male chauvinist attitudes of our predecessors. The [Court] stresses the lack of statistical evidence to support the widely held belief that, at least in certain types of cases, a juror's sex has some statistically significant predictive value as to how a juror will behave. This assertion seems to place the Court in opposition to its earlier Sixth Amendment 'fair cross-section' cases. But times and trends do change, and unisex is unquestionably in fashion. Personally, I am less inclined to demand statistics, and more inclined to credit the perceptions of experienced litigators who have had money on the line. But it does not matter. The Court's fervent defense of the proposition *il n'y a pas de différence entre les hommes et les femmes* (it stereotypes the opposite view as hateful stereotyping) turns out to be [utterly] irrelevant" because the complaining party has suffered no injury. If "men and women jurors are (as the Court thinks) fungible, then the only arguable injury from the prosecutor's 'impermissible' use of male sex as the basis for his peremptories is injury to the stricken juror, not to the defendant. [Although] the Court's legal reasoning in this case is largely obscured by anti-male-chauvinist oratory, to the extent such reasoning is discernible it invalidates much more than sex-based strikes. [The] Court applies the "heightened scrutiny" mode of equal-protection analysis used for sex-based discrimination, and concludes that the strikes fail heightened scrutiny because they do not substantially further an important government interest. [The] Court refuses to accept [the state's] argument that these strikes further [an interest in securing a fair and impartial jury] by eliminating a group (men) which may be partial to male defendants, because it will not accept any argument based on 'the very stereotype the law condemns.' This [implies] that sex-based strikes do not even rationally further a legitimate government interest, let alone pass heightened scrutiny. That places *all* peremptory strikes at risk, since they can all be denominated 'stereotypes.' Perhaps, however (although I do not see why it should be so), only the stereotyping of groups entitled to heightened or strict scrutiny constitutes 'the very stereotype the law condemns'—so that other stereotyping (e.g., wide-eyed blondes and football players are dumb) remains OK. Or perhaps when the Court refers to 'impermissible stereotypes,' it means the adjective to be limiting rather than descriptive—so that we can expect to learn from the Court's peremptory/stereotyping jurisprudence in the future which stereotypes the Constitution frowns on and which it does not."

12th ED., p. 679; IND. RTS., p. 350

Add to end to footnote 11 (on p. 680):

Similar issues were before the Court in the highly-publicized decision in International Union, United Automobile, Aerospace and Agricultural Implement Workers of America v. Johnson Controls, Inc., 499 U.S. 187 (1991), in which Justice Blackmun's opinion for the Court held it to be a violation of Title VII for an employer to preclude women from holding certain jobs because of a fear that those jobs would endanger the health of a fetus. In addition to relying on evidence showing male exposure to the same conditions could also have effects on future children, Justice Blackmun made clear that even a statistically-based distinction between men and women in this respect would be insufficient to justify the gender-based policy. "[T]he absence of a malevolent motive does not convert a facially discriminatory policy into a neutral policy with a discriminatory effect. Whether an employment practice involves disparate treatment does not depend on why the employer discriminates but rather on the explicit terms of the discrimination." He went on to conclude that neither the heavier incidence of the risk for women nor the desire to avoid civil liability constituted a bona fide occupational qualification (BFOQ), which would, pursuant to Title VII, make permissible an otherwise unlawful discrimination on the basis of gender.

12th ED., p. 701; IND. RTS., p. 372

Add as footnote at end of Cleburne case:

* Note also Heller v. Doe, 510 U.S. ___ (1993), described above, addition to 12th Ed., p. 635; Ind.Rts., p. 306, in which the Court, for procedural reasons, refused to consider the question whether a distinction between the procedures for commitment of the mentally retarded and those for commitment of the mentally ill should be evaluated against a standard higher than mere rationality. And consider whether Justice SOUTER's dissent, arguing that a differential burden of proof did not even satisfy rational basis scrutiny, was based on an implicit elevation of the level of scrutiny.

12th ED., p. 701; IND. RTS., p. 372

Add at end of footnote 2:

For a specific reaffirmance and application of the deferential standard of Murgia, see Gregory v. Ashcroft, 501 U.S. 452 (1991), described at length above and below, addition to 12th Ed., p. 175; addition to 12th Ed., p. 993, upholding against an equal protection challenge the section of the Missouri Constitution requiring state judges to retire at age 70.

12th ED., p. 705; IND. RTS., p. 376

Add at end of footnote 3:

In Powers v. Ohio, 499 U.S. 400 (1991), the Court held that claims pursuant to Batson were not limited to those cases in which the objector is the same race as the excluded jurors. Justice Kennedy's opinion for the Court concluded that a white defendant could object to the exclusion of black jurors, because "a prosecutor's discriminatory use of peremptory challenges harms the excluded jurors and the community at large." He went on to hold that the defendant had standing as *jus tertii* (see below, 12th Ed., pp. 1624–26; Ind. Rts., pp. 1295–97) to raise these claims, both because the defendant had sufficient motivation to be an effective advocate for them, and because it was unlikely that they could be raised effectively in any other way. Justice Scalia, joined by Chief Justice Rehnquist, dissented, objecting both to the allowance of standing and to the related merits of the equal protection determination. "[I]t is intolerably offensive for the State to imprison a person on the basis of a conviction rendered by a jury from which members of that person's minority race were carefully excluded. I am unmoved, however, and I think most Americans would be, by this white defendant's complaint that he was sought to be tried by an all-white jury, or that he should be permitted to press black jurors' unlodged complaint that they were not allowed to sit in judgment of him."

And in Hernandez v. New York, 500 U.S. 352 (1991), a claim under Batson suggested but did not resolve a number of more pervasive equal protection issues. At issue was the action of a prosecutor in striking several Hispanic jurors because he feared that their Spanish-language abilities would interfere with their ability to rely exclusively on the official translation of the testimony of Spanish-speaking witnesses. Justice Kennedy's plurality opinion, joined by Chief Justice Rehnquist and Justices White and Souter, upheld the trial judge's determination that no intentional race-based discrimination was present here, and said that the disproportionate impact of exclusions would not itself necessarily constitute intentional discrimination based on race. Justice Kennedy's opinion, however, left open the issue of when decisions based on language might either be evidence of or themselves constitute intentional discrimination based on race. Justice O'Connor, joined by Justice Scalia, concurred only in the judgment, explicitly denying that a language-based governmental decision, however intentional and however disproportionate in its impact, could ever constitute discrimination on the basis of race. "[These strikes based on doubts about the abilities of these jurors to accept the official translation] may have acted like strikes based on race, but they were *not* based on race. No matter how closely tied or significantly correlated to race the explanation for a peremptory strike may be, the strike does not implicate the Equal Protection Clause unless it is based on race. That is the distinction between disproportionate effect, which is not sufficient to constitute an equal protection violation, and intentional discrimination, which is." Justice Stevens, joined by Justice Marshall and in part by Justice Blackmun, dissented, arguing that in light of the disproportionate impact of the strikes, the burden of justification fell to the prosecutor, whose explanation "should have been rejected as a matter of law." (See also Edmonson v. Leesville Concrete Co., 500 U.S. 614 (1991), described at length below, addition to 12th Ed., p. 924; Ind. Rts., p. 595, holding Batson and Powers applicable to peremptory strikes by private litigants in civil litigation). And see especially J.E.B. v. ALABAMA ex rel. T.B., 508 U.S. ___ (1994), described at length above, addition to 12th Ed., p. 675; Ind.Rts., p. 346, applying Batson to peremptory challenges exercised on the basis of gender.

12th ED., p. 707; IND. RTS., p. 378

Add at end of footnote 7:

Gomillion and Wright figured prominently in the Court's most recent racial gerrymandering case, Shaw v. Reno, 510 U.S. ___ (1993), set out below, addition to 12th Ed., p. 819; Ind.Rts., p. 490.

12th ED., p. 708; IND. RTS., p. 379

Add at end of footnote 10 (on p. 709):

After several years of debate centering around the appropriate legislative response to a number of Supreme Court decisions, Congress in 1991 finally passed a comprehensive civil rights bill (S. 1745), signed into law by President Bush on November 22, 1991. This legislation, the Civil Rights Act of 1991 (P.L. 102–166, 105 Stat. 1071), codified Griggs v. Duke Power (1971; 12th Ed., p. 708; Ind.Rts., p. 379) and reversed Wards Cove Packing Co. v. Atonio (1989; 12th Ed., p. 708; Ind.Rts., p. 379). Numerous compromises preceded the passage of the legislation, and equally numerous issues remain open. Most significantly, Congress failed to define the "justified by business necessity" defense, and did not state specifically whether the legislation applied retroactively. The Act places caps on the amount of monetary damages recoverable in sex discrimination cases. Ironically, the Wards Cove workers themselves were exempted from the legislation at the insistence of the Alaska delegation.

In addition to reversing Wards Cove, the legislation also reversed or changed five other recent Supreme Court decisions: Patterson v. McLean Credit Union (1989; 12th Ed., p. 951; Ind.Rts., p. 622) (statute bars racial harassment and other forms of bias even after a person is hired); Martin v. Wilks (1989; 12th Ed., p. 782; Ind.Rts., p. 453) (statute allows third party challenges to consent decrees); Price Waterhouse v. Hopkins (1989; 12th Ed., p. 726; Ind.Rts., p. 397) (statute says race, color, religion, sex, national origin cannot be a factor regardless of whether other factors also motivated the decision); Lorance v. AT & T Technologies, Inc., 490 U.S. 900 (1990) (statute provides deadline for bringing suit on a seniority policy not tied to date of company's adoption of policy); and EEOC v. Arabian American Oil Co., 499 U.S. 244 (1991) (statute allows employment discrimination suits by American workers abroad against U.S.-based companies). The legislation also bars "race norming" of test scores, an issue which had not yet reached the Supreme Court.

Another controversial aspect of the legislation was the explicit attempt to shape the legislative history and limit the parts of that history that could be used by an interpreting court. On October 25, 1991, some sponsors of the bill inserted a three paragraph memorandum into the Congressional Record which they maintained represented the bill's "exclusive legislative history". Given the repudiation of that claimed exclusivity by others later in the Congressional debate, and given Justice Scalia's oft-expressed hostility to the use of legislative history as an important basis for statutory interpretation (see, e.g., Wisconsin Public Intervenor v. Mortier (1991; addition to 12th Ed., p. 300: "we are a Government of laws not of committee reports"), this attempt at conscious manipulation of the legislative history is likely to be raised in future litigation.

In Landgraf v. USI Film Products, 509 U.S. ___ (1994), and Rivers v. Roadway Express, Inc., 509 U.S. ___ (1994), discussed at greater length above, addition to 12th Ed. and Ind.Rts., p. 28, the Supreme Court, by a vote of eight to one, held that the provisions of the Civil Rights Act of 1991 did not apply to cases arising before its enactment. Justice Stevens wrote the majority opinion, analyzing in detail the history and rationale of the presumption against statutory retroactivity, a presumption requiring specific congressional intent to overcome. The Court did not find such an intent here, even with respect to the section of the Act designed to "overrule" Patterson v. McLean Credit Union.

Political commitment to end affirmative action was one of the hallmarks of the Republican 1994 election campaign, and the 104th Congress has before it several proposals both to uphold and to eliminate affirmative action. The House Subcommittee on Employer–Employee Relations held hearings March 24, 1995, on the issue of affirmative action. House bills which would support affirmative action include H.R. 177, the Diversity in Media Act of 1995, H.R. 187, and H.R. 503, all of which would mandate the F.C.C. to increase minority and female presence among telecommunications licensees. H.R. 382 would prohibit discrimination based on sexual orientation, and H.R. 190 would strengthen the E.E.O.C. H.R. 658, the Justice for Wards Cove Workers Act, would specifically overturn the Wards Cove decision. On the other hand, H.R. 1764, the Act to End Unfair Preferential Treatment, and H.R. 1840, the American Action Act of 1995, would eliminate affirmative action in all federal programs. Senate bills to eliminate affirmative action, all introduced by Senator Helms, include the Civil Rights Restoration Act of 1995 (S. 26, S. 318) and his version of the Act to End Unfair Preferential Treatment (S. 497). A Department of Labor review of affirmative action programs is to be submitted to President Clinton during the summer of 1995. The most notable accomplishment of the 104th Congress regarding civil rights may be the passage of the Congressional Accountability Act of 1995 (P.L. 104–1), which applies the major civil rights statutory requirements to Congress itself for the first time.

12th ED., p. 727; IND. RTS., p. 398
Add as new footnote at end of Hunter v. Underwood:

2. The age of the constitutional provision at issue in Hunter raises the question of the circumstances under which governmental action has been "cleansed" of prior discriminatory intent. On this issue as it arises in the context of school desegregation, see Board of Education of Oklahoma City Public Schools v. Dowell, 498 U.S. 237 (1991), described at length below, addition to 12th Ed., p. 750, Ind. Rts., p. 421.

12th ED., p. 750; IND. RTS., p. 421
Add as new footnote after "showing" at end of first paragraph:

13. In response to Missouri v. Jenkins, various bills have been proposed that would bar federal judges from mandating tax expenditures as a remedy. H.R. 212, S. 51.

12th ED., p. 750; IND. RTS., p. 421
Add after Note 4b (enforcing compliance):

c. *Measuring compliance with long-standing decrees.* As the years pass, and as overt resistance becomes rarer, questions arise about the temporal limits of a desegregation decree. At what point is it possible to say that a decree, originally entered to remedy de jure segregation, is no longer necessary? Does compliance with a decree bring judicial involvement to an end unless there is evidence of new de jure segregation?

These questions came to the Court in BOARD OF EDUCATION OF OKLAHOMA CITY PUBLIC SCHOOLS v. DOWELL, 498 U.S. 237 (1991). Oklahoma City had at the time of Brown v. Board of Education operated an explicitly segregated school system. Suit challenging that system was first filed in 1961, and the District Court in 1963 ordered relief aimed at dismantling the intentionally created system of segregated schools. After finding previous school board efforts unsuccessful, in 1972 the District Court ordered system-wide busing. That plan produced substantial integration in the public schools, and in 1977 the court entered an order terminating the case and ending its jurisdiction, saying that "The School Board, under the oversight of the Court, has operated the Plan properly, and the Court does not foresee that the termination of its jurisdiction will result in the dismantlement of the Plan or any affirmative action by the defendant to undermine the unitary school system so slowly and painfully accomplished over the 16 years during which the cause has been pending before this court."

In part because of demographic changes that had "led to greater burdens on young black children," the school board in 1984 reintroduced a neighborhood school system for grades K–4, although allowing any student to transfer from a school in which he or she was in the majority to a school in which he or she would be in the minority. A year later a "Motion to Reopen the Case" was filed with the District Court, the petitioners arguing that the new plan would reinstitute segregation. The District Court refused to reopen the case, but the Court of Appeals reversed, holding that the 1972 decree remained in force and imposed an "affirmative duty ... not to take any action that would impede the process of disestablishing the dual system and its effects." The Supreme Court, however, reversed the Tenth Circuit, with Chief Justice REHN-QUIST writing for the majority. "From the very first, federal supervision of local school systems was intended as a temporary measure to remedy past discrimination." Emphasizing that both Brown and Green had stressed the idea of a "transition," the Chief Justice rejected the Court of Appeals' reliance on precedents from antitrust cases like United States v. Swift, 286 U.S. 106 (1932), and concluded instead that "injunctions entered in school desegregation cases [are] not intended to operate in perpetuity. [The] legal justification for displacement of local authority by an injunctive decree in a school desegregation case is a violation of the Constitution by the local authorities. Dissolving a desegregation decree after the local authorities have operated in compliance with it for a reasonable period of time recognizes that 'necessary concern for the important values of local control of public school systems dictates that a federal court's regulatory control of such systems not extend beyond the time required to remedy the effects of past intentional discrimination. See Milliken II.' Spangler v. Pasadena City Bd. of Education, 611 F.2d 1239, 1245 (9th Cir.1979) (Kennedy, J., concurring)."

The Court acknowledged that a "district court need not accept at face value the profession of a school board which has intentionally discriminated that it will cease to do so in the future." But it noted that the personnel of school boards changes over time, and that "a school board's compliance with previous court orders is obviously relevant" in determining whether to modify or dissolve a desegregation decree. The Court remanded the case for just such a determination of good faith compliance as of 1985. If such good faith compliance were found, however, and if "the vestiges of past discrimination" had as of that date been eliminated, then the school board could be deemed to have been released from the injunction. "A school district which has been released from an injunction imposing a desegregation plan no longer requires court authorization for the promulgation of policies and rules regulating matters such as assignment of students and the like, but of course remains subject to the mandates of the Equal Protection Clause of the Fourteenth Amendment. If the Board was entitled to have the decree terminated as of 1985, the District Court should then evaluate the Board's decision to implement [the neighborhood schools program] under appropriate equal protection principles. Washington v. Davis. Arlington Heights v. Metropolitan Housing Development Corp."

Justice MARSHALL, joined by Justices Blackmun and Stevens, dissented, chastising the majority for suggesting that after 65 years of official segregation, "13 years of desegregation was enough. [I] believe a desegregation decree cannot be lifted so long as conditions likely to inflict the stigmatic injury condemned in Brown I persist and there remain feasible methods of eliminating such conditions. [By] focusing heavily on present and future compliance with the Equal Protection Clause, the majority's standard ignores how the stigmatic harm identified in Brown I can persist even after the State ceases actively to enforce segregation. [Our] school-desegregation jurisprudence establishes that the *effects* of past discrimination remain chargeable to the school district regardless of its lack of continued enforcement of segregation, and the remedial decree is required until those effects have been finally eliminated. [Our] cases have imposed on school districts an unconditional duty to eliminate *any* condition that perpetuates the message of racial inferiority inherent in the policy of state-sponsored segregation. The racial identifiability of a district's schools is such a condition. [In] a district with a history of state-sponsored school segregation, racial separation, in my view, *remains* inherently unequal."

The Court returned to the issue a year later in FREEMAN v. PITTS, 503 U.S. 467 (1992), and followed Dowell in approving partial withdrawal of judicial supervision of a school system that had long operated under a desegregation order.

The school system at issue was the DeKalb County (Georgia) School System, serving approximately 73,000 students. The system entered a consent decree in 1969, and had operated under relatively inactive judicial supervision from that date until 1986, when it moved to dismiss the decree, contending that it had successfully desegregated its school system and replaced a dual school system with a unitary one. The District Court found that although there was considerably greater racial imbalance in the schools than there had been in 1969, this was a function of demographic changes rather than any of the vestiges of a previously dual system. In 1969 the System had 5.6% black students, and in 1986 it had 47%. Although there was considerable racial imbalance, the District Court attributed that to the residential patterns of the demographic changes, noting that the existence of effective desegregation for a few years after 1969 was strong evidence of the lack of a connection between the previous segregation and the current racial imbalance. But although the District Court concluded that no current vestiges of the dual school system existed with respect to student assignments and physical facilities, there was as yet no unitary system in the areas of teacher and principal assignments, resource allocation, and some aspects of quality of education. As a result, it withdrew from supervision in the former areas, but refused to dismiss the decree.

The school system appealed from the refusal to dismiss, and a group of objecting parents appealed from the finding of effective desegregation. The Court of Appeals upheld the District Court's refusal to dismiss, but reversed on the issue of the unitary status of the system, holding that only when all of the factors specified in Green had been satisfied simultaneously could a school district be considered to have desegregated its system. The Supreme Court, however, with Justice KENNEDY writing for the majority, concluded both that the District Court's views about desegregation were substantially correct, and that a partial dismissal of the decree would therefore be appropriate.

Justice Kennedy focused on Green as the watershed case in desegregation compliance, but emphasized that the terms "dual" and "unitary" should not be taken as overriding a court's equitable responsibilities, nor as substitutes for the remedial court's power focused only on the correction of the condition that had violated the Constitution. "The essence of a court's equity power lies in its inherent capacity to adjust remedies in a feasible and practical way to eliminate the conditions or redress the injuries caused by unlawful action." Stressing the limitation of the remedy to those conditions that violated the Constitution, Justice

Kennedy relied heavily on Pasadena City Bd. of Educ. v. Spangler (1976, noted above, 12th Ed., p. 733; Ind. Rts., p. 404) in reaffirming the proposition that a District Court "exceed[s] its remedial authority in requiring annual readjustment of school attendance zones [when] changes in the racial makeup of the schools were caused by demographic shifts 'not attributed to any segregative acts on the part of the [school district.' [A] federal court in a school desegregation case has the discretion to order an incremental or partial withdrawal of its supervision and control. This discretion derives both from the constitutional authority which justified its intervention in the first instance and its ultimate objectives in formulating the decree. The authority of the court is invoked at the outset to remedy particular constitutional violations. In construing the remedial authority of the district courts, we have been guided by the principle[ ] [that a] remedy is justifiable only insofar as it advances the ultimate objective of alleviating the initial constitutional violation."

The Court focused on the value of the goal of local control over schools, and on the consequent necessity of seeing federal judicial supervision as temporary. "We hold that [federal] courts have the authority to relinquish supervision and control of school districts in incremental stages, before full compliance has been achieved in every area of school operations. [The] court in appropriate cases may return control to the school system in those areas where compliance has been achieved, limiting further judicial supervision to operations that are not yet in full compliance with the court decree. In particular, the district court may determine that it will not order further remedies in the area of student assignments where racial imbalance is not traceable, in a proximate way, to constitutional violations. [Where] resegregation is a product not of state action but of private choices, it does not have constitutional implications. It is beyond the authority and beyond the practical ability of the federal courts to try to counteract these kinds of continuous and massive demographic shifts. [In] one sense of the term, vestiges of past segregation by state decree do remain in our society and in our schools. Past wrongs to the black race, wrongs committed by the State and in its name, are a stubborn fact of history. And stubborn facts of history linger and persist. But though we cannot escape our history, neither must we overstate its consequences in fixing legal responsibilities. The vestiges of segregation that are the concern of the law in a school case may be subtle and intangible but nonetheless they must be so real that they have a causal link to the de jure violation being remedied. It is simply not always the case that demographic forces causing population change bear any real and substantial relation to a de jure violation. And the law need not proceed on that premise."

Justice SCALIA concurred, warning that this judgment would not do as much as he thought ought to be done in returning schools to local control. This case "will have little [effect] upon the many other school districts throughout the country that are still supervised by federal judges, since it turns upon the extraordinarily rare circumstances of a *finding* that no portion of the current racial imbalance is a remnant of prior de jure discrimination. [We] must resolve—if not today, then soon—what is to be done in the vast majority of other districts, where, though our cases continue to profess that judicial oversight of school operations is a temporary expedient, democratic processes remain suspended, with no prospect of restoration, 38 years after Brown. [At] some time, we must acknowledge that it has become absurd to assume, without any further proof, that violations of the Constitution dating from the days when Lyndon Johnson was President, or earlier, continue to have an appreciable effect upon current operation of schools. We are close to that time. While we must continue to prohibit, without qualification, all racial discrimination in the operation of the public schools, and to afford remedies that eliminate not only the discrimination but its identified consequences, we should consider laying aside the extraordinary, and increasingly counterfactual, presumption [of de jure effect] of Green. We must soon revert to the ordinary principles of law [and require] that plaintiffs alleging Equal Protection violations [ ] prove intent and causation and not merely the existence of racial disparity.''

Justice SOUTER also issued a concurring opinion, mainly to note several possibilities in which racial imbalance may be an indication of other constitutionally cognizable factors. One is where a residential or demographic change does not occur independently of school segregation, but is instead itself a product of prior unconstitutional school segregation. In those cases, he urged, racial imbalance should not be considered immune from continued judicial supervision. And where there is a risk that those aspects of segregation that have yet to be completely remedied (as with teacher and principal assignments in this case) might prompt resegregation in the event of judicial withdrawal, a court withdrawing partially should satisfy itself that the area from which it withdraws should not be at risk from those areas in which compliance has yet to be achieved.

Justice BLACKMUN, joined by Justices Stevens and O'Connor, concurred in the judgment, first emphasizing that judicial withdrawal from active supervision in some area did not indicate withdrawal of jurisdiction, and that the courts could without issuing new plans still oversee the transition to a fully unitary system. He then went on to conclude, on the issues of demographic change and residential segregation, that it should be the obligation of the school system to demonstrate affirmatively that its policies did not contribute to any existing racial imbalance in the schools. Thus, a school system would have to demonstrate not only that, as Justice Souter had suggested, its segregation of schools did not contribute to demographic changes, but also that its other decisions in the areas of school placement, school construction, school closings, and the like did not contribute to the racial imbalance. "The District Court apparently has concluded that [the school system] should be relieved of the responsibility to desegregate because such responsibility would be burdensome. To be sure, changes in demographic patterns aggravated the vestiges of segregation and made it more difficult for [the system] to desegregate. But an integrated school system is no less desirable because it is difficult to achieve, and it is no less a constitutional imperative because that imperative has gone unmet for 38 years. [I] would remand for the Court of Appeals to review [the]

District Court's finding that [the system] has met its burden of proving the racially identifiable schools are in no way the result of past segregative action." *

In UNITED STATES v. FORDICE, 505 U.S. ___ (1992), the Court refused to distinguish colleges and universities from primary and secondary schools in holding that the state college and university system of Mississippi had the same affirmative obligation to dismantle its dual system that primary and secondary school systems had under Green. Writing for the Court, Justice WHITE outlined the history of segregation in higher education in Mississippi, and relied heavily on statistics showing that the state still maintained a system of higher education dominated by racially identifiable institutions. He rejected the state's argument that establishing a true freedom of choice system was sufficient in the higher education context even though not in the primary and secondary school context. "We do not agree that the adoption and implementation of race-neutral policies alone suffice to demonstrate that the State has completely abandoned its prior dual system. That college attendance is by choice and not by assignment does not mean that a race-neutral admissions policy eliminates the constitutional violation of a dual system. In a system based on choice, student attendance is determined not simply by admissions policies, but also by many other factors." As a result, Justice White made clear that the state had an obligation to eliminate all practices and procedures (including use of certain tests, and the financing of some organizations) that had originally been employed for discriminatory purposes and that now had discriminatory effects, even if race-neutral justifications could now be offered for them. Moreover, he emphasized that the burden of proof remained with the state to demonstrate both that it had dismantled its dual system and that current practices having discriminatory impact could not be replaced with others. "If the State perpetuates policies and practices traceable to its prior system that continue to have segregative effects—whether by influencing student enrollment decisions or by fostering segregation in other facets of the university system—and such policies are without sound educational justification and can be practicably eliminated, the State has not satisfied its burden of proving that it has dismantled its prior system. Such policies run afoul of the Equal Protection Clause, even though the State has abolished the legal requirement that whites and blacks be educated separately and has established racially neutral policies not animated by a discriminatory purpose."

Justice O'CONNOR concurred, and wrote separately to make clear that even "if the State shows that maintenance of certain remnants of its prior system is essential to accomplish its legitimate goals, then it still must prove that it has counteracted and minimized the segregative impact of such policies to the extent possible." Justice THOMAS also concurred, agreeing with the Court's approach, but noting both that the Court had not specified what would count as an "adequate justification," and that in his view there could be a " 'sound educational justification' for maintaining historically black colleges as such. Despite the shameful

---

* Justice Thomas took no part in the consideration or decision of the case.

history of state-enforced segregation, these institutions have survived and flourished. [It] would be ironic, to say the least, if the institutions that sustained blacks during segregation were themselves destroyed in an attempt to combat its vestiges." Justice SCALIA concurred in the judgment in part and dissented in part, objecting to the application of the Green standards to colleges and universities. "The requirement of compelled integration [does] not apply to higher education. Only one aspect of an historically segregated university system need be eliminated: discriminatory admissions standards."

In 1995 Missouri v. Jenkins returned to the Supreme Court for the third time. MISSOURI v. JENKINS, 518 U.S. ___ (1995). Now the central issue was further mandated expenditures, for teacher salaries, magnet schools, and related programs, all designed to make the Kansas City schools more attractive, diminish "white flight," and deal with the fact that the school district's enrollment remained 68.3% black, a figure substantially above the percentage of black population in the district. Missouri challenged the district judge's remedial authority, arguing that the remedies went beyond the scope of any of the original violations. Writing for the Court, Chief Justice REHNQUIST relied heavily on Milliken v. Bradley and concluded that many of the goals identified by the district judge were interdistrict goals, such as the goal of using magnet schools to attract more nonminority students to the district, which were "beyond the scope of the *intra*district violation identified by the District Court. [The] District Court's pursuit of 'desegregative attractiveness' is beyond the scope of its broad remedial authority. [A] district court seeking to remedy an *intra*district violation that has not 'directly caused' significant interdistrict effects, Milliken, exceeds its remedial authority if it orders a remedy with an interdistrict purpose. [Similar] considerations lead us to conclude that the District Court's order requiring the State to continue to fund the quality education programs because student achievement levels were 'still at or below national norms at many grade levels' cannot be sustained. [While] a mandate for significant educational improvement, both in teaching and in facilities, may have been justified originally, its indefinite extension is not. [On] remand, the District Court must bear in mind that its end purpose is not only 'to remedy the violation' to the extent practicable, but also 'to restore state and local authorities to the control of the school system that is operating in compliance with the Constitution.' Freeman v. Pitts."

Justice O'CONNOR joined the opinion of the Court, and also wrote separately to stress her views about the limits of judicial power. This case, like other school desegregation litigation, is concerned with "the elimination of the discrimination inherent in the dual school systems, not with myriad factors of human existence which can cause discrimination in a multitude of ways on racial, religious, or ethnic grounds." Swann. Those myriad factors are not readily corrected by judicial intervention, but are best addressed by the representative branches. [Courts,] however, are different. The necessary restrictions on our jurisdiction and authority contained in Article III [limit] the judiciary's institutional capacity to prescribe palliatives for societal ills. The unfortunate fact of racial imbalance and bias in our society, however pervasive and invidious, does not admit of judicial intervention absent a constitutional violation.

Justice THOMAS also concurred, opening with the statement that "It never ceases to amaze me that the courts are so willing to assume that anything that is predominantly black must be inferior. Instead of focusing on remedying the harm done to those black schoolchildren injured by segregation, the District Court here sought to convert the Kansas City [School] District into a 'magnet district' that would reverse the 'white flight' caused by *de*segregation." He then continued in the same vein. "Two threads in our jurisprudence have produced this unfortunate situation, in which a District Court has taken it upon itself to experiment with the education of [the school district's] black youth. First, the court has read our cases to support the theory that black students suffer an unspecified psychological harm from segregation that retards their mental and educational development. This approach not only relies upon questionable social science research rather than constitutional principle, but it also rests on an assumption of black inferiority. Second, we have permitted the Federal Courts to exercise virtually unlimited equitable powers to remedy this alleged constitutional violation. The exercise of this authority has trampled upon principles of federalism and the separation of powers and has freed courts to pursue other agendas unrelated to the narrow purpose of precisely remedying a constitutional harm. When a District Court holds the State liable for discrimination almost 30 years after the last official state action, it must do more than show that there are schools with high black populations or low test scores. Here, the district judge did not make clear how the high black enrollments in certain schools were fairly traceable to the State of Missouri's actions. I do not doubt that Missouri maintained the despicable system of segregation until 1954. But I question the District Court's conclusion that because the State had enforced segregation until 1954, its actions, or lack thereof, proximately caused the 'racial isolation' of the predominantly black schools in 1984. [Without] a basis in any real finding of intentional government action, the District Court's imposition of liability on the State of Missouri rests upon a theory that racial imbalances are unconstitutional. [In] effect, the court found that racial imbalances constituted an ongoing constitutional violation that continued to inflict harm on black students. This position appears to rest upon the idea that any school that is black is inferior, and the blacks cannot succeed without the benefit of the company of whites. [Brown] did not say that 'racially isolated' schools were inherently inferior; the harm that it identified was tied purely to *de jure* segregation, not *de facto* segregation. [Brown] did not need to rely upon any psychological or social-science research in order to announce the simple, yet fundamental truth that the Government cannot discriminate among its citizens on the basis of race. [Segregation] was not unconstitutional because it might have caused psychological feelings of inferiority. [Psychological] injury or benefit is irrelevant to the question whether state actors have engaged in intentional discrimination—the critical inquiry for ascertaining violations of the Equal Protection Clause. [Given] that desegregation has not produced the predicted leaps forward in black educational achievement, there is no reason to think that black students cannot learn as well when surrounded by members of their own race as when they are in an integrated environment. Indeed, it may very well be that what has been true for historically black colleges is true for black middle and high schools. [If] separation is itself a harm, and if integration is the only way that blacks can receive a proper education, then there must be something inferior about blacks. Under this theory, segregation injures blacks because blacks, when left on their own, cannot achieve. To my way of thinking, that conclusion is the result of a jurisprudence based upon a theory of black inferiority." Justice Thomas then went on to question the broad use of the federal equitable remedial power. "Our willingness to unleash the federal equitable power has reached beyond school desegregation. Federal Courts have used 'structural injunctions,' as they are known, not only to supervise our Nation's schools, but also to manage prisons, mental hospitals, and public housing. Judges have directed or managed the reconstruction of entire institutions or bureaucracies, with little regard for the inherent limitations of their authority. Such extravagant uses of judicial power are at odds with the history and tradition of the equity power and the Framers' design. [At] some point, we must recognize that the judiciary is not omniscient, and that all problems do not require a remedy of constitutional proportions."

Justice SOUTER, joined by Justices Stevens, Ginsburg, and Breyer, dissented. Much of the dissent addressed the procedural posture of the case, and objected to the Court's taking on of issues not properly presented on the record. Justice Souter also took issue with the majority's treatment of the intradistrict-interdistrict issue. "[T]he District Court did not mean by an 'intradistrict violation' what the Court apparently means by it today. The District Court meant that the violation within the [district] had not led to segregation outside of it, and that no other school districts had played a part in the violation. It did not mean that the violation had not produced effects of any sort beyond the district. [The] record we have indicates that the District Court understood that the violation here did produce effects spanning district borders and leading to greater segregation, [the] reversal of which the District Court sought to accomplish by establishing magnet schools." In the same vein, Justice Souter challenged the majority's conclusion that "white flight" had been caused not by segregation, but by the desegregation orders. "When the [majority] quotes the District Court's reference to abundant evidence that integration caused the flight to the suburbs, [it] quotes nothing inconsistent with the District Court's other findings that segregation had caused the flight. The only difference between the statements lies in the point to which the District Court happened to trace the causal sequence. [Property] tax-paying parents of white children, seeing the handwriting on the wall in 1985, could well have decided that the inevitable cost of [school repair to the segregated schools] would produce an intolerable tax rate and could have moved to escape it. The District Court's remedial orders had not yet been put in place. Was the white flight caused by segregation or desegregation?

The distinction has no significance. Another example makes the same point. After Brown, white parents likely came to understand that the practice of spending more on white schools than on black ones would be stopped at some point. If they were unwilling to raise all expenditures to match the customary white school level, they must have expected the expenditures on white schools to drop to the level of those for the segregated black schools or to some level in between. If they thus believed that the white schools would deteriorate they might then have taken steps to establish private white schools, starting a practice of local private education that has endured. Again, what sense does it make to say of this example that the cause of white private education was desegregation (not yet underway), rather than the segregation that led to it?"

Justice GINSBURG filed a brief separate dissent, emphasizing the shortness of the remedial period so far compared to the length and the extent of the segregation that had preceded it.

12th ED., p. 819; IND. RTS., p. 490
Add after Metro Broadcasting v. FCC:

ADARAND CONSTRUCTORS, INC. v. PENA

518 U.S. ___, 115 S.Ct. 2097, 132 L.Ed.2d 158 (1995).

Justice O'CONNOR announced the judgment of the Court and delivered an opinion with respect to Parts I, II, III–A, III–B, III–D, and IV, which is for the Court except insofar as it might be inconsistent with the views expressed in Justice SCALIA's concurrence, and an opinion with respect to Part III–C in which Justice KENNEDY joins.

Petitioner Adarand Constructors, Inc., claims that the Federal Government's practice of giving general contractors on government projects a financial incentive to hire subcontractors controlled by "socially and economically disadvantaged individuals," and in particular, the Government's use of race-based presumptions in identifying such individuals, violates the equal protection component of the Fifth Amendment's Due Process Clause. The Court of Appeals rejected Adarand's claim. We conclude, however, that courts should analyze cases of this kind under a different standard of review than the one the Court of Appeals applied. We therefore vacate the Court of Appeals' judgment and remand the case for further proceedings.

I. In 1989, the Central Federal Lands Highway Division (CFLHD), which is part of the United States Department of Transportation (DOT), awarded the prime contract for a highway construction project in Colorado to Mountain Gravel & Construction Company. Mountain Gravel then solicited bids from subcontractors for the guardrail portion of the contract. Adarand, a Colorado-based highway construction company specializing in guardrail work, submitted the low bid. Gonzales Construction Company also submitted a bid.

The prime contract's terms provide that Mountain Gravel would receive additional compensation if it hired subcontractors certified as small businesses controlled by "socially and economically disadvantaged individuals." Gonzales is certified as such a business; Adarand is not. Mountain Gravel awarded the subcontract to Gonzales, despite Adarand's low bid, and Mountain Gravel's Chief Estimator has submitted an affidavit stating that Mountain Gravel would have accepted Adarand's bid, had it not been for the additional payment it received by hiring Gonzales instead. Federal law requires that a subcontracting clause similar to the one used here must appear in most federal agency contracts, and it also requires the clause to state that "[t]he contractor shall presume that socially and economically disadvantaged individuals include Black Americans, Hispanic Americans, Native Americans, Asian Pacific Americans, and other minorities, or any other individual found to be disadvantaged by the [Small Business] Administration pursuant to section 8(a) of the Small Business Act." Adarand claims that the presumption [discriminates] on the basis of race in violation of the Fifth Amendment obligation not to deny anyone equal protection of the laws.

These fairly straightforward facts implicate a complex scheme of federal statutes and regulations, to which we now turn. The Small Business Act, 15 U.S.C. § 631 et seq., declares it to be "the policy of the United States that small business concerns, [and] small business concerns owned and controlled by socially and economically disadvantaged individuals, ... shall have the maximum practicable opportunity to participate in the performance of contracts let by any Federal agency." The Act defines "socially disadvantaged individuals" as "those who have been subjected to racial or ethnic prejudice or cultural bias because of their identity as a member of a group without regard to their individual qualities," and it defines "economically disadvantaged individuals" as "those socially disadvantaged individuals whose ability to compete in the free enterprise system has been impaired due to diminished capital and credit opportunities as compared to others in the same business area who are not socially disadvantaged." [The] Act establishes "[t]he Government-wide goal for participation by small business concerns owned and controlled by socially and economically disadvantaged individuals" at "not less than 5 percent of the total value of all prime contract and subcontract awards for each fiscal year." It also requires the head of each Federal agency to set agency-specific goals for participation by businesses controlled by socially and economically disadvantaged individuals.

The Small Business Administration (SBA) has implemented these statutory directives in a variety of ways, two of which are relevant here. One is the "8(a) program," which is available to small businesses controlled by socially and economically disadvantaged individuals. [The] 8(a) program confers a wide range of benefits on participating businesses, one of which is automatic eligibility for subcontractor compensation provisions of the kind at issue in this case. To participate in the 8(a) program, a business must be "small," as defined in 13 CFR § 124.102 (1994); and it must be 51% owned by individuals who qualify as "socially and economically disadvantaged." The SBA presumes that Black, Hispanic, Asian Pacific, Subcontinent Asian, and Native Americans, as well as "members of other groups designated from time to time by SBA," are "socially disadvantaged." It also allows any individual not a member of a listed group to prove social disadvantage "on the basis of clear and convincing evidence." Social disadvantage is not enough to establish eligibility, however; SBA also requires each 8(a) program participant to prove "economic disadvantage."

The other SBA program relevant to this case is the "8(d) subcontracting program," which unlike the 8(a) program is limited to eligibility for subcontracting provisions like the one at issue here. In determining eligibility, the SBA presumes social disadvantage based on membership in certain minority groups, just as in the 8(a) program, and again appears to require an individualized, although "less restrictive," showing of economic disadvantage. A different set of regulations, however, says that members of minority groups wishing to participate in the 8(d) subcontracting program are entitled to a race-based presumption of social and economic disadvantage. [In both] the 8(a) and the 8(d) programs, the presumptions of disadvantage are rebuttable if a third party comes forward with evidence suggesting that the participant is not, in fact, either economically or socially disadvantaged.

The contract giving rise to the dispute in this case came about as a result of the Surface Transportation and Uniform Relocation Assistance Act of 1987 (STURAA), a DOT appropriations measure. Section 106(c)(1) of STURAA provides that "not less than 10 percent" of the appropriated funds "shall be expended with small business concerns owned and controlled by socially and economically disadvantaged individuals." STURAA adopts the Small Business Act's definition of "socially and economically disadvantaged individual," including the applicable race-based presumptions, and adds that "women shall be presumed to be socially and economically disadvantaged individuals for purposes of this subsection." STURAA also requires the Secretary of Transportation to establish "minimum uniform criteria for State governments to use in certifying whether a concern qualifies for purposes of this subsection." [Those] regulations say that the certifying authority should presume both social and economic disadvantage (i.e., eligibility to participate) if the applicant belongs to certain racial groups, or is a woman.

[The] operative clause in the contract in this case reads as follows:

"Subcontracting. This subsection is supplemented to include a Disadvantaged Business Enterprise (DBE) Development and Subcontracting Provision as follows:

"Monetary compensation is offered for awarding subcontracts to small business concerns owned and controlled by socially and economically disadvantaged individuals. . . .

"A small business concern will be considered a DBE after it has been certified as such by the U.S. Small Business Administration or any State Highway Agency. Certification by other Government agencies, counties, or cities may be acceptable on an individual basis. . . .

"The Contractor will be paid an amount computed as follows:

"1.   If a subcontract is awarded to one DBE, 10 percent of the final amount of the approved DBE subcontract, not to exceed 1.5 percent of the original contract amount.

"2.   If subcontracts are awarded to two or more DBEs, 10 percent of the final amount of the approved DBE subcontracts, not to exceed 2 percent of the original contract amount."

To benefit from this clause, Mountain Gravel had to hire a subcontractor who had been certified as a small disadvantaged business by the SBA, a state highway agency, or some other certifying authority acceptable to the Contracting Officer. Any of the three routes to such certification described above—SBA's 8(a) or 8(d) program, or certification by a State under the DOT regulations—would meet that requirement.

[After] losing the guardrail subcontract to Gonzales, Adarand filed suit [in] the United States District Court for the District of Colorado, claiming that the race-based presumptions involved in the use of subcontracting compensation clauses violate Adarand's right to equal protection. The District Court granted the Government's motion for summary judgment. The Court of Appeals for the Tenth Circuit affirmed. It understood our decision in Fullilove to have adopted "a lenient standard, resembling intermediate scrutiny, in assessing" the constitutionality of federal race-based action. Applying that "lenient standard," as further developed in Metro Broadcasting, the Court of Appeals upheld the use of subcontractor compensation clauses. We granted certiorari.

II.   [The Court held that Adarand had standing not only to sue for damages for a contract it had lost in the past, but also had standing to seek forward-looking injunctive and declaratory relief because of the actual likelihood that it would submit bids under similar circumstances in the future.]

III.   The Government urges that "[t]he Subcontracting Compensation Clause program is . . . a program based on disadvantage, not on race," and thus that it is subject only to "the most relaxed judicial scrutiny." To the extent that the statutes and regulations involved in this case are race neutral, we agree. The Government concedes, however, that "the race-based rebuttable presumption used in some certification determinations under the Subcontracting Compensation Clause" is subject to some heightened level of scrutiny. The parties disagree as to what that level should be.

[Adarand's] claim arises under the Fifth Amendment, which provides that "No person shall . . . be deprived of life, liberty, or property, without due process of law." Although this Court has always understood that Clause to provide [protection] against arbitrary treatment by the Federal Government, it is not as explicit a guarantee of equal treatment as the Fourteenth Amendment. [Our] cases have accorded varying degrees of significance to the difference in the language of those two Clauses. We think it necessary to revisit the issue here.

A.   Through the 1940s, this Court had routinely taken the view in non-race-related cases that, "[u]nlike the Fourteenth Amendment, the

Fifth contains no equal protection clause and it provides no guaranty against discriminatory legislation by Congress." Detroit Bank v. United States, 317 U.S. 329 (1943). When the Court first faced a Fifth Amendment equal protection challenge to a federal racial classification, it adopted a similar approach, with most unfortunate results. In Hirabayashi v. United States, 320 U.S. 81 (1943), the Court considered a curfew applicable only to persons of Japanese ancestry. The Court observed—correctly—that "[d]istinctions between citizens solely because of their ancestry are by their very nature odious to a free people whose institutions are founded upon the doctrine of equality," and that "racial discriminations are in most circumstances irrelevant and therefore prohibited." But it also cited Detroit Bank for the proposition that the Fifth Amendment "restrains only such discriminatory legislation by Congress as amounts to a denial of due process," and upheld the curfew because "circumstances within the knowledge of those charged with the responsibility for maintaining the national defense afforded a rational basis for the decision [ ]." Eighteen months later, the Court [in Koprematsu] again approved wartime measures directed at persons of Japanese ancestry. The Court did not address the view [that] the Federal Government's obligation to provide equal protection differs significantly from that of the States. Instead, it began by noting that "all legal restrictions which curtail the civil rights of a single racial group are immediately suspect ... [and] courts must subject them to the most rigid scrutiny." That promising dictum might be read to undermine the view that the Federal Government is under a lesser obligation to avoid injurious racial classifications than are the States. But in spite of the "most rigid scrutiny" standard it [set] forth, the Court then inexplicably relied on "the principles we announced in the Hirabayashi case" to conclude that [the] racially discriminatory order was [within] the Federal Government's power.

In Bolling v. Sharpe, the Court for the first time explicitly questioned the existence of any difference between the obligations of the Federal Government and the States to avoid racial classifications. Bolling [concluded] that, "[i]n view of [the] decision that the Constitution prohibits the states from maintaining racially segregated public schools, it would be unthinkable that the same Constitution would impose a lesser duty on the Federal Government." Bolling's facts concerned school desegregation, but its reasoning was not so limited. The Court's observations that "[d]istinctions between citizens solely because of their ancestry are by their very nature odious," and that "all legal restrictions which curtail the civil rights of a single racial group are immediately suspect," carry no less force in the context of federal action than in the context of action by the States—indeed, they first appeared in cases concerning action by the Federal Government. Bolling relied on those observations, and reiterated "that the Constitution of the United States, in its present form, forbids, so far as civil and political rights are concerned, discrimination by the General Government, or by the States, against any citizen because of his race." The Court's application of that general principle to the case before it, and the resulting imposition on the Federal Government of an obligation equivalent to that of the States, followed as a matter of course. Later cases in contexts other than school desegregation [continued] to treat the equal protection obligations imposed by the Fifth and the Fourteenth Amendments as indistinguishable.

B. Most of the cases discussed above involved classifications burdening groups that have suffered discrimination in our society. In 1978, the Court confronted the question whether race-based governmental action designed to benefit such groups should also be subject to "the most rigid scrutiny." [Bakke] did not produce an opinion for the Court, but Justice Powell [wrote] that "[t]he guarantee of equal protection cannot mean one thing when applied to one individual and something else when applied to a person of another color." He concluded that "[r]acial and ethnic distinctions of any sort are inherently suspect and thus call for the most exacting judicial examination." [Two] years after Bakke, the Court faced another challenge to remedial race-based action, this time involving action undertaken by the Federal Government. In Fullilove, [as] in Bakke, there was no opinion for the Court. Chief Justice Burger, in an opinion joined by Justices White and Powell, observed that "[a]ny preference based on racial or ethnic criteria must necessarily receive a most searching examination to make sure that it does not conflict with constitutional guarantees." [Justice] Marshall (joined by Justices Brennan and Blackmun) concurred in the judgment, reiterating the view of four Justices in Bakke that any race-based governmental action designed to "remed[y] the present effects of past racial discrimination" should be upheld if it was "substantially related" to the achievement of an "important governmental objective"—i.e., such action should be subjected only to what we now call "intermediate scrutiny." In Wygant, [Justice] Powell's plurality opinion observed that "the level of scrutiny does not change merely because the challenged classification operates against a group that historically has not been subject to governmental discrimination." [In] other words, "racial classifications of any sort must be subjected to 'strict scrutiny.'" [Justice] White concurred only in the judgment, although he agreed that the school board's asserted interests could not, "singly or together, justify this racially discriminatory layoff policy." Four Justices dissented, three of whom again argued for intermediate scrutiny of remedial race-based government action.

The Court's failure to produce a majority opinion in Bakke, Fullilove, and Wygant left unresolved the proper analysis for remedial race-based governmental action. [The] Court resolved the issue, at least in part, in 1989. With Richmond v. J.A. Croson, the Court finally agreed that the Fourteenth Amendment requires strict scrutiny of all race-based action by state and local governments. But Croson of course had no occasion to declare what standard of review the Fifth Amendment requires for such action taken by the Federal Government. Croson observed simply that the Court's "treatment of an exercise of congressional power in Fullilove cannot be dispositive here," because [the case] did not implicate Congress' broad power under § 5 of the Fourteenth Amendment.

[Despite] lingering uncertainty in the details, however, the Court's cases through Croson had established three general propositions with respect to governmental racial classifications. First, skepticism: " '[a]ny preference based on racial or ethnic criteria must necessarily receive a most searching examination,' " Wygant (plurality opinion of Powell, J.). Second, consistency: "the standard of review under the Equal Protection Clause is not dependent on the race of those burdened or benefited by a particular classification," Croson, i.e., all racial classifications reviewable under the Equal Protection Clause must be strictly scrutinized. And third, congruence: "[e]qual protection analysis in the Fifth Amendment area is the same as that under the Fourteenth Amendment." Taken together, these three propositions lead to the conclusion that any person, of whatever race, has the right to demand that any governmental actor subject to the Constitution justify any racial classification subjecting that person to unequal treatment under the strictest judicial scrutiny. [A] year later, however, the Court took a surprising turn. [In] Metro Broadcasting, the Court repudiated the long-held notion that "it would be unthinkable that the same Constitution would impose a lesser duty on the Federal Government" than it does on a State to afford equal protection of the laws. It did so by holding that "benign" federal racial classifications need only satisfy intermediate scrutiny, even though Croson had recently concluded that such classifications enacted by a State must satisfy strict scrutiny. [By] adopting intermediate scrutiny as the standard of review for congressionally mandated "benign" racial classifications, Metro Broadcasting departed from prior cases in two significant respects. First, it turned its back on Croson's explanation of why strict scrutiny of all governmental racial classifications is essential: "Absent searching judicial inquiry into the justification for such race-based measures, there is simply no way of determining what classifications are 'benign' or 'remedial' and what classifications are in fact motivated by illegitimate notions of racial inferiority or simple racial politics[ ]." We adhere to that view today, despite the surface appeal of holding "benign" racial classifications to a lower standard, because "it may not always be clear that a so-called preference is in fact benign," Bakke (Powell, J.). Second, Metro Broadcasting squarely rejected one of the three propositions established by the Court's earlier equal protection cases, namely, congruence between the standards applicable to federal and state racial classifications, and in so doing also undermined the other two—skepticism of all racial classifications, and consistency of treatment irrespective of the race of the burdened or benefited group. Under Metro Broadcasting, certain racial classifications ("benign" ones enacted by the Federal Government) should be treated less skeptically than others; and the race of the benefited group is critical to the determination of which standard of review to apply. Metro Broadcasting was thus a significant departure from much of what had come before it.

The three propositions undermined by Metro Broadcasting all derive from the basic principle that the Fifth and Fourteenth Amendments to the Constitution protect persons, not groups. It follows from that principle that all governmental action based on race [should] be subjected to detailed judicial inquiry to ensure that the personal right to equal protection of the laws has not been infringed. These ideas have long been central to this Court's understanding of equal protection, and holding "benign" state and federal racial classifications to different standards does not square with them. [Accordingly,] we hold today that all racial classifications, imposed by whatever federal, state, or local governmental actor, must be analyzed by a reviewing court under strict scrutiny. In other words, such classifications are constitutional only if they are narrowly tailored measures that further compelling governmental interests. To the extent that Metro Broadcasting is inconsistent with that holding, it is overruled. [By] requiring strict scrutiny of [all] racial classifications, we require courts to make sure that a governmental classification based on race, which "so seldom provide[s] a relevant basis for disparate treatment," Fullilove (Stevens, J., dissenting), is legitimate, before permitting unequal treatment based on race to proceed.

Justice Stevens chides us for our "supposed inability to differentiate between 'invidious' and 'benign' discrimination," because it is in his view sufficient that "people understand the difference between good intentions and bad." But, as we have just explained, the point of strict scrutiny is to "differentiate between" permissible and impermissible governmental use of race. And Justice Stevens himself has already' explained in his dissent in Fullilove why "good intentions" alone are not enough to sustain a supposedly "benign" racial classification: "[E]ven though it is not the actual predicate for this legislation, a statute of this kind inevitably is perceived by many as resting on an assumption that those who are granted this special preference are less qualified in some respect that is identified purely by their race. Because that perception—especially when fostered by the Congress of the United States—can only exacerbate rather than reduce racial prejudice, it will delay the time when race will become a truly irrelevant, or at least insignificant, factor. Unless Congress clearly articulates the need and basis for a racial classification, and also tailors the classification to its justification, the Court should not uphold this kind of statute." Fullilove (dissenting opinion).

[Perhaps] it is not the standard of strict scrutiny itself, but our use of the concepts of "consistency" and "congruence" in conjunction with it, that leads Justice Stevens to dissent. According to [him,] our view of consistency "equate[s] remedial preferences with invidious discrimination," and ignores the difference between "an engine of oppression" and an effort "to foster equality in society," or, more colorfully, "between a 'No Trespassing' sign and a welcome mat." It does nothing of the kind. The principle of consistency simply means that whenever the government treats any person unequally because of his or her race, that person has suffered an injury that falls squarely within the language and spirit of the Constitution's guarantee of equal protection. It says nothing about the ultimate validity of any particular law; that determination is the job of the court applying strict scrutiny. The principle of consistency explains the circumstances in which the injury requiring strict scrutiny occurs. The application of strict scrutiny, in turn, determines whether a compelling governmental interest justifies the infliction of that injury.

Consistency does recognize that any individual suffers an injury when he or she is disadvantaged by the government because of his or her race, whatever that race may be. [And] requiring that Congress, like the States, enact racial classifications only when doing so is necessary to further a "compelling interest" does not contravene any principle of appropriate respect for a co-equal Branch of the Government. It is true that various Members of this Court have taken different views of the authority § 5 of the Fourteenth Amendment confers upon Congress to deal with the problem of racial discrimination, and the extent to which courts should defer to Congress' exercise of that authority. We need not, and do not, address these differences today. For now, it is enough to observe that Justice Stevens' suggestion that any Member of this Court has repudiated in this case his or her previously expressed views on the subject is incorrect.

C. "Although adherence to precedent is not rigidly required in constitutional cases, any departure from the doctrine of stare decisis demands special justification." Arizona v. Rumsey, 467 U.S. 203, 212 (1984). In deciding whether this case presents such justification, we recall Justice Frankfurter's admonition that "stare decisis is a principle of policy and not a mechanical formula of adherence to the latest decision, however recent and questionable, when such adherence involves collision with a prior doctrine more embracing in its scope, intrinsically sounder, and verified by experience." Helvering v. Hallock, 309 U.S. 106 (1940). Remaining true to an "intrinsically sounder" doctrine established in prior cases better serves the values of stare decisis than would following a more recently decided case inconsistent with the decisions that came before it; the latter course would simply compound the recent error and would likely make the unjustified break from previously established doctrine complete. In such a situation, "special justification" exists to depart from the recently decided case.

As we have explained, Metro Broadcasting undermined important principles of this Court's equal protection jurisprudence, established in a line of cases stretching back over fifty years. [This] case therefore presents precisely the situation described by Justice Frankfurter in Helvering: we cannot adhere to our most recent decision without colliding with an accepted and established doctrine. [By] refusing to follow Metro Broadcasting, then, we do not depart from the fabric of the law; we restore it. We also note that reliance on a case that has recently departed from precedent is likely to be minimal, particularly where, as here, the rule set forth in that case is unlikely to affect primary conduct in any event. ["The] real problem," Justice Frank-further explained, "is whether a principle shall prevail over its later misapplications." Metro Broadcasting's untenable distinction between state and federal racial classifications lacks support in our precedent, and undermines the fundamental principle of equal protection as a personal right. In this case, as between that principle and "its later misapplications," the principle must prevail.

D. Our action today makes explicit what Justice Powell thought implicit in the Fullilove lead opinion: federal racial classifications, like those of a State, must serve a compelling governmental interest, and must be narrowly tailored to further that interest. Of course, it follows that to the extent (if any) that Fullilove held federal racial classifications to be subject to a less rigorous standard, it is no longer controlling. But we need not decide today whether the program upheld in Fullilove would survive strict scrutiny as our more recent cases have defined it.

Some have questioned the importance of debating the proper standard of review of race-based legislation. But we agree with Justice Stevens that, "[b]ecause racial characteristics so seldom provide a relevant basis for disparate treatment, and because classifications based on race are potentially so harmful to the entire body politic, it is especially important that the reasons for any such classification be clearly identified and unquestionably legitimate," and that "[r]acial classifications are simply too pernicious to permit any but the most exact connection between justification and classification." Fullilove (dissenting opinion). We think that requiring strict scrutiny is the best way to ensure that courts will consistently give racial classifications that kind of detailed examination, both as to ends and as to means. Korematsu demonstrates vividly that even "the most rigid scrutiny" can sometimes fail to detect an illegitimate racial classification. Any retreat from the most searching judicial inquiry can only increase the risk of another such error occurring in the future.

Finally, we wish to dispel the notion that strict scrutiny is "strict in theory, but fatal in fact." Fullilove (Marshall, J.). The unhappy persistence of both the practice and the lingering effects of racial discrimination against minority groups in this country is an unfortunate reality, and government is not disqualified from acting in response to it. [When] race-based action is necessary to further a compelling interest, such action is within constitutional constraints if it satisfies the "narrow tailoring" test this Court has set out in previous cases.

IV. Because our decision today alters the playing field in some important respects, we think it best to remand the case to the lower courts for further consideration in light of the principles we have announced. The Court of Appeals, following Metro Broadcasting and Fullilove, analyzed the case in terms of intermediate scrutiny [and] did not decide the question whether the interests served by the use of subcontractor compensation clauses are properly described as "compelling." [Moreover,] unresolved questions remain concerning the details of the complex regulatory regimes implicated by the use of subcontractor compensation clauses. [The] question whether any of the ways in which the Government uses subcontractor compensation clauses can survive strict scrutiny, and any relevance distinctions such as these may have to that question, should be addressed in the first instance by the lower courts.

[Remanded.]

Justice SCALIA, concurring in part and concurring in the judgment.

I join the opinion of the Court, except Part III–C, and except insofar as it may be inconsistent with the following: In my view, government can never have a "compelling interest" in discriminating on the basis of race in order to "make up" for past racial discrimination in the opposite direction. Individuals who have been wronged by unlawful racial discrimination should be made whole; but under our Constitution there can be no such thing as either a creditor or a debtor race. That concept is alien to the Constitution's focus upon the individual, and its rejection of dispositions based on race, or based on blood (see Art. III ("[N]o Attainder of Treason shall work Corruption of Blood"); Art. I, § 9 ("No Title of Nobility shall be granted by the United States")). To pursue the concept of racial entitlement—even for the most admirable and benign of purposes—is to reinforce and preserve for future mischief the way of thinking that produced race slavery, race privilege and race hatred. In the eyes of government, we are just one race here. It is American.

Justice THOMAS, concurring in part and concurring in the judgment.

I agree with the majority's conclusion that strict scrutiny applies to all government classifications based on race. I write separately, however, to express my disagreement with the premise underlying Justice Stevens' and Justice Ginsburg's dissents: that there is a racial paternalism exception to the principle of equal protection. I believe that there is a "moral [and] constitutional equivalence" between laws designed to subjugate a race and those that distribute benefits on the basis of race in order to foster some current notion of equality. Government cannot make us equal; it can only recognize, respect, and protect us as equal before the law.

That these programs may have been motivated, in part, by good intentions cannot provide refuge from the principle that under our Constitution, the government may not make distinctions on the basis of race. As far as the Constitution is concerned, it is irrelevant whether a government's racial classifications are drawn by those who wish to oppress a race or by those who have a sincere desire to help those thought to be disadvantaged. There can be no doubt that the paternalism that appears to lie at the heart of this program is at war with the principle of inherent equality that underlies and infuses our Constitution.

These programs not only raise grave constitutional questions, they also undermine the moral basis of the equal protection principle. Purchased at the price of immeasurable human suffering, the equal protection principle reflects our Nation's understanding that such classifications ultimately have a destructive impact on the individual and our society. Unquestionably, "[i]nvidious [racial] discrimination is an engine of oppression." It is also true that "[r]emedial" racial preferences may reflect "a desire to foster equality in society." But there can be no doubt that racial paternalism and its unintended consequences can be as poisonous and pernicious as any other form of discrimination. So-called "benign" discrimination teaches many that because of chronic and apparently immutable handicaps, minorities cannot compete with them without their patronizing indulgence. Inevitably, such programs engender attitudes of superiority or, alternatively, provoke resentment among those who believe that they have been wronged by the government's use of race. These programs stamp minorities with a badge of inferiority and may cause them to develop dependencies or to adopt an attitude that they are "entitled" to preferences. [In] my mind, government-sponsored racial discrimination based on benign prejudice is just as noxious as discrimination inspired by malicious prejudice.* In each instance, it is racial discrimination, plain and simple.

Justice STEVENS, with whom Justice GINSBURG joins, dissenting.

Instead of deciding this case in accordance with controlling precedent, the Court today delivers a disconcerting lecture about the evils of governmental racial classifications. For its text the Court has selected three propositions, represented by the bywords "skepticism," "consistency," and "congruence."

I. [The] Court's concept of skepticism is, at least in principle, a good statement of law and of common sense. Undoubtedly, a court should be wary of a governmental decision that relies upon a racial classification. This principle is explicit in Chief Justice Burger's opinion, in Justice Powell's concurrence, and in my dissent in Fullilove. I welcome its renewed endorsement by the Court today. But, as the opinions in Fullilove demonstrate, substantial agreement on the standard to be applied in deciding difficult cases does not necessarily lead to agreement on how those cases actually should or will be resolved. In my judgment, because uniform standards are often anything but uniform, we should evaluate the Court's comments on "consistency," "congruence," and stare decisis with the same type of skepticism that the Court advocates for the underlying issue.

II. The Court's concept of "consistency" assumes that there is no significant difference between a decision by the majority to impose a special burden on the members of a minority race and a decision by the majority to provide a benefit to certain members of that minority notwithstanding its incidental burden on some members of the majority. In my opinion that assumption is untenable. There is no moral or constitutional equivalence between a policy that is designed to perpetuate a caste system and one that seeks to eradicate racial subordination. Invidious discrimination is an engine of oppression, subjugating a disfavored group to enhance or maintain the power of the majority. Remedial race-based preferences reflect the opposite impulse: a desire to foster equality in society. No sensible conception of the Government's constitutional obligation to "govern impartially," Hampton v. Mow Sun Wong, 426 U.S. 88 (1976), should ignore this distinction.[1]

---

* It should be obvious that every racial classification helps, in a narrow sense, some races and hurts others. As to the races benefitted, the classification could surely be called "benign." Accordingly, whether a law relying upon racial taxonomy is "benign" or "malign," either turns on " 'whose ox is gored,' " or on distinctions found only in the eye of the beholder. [Footnote by Justice Thomas.]

1. As Justice Ginsburg observes, the majority's "flexible" approach to "strict scrutiny" may well take into account differences between benign and invidious programs. The majority specifically notes that strict scrutiny can accommodate " 'relevant differences,' " surely the intent of a government actor and the effects of a program are relevant to its constitutionality. Even if this is so, however, I think it is unfortunate that the majority insists on applying the label "strict scrutiny" to benign race-based programs. That label has usually been understood to spell the death of any governmental action to which a court may apply

To illustrate the point, consider our cases addressing the Federal Government's discrimination against Japanese Americans during World War II. The discrimination at issue in those cases was invidious because the Government imposed special burdens—a curfew and exclusion from certain areas on the West Coast [2]—on the members of a minority class defined by racial and ethnic characteristics. Members of the same racially defined class exhibited exceptional heroism in the service of our country during that War. Now suppose Congress decided to reward that service with a federal program that gave all Japanese–American veterans an extraordinary preference in Government employment. If Congress had done so, the same racial characteristics that motivated the discriminatory burdens in Hirabayashi and Korematsu would have defined the preferred class of veterans. Nevertheless, "consistency" surely would not require us to describe the incidental burden on everyone else in the country as "odious" or "invidious" as those terms were used in those cases. We should reject a concept of "consistency" that would view the special preferences that the National Government has provided to Native Americans since 1834 as comparable to the official discrimination against African Americans that was prevalent for much of our history.

The consistency that the Court espouses would disregard the difference between a "No Trespassing" sign and a welcome mat. It would treat a Dixiecrat Senator's decision to vote against Thurgood Marshall's confirmation in order to keep African Americans off the Supreme Court as on a par with President Johnson's evaluation of his nominee's race as a positive factor. It would equate a law that made black citizens ineligible for military service with a program aimed at recruiting black soldiers. An attempt by the majority to exclude members of a minority race from a regulated market is fundamentally different from a subsidy that enables a relatively small group of newcomers to enter that market. An interest in "consistency" does not justify treating differences as though they were similarities.

The Court's explanation for treating dissimilar race-based decisions as though they were equally objectionable is a supposed inability to differentiate between "invidious" and "benign" discrimination. But the term "affirmative action" is common and well understood. Its presence in everyday parlance shows that people understand the difference between good intentions and bad. As with any legal concept, some cases may be difficult to classify, but our equal protection jurisprudence has identified a critical difference between state action that imposes burdens on a disfavored few and state action that benefits the few "in spite of" its adverse effects on the many.

---

it. The Court suggests today that "strict scrutiny" means something different—something less strict—when applied to benign racial classifications. Although I agree that benign programs deserve different treatment than invidious programs, there is a danger that the fatal language of "strict scrutiny" will skew the analysis and place well-crafted benign programs at unnecessary risk. [Footnote by Justice Stevens.]

2. These were, of course, neither the sole nor the most shameful burdens the Government imposed on Japanese Americans during that War. They were, however, the only such burdens this Court had occasion to address in Hirabayashi and Korematsu. [Footnote by Justice Stevens.]

Indeed, our jurisprudence has made the standard to be applied in cases of invidious discrimination turn on whether the discrimination is "intentional," or whether, by contrast, it merely has a discriminatory "effect." Washington v. Davis. Surely this distinction is at least as subtle, and at least as difficult to apply, as the usually obvious distinction between a measure intended to benefit members of a particular minority race and a measure intended to burden a minority race. A state actor inclined to subvert the Constitution might easily hide bad intentions in the guise of unintended "effects"; but I should think it far more difficult to enact a law intending to preserve the majority's hegemony while casting it plausibly in the guise of affirmative action for minorities.

Nothing is inherently wrong with applying a single standard to fundamentally different situations, as long as that standard takes relevant differences into account. For example, if the Court in all equal protection cases were to insist that differential treatment be justified by relevant characteristics of the members of the favored and disfavored classes that provide a legitimate basis for disparate treatment, such a standard would treat dissimilar cases differently while still recognizing that there is, after all, only one Equal Protection Clause. Under such a standard, subsidies for disadvantaged businesses may be constitutional though special taxes on such businesses would be invalid. But a single standard that purports to equate remedial preferences with invidious discrimination cannot be defended in the name of "equal protection."

Moreover, the Court may find that its new "consistency" approach to race-based classifications is difficult to square with its insistence upon rigidly separate categories for discrimination against different classes of individuals. For example, as the law currently stands, the Court will apply "intermediate scrutiny" to cases of invidious gender discrimination and "strict scrutiny" to cases of invidious race discrimination, while applying the same standard for benign classifications as for invidious ones. If this remains the law, then today's lecture about "consistency" will produce the anomalous result that the Government can more easily enact affirmative-action programs to remedy discrimination against women than it can enact affirmative-action programs to remedy discrimination against African Americans—even though the primary purpose of the Equal Protection Clause was to end discrimination against the former slaves. When a court becomes preoccupied with abstract standards, it risks sacrificing common sense at the altar of formal consistency.

As a matter of constitutional and democratic principle, a decision by representatives of the majority to discriminate against the members of a minority race is fundamentally different from those same representatives' decision to impose incidental costs on the majority of their constituents in order to provide a benefit to a disadvantaged minority. [The] former is virtually always repugnant to the principles of a free and democratic society, whereas the latter is, in some circumstances, entirely consistent with the ideal of equality. By insisting on a doctrinaire notion of "consistency" in the standard applicable to all race-based governmental actions, the Court obscures this essential dichotomy.

III. The Court's concept of "congruence" assumes that there is no significant difference between a decision by the Congress of the United States to adopt an affirmative-action program and such a decision by a State or a municipality. In my opinion that assumption is untenable. It ignores important practical and legal differences between federal and state or local decisionmakers. These differences have been identified repeatedly and consistently both in opinions of the Court and in separate opinions authored by members of today's majority. Thus, in Metro Broadcasting, in which we upheld a federal program designed to foster racial diversity in broadcasting, we identified the special "institutional competence" of our National Legislature. [We] recalled the several opinions in Fullilove that admonished this Court to " 'approach our task with appropriate deference to the Congress, a co-equal branch charged by the Constitution with the power to "provide for the . . . general Welfare of the United States" and "to enforce, by appropriate legislation," the equal protection guarantees of the Fourteenth Amendment.' "

The majority in Metro Broadcasting and the plurality in Fullilove were not alone in relying upon a critical distinction between federal and state programs. In his separate opinion in Croson, Justice Scalia discussed the basis for this distinction. He observed that "it is one thing to permit racially based conduct by the Federal Government—whose legislative powers concerning matters of race were explicitly enhanced by the Fourteenth Amendment, and quite another to permit it by the precise entities against whose conduct in matters of race that Amendment was specifically directed."

[An] additional reason for giving greater deference to the National Legislature than to a local law-making body is that federal affirmative-action programs represent the will of our entire Nation's elected representatives, whereas a state or local program may have an impact on nonresident entities who played no part in the decision to enact it. Thus, in the state or local context, individuals who were unable to vote for the local representatives who enacted a race-conscious program may nonetheless feel the effects of that program. This difference recalls the goals of the Commerce Clause, which permits Congress to legislate on certain matters of national importance while denying power to the States in this area for fear of undue impact upon out-of-state residents.

Ironically, after all of the time, effort, and paper this Court has expended in differentiating between federal and state affirmative action, the majority today virtually ignores the issue. [Such] silence, however, cannot erase the difference between Congress' institutional competence and constitutional authority to overcome historic racial subjugation and the States' lesser power to do so.

Presumably, the majority is now satisfied that its theory of "congruence" between the substantive rights provided by the Fifth and Fourteenth Amendments disposes of the objection based upon divided constitutional powers. But it is one thing to say (as no one seems to dispute) that the Fifth Amendment encompasses a general guarantee of equal protection as broad as that contained within the Fourteenth Amendment. It is another thing entirely to say that Congress' institutional competence and constitutional authority entitles it to no greater deference when it enacts a program designed to foster equality than the deference due a State legislature. The latter is an extraordinary proposition; and [our] precedents have rejected it explicitly and repeatedly.

Our opinion in Metro Broadcasting relied on several constitutional provisions to justify the greater deference we owe to Congress when it acts with respect to private individuals. [When] Congress does this, it draws its power directly from § 5 of the Fourteenth Amendment, [which] directly empowers Congress at the same time it expressly limits the States. This is no accident. It represents our Nation's consensus, achieved after hard experience throughout our sorry history of race relations, that the Federal Government must be the primary defender of racial minorities against the States, some of which may be inclined to oppress such minorities. A rule of "congruence" that ignores a purposeful "incongruity" so fundamental to our system of government is unacceptable. In my judgment, the Court's novel doctrine of "congruence" is seriously misguided. Congressional deliberations about a matter as important as affirmative action should be accorded far greater deference than those of a State or municipality.

IV. The Court's concept of stare decisis treats some of the language we have used in explaining our decisions as though it were more important than our actual holdings. In my opinion that treatment is incorrect. This is the third time in the Court's entire history that it has considered the constitutionality of a federal affirmative-action program. On each of the two prior occasions, the first in 1980, Fullilove, and the second in 1990, Metro Broadcasting, the Court upheld the program. Today the Court explicitly overrules Metro Broadcasting (at least in part), and undermines Fullilove by recasting the standard on which it rested and by calling even its holding into question. By way of explanation, Justice O'Connor advises the federal agencies and private parties that have made countless decisions in reliance on those cases that "we do not depart from the fabric of the law; we restore it." A skeptical observer might ask whether this pronouncement is a faithful application of the doctrine of stare decisis.

[Prior] to Metro Broadcasting, the interest in diversity had been mentioned in a few opinions, but it is perfectly clear that the Court had not yet decided whether that interest had sufficient magnitude to justify a racial classification. Metro Broadcasting, of course, answered that question in the affirmative. The majority today overrules Metro Broadcasting only insofar as it is "inconsistent with [the] holding" that strict scrutiny applies to "benign" racial classifications promulgated by the Federal Government. The proposition that fostering diversity may provide a sufficient interest to justify such a program is not inconsistent with the Court's holding today—indeed, the question is not remotely presented in this case—and I do not take the Court's opinion to diminish that aspect of our decision in Metro Broadcasting....

V. The Court's holding in Fullilove surely governs the result in this case. [Unlike] the Public Works Employment Act of 1977, which this Court upheld in Fullilove, the present statutory scheme does not make race the sole criterion of eligibility for participation in the program. Race does give rise to a rebuttable presumption of social disadvantage which, at least under STURAA, gives rise to a second rebuttable presumption of economic disadvantage. But a small business may qualify as a DBE, by showing that it is both socially and economically disadvantaged, even if it receives neither of these presumptions. Thus, the current preference is more inclusive than the 1977 Act because it does not make race a necessary qualification.

More importantly, race is not a sufficient qualification. Whereas a millionaire with a long history of financial successes, who was a member of numerous social clubs and trade associations, would have qualified for a preference under the 1977 Act merely because he was an Asian American or an African American, neither the SBA nor STURAA creates any such anomaly. The DBE program excludes members of minority races who are not, in fact, socially or economically disadvantaged. The presumption of social disadvantage reflects the unfortunate fact that irrational racial prejudice—along with its lingering effects—still survives. The presumption of economic disadvantage embodies a recognition that success in the private sector of the economy is often attributable, in part, to social skills and relationships. Unlike the 1977 set-asides, the current preference is designed to overcome the social and economic disadvantages that are often associated with racial characteristics. If, in a particular case, these disadvantages are not present, the presumptions can be rebutted. The program is thus designed to allow race to play a part in the decisional process only when there is a meaningful basis for assuming its relevance. [Significantly,] the current program, unlike the 1977 set-aside, does not establish any requirement—numerical or otherwise—that a general contractor must hire DBE subcontractors. The program we upheld in Fullilove required that 10% of the federal grant for every federally funded project be expended on minority business enterprises. In contrast, the current program contains no quota. Although it provides monetary incentives to general contractors to hire DBE subcontractors, it does not require them to hire DBE's, and they do not lose their contracts if they fail to do so. The importance of this incentive to general contractors (who always seek to offer the lowest bid) should not be underestimated; but the preference here is far less rigid, and thus more narrowly tailored, than the 1977 Act.

VI. My skeptical scrutiny of the Court's opinion leaves me in dissent. The majority's concept of "consistency" ignores a difference, fundamental to the idea of equal protection, between oppression and assistance.[3] The majority's concept of "congruence" ignores a differ-

3. In his concurrence, Justice Thomas argues that the most significant cost associated with an affirmative-action program is its adverse stigmatic effect on its intended beneficiaries. Although I agree that this cost may be more significant than many people realize, I do not think it applies to the facts of this case. First, this is not an argument that petitioner Adarand, a white-owned business, has standing to advance. No beneficiaries of the specific program under attack today have challenged its constitutionality—perhaps because they do not find the preferences stigmatizing, or perhaps because their ability to opt out of the program provides them all the relief they

ence, fundamental to our constitutional system, between the Federal Government and the States. And the majority's concept of stare decisis ignores the force of binding precedent....

Justice SOUTER, with whom Justice GINSBURG and Justice BREYER join, dissenting.

[I] agree with Justice Stevens' conclusion that stare decisis compels the application of Fullilove. Although Fullilove did not reflect doctrinal consistency, its several opinions produced a result on shared grounds that petitioner does not attack: that discrimination in the construction industry had been subject to government acquiescence, with effects that remain and that may be addressed by some preferential treatment falling within the congressional power under § 5 of the Fourteenth Amendment. Once Fullilove is applied, [it] follows that the statutes in question here (which are substantially better tailored to the harm being remedied than the statute endorsed in Fullilove) pass muster under Fifth Amendment due process and Fourteenth Amendment equal protection.

[The] result in Fullilove was controlled by the plurality for whom Chief Justice Burger spoke in announcing the judgment. Although his opinion did not adopt any label for the standard it applied, and although it was later seen as calling for less than strict scrutiny, none other than Justice Powell joined the plurality opinion as comporting with his own view that a strict scrutiny standard should be applied to all injurious race-based classifications. Chief Justice Burger's noncategorical approach is probably best seen not as more lenient than strict scrutiny but as reflecting his conviction that the treble-tiered scrutiny structure merely embroidered on a single standard of reasonableness whenever an equal protection challenge required a balancing of justification against probable harm. Indeed, the Court's very recognition today that strict scrutiny can be compatible with the survival of a classification so

---

would need. Second, even if the petitioner in this case were a minority-owned business challenging the stigmatizing effect of this program, I would not find Justice Thomas' extreme proposition—that there is a moral and constitutional equivalence between an attempt to subjugate and an attempt to redress the effects of a caste system—at all persuasive. It is one thing to question the wisdom of affirmative-action programs: there are many responsible arguments against them, including the one based upon stigma, that Congress might find persuasive when it decides whether to enact or retain race-based preferences. It is another thing altogether to equate the many well-meaning and intelligent lawmakers and their constituents—whether members of majority or minority races—who have supported affirmative action over the years, to segregationists and bigots. Finally, although Justice Thomas is more concerned about the poten-

tial effects of these programs than the intent of those who enacted them, [I] am not persuaded that the psychological damage brought on by affirmative action is as severe as that engendered by racial subordination. That, in any event, is a judgment the political branches can be trusted to make. In enacting affirmative action programs, a legislature intends to remove obstacles that have unfairly placed individuals of equal qualifications at a competitive disadvantage. I do not believe such action, whether wise or unwise, deserves such an invidious label as "racial paternalism." If the legislature is persuaded that its program is doing more harm than good to the individuals it is designed to benefit, then we can expect the legislature to remedy the problem. Significantly, this is not true of a government action based on invidious discrimination. [Footnote by Justice Stevens.]

reviewed demonstrates that our concepts of equal protection enjoy a greater elasticity than the standard categories might suggest.

In assessing the degree to which today's holding portends a departure from past practice, it is also worth noting that nothing in today's opinion implies any view of Congress' § 5 power and the deference due its exercise that differs from the views expressed by the Fullilove plurality. The Court simply notes the observation in Croson "that the Court's 'treatment of an exercise of congressional power in Fullilove cannot be dispositive here,' because Croson's facts did not implicate Congress' broad power under § 5 of the Fourteenth Amendment," and explains that there is disagreement among today's majority about the extent of the § 5 power. There is therefore no reason to treat the opinion as affecting one way or another the views of § 5 power. [Thus,] today's decision should leave § 5 exactly where it is as the source of an interest of the national government sufficiently important to satisfy the corresponding requirement of the strict scrutiny test.

Finally, I should say that I do not understand that today's decision will necessarily have any effect on the resolution of an issue that was just as pertinent under Fullilove's unlabeled standard as it is under the standard of strict scrutiny now adopted by the Court. The Court has long accepted the view that constitutional authority to remedy past discrimination is not limited to the power to forbid its continuation, but extends to eliminating those effects that would otherwise persist and skew the operation of public systems even in the absence of current intent to practice any discrimination. This is so whether the remedial authority is exercised by a court, the Congress, or some other legislature. Indeed, a majority of the Court today reiterates that there are circumstances in which Government may, consistently with the Constitution, adopt programs aimed at remedying the effects of past invidious discrimination.

When the extirpation of lingering discriminatory effects is thought to require a catch-up mechanism, like the racially preferential inducement under the statutes considered here, the result may be that some members of the historically favored race are hurt by that remedial mechanism, however innocent they may be of any personal responsibility for any discriminatory conduct. When this price is considered reasonable, it is in part because it is a price to be paid only temporarily; if the justification for the preference is eliminating the effects of a past practice, the assumption is that the effects will themselves recede into the past, becoming attenuated and finally disappearing. [Surely] the transition from the Fullilove plurality view [to] today's strict scrutiny [does] not signal a change in the standard by which the burden of a remedial racial preference is to be judged as reasonable or not at any given time....

Justice GINSBURG, with whom Justice BREYER joins, dissenting.

For the reasons stated by Justice Souter, and in view of the attention the political branches are currently giving the matter of affirmative action, I see no compelling cause for the intervention the Court has made in this case. I further agree with Justice Stevens that [large] deference is owed by the Judiciary to "Congress' institutional competence and constitutional authority to overcome historic racial subjugation." I write separately to underscore not the differences the several opinions in this case display, but the considerable field of agreement—the common understandings and concerns—revealed in opinions that together speak for a majority of the Court.

I. The statutes and regulations at issue, as the Court indicates, were adopted by the political branches in response to an "unfortunate reality": "[t]he unhappy persistence of both the practice and the lingering effects of racial discrimination against minority groups in this country." The United States suffers from those lingering effects because, for most of our Nation's history, the idea that "we are just one race," was not embraced. For generations, our lawmakers and judges were unprepared to say that there is in this land no superior race, no race inferior to any other. In Plessy v. Ferguson, not only did this Court endorse the oppressive practice of race segregation, but even Justice Harlan, the advocate of a "color-blind" Constitution, stated: "The white race deems itself to be the dominant race in this country. And so it is, in prestige, in achievements, in education, in wealth and in power. So, I doubt not, it will continue to be for all time, if it remains true to its great heritage and holds fast to the principles of constitutional liberty." Not until Loving v. Virginia, which held unconstitutional Virginia's ban on interracial marriages, could one say with security that the Constitution and this Court would abide no measure "designed to maintain White Supremacy." The divisions in this difficult case should not obscure the Court's recognition of the persistence of racial inequality and a majority's acknowledgement of Congress' authority to act affirmatively, not only to end discrimination, but also to counteract discrimination's lingering effects. Those effects, reflective of a system of racial caste only recently ended, are evident in our workplaces, markets, and neighborhoods. Job applicants with identical resumes, qualifications, and interview styles still experience different receptions, depending on their race. White and African–American consumers still encounter different deals. People of color looking for housing still face discriminatory treatment by landlords, real estate agents, and mortgage lenders. Minority entrepreneurs sometimes fail to gain contracts though they are the low bidders, and they are sometimes refused work even after winning contracts. Bias both conscious and unconscious, reflecting traditional and unexamined habits of thought, keeps up barriers that must come down if equal opportunity and nondiscrimination are ever genuinely to become this country's law and practice. Given this history and its practical consequences, Congress surely can conclude that a carefully designed affirmative action program may help to realize, finally, the "equal protection of the laws" the Fourteenth Amendment has promised since 1868.

II. The lead opinion uses one term, "strict scrutiny," to describe the standard of judicial review for all governmental classifications by race. But that opinion's elaboration strongly suggests that the strict standard announced is indeed "fatal" for classifications burdening groups that have suffered discrimination in our society. That seems to me, and, I believe, to the Court, the enduring lesson one should draw from Korematsu; for in that case, scrutiny the Court described as "most rigid," nonetheless yielded a pass for an odious, gravely injurious racial classification. A Korematsu-type classification, as I read the opinions in this case, will never again survive scrutiny: such a classification, history and precedent instruct, properly ranks as prohibited.

For a classification made to hasten the day when "we are just one race," however, the lead opinion has dispelled the notion that "strict scrutiny" is "fatal in fact." Properly, a majority of the Court calls for review that is searching, in order to ferret out classifications in reality malign, but masquerading as benign. The Court's once lax review of sex-based classifications demonstrates the need for such suspicion. Today's decision thus usefully reiterates that the purpose of strict scrutiny "is precisely to distinguish legitimate from illegitimate uses of race in governmental decisionmaking," "to 'differentiate between' permissible and impermissible governmental use of race," to distinguish " 'between a "No Trespassing" sign and a welcome mat.' "

Close review also is in order for this further reason. As Justice Souter points out, and as this very case shows, some members of the historically favored race can be hurt by catch-up mechanisms designed to cope with the lingering effects of entrenched racial subjugation. Court review can ensure that preferences are not so large as to trammel unduly upon the opportunities of others or interfere too harshly with legitimate expectations of persons in once-preferred groups.

. . .

While I would not disturb the programs challenged in this case, and would leave their improvement to the political branches, I see today's decision as one that allows our precedent to evolve, still to be informed by and responsive to changing conditions.

SHAW v. RENO

510 U.S. ___, 113 S.Ct. 2816, 125 L.Ed.2d 511 (1993).

Justice O'CONNOR delivered the opinion of the Court.

This case involves two of the most complex and sensitive issues this Court has faced in recent years: the meaning of the constitutional "right" to vote, and the propriety of race-based state legislation designed to benefit members of historically disadvantaged racial minority groups. As a result of the 1990 census, North Carolina became entitled to a twelfth seat in the United States House of Representatives. The General Assembly enacted a reapportionment plan that included one majority-black congressional district. After the Attorney General of the United States objected to the plan pursuant to section 5 of the Voting Rights Act of 1965, the General Assembly passed new legislation creating a second majority-black district. Appellants allege that the revised plan, which contains district boundary lines of dramatically irregular shape, constitutes an unconstitutional racial gerrymander. The question before us is whether appellants have stated a cognizable claim.

I. The voting age population of North Carolina is approximately 78% white, 20% black, and 1% Native American; the remaining 1% is predominantly Asian. The black population is relatively dispersed; blacks constitute a majority of the general population in only 5 of the State's 100 counties. [The] largest concentrations of black citizens live in the Coastal Plain, primarily in the northern part. The General Assembly's first redistricting plan contained one majority-black district centered in that area of the State.

Forty of North Carolina's one hundred counties are covered by section 5 of the Voting Rights Act of 1965, which prohibits a jurisdiction subject to its provisions from implementing changes in a "standard, practice, or procedure with respect to voting" without federal authorization. [The] Attorney General, acting through the Assistant Attorney General for the Civil Rights Division, interposed a formal objection to the General Assembly's plan. [In] the Attorney General's view, the General Assembly could have created a second majority-minority district "to give effect to black and Native American voting strength in this area" by using boundary lines "no more irregular than [those] found elsewhere in the proposed plan," but failed to do so for "pretextual reasons." [The] General Assembly [then] enacted a revised redistricting plan that included a second majority-black district. The General Assembly located the second district [in] the north-central region along Interstate 85.

The first of the two majority-black districts contained in the revised plan is somewhat hook shaped. Centered in the northeast portion of the State, it moves southward until it tapers to a narrow band; then, with finger-like extensions, it reaches far into the southern-most part of the State near the South Carolina border. District 1 has been compared to a "Rorschach ink-blot test," Shaw v. Barr, 808 F.Supp. 461, and a "bug splattered on a windshield," Wall Street Journal, Feb. 4, 1992. The second majority-black district, District 12, is even more unusually shaped. It is approximately 160 miles long and, for much of its length, no wider than the I–85 corridor. It winds in snake-like fashion through tobacco country, financial centers, and manufacturing areas "until it gobbles in enough enclaves of black neighborhoods." Northbound and southbound drivers on I–85 sometimes find themselves in separate districts in one county, only to "trade" districts when they enter the next county. Of the 10 counties through which District 12 passes, five are cut into three different districts; even towns are divided. [One] state legislator has remarked that "[i]f you drove down the interstate with both car doors open, you'd kill most of the people in the district."

The Attorney General did not object to the [revised] plan. But numerous North Carolinians did. The North Carolina Republican Party and individual voters brought suit [alleging] that the plan constituted an unconstitutional political gerrymander under Davis v. Bandemer [1986, described below, 12th Ed., p. 1674; Ind.Rts., p. 1345.] That claim was dismissed, and this Court summarily affirmed. Shortly after [that] complaint was filed, appellants instituted the present action [alleging] that the State had created an unconstitutional racial gerrymander. [A three-judge court dismissed the complaint, and we] noted probable jurisdiction.

II. A. [For] much of our Nation's history, [the right to vote] sadly has been denied to many because of race. [Even after the passage of the Fifteenth Amendment,] ostensibly race-neutral devices such as literacy tests with "grandfather" clauses and "good character" provisos were devised to deprive black voters of the franchise. Another of the weapons in the States' arsenal was the racial gerrymander. [In] the 1870's, for example, opponents of Reconstruction in Mississippi "concentrated the bulk of the black population in a 'shoestring' Congressional district running the length of the Mississippi River, leaving five others with white majorities." E. Foner, Reconstruction: America's Unfinished Revolution, 1863–1877 (1988). Some 90 years later, Alabama redefined the boundaries of the city of Tuskegee "from a square to an uncouth twenty-eight-sided figure" in a manner that was alleged to exclude black voters, and only black voters, from the city limits. Gomillion v. Lightfoot [1960, described above, 12th Ed., p. 707; Ind.Rts., p. 378.]. Alabama's exercise in geometry was but one example of the racial discrimination in voting that persisted in parts of this country nearly a century after ratification of the Fifteenth Amendment. In some States, registration of eligible black voters ran 50% behind that of whites. Congress enacted the Voting Rights Act of 1965 as a dramatic and severe response to the situation. The Act proved immediately successful in ensuring racial minorities access to the voting booth; by the early 1970's, the spread between black and white registration in several of the targeted Southern States had fallen to well below 10%.

But it soon became apparent that guaranteeing equal access to the polls would not [root] out other racially discriminatory voting practices. [Accordingly,] the Court held that [multi-member or at-large voting] schemes violate the Fourteenth Amendment when they are adopted with a discriminatory purpose and have the effect of diluting minority voting strength. Rogers v. Lodge. [In] 1982, Congress amended section 2 of the Voting Rights Act to prohibit legislation that results in the dilution of a minority group's voting strength, regardless of the legislature's intent.

B. [The] appellants' argument strikes a powerful historical chord: It is unsettling how closely the North Carolina plan resembles the most egregious racial gerrymanders of the past. [In] their complaint, appellants did not claim that the General Assembly's reapportionment plan unconstitutionally "diluted" white voting strength. They did not even claim to be white. Rather, appellants' complaint alleged that the deliberate segregation of voters into separate districts on the basis of race violated their constitutional right to participate in a "color-blind" electoral process. Despite their invocation of the ideal of a "color-blind" Constitution, appellants appear to concede that race-conscious redistricting is not always unconstitutional. That concession is wise: This Court never has held that race-conscious state decisionmaking is impermissible in all circumstances. What appellants object to is redistricting legislation that is so extremely irregular on its face that it rationally can be viewed only as an effort to segregate the races for purposes of voting, without regard for traditional districting principles and without sufficiently compelling justification. [We] conclude that appellants have stated a claim upon which relief can be granted under the Equal Protection Clause.

III.   A.   [The] central purpose [of the Equal Protection Clause] is to prevent the States from purposefully discriminating between individuals on the basis of race. Laws that explicitly distinguish between individuals on racial grounds fall within the core of that prohibition. No inquiry into legislative purpose is necessary when the racial classification appears on the face of the statute. Express racial classifications are immediately suspect because [they] threaten to stigmatize individuals by reason of their membership in a racial group and to incite racial hostility. Accordingly, [the] Fourteenth Amendment requires state legislation that expressly distinguishes among citizens because of their race to be narrowly tailored to further a compelling governmental interest. These principles apply not only to legislation that contains explicit racial distinctions, but also to those "rare" statutes that, although race-neutral, are, on their face, "unexplainable on grounds other than race." Arlington Heights.

B.   Appellants contend that redistricting legislation that is so bizarre on its face that it is "unexplainable on grounds other than race," demands the same close scrutiny that we give other state laws that classify citizens by race. Our voting rights precedents support that conclusion. [Gomillion] supports appellants' contention that district lines obviously drawn for the purpose of separating voters by race require careful scrutiny under the Equal Protection Clause regardless of the motivations underlying their adoption. [Yet] redistricting differs from other kinds of state decisionmaking in that the legislature always is aware of race when it draws district lines, just as it is aware of age, economic status, religious and political persuasion, and a variety of other demographic factors. That sort of race consciousness does not lead inevitably to impermissible race discrimination. As Wright v. Rockefeller [1964, described above, 12th Ed., p. 707; Ind.Rts., 378] demonstrates, when members of a racial group live together in one community, a reapportionment plan that concentrates members of the group in one district and excludes them from others may reflect wholly legitimate purposes. The district lines may be drawn, for example, to provide for compact districts of contiguous territory, or to maintain the integrity of political subdivisions.

The difficulty of proof, of course, does not mean that a racial gerrymander, once established, should receive less scrutiny [than] other state legislation classifying citizens by race. Moreover, it seems clear to us that proof sometimes will not be difficult at all. In some exceptional cases, a reapportionment plan may be so highly irregular that, on its face, it rationally cannot be understood as anything other than an effort to "segregat[e] ... voters" on the basis of race. Gomillion [was] such a case. So, too, would be a case in which a State concentrated a dispersed minority population in a single district by disregarding traditional districting principles such as compactness, contiguity, and respect for political subdivisions. We emphasize that these criteria are important not because they are constitutionally required—they are not—but because they are objective factors that may serve to defeat a claim that a district has been gerrymandered on racial lines.

Put differently, we believe that reapportionment is one area in which appearances do matter. A reapportionment plan that includes in one district individuals who belong to the same race, but who are otherwise widely separated by geographical and political boundaries, and who may have little in common with one another but the color of their skin, bears an uncomfortable resemblance to political apartheid. It reinforces the perception that members of the same racial group—regardless of their age, education, economic status, or the community in which the live—think alike, share the same political interests, and will prefer the same candidates at the polls. We have rejected such perceptions elsewhere as impermissible racial stereotypes. By perpetuating such notions, a racial gerrymander may exacerbate the very patterns of racial bloc voting that majority-minority districting is sometimes said to counteract.

The message that such districting sends to elected representatives is equally pernicious. When a district obviously is created solely to effectuate the perceived common interests of one racial group, elected officials are more likely to believe that their primary obligation is to represent only the members of that group, rather than their constituency as a whole. This is altogether antithetical to our system of representative democracy. As Justice Douglas explained in his dissent in Wright v. Rockefeller: "Here the individual is important, not his race, his creed, or his color. The principle of equality is at war with the notion that District A must be represented by a Negro, as it is with the notion that District B must be represented by a Caucasian, District C by a Jew, District D by a Catholic, and so on ... That system, by whatever name it is called, is a divisive force in a community, emphasizing differences between candidates and voters that are irrelevant in the constitutional sense. . . . When racial or religious lines are drawn by the State, the multiracial, multireligious communities that our Constitution seeks to weld together as one become separatist; antagonisms that relate to race or to religion rather than to political issues are generated; communities seek not the best representative but the best racial or religious partisan. Since that system is at war with the democratic ideal, it should find no footing here." For these reasons, we conclude that a plaintiff challenging a reapportionment statute under the Equal Protection Clause may state a claim by alleging that the legislation, though race-neutral on its face, rationally cannot be understood as anything other than an effort to separate voters into different districts on the basis of race, and that the separation lacks sufficient justification. . . .

C. The dissenters consider the circumstances of this case "functionally indistinguishable" from multimember districting and at-large voting systems, which are loosely described as "other varieties of gerrymandering." At-large and multimember schemes, however, do not classify voters on the basis of race. Classifying citizens by race [threatens] special harms that are not present in our vote-dilution cases. It therefore warrants different analysis. Justice Souter apparently believes that racial gerrymandering is harmless unless it dilutes a racial group's voting strength. [But] reapportionment legislation that cannot be understood as anything other than an effort to classify and separate voters by race injures voters in other ways. It reinforces racial stereotypes and threatens to undermine our system of representative democracy by signaling to elected officials that they represent a particular racial group rather than their constituency as a whole. [The] dissenters make two other arguments that cannot be reconciled with our precedents. First, they suggest that a racial gerrymander of the sort alleged here is functionally equivalent to gerrymanders for nonracial purposes, such as political gerrymanders. [But] our country's long and persistent history of racial discrimination in voting—as well as our Fourteenth Amendment jurisprudence, which always has reserved the strictest scrutiny for discrimination on the basis of race—would seem to compel the opposite conclusion. Second, Justice Stevens argues that racial gerrymandering poses no constitutional difficulties when district lines are drawn to favor the minority, rather than the majority. We have made clear, however, that equal protection analysis "is not dependent on the race of those burdened or benefited by a particular classification." Croson....

IV. Justice Souter contends that exacting scrutiny of racial gerrymanders under the Fourteenth Amendment is inappropriate because reapportionment "nearly always require[s] some consideration of race for legitimate reasons." [That] racial bloc voting or minority political cohesion may be found to exist in some cases, [however,] is no reason to treat all racial gerrymanders differently from other kinds of racial classification. Justice Souter apparently views racial gerrymandering of the type presented here as a special category of "benign" racial discrimination that should be subject to relaxed judicial review. As we have said, however, the very reason that the Equal Protection Clause demands strict scrutiny of all racial classifications is because without it, a court cannot determine whether or not the discrimination truly is "benign." Thus, if appellants' allegations of a racial gerrymander are not contradicted on remand, the District Court must determine whether the reapportionment plan satisfies strict scrutiny. [The] state appellees suggest that a covered jurisdiction may have a compelling interest in creating majority-minority districts in order to comply with the Voting Rights Act. The States certainly have a very strong interest in complying with federal antidiscrimination laws that are constitutionally valid as interpreted and as applied. But in the context of a Fourteenth Amendment challenge, courts must bear in mind the difference between what the law permits, and what it requires. [A] reapportionment plan that satisfies section 5 still may be enjoined as unconstitutional....

V. Racial classifications of any sort pose the risk of lasting harm to our society. They reinforce the belief, held by too many for too much of our history, that individuals should be judged by the color of their skin. Racial classifications with respect to voting carry particular dangers. Racial gerrymandering, even for remedial purposes, may balkanize us into competing racial factions; it threatens to carry us further from the goal of a political system in which race no longer matters—a goal that the Fourteenth and Fifteenth Amendments embody, and to which the Nation continues to aspire. It is for these reasons that race-based districting by our state legislatures demands close judicial scrutiny. [We] hold [that] appellants have stated a claim under the Equal Protection Clause by alleging that the North Carolina General Assembly adopted a reapportionment scheme so irrational on its face that it can be understood only as an effort to segregate voters into separate voting districts because of their race, and that the separation lacks sufficient justification. . . .

[Reversed.]

Justice WHITE, with whom Justice BLACKMUN and Justice STEVENS join, dissenting.

The facts of this case mirror those presented in United Jewish Organizations of Williamsburgh, Inc. v. Carey [1977, described above, 12th Ed., p. 766; Ind.Rts., p. 437] (UJO), where the Court rejected a claim that creation of a majority-minority district violated the Constitution. [Of] particular relevance, five of the Justices reasoned that members of the white majority could not plausibly argue that their influence over the political process had been unfairly cancelled. [The] Court today chooses not to overrule, but rather to sidestep, UJO. It does so by glossing over the striking similarities, focusing on surface differences, most notably the (admittedly unusual) shape of the newly created district, and imagining an entirely new cause of action. [The] notion that North Carolina's plan, under which whites remain a voting majority in a disproportionate number of congressional districts, and pursuant to which the State has sent its first black representatives since Reconstruction to Congress, might have violated appellants' constitutional rights is both a fiction and a departure from settled equal protection principles. . . .

I. A. The grounds for my disagreement [are] simply stated: Appellants have not presented a cognizable claim, because they have not alleged a cognizable injury. To date, we have held that only two types of state voting practices could give rise to a constitutional claim. The first involves direct and outright deprivation of the right to vote, for example by means of a poll tax or literacy test. Plainly, this variety is not implicated by appellants' allegations. [The] second type of unconstitutional practice is that which "affects the political strength of various groups," Mobile v. Bolden, 446 U.S. 55 (1980), in violation of the Equal Protection Clause. As for this latter category, we have insisted that members of the political or racial group demonstrate that the challenged action have the intent and effect of unduly diminishing their influence on the political process. Although this severe burden has limited the number of successful suits, it was adopted for sound reasons.

The central explanation has to do with the nature of the redistricting process. As the majority recognizes, "redistricting differs from other kinds of state decisionmaking in that the legislature always is aware of race when it draws district lines, just as it is aware of age, economic status, religious and political persuasion, and a variety of other demographic factors." [Because] extirpating such considerations from the redistricting process is unrealistic, the Court has not invalidated all plans that consciously use race, but rather has looked at their impact.

Redistricting plans also reflect group interests and inevitably are conceived with partisan aims in mind. To allow judicial interference whenever this occurs would be to invite constant and unmanageable intrusion. Moreover, a group's power to affect the political process does not automatically dissipate by virtue of an electoral loss. Accordingly, we have asked that an identifiable group demonstrate more than mere lack of success at the polls to make out a successful gerrymandering claim....

B.   [The] State has made no mystery of its intent, which was to respond to the Attorney General's objections by improving the minority group's prospects of electing a candidate of its choice. I doubt that this constitutes a discriminatory purpose. [But] even assuming that it does, there is no question that appellants have not alleged the requisite discriminatory effects. Whites constitute roughly 76 percent of the total population and 79 percent of the voting age population in North Carolina. Yet, under the State's plan, they still constitute a voting majority in 10 (or 83 percent) of the 12 congressional districts. Though they might be dissatisfied at the prospect of casting a vote for a losing candidate—a lot shared by many, including a disproportionate number of minority voters—surely they cannot complain of discriminatory treatment.

II.   The majority attempts to distinguish UJO by imagining a heretofore unknown type of constitutional claim. [The] logic of its theory appears to be that race-conscious redistricting that "segregates" by drawing odd-shaped lines is qualitatively different from race-conscious redistricting that affects groups in some other way. The distinction is without foundation.

A.   The essence of the majority's argument is that UJO dealt with a claim of vote dilution—which required a specific showing of harm—and that cases such as Gomillion and Wright dealt with claims of racial segregation—which did not. I read these decisions quite differently. [In] Gomillion, [the] group that formed the majority at the state level purportedly set out to manipulate city boundaries in order to remove members of the minority, thereby denying them valuable municipal services. No analogous purpose or effect has been alleged in this case. [In] Wright, [the] facts might have supported the contention that the districts were intended to, and did in fact, shield the Seventeenth District from any minority influence and "pack" black and Puerto Rican voters in the Eighteenth, thereby invidiously minimizing their voting strength. In other words, the purposeful creation of a majority-minority district could have discriminatory effect if it is achieved by means of "packing"—i.e., over-concentration of minority voters. In the present case, the facts could sustain no such allegation.

B.   Lacking support in any of the Court's precedents, the majority's novel type of claim also makes no sense. As I understand the [majority's] theory, a redistricting plan that uses race to "segregate" voters by drawing "uncouth" lines is harmful in a way that a plan that uses race to distribute voters differently is not, for the former "bears an uncomfortable resemblance to political apartheid." The distinction is untenable.

Racial gerrymanders come in various shades: At-large voting schemes; the fragmentation of a minority group among various districts "so that it is a majority in none," otherwise known as "cracking,"; the "stacking" of "a large minority population concentration ... with a larger white population"; and, finally, the "concentration of [minority voters] into districts where they constitute an excessive majority," also called "packing." In each instance, race is consciously utilized by the legislature for electoral purposes; in each instance, we have put the plaintiff challenging the district lines to the burden of demonstrating that the plan was meant to, and did in fact, exclude an identifiable racial group from participation in the political process.

Not so, apparently, when the districting "segregates" by drawing odd-shaped lines. In that case, we are told, such proof no longer is needed. Instead, it is the State that must rebut the allegation that race was taken into account, a fact that, together with the legislators' consideration of ethnic, religious, and other group characteristics, I had thought we practically took for granted. Part of the explanation for the majority's approach has to do, perhaps, with the emotions stirred by words such as "segregation" and "political apartheid." But their loose and imprecise use by today's majority has, I fear, led it astray. [A] plan that "segregates" being functionally indistinguishable from any of the other varieties of gerrymandering, we should be consistent in what we require from a claimant: Proof of discriminatory purpose and effect.

The other part of the majority's explanation of its holding is related to its simultaneous discomfort and fascination with irregularly shaped districts. Lack of compactness or contiguity, like uncouth district lines, certainly is a helpful indicator that some form of gerrymandering (racial or other) might have taken place. [But] while district irregularities may provide strong indicia of a potential gerrymander, they do no more than that. In particular, they have no bearing on whether the plan ultimately is found to violate the Constitution. Given two districts drawn on similar, race-based grounds, the one does not become more injurious than the other simply by virtue of being snake-like. [By] focusing on looks rather than impact, the majority [in its approach] will unnecessarily hinder to some extent a State's voluntary effort to ensure a modicum of minority representation [where] the minority population is geographically dispersed. [When the] creation of a majority-minority district does not unfairly minimize the voting power of any other group, the Constitution does not justify, much less mandate, such obstruction.

III. Although I disagree [that] appellants' claim is cognizable, the Court's discussion of the level of scrutiny it requires warrants a few comments. I have no doubt that a State's compliance with the Voting Rights Act clearly constitutes a compelling interest. [The] Court [warns] that the State's redistricting effort must be "narrowly tailored" to further its interest in complying with the law. It is evident to me, however, that what North Carolina did was precisely tailored to meet the objection of the Attorney General to its prior plan. Hence, I see no need for a remand at all, even accepting the majority's basic approach.

Furthermore, how it intends to manage this standard, I do not know. Is it more "narrowly tailored" to create an irregular majority-minority district as opposed to one that is compact but harms other State interests such as incumbency protection or the representation of rural interests? Of the following two options—creation of two minority influence districts or of a single majority-minority district—is one "narrowly tailored" and the other not? [State] efforts to remedy minority vote dilution are wholly unlike what typically has been labeled "affirmative action." To the extent that no other racial group is injured, remedying a Voting Rights Act violation does not involve preferential treatment. It involves, instead, an attempt to equalize treatment, and to provide minority voters with an effective voice in the political process. The Equal Protection Clause of the Constitution, surely, does not stand in the way....

Justice BLACKMUN, dissenting.

I join Justice White's dissenting opinion. [It] is particularly ironic that the case in which today's majority chooses to abandon settled law and to recognize for the first time this "analytically distinct" constitutional claim, is a challenge by white voters to the plan under which North Carolina has sent black representatives to Congress for the first time since Reconstruction....

Justice STEVENS, dissenting.

For the reasons stated by Justice White, the decision of the District Court should be affirmed. I add these comments to emphasize that the two critical facts in this case are undisputed: first, the shape of District 12 is so bizarre that it must have been drawn for the purpose of either advantaging or disadvantaging a cognizable group of voters; and, second, regardless of that shape, it was drawn for the purpose of facilitating the election of a second black representative from North Carolina. These unarguable facts, which the Court devotes most of its opinion to proving, give rise to three constitutional questions: Does the Constitution impose a requirement of contiguity or compactness on how the States may draw their electoral districts? Does the Equal Protection Clause prevent a State from drawing district boundaries for the purpose of facilitating the election of a member of an identifiable group of voters? And, finally, if the answer to the second question is generally "No," should it be different when the favored group is defined by race?

[The] first question is easy. There is no independent constitutional requirement of compactness or contiguity, and the Court's opinion (despite its many references to the shape of District 12) does not suggest otherwise. The existence of bizarre and uncouth district boundaries is powerful evidence of an ulterior purpose behind the shaping of those boundaries—usually a purpose to advantage the political party in control of the districting process. [In] this case, however, we know what the legislators' purpose was: The North Carolina Legislature drew District 12 to include a majority of African–American voters. Evidence of the district's shape is therefore convincing, but it is also cumulative, and, for our purposes, irrelevant.

As for the second question, I believe that the Equal Protection Clause is violated when the State creates the kind of uncouth district boundaries seen in Gomillion and this case for the sole purpose of making it more difficult for members of a minority group to win an election. The duty to govern impartially is abused when a group with power over the electoral process defines electoral boundaries solely to enhance its own political strength at the expense of any weaker group. That duty, however, is not violated when the majority acts to facilitate the election of a member of a group that lacks such power because it remains underrepresented in the state legislature—whether that group is defined by political affiliation, by common economic interests, or by religious, ethnic, or racial characteristics. The difference between constitutional and unconstitutional gerrymanders has nothing to do with whether they are based on assumptions about the groups they affect, but whether their purpose is to enhance the power of the group in control of the districting process at the expense of any minority group, and thereby to strengthen the unequal distribution of electoral power. When an assumption that people in particular a minority group (whether they are defined by the political party, religion, ethnic group, or race to which they belong) will vote in a particular way is used to benefit that group, no constitutional violation occurs. Politicians have always relied on assumptions that people in particular groups are likely to vote in a particular way when they draw new district lines, and I cannot believe that anything in today's opinion will stop them from doing so in the future. Finally, we must ask whether otherwise permissible redistricting to benefit an underrepresented minority group becomes impermissible when the minority group is defined by its race. The Court today answers this question in the affirmative, and its answer is wrong. If it is permissible to draw boundaries to provide adequate representation for rural voters, for union members, for Hasidic Jews, for Polish Americans, or for Republicans, it necessarily follows that it is permissible to do the same thing for members of the very minority group whose history in the United States gave birth to the Equal Protection Clause. A contrary conclusion could only be described as perverse....

Justice SOUTER, dissenting.

Today, the Court recognizes a new cause of action under which a State's electoral redistricting plan that includes a configuration "so bizarre" that it "rationally cannot be understood as anything other than an effort to separate voters into different districts on the basis of race [without] sufficient justification," will be subjected to strict scrutiny. In my view there is no justification [to] depart from our prior decisions by carving out this narrow group of cases for strict scrutiny in place of the review customarily applied in cases dealing with discrimination in electoral districting on the basis of race.

I. Until today, the Court has analyzed equal protection claims involving race in electoral districting differently from equal protection claims involving other forms of governmental conduct. [Unlike] other contexts in which we have addressed the State's conscious use of race, electoral districting calls for decisions that nearly always require some consideration of race for legitimate reasons where there is a racially mixed population. As long as members of racial groups have the commonality of interest implicit in our ability to talk about concepts like "minority voting strength," and "dilution of minority votes," and as long as racial bloc voting takes place, legislators will have to take race into account in order to avoid dilution of minority voting strength in the districting plans they adopt. [A] second distinction between districting and most other governmental decisions in which race has figured is that those other decisions using racial criteria characteristically occur in circumstances in which the use of race to the advantage of one person is necessarily at the obvious expense of a member of a different race. Thus, for example, awarding government contracts on a racial basis excludes certain firms from competition on racial grounds. And when race is used to supplant seniority in layoffs, someone is laid off who would not be otherwise. The same principle pertains in nondistricting aspects of voting law, where race-based discrimination places the disfavored voters at the disadvantage of exclusion from the franchise without any alternative benefit. In districting, by contrast, the mere placement of an individual in one district instead of another denies no one a right or benefit provided to others. All citizens may register, vote, and be represented. In whatever district, the individual voter has a right to vote in each election, and the election will result in the voter's representation. [One's] constitutional rights are not violated merely because the candidate one supports loses the election or because a group (including a racial group) to which one belongs winds up with a representative from outside that group. . . .

II. Our different approaches to equal protection in electoral districting and nondistricting cases reflect these differences. [Because] the legitimate consideration of race in a districting decision is usually inevitable under the Voting Rights Act when communities are racially mixed, however, and because, without more, it does not result in diminished political effectiveness for anyone, we have not taken the approach of applying the usual standard of such heightened "scrutiny" to race-based districting decisions. [If] a cognizable harm like dilution or the abridgment of the right to participate in the electoral process is shown, the districting plan violates the Fourteenth Amendment. If not, it does not. Under this approach, in the absence of an allegation of such cognizable harm, there is no need for further scrutiny because a gerrymandering claim cannot be proven without the element of harm. Nor if dilution is proven is there any need for further constitutional scrutiny; there has never been a suggestion that such use of race could be justified under any type of scrutiny, since the dilution of the right to vote can not be said to serve any legitimate governmental purpose.

There is thus no theoretical inconsistency in having two distinct approaches to equal protection analysis, one for cases of electoral districting and one for most other types of state governmental decisions. Nor, because of the distinctions between the two categories, is there any risk that Fourteenth Amendment districting law as such will be taken to imply anything for purposes of general Fourteenth Amendment scrutiny about "benign" racial discrimination, or about group entitlement as distinct from individual protection, or about the appropriateness of strict or other heightened scrutiny.

III. The Court appears to accept this, and it does not purport to disturb the law of vote dilution in any way. Instead, the Court creates a new "analytically distinct" cause of action, the principal element of which is that a districting plan be "so bizarre on its face," or "irrational on its face," or "extremely irregular on its face," that it "rationally cannot be understood as anything other than an effort to segregate citizens into separate voting districts on the basis of race without sufficient justification." Pleading such an element, the Court holds, suffices without a further allegation of harm, to state a claim upon which relief can be granted under the Fourteenth Amendment.

[The] Court offers no adequate justification for treating the narrow category of bizarrely shaped district claims differently from other districting claims. The only justification I can imagine would be the preservation of "sound districting principles," UJO, such as compactness and contiguity. But [such] principles are not constitutionally required, with the consequence that their absence cannot justify the distinct constitutional regime put in place by the Court today. Since there is no justification for the departure here from the principles that continue to govern electoral districting cases generally in accordance with our prior decisions, I would not respond to the seeming egregiousness of the redistricting now before us by untethering the concept of racial gerrymander in such a case from the concept of harm exemplified by dilution. . . . *

Probably the most significant doctrinal question remaining open after Shaw v. Reno was whether the existence of a bizarrely shaped district, as in Shaw, was a necessary condition for a finding of unconstitutionality. Two years later, in MILLER v. JOHNSON, 519 U.S. ___ (1995), the Court answered that question in the negative. As in Shaw,

---

* One legislative response to Shaw v. Reno is H.R. 1096, which would forbid legislative redistricting on the basis of race. In connection with Shaw, note the two Voting Rights Act cases of the 1993 Term that dealt with related issues in a statutory context. In particular, the views expressed in Justice O'Connor's opinion in Shaw should be compared to those expressed by Justice Thomas in Holder v. Hall, 514 U.S. ___ (1994), described below, addition to 12th Ed., p. 959; Ind.Rts., p. 630. And in Johnson v. De Grandy, 514 U.S. ___ (1994), the Court's rejection of a Voting Rights Act claim was accompanied by Justice Kennedy's explicit warning about the importance of evaluating Voting Rights Act-inspired redistricting plans against the constitutional commands of Shaw v. Reno. "[T]he number of minorities elected to office [and] the number of districts in which minorities constitute a voting majority [are] not synonymous, and it would be an affront to our constitutional traditions to treat them as such. [Given] our decision in Shaw, there is good reason for state and federal officials with responsibilities related to redistricting, as well as reviewing courts, to recognize that explicit race-based redistricting embarks us on a most dangerous course. It is necessary to bear in mind that redistricting must comply with the overriding demands of the Equal Protection Clause."

the case concerned a congressional district, in this case the newly created Eleventh District in Georgia. After two previous attempts at congressional redistricting had failed to receive United States Department of Justice preclearance under the Voting Rights Act, largely for failure to locate certain concentrations of black citizens within a majority-black district and for failure to take the opportunity to create three rather than two majority-black districts. When Georgia responded by creating three majority-black districts, including the Eleventh, the Justice Department gave clearance, but suit was filed by white voters in the District, claiming the existence of a gerrymandered district as in Shaw. With Justice KENNEDY writing for the majority, the Court held the districting unconstitutional, largely on the authority of Shaw, and confronted directly the question of the relevance of the shape of the District. "The essence of the equal protection claim recognized in Shaw is that the State has used race as a basis for separating voters into districts. Just as the State may not, absent extraordinary justification, segregate citizens on the basis of race in its public parks, buses, golf courses, beaches, and schools, so did we recognize in Shaw that it may not separate its citizens into different voting districts on the basis of race. [Our] observation in Shaw of the consequences of racial stereotyping was not meant to suggest that a district must be bizarre on its face before there is a constitutional violation. Nor was our conclusion in Shaw that in certain instances a district's appearance [can] give rise to an equal protection claim, a holding that bizarreness was a threshold showing. [Shape] is relevant not because bizarreness is a necessary element of the constitutional wrong or a threshold requirement of proof, but because it may be persuasive circumstantial evidence that race for its own sake, and not other districting principles, was the legislature's dominant and controlling rationale in drawing its district lines. The logical implication [is] that parties may rely on evidence other than bizarreness to establish race-based districting."

Justice Kennedy went on to specify the standard to be applied to make out a claim after Shaw. "Parties alleging that a State has assigned voters on the basis of race are neither confined in their proof to evidence regarding the district's geometry and makeup nor required to make a threshold showing of bizarreness. Although race-based decision-making is inherently suspect, Adarand, until a claimant makes a showing sufficient to support that allegation the good faith of a state legislature must be presumed. [Redistricting] legislatures will, for example, almost always be aware of racial demographics, but it does not follow that race predominates in the redistricting process. [The] plaintiff's burden is to show, either through circumstantial evidence of a district's shape and demographics or more direct evidence going to legislative purpose, that race was the predominant factor motivating the legislature's decision to place a significant number of voters within or without a particular district. To make this showing, a plaintiff must prove that the legislature subordinated traditional race-neutral districting principles, including but not limited to compactness, contiguity, respect for political subdivisions or communities defined by actual shared interests, to racial considerations. [Although] by comparison with other districts the geometric shape of the Eleventh District may not seem bizarre on its face, when shape is considered in conjunction with its racial and population densities, [and in conjunction with] evidence showing that the General Assembly was motivated by a predominant, overriding desire to assign black populations to the Eleventh District and thereby permit the creation of a third majority-black district[, Georgia's] congressional redistricting plan cannot be upheld unless it satisfies strict scrutiny, our most rigorous and exacting standard of constitutional review." Finding that standard satisfied neither by the attempted acquiescence with the Department of Justice, nor by any other interest, the Court upheld the judgment of unconstitutionality.

Justice O'CONNOR issued a brief concurring opinion, explaining the evidentiary importance of "substantial disregard of customary and traditional districting practices." Consequently, she argued, "application of the Court's standard does not throw into doubt the vast majority of the Nation's 435 congressional districts [even] though race may well have been considered in the redistricting process." Justice STEVENS dissented on the grounds that in his view the plaintiffs had no standing to sue, and in addition he, along with Justices Breyer and Souter (in part), joined the dissenting opinion of Justice GINSBURG. Her dissent was based largely on disagreement with what she described as the majority's new "race-as-predominant-factor" standard. She emphasized the history of racial districting to prevent black representation, and noted that "only 14 years ago" the Chairman of the Georgia House Reapportionment Committee had said, " 'I don't want to draw nigger districts.' " Yet in addition to the affirmative action dimension, she focused on the way in which taking "ethnicity" into account, even as a predominant factor, was very much part of a traditional approach to districting. "Ethnicity itself can tie people together, as volumes of social science literature have documented. [The] creation of ethnic districts reflecting felt identity is not ordinarily viewed as offensive or demeaning to those included in the delineation. [That] ethnicity defines some [voting] groups is a political reality. Until now, no constitutional infirmity has been seen in districting Irish or Italian voters together, for example, so long as the delineation does not abandon traditional apportionment practices. If Chinese–Americans and Russian–Americans may seek and secure group recognition in the delineation of voting districts, then African–Americans should not be dissimilarly treated."

12th ED., p. 851; IND. RTS., p. 522
Add as new footnote at end of Note 3:

   4a. Illinois Elections Board v. Socialist Workers Party was applied in Norman v. Reed, 502 U.S. 279 (1992). In striking down various restrictions on the efforts of the Harold Washington Party to expand from Chicago out into all of Cook County, Justice Souter's majority opinion (Justice Scalia was the only dissenter) again required that signature and related restrictions on new parties "be narrowly drawn to advance a state interest of compelling importance."

12th ED., p. 854; IND. RTS., p. 525
Add as new Note at end of Ballot Access materials:

   8. *Write-in voting.* The focus on the First Amendment was even more apparent in BURDICK v. TAKUSHI, 504 U.S. 428 (1992), in which

the Court upheld Hawaii's prohibition on write-in voting. Although Hawaii's election laws satisfied the ballot access requirements of Anderson v. Celebrezze and other cases, the challenger claimed he still had a First Amendment right to write in the candidate of his choice at the election, even if only as a protest, and even if the vote were to be cast for "Donald Duck."

In rejecting the claim, Justice WHITE's opinion for the Court first rejected the idea that all restrictions on the right to vote were to be subject to strict scrutiny. "Election laws will invariably impose some burden on individual voters. [Consequently,] to subject every voting regulation to strict scrutiny and to require that the regulation be narrowly tailored to advance a compelling state interest [would] tie the hands of States seeking to assure that elections are operated equitably and efficiently. [Instead, a] more flexible standard applies. [Anderson v. Celebrezze.] [Under] this standard, the rigorousness of our inquiry into the propriety of a state election law depends upon the extent to which a challenged regulation burdens First and Fourteenth Amendment rights. [When] those rights are subject to 'severe' restrictions, the regulation must be 'narrowly drawn to advance a state interest of compelling importance.' Norman v. Reed, 502 U.S. ___ (1992) [noted briefly above, addition to 12th Ed., p. 851; Ind.Rts., p. 522]. But when a state election law provision imposes only 'reasonable, nondiscriminatory restrictions' upon the First and Fourteenth Amendment rights of voters, 'the State's important regulatory interests are generally sufficient to justify' the restrictions. Anderson."

Applying this standard, Justice White found the prohibition on write-in voting constitutionally permissible. Given that the access of candidates to the ballot satisfied constitutional standards, "any burden on voters' freedom of choice and association is borne only by those who fail to identify their candidate of choice until days before the primary. [Attributing] to elections a [generalized] expressive function would undermine the ability of States to operate elections fairly and efficiently. [When] a State's ballot access laws pass constitutional muster, [a] prohibition on write-in voting will be presumptively valid. [In] such situations, the objection [amounts] to nothing more than the insistence that the State record, count, and publish individual protests against the election system or the choices presented on the ballot through the efforts of those who actively participate in the system."

Justice KENNEDY, joined by Justices Blackmun and Stevens, dissented. Noting that "Democratic candidates often run unopposed, especially in state legislative races," he concluded that because the challenger "could not write in the name of a candidate he preferred, he had no way to cast a meaningful vote. [The] majority's approval of Hawaii's ban is ironic at a time when the new democracies in foreign countries strive to emerge from an era of sham elections in which the name of the ruling party candidate was the only one on the ballot. Hawaii does not impose as severe a restriction on the right to vote, but it imposes a restriction that has a haunting similarity in its tendency to exact severe similarities for one who does anything but vote the dominant party ballot." Although Justice Kennedy agreed that there was no independent right to cast a protest vote, and agreed as well with the majority's general standard for ballot access cases, he disagreed with the Court's presumption in favor of the constitutionality of restrictions on write-in voting, and offered a more specific application of that standard: a ban on write-in votes is impermissible when it operates as part of a general ballot access mechanism that "deprives some voters of any substantial voice in selecting candidates for the entire range of offices at issue in a particular election."

12th ED., p. 870; IND. RTS., p. 541

Add at end of footnote 2:

Note Nordlinger v. Hahn, 505 U.S. 1 (1992), described above, addition to 12th Ed., p. 635; Ind.Rts., p. 306, applying a particularly deferential version of rational-basis review in upholding California's Proposition 13, whose acquisition-value method of taxation benefited long-term residents over newer property owners. Finding that the plaintiff had been a California resident (in an apartment) before purchasing property, the Court held that she had no standing to maintain a heightened scrutiny right to travel claim.

Chapter 10(5)

THE POST–CIVIL WAR AMENDMENTS AND CIVIL LEGISLATION: CONSTITUTIONAL RESTRAINTS ON PRIVATE CONDUCT; CONGRESSIONAL POWER TO IMPLEMENT THE AMENDMENTS

12th ED., p. 922; IND. RTS., p. 593

Add at end of footnote 5:

The non-governmental defendants in Lugar claimed that even if their conduct violated the Constitution, they enjoyed a qualified immunity from suit for damages under section 1983. The Court did not deal with that issue in Lugar itself, but revisited it in Wyatt v. Cole, 504 U.S. 158 (1992), there rejecting the claim that private parties whose conduct was found to deprive others of constitutional rights had even a qualified immunity from suit for damages.

12th ED., p. 924; IND. RTS., p. 595

Add as new Note after Note 5 (U.S.O.C.):

5A. *Edmonson.* In contrast to most of its recent state action decisions, the Court in EDMONSON v. LEESVILLE CONCRETE CO., 500 U.S. 614 (1991), found the requisite state action in a decision taken by a non-governmental actor. In holding that race-based peremptory challenges (see Batson v. Kentucky, 1986, described above, 12th Ed., p. 705; Ind. Rts., p. 376, and subsequent cases, described above, addition to 12th Ed., p. 705; Ind. Rts., p. 376) to jurors by private litigants in civil litigation constituted state action for Fourteenth Amendment equal protection purposes, Justice KENNEDY's opinion for the Court relied heavily on the analytical approach of Lugar v. Edmondson. Turning first to the question "whether the claimed constitutional deprivation resulted from the exercise of a right or privilege having its source in state authority," Justice Kennedy found this standard easily satisfied because peremptory challenges in civil litigation were here the creatures of "statutory authorization" and because the very idea of a peremptory challenge has "no significance outside a court of law." He then turned to the second part of the "Lugar test, whether a private litigant in all fairness must be deemed a government actor." Recognizing that this is "often a factbound inquiry," Justice Kennedy nevertheless asserted that "our cases disclose certain principles of general application, [including] the extent to which the actor relies on governmental assistance and benefits [Burton]; whether the actor is performing a traditional governmental function [Terry v. Adams; Marsh v. Alabama; U.S.O.C.]; and whether the injury caused is aggravated in a unique way by the incidents of governmental authority [Shelley v. Kraemer]."

Applying these principles, the Court relied on the "overt, significant participation of the government" in both the peremptory challenge system and civil litigation generally; on the pervasive statutory regulation of the jury system generally; and on the active involvement of the judge in voir dire examination of jurors and in administering the peremptory challenge system. It also found the jury system in general and the peremptory challenge system in particular the very embodiment of a traditional governmental function. "The peremptory challenge is used in selecting an entity that is a quintessential governmental body, having no attributes of a private actor. [If] the government confers on a private body the power to choose the government's employees or officials, the private body will be bound by the constitutional mandate of race-neutrality [Tarkanian; Rendell–Baker; Terry]. [Finally,] we note that the injury caused by the discrimination is made more severe because the government permits it to occur within the courthouse itself. Few places are a more real expression of the constitutional authority of the government, where the law unfolds. [To] permit racial exclusion in this official forum compounds the racial insult inherent in judging a citizen by the color of his or her skin."

Justice O'CONNOR, joined by Chief Justice Rehnquist and Justice Scalia, dissented, maintaining that it was necessary after Jackson v. Metropolitan Edison and Blum v. Yaretsky for it to be shown that the government was involved in the specific decision challenged, a showing not made here. She maintained that the involvement of government in setting up the process of peremptory challenges was "irrelevant to the issue at hand. [All] of this government action [is] merely prerequisite[ ] to the use of a peremptory challenge; [it does not constitute] participation *in* the challenge. That these actions may be necessary to a peremptory challenge [no] more makes the challenge state action than the building of roads and provision of public transportation makes state action of riding on a bus." Similarly, she argued, because the choice of whom, if anyone, to strike peremptorily is and always has been a private choice, there was no warrant for concluding that this was a traditional governmental function. "Trials in this country are adversarial proceedings. Attorneys for private litigants do not act on behalf of the government, or even the public as a whole; attorneys represent their clients. [The] actions of a lawyer in a courtroom do not become those of the government by virtue of their location[, even] if those actions are based on race. Racism is a terrible thing. It is irrational, destructive, and mean. [But] not every opprobrious act is a constitutional violation."

Justice SCALIA's separate dissent, echoing criticisms made earlier of Shelley v. Kraemer and Burton v. Wilmington Parking Authority, chastised the majority for distorting state action doctrine where race was at issue. "To overhaul the doctrine of state action in this fashion—what a magnificent demonstration of this institution's hostility to race-based judgments, even by private actors! The price of the demonstration is, alas, high, and much of it will be paid by the minority litigants who use our courts." *

---

* A Term later, the Court followed Edmonson in holding that the race-based peremptory challenges of a criminal defendant constituted state action and consequently a

5B. *Amtrak.* In most state action cases, the question is whether an admittedly non-governmental entity is sufficiently involved with or controlled by government as to take on the constitutional obligations of the state. Occasionally, however, the question is more straightforward, with the issue being whether some entity simply *is* the state. That was the issue in LEBRON v. NATIONAL RAILROAD PASSENGER CORPO-RATION, 516 U.S. ___ (1995), involving the question whether the National Railroad Passenger Corporation (Amtrak) could, as operator of Pennsylvania Station in New York City, impose content-based restrictions on the leasing of billboard space for political purposes. The United States Court of Appeals for the Second Circuit had held that Amtrak was not a governmental entity, relying largely on provisions to that effect in the Act of Congress that created and incorporated it. Writing for an 8–1 majority, however, Justice SCALIA rejected this claim, concluding that the status of an entity as governmental or not was not, for constitutional purposes, to be determined by its authorizing statutes or regulations. "If Amtrak is, by its very nature, what the Constitution regards as the Government, congressional pronouncement can no more relieve it of its First Amendment restrictions than a similar pronouncement could exempt the Federal Bureau of Investigation from the Fourth Amendment." Justice Scalia then looked directly at Amtrak's status, and determined that it was "an agency or instrumentality of the United States.... [W]here, as here, the Government creates a corporation by special law, for the furtherance of governmental objectives, and retains for itself permanent authority to appoint a majority of the directors of that corporation, the corporation is part of the Government for purposes of the First Amendment." Justice O'CONNOR was the only dissenter. Believing that the question of Amtrak's status as a governmental entity was not properly before the Court, she treated the case as a more traditional one involving a private entity involved with the government, and concluded that in the absence of any governmental involvement with the challenged decision, there was no basis for a state action finding in light of Jackson and subsequent cases.

12th ED., p. 945; IND. RTS., p. 616
Add as new Note after Note 2 on Carpenters v. Scott:

3. *Section 1985(c), abortion, and the Bray case.* In 1993 blockades of abortion clinics served as the arena for the disputes about the scope of

violation of the Equal Protection Clause. Georgia v. McCollum, 505 U.S. 42 (1992). Justice Blackmun's majority opinion found that "the defendant in a Georgia criminal case relies on 'governmental assistance and benefits' that are equivalent to those found in the civil context in Edmonson." Chief Justice Rehnquist concurred, noting his dissent in Edmonson, but joining the majority here because Edmonson "remains the law" and thus "controls the disposition of this case." Justice Thomas concurred in the judgment, agreeing with Chief Justice Rehnquist that Edmonson controls, but disagreeing with Batson and its progeny on

the general issue of whether peremptory challenges are subject to constitutional constraint. Justice O'Connor's dissent drew on the difference between civil and criminal cases, and the adversarial role between the defendant and the state in the latter, in distinguishing Edmonson. And Justice Scalia's brief dissent reiterated his belief in the wrongness of Edmonson, and in the wrongness of using "the interest of promoting the supposedly greater good of race relations in the society as a whole [to] destroy the ages-old right of criminal defendants to exercise peremptory challenges as they wish."

Griffin v. Breckinridge and the ability of the federal civil rights laws to reach private conspiracies. In the wake of numerous obstructions of access to abortion clinics by groups such as Operation Rescue, a group of abortion clinics and supporting organizations brought suit under 42 U.S.C. 1985(3) (the renumbered 1985(c)) seeking a federal court injunction against those who would obstruct access to abortion clinics, as well as attorney's fees and costs. The plaintiffs prevailed in the United States District Court for the Eastern District of Virginia, and then in the Court of Appeals for the Fourth Circuit, but in BRAY v. ALEXANDRIA WOMEN'S HEALTH CLINIC, 506 U.S. ___ (1993), the Supreme Court reversed, holding that animus towards abortion did not constitute a class-based animus towards women, and thus that the class-based animus required by section 1985(3) was not present.

Writing for the majority, Justice SCALIA again, as in Carpenters, refused either to affirm or to reject the suggestion in Griffin that forms of class-based animus other than race-based would fall within the domain of section 1985(3). Whatever the reach of section 1985(3) as interpreted in Griffin, he said, it did not extend as far as to include within the notion of a "class" those whose connections were only in a common "desire to engage in conduct that the section 1985(3) defendant disfavors. [This] definitional ploy would convert the statute into the 'general federal tort law' it was the very purpose of the animus requirement to avoid. ['Women] seeking abortion' is not a qualifying class."

Justice Scalia went on to reject the argument that animus towards women seeking abortions constituted animus directed at women in general, even assuming, *arguendo*, that animus against women was sufficient to make out a section 1985(3) claim. "We do not think that the 'animus' requirement can be met only by maliciously motivated, as opposed to assertedly benign (though objectively invidious), discrimination against women. It does demand, however, at least a purpose that focuses upon women *by reason of their sex*—for example (to use an illustration of assertedly benign discrimination), the purpose of 'saving' women *because they are women* from a combative, aggressive profession such as the practice of law. The record in this case does not indicate that petitioners' demonstrations are motivated by a purpose (malevolent *or* benign) directed specifically to women as a class; to the contrary, the District Court found that petitioners define their 'rescues' not with reference to women, but as physical intervention 'between abortionists and the innocent victims.' [Given] this record, respondents' contention that a class-based animus has been established can be true only if one of two suggested propositions is true: (1) that opposition to abortion can reasonably be presumed to reflect a sex-based intent, or (2) that intent is irrelevant, and a class-based animus can be determined solely by effect. Neither proposition is supportable."

Turning to the connection between opposition to abortion and opposition to women as a class, Justice Scalia acknowledged that "[s]ome activities may be such an irrational object of disfavor that, if they are targeted, and if they also happen to be engaged in exclusively or predominantly by a particular class of people, an intent to disfavor that class can readily be presumed. A tax on wearing yarmulkes is a tax on

Jews. But opposition to voluntary abortion cannot possibly be considered such an irrational surrogate for opposition to (or paternalism towards) women. Whatever one thinks of abortion, it cannot be denied that there are common and respectable reasons for opposing it, other than hatred of or condescension toward (or indeed any view at all concerning) women as a class—as is evident from the fact that men and women are on both sides of the issue, just as men and women are on both sides of petitioners' unlawful demonstrations. [Whether] one agrees or disagrees with the goal of preventing abortion, that goal in itself (apart from the use of unlawful means to achieve it, which is not relevant to our discussion of animus) does not remotely qualify for [a] derogatory association with racism."

Turning to the issue that was the focus of Carpenters v. Scott, the Court also concluded that the facts of this case showed no possible intent to deprive anyone of a right guaranteed against federal impairment. Justice Scalia rejected the right to travel argument, maintaining that there was no connection between the fact of the interstate travel and the reasons for the obstructions of the abortion clinics. "Petitioners oppose abortion, and it is irrelevant to their opposition whether the abortion is performed after interstate travel." Moreover, Justice Scalia argued, the right at issue was like the First Amendment right in Carpenters, protected by the Constitution only against state and not against private interference. As a result, no conspiracy with an intent to interfere with a right protected against private action could be shown.

In a lengthy opinion concurring in the judgment and dissenting in part, Justice SOUTER took issue with the majority's suggestion that the issues were likely to be the same under the second clause of 1985(3), reaching conspiracies "for the purpose of preventing or hindering [state authorities] from giving or securing to all persons [the] equal protection of the laws." To Justice Souter this clause was more different from the first clause (the deprivation clause) of 1985(3) than the majority acknowledged. Even if the equal protection component of the deprivation clause was to be read more narrowly than the equal protection component of the Fourteenth Amendment, the arguments for doing so (arguments he found less than persuasive) did not apply to the prevention clause. Because the prevention clause was limited in its application to hindrances with state authorities, it contained its own safeguards against undue expansion, safeguards less apparent in the deprivation clause. Thus, "the prevention clause may be applied to a conspiracy intended to hobble or overwhelm the capacity of duly constituted state police authorities to secure equal protection of the laws, even when the conspirators' animus is not based on race or a like class characteristic, and even when the ultimate object of the conspiracy is to violate a constitutional guarantee that applies solely against state action." Justice Souter thus agreed with the Court's decision to remand, but for him all that was necessary on remand, in addition to what was already contained in the record, was a determination of whether there was a purpose to interfere with the appropriate state or local officials. If that were found, he concluded, a cause of action would have been made out.

Justice STEVENS, joined by Justice Blackmun, dissented, detailing at length the activities of Operation Rescue in violation of law throughout the country. Because of the size and fervor of the organization, he argued, state and local law enforcement was not and could not be expected to be effective against their activities. Dealing with problems such as this was to him the very purpose of the federal civil rights laws, a purpose that in this case was embodied in the particular words of the relevant statute. Taking issue with the successive narrowing of 1985(3) in Collins, Griffin, and Carpenters, he chided the majority for its selective reliance on statutory language. "[I]f, as it sometimes does, the Court limited its analysis to the statutory text, it would certainly affirm the Court of Appeals. [Instead, the] Court bypasses the statute's history, intent, and plain language in its misplaced reliance on prior precedent." Moreover, he argued, the narrowness of the previous decisions was based in part on a sensitivity to constitutional questions of federal power not presented in a case dealing with what was plainly a conspiracy large and national in scope. Thus he argued that this statute could, and did, "offer relief from discriminatory effects even if the Fourteenth Amendment prevents only discriminatory intent."

But even if there were to be an intent requirement, to Justice Stevens it was, at the very least, clear that the statute reached gender as well as racial bias, and equally clear that intentional gender bias was present here and constituted class-based animus. "The immediate and intended effect of this conspiracy was to prevent women from obtaining abortions. Even assuming that the ultimate and indirect consequence of petitioners' blockade was the legitimate and nondiscriminatory goal of saving potential life, it is undeniable that the conspirators' immediate purpose was to affect the conduct of women. Moreover, petitioners target women *because* of their sex, specifically, because of their capacity to become pregnant and to have an abortion. [Petitioners'] conduct is designed to deny *every* woman the opportunity to exercise a constitutional right that *only* women possess. [The] activity of traveling to a clinic to obtain an abortion is, of course, exclusively performed by women. Opposition to that activity may not be 'irrational,' but violent interference with it is unquestionably 'aimed at' women. The Court offers no justification for its newly crafted suggestion that *deliberately* imposing a burden on an activity exclusively performed by women is not class-based discrimination unless opposition to that activity is also irrational. [It] is irrelevant whether the Court is correct in its assumption that 'opposition to abortion' does not necessarily evidence an intent to disfavor women. Many opponents of abortion respect both the law and the rights of others to make their own decisions on this important matter. Petitioners, however, are not mere opponents of abortion; they are defiant lawbreakers who have engaged in massive concerted conduct that is designed to prevent all women from making up their own minds about not only the issue of abortion in general, but also whether they should (or will) exercise a right that all women—and only women—possess. Indeed, the error that infects the Court's entire opinion is the unstated and mistaken assumption that this is a case about opposition to abortion. It is not. It is a case about the exercise of Federal power to control an interstate conspiracy to commit illegal acts. I have no doubt that most opponents of abortion, like most members of the citizenry at large, understand why the existence of federal jurisdiction is appropriate in a case of this kind."

Justice O'CONNOR, joined by Justice Blackmun, also dissented. She reaffirmed her dissent in Carpenters, and reemphasized her belief that the class-based animus described in Griffin could extend to groups joined by their "affiliations and activities," and plainly to any class covered as a class by the Equal Protection Clause. Concluding therefore that gender was undeniably such a class, she argued that the scope of 1985(3) must extend to "conspiracies whose motivation is directly related to characteristics unique to that class. The victims of petitioners' tortious actions are linked by their ability to become pregnant and by their ability to terminate their pregnancies, characteristics unique to the class of women. [I] cannot agree with the Court that the use of unlawful means to achieve one's goal 'is not relevant to [the] discussion of animus.' To the contrary, the deliberate decision to isolate members of a vulnerable group and physically prevent them from conducting legitimate activities cannot be irrelevant in assessing motivation." [1]

A year after Bray, however, a unanimous Court, applying a different statute, upheld the availability of civil remedies against those who would unlawfully obstruct access to abortion clinics. In NATIONAL ORGANIZATION FOR WOMEN, INC. v. SCHEIDLER, 507 U.S. ___ (1994), the Court addressed the question whether the civil damages provisions section 1962(c) of the Racketeer Influenced and Corrupt Organizations (RICO) chapter of the Organized Crime Control Act of 1970 could be applied to those who would repeatedly and unlawfully block access to abortion services. Among the defendants in the case were Randall A. Terry, the Pro–Life Action League, the Pro–Life Direct Action League, Operation Rescue, and Project Life. The statute provided remedies against those engaged in a "pattern of racketeering activity." "Racketeering activity" was defined in the statute to include a wide range of crimes, including various crimes of intimidation and obstruction, and so the primary contested issue was whether the word "enterprise" in the statute served to restrict application of the RICO law to those whose illegal activities were economically motivated. Writing for the Court, Chief Justice REHNQUIST concluded that the word "enterprise" did not require such an economic motive, and thus the RICO law could be applied to those whose unlawful activities were based on ideological rather than financial motivations.

Justice SOUTER, joined by Justice Kennedy, concurred in the Court's opinion, but issued a separate concurring opinion to explain why

---

1. In a brief concurrence, Justice KENNEDY, who joined the opinion of the Court, noted that federal law enforcement assistance is available in the event that state and local officials are unable sufficiently to protect lives and property within their jurisdiction. The statutory authorization for this assistance, he argued, demonstrated that Congress had provided multiple means for federal assistance in state law enforcement, and that the unavailability of a 1985(3) remedy should not be equated with the unavailability of any federal assistance.

he did not believe that the First Amendment required that the word "enterprise" be defined to include an economic motivation. "[Such] a requirement would correspond only poorly to free-speech concerns. [Respondents] complain that, unless so limited, the statute permits an ideological organization's opponents to label its vigorous expression as RICO predicate acts, thereby availing themselves of powerful remedial provisions that could destroy the organization. But an economic-motive requirement would protect too much with respect to First Amendment interests, since it would keep RICO from reaching ideological entities whose members commit acts of violence we need not fear chilling. An economic-motive requirement might also prove to be underprotective, in that entities engaging in vigorous but fully protected expression might fail the proposed economic-motive test (for even protest movements need money) and so be left exposed to harassing RICO suits." H.R. 230, introduced in the 104th Congress by Rep. Dornan, would redefine the pattern of racketeering definition in the RICO statute to require a profit-seeking purpose, thus presumably exempting organizations such as Operation Rescue from RICO coverage. (For other cases on the free speech dimensions of the abortion-protest issue, see Frisby v. Schultz, 487 U.S. 474 (1988), described at length below, 12th Ed., p. 1266; Ind.Rts., p. 937, and especially Madsen v. Women's Health Center, Inc., set out below, addition to 12th Ed., p. 1268; Ind.Rts., p. 939.)

———

With respect to the specific issue of remedies against those who would unlawfully obstruct access to abortion clinics, the Court's decision in Bray has not only been rendered less important by virtue of NOW v. Scheidler, but has also been substantially superseded by the Freedom of Access to Clinic Entrances Act of 1994, signed into law on May 26, 1994 (P.L. 103–259). The Act, whose final version is the product of much public controversy since Bray was decided, relies for its authority both on the commerce clause and on section 5 of the Fourteenth Amendment. Its stated purpose is to "protect and promote the public safety and activities affecting interstate commerce by establishing Federal criminal penalties and civil remedies for certain violent, threatening, obstructive and destructive conduct that is intended to injure, intimidate or interfere with persons seeking to obtain or provide reproductive health services." The Act makes it unlawful to physically obstruct, intentionally injure, intimidate or interfere with any person seeking to obtain or provide reproductive health services, and also makes it unlawful to engage in such obstruction, injury, intimidation or interference "with any person lawfully exercising or seeking to exercise the First Amendment right of religious freedom at a place of religious worship." The Act also reaches anyone damaging or destroying the property of "a facility [that] provides reproductive health services" or is "a place of religious worship." By way of enforcement, the Act provides for civil remedies brought by any person injured, or by the Attorney General of the United States, to recover compensatory and punitive damages, and also allows for injunctive relief. The Act also allows for criminal enforcement, with fines and a term of imprisonment not exceeding one year for a first offense and three years for subsequent offenses. In cases involving "exclusively a nonviolent physical obstruction," the penalties are lessened to a maximum of six months and eighteen months, respectively, and in cases of bodily injury or death the penalties are increased to maximums of ten years and life imprisonment, respectively. In light of the First Amendment freedom of speech issues surrounding the abortion clinic protest question, it is interesting to note that the Act also contains rules of construction providing that "nothing in this section shall be construed (1) to 'prohibit any expressive conduct (including peaceful picketing or other peaceful demonstration) protected from legal prohibition by the First Amendment [ ]; [or] (2) to create new remedies for interference with activities protected by the free speech or free exercise clauses of the First Amendment [ ], occurring outside a facility, regardless of the point of view expressed, or to limit any existing legal remedies for such interference."

12th ED., p. 946; IND. RTS., p. 617
Add at end of carryover footnote 2:

Under many circumstances, the primary import of sec. 1983 is in holding officials *personally* liable for unconstitutional actions taken "under color" of their official position. See, most recently, Hafer v. Melo, 502 U.S. 21 (1991). Where the defendants in a section 1983 action are private parties, the Court has held that the defendants do not enjoy even a qualified immunity from suit. Wyatt v. Cole, 504 U.S. 158 (1992).

12th ED., p. 958; IND. RTS., p. 629
Add at end of first paragraph of footnote 6:

In Presley v. Etowah County Commission, 502 U.S. 491 (1992), however, the Court, in its most recent decision on the types of changes that required preclearance, gave section 5 a somewhat narrower reading, refusing to hold that changes in the responsibilities of elected county commissioners were changes "with respect to voting."

12th ED., p. 959; IND. RTS., p. 630
Add at end of footnote 9:

For an example of recent litigation under the 1982 extension, see Chisom v. Roemer, 501 U.S. 380 (1991), holding that "the coverage provided by the 1982 amendment is coextensive with the coverage provided by the Act prior to 1982 and that judicial elections are embraced within that coverage." Note also HOLDER v. HALL, 514 U.S. ___ (1994), in which a complex array of opinions produced the conclusion of a majority of Justices that the mere fact of the size of the governing authority could not form the basis for a claim under section 2. Thus, the "single commissioner" system of Bleckley County, Georgia, was not, according to a majority of the Justices, open to section 2 challenge just because a single commissioner system would almost necessarily produce less minority representation than the five-commissioner (and district-based) system that had been defeated at a recent election. Of particular note is the lengthy separate opinion of Justice THOMAS. He not only argued that no vote dilution claim could ever come within the "standard, practice or procedure" language of section 2, but also maintained that a vote dilution claim necessarily presupposed some notion of the "correct" degree of minority representation, and that this in turn presupposed an essentially "proportional representation" view of voting that was neither the intention of the drafters of the Voting Rights Act nor the type of task— essentially one of political theory—in which the Court should be engaged. "If a minority group is unable to control seats, that result may plausibly be attributed to the inescapable fact that, in a majoritarian system, numerical minorities lose elections. There are undoubtedly an infinite number of theories of effective suffrage, representation, and the proper apportionment of political power in a representative democracy. [Such] matters of political theory are beyond the ordinary sphere of federal judges. [The] dabbling in political theory that dilution cases have prompted, however, is hardly the worst aspect of our vote dilution jurisprudence. Far more pernicious has been the Court's willingness to accept the one underlying premise that must inform every vote dilution claim: the assumption that the group asserting dilution is not merely a racial or ethnic group, but a group having distinct political interests as well. Of necessity, in resolving vote dilution acts we have given credence to the view that race defines political interest. We have acted on the implicit assumption that members of racial and ethnic groups must think alike on important matters of public policy and must have their own 'minority preferred' representatives holding seats in elected bodies if they are to be considered represented at all. [The] assumptions upon which our vote dilution decisions have been based should be repugnant to any nation that strives for the ideal of a color-blind Constitution. [As] a practical political matter, our drive to segregate political districts by race can only serve to deepen racial divisions by destroying any need for voters or candidates to build bridges between racial groups or to form voting coalitions. [Nothing] in our present understanding of the Voting Rights Act places a principled limit on the authority of federal courts that would prevent them from instituting a system of cumulative voting as a remedy under section 2, or even from establishing a more elaborate mechanism for securing proportional representation based on transferable votes. [We] would be mighty Platonic guardians indeed if Congress had granted us the authority to determine the best form of local government for every county, city, town, or village in America. But under our constitutional system, this Court is not a centralized politburo appointed for life to dictate to the provinces the 'correct' theories of democratic representation, the 'fairest' proportions of minority political influence, or, as respondents would have us hold today, the 'proper' size for local governing bodies.''

12th ED., p. 993; IND. RTS., p. 664

Add at end of Note 5c (EEOC v. Wyoming):

In GREGORY v. ASHCROFT, 501 U.S. 452 (1991), however, described at length above, addition to 12th Ed., p. 175, Justice O'CONNOR's majority opinion returned to the Section 5 question, and relied specifically on Pennhurst in holding the "plain statement" rule applicable to congressional restriction on certain central state political functions even when the Fourteenth Amendment rather than the commerce clause was the basis for congressional authority. "[T]he Court has recognized that the States' power to define the qualifications of their officeholders has force even as against the proscriptions of the Fourteenth Amendment. [The] Fourteenth Amendment does not override all principles of federalism. [We] will not attribute to Congress [without a plain statement] an intent to intrude on state governmental functions regardless of whether Congress acted pursuant to its Commerce Clause powers or Section 5 of the Fourteenth Amendment."

Justice WHITE, joined by Justice Stevens, found especially "disturbing" the majority's "failure to recognize the special status of legislation enacted pursuant to Section 5. [The] Pennhurst presumption was designed only to answer the question whether a particular piece of legislation was enacted pursuant to Section 5. That is very different from the majority's apparent holding that even when Congress is acting pursuant to section 5, it nevertheless must specify the precise details of its enactment." [19]

19. The dissenting opinion of Justice BLACKMUN, joined by Justice Marshall, indicated "entire" agreement with this part of Justice White's opinion.

Chapter 11(6)

FREEDOM OF EXPRESSION—SOME BASIC THEMES: REGULATION OF SPEECH BECAUSE OF ITS CONTENT

12th ED., p. 1069; IND. RTS., p. 740

Add at end of first paragraph of footnote 4:

On the question whether there are "compelling interests" not fitting the Brandenburg formula, see Justice Kennedy's opinion concurring in the judgment in Simon & Schuster, Inc. v. New York State Crime Victims Board, 502 U.S. 105 (1991), described and quoted at length below, addition to 12th Ed., p. 1499; Ind.Rts., p. 1170. There Justice Kennedy objected to the use of "compelling interest" analysis in First Amendment cases, arguing that the "traditional" categories of non-protection ought to be taken as presumptively exhaustive, such that even compelling interests would be generally insufficient for regulation of speech not within one of these categories.

12th ED., p. 1070; IND. RTS., p. 741

Add as new footnote at end of carryover paragraph (before 2.A.):

* For a broad-based endorsement of a strong categorization approach throughout the First Amendment, and a warning of the dangers to speech of using an "ad hoc" "compelling interest" analysis, see Justice Kennedy's opinion concurring in the judgment in Simon & Schuster, Inc. v. New York State Crime Victims Board, 502 U.S. 105 (1991), described and quoted at length below, addition to 12th Ed., p. 1499; Ind.Rts., p. 1170.

12th ED., p. 1088; IND. RTS., p. 759

Add at end of footnote 10 (on p. 1089):

In Masson v. New Yorker Magazine, Inc., 501 U.S. 496 (1991), the Court was called upon to determine the contours of the "actual malice" rule in the context of statements attributed to the plaintiff and placed in quotation, but which the plaintiff claimed were both inaccurate quotations and presented the plaintiff in an unfavorable light. The plaintiff, a psychiatrist who had written a widely publicized book about Freud, was said in a New Yorker article by Janet Malcolm to have described himself as an "intellectual gigolo" and "the greatest analyst who ever lived," as well as having made a number of other statements he denied having made. Masson argued that, except for trivial changes of grammar or punctuation, any false attribution contained in quotation marks necessarily satisfied the actual malice standard, since the author knew the plaintiff had not made the exact statements quoted. With the opinion written by Justice Kennedy, however, the Court refused to recognize such a broad principle of liability for inaccurate quotation, holding instead that where, as here, the plaintiff was a public figure, a fabricated quotation may be the basis of liability only if there has been a "material change in meaning."

Justice Kennedy made clear that the term "actual malice" is "unfortunate" and potentially confusing, being different from "the concept of malice as an evil intent or a motive arising from spite or ill will. [The term is] shorthand to describe the First Amendment protections for speech injurious to reputation." He emphasized that actual malice meant only knowledge of falsity or reckless disregard as to truth or falsity, the latter not being satisfied by mere negligence, but only by actual doubts about truth or actual awareness of probable falsity. "We must consider whether the requisite falsity inheres in the attribution of words to the petitioner which he did not speak. [But if] every alteration constituted the falsity required to prove actual malice, the practice of journalism, which the First Amendment is designed to protect, would require radical change. [We reject] the idea that any alteration beyond correction of grammar or syntax by itself proves falsity in the sense relevant to determining actual malice. [If] an author alters a speaker's words but effects no material change in meaning, including any meaning conveyed by the manner or fact of expression, the speaker suffers no injury to reputation that is compensable as a defamation." Rejecting the defense's proposed "rational interpretation" standard as well as the plaintiff's "grammar and syntax only" view, the Court concluded that "a deliberate alteration of the words uttered by a plaintiff does not equate with knowledge of falsity for purposes of [New York Times and Gertz] unless the alteration results in a material change in the meaning conveyed by the statement." Applying this standard, the Court determined that that standard could possibly be found by a jury to have been met for five of the six misquotations at issue, and reversed the grant of summary judgment in favor of the defendants. Justice White, joined by Justice Scalia, concurred in part and dissented in part, disagreeing with the "material alteration" rule and arguing that a "knowingly false attribution" should be sufficient under New York Times for the case to go to a jury. When "the author deliberately put within quotation marks and attributed to the speaker words that the author knew the speaker did not utter," actual malice in the constitutional sense exists. [After remand (see 960 F.2d 896 (1992), Masson v. New Yorker finally went to trial in San Francisco on May 10, 1993. On June 3, the jury found for Masson against Janet Malcolm (but not against The New Yorker) in respect to two of the five quotes at issue, but were unable to agree on damages. With the plaintiff urging a new trial solely on the issue of damages, and the defendant arguing for an entirely new trial, post-trial motions are now awaiting decision.]

12th ED., p. 1093; IND.RTS., p. 763
Add at end of footnote 12:

In Campbell v. Acuff–Rose Music, Inc., 508 U.S. __ (1994), noted briefly below, addition to 12th Ed., p. 1093; Ind.Rts., p. 764, a unanimous Supreme Court held likely protected as a "fair use" under copyright law a parody of Roy Orbison's "Oh, Pretty Woman" by the rap group 2 Live Crew. Justice Souter's opinion relied on copyright principles and not on the First Amendment. The themes in the opinion, however, were similar to those articulated in Hustler v. Falwell, including the protection of the parody in part because "2 Live Crew's song reasonably could be perceived as commenting on the original or criticizing it, to some degree," and the irrelevance to the fair use question of the fact that the parody may have been "shocking" or in "bad taste."

12th ED., p. 1093; IND.RTS., p. 764
Add at end of footnote 3 (on p. 1094; 764) inside brackets:

In Campbell v. Acuff–Rose Music, Inc., 508 U.S. __ (1994), the Court held that a parody by the rap group 2 Live Crew of "Oh, Pretty Woman," by Roy Orbison was likely protected as fair use and thus not open to a charge of copyright violation. Although Justice Souter's opinion for a unanimous Court made no reference to the First Amendment, his articulation of the rationale for and application of fair use principles in copyright law tracked a number of familiar First Amendment themes. Justice Souter stressed the way in which a parody could be viewed as a work "commenting on and criticizing the original work." He also stressed that the fact that a parody might be in bad taste (a not unreasonable characterization in the case at hand) "does not and should not matter to fair use."

12th ED., p. 1121; IND. RTS., p. 792
Add after Note 3c:

d. Consider the implications of a finding of obscenity. Are obscene materials totally beyond First Amendment interest, or does some residuum of First Amendment concern remain distinguishing obscene materials from other forms of contraband? In ALEXANDER v. UNITED STATES, 511 U.S. __ (1993), noted at greater length below, 12th Ed., p. 1211; Ind.Rts., p. 882, the Court divided on whether a massive Racketeer Influenced and Corrupt Organizations (RICO) seizure of non-obscene publications, as well as other assets, consequent upon an obscenity conviction, was a violation of the First Amendment. Writing for a 5–4 majority, Chief Justice REHNQUIST reaffirmed the Roth–Paris non-speech approach, and concluded that upon a conviction for obscenity there was no more of a bar on forfeiture of related assets than there would be for any other conviction. In dissent, however, Justice KENNE-DY, joined by Justices Blackmun, Stevens, and (on this point) Souter, noted the chilling effect that would come from the possibility that all of one's assets might be forfeited upon an obscenity conviction based on merely one publication. Decrying the majority's approach as "formalistic," Justice Kennedy maintained that the nature of the materials and the business was relevant, and that even after an obscenity conviction the courts must remain sensitive to the expression-inhibiting effects of massive seizures such as that involved in this case.

12th ED., p. 1125; IND. RTS., p. 796

Add as footnote at end of child pornography materials:

* Note also Jacobson v. United States, 503 U.S. 540 (1992), in which the Court invalidated on entrapment grounds a conviction under the federal child pornography statute, the Child Protection Act of 1984. In United States v. X–Citement Video, Inc., 515 U.S. ___ (1994), the Court interpreted the Protection of Children Against Sexual Exploitation Act of 1977, which prohibits the interstate transportation of visual depictions of minors engaged in sexually explicit conduct, as requiring the prosecution to prove that a defendant knew that one of the performers was a minor. Failure to read such a scienter (see Smith v. California, 1959, noted below, 12th Ed., p. 1207; Ind.Rts., p. 878) requirement into the statute, Chief Justice Rehnquist's majority maintained, would raise substantial constitutional problems that could be avoided by interpreting the statute to impose such a requirement. In dissent Justice Scalia, joined by Justice Thomas, objected that the Court had rewritten the statute because of an unjustified question about constitutionality, since in Justice Scalia's view the imposition of strict liability vis-vis-age in child pornography cases would not offend the First Amendment.

12th ED., p. 1126; IND. RTS., p. 797

Add to footnote 2:

In considering the constitutionality of these proposals, and in considering the case immediately following, consider as well the effect of R.A.V. v. City of St. Paul, 504 U.S. ___ (1992), set out below, addition to 12th Ed., p. 1248; Ind.Rts., p. 919. Can Justice Scalia's majority opinion in R.A.V. be said to affirm or endorse Judge Easterbrook's opinion in American Booksellers v. Hudnut?

12th ED., p. 1137; IND. RTS., p. 808

Add at end of discussion of Regulating Racist Speech on Campus:

Representative Hyde of Illinois introduced in the 102nd Congress the Collegiate Speech Protection Act of 1991, which would amend Title VI of the Civil Rights Act of 1964 by providing that "A postsecondary educational institution [covered by the Act] shall not make or enforce any rule subjecting any student to disciplinary sanctions solely on the basis of conduct that is speech or other communication protected from governmental restriction by the first article of amendment to the Constitution of the United States." The bill further provided for injunctive and declaratory relief, costs and attorneys' fees to a successful plaintiff, and contained an exemption for "an educational institution that is controlled by a religious organization, to the extent that the application of this section would not be consistent with the religious tenet of such organization." The bill attracted 17 cosponsors from both parties and support from a range of civil liberties and conservative organizations. It was referred to the House Judiciary Committee on March 12, 1991, but was not pressed further by its sponsors.

12th ED., p. 1137; IND. RTS., p. 808
Add at end of hate speech materials:

R.A.V. v. CITY OF ST. PAUL, MINNESOTA

504 U.S. ___, 112 S.Ct. 2538, 120 L.Ed.2d 305 (1992).

[This case involves the St. Paul Bias–Motivated Crime Ordinance, focused on racist and related graffiti, cross-burnings, and the like, and interpreted by the Minnesota Supreme Court to reach otherwise unprotected fighting words that would arouse "anger, alarm, or resentment on the basis of race, color, creed, religion, or gender." Writing for a 5–4 majority, Justice Scalia's opinion held the ordinance, even when restricted to fighting words, an unconstitutional regulation on the basis of content and viewpoint. The decision is consequently directly relevant to the hate speech issue, and to several of the proposals discussed here. Because the various opinions take on a number of pervasive issues of content regulation, overbreadth, and symbolic behavior, however, and draw heavily on commercial speech and obscenity issues, detailed consideration of the case is best deferred until after those topics are treated, and the full case is thus set out below, addition to 12th Ed., p. 1248; Ind.Rts., p. 919.]

12th ED., p. 1163; IND.RTS., p. 834
Add after discussion of Sable Communications:

The strength of the Court's unanimous conclusion about "indecency" in Sable Communications is likely to be tested in the context of new regulations of computerized communications, in particular the Internet, electronic bulletin boards, and related communications media. In the wake of considerable publicity about the ready availability on the Internet of sexually explicit material, material promoting violence against women, racist communications, and material promoting violence against government officials, various regulatory proposals have surfaced. The most widely discussed is Senator Exon's addition to the proposed Telecommunications Competition and Deregulation Act of 1995. Sections 401 et seq. of the Bill, entitled the Communications Decency Act of 1994, prohibits the use of a telecommunications device to "initiate[ ] the transmission of any comment, request, suggestion, proposal, image, or other communication which is obscene, lewd, lascivious, filthy, or indecent, with intent to annoy, abuse, threaten, or harass another person." The Act also would impose criminal penalties on anyone who "knowingly [by] means of a telecommunications device makes or makes available any indecent communication in any form including any comment, request, suggestion, proposal or image, to any person under 18 years of age regardless of whether the maker of such communication [initiated] the communication." Some defenses are provided for those who only operate communications networks for use by others. Can the "indecency" restrictions survive Sable?

12th ED., p. 1164; IND.RTS., p. 835
Add as Note 3 after Pacifica:

 3. *The question of television violence.* There has been a recent flurry of concern about violence on television. Some of this has been in the form of calls for greater "responsibility" or self-regulation by the television industry, but the Attorney General of the United States has offered her support, and her opinion about their constitutionality under, especially, Pacifica, for several pending bills seeking more direct control. One, the Children's Protection from Violent Programming Act of 1995, S. 470, introduced by Sen. Hollings, states that it is based on "empirical evidence that children exposed to violent video programming at a young age have a higher tendency for violent and aggressive behavior later in life than those children not so exposed." It also asserts a "compelling governmental interest in limiting the negative influences of violent video programming on children," and "a compelling governmental interest in channeling programming with violent content to periods of the day when children are not likely to comprise a substantial portion of the television audience." It goes on to claim that "restricting the hours when violent video programming is shown is the least restrictive and most narrowly tailored means to achieve that compelling governmental interest." The bill makes unlawful broadcast or cable distribution of violent programming during hours when children "are reasonably likely to comprise a substantial portion of the audience," and mandates that the Federal Communications Commission enact implementing rules, including rules defining "violent ... programming." Consider the constitutionality of the proposed legislation. Does Pacifica make the bill constitutional? Does it make available an argument for its constitutionality? What are the arguments against the bill's constitutionality?

 Other proposals in the 104th Congress concerning violence on television include sections in the Telecommunications Competition and Deregulation Act of 1995 (S. 652), particularly Title V, entitled Parental Choice in Television, which was passed by the Senate on June 22, 1995. Bills awaiting action in committee include the Children's Media Protection Act of 1995 (H.R. 1390), H.R. 1807, S. 306, S. 332 and S. 772. Unlike Senator Hollings' bill, many of these proposals focus on providing technical means for parental control over what children watch rather than direct FCC control over programming.

 In June, 1995 both President Clinton and Presidential candidate Robert Dole took up the issue of violence in the media generally, not just television, in widely-publicized speeches. The film "Natural–Born Killers" was the focus of much of the commentary in both politics and the media.

12th ED., p. 1177; IND.RTS., p. 848
Add new footnote at end of Note 1 on the legal profession:

 5a. For a case following Peel in disallowing prohibitions on the accurate advertising of professional qualifications and certifications, but in the context of accountants and not lawyers, see Ibanez v. Florida Board of Accountancy, 510 U.S. ___ (1994). Justice Ginsburg wrote the majority opinion, finding the Board's broad assertions of potential misleadingness insufficient to justify a restriction on accurate information in professional advertising. Justice O'Connor, joined by Chief Justice Rehnquist, dissented in part, arguing that some restrictions on even potentially misleading professional advertising should be permitted.

12th ED., p. 1189; IND. RTS., p. 860
Add as new Note at end of commercial speech materials:

5. *New vitality for the protection of commercial speech?* Although Posadas and Fox appeared to signal increasingly deferential review in the commercial speech area, a series of cases in the 1992 Term indicated a possible reversal of this trend. Most important was CITY OF CINCINNATI v. DISCOVERY NETWORK, INC., 507 U.S. ___ (1993), in which the Court struck down a Cincinnati practice of barring from public property newsracks distributing commercial handbills but not newsracks distributing ordinary newspapers. A municipal ordinance prohibited the distribution of any commercial handbill on public property, and another ordinance explicitly allowed the distribution of newspapers. Claiming that an excess number of newsracks would impede safety and increase "visual blight," and fearing that a total ban on all newsracks would be unconstitutional, Cincinnati argued that the lesser protection afforded to commercial speech allowed it to restrict publications consisting wholly of commercial speech while it did not restrict the distribution of noncommercial speech, such as ordinary newspapers. Distributors of free newspapers and magazines advertising real estate and various services challenged the prohibition, however, arguing that Cincinnati's asserted safety and aesthetic interests could not justify the restriction on commercial speech or the distinction here between the commercial and the noncommercial.

With the majority opinion written by Justice STEVENS, the Court upheld the claims of the newsrack distributors. Although Justice Stevens raised some questions about the clarity of the distinction between commercial and noncommercial speech, especially given that the advertising newspapers did contain some editorial content, he proceeded to assume both that these publications were "core commercial speech" and that there was no claim that they were in any way false or misleading. Commencing with the observation that Cincinnati had "attached more importance to the distinction between commercial and noncommercial speech than our cases warrant and seriously underestimate[d] the value of commercial speech," Justice Stevens then turned to the application of the commercial speech standard itself. Making no reference whatsoever to Posadas, Justice Stevens proceeded to apply the "reasonable fit" standard of Fox. In applying this test, however, he rejected Cincinnati's argument that the fit between its safety and aesthetic interests and its prohibition on commercial newsracks was close because every excluded newsrack produced an incremental increase in safety and aesthetic quality. Rather, he said that the fit must be between the city's interest and the *distinction* embodied in the city's regulatory approach. This, the Court concluded, could not be shown. "The city has asserted an interest in esthetics, but respondent publishers' newsracks are no greater an eyesore than the newsracks permitted to remain on Cincinnati's sidewalks. [The] city's primary concern [is] with the aggregate number of newsracks on its streets. On that score, however, all newsracks, regardless of whether they contain commercial or noncommercial publications, are equally at fault. In fact, the newspapers are arguably the greater culprit because of their superior number. [In] the absence of some basis for distinguishing between 'newspapers' and 'commercial handbills' that is relevant to an interest asserted by the city, we are unwilling to recognize Cincinnati's bare assertion that the 'low value' of commercial speech is a sufficient justification for its selective and categorical ban on newsracks dispensing 'commercial handbills.' [Because] the distinction Cincinnati has drawn has absolutely no bearing on the interests it has asserted, we have no difficulty concluding [that] the city has not established a 'fit' between its goals and its chosen means that is required by Fox. [Moreover,] because the ban is predicated on the content of the publications distributed by the subject newsracks, it is not a valid time, place, or manner restriction on protected speech."

Justice BLACKMUN concurred, reiterating the concerns he expressed both in Central Hudson and in Fox that in his view there was no justification for distinguishing true and not misleading commercial speech from any other sort of protected speech. Chief Justice REHNQUIST, joined by Justices White and Thomas, dissented, relying in part on Posadas. And in addition to arguing that the regulatory scheme satisfied the fit standards of Central Hudson and Fox, he questioned the majority's focus on the distinction between commercial and noncommercial speech. "If (as I am certain) Cincinnati may regulate newsracks that disseminate commercial speech based on the interests it has asserted, I am at a loss as to why its scheme is unconstitutional because it does not also regulate newsracks that disseminate noncommercial speech. One would have thought that the city, perhaps even following the teachings of our commercial speech jurisprudence, could have decided to place the burden of its regulatory scheme on less protected speech (i.e., commercial handbills) without running afoul of the First Amendment. Today's decision, though, places the city in the position of having to decide to restrict more speech—fully protected speech—and allowing the proliferation of newsracks on its street corners to continue unabated. It scarcely seems logical that the First Amendment compels such a result," and that Cincinnati is prohibited from restricting "less speech than necessary to fully accomplish its objective."

In EDENFIELD v. FANE, 508 U.S. ___ (1993), the Court also upheld a claim for the protection of commercial speech, here in the context of striking down Florida's ban on any form of client solicitation by Certified Public Accountants. Although Justice KENNEDY's majority opinion evaluated the prohibition by use of the tests set forth in Central Hudson and Fox, he relied even more heavily on earlier cases dealing with lawyer solicitation and advertising. Florida had attempted to distinguish those cases on the basis of the special responsibilities of CPA's to the public as well as to their clients, but Justice Kennedy found no evidence to support that argument. Moreover, he found Florida's reliance on Ohralik misplaced, for none of the dangers associated with face-to-face lawyer solicitation of clients were likely to be present in the case of accountants. Justice BLACKMUN concurred, again noting his objection to treating truthful and nonmisleading commercial speech as anything other than "pure" speech. Justice O'CONNOR was the only dissenter. She questioned the majority's application of the Central Hudson and Fox tests, but her main concern was the whole line of professional advertising cases going back to Bates. "In my view, the States have the broader authority to prohibit commercial speech that, albeit not directly harmful to the listener, is inconsistent with the speaker's membership in a learned profession and therefore damaging to the profession and society at large." Reiterating concerns she expressed in earlier attorney advertising cases, she thought it appropriate for a state to regulate professional advertising on the basis of a belief that "pure profit seeking degrades the public-spirited culture of [a] profession. [Commercialism] has an incremental, indirect, yet profound effect on professional culture, as lawyers know all too well."

In UNITED STATES v. EDGE BROADCASTING CO., 510 U.S. ___ (1993), however, Posadas and its approach were somewhat more present than in either Edenfield or Discovery Network. At issue were applications of 18 U.S.C. 1304 and 1307, which prohibit the broadcasting of advertisements for lotteries, but contain exemptions for advertising state-run lotteries by broadcast licensees located within states having such lotteries. Edge Broadcasting operated WMYK–FM, located in Elizabeth City, North Carolina. But although WMYK operated out of Elizabeth City, North Carolina, a non-lottery state, and therefore did not have the benefit of the exemption, its primary broadcast audience— 92.2% of its listenership and 95.9% of its advertising revenues—was in Virginia, a lottery state. Edge argued that the application of the federal prohibitions to it constituted an unconstitutional abridgment of its First Amendment rights with respect to commercial advertising, in particular its right to broadcast advertisements for the Virginia lottery. Although the lower courts had agreed, the Supreme Court, with Justice WHITE writing for the majority, rejected the First Amendment argument. Because the lower courts did not decide whether the fact of lotteries being a "vice" put their advertisement out of the commercial speech arena entirely, the Court did not discuss this possibility either, although Justice White's phrasing in several points suggests that a majority of the Court may now see Posadas as specially related to this "vice" category, and viable for that category, although not relevant for other unlawful activities that might be advertised.

The Court's main focus, therefore, was on the application of the Central Hudson test, in particular on the "fit" question. Rejecting the lower court's view that the purpose of the law would not be served very well by applying it in the particular circumstances of WMYK's audience, Justice White made it clear that the third and fourth prongs of the Central Hudson standard are not to be applied with reference to each particular person or entity falling within a regulation of commercial speech. Rather, relying heavily on Ward v. Rock Against Racism (1989, described below, 12th Ed., p. 1345; Ind.Rts., p. 1016), Justice White made it clear that in general, and in this case, the fit requirement of

Central Hudson could be satisfied if the fit were sufficiently close vis-a-vis the class of addressees of the law, even if there were a less close fit in the circumstances of the individual case. And thus, noting again the relevance of Posadas, the Court held that at least as for activities of the "vice" variety, the closeness of fit between the goal of lessening the incidence of lotteries and the particular statutory scheme was sufficient to satisfy the requirements of Central Hudson. Justice SOUTER, joined by Justice Kennedy, concurred in the judgment and in part of Justice White's opinion, but did not feel it necessary to reach the question of generality that was most of the Court's focus. And Justice STEVENS, joined by Justice Blackmun, dissented, maintaining that the case was controlled by Bigelow, and that it was a mistake to suppose that the result in Bigelow turned on the independent constitutional protection of the activity—abortion—that had been the subject of the advertisement.*

In RUBIN v. COORS BREWING CO., 517 U.S. ___ (1995), the Court was unanimous in striking down a federal law prohibiting beer labels from displaying the alcohol content of the beer. Applying the Central Hudson analysis to the restriction, Justice THOMAS's opinion evaluated the government's argument that the restriction was necessary to prevent "strength wars," particularly with respect to malt liquor and related beverages. Justice Thomas relied heavily on the inconsistency in the full regulatory scheme. "To be sure, the Government's interest in combatting strength wars remains a valid goal. But [one] would think that if the Government sought to suppress strength wars by prohibiting numerical disclosures of alcohol content, it also would preclude brewers from indicating higher alcohol beverages by using descriptive terms. [The] irrationality of this unique and puzzling regulatory framework ensures that the labeling ban will fail to achieve [the] end [of reducing strength wars]. There is little chance that [this restriction] can directly and materially advance its aim, while other provisions of the same act directly undermine and counteract its effects." Justice STEVENS concurred in the judgment, but disagreed with the application of the Central Hudson analysis. "In my opinion the 'commercial speech doctrine' is unsuited to this case, because the Federal Alcohol Administration Act neither prevents misleading speech nor protects consumers from the dangers of incomplete information. [If] varying alcohol strengths are lawful, I see no reason why brewers may not advise customers that their beverages are stronger—or weaker—than competing products."

Although the Court has, since Bates, struck down most restrictions on lawyer advertising as violative of the First Amendment, it upheld a restriction in FLORIDA BAR v. WENT FOR IT, 518 U.S. ___ (1995). At issue was a Florida bar regulation prohibiting personal injury lawyers from sending targeted direct-mail solicitations to accident victims for 30 days following an accident or disaster. Writing for a 5–4 majority, Justice O'CONNOR explained why the restriction did not violate the

---

* Note also IBANEZ v. FLORIDA BOARD OF ACCOUNTANCY, 510 U.S. ___ (1994), in which Justice GINSBURG's decision for a 7–2 majority struck down Florida's attempts to restrict the designations and special qualifications that Certified Public Accountants could use in their advertisements. See the further note on the case above, addition to 12th Ed., p. 1177; Ind.Rts., p. 848.

First Amendment's protection of commercial advertising. Applying the Central Hudson test, she accepted as substantial Florida's interest in protecting the privacy of accident victims and its related (because of public perception about lawyer invasions of privacy) interest in protecting the reputation and image of the legal profession. As to the second prong of the Central Hudson test, requiring a "direct and material" connection between the regulation and the state interest, Justice O'Connor distinguished Edenfield, and noted the extensive and well-documented Florida study that preceded adoption of the regulation and that supported the view that direct mail solicitation of accident victims was extensive and perceived by the public in a highly negative way. Most of her opinion stressed the detail of this study, a degree of factual documentation she concluded not only satisfied the second prong of Central Hudson, but also distinguished this case from others striking down restrictions on various forms of professional solicitation. As to the third prong, the Court reiterated that "least restrictive alternative" standards are no part of the evaluation of restrictions on commercial speech, and found the Florida restriction to have a sufficiently close fit, to be sufficiently narrowly tailored, and to leave open sufficient alternative channels of information, as to constitute a permissible restriction. "We believe that the Florida Bar's 30–day restriction on targeted direct-mail solicitation of accident victims withstands scrutiny under the three-part Central Hudson test. [The] Bar has substantial interest both in protecting injured Floridians from invasive conduct by lawyers and in preventing the erosion of confidence in the profession that such repeated invasions have engendered. The Bar's proffered study, unrebutted by respondents below, provides evidence indicating that the harms it targets are far from illusory. The palliative devised by the Bar to address these harms is narrow both in scope and in duration. The Constitution [requires] nothing more.

Justice KENNEDY, joined by Justices Stevens, Souter, and Ginsburg, dissented, arguing that "when an accident results in death or injury, it is often urgent at once to investigate the occurrence, identify witnesses, and preserve evidence. Vital interests in speech and expression are, therefore, at stake when by law an attorney cannot direct a letter to the victim or the family explaining this simple fact and offering competent legal assistance. Meanwhile, represented and better informed parties, or parties who have been solicited in ways more sophisticated and indirect, may be at work. [To] the extent the bar seeks to protect lawyers' reputations by preventing them from engaging in speech some deem offensive, the State is doing nothing more [than] manipulating the public's opinion by suppressing speech that informs us how the legal system works. The disrespect argument thus proceeds from the very assumption it tries to prove, which is to say that solicitations within 30 days serve no legitimate purpose. This, of course, is censorship pure and simple; and censorship is antithetical to the first principles of free expression. [The] Court's opinion reflects a new-found and illegitimate confidence that it, along with the Supreme Court of Florida, knows what is best for the Bar and its clients. Self-assurance has always been the hallmark of a censor. [By] validating Florida's rule, today's majority is complicit in the Bar's censorship."

Chapter 12(7)

FREEDOM OF EXPRESSION: ADDITIONAL PERVASIVE THEMES; THE PUBLIC FORUM PROBLEM

12th ED., p. 1208; IND. RTS., p. 779
Add to footnote 1:

For an application of the principles of Freedman and Lakewood in the context of demonstration permits, see Forsyth County, Georgia v. Nationalist Movement, 505 U.S. 123 (1992), described below, addition to 12th Ed., p. 1292; Ind.Rts., p. 963.

12th ED., p. 1211; IND. RTS., p. 882
Add at end of Note 3:

In ALEXANDER v. UNITED STATES, 511 U.S. ___ (1993), however, the Court, while acknowledging some of the questions about the viability of a distinction between prior restraints and subsequent punishments, explicitly reaffirmed the distinction and its importance. The case, also noted above in connection with the obscenity materials, addition to 12th Ed., p. 1121; Ind.Rts., p. 792, involved the claim that some forfeitures under the Racketeer Influenced and Corrupt Organizations Act (RICO), 18 U.S.C. 1963, constituted unlawful prior restraints in light of the principles set forth in Near and subsequent cases. Alexander had been for thirty years a large-scale dealer and distributor, owning and operating thirteen different outlets in Minnesota, in the "adult entertainment" business. Upon his conviction on seventeen counts of federal obscenity violations, RICO proceedings to forfeit assets connected with and gained as a result of his unlawful activities were instituted. The resulting forfeiture included nine million dollars in cash, as well as Alexander's business assets, assets including theatres, bookstores, and publications not themselves adjudicated obscene. As a result, Alexander argued that the seizure of these non-obscene publications and facilities for distributing them constituted a prior restraint.

Writing for the Court, Chief Justice REHNQUIST rejected the claim that the seizures constituted a prior restraint, and argued that Alexander's contention would "obliterate" the distinction between prior restraints and subsequent punishments, to the detriment of the prior restraint doctrine itself. Unlike cases in which there is an injunction prohibiting the sale of distribution of presumptively lawful material, here Alexander remained "perfectly free to open an adult bookstore or otherwise engage in the production and distribution of erotic materials; he just cannot finance these enterprises with assets derived from his prior racketeering offenses." And because the assets seized here were seized not because they might be obscene, but rather just because they were assets, the fact that they were constitutionally protected made no difference. The statute, the Court noted, is "oblivious to the expressive or nonexpressive nature of the assets forfeited; books, sports cars, narcotics, and cash are all forfeitable alike under RICO."

JUSTICE KENNEDY, joined by Justices Blackmun and Stevens, and in part by Justice Souter, argued that seizure of expressive materials prior to a determination of obscenity constituted a prior restraint. Questioning the rigid distinction between prior restraints and subsequent punishments, he urged that the definition of prior restraint be flexible enough to accommodate changing conceptions of the threats that governmental action might constitute to freedom of speech. Here, he argued, the fact that materials protected by the Constitution were seized (and subsequently destroyed) without any hearing on *their* illegality produced the kinds of elimination of speech in advance that the prior restraint doctrine was designed to combat, even though there was not an injunction. Justice SOUTER, although disagreeing with him that this seizure constituted a prior restraint, agreed with him that the risk of forfeiting all of one's business assets because one publication might be found obscene created an excessive chill on freedom of speech, and was thus unconstitutional even if not a prior restraint. (Is an injunction always a prior restraint? See Madsen v. Women's Health Center, Inc., below, addition to 12th Ed., p. 1268; Ind.Rts., p. 939).

12th ED., p. 1217; IND. RTS., p. 888

Add as new Note after Note 3 in Section 2:

4. *The scope of the presumption against content discrimination.* Although it is moderately well-settled that the Mosley principle is relevant with respect to communications otherwise fully covered by the First Amendment, the issue has not been so clear with respect to communications held to have less or no First Amendment value. Can regulation of no value (obscenity; fighting words) or low value (commercial speech) speech be based on viewpoint or subject-matter in a way that full value speech could not be. This is the issue heatedly debated by the Court in R.A.V. v. City of St. Paul, Minnesota, 504 U.S. ___ (1992), in the context of a restriction on racist (and related) fighting words. Because the case arose in the context of so-called "symbolic behavior" (in this case a cross-burning), and because the various opinions rely heavily on a number of symbolic behavior cases and doctrines, the full case is set out not here, but instead at the end of the symbolic behavior materials, addition to 12th Ed., p. 1248; Ind.Rts., p. 919.

12th ED., p. 1227; IND. RTS., p. 898

Add after Arcara:

Consider also ALEXANDER v. UNITED STATES, 511 U.S. ___ (1993), described and discussed above, addition to 12th Ed., pp. 1121 and 1211; Ind.Rts., pp. 792 and 882, in which Chief Justice REHNQUIST's opinion for the Court relied heavily on Arcara in finding no violation of the First Amendment in a RICO seizure of books, magazines, and films consequent to an obscenity conviction. The statute, he maintained, "is oblivious to the expressive or nonexpressive nature of the assets forfeited; books, sports cars, narcotics, and cash are all forfeitable alike under RICO." Justice KENNEDY's dissent is described above.

BARNES v. GLEN THEATRE, INC.

501 U.S. 560, 111 S.Ct. 2456, 115 L.Ed.2d 504 (1991).

Chief Justice REHNQUIST announced the judgment of the Court and delivered an opinion in which Justice O'CONNOR and Justice KENNEDY join.

Respondents are two establishments in South Bend, Indiana, that wish to provide totally nude dancing as entertainment, and individual dancers who are employed at these establishments. They claim that the First Amendment [prevents] the State of Indiana from enforcing its public indecency law to prevent this form of dancing. We reject their claim.

The facts [are] uncontested here. The Kitty Kat Lounge, Inc. [sells] alcoholic beverages and presents "go-go dancing." Its proprietor desires to present "totally nude dancing," but an applicable Indiana statute regulating public nudity requires that the dancers wear "pasties" and a "G-string" when they dance. The dancers are not paid an hourly wage, but work on commission. They receive a 100 percent commission on the first $60 in drink sales during their performances. Darlene Miller, one of the respondents in the action, had worked at the Kitty Kat for about two years at the time this action was brought. Miller wishes to dance nude because she believes she would make more money doing so.

Respondent Glen Theatre, Inc.['s primary] business is supplying so-called adult entertainment through written and printed materials, movie showings, and live entertainment at an enclosed "bookstore." The live entertainment at the "bookstore" consists of nude and seminude performances and showings of the female body through glass panels. Customers sit in a booth and insert coins into a timing mechanism that permits them to observe the live nude and seminude dancers for a period of time. One of Glen Theatre's dancers, Gayle Ann Marie Sutro, has danced, modeled, and acted professionally for more than 15 years [and] can be seen in a pornographic movie at a nearby theater.

Respondents sued [to] enjoin the enforcement of the Indiana public indecency statute, asserting that its prohibition against complete nudity in public places violated the First Amendment. The District Court originally granted respondents' prayer for an injunction, finding that the statute was facially overbroad. The Court of Appeals for the Seventh Circuit reversed, deciding that previous litigation [precluded] the possibility of such a challenge. [On] remand, the District Court concluded that "the type of dancing these plaintiffs wish to perform is not expressive activity protected by the Constitution of the United States," and rendered judgment in favor of the defendants. The case was again appealed to the Seventh Circuit, and a panel [reversed] the District Court, holding that the nude dancing involved here was expressive conduct protected by the First Amendment. The Court of Appeals then heard the case en banc, and [the] majority concluded that non-obscene nude dancing performed for entertainment is expression protected by the First Amendment, and that the public indecency statute was an improper infringement of that expressive activity because its purpose was to prevent the message of eroticism and sexuality conveyed by the dancers. Miller v. Civil City of South Bend, 904 F.2d 1081. We granted certiorari, and now hold that the Indiana statutory requirement that the dancers in the establishments involved in this case must wear pasties and a G-string does not violate the First Amendment.

Several of our cases [support] the conclusion of the Court of Appeals that nude dancing of the kind sought to be performed here is expressive conduct within the outer perimeters of the First Amendment, though we view it as only marginally so. This, of course, does not end our inquiry. We must determine the level of protection to be afforded, [and whether] the Indiana statute is an impermissible infringement of that protected activity.

Indiana, of course, has not banned nude dancing as such, but has proscribed public nudity across the board. The Supreme Court of Indiana has construed the [statute] to preclude nudity in what are essentially places of public accommodation such as the Glen Theatre and the Kitty Kat Lounge. In such places, respondents point out, minors are excluded and there are no non-consenting viewers. Respondents contend that while the state may license [such] establishments, and limit the geographical area in which they do business, it may not in any way limit the performance of the dances within them without violating the First Amendment. The petitioner contends, on the other hand, that Indiana's restriction on nude dancing is a valid "time, place or manner" restriction under cases such as Clark v. Community for Creative Non-Violence [1984; below, 12th Ed., p. 1333; Ind. Rts., p. 1004].

The "time, place, or manner" test was developed for evaluating restrictions on expression taking place on public property which had been dedicated as a "public forum." [In] Clark we observed that this test has been interpreted to embody much the same standards as those set forth in [O'Brien.] [Applying] the [O'Brien test,] we find that Indiana's public indecency statute is justified despite its incidental limitations on some expressive activity. The public indecency statute is clearly within the constitutional power of the State and furthers substantial governmental interests. It is impossible to discern [exactly] what governmental interest the Indiana legislators had in mind when they enacted this statute, for Indiana does not record legislative history, and the state's highest court has not shed additional light on the statute's purpose. Nonetheless, the statute's purpose of protecting societal order and morality is clear from its text and history. Public indecency statutes of this sort are of ancient origin, and presently exist in at least 47 States. Public indecency, including nudity, was a criminal offense at common law. [Statutes] such as the one before us reflect moral disapproval of people appearing in the nude among strangers in public places.

This public indecency statute follows a long line of earlier Indiana statutes banning all public nudity. The history of Indiana's public indecency statute shows that it predates barroom nude dancing and was enacted as a general prohibition. At least as early as 1831, Indiana had a statute punishing "open and notorious lewdness, or . . . any grossly scandalous and public indecency." [This] [1] and other public indecency statutes were designed to protect morals and public order. The traditional police power of the States is defined as the authority to provide for the public health, safety, and morals, and we have upheld such a basis for legislation. [Paris Adult Theatre I v. Slaton; Bowers v. Hardwick.] Thus, the public indecency statute furthers a substantial government interest in protecting order and morality.

This interest is unrelated to the suppression of free expression. Some may view restricting nudity on moral grounds as necessarily related to expression. We disagree. It can be argued, of course, that almost limitless types of conduct—including appearing in the nude in public—are "expressive," and in one sense of the word this is true. People who go about in the nude in public may be expressing something about themselves by so doing. But the court rejected this expansive notion of "expressive conduct" in O'Brien.

[Respondents] contend that even though prohibiting nudity in public generally may not be related to suppressing expression, prohibiting the performance of nude dancing is related to expression because the state seeks to prevent its erotic message. Therefore, they reason that the application of the Indiana statute [fails] the third part of the O'Brien test, viz: the governmental interest must be unrelated to the suppression of free expression.

But we do not think that when Indiana applies its statute to the nude dancing in these nightclubs it is proscribing nudity because of the erotic message conveyed by the dancers. Presumably numerous other erotic performances are presented at these establishments and similar clubs without any interference from the state, so long as the performers wear a scant amount of clothing. Likewise, the requirement that the dancers don pasties and a G-string does not deprive the dance of whatever erotic message it conveys; it simply makes the message slightly less graphic. The perceived evil that Indiana seeks to address is not erotic dancing, but public nudity. The appearance of people of all shapes, sizes and ages in the nude at a beach, for example, would convey little if any erotic message, yet the state still seeks to prevent it. Public nudity is the evil the state seeks to prevent, whether or not it is combined with expressive activity. [It] was assumed that O'Brien's act in burning the certificate had a communicative element in it sufficient to bring into play the First Amendment, but it was for the noncommunica-

---

1. Indiana Code section 35–45–4–1 (1988) provides: "Public Indecency "Sec. 1. (a) A person who knowingly or intentionally, in a public place: "(1) engages in sexual intercourse; "(2) engages in deviate sexual conduct; "(3) appears in a state of nudity; or "(4) fondles the genitals of himself or another person; commits public indecency, a Class A misdemeanor. "(b) 'Nudity' means the showing of the human male or female genitals, pubic area, or buttocks with less than a fully opaque covering, the showing of the female breast with less than a fully opaque covering of any part of the nipple, or the showing of the covered male genitals in a discernibly turgid state." [Footnote by Chief Justice Rehnquist.]

tive element that he was prosecuted. So here with the Indiana statute; while the dancing to which it was applied had a communicative element, it was not the dancing that was prohibited, but simply its being done in the nude.

The fourth part of the O'Brien test requires that the incidental restriction on First Amendment freedom be no greater than is essential to the furtherance of the governmental interest. As indicated in the discussion above, the governmental interest served by the text of the prohibition is societal disapproval of nudity in public places and among strangers. The statutory prohibition is not a means to some greater end, but an end in itself. It is without cavil that the public indecency statute is "narrowly tailored;" Indiana's requirement that the dancers wear at least pasties and a G-string is modest, and the bare minimum necessary to achieve the state's purpose.

[Reversed.]

Justice SCALIA, concurring in the judgment.

I agree that the judgment of the Court of Appeals must be reversed. In my view, however, the challenged regulation must be upheld, not because it survives some lower level of First–Amendment scrutiny, but because, as a general law regulating conduct and not specifically directed at expression, it is not subject to First–Amendment scrutiny at all.

I. [On] its face, [the Indiana] law is not directed at expression in particular. [The] intent to convey a "message of eroticism" (or any other message) is not a necessary element of the statutory offense of public indecency; nor does one commit that statutory offense by conveying the most explicit "message of eroticism," so long as he does not commit [in public] any of the four specified acts.

Indiana's statute is in the line of a long tradition of laws against public nudity, which have never been thought to run afoul of traditional understanding of "the freedom of speech." [Indiana's] first public nudity statute predated by many years the appearance of nude barroom dancing. It was general in scope, directed at all public nudity, and not just at public nude expression; and all succeeding statutes, down to the present one, have been the same. Were it the case that Indiana in practice targeted only expressive nudity, while turning a blind eye to nude beaches and unclothed purveyors of hot dogs and machine tools, it might be said that what posed as a regulation of conduct in general was in reality a regulation of only communicative conduct. Respondents have adduced no evidence of that. Indiana officials have brought many public indecency prosecutions for activities having no communicative element.

The dissent confidently asserts that the purpose of restricting nudity in public places in general is to protect nonconsenting parties from offense; and argues that since only consenting, admission-paying patrons see respondents dance, that purpose cannot apply and the only remaining purpose must relate to the communicative elements of the performance. Perhaps the dissenters believe that "offense to others" ought to be the only reason for restricting nudity in public places generally, but there is no basis for thinking that our society has ever shared that Thoreauvian "you-may-do-what-you-like-so-long-as-it-does-not-injure-someone-else" beau ideal—much less for thinking that it was written into the Constitution. The purpose of Indiana's nudity law would be violated, I think, if 60,000 fully consenting adults crowded into the Hoosierdome to display their genitals to one another, even if there were not an offended innocent in the crowd. Our society prohibits, and all human societies have prohibited, certain activities not because they harm others but because they are considered, in the traditional phrase, "contra bonos mores," i.e., immoral. In American society, such prohibitions have included, for example, sadomasochism, cockfighting, bestiality, suicide, drug use, prostitution, and sodomy. While there may be great diversity of view on whether various of these prohibitions should exist (though I have found few ready to abandon, in principle, all of them) there is no doubt that, absent specific constitutional protection for the conduct involved, the Constitution does not prohibit them simply because they regulate "morality." The purpose of the Indiana statute, as both its text and the manner of its enforcement demonstrate, is to enforce the traditional moral belief that people should not expose their private parts indiscriminately, regardless of whether those who see them are disedified. Since that is so, the dissent has no basis for positing that, where only thoroughly edified adults are present, the purpose must be repression of communication.[1]

II. Since the Indiana regulation is a general law not specifically targeted at expressive conduct, its application to such conduct does not in my view implicate the First Amendment.

The First Amendment explicitly protects "the freedom of speech [and] of the press"—oral and written speech—not "expressive conduct." When any law restricts speech, even for a purpose that has nothing to do with the suppression of communication (for instance, to reduce noise [or] to prevent littering), we insist that it meet the high, First–Amendment standard of justification. But virtually every law restricts conduct, and virtually any prohibited conduct can be performed for an expressive purpose—if only expressive of the fact that the actor disagrees with the prohibition. It cannot reasonably be demanded, therefore, that every restriction of expression incidentally produced by a general law regulating conduct pass normal First–Amendment scrutiny, or even—as some of our cases have suggested, see e.g. [O'Brien]—that it be justified by an "important or substantial" government interest. Nor do our holdings require such justification: we have never invalidated the application of a general law simply because the conduct that it reached was being

---

1. The dissent also misunderstands what is meant by the term "general law." I do not mean that the law restricts the targeted conduct in all places at all times. A law is "general" for the present purposes if it regulates conduct without regard to whether that conduct is expressive. Concededly, Indiana bans nudity in public places, but not within the privacy of the home. That is not surprising, since the common law offense, and the traditional moral prohibition, runs against public nudity, not against all nudity. But that confirms, rather than refutes, the general nature of the law: one may not go nude in public, whether or not one intends thereby to convey a message, and similarly one may go nude in private, again whether or not that nudity is expressive. [Footnote by Justice Scalia.]

engaged in for expressive purposes and the government could not demonstrate a sufficiently important state interest.

This is not to say that the First Amendment affords no protection to expressive conduct. Where the government prohibits conduct precisely because of its communicative attributes, we hold the regulation unconstitutional. See, e.g., United States v. Eichman (burning flag); Texas v. Johnson (same); Spence v. Washington (defacing flag); Tinker v. Des Moines Independent Community School District [immediately following] (wearing black arm bands).[2] In each of the foregoing cases, we explicitly found that suppressing communication was the object of the regulation of conduct. Where that has not been the case, however—where suppression of communicative use of the conduct was merely the incidental effect of forbidding the conduct for other reasons—we have allowed the regulation to stand. [Such] a regime ensures that the government does not act to suppress communication, without requiring that all conduct-restricting regulation (which means in effect all regulation) survive an enhanced level of scrutiny.

We have explicitly adopted such a regime in another First Amendment context: that of Free Exercise. In Employment Division, Oregon Dept. of Human Resources v. Smith [1990; below, 12th Ed., p. 1573; Ind. Rts., p. 1244], we held that general laws not specifically targeted at religious practices did not require heightened First Amendment scrutiny even though they diminished some people's ability to practice their religion. [There] is even greater reason to apply this approach to the regulation of expressive conduct. Relatively few can plausibly assert that their illegal conduct is being engaged in for religious reasons; but almost anyone can violate almost any law as a means of expression. In the one case, as in the other, if the law is not directed against the protected value (religion or expression) the law must be obeyed.

III. [I] cannot entirely endorse [the plurality's] reasoning. The plurality purports to apply to this general law, insofar as it regulates this allegedly expressive conduct, an intermediate level of First Amendment scrutiny. [I] do not believe such a heightened standard exists. I think we should avoid wherever possible [a] method of analysis that requires judicial assessment of the "importance" of government interests—and especially of government interests in various aspects of morality.

Neither of the cases that the plurality cites to support the "importance" of the State's interest here is in point. Paris Adult Theatre I v. Slaton and Bowers v. Hardwick did uphold laws prohibiting private conduct based on concerns of decency and morality; but neither opinion held that those concerns were particularly "important" or "substantial,"

---

2. It is easy to conclude that conduct has been forbidden because of its communicative attributes when the conduct in question is what the Court has called "inherently expressive," and what I would prefer to call "conventionally expressive"—such as flying a red flag. I mean by that phrase (as I assume the Court means by "inherently expressive") conduct that is normally engaged in for the purpose of communicating an idea, or perhaps an emotion, to someone else. I am not sure whether dancing fits that description. But even if it does, this law is directed against nudity, not dancing. Nudity is not normally engaged in for the purpose of communicating an idea or an emotion. [Footnote by Justice Scalia.]

or amounted to anything more than a rational basis for regulation. [I] would uphold the Indiana statute on precisely the same ground: moral opposition to nudity supplies a rational basis for its prohibition, and since the First Amendment has no application to this case no more than that is needed. . . .

Justice SOUTER, concurring in the judgment.

Not all dancing is entitled to First Amendment protection as expressive activity. [But] dancing as a performance directed to an actual or hypothetical audience gives expression at least to generalized emotion or feeling, and where the dancer is nude or nearly so the feeling expressed, in the absence of some contrary clue, is eroticism, carrying an endorsement of erotic experience. Such is the expressive content of the dances described in the record.

Although such performance dancing is inherently expressive, nudity per se is not. It is a condition, not an activity, and the voluntary assumption of that condition, without more, apparently expresses nothing beyond the view that the condition is somehow appropriate to the circumstances. But every voluntary act implies some such idea, and the implication is thus so common and minimal that calling all voluntary activity expressive would reduce the concept of expression to the point of the meaningless. A search for some expression beyond the minimal in the choice to go nude will often yield nothing: a person may choose nudity, for example, for maximum sunbathing. But when nudity is combined with expressive activity, its stimulative and attractive value certainly can enhance the force of expression, and a dancer's acts in going from clothed to nude, as in a strip-tease, are integrated into the dance and its expressive function. Thus I agree with the plurality and the dissent that an interest in freely engaging in the nude dancing at issue here is subject to a degree of First Amendment protection.

I also agree [that] the appropriate analysis to determine the actual protection required by the First Amendment is the four-part enquiry described in O'Brien for judging the limits of appropriate state action burdening expressive acts as distinct from pure speech or representation. I nonetheless write separately to rest my concurrence in the judgment, not on the possible sufficiency of society's moral views to justify the limitations at issue, but on the State's substantial interest in combating the secondary effects of adult entertainment establishments of the sort typified by respondents' establishments. [This] asserted justification for the statute may not be ignored merely because it is unclear to what extent this purpose motivated the Indiana Legislature in enacting the statute. Our appropriate focus is not an empirical enquiry into the actual intent of the enacting legislature, but rather the existence or not of a current governmental interest in the service of which the challenged application of the statute may be constitutional. [In] my view, the interest asserted by petitioners in preventing prostitution, sexual assault, and other criminal activity, although presumably not a justification for all applications of the statute, is sufficient under O'Brien to justify the State's enforcement of the statute against [this] type of adult entertainment.

[It] is clear that the prevention of such evils falls within the constitutional power of the State, which satisfies the first O'Brien criterion. The second [asks] whether the regulation "furthers an important or substantial governmental interest." The asserted state interest is plainly a substantial one; the only question is whether prohibiting nude dancing of the sort at issue here "furthers" that interest. I believe that our cases [establish] that it does. [The] type of entertainment respondents seek to provide is [of] the same character as that [in] Renton [and] American Mini Theatres. [It] therefore is no leap to say that live nude dancing of the sort [here] is likely to produce the same pernicious secondary effects as the adult films displaying "specified anatomical areas" [in] Renton. In light of Renton's recognition that legislation seeking to combat the secondary effects of adult entertainment need not await localized proof of those effects, [Indiana] could reasonably conclude that forbidding nude entertainment of the type [at issue here] furthers its interest in preventing prostitution, sexual assault, and associated crimes. [I] do not believe that a State is required affirmatively to undertake to litigate this issue repeatedly in every case.[1]

[The] third O'Brien condition is that the governmental interest be "unrelated to the suppression of free expression," and, on its face, the governmental interest in combating prostitution and other criminal activity is not at all inherently related to expression. The dissent contends, however, that Indiana seeks to regulate nude dancing as its means of combating such secondary effects "because . . . creating or emphasizing [the] thoughts and ideas [expressed by nude dancing] in the minds of the spectators may lead to increased prostitution," and that regulation of expressive conduct because of the fear that the expression will prove persuasive is inherently related to the suppression of free expression. The major premise of the dissent's reasoning may be correct, but its minor premise describing the causal theory of Indiana's regulatory justification is not. To say that pernicious secondary effects are associated with nude dancing establishments is not necessarily to say that such effects result from the persuasive effect of the expression inherent in nude dancing. It is to say, rather, only that the effects are correlated with the existence of establishments offering such dancing, without deciding what the precise causes of the correlation actually are. It is possible, for example, that the higher incidence of prostitution and sexual assault in the vicinity of adult entertainment locations results from the concentration of crowds of men predisposed to such activities, or from the simple viewing of nude bodies regardless of whether those

---

1. Because there is no overbreadth challenge before us, we are not called upon to decide whether the application of the statute would be valid in other contexts. It is enough, then, to say that the secondary effects rationale on which I rely here would be open to question if the State were to seek to enforce the statute by barring expressive nudity in classes of productions that could not readily be analogized to the adult films at issue in Renton. It is diffi- cult to see, for example, how the enforcement of Indiana's statute against nudity in a production of "Hair" or "Equus" somewhere other than an "adult" theater would further the State's interest in avoiding harmful secondary effects, in the absence of evidence that expressive nudity outside the context of Renton-type adult entertainment was correlated with such secondary effects. [Footnote by Justice Souter.]

bodies are engaged in expression or not. In neither case would the chain of causation run through the persuasive effect of the expressive component of nude dancing. Because the State's interest in banning nude dancing results from a simple correlation of such dancing with other evils, rather than from a relationship between the other evils and the expressive component of the dancing, the interest is unrelated to the suppression of free expression.[2]

[The] fourth O'Brien condition, that the restriction be no greater than essential to further the governmental interest, requires little discussion. Pasties and a G-string moderate the expression to some degree, to be sure, but only to a degree. Dropping the final stitch is prohibited, but the limitation is minor when measured against the dancer's remaining capacity and opportunity to express the erotic message. Nor, so far as we are told, is the dancer or her employer limited by anything short of obscenity laws from expressing an erotic message by articulate speech or representational means; a pornographic movie featuring one of respondents, for example, was playing nearby without any interferences from the authorities at the time these cases arose.

Accordingly, I find O'Brien satisfied and concur in the judgment.

Justice WHITE, with whom Justice MARSHALL, Justice BLACKMUN, and Justice STEVENS join, dissenting.

The first question presented [is] whether nonobscene nude dancing performed as entertainment is expressive conduct protected by the First Amendment. The Court of Appeals held that [our] prior decisions permit no other conclusion. Not surprisingly, then, the Court now concedes that "nude dancing of the kind sought to be performed here is expressive conduct within the outer perimeters of the First Amendment...." This is no more than recognizing, as the Seventh Circuit observed, that dancing is an ancient art form and "inherently embodies the expression and communication of ideas and emotions."[1] Having arrived at the conclusion that nude dancing performed as entertainment enjoys First Amendment protection, [the] Court turns to O'Brien [and] finds that the Indiana statute satisfies the O'Brien test in all respects.

---

2. I reach this conclusion again mindful, as was the Court in Renton, that the protection of sexually explicit expression may be of lesser societal importance than the protection of other forms of expression. [Footnote by Justice Souter.]

1. Justice Scalia suggests that performance dancing is not inherently expressive activity, but the Court of Appeals has the better view: "Dance has been defined as 'the art of moving the body in a rhythmical way, usually to music, to express an emotion or idea, to narrate a story, or simply to take delight in the movement itself.' Encyclopedia Britannica. Inherently, it is the communication of emotion or ideas. At the root of all '[t]he varied manifestations of dancing ... lies the common impulse to resort to movement to externalise states which we cannot externalise by rational means. This is basic dance.' Martin, J. Introduction to the Dance (1939). Aristotle recognized in Poetics that the purpose of dance is 'to represent men's character as well as what they do and suffer.' The raw communicative power of dance was noted by the French poet Stephane Mallarme who declared that the dancer 'writing with her body ... suggests things which the written work could express only in several paragraphs of dialogue or descriptive prose.'" 904 F.2d at 1085–1086. [The] Justice also asserts that even if dancing is inherently expressive, nudity is not. The statement may be true, but it tells us nothing about dancing in the nude. [Footnote by Justice White.]

The Court acknowledges that it is impossible to discern the exact state interests which the Indiana legislature had in mind when it enacted the Indiana statute, but [nonetheless] concludes [that] the law's purpose is to protect "societal order and morality." [The] Court's analysis is erroneous in several respects. Both the Court and Justice Scalia [overlook] a [critical] aspect of our cases upholding the States' exercise of their police powers. None of the cases they rely upon, including O'Brien and Bowers v. Hardwick, involved anything less than truly general proscriptions on individual conduct. In O'Brien, for example, individuals were prohibited from destroying their draft cards at any time and in any place, even in completely private places such as the home. Likewise, in Bowers, the State prohibited sodomy, regardless of where the conduct might occur, including the home as was true in that case. [By] contrast, [Indiana] does not suggest that its statute applies to, or could be applied to, nudity wherever it occurs, including the home. We do not understand the Court or Justice Scalia to be suggesting that Indiana could constitutionally enact such an intrusive prohibition [in] light of our decision in Stanley v. Georgia.

[We] are told [that] the Indiana Supreme Court held that the statute at issue here cannot and does not prohibit nudity as a part of some larger form of expression meriting protection when the communication of ideas is involved. Petitioners also state that the evils sought to be avoided by applying the statute in this case would not obtain in the case of theatrical productions, such as Salome or Hair. Neither is there any evidence that the State has attempted to apply the statute to nudity in performances such as plays, ballets or operas. [Thus,] the Indiana statute is not a general prohibition of the type we have upheld in prior cases. As a result, [simple] references to the State's general interest in promoting societal order and morality is not sufficient justification for a statute which concededly reaches a significant amount of protected expressive activity. Instead, [we] are obligated to carefully examine the reasons the State has chosen to regulate this expressive conduct in a less than general statute. In other words, when the State enacts a law which draws a line between expressive conduct which is regulated and nonexpressive conduct of the same type which is not regulated, O'Brien places the burden on the State to justify the distinctions it has made.

[Legislators] do not just randomly select certain conduct for proscription; they have reasons for doing so and those reasons illuminate the purpose of the law that is passed. Indeed, a law may have multiple purposes. The purpose of forbidding people from appearing nude in parks, beaches, hot dog stands, and like public places is to protect others from offense. But that could not possibly be the purpose of preventing nude dancing in theaters and barrooms since the viewers are exclusively consenting adults who pay money to see these dances. The purpose of the proscription in these contexts is to protect the viewers from what the State believes is the harmful message that nude dancing communicates. [As] the State now tells us, and as Justice Souter agrees, the State's goal in applying what it describes as its "content neutral" statute to the nude dancing in this case is "deterrence of prostitution, sexual assaults, criminal activity, degradation of women, and other activities which break down family structure." The attainment of these goals, however, depends on preventing an expressive activity.

The Court nevertheless holds that the third requirement of the O'Brien test [is] satisfied because [the] State is not "proscribing nudity because of the erotic message conveyed by the dancers." The Court suggests that this is so because the State does not ban dancing that sends an erotic message; it is only nude erotic dancing that is forbidden. The perceived evil is not erotic dancing but public nudity, which may be prohibited despite any incidental impact on expressive activity. This analysis is transparently erroneous.

[The] Court concedes that nude dancing conveys an erotic message and [that] the message would be muted if the dancers wore pasties and G-strings. Indeed, the emotional or erotic impact of the dance is intensified by the nudity of the performers. [The] nudity is itself an expressive component of the dance, not merely incidental "conduct." [It] is only because nude dancing performances may generate emotions and feelings of eroticism and sensuality among the spectators that the State seeks to regulate such expressive activity, apparently on the assumption that creating or emphasizing such thoughts and ideas in the minds of the spectators may lead to increased prostitution and the degradation of women. But generating thoughts, ideas, and emotions is the essence of communication. The nudity element of nude dancing performances cannot be neatly pigeonholed as mere "conduct" independent of any expressive component of the dance.[2] [That] the performances [may] not be high art, to say the least, and may not appeal to the Court, is hardly an excuse for distorting and ignoring settled doctrine. The Court's assessment of the artistic merits of nude dancing performances should not be the determining factor in deciding this case. [Our] cases require us to affirm absent a compelling state interest supporting the statute. Neither the Court nor the State suggest that the statute could withstand scrutiny under that standard.

[We] agree with Justice Scalia that the Indiana statute would not permit 60,000 consenting Hoosiers to expose themselves to each other in the Hoosierdome. No one can doubt, however, that those same 60,000 Hoosiers would be perfectly free to drive to their respective homes all across Indiana and, once there, to parade around, cavort, and revel in the nude for hours in front of relatives and friends. It is difficult to see why the State's interest in morality is any less in that situation, especially if, as Justice Scalia seems to suggest, nudity is inherently evil, but clearly the statute does not reach such activity. The State's failure

---

2. Justice Souter agrees with the Court that the third requirement of the O'Brien test is satisfied, but only because he is not certain that there is a causal connection between the message conveyed by nude dancing and the evils which the State is seeking to prevent. [If he] is correct that there is no causal connection between the message conveyed by the nude dancing at issue here and the negative secondary effects that the State desires to regulate, the State does not have even a rational basis for its absolute prohibition on nude dancing that is admittedly expressive. Furthermore, if the real problem is the "concentration of crowds of men predisposed to the" designated evils, then the First Amendment requires that the State address that problem in a fashion that does not include banning an entire category of expressive activity. [Footnote by Justice White.]

to enact a truly general proscription requires closer scrutiny of the reasons for the distinctions the State has drawn.

[I] would affirm the judgment of the Court of Appeals ...

12th ED., p. 1248; IND.RTS., p. 919
Add at end of footnote *:

The drive to reverse the Supreme Court's flag-burning decisions has gained new momentum in the 104th Congress. The two leading constitutional amendment proposals would grant to Congress and the States the power to prohibit "physical desecration of the flag of the United States." S.J.Res. 31, with 54 cosponsors, was introduced March 21, 1995 and on June 6, 1995, the Senate Subcommittee on the Constitution, Federalism and Property Rights concluded hearings on this legislation. Hearings were concluded on May 24, 1995 on H.J.Res. 79, a companion bill, with 280 cosponsors. That resolution was reported favorably out of the full House Judiciary Committee on June 7, 1995. On June 28, 1995, the flag desecration amendment was passed by the full House by a vote of 312–120 and sent to the Senate. Other proposals concerning flag desecration in the 104th Congress include H.J.Res. 13, 14, 32 and 41.

12th ED., p. 1248; IND. RTS., p. 919
Add after materials on flag desecration:

R.A.V. v. CITY OF ST. PAUL, MINNESOTA

504 U.S. __, 112 S.Ct. 2538, 120 L.Ed.2d 305 (1992).

Justice SCALIA delivered the opinion of the Court.

In the predawn hours of June 21, 1990, petitioner and several other teenagers allegedly assembled a crudely-made cross by taping together broken chair legs. They then allegedly burned the cross inside the fenced yard of a black family that lived across the street from the house where petitioner was staying. Although this conduct could have been punished under any of a number of laws,[1] one of the two provisions under which [St. Paul] chose to charge petitioner (then a juvenile) was the St. Paul Bias–Motivated Crime Ordinance, which provides:

"Whoever places on public or private property a symbol, object, appellation, characterization or graffiti, including, but not limited to, a burning cross or Nazi swastika, which one knows or has reasonable grounds to know arouses anger, alarm or resentment in others on the basis of race, color, creed, religion or gender commits disorderly conduct and shall be guilty of a misdemeanor."

Petitioner moved to dismiss this count on the ground that the [ordinance] was substantially overbroad and impermissibly content-based and therefore facially invalid under the First Amendment.[2] The trial court granted this motion, but the Minnesota Supreme Court reversed. That

---

1. The conduct might have violated Minnesota statutes carrying significant penalties. E.g., Minn.Stat. 609.713(1) (providing for up to five years in prison for terroristic threats); 609.563 (arson) (providing for up to five years and a $10,000 fine ...); 606.595 (criminal damage to property) (pro-viding for up to one year and a $3,000 fine ...) [Footnote by Justice Scalia.]

2. Petitioner has also been charged [with] a violation of Minn.Stat. 609.2231(4) (racially motivated assaults). Petitioner did not challenge this count. [Footnote by Justice Scalia.]

court rejected petitioner's overbreadth claim because, as construed in prior Minnesota cases, the modifying phrase "arouses anger, alarm or resentment in others" limited the reach of the ordinance to conduct that amounts to "fighting words," i.e., "conduct that itself inflicts injury or tends to incite immediate violence ..." [Chaplinsky,] and therefore the ordinance reached only expression "that the first amendment does not protect." The court also concluded that the ordinance was not impermissibly content-based because, in its view, "the ordinance is a narrowly tailored means toward accomplishing the compelling governmental interest in protecting the community against bias-motivated threats to public safety and order." ...

I. In construing the St. Paul ordinance, we are bound by the construction given to it by the Minnesota court. Accordingly, we accept the [authoritative] statement that the ordinance reaches only those expressions that constitute "fighting words" within the meaning of Chaplinsky. Petitioner [urges] us to [invalidate] the ordinance as "substantially overbroad," Broadrick v. Oklahoma [1973; above, 12th Ed., p. 1194; Ind.Rts., p. 865.] We find it unnecessary to consider this issue. Assuming, arguendo, that all of the expression reached by the ordinance is proscribable under the "fighting words" doctrine, we nonetheless conclude that the ordinance is facially unconstitutional in that it prohibits otherwise permitted speech solely on the basis of the subjects the speech addresses.[3]

The First Amendment generally prevents government from proscribing speech [or expressive conduct] because of disapproval of the ideas expressed. Content-based regulations are presumptively invalid. From 1791 to the present, however, our society, like other free but civilized societies, has permitted restrictions upon the content of speech in a few limited areas, which are "of such slight social value as a step to truth that any benefit that may be derived from them is clearly outweighed by the social interest in order and morality." Chaplinsky. We have recognized that "the freedom of speech" [does] not include a freedom to disregard these traditional limitations. Roth v. United States [1957; 12th Ed., p. 1099; Ind.Rts., p. 770]; Beauharnais v. Illinois [1952; 12th Ed., p. 1075; Ind.Rts., p. 746]; Chaplinsky. Our decisions since the 1960's have narrowed the scope of the traditional categorical exceptions for defamation and for obscenity, but a limited categorical approach has remained an important part of our First Amendment jurisprudence.

We have sometimes said that these categories of expression are "not within the area of constitutionally protected speech," [Roth; Beauharnais; Chaplinsky], or that the "protection of the First Amendment does not extend" to them, Bose Corp. v. Consumers Union, 466 U.S. 485

3. Contrary to Justice White's suggestion, petitioner's claim is "fairly included" within the [petition] for certiorari. It was clear from [petitioner's filings] in this Court (and in the courts below) that his assertion that the St. Paul ordinance "violat[es] overbreadth ... principles of the First Amendment," was not just a technical "overbreadth" claim—i.e., a claim that the ordinance violated the rights of too many third parties—but included the contention that the ordinance was "overbroad" in the sense of restricting more speech than the Constitution permits, even in its application to him, because it is content-based.... [Footnote by Justice Scalia.]

(1984). Such statements must be taken in context, however, and are no more literally true than is the occasionally repeated shorthand characterizing obscenity "as not ɔeing speech at all." Sunstein, Pornography and the First Amendment, 1986 Duke L.J. 589. What they mean is that these areas of speech can [be] regulated because of their constitutionally proscribable content (obscenity, defamation, etc.)—not that they are categories of speech entirely invisible to the Constitution, so that they may be made the vehicles for content discrimination unrelated to their distinctively proscribable content. Thus, the government may proscribe libel; but it may not make the further content discrimination of proscribing only libel critical of the government. [Our] cases surely do not establish the proposition that the First Amendment imposes no obstacle whatsoever to regulation of particular instances of such proscribable expression. [That] would mean that a city council could enact an ordinance prohibiting only those legally obscene works that contain criticism of the city government or, indeed, that do not include endorsement of the city government. Such a simplistic, all-or-nothing-at-all approach [is] at odds with common sense and with our jurisprudence as well.[4] It is not true that "fighting words" have at most a "de minimis" expressive content, or that their content is in all respects "worthless and undeserving of constitutional protection"; sometimes they are quite expressive indeed. We have not said that they constitute "no part of the expression of ideas," but only that they constitute "no *essential* part of any exposition of ideas."

The proposition that a particular instance of speech can be proscribable on the basis of one feature (e.g., obscenity) but not on the basis of another (e.g., opposition to the city government) is commonplace, and has found application in many contexts. [Nonverbal] expressive activity can be banned because of the action it entails, but not because of the ideas it expresses—so that burning a flag in violation of an ordinance against outdoor fires could be punishable, whereas burning a flag in violation of an ordinance against dishonoring the flag is not. Similarly, we have upheld reasonable "time, place, or manner" restrictions, but only if they are "justified without reference to the content of the

---

4. Justice White concedes that a city council cannot prohibit only those legally obscene works that contain criticism of the city government, but asserts that to be the consequence [of] the Equal Protection Clause. Such content-based discrimination would not, he asserts, "be rationally related to a legitimate government interest." But of course the only reason that government interest is not a "legitimate" one is that it violates the First Amendment. This Court itself has occasionally [e.g., Mosley] fused the First Amendment into the Equal Protection Clause, [but] at least with the acknowledgment (which Justice White cannot afford to make) that the First Amendment underlies its analysis. Justice Stevens seeks to avoid the point by dismissing the notion of obscene anti-government speech as "fantastical," apparently believing that any reference to politics prevents a finding of obscenity. Unfortunately for the purveyors of obscenity, that is obviously false. A shockingly hard core pornographic movie that contains a model sporting a political tattoo can be found, "taken as a whole [to] lac[k] serious literary, artistic, political, or scientific value," Miller v. California [1973; above, 12th Ed., p. 1108; Ind.Rts., p. 779.] Anyway, it is easy enough to come up with other illustrations of a content-based restriction upon "unprotected speech" that is obviously invalid: the anti-government libel illustration mentioned earlier, for one. And of course the concept of racist fighting words is, unfortunately, anything but a "highly speculative hypothetica[l]." [Footnote by Justice Scalia.]

regulated speech." Ward v. Rock Against Racism [1989; below, 12th Ed., p. 1345; Ind.Rts., p. 1016]; Clark v. Community for Creative Non–Violence [1984; immediately below]. And just as the power to proscribe particular speech on the basis of a noncontent element (e.g., noise) does not entail the power to proscribe the same speech on the basis of a content element; so also, the power to proscribe it on the basis of one content element (e.g., obscenity) does not entail the power to proscribe it on the basis of other content elements.

In other words, the exclusion of "fighting words" from the scope of the First Amendment simply means that [the] unprotected features of the words are [essentially] a "nonspeech" element of communication. Fighting words are thus analogous to a noisy sound truck: [both] can be used to convey an idea; but neither has, in and of itself, a claim upon the First Amendment. As with the sound truck, however, so also with fighting words: The government may not regulate use based on hostility—or favoritism—towards the underlying message expressed.[5]

The concurrences describe us as setting forth a new First Amendment principle that prohibition of constitutionally proscribable speech cannot be "underinclusiv[e],"—a First Amendment "absolutism" whereby "within a particular 'proscribable' category of expression, ... a government must either proscribe all speech or no speech at all." That easy target is of the concurrences' own invention. [The] First Amendment imposes not an "underinclusiveness" limitation but a "content discrimination" limitation upon a State's prohibition of proscribable speech. There is no problem [with] a State's prohibiting obscenity (and other forms of proscribable expression) only in certain media or markets, for although that prohibition would be "underinclusive," it would not discriminate on the basis of content.

Even the prohibition against content discrimination [is] not absolute. It applies differently in the context of proscribable speech than in the area of fully protected speech. The rationale of the general prohibition, after all, is that content discrimination "rais[es] the specter that the Government may effectively drive certain ideas or viewpoints from the marketplace," Simon & Schuster v. New York Crime Victims Board [1991; below, addition to 12th Ed., p. 1499; Ind.Rts., p. 1170.] But content discrimination among various instances of a class of proscribable speech often does not pose this threat.

When the basis for the content discrimination consists entirely of the very reason the entire class of speech at issue is proscribable, no significant danger of idea or viewpoint discrimination exists. Such a reason, having been adjudged neutral enough to support exclusion of the entire class of speech from [protection,] is also neutral enough to form the basis of distinction within the class. To illustrate: A State might

5. Although Justice White asserts that our analysis disregards "established principles of First Amendment law," he cites not a single case (and we are aware of none) that even involved, much less considered and resolved, the issue of content discrimination through regulation of "unprotected" speech—though we plainly recognized that as an issue in Ferber. It is of course contrary to all traditions of our jurisprudence to consider the law on this point conclusively resolved by broad language in cases where the issue was not presented or even envisioned. [Footnote by Justice Scalia.]

choose to prohibit only that obscenity which is the most patently offensive in its prurience—i.e., that which involves the most lascivious displays of sexual activity. But it may not prohibit [only] that obscenity which includes offensive political messages. And the Federal Government can criminalize only those threats of violence that are directed against the President, since the reasons why threats of violence are outside the First Amendment (protecting individuals from the fear of violence, from the disruption that fear engenders, and from the possibility that the threatened violence will occur) have special force when applied to the person of the President. Watts v. United States [1969; above, 12th Ed., p. 1068; Ind.Rts., p. 739.] But the Federal Government may not criminalize only those threats against the President that mention his policy on aid to inner cities. And to take a final example, [a] State may choose to regulate price advertising in one industry but not in others, because the risk of fraud (one of the characteristics of commercial speech that justifies depriving it of full First Amendment protection) is in its view greater there. But a State may not prohibit only that commercial advertising that depicts men in a demeaning fashion.

Another valid basis for according differential treatment to even a content-defined subclass of proscribable speech is that the subclass happens to be associated with particular "secondary effects" of the speech, so that the regulation is "justified without reference to the content of the ... speech," Renton v. Playtime Theatres [1986; above, 12th Ed., p. 1151; Ind.Rts., p. 822.] A State could, for example, permit all obscene live performances except those involving minors. Moreover, since words can [violate] laws directed not against speech but against conduct (a law against treason, for example, is violated by telling the enemy the nation's defense secrets), a particular content-based subcategory of a proscribable class of speech can be swept up incidentally within the reach of a statute directed at conduct rather than speech. Thus [sexually] derogatory "fighting words," among other words, may produce a violation of Title VII's general prohibition against sexual discrimination in employment practices. Where the government does not target conduct on the basis of its expressive content, acts are not shielded from regulation merely because they express a discriminatory idea or philosophy.

These bases for distinction refute the proposition that the selectivity of the restriction is "even arguably 'conditioned upon the sovereign's agreement with what a speaker may intend to say.'" Metromedia, Inc. v. San Diego [1981; below, 12th Ed., p. 1330; Ind.Rts., p. 1001] (Stevens, dissenting in part). There may be other such bases as well. Indeed, to validate such selectivity (where totally proscribable speech is at issue) it may not even be necessary to identify any particular "neutral" basis, so long as the nature of the content discrimination is such that there is no realistic possibility that official suppression of ideas is afoot. (We cannot think of any First Amendment interest that would stand in the way of a State's prohibiting only those obscene motion pictures with blue-eyed actresses.) Save for that limitation, the regulation of "fighting words," like the regulation of noisy speech, may address some offensive instances and leave other, equally offensive, instances alone.[6]

II.   Applying these principles, we conclude that, even as narrowly construed, [the ordinance] is facially unconstitutional. Although the phrase "arouses anger, alarm or resentment in others" has been limited [to] reach only those symbols or displays that amount to "fighting words," the remaining, unmodified terms make clear that the ordinance applies only to "fighting words" that insult, or provoke violence, "on the basis of race, color, creed, religion or gender."   Displays containing abusive invective, no matter how vicious or severe, are permissible unless they are addressed to one of the specified disfavored topics. Those who wish to use "fighting words" in connection with other ideas—to express hostility, for example, on the basis of political affiliation, union membership, or homosexuality—are not covered.   The First Amendment does not permit [special] prohibitions on those speakers who express views on disfavored subjects.   In its practical operation, moreover, the ordinance goes even beyond mere content discrimination, to actual viewpoint discrimination.   Displays containing some words— odious racial epithets, for example—would be prohibited to proponents of all views.   But "fighting words" that do not themselves invoke race, color, creed, religion, or gender—aspersions upon a person's mother, for example—would seemingly be usable ad libitum in the placards of those arguing in favor of racial, color, etc. tolerance and equality, but could not be used by that speaker's opponents.   One could hold up a sign saying, for example, that all "anti-Catholic bigots" are misbegotten; but not that all "papists" are, for that would insult and provoke violence "on the basis of religion."   St. Paul has no such authority to license one side of a debate to fight freestyle, while requiring the other to follow Marquis of Queensbury Rules.

What we have here [is] not a prohibition of fighting words [directed] at certain persons or groups (which would be facially valid if it met the requirements of the Equal Protection Clause); but rather, a prohibition of fighting words that contain (as the Minnesota Supreme Court repeatedly emphasized) messages of "bias-motivated" hatred and in particular, as applied to this case, messages "based on virulent notions of racial supremacy."   One must wholeheartedly agree [that] "[i]t is the responsibility, even the obligation, of diverse communities to confront such notions in whatever form they appear," but the manner of that confrontation cannot consist of selective limitations upon speech.   St.

---

6. Justice Stevens cites a string of opinions as supporting his assertion that "selective regulation of speech based on content" is not presumptively invalid. Analysis reveals, however, that they do not support it. To begin with, three of them did not command a majority of the Court, Young v. American Mini Theatres, Inc. [1976; above, 12th Ed., p. 1147; Ind.Rts., p. 818] (plurality); FCC v. Pacifica Foundation [1978; above, 12th Ed., p. 1154; Ind.Rts., p. 825] (plurality); Lehman v. City of Shaker Heights [1974; below, 12th Ed., p. 1299; Ind.Rts., p. 970] (plurality), and two others did not even discuss the First Amendment, Morales v. Trans World Airlines, Inc., 504 U.S. __ (1992); Jacob Siegel Co. v. FTC, 327 U.S. 608 (1946).   In any event, all [they] establish is what we readily concede: that presumptive invalidity does not mean invariable invalidity, leaving room for such exceptions as reasonable and viewpoint-neutral content-based discrimination in nonpublic forums, or with respect to certain speech by government employees. [Footnote by Justice Scalia.]

Paul [asserts] that a general "fighting words" law would not meet the city's needs because only a content-specific measure can communicate to minority groups that the "group hatred" aspect of such speech "is not condoned by the majority." The point of the First Amendment is that majority preferences must be expressed other than [by] silencing speech on the basis of its content.

Despite the fact that the Minnesota Supreme Court and St. Paul acknowledge that the ordinance is directed at expression of group hatred, Justice Stevens suggests that this "fundamentally misreads" the ordinance. It is directed, he claims, not to speech of a particular content, but to particular "injur[ies]" that are "qualitatively different" from other injuries. This is word-play. What makes the anger, fear, sense of dishonor, etc. produced by violation of this ordinance distinct from the anger, fear, sense of dishonor, etc. produced by other fighting words is nothing other than the fact that it is caused by a distinctive idea, conveyed by a distinctive message. The First Amendment cannot be evaded that easily. It is obvious that the symbols which will arouse "anger, alarm or resentment in others on the basis of race, color, creed, religion or gender" are those symbols that communicate a message of hostility based on one of these characteristics. St. Paul concedes [that] the ordinance applies only to "racial, religious, or gender-specific symbols" such as "a burning cross, Nazi swastika or other instrumentality of like import." Indeed, St. Paul argued in the Juvenile Court that "[t]he burning of a cross does express a message and it is, in fact, the content of that message which the St. Paul Ordinance attempts to legislate." The content-based discrimination reflected in the ordinance comes within neither any of the specific exceptions to the First Amendment prohibition, [nor] within a more general exception for content discrimination that does not threaten censorship of ideas. It assuredly does not fall within the exception for content discrimination based on the very reasons why the particular class of speech at issue (here, fighting words) is proscribable. [The] reason why fighting words are categorically excluded from [protection] is not that their content communicates any particular idea, but that their content embodies a particularly intolerable (and socially unnecessary) mode of expressing whatever idea the speaker wishes to convey. St. Paul has not singled out an especially offensive mode of expression—it has not, for example, selected for prohibition only those fighting words that communicate ideas in a threatening (as opposed to a merely obnoxious) manner. Rather, it has proscribed fighting words of whatever manner that communicate messages of racial, gender, or religious intolerance. Selectivity of this sort creates the possibility that the city is seeking to handicap the expression of particular ideas. That possibility would alone be enough to render the ordinance presumptively invalid, but St. Paul's [concessions] in this case elevate the possibility to a certainty.

St. Paul argues that the ordinance comes within another of the specific exceptions we mentioned, the one that allows content discrimination aimed only at the "secondary effects" of the speech. Renton. According to St. Paul, the ordinance is intended, "not to impact on [sic] the right of free expression of the accused," but rather to "protect against the victimization of a person or persons who are particularly vulnerable because of their membership in a group that historically has been discriminated against." Even assuming that an ordinance that completely proscribes, rather than merely regulates, a specified category of speech can ever be considered to be directed only to the secondary effects of such speech, it is clear that the [ordinance] is not directed to secondary effects within the meaning of Renton. As we said in Boos v. Barry [1988; above, 11th Ed., p. 1153; Ind.Rts., p. 824], "[l]isteners' reactions to speech are not the type of 'secondary effects' we referred to in Renton." [7]

[Finally,] St. Paul [argues] that, even if the ordinance regulates expression based on hostility towards its protected ideological content, this discrimination is nonetheless justified because it is narrowly tailored to serve compelling state interests. [It asserts] that the ordinance helps to ensure the basic human rights of members of groups that have historically been subjected to discrimination, including the right of such group members to live in peace where they wish. We do not doubt that these interests are compelling, and that the ordinance can be said to promote them. But the "danger of censorship" presented by a facially content-based statute requires that that weapon be employed only where it is "necessary to serve the asserted [compelling] interest," Burson v. Freeman [1992; below, addition to 12th Ed., p. 1374; Ind.Rts., p. 1045.] [The] dispositive question in this case [is] whether content discrimination is reasonably necessary to achieve St. Paul's compelling interests; it plainly is not. An ordinance not limited to the favored topics, for example, would have precisely the same beneficial effect. In fact the only interest distinctively served by the content limitation is that of displaying the city council's special hostility towards the particular biases thus singled out. That is precisely what the First Amendment forbids. The politicians of St. Paul are entitled to express that hostility—but not through the means of imposing unique limitations upon speakers who (however benightedly) disagree.

Let there be no mistake about our belief that burning a cross in someone's front yard is reprehensible. But St. Paul has sufficient means at its disposal to prevent such behavior without adding the First Amendment to the fire.

[Reversed.]

Justice WHITE, with whom Justice BLACKMUN and Justice O'CONNOR join, and with whom Justice STEVENS joins except as to Part I(A), concurring in the judgment.

---

7. St. Paul has not argued [that] the ordinance merely regulates that subclass of fighting words [most] likely to provoke a violent response. But even if one assumes (as appears unlikely) that the categories selected may be so described, that would not justify selective regulation under a "secondary effects" theory. The only reason why such expressive conduct would be especially correlated with violence is that it conveys a particularly odious message; because the "chain of causation" thus necessarily "run[s] through the persuasive effect of the expressive component" of the conduct, Barnes v. Glen Theatre [1991; below, addition to 12th Ed., p. 1227; Ind.Rts., p. 898] (Souter, concurring in judgment), it is clear that the ordinance regulates on the basis of the "primary" effect of the speech—i.e., its persuasive (or repellant) force. [Footnote by Justice Scalia.]

I agree with the majority that the judgment [should] be reversed. However, our agreement ends there. This case could easily be decided within the contours of established [law] by holding [that] the ordinance is fatally overbroad because it criminalizes [expression] protected by the First Amendment. Instead, "find[ing] it unnecessary" to consider the questions upon which we granted review,[1] the Court holds the ordinance facially unconstitutional on a ground [never] presented to the Minnesota Supreme Court, [not briefed] by the parties before this Court, [and seriously departing] from the teaching of prior cases. This Court ordinarily is not so eager to abandon its precedents. But [here] the majority casts aside long-established [doctrine] without the benefit of briefing and adopts an untried theory. This is hardly a judicious way of proceeding, and the Court's reasoning [is] transparently wrong.

I. A. This Court's decisions have plainly stated that expression falling within certain limited categories so lacks the values the First Amendment was designed to protect that the Constitution affords no protection to that expression. Chaplinsky. [Thus] this Court has long held certain discrete categories of expression to be proscribable on the basis of their content. For instance, [the] individual who falsely shouts "fire" in a crowded theatre may not claim the protection of the First Amendment. Schenck. [Neither] child pornography, nor obscenity, is protected by the First Amendment. Ferber; Miller; Roth. And ["leaving] aside the special considerations when public officials [and public figures] are the target, a libelous publication is not protected by the Constitution." Ferber. All of these categories are content based. But [the] First Amendment does not apply to them because their expressive content is worthless or of de minimis value to society. [This] categorical approach has provided a principled and narrowly focused means for distinguishing between expression that the government may regulate freely and that which it may regulate on the basis of content only upon a showing of compelling need.

1. The Court granted certiorari to review the following questions:

"1. May a local government enact a content-based, 'hate-crime' ordinance prohibiting the display of symbols, including a Nazi swastika or a burning cross, on public or private property, which one knows or has reason to know arouses anger, alarm, or resentment in others on the basis of race, color, creed, religion, or gender without violating overbreadth and vagueness principles of the First Amendment to the United States Constitution?

"2. Can the constitutionality of such a vague and substantially overbroad content-based restraint of expression be saved by a limiting construction, like that used to save the vague and overbroad content-neutral laws, restricting its application to 'fighting words' or 'imminent lawless action?'"

It has long been the rule of this Court that "[o]nly the questions set forth in the petition, or fairly included therein, will be considered by the Court." [Rule 14.1a] has served to focus the issues presented for review. But the majority reads the Rule so expansively that any First Amendment theory would appear to be "fairly included" within the questions quoted above.

Contrary to the impression the majority attempts to create through its selective quotation of petitioner's briefs, petitioner did not present to this Court or the Minnesota Supreme Court anything approximating the novel theory the majority adopts today. [Previously,] this Court has shown the restraint to refrain from deciding cases on the basis of its own theories when they have not been pressed or passed upon by a state court of last resort ... [Footnote by Justice White.]

Today, however, the Court announces that earlier Courts did not mean their repeated statements that certain categories of expression are "not within the area of constitutionally protected speech." Roth. The present Court submits that such clear statements "must be taken in context" and are not "literally true." To the contrary, those statements meant precisely what they said: The categorical approach is a firmly entrenched part of our First Amendment jurisprudence. Indeed, the Court in Roth reviewed the guarantees of freedom of expression in effect at the time of the ratification of the Constitution and concluded, "[i]n light of this history, it is apparent that the unconditional phrasing of the First Amendment was not intended to protect every utterance." [Nevertheless,] the majority holds that the First Amendment protects those narrow categories of expression long held to be undeserving of protection—at least to the extent that lawmakers may not regulate some fighting words more strictly than others because of their content. The Court announces that such content-based distinctions violate the First Amendment because "the government may not regulate use based on hostility—or favoritism—towards the underlying message expressed." Should the government want to criminalize certain fighting words, the Court now requires it to criminalize all fighting words.

To borrow a phrase, "Such a simplistic, all-or-nothing-at-all approach to First Amendment protection is at odds with common sense and with our jurisprudence as well." It is inconsistent to hold that the government may proscribe an entire category of speech because the content of that speech is evil, Ferber, but that the government may not treat a subset of that category differently without violating the First Amendment; the content of the subset is by definition worthless and undeserving of [protection.]

The majority's observation that fighting words are "quite expressive indeed" is no answer. Fighting words are not a means of exchanging views, rallying supporters, or registering a protest; they are directed against individuals to provoke violence or to inflict injury. Therefore, a ban on all [or a] subset of the fighting words category would restrict only the social evil of hate speech, without [the] danger of driving viewpoints from the marketplace.

[The] Court's insistence on inventing its brand of First Amendment underinclusiveness puzzles me. The overbreadth doctrine has the redeeming virtue of attempting to avoid the chilling of protected expression, but the Court's new "underbreadth" creation serves no desirable function. Instead, it permits, indeed invites, the continuation of expressive conduct that in this case is evil and worthless in First Amendment terms until [St. Paul] cures the underbreadth by adding to its ordinance a catch-all phrase such as "and all other fighting words that may constitutionally be subject to this ordinance." Any contribution of this holding to First Amendment jurisprudence is surely [negative], since it necessarily signals that expressions of violence, such as the message of intimidation and racial hatred conveyed by burning a cross on someone's lawn, are of sufficient value to outweigh the social interest in order and morality that has traditionally placed such fighting words outside the

First Amendment.[2] Indeed, by characterizing fighting words as a form of "debate," the majority legitimates hate speech as a form of public discussion.

Furthermore, the Court obscures the line between speech that could be regulated freely on the basis of content (i.e., the narrow categories of expression falling outside the First Amendment) and that which could be regulated on the basis of content only upon a showing of a compelling state interest (i.e., all remaining expression). By placing fighting words, [long] held to be valueless, on at least equal constitutional footing with political discourse and other forms of speech [deemed] to have the greatest social value, the majority devalues the latter category.

B. In a second break with precedent, the Court refuses to sustain the ordinance even though it would survive under the strict scrutiny applicable to other protected expression. Assuming, arguendo, that the [ordinance] is a content-based regulation of protected expression, it nevertheless would pass First Amendment review under settled law upon a showing that the regulation " 'is necessary to serve a compelling state interest and is narrowly drawn to achieve that end.' " Simon & Schuster. St. Paul has urged that its ordinance "[helps] to ensure the basic human rights of members of groups that have historically been subjected to discrimination...." The Court expressly concedes that this interest is compelling and is promoted by the ordinance. Nevertheless, the Court treats strict scrutiny analysis as irrelevant. [Under] the majority's view, a narrowly drawn, content-based ordinance could never pass constitutional muster if the object of that legislation could be accomplished by banning a wider category of speech. This appears to be a general renunciation of strict scrutiny review, a fundamental tool of First Amendment analysis.

[As] with its rejection of the Court's categorical analysis, the majority offers no reasoned basis for discarding our firmly established strict scrutiny analysis. [The] majority appears to believe that its doctrinal revisionism is necessary to prevent our elected lawmakers from prohibiting libel against members of one political party but not another and from enacting similarly preposterous laws. The majority is misguided. Although the First Amendment does not apply to categories of unprotected speech, [the] Equal Protection Clause requires that the regulation of unprotected speech be rationally related to a legitimate government interest. A defamation statute that drew distinctions on the basis of political affiliation or "an ordinance prohibiting only those legally obscene works that contain criticism of the city government" would unquestionably fail rational basis review.[3]

2. This does not suggest, of course, that cross burning is always unprotected. Burning a cross at a political rally would almost certainly be protected expression. But in such a context, the cross burning could not be characterized as a "direct personal insult or an invitation to exchange fisticuffs," Texas v. Johnson, to which the fighting words doctrine applies. [Footnote by Justice White.]

3. The majority is mistaken in stating that a ban on obscene works critical of government would fail equal protection review only because the ban would violate the First Amendment. While decisions such as Mosley recognize that First Amendment principles may be relevant to an equal pro-

[There] is no question that [the St. Paul ordinance] would pass equal protection review. [It] proscribes a subset of "fighting words," those that injure "on the basis of race, color, creed, religion or gender." This selective regulation reflects the [judgment] that harms based on race, color, creed, religion, or gender are more pressing public concerns than the harms caused by other fighting words. In light of our Nation's long and painful experience with discrimination, this determination is plainly reasonable. Indeed, as the majority concedes, the interest is compelling.

C. The Court has patched up its argument with an apparently nonexhaustive list of ad hoc exceptions, in what can be viewed either as an attempt to confine the effects of its decision, [or] as an effort to anticipate some of the questions that will arise from its radical revision of First Amendment law. For instance, if the majority were to give general application to the rule on which it decides this case, today's decision would call into question the constitutionality of the statute making it illegal to threaten the life of the President. Surely, this statute, by singling out certain threats, incorporates a content-based distinction; it indicates that the Government especially disfavors threats against the President as opposed to threats against all others. But because the Government could prohibit all threats and not just those directed against the President, under the Court's theory, the compelling reasons justifying the enactment of special legislation to safeguard the President would be irrelevant, and the statute would fail. [To] save the statute, the majority has engrafted the following exception onto its newly announced [rule:] Content-based distinctions may be drawn within an unprotected category of speech if the basis for the distinctions is "the very reason the entire class of speech at issue is proscribable." [The] exception swallows the [rule.] Certainly, it should apply to the St. Paul ordinance, since "the reasons why [fighting words] are outside the First Amendment ... have special force when applied to [groups that have historically been subjected to discrimination]." To avoid the result of its own analysis, the Court suggests that fighting words are simply a mode of communication, rather than a content-based category, and that the ordinance has not singled out a particularly objectionable mode of communication. Again, the majority confuses the issue. A prohibition on fighting words is not a time, place, or manner restriction; it is a ban on a class of speech that conveys an overriding message of personal injury and imminent violence, a message that is at its ugliest when directed against groups that have long been the targets of discrimination. Accordingly, the ordinance falls within the first exception to the majority's theory.

As its second exception, the Court posits that certain content-based regulations will survive under the new regime if the regulated subclass "happens to be associated with particular 'secondary effects' of the

tection claim challenging distinctions that impact on protected expression, there is no basis for linking First and Fourteenth Amendment analysis in a case involving unprotected expression. Certainly, one need not resort to First Amendment principles to conclude that the sort of improbable legislation the majority hypothesizes is based on senseless distinctions. [Footnote by Justice White.]

speech ...," which the majority treats as encompassing instances in which "words can ... violate laws directed not against speech but against conduct ..."[4] Again, there is a simple explanation for the Court's eagerness to craft an exception to its new rule: Under the general rule the Court applies in this case, Title VII hostile work environment claims would suddenly be unconstitutional. Title VII makes it unlawful to discriminate "because of [an] individual's race, color, religion, sex, or national origin," and the regulations covering hostile workplace claims forbid "sexual harassment," which includes "[u]nwelcome sexual advances, requests for sexual favors, and other verbal or physical conduct of a sexual nature" which creates "an intimidating, hostile, or offensive working environment." 29 CFR 1604.11(a). The regulation does not prohibit workplace harassment generally; it focuses on what the majority would characterize as the "disfavored topi[c]" of sexual harassment. In this way, Title VII is similar to the ordinance that the majority condemns because it "impose[s] special prohibitions on those speakers who express views on disfavored subjects." Under the broad principle the Court uses to decide the present case, hostile work environment claims based on sexual harassment should fail First Amendment review; because a general ban on harassment in the workplace would cover the problem of sexual harassment, any attempt to proscribe the subcategory of sexually harassing expression would violate the First Amendment.

Hence, the majority's second exception, which the Court indicates would insulate a Title VII hostile work environment claim from an underinclusiveness challenge because "sexually derogatory 'fighting words' ... may produce a violation of Title VII's general prohibition against sexual discrimination in employment practices." But application of this exception to a hostile work environment claim does not hold up under close examination. First, the hostile work environment regulation is not keyed to the presence or absence of an economic quid pro quo, but to the impact of the speech on the victimized worker. Consequently, the regulation would no more fall within a secondary effects exception than does the St. Paul ordinance. Second, the majority's focus on the statute's general prohibition on discrimination glosses over the language of the specific regulation governing hostile working environment, which reaches beyond any "incidental" effect on speech. If the relationship between the broader statute and specific regulation is sufficient to bring the Title VII regulation within [O'Brien], then all St. Paul need do to bring its ordinance within this exception is to add some prefatory language concerning discrimination generally.[5] ...

4. The consequences of the majority's conflation of the rarely-used secondary effects standard and the O'Brien test for conduct incorporating "speech" and "nonspeech" elements present another question that I fear will haunt us and the lower courts in the aftermath of the majority's opinion. [Footnote by Justice White.]

5. The focus on possible First Amendment defenses to sexual harassment claims may have been inspired by existing litigation in which just such defenses have been raised. In particular, Robinson v. Jacksonville Shipyards, Inc., 760 F.Supp. 1486 (M.D.Fla.1991), involved the claim by a woman that a significant contributing factor in the creation of a "hostile and intimidating" workplace environment was the prevalence of sexually explicit photographs in various parts of the shipyard. Although

II. [I] do agree [that the] ordinance is unconstitutional. However, I would decide the case on overbreadth grounds. [Although] the ordinance as construed reaches categories of speech that are constitutionally unprotected, it also criminalizes a substantial amount of expression that—however repugnant—is shielded by the First Amendment. In attempting to narrow the scope of the [ordinance], the Minnesota Supreme Court relied upon two of the categories of speech and expressive conduct that fall outside the First Amendment's protective sphere: words that incite "imminent lawless action," Brandenburg, and "fighting" words, Chaplinsky. The [court] erred in its application of the Chaplinsky fighting words test and consequently interpreted the [ordinance] in a fashion that rendered [it] facially overbroad. [The] Minnesota Supreme Court drew upon [Chaplinsky]—words "which by their very utterance inflict injury or tend to incite an immediate breach of the peace." However, the [court] was far from clear in identifying the "injur[ies]" inflicted by the expression that St. Paul sought to regulate. Indeed, the [court] emphasized [that] "the ordinance censors only those displays that one knows or should know will create anger, alarm or resentment based on racial, ethnic, gender or religious bias." I therefore understand the court to have ruled that St. Paul may constitutionally prohibit expression that "by its very utterance" causes "anger, alarm or resentment."

Our [cases] have made clear, however, that such generalized reactions are not sufficient to strip expression of its [protection.] The mere fact that expressive activity causes hurt feelings, offense, or resentment does not render the expression unprotected. United States v. Eichman; Texas v. Johnson; Hustler Magazine v. Falwell; FCC v. Pacifica Foundation; Cohen v. California; Terminiello v. Chicago. [Although] the ordinance reaches conduct that is unprotected, it also makes criminal expressive conduct that causes only hurt feelings, offense, or resentment,

some of the photographs (most of which would be unlikely to be judged legally obscene) had been attached to her locker as a deliberate attempt to intimidate her, others were posted by male workers on their own lockers, and still others were posted in various places used by all workers. The District Court rejected the employer's attempted First Amendment defense. More recently, the Court's unanimous decision in Harris v. Forklift Systems, Inc., 508 U.S. ___ (1993), is potentially relevant to this issue. The complainant alleged sexual harassment by virtue of a "discriminatorily abusive work environment." Although not all of the conduct the lower court found to have taken place was verbal, much of it involved various sexually-oriented insults and comments made to Harris by the president of the company for which she worked. Justice O'Connor's opinion for the Court rejected the company's claim that the complainant was required to demonstrate "concrete psychological harm." Rather, reaffirming the approach of Meritor Savings Bank v. Vinson, 477 U.S. 57 (1986), Justice O'Connor concluded that although "a mere offensive utterance" would be insufficient to establish an abusive work environment, a complainant could prove the existence of an abusive work environment by showing that the conduct, including verbal conduct, was "severe or pervasive enough to create an objectively hostile or abusive work environment—an environment that a reasonable person would find hostile or abusive. [But] Title VII comes into play before the harassing conduct leads to a nervous breakdown. A discriminatorily abusive work environment, even one that does not seriously affect employees' psychological well-being, can and often will detract from employees' job performance, discourage employees from remaining on the job, or keep them from advancing in their careers." [Ed.]

and is protected by the First Amendment. The ordinance is therefore fatally overbroad and invalid on its face.

III. Today, the Court has disregarded two established principles of First Amendment law without providing a coherent replacement theory. Its decision is an arid, doctrinaire interpretation, driven by the frequently irresistible impulse of judges to tinker with the First Amendment. The decision is mischievous at best and will surely confuse the lower courts. I join the judgment, but not the folly of the opinion.

JUSTICE BLACKMUN, concurring in the judgment.

I regret what the Court has done in this case. The majority opinion signals one of two possibilities: it will serve as precedent for future cases, or it will not. Either result is disheartening.

In the first instance, by deciding that a State cannot regulate speech that causes great harm unless it also regulates speech that does not (setting law and logic on their heads), the Court seems to abandon the categorical approach, and inevitably to relax the level of scrutiny applicable to content-based laws. As Justice White points out, this weakens the traditional protections of speech. If all expressive activity must be accorded the same protection, that protection will be scant. The simple reality is that the Court will never provide child pornography or cigarette advertising the level of protection customarily granted political speech. If we are forbidden from categorizing, [we] shall reduce protection across the board. It is sad that in its effort to reach a satisfying result in this case, the Court is willing to weaken First Amendment protections.

In the second instance is the possibility that this case will not significantly alter First Amendment jurisprudence, but, instead, will be regarded as an aberration—a case where the Court manipulated doctrine to strike down an ordinance whose premise it opposed, namely, that racial threats and verbal assaults are of greater harm than other fighting words. I fear that the Court has been distracted from its proper mission by the temptation to decide the issue over "politically correct speech" and "cultural diversity," neither of which is presented here. If this is the meaning of today's opinion, it is perhaps even more regrettable.

I see no First Amendment values that are compromised by a law that prohibits hoodlums from driving minorities out of their homes by burning crosses on their lawns, but I see great harm in preventing the people of Saint Paul from specifically punishing the race-based fighting words that so prejudice their community. I concur in the judgment, however, because I agree [that] the ordinance reaches beyond fighting words to [protected speech.]

Justice STEVENS, with whom Justice WHITE and Justice BLACKMUN join as to Part I, concurring in the judgment.

Conduct that creates special risks or causes special harms may be prohibited by special rules. Lighting a fire near an ammunition dump or a gasoline storage tank is especially dangerous; such behavior may be punished more severely than burning trash in a vacant lot. Threatening someone because of her race or religious beliefs may cause particularly severe trauma or touch off a riot, and threatening a high public official may cause substantial social disruption; such threats may be punished more severely than threats against someone based on, say, his support of a particular athletic team. There are legitimate, reasonable, and neutral justifications for such special rules. This case involves [one] such ordinance. Because the regulated conduct has some communicative content—a message of racial, religious or gender hostility—the ordinance raises two quite different First Amendment questions. Is the ordinance "overbroad" because it prohibits too much speech? If not, is it "under-broad" because it does not prohibit enough speech?

In answering these questions, my colleagues today wrestle with two broad principles: first, that certain "categories of expression are [not] within the area of constitutionally protected speech," and second, that "[c]ontent-based regulations [of expression] are presumptively invalid." Although in past opinions the Court has repeated [these] maxims, it has—quite rightly—adhered to neither with the absolutism suggested by my colleagues. Thus [I] write separately to suggest how the allure of absolute principles has skewed the analysis of both the majority and concurring opinions.

I. Fifty years ago, [Chaplinsky] articulated a categorical approach to First Amendment jurisprudence. [The] Court today revises this categorical approach. It is not [that] certain "categories" of expression are "unprotected," but rather that certain "elements" of expression are wholly "proscribable." To the Court, an expressive act, like a chemical compound, consists of more than one element. Although the act may be regulated because it contains a proscribable element, it may not be regulated on the basis of another (nonproscribable) element it also contains. Thus, obscene antigovernment speech may be regulated because it is obscene, but not because it is antigovernment. It is this revision of the categorical approach that allows the Court to assume that the ordinance proscribes only fighting words, while at the same time concluding that the ordinance is invalid because it imposes a content-based regulation on expressive activity.

[The] Court's revision of the categorical approach seems [something] of an adventure in a doctrinal wonderland, for the concept of "obscene antigovernment" speech is fantastical. The category of the obscene is very narrow; to be obscene, expression must "[lack] serious literary, artistic, political or scientific value." Miller. "Obscene antigovernment" speech, then, is a contradiction in terms: If expression is anti-government, it does not "lac[k] serious ... political ... value" and cannot be obscene.

The Court [likens] its novel analysis to that applied to restrictions on the time, place, or manner of expression or on expressive conduct. It is true that loud speech in favor of the Republican Party can be regulated because it is loud, but not because it is pro-Republican; and it is true that the public burning of the American flag can be regulated because it involves public burning and not because it involves the flag. But these analogies are inapposite. In each of these examples, the two elements (e.g., loudness and pro-Republican orientation) can coexist; in the case of "obscene antigovernment" speech, however, the presence of one element ("obscenity") by definition means the absence of the other. [It] is unwise and unsound to craft a new doctrine based on such highly speculative hypotheticals.

I am [even] more troubled by the [conclusion] that the ordinance is an unconstitutional content-based regulation of speech. Drawing on broadly worded dicta, the Court establishes a near-absolute ban on content-based regulations of expression and holds that the First Amendment prohibits the regulation of fighting words by subject matter. Thus, while the Court rejects the "all-or-nothing-at-all" nature of the categorical approach, it promptly embraces an absolutism of its own: within a particular "proscribable" category of expression, the Court holds, a government must either proscribe all speech or no speech at all.[1]

[Although] the Court has, on occasion, declared that content-based regulations of speech are "never permitted," such claims are overstated. [Contrary] to the broad dicta in Mosley and elsewhere, our decisions demonstrate that content-based distinctions [are] an inevitable and indispensable aspect of a coherent understanding of the First Amendment. This is true at every level of First Amendment law. In broadest terms, our entire First Amendment jurisprudence creates a regime based on the content of speech. [Although] the First Amendment broadly protects "speech," it does not protect the right to "fix prices, breach contracts, make false warranties, place bets with bookies, threaten, [or] extort." Schauer, Categories and the First Amendment: A Play in Three Acts, 34 Vand.L.Rev. 265 (1981). Whether an agreement among competitors is a violation of the Sherman Act or protected activity under the Noerr–Pennington doctrine[2] hinges upon the content of the agreement. Similarly, "the line between permissible advocacy and impermissible incitation to crime or violence depends, not merely on the setting in which the speech occurs, but also on exactly what the speaker had to say." Young v. American Mini Theatres. [Whether] a magazine is obscene, a gesture a fighting word, or a photograph child pornography is determined, in part, by its content. Even within categories of protected expression, the First Amendment status of speech is fixed by its content. New York Times v. Sullivan and Dun & Bradstreet v. Greenmoss Builders [1984; above, 12th Ed., p. 1089; Ind.Rts., p. 760] establish that [speech] about public officials or matters of public concern receives greater protection than speech about other topics. It can, therefore,

1. The Court disputes this characterization because it has crafted two exceptions, one for "certain media or markets" and the other for content discrimination based upon "the very reason that the entire class of speech at issue is proscribable." These exceptions are, at best, ill-defined. The Court does not tell us whether, with respect to the former, fighting words such as cross-burning could be proscribed only in certain neighborhoods where the threat of violence is particularly severe, or whether, with respect to the second category, fighting words that create a particular risk of harm (such as a race riot) would be proscribable. The hypothetical and illusory category of these two exceptions persuades me that either my description of the Court's analysis is accurate or that the Court does not in fact mean much of what it says in its opinion. [Footnote by Justice Stevens.]

2. Mine Workers v. Pennington, 381 U.S. 657 (1965); Eastern Railroad Presidents Conference v. Noerr Motor Freight, 365 U.S. 127 (1961). [Footnote by Justice Stevens.]

scarcely be said that the regulation of expressive activity cannot be predicated on its content: much of our First Amendment jurisprudence is premised on the assumption that content makes a difference.

Consistent with this general premise, we have frequently upheld content-based regulations of speech. [In] Young v. American Mini Theatres, the Court upheld zoning ordinances that regulated movie theaters based on the content of the films shown. In FCC v. Pacifica Foundation, we upheld a restriction on the broadcast of specific indecent words. In Lehman v. City of Shaker Heights, we upheld a city law that permitted commercial advertising, but prohibited political advertising, on city buses. In Broadrick, we upheld a state law that restricted the speech of state employees, but only as concerned partisan political matters. We have long recognized the power of the Federal Trade Commission to regulate misleading advertising and labeling, Jacob Siegel Co. v. FTC, 327 U.S. 608 (1946), and the National Labor Relations Board's power to regulate an employer's election-related speech on the basis of its content. NLRB v. Gissel Packing Co., 395 U.S. 575 (1969). [The] Government may choose to limit advertisements for cigarettes, 15 U.S.C. 1331–1340, but not for cigars; choose to regulate airline advertising, see Morales v. Trans World Airlines, 504 U.S. ___ (1992), but not bus advertising; or choose to monitor solicitation by lawyers, see Ohralik v. Ohio State Bar Assn., 436 U.S. 447 (1978), but not by doctors. All of these cases involved the selective regulation of speech based on content—precisely the sort of regulation the Court invalidates today. Such selective regulations are unavoidably content based, but they are not ["presumptively] invalid."

[Disregarding] this vast body of case law, the Court today goes beyond even the overstatement in Mosley and applies the prohibition on content-based regulation to speech that the Court had until today considered wholly "unprotected" by the First Amendment. [This] new absolutism [severely] contorts the fabric of settled [law.] Our [decisions] have created a rough hierarchy in the constitutional protection of speech. Core political speech occupies the highest, most protected position; commercial speech and nonobscene, sexually explicit speech are regarded as a sort of second-class expression; obscenity and fighting words receive the least protection of all. Assuming that the Court is correct that this last class of speech is not wholly "unprotected," it certainly does not follow that fighting words and obscenity receive the same sort of protection afforded core political speech. Yet in ruling that proscribable speech cannot be regulated based on subject matter, the Court does just that. Perversely, this gives fighting words greater protection than is afforded commercial speech. If Congress can prohibit false advertising directed at airline passengers without also prohibiting false advertising directed at bus passengers and if a city can prohibit political advertisements in its buses while allowing other advertisements, it is ironic to hold that a city cannot regulate fighting words based on "race, color, creed, religion or gender" while leaving unregulated fighting words based on "union membership or homosexuality." The Court today turns First Amendment law on its head: Communication that was once entirely unprotected (and that still can be wholly proscribed) is now entitled to greater protection than commercial speech—and possibly greater protection than core political speech.

Perhaps because the Court recognizes these perversities, it quickly offers some ad hoc limitations on its newly extended prohibition on content-based regulations. First, the Court states that a content-based regulation is valid "[w]hen the content discrimination is based upon the very reason the entire class of speech ... is proscribable." In a pivotal passage, the Court writes "the Federal Government can criminalize only those physical threats that are directed against the President, see 18 U.S.C. 871—since the reasons why threats of violence are outside the First Amendment (protecting individuals from the fear of violence, from the disruption that fear engenders, and from the possibility that the threatened violence will occur) have special force when applied to the ... President." As I understand this opaque passage, Congress may choose from the set of unprotected speech (all threats) to proscribe only a subset (threats against the President) because those threats are particularly likely to cause "fear of violence," "disruption," and actual "violence." Precisely this same reasoning, however, compels the conclusion that St. Paul's ordinance is constitutional. Just as Congress may determine that threats against the President entail more severe consequences than other threats, so St. Paul [may] determine that threats based on the target's race, religion, or gender cause more severe harm to both the target and to society than other threats. This latter judgment—that harms caused by racial, religious, and gender-based invective are qualitatively different from that caused by other fighting words—seems to me eminently reasonable and realistic.

Next, the Court recognizes that a State may regulate advertising in one industry but not another because "the risk of fraud (one of the characteristics that justifies depriving [commercial speech] of full First Amendment protection ...)" in the regulated industry is "greater" than in other industries. Again, the same reasoning demonstrates the constitutionality of St. Paul's ordinance. [Certainly] a legislature that may determine that the risk of fraud is greater in the legal trade than in the medical trade may determine that the risk of injury or breach of peace created by race-based threats is greater than that created by other threats.

Similarly, it is impossible to reconcile the Court's analysis of the ordinance with its recognition that "a prohibition of fighting words that are directed at certain persons or groups ... would be facially valid." A selective proscription of unprotected expression designed to protect "certain persons or groups" (for example, a law proscribing threats directed at the elderly) would be constitutional if it were based on a legitimate determination that the harm created by the regulated expression differs from that created by the unregulated expression (that is, if the elderly are more severely injured by threats than are the nonelderly). Such selective protection is no different from a law prohibiting minors (and only minors) from obtaining obscene publications. See Ginsberg v. New York, 390 U.S. 629 (1968). St. Paul has determined—reasonably in my judgment—that fighting-word injuries "based on race, color, creed, religion or gender" are qualitatively different and more severe than fighting-word injuries based on other characteristics. Whether the selective proscription of proscribable speech is defined by the protected target ("certain persons or groups") or the basis of the harm (injuries "based on race, color, creed, religion or gender") makes no constitutional difference: what matters is whether the legislature's selection is based on a legitimate, neutral, and reasonable distinction.

II. [I] do not join Part I-A of [Justice White's] opinion because I have reservations about the "categorical approach" to the First Amendment. [Admittedly,] the categorical approach to the First Amendment has some appeal: either expression is protected or it is not—the categories create safe harbors for governments and speakers alike. But this approach sacrifices subtlety for clarity and is [ultimately] unsound. As an initial matter, the concept of "categories" fits poorly with the complex reality of expression. [Moreover,] the categorical approach does not take seriously the importance of context. The meaning of any expression and the legitimacy of its regulation can only be determined in context. Whether [a] picture or a sentence is obscene cannot be judged in the abstract, but rather only in the context of its setting, its use, and its audience. [Although] legislatures may freely regulate most nonobscene child pornography, such pornography that is part of "a serious work of art, a documentary on behavioral problems, or a medical or psychiatric teaching device," may be entitled to constitutional protection. [The] categorical approach sweeps too broadly when it declares that all such expression is beyond the protection of the First Amendment.

Perhaps sensing the limits of such an all-or-nothing approach, the Court has applied its analysis less categorically than its doctrinal statements suggest. The Court has recognized intermediate categories of speech (for example, for indecent nonobscene speech and commercial speech) and geographic categories of speech (public fora, limited public fora, nonpublic fora) entitled to varying levels of protection. The Court has also stringently delimited the categories of unprotected speech. While we once declared that "[l]ibelous utterances [are] not . . . within the area of constitutionally protected speech," Beauharnais, our rulings in New York Times v. Sullivan, Gertz v. Welch, and Dun & Bradstreet v. Greenmoss Builders have substantially qualified this broad claim. Similarly, we have consistently construed the "fighting words" exception set forth in Chaplinsky narrowly. In the case of commercial speech, our ruling that "the Constitution imposes no . . . restraint on government [regulation] as respects purely commercial advertising," Valentine v. Chrestensen, was expressly repudiated in Virginia Bd. of Pharmacy v. Virginia Citizens Consumer Council. In short, the history of the categorical approach is largely the history of narrowing the categories of unprotected speech. This evolution [indicates] that the categorical approach is unworkable and the quest for absolute categories of "protected" and "unprotected" speech ultimately futile. . . .

III. [Our] decisions clearly recognize that some content-based restrictions raise more constitutional questions than others. [Thus,] although a regulation that on its face regulates speech by subject matter may in some instances effectively suppress particular viewpoints, in general, viewpoint-based restrictions on expression require greater scrutiny than subject-matter based restrictions. [Whatever] the allure of absolute doctrines, it is just too simple to declare expression "protected" or "unprotected" or to proclaim a regulation "content-based" or "content-neutral." [Looking] to the content and character of the [activity regulated by the ordinance,] two things are clear. First, by hypothesis the ordinance bars only low-value speech, namely, fighting words. [Second,] the ordinance regulates "expressive conduct [rather] than ... the written or spoken word." Texas v. Johnson. Looking to the context of the regulated activity, it is again significant that the statute (by hypothesis) regulates only fighting words. [Fighting] words are not words that merely cause offense; fighting words must be directed at individuals so as to "by their very utterance inflict injury." By hypothesis, then, the ordinance restricts speech in confrontational and potentially violent situations. The case at hand is illustrative. The cross-burning in this case—directed as it was to a single African–American family trapped in their home—was nothing more than a crude form of physical intimidation. That this cross-burning sends a message of racial hostility does not automatically endow it with complete constitutional protection.[3]

[The] ordinance regulates speech not on the basis of its subject matter or the viewpoint expressed, but rather on the basis of the harm the speech causes. In this regard, the Court fundamentally misreads the ordinance. The Court describes the ordinance as regulating expression "addressed to one of [several] specified disfavored topics," as policing "disfavored subjects," and as "prohibit[ing] ... speech solely on the basis of the subjects the speech addresses." Contrary to the Court's suggestion, the ordinance regulates only a subcategory of expression that causes injuries based on "race, color, creed, religion or gender," not a subcategory that involves discussions that concern those characteristics.[4]

3. The Court makes much of St. Paul's description of the ordinance as regulating "a message." As always, however, St. Paul's argument must be read in context: "Finally, we ask the Court to reflect on the 'content' of the 'expressive conduct' represented by a 'burning cross.' It is no less than the first step in an act of racial violence. It was and unfortunately still is the equivalent of [the] waving of a knife before the thrust, the pointing of a gun before it is fired, the lighting of the match before the arson, the hanging of the noose before the lynching. It is not a political statement, or even a cowardly statement of hatred. It is the first step in an act of assault. It can be no more protected than holding a gun to a victim['s] head. It is perhaps the ultimate expression of 'fighting words.' " [Footnote by Justice Stevens.]

4. The Court contends that this distinction is "wordplay," reasoning that "[w]hat makes [the harms caused by race-based threats] distinct from [the harms] produced by other fighting words is ... the fact that

[the former are] caused by a distinctive idea." In this way, the Court concludes that regulating speech based on the injury it causes is no different from regulating speech based on its subject matter. This analysis fundamentally miscomprehends the role of "race, color, creed, religion [and] gender" in contemporary American society. One need look no further than the recent social unrest in the Nation's cities to see that race-based threats may cause more harm to society and to individuals than other threats. Just as the statute prohibiting threats against the President is justifiable because of the place of the President in our social and political order, so a statute prohibiting race-based threats is justifiable because of the place of race in our social and political order. Although it is regrettable that race occupies such a place and is so incendiary an issue, until the Nation matures beyond that condition, laws such as St. Paul's ordinance will remain reasonable and justifiable. [Footnote by Justice Stevens.]

Moreover, even if the [ordinance] did regulate fighting words based on [subject] matter, such a regulation would [be] constitutional. [Subject-matter] regulations generally do not raise the same concerns of government censorship and the distortion of public discourse presented by viewpoint regulations. [The] Court contends that the ordinance requires proponents of racial intolerance to "follow the Marquis of Queensbury Rules" while allowing advocates of racial tolerance to "fight freestyle." The law does no such thing. The Court writes: "One could hold up a sign saying, for example, that all 'anti-Catholic bigots' are misbegotten; but not that all 'papists' are, for that would insult and provoke violence 'on the basis of religion.'" This may be true, but it hardly proves the Court's point. The Court's reasoning is asymmetrical. The response to a sign saying that "all [religious] bigots are misbegotten" is a sign saying that "all advocates of religious tolerance are misbegotten." [In] a battle between advocates of tolerance and advocates of intolerance, the ordinance does not prevent either side from hurling fighting words at the other on the basis of their conflicting ideas, but it does bar both sides from hurling such words on the basis of the target's "race, color, creed, religion or gender." To extend the Court's pugilistic metaphor, the ordinance simply bans punches "below the belt"—by either party. It does not [favor] one side of any debate. [As] construed by the Court today, [the] ordinance does not ban all "hate speech," nor does it ban, say, all cross-burnings or all swastika displays. Rather it only bans a subcategory of the already narrow category of fighting words. [Petitioner] is free to burn a cross to announce a rally or to express his views about racial supremacy, he may do so on private property or public land, at day or at night, so long as the burning is not so threatening and so directed at an individual as to "by its very [execution] inflict injury." [In] sum, the ordinance (as construed by the Court) regulates expressive activity that is wholly proscribable and does so not on the basis of viewpoint, but rather in recognition of the different harms caused by such activity. [Were] the ordinance not overbroad, I would vote to uphold it.[5]

WISCONSIN v. MITCHELL

506 U.S. ___, 113 S.Ct. 2194, 124 L.Ed.2d 436 (1993).

Chief Justice REHNQUIST delivered the opinion of the Court.

Respondent Todd Mitchell's sentence for aggravated battery was enhanced because he intentionally selected his victim on account of the victim's race. The question presented [is] whether this penalty enhancement is prohibited by the First and Fourteenth Amendments. We hold that it is not.

5. The issue whether otherwise unprotected speech may be the subject of viewpoint-inspired regulation, and the majority's resolution of that issue, was foreshadowed in Alexander, Low Value Speech, 83 Nw.U.L.Rev. 547 (1988). Compare Schauer, The Aim and the Target in Free Speech Methodology, 83 Nw.U.L.Rev. 562 (1988). [Ed.]

On the evening of October 7, 1989, a group of young black men and boys, including Mitchell, gathered at an apartment complex in Kenosha, Wisconsin. Several members of the group discussed a scene from the motion picture "Mississippi Burning," in which a white man beat a young black boy who was praying. The group moved outside and Mitchell asked them: "Do you all feel hyped up to move on some white people?" Shortly thereafter, a young white boy approached the group on the opposite side of the street where they were standing. As the boy walked by, Mitchell said: "You all want to fuck somebody up? There goes a white boy; go get him." Mitchell counted to three and pointed in the boy's direction. The group ran towards the boy, beat him severely, and stole his tennis shoes. The boy was rendered unconscious and remained in a coma for four days.

After a jury trial, [Mitchell] was convicted of aggravated battery. That offense ordinarily carries a maximum sentence of two years' imprisonment. But because the jury found that Mitchell had intentionally selected his victim because of the boy's race, the maximum sentence for Mitchell's offense was increased to seven years under Wis.Stat. 939.645. That provision enhances the maximum penalty for an offense whenever the defendant "[i]ntentionally selects the person against whom the crime ... is committed ... because of the race, religion, color, disability, sexual orientation, national origin or ancestry of that person ...". The Circuit Court sentenced Mitchell to four years' imprisonment....

Mitchell [appealed,] challenging the constitutionality of Wisconsin's penalty-enhancement provision on First Amendment grounds.[1] The Wisconsin Court of Appeals rejected Mitchell's challenge, but the Wisconsin Supreme Court reversed. [It] held that the statute "violates the First Amendment directly by punishing what the legislature has deemed to be offensive thought." 485 N.W.2d 807 (1992). It rejected the State's contention "that the statute punishes only the 'conduct' of intentional selection of a victim." According to the court, "[t]he statute punishes the 'because of' aspect of the defendant's selection, the reason the defendant selected the victim, the motive behind the selection." And under R.A.V. v. St. Paul, "the Wisconsin legislature cannot criminalize bigoted thought with which it disagrees." The Supreme Court also held that the penalty-enhancement statute was unconstitutionally overbroad. It reasoned that, in order to prove that a defendant intentionally selected his victim because of the victim's protected status, the State would often have to introduce evidence of the defendant's prior speech, such as racial epithets he may have uttered before the commission of the offense. This evidentiary use of protected speech, the court

---

1. Mitchell also challenged the statute on Fourteenth Amendment equal protection and vagueness grounds. The Wisconsin Court of Appeals held that Mitchell waived his equal protection claim and rejected his vagueness challenge outright. The Wisconsin Supreme Court declined to address both claims. Mitchell renews his Fourteenth Amendment claims in this Court. But since they were not developed below and plainly fall outside of the question on which we granted certiorari, we do not reach them either. [Footnote by Chief Justice Rehnquist.]

thought, would have a "chilling effect" on those who feared the possibility of prosecution for offenses subject to penalty enhancement. . . .

We granted certiorari because of the importance of the question presented and the existence of a conflict of authority among state high courts on the constitutionality of statutes similar to Wisconsin's penalty-enhancement provision.[2] We reverse.

Mitchell argues that we are bound by the Wisconsin Supreme Court's conclusion that the statute punishes bigoted thought and not conduct. There is no doubt that we are bound by a state court's construction of a state statute. [But] here the Wisconsin Supreme Court did not, strictly speaking, construe the Wisconsin statute in the sense of defining the meaning of a particular statutory word or phrase. Rather, it merely characterized the "practical effect" of the statute for First Amendment purposes. ("Merely because the statute refers in a literal sense to the intentional 'conduct' of selecting, does not mean the court must turn a blind eye to the intent and practical effect of the law—punishment of motive or thought"). This assessment does not bind us. Once any ambiguities as to the meaning of the statute are resolved, we may form our own judgment as to its operative effect.

The State argues that the statute does not punish bigoted thought, [but] instead punishes only conduct. While this argument is literally correct, it does not dispose of Mitchell's First Amendment challenge. To be sure, our cases reject the "view that an apparently limitless variety of conduct can be labeled 'speech' whenever the person engaging in the conduct intends thereby to express an idea." O'Brien. Thus, a physical assault is not by any stretch of the imagination expressive conduct protected by the First Amendment. Roberts v. United States Jaycees [1984; described above and below, 12th Ed., pp. 574, 1408; Ind.Rts., pp. 245, 1069] ("[V]iolence or other types of potentially expressive activities that produce special harms distinct from their communicative impact . . . are entitled to no constitutional protection").

---

2. Several States have enacted penalty-enhancement provisions similar to the Wisconsin statute at issue in this case. See, e.g., Cal. Penal Code Ann. 422.7 (1993); Fla.Stat. 775.085 (1991); Mont. Code Ann. 45–5–222 (1992); Vt.Stat.Ann., Tit. 13, 1455 (1992). Proposed federal legislation to the same effect passed the House of Representatives in 1992, H.R. 4797, 102d Cong., 2d Sess. (1992), but failed to pass the Senate, S. 2522, 102d Cong., 2d Sess. (1992). The state high courts are divided over the constitutionality of penalty-enhancement statutes and analogous statutes covering bias-motivated offenses. Compare, e.g., State v. Plowman, 838 P.2d 558 (1992) (upholding Oregon statute), with State v. Wyant, 597 N.E.2d 450 (1992) (striking down Ohio statute). According to amici, bias-motivated violence is on the rise throughout the United States. See Brief for the National Asian Pacific American Legal Consortium et al. as Amici Curiae; Brief for the Anti–Defamation League et al. as Amici Curiae; Brief for Atlanta et al. as Amici Curiae. In 1990, Congress enacted the Hate Crimes Statistics Act, 28 U.S.C. 534 (note), directing the Attorney General to compile data "about crimes that manifest evidence of prejudice based on race, religion, sexual orientation, or ethnicity." Pursuant to the Act, the Federal Bureau of Investigation reported in January 1993, that 4,558 bias-motivated offenses were committed in 1991, including 1,614 incidents of intimidation, 1,301 incidents of vandalism, 796 simple assaults, 773 aggravated assaults, and 12 murders. [Footnote by Chief Justice Rehnquist.]

But the fact remains that under the Wisconsin statute the same criminal conduct may be more heavily punished if the victim is selected because of his race or other protected status than if no such motive obtained. Thus, although the statute punishes criminal conduct, it enhances the maximum penalty for conduct motivated by a discriminatory point of view more severely than the same conduct engaged in for some other reason or for no reason at all. Because the only reason for the enhancement is the defendant's discriminatory motive for selecting his victim, Mitchell argues (and the Wisconsin Supreme Court held) that the statute violates the First Amendment by punishing offenders' bigoted beliefs.

Traditionally, sentencing judges have considered a wide variety of factors in addition to evidence bearing on guilt in determining what sentence to impose on a convicted defendant. The defendant's motive for committing the offense is one important factor. See 1 W. LaFave & A. Scott, Substantive Criminal Law sec. 3.6(b) (1986) ("Motives are most relevant when the trial judge sets the defendant's sentence, and it is not uncommon for a defendant to receive a minimum sentence because he was acting with good motives, or a rather high sentence because of his bad motives"). Thus, in many States the commission of a murder, or other capital offense, for pecuniary gain is a separate aggravating circumstance under the capital-sentencing statute.

But it is equally true that a defendant's abstract beliefs, however obnoxious to most people, may not be taken into consideration by a sentencing judge. In Dawson v. Delaware [1992; described below, addition to 12th Ed., p. 1437; Ind.Rts., p. 1108], the State introduced evidence at a capital-sentencing hearing that the defendant was a member of a white supremacist prison gang. Because "the evidence proved nothing more than [the defendant's] abstract beliefs," we held that its admission violated the defendant's First Amendment rights. In so holding, however, we emphasized that "the Constitution does not erect a per se barrier to the admission of evidence concerning one's beliefs and associations at sentencing simply because those beliefs and associations are protected by the First Amendment." Thus, in Barclay v. Florida, 463 U.S. 939 (1983) (plurality opinion), we allowed the sentencing judge to take into account the defendant's racial animus towards his victim. The evidence in that case showed that the defendant's membership in the Black Liberation Army and desire to provoke a "race war" were related to the murder of a white man for which he was convicted. Because "the elements of racial hatred in [the] murder" were relevant to several aggravating factors, we held that the trial judge permissibly took this evidence into account in sentencing the defendant to death.

Mitchell suggests that Dawson and Barclay are inapposite because they did not involve application of a penalty-enhancement provision. But in Barclay we held that it was permissible for the sentencing court to consider the defendant's racial animus in determining whether he should be sentenced to death, surely the most severe "enhancement" of all. And the fact that the Wisconsin Legislature has decided, as a general matter, that bias-motivated offenses warrant greater maximum penalties across the board does not alter the result here. For the primary responsibility for fixing criminal penalties lies with the legislature.

Mitchell argues that the Wisconsin penalty-enhancement statute is invalid because it punishes the defendant's discriminatory motive, or reason, for acting. But motive plays the same role under the Wisconsin statute as it does under federal and state antidiscrimination laws, which we have previously upheld against constitutional challenge. Roberts v. Jaycees. Title VII, for example, makes it unlawful for an employer to discriminate against an employee "because of such individual's race, color, religion, sex, or national origin." 42 U.S.C. 2000e–2(a)(1). In Hishon v. King & Spaulding, 467 U.S. 69 (1984), we rejected the argument that Title VII infringed employers' First Amendment rights. And [in] R.A.V. v. St. Paul, we cited Title VII (as well as 18 U.S.C. 242 and 42 U.S.C. 1981 and 1982) as an example of a permissible content-neutral regulation of conduct. Nothing in our decision [in] R.A.V. compels a different result here. [Whereas] the ordinance struck down in R.A.V. was explicitly directed at expression (i.e., "speech" or "messages"), the statute in this case is aimed at conduct unprotected by the First Amendment.

Moreover, the Wisconsin statute singles out for enhancement bias-inspired conduct because this conduct is thought to inflict greater individual and societal harm. For example, according to the State and its amici, bias-motivated crimes are more likely to provoke retaliatory crimes, inflict distinct emotional harms on their victims, and incite community unrest. The State's desire to redress these perceived harms provides an adequate explanation for its penalty-enhancement provision over and above mere disagreement with offenders' beliefs or biases. As Blackstone said long ago, "it is but reasonable that among crimes of different natures those should be most severely punished, which are the most destructive of the public safety and happiness." 4 Commentaries *16.

Finally, there remains to be considered Mitchell's argument that the Wisconsin statute is unconstitutionally overbroad because of its "chilling effect" on free speech. Mitchell argues (and the Wisconsin Supreme Court agreed) that the statute is "overbroad" because evidence of the defendant's prior speech or associations may be used to prove that the defendant intentionally selected his victim on account of the victim's protected status. Consequently, the argument goes, the statute impermissibly chills free expression with respect to such matters by those concerned about the possibility of enhanced sentences if they should in the future commit a criminal offense covered by the statute. We find no merit in this contention.

The sort of chill envisioned here is far more attenuated and unlikely than that contemplated in traditional "overbreadth" cases. We must conjure up a vision of a Wisconsin citizen suppressing his unpopular bigoted opinions for fear that if he later commits an offense covered by the statute, these opinions will be offered at trial to establish that he selected his victim on account of the victim's protected status, thus qualifying him for penalty-enhancement. To stay within the realm of rationality, we must surely put to one side minor misdemeanor offenses covered by the statute, such as negligent operation of a motor vehicle, for it is difficult, if not impossible, to conceive of a situation where such offenses would be racially motivated. We are left, then, with the prospect of a citizen suppressing his bigoted beliefs for fear that evidence of such beliefs will be introduced against him at trial if he commits a more serious offense against person or property. This is simply too speculative a hypothesis to support Mitchell's overbreadth claim.

The First Amendment, moreover, does not prohibit the evidentiary use of speech to establish the elements of a crime or to prove motive or intent. Evidence of a defendant's previous declarations or statements is commonly admitted in criminal trials subject to evidentiary rules dealing with relevancy, reliability, and the like. Nearly half a century ago, in Haupt v. United States, 330 U.S. 631 (1947), we rejected a contention similar to that advanced by Mitchell here. Haupt was tried for the offense of treason, which, as defined by the Constitution (Art. III, § 3), may depend very much on proof of motive. To prove that the acts in question were committed out of "adherence to the enemy" rather than "parental solicitude," the Government introduced evidence of conversations that had taken place long prior to the indictment, some of which consisted of statements showing Haupt's sympathy with Germany and Hitler and hostility towards the United States. We rejected Haupt's argument that this evidence was improperly admitted. While "[s]uch testimony is to be scrutinized with care to be certain the statements are not expressions of mere lawful and permissible difference of opinion with our own government or quite proper appreciation of the land of birth," we held that "these statements ... clearly were admissible on the question of intent and adherence to the enemy." See also Price Waterhouse v. Hopkins, 490 U.S. 228 (1989) (plurality opinion) (allowing evidentiary use of defendant's speech in [Title] VII discrimination claim).

For the foregoing reasons, we hold that Mitchell's First Amendment rights were not violated by the application of the Wisconsin penalty-enhancement provision in sentencing him. The judgment of the Supreme Court of Wisconsin is [reversed.] *

12th ED., p. 1268; IND.RTS., p. 939

Add as new footnote at end of Frisby v. Schultz:

10. On demonstrations in opposition to abortion, note the related issue of unlawful blockades and other forms of demonstrations more physically obstructive than those at issue in Frisby. The control of such unlawful activities was before the Court in a different context in Bray v. Alexandria Women's Health Clinic, 1993, and National Organization for Women v. Scheidler, 1994, described (along with related legislation in Congress) above, addition to 12th Ed., p. 945; Ind.Rts., p 616.

* After the decision in Wisconsin v. Mitchell, on September 13, 1994, Congress passed the Violent Crime Control and Law Enforcement Act (P.L. 103–322). Section 280003 of that act directed the United States Sentencing Commission to enhance sentences for hate crimes up to three sentencing levels.

12th ED., p. 1268; IND. RTS., p. 939
Add after Frisby v. Schultz:

MADSEN v. WOMEN'S HEALTH CENTER, INC.

514 U.S. ___, 114 S.Ct. 2516, 129 L.Ed.2d 593 (1994).

Chief Justice REHNQUIST delivered the opinion of the Court.

Petitioners challenge the constitutionality of an injunction entered by a Florida state court which prohibits antiabortion protestors from demonstrating in certain places and in various ways outside of a health clinic that performs abortions. We hold that the establishment of a 36–foot buffer zone on a public street from which demonstrators are excluded passes muster under the First Amendment, but that several other provisions of the injunction do not.

I.   Respondents operate abortion clinics throughout central Florida. Petitioners [are] engaged in activities near the site of one such clinic in Melbourne, Florida. They picketed and demonstrated where the public street gives access to the clinic. In September 1992, a Florida state court permanently enjoined petitioners from blocking or interfering with public access to the clinic, and from physically abusing persons entering or leaving the clinic. Six months later, respondents sought to broaden the injunction, complaining that access to the clinic was still impeded by petitioners' activities and that such activities had also discouraged some potential patients from entering the clinic, and had deleterious physical effects on others. The trial court thereupon issued a broader injunction, which is challenged here.[1]

The court found that, despite the initial injunction, protesters continued to impede access to the clinic by congregating on the paved portion of the street—Dixie Way—leading up to the clinic, and by marching in front of the clinic's driveways. It found that as vehicles heading toward the clinic slowed to allow the protesters to move out of the way, "sidewalk counselors" would approach and attempt to give the vehicle's occupants antiabortion literature. The number of people congregating varied from a handful to 400, and the noise varied from singing and chanting to the use of loudspeakers and bullhorns.

The protests, the court found, took their toll on the clinic's patients. A clinic doctor testified that, as a result of having to run such a gauntlet to enter the clinic, the patients "manifested a higher level of anxiety and hypertension causing those patients to need a higher level of sedation to undergo the surgical procedures, thereby increasing the risk associated with such procedures." The noise produced by the protestors could be heard within the clinic, causing stress in the patients both during surgical procedures and while recuperating in the recovery rooms. And those patients who turned away because of the crowd to return at a later

---

1. In addition to petitioners, the state court's order was directed at "Operation Rescue, Operation Rescue America, Operation Goliath, their officers, agents, members, employees and servants, and ... Bruce Cadle, Pat Mahoney, Randall Terry, ... and all persons acting in concert or participation with them, or on their behalf." [Footnote by Chief Justice Rehnquist.]

date, the doctor testified, increased their health risks by reason of the delay.

Doctors and clinic workers, in turn, were not immune even in their homes. Petitioners picketed in front of clinic employees' residences; shouted at passersby; rang the doorbells of neighbors and provided literature identifying the particular clinic employee as a "baby killer." Occasionally, the protestors would confront minor children of clinic employees who were home alone. This and similar testimony led the state court to [amend] its prior order, enjoining a broader array of activities. The amended injunction prohibits petitioners from engaging in the following acts: "(1) At all times on all days, from entering the premises and property of the Aware Woman Center for Choice [the Melbourne clinic]. . . .

"(2) At all times on all days, from blocking, impeding, inhibiting, or in any other manner obstructing or interfering with access to, ingress into and egress from any building or parking lot of the Clinic.

"(3) At all times on all days, from congregating, picketing, patrolling, demonstrating or entering that portion of public right-of-way or private property within 36 feet of the property line of the Clinic. . . . An exception to the 36 foot buffer zone is the area immediately adjacent to the Clinic on the east. . . . The [petitioners] . . . must remain at least 5 feet from the Clinic's east line. Another exception to the 36 foot buffer zone relates to the record title owners of the property to the north and west of the Clinic.

The prohibition against entry into the 36 foot buffer zones does not apply to such persons and their invitees. The other prohibitions contained herein do apply, if such owners and their invitees are acting in concert with the [petitioners]. . . .

"(4) During the hours of 7:30 a.m. through noon, on Mondays through Saturdays, during surgical procedures and recovery periods, from singing, chanting, whistling, shouting, yelling, use of bullhorns, auto horns, sound amplification equipment or other sounds or images observable to or within earshot of the patients inside the Clinic.

"(5) At all times on all days, in an area within 300 feet of the Clinic, from physically approaching any person seeking the services of the Clinic unless such person indicates a desire to communicate by approaching or by inquiring of the [petitioners]. . . .

"(6) At all times on all days, from approaching, congregating, picketing, patrolling, demonstrating or using bullhorns or other sound amplification equipment within [300] feet of the residence of any of the [respondents'] employees, staff, owners or agents, or blocking or attempting to block, barricade, or in any other manner, temporarily or otherwise, obstruct the entrances, exits or driveways of the residences of any of the [respondents'] employees, staff, owners or agents. The [petitioners] and those acting in concert with them are prohibited from inhibiting or impeding or attempting to impede, temporarily or otherwise, the free ingress or egress of persons to any street that provides the sole access to the street on which those residences are located.

"(7) At all times on all days, from physically abusing, grabbing, intimidating, harassing, touching, pushing, shoving, crowding or assaulting persons entering or leaving, working at or using services at the [respondents'] Clinic or trying to gain access to, or leave, any of the homes of owners, staff or patients of the Clinic.

"(8) At all times on all days, from harassing, intimidating or physically abusing, assaulting or threatening any present or former doctor, health care professional, or other staff member, employee or volunteer who assists in providing services at the [respondents'] Clinic.

"(9) At all times on all days, from encouraging, inciting, or securing other persons to commit any of the prohibited acts listed herein." Operation Rescue v. Women's Health Center, Inc., 626 So.2d 664 (Fla. 1993).

The Florida Supreme Court upheld the constitutionality of the trial court's amended injunction. [Shortly] before the Florida Supreme Court's opinion was announced, the United States Court of Appeals for the Eleventh Circuit heard a separate challenge to the same injunction. The Court of Appeals struck down the injunction, characterizing the dispute as a clash "between an actual prohibition of speech and a potential hinderance [sic] to the free exercise of abortion rights." Cheffer v. McGregor, 6 F.3d 705 (1993). [We] granted certiorari to resolve the conflict between the Florida Supreme Court and the Court of Appeals over the constitutionality of the state court's injunction.

II.   We begin by addressing petitioners' contention that the state court's order, because it is an injunction that restricts only the speech of antiabortion protesters, is necessarily content or viewpoint based. Accordingly, they argue, we should examine the entire injunction under the strictest standard of scrutiny. We disagree. To accept petitioners' claim would be to classify virtually every injunction as content or viewpoint based. An injunction, by its very nature, applies only to a particular group (or individuals) and regulates the activities, and perhaps the speech, of that group. It does so, however, because of the group's past actions in the context of a specific dispute between real parties. [The] court hearing the action is charged with fashioning a remedy for a specific deprivation, not with the drafting of a statute addressed to the general public.

The fact that the injunction in the present case did not prohibit activities of those demonstrating in favor of abortion is justly attributable to the lack of any similar demonstrations by those in favor of abortion, and of any consequent request that their demonstrations be regulated by injunction. There is no suggestion in this record that Florida law would not equally restrain similar conduct directed at a target having nothing to do with abortion; none of the restrictions imposed by the court were directed at the contents of petitioner's message.

Our principal inquiry in determining content neutrality is whether the government has adopted a regulation of speech "without reference to the content of the regulated speech." Ward v. Rock Against Racism [1989; below, 12th Ed., p. 1345; Ind.Rts., p. 1016.] We thus look to governmental purpose as the primary consideration. Here, the state court imposed restrictions on petitioners incidental to their antiabortion message because they repeatedly violated the court's original order. That petitioners all share the same viewpoint regarding abortion does not in itself demonstrate that some invidious content or viewpoint-based purpose motivated the issuance of the order. It suggests only that those in the group whose conduct violated the court's order happen to share the same opinion regarding abortions being performed at the clinic. In short, the fact that the injunction covered people with a particular viewpoint does not itself render the injunction content or viewpoint based. Accordingly, the injunction issued in this case does not demand [heightened] scrutiny.[2] [And] we proceed to discuss the standard which does govern.

III. If this were a content-neutral, generally applicable statute, instead of an injunctive order, its constitutionality would be assessed under the standard set forth in Ward v. Rock Against Racism and similar cases. Given that the forum around the clinic is a traditional public forum, see Frisby v. Schultz, we would determine whether the time, place, and manner regulations were "narrowly tailored to serve a significant governmental interest." There are obvious differences, however, between an injunction and a generally applicable ordinance. Ordinances represent a legislative choice regarding the promotion of particular societal interests. Injunctions, by contrast, are remedies imposed for violations (or threatened violations) of a legislative or judicial decree. Injunctions also carry greater risks of censorship and discriminatory application than do general ordinances. "[T]here is no more effective practical guaranty against arbitrary and unreasonable government than to require that the principles of law which officials would impose upon a minority must be imposed generally." Railway Express Agency, Inc. v. New York, 336 U.S. 106 (1949). Injunctions, of course, have some advantages over generally applicable statutes in that they can be tailored by a trial judge to afford more precise relief than a statute where a violation of the law has already occurred.

We believe that these differences require a somewhat more stringent application of general First Amendment principles in this context. In past cases evaluating injunctions restricting speech, we have relied upon such general principles while also seeking to ensure that the injunction was no broader than necessary to achieve its desired goals. Carroll v. President and Comm'rs of Princess Anne [1968; below; 12th Ed., p. 1291; Ind.Rts., p. 962.] [Accordingly,] when evaluating a content-

---

2. We also decline to adopt the prior restraint analysis urged by petitioners. Prior restraints do often take the form of injunctions. See, e.g., New York Times Co. v. United States [1971; below, 12th Ed., p. 1459; Ind.Rts., p. 1130]; Vance v. Universal Amusement Co., 445 U.S. 308 (1980) (per curiam). Not all injunctions which may incidentally affect expression, however, are "prior restraints" in the sense that that term was used in New York Times Co. or Vance. Here petitioners are not prevented from expressing their message in any one of several different ways; they are simply prohibited from expressing it within the 36-foot buffer zone. Moreover, the injunction was issued not because of the content of petitioners' expression, as was the case in New York Times Co. and Vance, but because of their prior unlawful conduct. [Footnote by Chief Justice Rehnquist.]

neutral injunction, we think that our standard time, place, and manner analysis is not sufficiently rigorous. We must ask instead whether the challenged provisions of the injunction burden no more speech than necessary to serve a significant government interest. [Consistent with our cases,] we think [this] standard [exemplifies] "precision of regulation."

The Florida Supreme Court concluded that numerous significant government interests are protected by the injunction. It noted that the State has a strong interest in protecting a woman's freedom to seek lawful medical or counseling services in connection with her pregnancy. The State also has a strong interest in ensuring the public safety and order, in promoting the free flow of traffic on public streets and sidewalks, and in protecting the property rights of all its citizens. In addition, the court believed that the State's strong interest in residential privacy, acknowledged in Frisby, applied by analogy to medical privacy. The court observed that while targeted picketing of the home threatens the psychological well-being of the "captive" resident, targeted picketing of a hospital or clinic threatens not only the psychological, but the physical well-being of the patient held "captive" by medical circumstance. We agree [that] the combination of these governmental interests is quite sufficient to justify an appropriately tailored injunction to protect them. We now examine each contested provision of the injunction to see if it burdens more speech than necessary to accomplish its goal.

A. 1. We begin with the 36–foot buffer zone. The state court prohibited petitioners from "congregating, picketing, patrolling, demonstrating or entering" any portion of the public right-of-way or private property within 36 feet of the property line of the clinic as a way of ensuring access to the clinic. This speech-free buffer zone requires that petitioners move to the other side of Dixie Way and away from the driveway of the clinic, where the state court found that they repeatedly had interfered with the free access of patients and staff. The buffer zone also applies to private property to the north and west of the clinic property.

We examine each portion of the buffer zone separately. We have noted a distinction between the type of focused picketing banned from the buffer zone and the type of generally disseminated communication that cannot be completely banned in public places, such as handbilling and solicitation. Frisby. Here the picketing is directed primarily at patients and staff of the clinic. The 36–foot buffer zone protecting the entrances to the clinic and the parking lot is a means of protecting unfettered ingress to and egress from the clinic, and ensuring that petitioners do not block traffic on Dixie Way. The state court seems to have had few other options to protect access given the narrow confines around the clinic. As the Florida Supreme Court noted, Dixie Way is only 21 feet wide in the area of the clinic. The state court was convinced that allowing the petitioners to remain on the clinic's sidewalk and driveway was not a viable option in view of the failure of the first injunction to protect access. And allowing the petitioners to stand in the middle of Dixie Way would obviously block vehicular traffic.

The need for a complete buffer zone near the clinic entrances and driveway may be debatable, but some deference must be given to the state court's familiarity with the facts and the background of the dispute between the parties even under our heightened review. Moreover, one of petitioners' witnesses during the evidentiary hearing before the state court conceded that the buffer zone was narrow enough to place petitioners at a distance of no greater than 10 to 12 feet from cars approaching and leaving the clinic. Protesters standing across the narrow street from the clinic can still be seen and heard from the clinic parking lots. We also bear in mind the fact that the state court originally issued a much narrower injunction, providing no buffer zone, and that this order did not succeed in protecting access to the clinic. The failure of the first order to accomplish its purpose may be taken into consideration in evaluating the constitutionality of the broader order. On balance, we hold that the 36-foot buffer zone around the clinic entrances and driveway burdens no more speech than necessary to accomplish the governmental interest at stake....

2. The inclusion of private property on the back and side of the clinic in the 36-foot buffer zone raises different concerns. The accepted purpose of the buffer zone is to protect access to the clinic and to facilitate the orderly flow of traffic on Dixie Way. Patients and staff wishing to reach the clinic do not have to cross the private property abutting the clinic property on the north and west, and nothing in the record indicates that petitioners' activities on the private property have obstructed access to the clinic. Nor was evidence presented that protestors located on the private property blocked vehicular traffic on Dixie Way. Absent evidence that petitioners standing on the private property have obstructed access to the clinic, blocked vehicular traffic, or otherwise unlawfully interfered with the clinic's operation, this portion of the buffer zone fails to serve the significant government interests relied on by the Florida Supreme Court. We hold that on the record before us the 36-foot buffer zone as applied to the private property to the north and west of the clinic burdens more speech than necessary to protect access to the clinic.

B. In response to high noise levels outside the clinic, the state court restrained the petitioners from "singing, chanting, whistling, shouting, yelling, use of bullhorns, auto horns, sound amplification equipment or other sounds or images observable to or within earshot of the patients inside the [c]linic" during the hours of 7:30 a.m. through noon on Mondays through Saturdays. We must, of course, take account of the place to which the regulations apply in determining whether these restrictions burden more speech than necessary. [Noise] control is particularly important around hospitals and medical facilities during surgery and recovery periods, and in evaluating another injunction involving a medical facility, we stated: "Hospitals, after all are not factories or mines or assembly plants. They are hospitals, where human ailments are treated, where patients and relatives alike often are under emotional strain and worry, where pleasing and comforting patients are principal facets of the day's activity, and where the patient and his family ... need a restful, uncluttered, relaxing, and helpful atmosphere." ' NLRB v. Baptist Hospital, Inc., 442 U.S. 773 (1979), quoting Beth Israel Hospital v. NLRB, 437 U.S. 483 (1978) (Blackmun, J., concurring in judgment). We hold that the limited noise restrictions imposed by the state court order burden no more speech than necessary to ensure the health and well-being of the patients at the clinic....

C. The same, however, cannot be said for the "images observable" provision of the state court's order. Clearly, threats to patients or their families, however communicated, are proscribable under the First Amendment. But rather than prohibiting the display of signs that could be interpreted as threats or veiled threats, the state court issued a blanket ban on all "images observable." This broad prohibition on all "images observable" burdens more speech than necessary to achieve the purpose of limiting threats to clinic patients or their families. Similarly, if the blanket ban on "images observable" was intended to reduce the level of anxiety and hypertension suffered by the patients inside the clinic, it would still fail. The only plausible reason a patient would be bothered by "images observable" inside the clinic would be if the patient found the expression contained in such images disagreeable. But it is much easier for the clinic to pull its curtains than for a patient to stop up her ears, and no more is required to avoid seeing placards through the windows of the clinic. This provision of the injunction violates the First Amendment.

D. The state court ordered that petitioners refrain from physically approaching any person seeking services of the clinic "unless such person indicates a desire to communicate" in an area within 300 feet of the clinic. The state court was attempting to prevent clinic patients and staff from being "stalked" or "shadowed" by the petitioners as they approached the clinic. But it is difficult, indeed, to justify a prohibition on all uninvited approaches of persons seeking the services of the clinic, regardless of how peaceful the contact may be, without burdening more speech than necessary to prevent intimidation and to ensure access to the clinic. Absent evidence that the protesters' speech is independently proscribable (i.e., "fighting words" or threats), or is so infused with violence as to be indistinguishable from a threat of physical harm, this provision cannot stand....

E. The final substantive regulation challenged by petitioners relates to a prohibition against picketing, demonstrating, or using sound amplification equipment within 300 feet of the residences of clinic staff. The prohibition also covers impeding access to streets that provide the sole access to streets on which those residences are located. The same analysis applies to the use of sound amplification equipment here as that discussed above: the government may simply demand that petitioners turn down the volume if the protests overwhelm the neighborhood.

As for the picketing, [Frisby upheld] a law banning targeted residential picketing [and] remarked on the unique nature of the home as "the last citadel of the tired, the weary, and the sick." [But] the 300–foot zone around the residences in this case is much larger than the zone provided for in the ordinance which we approved in Frisby. [Here] the 300–foot zone would ban "[g]eneral marching through residential neighborhoods, or even walking a route in front of an entire block of houses." The record before us does not contain sufficient justification for this broad a ban on picketing; it appears that a limitation on the time, duration of picketing, and number of pickets outside a smaller zone could have accomplished the desired result.

IV. Petitioners also challenge the state court's order as being vague and overbroad. [The Court rejected both of these challenges, as well as a claim that the "in concert" portion of the injunction violated the freedom of association protected by the First Amendment.]

V. In sum, we uphold the noise restrictions and the 36–foot buffer zone around the clinic entrances and driveway because they burden no more speech than necessary to eliminate the unlawful conduct targeted by the state court's injunction. We strike down as unconstitutional the 36–foot buffer zone as applied to the private property to the north and west of the clinic, the "images observable" provision, the 300–foot no-approach zone around the clinic, and the 300–foot buffer zone around the residences, because these provisions sweep more broadly than necessary to accomplish the permissible goals of the injunction.

[Affirmed in part, and reversed in part.]

Justice SOUTER, concurring.

I join the Court's opinion and write separately only to clarify two matters in the record. First, the trial judge made reasonably clear that the issue of who was acting "in concert" with the named defendants was a matter to be taken up in individual cases, and not to be decided on the basis of protesters' viewpoints. Second, petitioners themselves acknowledge that the governmental interests in protection of public safety and order, of the free flow of traffic, and of property rights are reflected in Florida law.

Justice STEVENS, concurring in part and dissenting in part.

The certiorari petition presented three questions, corresponding to petitioners' three major challenges to the trial court's injunction. The Court correctly and unequivocally rejects petitioners' argument that the injunction is a "content-based restriction on free speech," as well as their challenge to the injunction on the basis that it applies to persons acting "in concert" with them. I therefore join Parts II and IV of the Court's opinion, which properly dispose of the first and third questions presented. I part company with the Court, however, on its treatment of the second question presented, including its enunciation of the applicable standard of review.

I. I agree with the Court that a different standard governs First Amendment challenges to generally applicable legislation than the standard that measures such challenges to judicial remedies for proven wrongdoing. Unlike the Court, however, I believe that injunctive relief should be judged by a more lenient standard than legislation. As the Court notes, legislation is imposed on an entire community, regardless of individual culpability. By contrast, injunctions apply solely to an individual or a limited group of individuals who, by engaging in illegal conduct, have been judicially deprived of some liberty—the normal consequence of illegal activity. Given this distinction, a statute prohibiting demonstrations within 36 feet of an abortion clinic would probably violate the First Amendment, but an injunction directed at a limited group of persons who have engaged in unlawful conduct in a similar zone might well be constitutional.

The standard governing injunctions has two obvious dimensions. On the one hand, the injunction should be no more burdensome than necessary to provide complete relief. In a First Amendment context, as in any other, the propriety of the remedy depends almost entirely on the character of the violation and the likelihood of its recurrence. For this reason, standards fashioned to determine the constitutionality of statutes should not be used to evaluate injunctions. On the other hand, even when an injunction impinges on constitutional rights, more than "a simple proscription against the precise conduct previously pursued" may be required; the remedy must include appropriate restraints on "future activities both to avoid a recurrence of the violation and to eliminate its consequences." National Society of Professional Engineers v. United States, 435 U.S. 679 (1978). [As] such, repeated violations may justify sanctions that might be invalid if applied to a first offender or if enacted by the legislature.

In this case, the trial judge heard three days of testimony and found that petitioners not only had engaged in tortious conduct, but also had repeatedly violated an earlier injunction. The injunction is thus twice removed from a legislative proscription applicable to the general public and should be judged by a standard that gives appropriate deference to the judge's unique familiarity with the facts.

II. The second question presented by the certiorari petition asks whether the "consent requirement before speech is permitted" within a 300–foot buffer zone around the clinic unconstitutionally infringes on free speech. Petitioners contend that these restrictions create a "no speech" zone in which they cannot speak unless the listener indicates a positive interest in their speech. And, in Part III–D of its opinion, the Court seems to suggest that, even in a more narrowly defined zone, such a consent requirement is constitutionally impermissible. Petitioners' argument and the Court's conclusion, however, are based on a misreading of ¶ (5) of the injunction. That paragraph does not purport to prohibit speech; it prohibits a species of conduct. Specifically, it prohibits petitioners "from physically approaching any person seeking the services of the Clinic unless such person indicates a desire to communicate by approaching or by inquiring" of petitioners. The meaning of the term "physically approaching" is explained by the detailed prohibition that applies when the patient refuses to converse with, or accept delivery of literature from, petitioners. Absent such consent, the petitioners "shall not accompany such person, encircle, surround, harass, threaten or physically or verbally abuse those individuals who choose not to communicate with them." As long as petitioners do not physically approach patients in this manner, they remain free not only to communicate with the public but also to offer verbal or written advice on an individual basis to the clinic's patients through their "sidewalk counseling."

Petitioners' "counseling" of the clinic's patients is a form of expression analogous to labor picketing. It is a mixture of conduct and communication. As with picketing, the principal reason why handbills containing the same message are so much less effective than "counseling" is that "the former depend entirely on the persuasive force of the idea." Just as it protects picketing, the First Amendment protects the speaker's right to offer "sidewalk counseling" to all passersby. That protection, however, does not encompass attempts to abuse an unreceptive or captive audience, at least under the circumstances of this case. One may register a public protest by placing a vulgar message on his jacket and, in so doing, expose unwilling viewers, Cohen v. California. Nevertheless, that does not mean that he has an unqualified constitutional right to follow and harass an unwilling listener, especially one on her way to receive medical services.

The "physically approaching" prohibition entered by the trial court is no broader than the protection necessary to provide relief for the violations it found. The trial judge entered this portion of the injunction only after concluding that the injunction was necessary to protect the clinic's patients and staff from "uninvited contacts, shadowing and stalking" by petitioners. The protection is especially appropriate for the clinic patients given that the trial judge found that petitioners' prior conduct caused higher levels of "anxiety and hypertension" in the patients, increasing the risks associated with the procedures that the patients seek. Whatever the proper limits on a court's power to restrict a speaker's ability to physically approach or follow an unwilling listener, surely the First Amendment does not prevent a trial court from imposing such a restriction given the unchallenged findings in this case.

The Florida Supreme Court correctly concluded: "While the First Amendment confers on each citizen a powerful right to express oneself, it gives the picketer no boon to jeopardize the health, safety, and rights of others. No citizen has a right to insert a foot in the hospital or clinic door and insist on being heard—while purposefully blocking the door to those in genuine need of medical services. No picketer can force speech into the captive ear of the unwilling and disabled." Operation Rescue v. Women's Health Center, Inc., 626 So.2d 664 (1993). I thus conclude that, under the circumstances of this case, the prohibition against "physically approaching" in the 300-foot zone around the clinic withstands petitioners' First Amendment challenge. I therefore dissent from Part III-D.

III. Because I have joined Parts I, II, III-E, and IV of the Court's opinion and have dissented as to Part III-D after concluding that the 300-foot zone around the clinic is a reasonable time, place, and manner restriction, no further discussion is necessary. The Court, however, proceeds to address challenges to the injunction that, although arguably raised by petitioners' briefs, are not properly before the Court.

After correctly rejecting the content-based challenge to the 36-foot buffer zone raised by the first question in the certiorari petition, the Court nevertheless decides to modify the portion of that zone that it believes does not protect ingress to the clinic. Petitioners, however, presented only a content-based challenge to the 36–foot zone; they did not present a time, place, and manner challenge. They challenged only the 300–foot zones on this ground. The scope of the 36–foot zone is thus not properly before us. The same is true of the noise restrictions and the "images observable" provision of ¶ (4). That paragraph does not refer to the 36–foot or the 300–foot buffer zones, nor does it relate to the constitutionality of the "in concert" provision. As such, although I am inclined to agree with the Court's resolution respecting the noise and images restrictions, I believe the Court should refrain from deciding their constitutionality because they are not challenged by the questions on which certiorari was granted.

IV. For the reasons stated, I concur in Parts I, II, III–E, and IV of the Court's opinion, and respectfully dissent from the remaining portions.

Justice SCALIA, with whom Justices KENNEDY and THOMAS join, concurring in the judgment in part and dissenting in part.

The judgment in today's case has an appearance of moderation and Solomonic wisdom, upholding as it does some portions of the injunction while disallowing others. That appearance is deceptive. The entire injunction in this case departs so far from the established course of our jurisprudence that in any other context it would have been regarded as a candidate for summary reversal.

But the context here is abortion. A long time ago, in dissent from another abortion-related case, Justice O'Connor, joined by then-Justice Rehnquist, wrote: "This Court's abortion decisions have already worked a major distortion in the Court's constitutional jurisprudence. Today's decision goes further, and makes it painfully clear that no legal rule or doctrine is safe from ad hoc nullification by this Court when an occasion for its application arises in a case involving state regulation of abortion. The permissible scope of abortion regulation is not the only constitutional issue on which this Court is divided, but—except when it comes to abortion—the Court has generally refused to let such disagreements, however longstanding or deeply felt, prevent it from evenhandedly applying uncontroversial legal doctrines to cases that come before it." Thornburgh v. American College of Obstetricians and Gynecologists [1986; above, 12th Ed., p. 525; Ind.Rts., p. 196.] Today the ad hoc nullification machine claims its latest, greatest, and most surprising victim: the First Amendment.

Because I believe that the judicial creation of a 36–foot zone in which only a particular group, which had broken no law, cannot exercise its rights of speech, assembly, and association, and the judicial enactment of a noise prohibition, applicable to that group and that group alone, are profoundly at odds with our First Amendment precedents and traditions, I dissent.

I. The record of this case contains a videotape, with running caption of time and date, displaying what one must presume to be the worst of the activity justifying the injunction issued by Judge McGregor and partially approved today by this Court. The tape was shot by employees of, or volunteers at, the Aware Woman Clinic on three

Saturdays in February and March 1993; the camera location, for the first and third segments, appears to have been an upper floor of the clinic. The tape was edited down (from approximately 6 to 8 hours of footage to ½ hour) by Ruth Arick, a management consultant employed by the clinic and by the Feminist Majority Foundation. Anyone seriously interested in what this case was about must view that tape. And anyone doing so who is familiar with run-of-the-mine labor picketing, not to mention some other social protests, will be aghast at what it shows we have today permitted an individual judge to do. I will do my best to describe it.

On Saturday, March 6, 1993, a group of antiabortion protesters is gathered in front of the clinic, arrayed from east (camera-left) to west (camera-right) on the clinic side of Dixie Way, a small, nonartery street. Men, women, and children are also visible across the street, on the south side of Dixie Way; some hold signs and appear to be protesters, others may be just interested onlookers. On the clinic side of the street, two groups confront each other across the line marking the south border of the clinic property—although they are so close together it is often impossible to tell them apart. On the clinic property (and with their backs to the camera) are a line of clinic and abortion-rights supporters, stretching the length of the property. Opposite them, and on the public right-of-way between the clinic property and Dixie Way itself, is a group of abortion opponents, some standing in place, others walking a picket line in an elongated oval pattern running the length of the property's south border. Melbourne police officers are visible at various times walking about in front of the clinic, and individuals can be seen crossing Dixie Way at various times. Clinic supporters are more or less steadily chanting the following slogans: "Our right, our right, our right, to decide"; "Right to life is a lie, you don't care if women die." Then abortion opponents can be heard to sing: "Jesus loves the little children, all the children of the world, red and yellow, black and white, they are precious in His sight, Jesus loves the little children of the world." Clinic supporters respond with: Q: "What do we want?" A: "Choice." Q: "When do we want it?" A: "Now." ("Louder!") And that call and response is repeated. Later in the tape, clinic supporters chant "1-2-3-4, we won't take it anymore; 5-6-7-8, Separate the Church and State." On placards held by picketers and by stationary protestors on both sides of the line, the following slogans are visible: "Abortionists lie to women." "Choose Life: Abortion Kills." "N.O.W. Violence." "The God of Israel is Pro-life." "RU 486 Now." "She Is a Child, Not a Choice." "Abortion Kills Children." "Keep Abortion Legal." "Abortion: God Calls It Murder." Some abortion opponents wear T-shirts bearing the phrase "Choose Life."

As the abortion opponents walk the picket line, they traverse portions of the public right-of-way that are crossed by paved driveways, on each side of the clinic, connecting the clinic's parking lot to the street. At one point an automobile moves west on Dixie Way and slows to turn into the westernmost driveway. There is a 3-to-4-second delay as the picketers, and then the clinic supporters, part to allow the car to enter. The camera cuts to a shot of another, parked car with a potato jammed onto the tailpipe. There is no footage of any person putting the potato on to the tailpipe. Later, at a point when the crowd appears to be larger and the picketers more numerous, a red car is delayed approximately 10 seconds as the picketers (and clinic supporters) move out of the driveway. Police are visible helping to clear a path for the vehicle to enter. As the car waits, two persons appearing to bear leaflets approach, respectively, the driver and front passenger doors. They appear to elicit no response from the car's occupants and the car passes safely onto clinic property. Later, a blue minivan enters the driveway and is also subject to the same delay. Still later a jeep-type vehicle leaves the clinic property and slows down slightly where the driveway crosses the public right-of-way. At no time is there any apparent effort to prevent entry or exit, or even to delay it, except for the time needed for the picketers to get out of the way. There is no sitting down, packing en masse, linking of hands or any other effort to blockade the clinic property. The persons standing but not walking the picket line include a woman with a child in a stroller, and a man shouting the Book of Daniel's account of Meshach, Shadrach, and Abednego. A woman on a stepladder holds up a sign in the direction of the clinic; a clinic supporter counters with a larger sign held up between the other and the clinic. A brief shot reveals an older man in a baseball cap—head, shoulders, and chest visible above the clinic fence—who appears to be reading silently from a small book. A man on clinic property holds a boom box out in the direction of the abortion opponents. As the crowd grows it appears at various points to have spilled over into the north-side, westbound lane of Dixie Way.

At one point, Randall Terry arrives and the press converge upon him, apparently in Dixie Way itself. A sign is held near his head reading "Randall Terry Sucks." Terry appears to be speaking to the press and at one point tears pages from a notebook of some kind. Through all of this, abortion opponents and abortion-rights supporters appear to be inches from one another on each side of the south border of the property. They exchange words, but at no time is there any violence or even any discernible jostling or physical contact between these political opponents. The scene shifts to early afternoon of the same day. Most of the press and most of the abortion opponents appear to have departed. The camera focuses on a woman who faces the clinic and, hands cupped over her mouth, shouts the following: "Be not deceived; God is not mocked.... Ed Windle, God's judgment is on you, and if you don't repent, He will strike you dead. The baby's blood flowed over your hands, Ed Windle.... You will burn in hell, Ed Windle, if you don't repent. There were arms and legs pulled off today.... An innocent little child, a little boy, a little girl, is being destroyed right now." Cheering is audible from the clinic grounds. A second person shouts "You are responsible for the deaths of children.... You are a murderer. Shame on you." From the clinic grounds someone shouts "Why don't you go join the wacko in Waco?" The first woman says "You are applauding the death of your children. We will be everywhere.... There will be no peace and no rest for the wicked.... I pray that you will give them dreams and nightmares, God."

The second segment of the videotape displays a group of approximately 40 to 50 persons walking along the side of a major highway. It is Saturday, March 13, 1993, at 9:56 a.m. The demonstrators walk in an oval pattern, carrying no signs or other visible indicators of their purpose. According to Ruth Arick, this second portion was filmed in front of the condominium where clinic owner Ed Windle lived.

A third segment begins. The date-time register indicates that it is the morning of Saturday, February 20, 1993. A teenage girl faces the clinic and exclaims: "Please don't let them kill me, Mommy. Help me, Daddy, please." Clinic supporters chant, "We won't go back." A second woman, the one who spoke at greatest length in the first segment calls, "If you [inaudible], help her through it." Off camera, a group sings "Roe, Roe, Roe v. Wade, we will never quit, Freedom of choice is the law of the land, better get used to it." The woman from the first segment appears to address specific persons on clinic property: "Do you ever wonder what your baby would have looked like? Do you wonder how old it would have been? Because I did the same thing...." Then a police officer is visible writing someone a citation. The videotape ends with a shot of an automobile moving eastbound on Dixie Way. As it slows to a stop at the intersection of U.S. 1, two leafletters approach the car and then pull back as it passes on.

The videotape and the rest of the record, including the trial court's findings, show that a great many forms of expression and conduct occurred in the vicinity of the clinic. These include singing, chanting, praying, shouting, the playing of music both from the clinic and from handheld boom boxes, speeches, peaceful picketing, communication of familiar political messages, handbilling, persuasive speech directed at opposing groups on the issue of abortion, efforts to persuade individuals not to have abortions, personal testimony, interviews with the press, and media efforts to report on the protest. What the videotape, the rest of the record, and the trial court's findings do not contain is any suggestion of violence near the clinic, nor do they establish any attempt to prevent entry or exit.

II. A. Under this Court's jurisprudence, there is no question that this public sidewalk area is a "public forum," where citizens generally have a First Amendment right to speak. The parties to this case invited the Court to employ one or the other of the two well established standards applied to restrictions upon this First Amendment right. Petitioners claimed the benefit of so-called "strict scrutiny," the standard applied to content-based restrictions: the restriction must be "necessary to serve a compelling state interest and . . . narrowly drawn to achieve that end." Perry Education Ass'n v. Perry Local Educators' Ass'n [1983; below, 12th Ed., p. 1317; Ind.Rts., p. 986.] Respondents, on the other hand, contended for what has come to be known as "intermediate scrutiny" (midway between the "strict scrutiny" demanded for content-based regulation of speech, and the "rational basis" standard that is applied—under the Equal Protection Clause—to government regulation of non-speech activities). That standard, applicable to so-called "time, place and manner regulations" of speech, provides that the regulations are permissible so long as they "are content-neutral, are narrowly tailored to serve a significant government interest, and leave open ample alternative channels of communication." Perry. The Court adopts neither of these, but creates, brand-new for this abortion-related case, an additional standard that is (supposedly) "somewhat more stringent" than intermediate scrutiny, yet not as "rigorous" as strict scrutiny. The Court does not give this new standard a name, but perhaps we could call it intermediate-intermediate scrutiny. The difference between it and intermediate scrutiny (which the Court acknowledges is inappropriate for injunctive restrictions on speech) is frankly too subtle for me to describe, so I must simply recite it: whereas intermediate scrutiny requires that the restriction be "narrowly tailored to serve a significant government interest," the new standard requires that the restriction "burden no more speech than necessary to serve a significant government interest."

I shall discuss the Court's mode of applying this supposedly new standard presently, but first I must remark upon the peculiar manner in which the standard was devised. The Court begins, in Part II of the opinion, by considering petitioners' contention that, since the restriction is content based, strict scrutiny should govern. It rejects the premise, and hence rejects the conclusion. It then proceeds, in Part III, to examination of respondents' contention that plain old intermediate scrutiny should apply. It says no to that, too, because of the distinctive characteristics of injunctions that it discusses, and hence decides to supplement intermediate scrutiny with intermediate-intermediate scrutiny. But this neatly staged progression overlooks an obvious option. The real question in this case is not whether intermediate scrutiny, which the Court assumes to be some kind of default standard, should be supplemented because of the distinctive characteristics of injunctions; but rather whether those distinctive characteristics are not, for reasons of both policy and precedent, fully as good a reason as "content-basis" for demanding strict scrutiny. That possibility is simply not considered. Instead, the Court begins Part III with the following optical illusion: "If this were a content-neutral, generally applicable statute, instead of an injunctive order, its constitutionality would be assessed under the [intermediate scrutiny] standard"—and then proceeds to discuss whether petitioners can sustain the burden of departing from that presumed disposition.

But this is not a statute, [ ] it is an injunctive order. The Court might just as logically (or illogically) have begun Part III "If this were a content-based injunction, rather than a non-content-based injunction, its constitutionality would be assessed under the strict scrutiny standard"— and have then proceeded to discuss whether respondents can sustain the burden of departing from that presumed disposition. The question should be approached, it seems to me, without any such artificial loading of the dice. And the central element of the answer is that a restriction upon speech imposed by injunction (whether nominally content based or nominally content neutral) is at least as deserving of strict scrutiny as a statutory, content-based restriction.

That is so for several reasons: The danger of content-based statutory restrictions upon speech is that they may be designed and used precisely to suppress the ideas in question rather than to achieve any other proper governmental aim. But that same danger exists with injunctions. Although a speech-restricting injunction may not attack content as content (in the present case, as I shall discuss, even that is not true), it lends itself just as readily to the targeted suppression of particular ideas. When a judge, on the motion of an employer, enjoins picketing at the site of a labor dispute, he enjoins (and he knows he is enjoining) the expression of pro-union views. Such targeting of one or the other side of an ideological dispute cannot readily be achieved in speech-restricting general legislation except by making content the basis of the restriction; it is achieved in speech-restricting injunctions almost invariably. The proceedings before us here illustrate well enough what I mean. The injunction was sought against a single-issue advocacy group by persons and organizations with a business or social interest in suppressing that group's point of view.

The second reason speech-restricting injunctions are at least as deserving of strict scrutiny is obvious enough: they are the product of individual judges rather than of legislatures—and often of judges who have been chagrined by prior disobedience of their orders. The right to free speech should not lightly be placed within the control of a single man or woman. And the third reason is that the injunction is a much more powerful weapon than a statute, and so should be subjected to greater safeguards. Normally, when injunctions are enforced through contempt proceedings, only the defense of factual innocence is available. The collateral bar rule of Walker v. Birmingham [1967; below, 12th Ed., p. 1290; Ind.Rts., p. 961] eliminates the defense that the injunction itself was unconstitutional. Thus, persons subject to a speech-restricting injunction who have not the money or not the time to lodge an immediate appeal face a Hobson's choice: they must remain silent, since if they speak their First Amendment rights are no defense in subsequent contempt proceedings. This is good reason to require the strictest standard for issuance of such orders.

The Court seeks to minimize the similarity between speech-restricting injunctions and content-based statutory proscriptions by observing that the fact that "petitioners all share the same viewpoint regarding abortion does not in itself demonstrate that some invidious content or viewpoint-based purpose motivated the issuance of the order," but rather "suggests only that those in the group whose conduct violated the court's order happen to share the same opinion regarding abortions." But the Court errs in thinking that the vice of content-based statutes is that they necessarily have the invidious purpose of suppressing particular ideas. The vice of content-based legislation—what renders it deserving of the high standard of strict scrutiny—is not that it is always used for invidious, thought-control purposes, but that it lends itself to use for those purposes. And, because of the unavoidable "targeting" discussed above, precisely the same is true of the speech-restricting injunction.

Finally, though I believe speech-restricting injunctions are dangerous enough to warrant strict scrutiny even when they are not technically content based, I think the injunction in the present case was content based (indeed, viewpoint based) to boot. The Court claims that it was

directed, not at those who spoke certain things (anti-abortion senti-
ments), but at those who did certain things (violated the earlier injunction). If that were true, then the injunction's residual coverage of "all
persons acting in concert or participation with [the named individuals
and organizations], or on their behalf" would not include those who
merely entertained the same beliefs and wished to express the same
views as the named defendants. But the construction given to the
injunction by the issuing judge, which is entitled to great weight, is to
the contrary: all those who wish to express the same views as the named
defendants are deemed to be "acting in concert or participation." Following issuance of the amended injunction, a number of persons were
arrested for walking within the 36–foot speech-free zone. At an April
12, 1993, hearing before the trial judge who issued the injunction, the
following exchanges occurred: Mr. Lacy: "I was wondering how we
can—why we were arrested and confined as being in concert with these
people that we don't know, when other people weren't, that were in that
same buffer zone, and it was kind of selective as to who was picked and
who was arrested and who was obtained for the same buffer zone in the
same public injunction." The Court: "Mr. Lacy, I understand that
those on the other side of the issue [abortion-rights supporters] were
also in the area. If you are referring to them, the Injunction did not
pertain to those on the other side of the issue, because the word in
concert with means in concert with those who had taken a certain
position in respect to the clinic, adverse to the clinic. If you are saying
that is the selective basis that the pro-choice were not arrested when
pro-life was arrested, that's the basis of the selection." And: John Doe
No. 16: "This was the first time that I was in this area myself and I had
not attempted to block an entrance to a clinic in that town or anywhere
else in the State of Florida in the last year or ever. I also understand
that the reason why I was arrested was because I acted in concert with
those who were demonstrating pro-life. I guess the question that I'm
asking is were the beliefs in ideologies of the people that were present,
were those taken into consideration when we were arrested? When you
issued the Injunction did you determine that it would only apply to—
that it would apply only to people that were demonstrating that were
pro-life?" The Court: "In effect, yes."

[These] colloquys leave no doubt that the revised injunction here is
tailored to restrain persons distinguished, not by proscribable conduct,
but by proscribable views.

B. I have discussed, in the prior subsection, the policy reasons for
giving speech-restricting injunctions, even content-neutral ones, strict
scrutiny. There are reasons of precedent as well, which are essentially
ignored by the Court. To begin with, an injunction against speech is the
very prototype of the greatest threat to First Amendment values, the
prior restraint. [We] have said that a "prior restraint on expression
comes to this Court with a 'heavy presumption' against its constitutional
validity," Organization for a Better Austin v. Keefe, and have repeatedly
struck down speech-restricting injunctions. At oral argument neither
respondents nor the Solicitor General, appearing as amicus for respondents, could identify a single speech-injunction case applying mere

intermediate scrutiny (which differs little if at all from the Court's intermediate-intermediate scrutiny). We have, in our speech-injunction cases, affirmed both requirements that characterize strict scrutiny: compelling public need and surgical precision of restraint. Even when (unlike in the present case) the First Amendment activity is intermixed with violent conduct, "precision of regulation is demanded." NAACP v. Claiborne Hardware Co. [1982; below, 12th Ed., p. 1394; Ind.Rts., p. 1065.] [The] utter lack of support for the Court's test in our jurisprudence is demonstrated by the two cases the opinion relies upon. For the proposition that a speech restriction is valid when it "burden[s] no more speech than necessary to accomplish a significant government interest," the Court cites NAACP v. Claiborne Hardware and Carroll v. President and Commissioners of Princess Anne. But [Claiborne] applied a much more stringent test; and the very text of Carroll contradicts the Court. In the passage cited, Carroll says this: "An order issued in the area of First Amendment rights must be couched in the narrowest terms that will accomplish the pin-pointed objective permitted by constitutional mandate and the essential needs of the public order." That, of course, is strict scrutiny; and it does not remotely resemble the Court's new proposal, for which it is cited as precedential support. "Significant government interest[s]" (referred to in the Court's test) are general, innumerable, and omnipresent—at least one of them will be implicated by any activity set in a public forum. "Essential needs of the public order," on the other hand, are factors of exceptional application. And that an injunction "burden no more than necessary" is not nearly as demanding as the requirement that it be couched in the "narrowest terms that will accomplish [a] pin-pointed objective." That the Court should cite this case as its principal authority is an admission that what it announces rests upon no precedent at all.

III. A. I turn now from the Court's selection of a constitutional test to its actual application of that test to the facts of the present case. Before doing that, however, it will be helpful—in order to demonstrate how far the Court has departed from past practice—to consider how we proceeded in a relatively recent case that did not involve the disfavored class of abortion protesters. NAACP v. Claiborne Hardware involved, like this case, protest demonstrations against private citizens mingling political speech with (what I will assume for the time being existed here) significant illegal behavior. Writing for the Court, Justice Stevens summarized the events giving rise to the Claiborne litigation: A local chapter of the NAACP, rebuffed by public officials of Port Gibson and Claiborne County in its request for redress of various forms of racial discrimination, began a boycott of local businesses. During the boycott, a young black man was shot and killed in an encounter with [police] and "sporadic acts of violence ensued." The following day, boycott leader Charles Evers told a group that boycott violators would be disciplined by their own people and warned that the Sheriff "could not sleep with boycott violators at night." He stated at a second gathering that "If we catch any of you going in any of them racist stores, we're gonna break your damn neck." In connection with the boycott, there were marches and picketing (often by small children). "Store watchers" were posted outside boycotted stores to identify those who traded, and their names were read aloud at meetings of the [NAACP] and published in a mimeographed paper. The chancellor found that those persons were branded traitors, called demeaning names, and socially ostracized. Some had shots fired at their houses, a brick was thrown through a windshield and a garden damaged. Other evidence showed that persons refusing to observe the boycott were beaten, robbed and publicly humiliated (by spanking).

The merchants brought suit against two groups involved in organizing the boycott and numerous individuals. The trial court found tort violations, violations of a state statute prohibiting secondary boycotts, and state antitrust violations. It issued a broad permanent injunction against the boycotters, enjoining them from stationing "store watchers" at the plaintiffs' business premises; from persuading any person to withhold patronage; from using demeaning and obscene language to or about any person because of his patronage; from picketing or patrolling the premises of any of the respondents; and from using violence against any person or inflicting damage upon any real or personal property. The Mississippi Supreme Court upheld the assessment of liability and the injunction, but solely on the tort theory. [The] legal analysis of this Court proceeded along the following lines: "[T]he boycott ... took many forms. [It] was launched at a meeting of the local branch of the NAACP. [It] was attended by several hundred persons. Its acknowledged purpose was to secure compliance ... with a lengthy list of demands for racial equality and racial justice. The boycott was supported by speeches and nonviolent picketing. Participants repeatedly encouraged others to join its cause. Each of these elements of the boycott is a form of speech or conduct that is ordinarily entitled to protection under the First and Fourteenth Amendments ... '[T]he practice of persons sharing common views banded together to achieve a common end is deeply embedded in the American political process.' We recognize that 'by collective effort individuals can make their views known, when, individually, their voices would be faint or lost.'" We went on to say that "[t]he right to associate does not lose all constitutional protection merely because some members of the group may have participated in conduct or advocated doctrine that is not itself protected," and held that the nonviolent elements of the protestors' activities were entitled to the protection of the First Amendment.

Because we recognized that the boycott involved elements of protected First Amendment speech and other elements not so protected, we took upon ourselves a highly particularized burden of review, recognizing a "special obligation on this Court to examine critically the basis on which liability was imposed." "The First Amendment," we noted, "does not protect violence," but when conduct sanctionable by tort liability "occurs in the context of constitutionally protected activity ... 'precision of regulation' is demanded." Then, criticizing the Mississippi Supreme Court for "broadly assert[ing]—without differentiation—that intimidation, threats, social ostracism, vilification, and traduction were devices used by the defendants to effectuate the boycott," we carefully examined the record for factual support of the findings of liability. While affirming that a "judgment tailored to the consequences of [individuals'] unlawful conduct may be sustained," we said that "mere association with [a] group—absent a specific intent to further an unlawful aim embraced by that group—is an insufficient predicate for liability." We said in conclusion that any characterization of a political protest movement as a violent conspiracy "must be supported by findings that adequately disclose the evidentiary basis for concluding that specific parties agreed to use unlawful means, that carefully identify the impact of such unlawful conduct, and that recognize the importance of avoiding the imposition of punishment for constitutionally protected activity." Because this careful procedure had not been followed by the Mississippi courts, we set aside the entire judgment, including the injunction.

B. I turn now to the Court's performance in the present case. I am content to evaluate it under the lax (intermediate-intermediate scrutiny) standard that the Court has adopted, because even by that distorted light it is inadequate. [In this and the following subsection Justice Scalia argued that the Court's conclusions were unwarranted even under its own standard, and that neither in the courts below or in the Supreme Court was there any basis for the finding about prior violations of law.]

. . .

In his dissent in Korematsu v. United States [1944; above, 12th Ed., p. 638; Ind.Rts., p. 309], the case in which this Court permitted the wartime military internment of Japanese–Americans, Justice Jackson wrote the following: "A military order, however unconstitutional, is not apt to last longer than the military emergency . . . But once a judicial opinion . . . rationalizes the Constitution to show that the Constitution sanctions such an order, the Court for all time has validated the principle of racial discrimination in criminal procedure and of transplanting American citizens. The principle then lies about like a loaded weapon ready for the hand of any authority that can bring forward a plausible claim of an urgent need." What was true of a misguided military order is true of a misguided trial-court injunction. And the Court has left a powerful loaded weapon lying about today.

What we have decided seems to be, and will be reported by the media as, an abortion case. But it will go down in the lawbooks, it will be cited, as a free-speech injunction case—and the damage its novel principles produce will be considerable. The proposition that injunctions against speech are subject to a standard indistinguishable from (unless perhaps more lenient in its application than) the "intermediate scrutiny" standard we have used for "time, place, and manner" legislative restrictions; the notion that injunctions against speech need not be closely tied to any violation of law, but may simply implement sound social policy; and the practice of accepting trial-court conclusions permitting injunctions without considering whether those conclusions are supported by any findings of fact—these latest by-products of our abortion jurisprudence ought to give all friends of liberty great concern.

For these reasons, I dissent from that portion of the judgment upholding parts of the injunction.

12th ED., p. 1270; IND. RTS., p. 941

Add to Footnote 6:

The First Amendment right to engage in anonymous political speech was reaffirmed in McINTYRE v. OHIO ELECTIONS COMMISSION, 517 U.S. ___ (1995). At issue was an Ohio statute that required that anyone distributing written or printed election material (other than personal correspondence) include on the material the name and address of the person "responsible" for it. McIntyre was convicted of violating the statute for distributing an anonymous handbill in connection with a local school tax referendum, but the Supreme Court, with Justice STEVENS writing for the majority, reversed the conviction, held the statute unconstitutional, and made clear that the identification requirement in the context of political advocacy was a First Amendment violation. Relying on such diverse exemplars as the Federalist Papers, pseudonymous literature such as that produced by Mark Twain, O. Henry, Voltaire, George Eliot, and George Sand, and the anonymous grading of law school examinations, Justice Stevens reaffirmed Talley and made clear that in it "the Court's reasoning embraced a respected tradition of anonymity in the advocacy of political causes. This tradition is perhaps best exemplified by the secret ballot, the hard-won right to vote one's conscience without fear of retaliation."

Finding that the law burdened "core political speech," Justice Stevens went on to apply "exacting scrutiny" and concluded that none of the state's purported justifications for the requirement were sufficient. Ohio had argued that it had an interest in making sure that more information was provided to the electorate, but the Court held that "the identity of the speaker is no different from other components of the document's content that the author is free to include or exclude." And the Court also determined that Ohio's interest in preventing libelous and fraudulent campaign literature could be (and in fact was) served by direct prohibitions on libelous and fraudulent statements, prohibitions that would not, as did this requirement, "encompass[ ] documents that are not even arguably false or misleading. [Under] our Constitution, anonymous pamphleteering is not a pernicious, fraudulent, practice, but an honorable tradition of advocacy and dissent. Anonymity is a shield from the tyranny of the majority."

Justice GINSBURG wrote a brief concurring opinion, making it clear that in other cases the interest in the integrity of the electoral process might justify a more limited identification requirement. Justice THOMAS concurred in the judgment, saying that he would "apply [a] different methodology to this case. Instead of asking whether an 'honorable tradition' of anonymous speech has existed throughout American history, or what the 'value' of anonymous speech might be, we should determine whether the phrase 'freedom of speech, or of the press,' as originally understood, protected anonymous political leafletting. I believe that it did." Justice Thomas noted the Federalist Papers and the trial of John Peter Zenger to establish "the extent to which anonymity and the freedom of the press were intertwined in the early American mind," and also described a number of late eighteenth century colonial cases that supported the view that at the time of the drafting of the First Amendment it was well accepted that "anonymity was protected by the freedom of the press. [I] must conclude that both Anti–Federalists and Federalists believed that the freedom of the press included the right to publish without revealing the author's name. [It] is only an innovation of modern times that has permitted the regulation of anonymous speech."

Justice SCALIA, joined by Chief Justice Rehnquist, dissented, objecting to the majority's "preferring the views of the English utilitarian philosopher John Stuart Mill to the considered judgment of the American people's elected representatives from coast to coast." Although agreeing with Justice Thomas about much of the history of anonymous political advocacy, Justice Scalia argued that "to prove that anonymous electioneering was used frequently is not to establish that it is a constitutional right. [The] issue of a governmental prohibition upon anonymous electioneering in particular (as opposed to a government prohibition on anonymous publication in general) simply never arose. [What] we have, then, is the most difficult case for determining the meaning of the Constitution. No accepted existence of governmental restrictions of the sort at issue here demonstrates their constitutionality, but neither can their nonexistence clearly be attributed to constitutional objections." Relying then on widespread state practice for the last hundred years, Justice Scalia concluded that "[s]uch a universal and long established American legislative practice must be given precedence [over] historical and academic speculation regarding a restriction that assuredly does not go to the heart of free speech." And rejecting most of the majority's sympathy for the practice of anonymous speech, he argued that "I can imagine no reason why an anonymous leaflet is more honorable, as a general matter, than an anonymous phone call or an anonymous letter. It facilitates wrong by eliminating accountability, which is ordinarily the very purpose of anonymity."

12th ED., p. 1292; IND. RTS., p. 963

Add at end of Permit Requirements materials:

5. *Forsyth County.* In FORSYTH COUNTY, GEORGIA v. NA-TIONALIST MOVEMENT, 505 U.S. 123 (1992), a majority of the Court struck down a parade permit ordinance that in the Court's view allowed officials too much discretion to vary the permit fee with the content of the paraders' expression. The ordinance was enacted in the wake of a widely-publicized civil rights demonstration in 1987 in a predominantly white county widely known for Ku Klux Klan activity. Two parades and demonstrations, the second much larger than the first, attracted a large number of Ku Klux Klan and other counter-demonstrators, and resulted in a cost for police protection of $670,000. Forsyth County then passed an ordinance providing for a sum of up to $1000 per day for a parade permit, and providing as well that the county administrator could "adjust" the amount of the fee based on the expected expense of processing the application and of maintaining order in connection with the demonstration or parade. The ordinance was challenged in 1989 by a group called The Nationalist Movement, in connection with its plans to demonstrate in opposition to the federal holiday commemorating the birthday of Dr. Martin Luther King, Jr.

Although the ordinance resembled the one upheld by the Court in Cox v. New Hampshire, Justice BLACKMUN's opinion for the Court upheld a facial challenge to the ordinance largely on the basis of more recent cases such as Lakewood v. Plain Dealer Publishing Co. [1988; above, 12th Ed., p. 1208; Ind.Rts., p. 879.] Because the ordinance "did not prescribe adequate standards for the administrator to apply when he sets a permit fee," the Court ruled, the potential for arbitrary application was too high to satisfy First Amendment scrutiny. "Nothing in the law or its application prevents the official from encouraging some views and discouraging others through the arbitrary application of fees."

Justice Blackmun also found the ordinance's requirement that the amount of the fee turn on the cost of police protection an even more direct form of control based on the content of the expression. "The fee assessed will depend on the administrator's measure of the amount of hostility likely to be created by the speech based on its content. Those wishing to express views unpopular with bottle-throwers, for example, may have to pay more for their permit." Rejecting the County's "secondary effects" argument [above, 12th Ed., pp. 1151–54; Ind.Rts., pp. 822–25], Justice Blackmun made clear that "listeners' reaction to speech is not a content-neutral basis for regulation. [Speech] cannot be financially burdened, any more than it can be punished or banned, simply because it might offend a hostile mob. [Neither] the $1,000 cap on the fee charged, nor even some lower nominal cap, could save the ordinance because in this context, the level of the fee is irrelevant. A tax based on the content of speech does not become more constitutional because it is a small tax."

Chief Justice REHNQUIST, joined by Justices White, Scalia, and Thomas, dissented, arguing that Cox settled the issue of the facial validity of such an ordinance, and that questions about potential content-based application should not be reached in the absence of any evidence of an authoritative construction by the Georgia courts, and in the absence of any evidence of content-based enforcement.

12th ED., p. 1316; IND. RTS., p. 987
Add after Widmar v. Vincent:

LAMB'S CHAPEL v. CENTER MORICHES UNION FREE SCHOOL DISTRICT, 509 U.S. ___ (1993): Although Justice WHITE was the sole dissenter in Widmar, he wrote for a unanimous Supreme Court in striking down on free speech grounds a somewhat similar restriction on the after-hours use of public school facilities by religious organizations. At issue was a rule of the Center Moriches (New York) Union Free School District, consonant with and arguably required by New York state law, allowing use of school facilities by various groups for various purposes, but at the same time providing that "school premises shall not be used by any group for religious purposes." Lamb's Chapel, an evangelical church, requested permission to use school facilities, out of school hours, to show a six-part series of films by Dr. James Dobson, a series that would discuss various social issues in the context of "traditional, Christian family values." The school district denied the application for permission to use the premises, relying on the rule prohibiting the use of the school for religious purposes, and saying that "[t]his film does appear to be church related and therefore your request must be refused."

Justice White's opinion accepted the conclusion of the court of appeals that the school facilities were neither a traditional nor a designated public forum. Nevertheless, it was clear that films dealing with the same subject matter would have been permitted if only that subject matter had not been treated from a religious perspective, and sponsored by a religious group. This, Justice White concluded, rendered the exclusion impermissible, for even a total exclusion of all religious groups and perspectives was a viewpoint and not subject-matter restriction. Thus the exclusion's fatal flaw was that it was "discriminat[ion] on the basis of viewpoint to permit school property to be used for the presentation of all views about family issues and child-rearing except those dealing with the subject matter from a religious standpoint." [6]

ROSENBERGER v. UNIVERSITY OF VIRGINIA, 519 U.S. ___ (1995): The Court relied heavily on Lamb's Chapel in invalidating the University of Virginia's refusal to pay the printing bills of a student

---

6. As in Widmar, the Court relied on free speech and not on free exercise of religion arguments. And as in Widmar, the Court rejected the argument that the exclusion of religious groups was required by the establishment clause of the first amendment. This aspect of the case is discussed below, addition to 12th Ed., p. 1531; Ind. Rts., p. 1202, including the separate opinions of Justices SCALIA, Thomas, and Kennedy on the establishment clause issues.

publication whose perspective was expressly religious. Under the applicable procedures of the University, student organizations could become eligible to have some of their expenses, such as printing expenses for publications, paid out of the mandatory Student Activities Fund. The guidelines for the disbursement of moneys by the Fund on behalf of student organizations were in general widely inclusive, and explicitly extended to "student organizations ... which espouse[ ] particular positions or ideological viewpoints, including those that may be unpopular or are not generally accepted." Under the guidelines, however, funds could not be used to support "religious activity," defined as an activity that "primarily promotes or manifests a particular belie[f] in or about a deity or an ultimate reality." On the basis of these guidelines, the Student Council refused to pay the printing expenses ($5862) of a student publication entitled Wide Awake: A Christian Perspective at the University of Virginia, which discussed world, national, and university events from an explicitly Christian perspective. The students who ran Wide Awake challenged the exclusion of religious activities as viewpoint discrimination in violation of the First Amendment's free speech clause, and the Supreme Court, with Justice KENNEDY, writing for the majority, agreed.

Relying substantially on Lamb's Chapel, and to some extent on Widmar v. Vincent, Justice Kennedy noted that the Student Activities Fund was a "forum more in a metaphysical than in a spatial or geographic sense, but the same principles are applicable. Consequently, [in] determining whether the State is acting to preserve the limits of the forum it has created so that the exclusion of a class of speech is legitimate, we have observed a distinction between, on the one hand, content discrimination, which may be permissible if it preserves the purposes of that limited forum, and, on the other hand, viewpoint discrimination, which is presumed impermissible when directed against speech otherwise within the forum's limitations. [It] is, in a sense, something of an understatement to speak of religious thought and discussion as just a viewpoint, as distinct from a comprehensive body of thought. [We] conclude, nonetheless, that here, as in Lamb's Chapel, viewpoint discrimination is the proper way to interpret the University's objections to Wide Awake. By the very terms of the [prohibition,] the University does not exclude religion as a subject matter but selects for disfavored treatment those student journalistic efforts with religious editorial viewpoints. Religion may be a vast area of inquiry, but it also provides, as it did here, a specific premise, a perspective, a standpoint from which a variety of subjects may be discussed and considered. The prohibited perspective, not the general subject matter, resulted in the refusal to make third-party payments, for the subjects discussed were otherwise within the approved category of publications. [The] assertion that no viewpoint discrimination occurs because the Guidelines discriminate against an entire class of viewpoints reflects an unsupportable assumption that all debate is bipolar and that anti-religious speech is the only response to religious speech. Our understanding of the complex and multifaceted nature of public discourse has not embraced such a contrived description of the marketplace of ideas. If the topic of the debate is, for example, racism, then exclusion of several views on that problem is just as offensive to the First Amendment as exclusion of only one. It is as objectionable to exclude both a theistic and an atheistic perspective on the debate as it is to exclude one, the other, or yet another political, economic, or social viewpoint."

The University's primary defense of the exclusion was based on the ability of a university to make the necessary content-based distinctions and academic judgments that are essential to and virtually definitional of its mission. Justice Kennedy accepted the justification in the context of the University's own teaching and related communicative activities, but found that justification inapplicable to the funding of student speech. Distinguishing Rust v. Sullivan and numerous other cases involving government subsidies of its own message, Justice Kennedy observed that "a holding that the University may not discriminate based on the viewpoint of private persons whose speech it facilitates does not restrict the University's own speech, which is controlled by different principles. [The] distinction between the University's own favored message and the private speech of students is evident in the case before us. [Having] offered to pay the third-party contractors [such as printers] on behalf of private speakers who convey their own messages, the University may not silence the expression of selected viewpoints."

Although the University had in its brief and oral argument defended its policy solely on the grounds of its claimed power to make content-based choices within its educational mission, it had earlier defended the exclusion as required by the Establishment Clause of the First Amendment, and the Court's grant of certiorari had included the Establishment Clause issue. Consequently, Justice Kennedy went on to conclude, even though the University had not pressed the point, that the exclusion was not required by the Establishment Clause. This aspect of the opinion is discussed below, addition to 12th Ed., p. 1531; Ind.Rts., p. 1202. The various other opinions in the case focused on the Establishment Clause question, but part of the dissenting opinion of Justice SOUTER, joined by Justices Stevens, Ginsburg, and Breyer, addressed the free speech issue as well, arguing that the majority had misconceived the prohibition on viewpoint discrimination. "If the Guidelines were written or applied so as to limit only [Christian] advocacy and no other evangelical efforts that might compete with it, the discrimination would be based on viewpoint. But [the regulation] applies to Muslim and Jewish and Buddhist advocacy as well as to Christian. [The] Guidelines [thus] do not skew debate by funding one position but not its competitors; [they] deny funding for the entire subject matter of religious apologetics. [To] put the point another way, the Court's decision equating a categorical exclusion of both sides of the religious debate with viewpoint discrimination suggests the Court has concluded that primarily religious and antireligious speech, grouped together, always provides an opposing (and not merely a related) viewpoint to any speech about any secular topic. Thus, the Court's reasoning requires a university that funds private publications about any primarily nonreligious topic also to fund publications primarily espousing adherence to or rejection of religion. But a university's decision to fund a magazine about racism, and not to fund publications aimed at urging repentance before God does not skew the debate either about racism or the desirability of religious conversion. The Court's contrary holding amounts to a significant reformulation of our viewpoint discrimination precedents."

12th ED., p. 1323; IND. RTS., p. 994
Add at end of What is Left of Access section:

INTERNATIONAL SOCIETY FOR KRISHNA CONSCIOUSNESS, INC. v. LEE, 504 U.S. ___ (1992); LEE v. INTERNATIONAL SOCIETY FOR KRISHNA CONSCIOUSNESS, 504 U.S. ___ (1992): After years of lower court litigation, and after dealing with one case on overbreadth grounds (Board of Airport Commissioners v. Jews for Jesus, 1987; 12th Ed., p. 1201; Ind.Rts., p. 872), the Court finally confronted the question whether airports would be considered public fora for access purposes. The Port Authority of New York, which operates Kennedy, LaGuardia, and Newark airports, prohibited (other than in rented stores and the like) the distribution of literature and the solicitation of funds, a prohibition challenged by the International Society for Krishna Consciousness (Hare Krishna). In companion cases, the Court upheld the restriction on solicitation of funds, but struck down the prohibition on distribution of literature.

Chief Justice REHNQUIST wrote the opinion of the Court upholding the restriction on solicitation of funds. He relied on the Court's recent "forum analysis," reiterating that "the government need not permit all forms of speech on property that it owns and controls. Where the government is acting as a proprietor, managing its internal operations, rather than acting as lawmaker with the power or license, its actions will not be subject to the heightened review to which its actions as a lawmaker may be subject. [Regulation] of speech on government property that has traditionally been available for public expression is subject to the highest scrutiny." He also noted that the parties agreed on the division of fora into categories of public forum, designated public forum, and nonpublic forum, as set out in Cornelius, but "disagree[d] whether the airport terminals are public fora or nonpublic fora." Addressing this question, Chief Justice Rehnquist again rejected the notion that widespread public use and generally uncontrolled public access were sufficient to create a public forum. Rather, he stressed that airports are relatively recent innovations, that in their current size and scope they are even more recent, and that they were created for a primary purpose other than public discourse. "The tradition of airport activity does not demonstrate that airports have historically been made available for speech activity. Nor can we say that [airport] terminals [have] been intentionally opened by their operators to such activity; the frequent and continuing litigation evidencing the operators' objections belies any such claim." The Chief Justice also rejected the relevance of historical practices regarding other forms of transportation terminals. Noting the differences between different forms of transportation, and commenting on the special security problems at airports, he concluded that "the relevant unit for our inquiry in an airport, not 'transportation nodes' generally. [Although] many airports have expanded their function beyond merely contributing to efficient air travel, few have included among their purposes the designation of a forum for solicitation and distribution activities. [Neither] by tradition nor purpose can the terminals be described as satisfying the standards we have previously set out for identifying a public forum. The restrictions here challenged, therefore, need only satisfy a requirement of reasonableness."

Applying this standard, the Court had little difficulty upholding the restriction on solicitation. In addition to creating the possibility of delay for passengers in a hurry, "face-to-face solicitation presents risks of duress that are an appropriate target of regulation. The solicitor [can] target the most vulnerable, including those accompanying children or those suffering physical impairment and who cannot easily avoid the solicitation. The unsavory solicitor can also commit fraud through concealment of his affiliation or through deliberate efforts to short-change those who agree to purchase. Compounding this problem is the fact that, in an airport, the targets of such activity frequently are on tight schedules[, and are thus] unlikely to stop and formally complain to airport authorities." Because the Port Authority had not restricted use of the sidewalk areas outside the terminal, and because solicitors thus had access to virtually all people coming to use the airport, Chief Justice Rehnquist concluded that the restriction on solicitation satisfied the reasonableness standard.

Justice KENNEDY, joined by Justices Blackmun, Stevens, and Souter, concurred in this judgment, but offered an importantly different approach. He started by taking issue with the majority's conclusion that the airports (except for security areas) were not public fora, and with the majority's method of reaching that conclusion. "Our public forum doctrine ought not to be a jurisprudence of categories rather than ideas or convert what was once an analysis protective of expression into one which grants the government authority to restrict speech by fiat." Retracing the guaranteed access roots of public forum doctrine dating back to Hague v. CIO, Justice Kennedy found the recent categorization approach, and even more the reliance of that approach on the government's own characterization of the property, to be unfaithful to the goals of providing areas where access would be assured. "The Court's error lies in its conclusion that the public-forum status of public property depends on the government's defined purpose for the property, or on an explicit decision by the government to dedicate the property to expressive activity. In my view, the inquiry must be an objective one, based on the actual, physical characteristics and uses of the property. [The] First Amendment is a limitation on government, not a grant of power. Its design is to prevent the government from controlling speech. Yet under the Court's view the authority of the government to control speech on its property is paramount, for in almost all cases the critical step in the Court's analysis is a classification of the property that turns on the government's own definition or decision, unconstrained by an independent duty to respect the speech its citizens can voice there. The Court acknowledges as much. by reintroducing today [a] strict doctrinal line between the proprietary and regulatory functions of government which I thought had been abandoned long ago [in Hague.]"

"The Court's approach is contrary to the underlying purposes of the public forum doctrine. The liberties protected by our doctrine derive from the Assembly, as well as the Speech and Press Clauses of the First Amendment, and are essential to a functioning democracy. Public places are of necessity the locus for discussion of public issues, as well as protest against arbitrary government action. [In] a free nation citizens must have the right to gather and speak with other persons in public places. The recognition that certain government-owned property is a public forum provides open notice to citizens that their freedoms may be exercised there without fear of a censorial government, adding tangible reinforcement to the idea that we are a free people."

Justice Kennedy questioned the Court's recent inclination to limit public forum doctrine to streets, parks, and sidewalks, arguing that it "rests on an inaccurate view of history. [The] principal purpose of streets and sidewalks, like airports, is to facilitate transportation, not public discourse. [Similarly,] the purpose for the creation of public parks may be as much for beauty and open space as for discourse." Because traditional public forums were recognized as such despite having primary purposes other than discourse, he argued, "the policies underlying [public forum] doctrine cannot be given effect unless we recognize that open, public spaces and thoroughfares which are suitable for discourse may be public forums, whatever their historical pedigree and without concern for a precise classification of the property. [In] a country where most citizens travel by automobile, and parks all too often become locales for crime rather than social intercourse, our failure to recognize that new types of government property may be appropriate forums for speech will lead to a serious curtailment of our expressive activity."

Thus, "regardless of ancient or contemporary origins and whether or not it fits within a narrow historic tradition," Justice Kennedy would grant public forum status to other forms of property "if the objective, physical characteristics of the property at issue and the actual public access and uses which have been permitted by the government indicate that expressive activity would be appropriate and compatible with those uses. [The] most important considerations [are] whether the property shares physical similarities with more traditional public forums, whether the government has permitted or acquiesced in broad public access to the property, and whether expressive activity would tend to interfere in a significant way with the uses to which the government has as a factual matter dedicated the property. In conducting the last inquiry, courts must consider the consistency of those uses with expressive activity in general, rather than the specific sort of speech at issue in the case before it."

This standard led Justice Kennedy to find that the public spaces in the airports qualified as public forums. The airports' main thoroughfares bore significant resemblance to public streets and sidewalks, they are open to the public without restriction, and, subject to time, place, and manner restrictions, expressive activity is consistent with the airport's primary use. But although this led him to strike down the prohibition on distribution of flyers and other literature, he agreed with the Chief Justice on the permissibility of the restriction on solicitation of funds. This he found either to be a reasonable time, place, and manner restriction in the public forum, or a restriction on the nonspeech elements of expressive conduct. (On the latter, see R.A.V. v. St. Paul, 1992; set out above, addition to 12th Ed., p. 1248; Ind.Rts., p. 919). Although he agreed that solicitation in general was a form of protected speech, he found that the solicitation for the immediate payment of money, which is what was prohibited here, was of a different character than sales in general, and thus subject to regulation, largely for the reasons set out by Chief Justice Rehnquist. And when measured against a standard requiring that regulations must be narrowly drawn "and leave open ample alternative channels of communication," Justice Kennedy found that the prohibition within the airport on the solicitation for the immediate payment of money constitutionally permissible. Thus although making clear that he would not countenance a general restriction on sales, largely because that would "close the marketplace of ideas to less affluent organizations," this narrower regulation on the solicitation and immediate receipt of funds was within the airport's constitutional power.

Justice O'CONNOR, in a separate opinion, concurred in Chief Justice Rehnquist's opinion and his conclusion that the airport was not a public forum. She wrote separately to emphasize, however, that for her the reasonableness standard applied to nonpublic fora had some bite. Thus, she concluded that in reality the Port Authority was here "operating a shopping mall as well as an airport," and the standard of compatibility had to measured in that light. In doing so, she agreed that the ban on solicitation was reasonable, but that the prohibition on leafletting and distribution of written material did not qualify under her standard of reasonableness, especially in light of the other activities permitted at the airport.

Justice SOUTER, joined by Justices Blackmun and Stevens, concurred in the judgment on the impermissibility of the restriction on distribution of literature, and, more significantly, agreed with the standard offered by Justice Kennedy and its application to these airports. Thus he agreed that these airports were public forums, and that only reasonable time, place, and manner restrictions were permitted. But to Justice Souter this standard also compelled invalidation of the restriction on solicitation of funds, as he was not convinced that other and less restrictive means could equally well satisfy the interests in preventing fraud and coercion.

Chief Justice REHNQUIST, in a separate opinion joined by Justices White, Scalia, and Thomas, dissented from the conclusion (comprised of Justice Kennedy's opinion on this issue joined by Justices Souter, Blackmun, and Stevens, and Justice O'Connor's reaching the same result on her application of traditional forum analysis) that distribution of literature could not be prohibited. He found the interest in preventing congestion reasonable, the distinction between solicitation and distribution untenable, and the goals of the Port Authority in traveler convenience justifiable. "The weary, harried, or hurried traveler may have no less desire and need to avoid the delays generated by having literature foisted upon him than he does to avoid delays from a financial solicitation."

12th ED., p. 1333; IND.RTS., p. 1004
Add after Note on Visual Pollution:

CITY OF LADUE v. GILLEO

514 U.S. ___, 114 S.Ct. 2038, 129 L.Ed.2d 36 (1994).

Justice STEVENS delivered the opinion of the Court.

An ordinance of the City of Ladue prohibits homeowners from displaying any signs on their property except "residence identification" signs, "for sale" signs, and signs warning of safety hazards. The ordinance permits commercial establishments, churches, and nonprofit organizations to erect certain signs that are not allowed at residences. The question presented is whether the ordinance violates a Ladue resident's right to free speech.

I. Respondent Margaret P. Gilleo owns one of the 57 single-family homes in the Willow Hill subdivision of Ladue. On December 8, 1990, she placed on her front lawn a 24– by 36–inch sign printed with the words "Say No to War in the Persian Gulf, Call Congress Now." After that sign disappeared, Gilleo put up another but it was knocked to the ground. When Gilleo reported these incidents to the police, they advised her that such signs were prohibited in Ladue. The City Council denied her petition for a variance. Gilleo then filed this action, [alleging] that Ladue's sign ordinance violated her First Amendment right of free speech. The District Court issued a preliminary injunction against enforcement of the ordinance. Gilleo then placed an 8.5– by 11–inch sign in the second story window of her home stating, "For Peace in the Gulf." The Ladue City Council responded to the injunction by repealing its ordinance and enacting a replacement. Like its predecessor, the new ordinance contains a general prohibition of "signs" and defines that term broadly. The ordinance prohibits all signs except those that fall within one of ten exemptions. Thus, "residential identification signs" no larger than one square foot are allowed, as are signs advertising "that the property is for sale, lease or exchange" and identifying the owner or agent. Also exempted are signs "for churches, religious institutions, and schools," "[c]ommercial signs in commercially or industrial zoned districts," and on-site signs advertising "gasoline filling stations." Unlike its predecessor, the new ordinance contains a lengthy "Declaration of Findings, Policies, Interests, and Purposes," part of which recites that the "proliferation of an unlimited number of signs in private, residential, commercial, industrial, and public areas of the City of Ladue would create ugliness, visual blight and clutter, tarnish the natural beauty of the landscape as well as the residential and commercial architecture, impair property values, substantially impinge upon the privacy and special ambience of the community, and may cause safety and traffic hazards to motorists, pedestrians, and children[.]"

Gilleo amended her complaint to challenge the new ordinance, which explicitly prohibits window signs like hers. The District Court held the ordinance unconstitutional, and the Court of Appeals affirmed. Relying on the plurality opinion in Metromedia, Inc. v. San Diego, the Court of Appeals held the ordinance invalid as a "content based" regulation because the City treated commercial speech more favorably than non-commercial speech and favored some kinds of noncommercial speech over others. [We] granted the City of Ladue's petition for certiorari, and now affirm.

II. While signs are a form of expression protected by the Free Speech Clause, they pose distinctive problems that are subject to municipalities' police powers. Unlike oral speech, signs take up space and may obstruct views, distract motorists, displace alternative uses for land, and pose other problems that legitimately call for regulation. It is common ground that governments may regulate the physical characteristics of signs—just as they can, within reasonable bounds and absent censorial purpose, regulate audible expression in its capacity as noise. Ward v. Rock Against Racism [1989; below, 12th Ed., p. 1345; Ind.Rts., p. 1016]; Kovacs v. Cooper [1949; above, 12th Ed., p. 1262; Ind.Rts., p. 933.]. However, because regulation of a medium inevitably affects communication itself, it is not surprising that we have had occasion to review the constitutionality of municipal ordinances prohibiting the display of certain outdoor signs.

In Linmark Associates, Inc. v. Willingboro [1977; above, 12th Ed., p. 1777; Ind.Rts., p. 848], we addressed an ordinance that sought to maintain stable, integrated neighborhoods by prohibiting homeowners from placing "For Sale" or "Sold" signs on their property. Although we recognized the importance of Willingboro's objective, we held that the First Amendment prevented the township from "achieving its goal by restricting the free flow of truthful information." In some respects Linmark is the mirror image of this case. For instead of prohibiting "For Sale" signs without banning any other signs, Ladue has exempted such signs from an otherwise virtually complete ban. Moreover, whereas in Linmark we noted that the ordinance was not concerned with the promotion of aesthetic values unrelated to the content of the prohibited speech, here Ladue relies squarely on that content-neutral justification for its ordinance.

In Metromedia, we reviewed an ordinance imposing substantial prohibitions on outdoor advertising displays [in] the interest of traffic safety and aesthetics. [The] Court concluded that the City's interest in traffic safety and its aesthetic interest in preventing "visual clutter" could justify a prohibition of off-site commercial billboards even though similar on-site signs were allowed. Nevertheless, the Court's judgment in Metromedia, supported by two different lines of reasoning, invalidated the San Diego ordinance in its entirety. [In] City Council of Los Angeles v. Taxpayers for Vincent [1984; immediately above], we upheld a Los Angeles ordinance that prohibited the posting of signs on public property. Noting the conclusion shared by seven Justices in Metromedia that San Diego's "interest in avoiding visual clutter" was sufficient to justify a prohibition of commercial billboards, in Vincent we upheld the Los Angeles ordinance, which was justified on the same grounds.

[These] decisions identify two analytically distinct grounds for challenging the constitutionality of a municipal ordinance regulating the display of signs. One is that the measure in effect restricts too little speech because its exemptions discriminate on the basis of the signs' messages. Alternatively, such provisions are subject to attack on the ground that they simply prohibit too much protected speech. The City of Ladue contends, first, that the Court of Appeals' reliance on the former rationale was misplaced because the City's regulatory purposes are content-neutral, and, second, that those purposes justify the comprehensiveness of the sign prohibition. A comment on the former contention will help explain why we ultimately base our decision on a rejection of the latter.

III. While surprising at first glance, the notion that a regulation of speech may be impermissibly underinclusive is firmly grounded in basic First Amendment principles. Thus, an exemption from an otherwise permissible regulation of speech may represent a governmental "attempt to give one side of a debatable public question an advantage in expressing its views to the people." First Nat. Bank of Boston v. Bellotti [1978; below, 12th Ed., p. 1368; Ind.Rts., p. 1039.] Alternatively, through the combined operation of a general speech restriction and its exemptions, the government might seek to select the "permissible subjects for public debate" and thereby to "control ... the search for political truth." Consolidated Edison Co. of N.Y. v. Public Service Comm'n of N.Y. [1980; above, 12th Ed., p. 1163; Ind.Rts., p. 834.]

The City argues that its sign ordinance implicates neither of these concerns, and that the Court of Appeals therefore erred in demanding a "compelling" justification for the exemptions. The mix of prohibitions and exemptions in the ordinance, Ladue maintains, reflects legitimate differences among the side effects of various kinds of signs. These differences are only adventitiously connected with content, and supply a sufficient justification, unrelated to the City's approval or disapproval of specific messages, for carving out the specified categories from the general ban. Thus, according to the Declaration of Findings, Policies, Interests, and Purposes supporting the ordinance, the permitted signs, unlike the prohibited signs, are unlikely to contribute to the dangers of "unlimited proliferation" associated with categories of signs that are not inherently limited in number. Because only a few residents will need to display "for sale" or "for rent" signs at any given time, permitting one such sign per marketed house does not threaten visual clutter. Because the City has only a few businesses, churches, and schools, the same rationale explains the exemption for on-site commercial and organizational signs. Moreover, some of the exempted categories (e.g., danger signs) respond to unique public needs to permit certain kinds of speech. Even if we assume the validity of these arguments, the exemptions in Ladue's ordinance nevertheless shed light on the separate question of whether the ordinance prohibits too much speech.

Exemptions from an otherwise legitimate regulation of a medium of speech may be noteworthy for a reason quite apart from the risks of viewpoint and content discrimination: they may diminish the credibility of the government's rationale for restricting speech in the first place. In this case, at the very least, the exemptions from Ladue's ordinance demonstrate that Ladue has concluded that the interest in allowing certain messages to be conveyed by means of residential signs outweighs the City's aesthetic interest in eliminating outdoor signs. Ladue has not imposed a flat ban on signs because it has determined that at least some of them are too vital to be banned.

Under the Court of Appeals' content discrimination rationale, the City might theoretically remove the defects in its ordinance by simply repealing all of the exemptions. If, however, the ordinance is also vulnerable because it prohibits too much speech, that solution would not save it. Moreover, if the prohibitions in Ladue's ordinance are impermissible, resting our decision on its exemptions would afford scant relief for respondent Gilleo. She is primarily concerned not with the scope of the exemptions available in other locations, such as commercial areas and on church property. She asserts a constitutional right to display an antiwar sign at her own home. Therefore, we first ask whether Ladue may properly prohibit Gilleo from displaying her sign, and then, only if necessary, consider the separate question whether it was improper for the City simultaneously to permit certain other signs. In examining the propriety of Ladue's near-total prohibition of residential signs, we will assume, arguendo, the validity of the City's submission that the various exemptions are free of impermissible content or viewpoint discrimination. The inquiry we undertake below into the adequacy of alternative channels of communication would also apply to a provision justified on those grounds.

IV. In Linmark we held that the City's interest in maintaining a stable, racially integrated neighborhood was not sufficient to support a prohibition of residential "For Sale" signs. We recognized that even such a narrow sign prohibition would have a deleterious effect on residents' ability to convey important information because alternatives were "far from satisfactory." Ladue's sign ordinance is supported principally by the City's interest in minimizing the visual clutter associated with signs, an interest that is concededly valid but certainly no more compelling than the interests at stake in Linmark. Moreover, whereas the ordinance in Linmark applied only to a form of commercial speech, Ladue's ordinance covers even such absolutely pivotal speech as a sign protesting an imminent governmental decision to go to war.

The impact on free communication of Ladue's broad sign prohibition, moreover, is manifestly greater than in Linmark. Gilleo and other residents of Ladue are forbidden to display virtually any "sign" on their property. The ordinance defines that term sweepingly. A prohibition is not always invalid merely because it applies to a sizeable category of speech; the sign ban we upheld in Vincent, for example, was quite broad. But in Vincent we specifically noted that the category of speech in question—signs placed on public property—was not a "uniquely valuable or important mode of communication," and that there was no evidence that "appellees' ability to communicate effectively is threatened by ever-increasing restrictions on expression." Here, in contrast, Ladue has almost completely foreclosed a venerable means of communication that is both unique and important. It has totally foreclosed that medium to political, religious, or personal messages. Signs that react to a local happening or express a view on a controversial issue both reflect and animate change in the life of a community. Often placed on lawns or in windows, residential signs play an important part in political campaigns, during which they are displayed to signal the resident's support for particular candidates, parties, or causes. They may not afford the same opportunities for conveying complex ideas as do other media, but residential signs have long been an important and distinct medium of expression.

Our prior decisions have voiced particular concern with laws that foreclose an entire medium of expression. Thus, we have held invalid ordinances that completely banned the distribution of pamphlets within the municipality, Lovell v. Griffin [1938; above, 12th Ed., p. 1254; Ind.Rts., p. 925], handbills on the public streets, Jamison v. Texas, 318 U.S. 413 (1943); the door-to-door distribution of literature, Martin v. Struthers [1943; above, 12th Ed., p. 1269; Ind.Rts., p. 940], and live entertainment, Schad v. Mount Ephraim [1981; above, 12th Ed., p. 1164; Ind.Rts., p. 835.] Although prohibitions foreclosing entire media may be completely free of content or viewpoint discrimination, the danger they pose to the freedom of speech is readily apparent—by eliminating a common means of speaking, such measures can suppress too much speech.

Ladue contends, however, that its ordinance is a mere regulation of the "time, place, or manner" of speech because residents remain free to convey their desired messages by other means, such as hand-held signs, "letters, handbills, flyers, telephone calls, newspaper advertisements, bumper stickers, speeches, and neighborhood or community meetings." However, even regulations that do not foreclose an entire medium of expression, but merely shift the time, place, or manner of its use, must "leave open ample alternative channels for communication." Clark v. Community for Creative Non–Violence [1984; immediately below.] In this case, we are not persuaded that adequate substitutes exist for the important medium of speech that Ladue has closed off. Displaying a sign from one's own residence often carries a message quite distinct from placing the same sign someplace else, or conveying the same text or picture by other means. Precisely because of their location, such signs provide information about the identity of the "speaker." As an early and eminent student of rhetoric [Aristotle] observed, the identity of the speaker is an important component of many attempts to persuade. A sign advocating "Peace in the Gulf" in the front lawn of a retired general or decorated war veteran may provoke a different reaction than the same sign in a 10–year–old child's bedroom window or the same message on a bumper sticker of a passing automobile. An espousal of socialism may carry different implications when displayed on the grounds of a stately mansion than when pasted on a factory wall or an ambulatory sandwich board.

Residential signs are an unusually cheap and convenient form of communication. Especially for persons of modest means or limited mobility, a yard or window sign may have no practical substitute. Even for the affluent, the added costs in money or time of taking out a newspaper advertisement, handing out leaflets on the street, or standing in front of one's house with a handheld sign may make the difference between participating and not participating in some public debate. Furthermore, a person who puts up a sign at her residence often intends to reach neighbors, an audience that could not be reached nearly as well by other means.

A special respect for individual liberty in the home has long been part of our culture and our law); that principle has special resonance when the government seeks to constrain a person's ability to speak there. Most Americans would be understandably dismayed, given that tradition, to learn that it was illegal to display from their window an 8- by 11-inch sign expressing their political views. Whereas the government's need to mediate among various competing uses, including expressive ones, for public streets and facilities is constant and unavoidable, its need to regulate temperate speech from the home is surely much less pressing.

Our decision that Ladue's ban on almost all residential signs violates the First Amendment by no means leaves the City powerless to address the ills that may be associated with residential signs. It bears mentioning that individual residents themselves have strong incentives to keep their own property values up and to prevent "visual clutter" in their own yards and neighborhoods—incentives markedly different from those of persons who erect signs on others' land, in others' neighborhoods, or on public property. Residents' self-interest diminishes the danger of the "unlimited" proliferation of residential signs that concerns the City of Ladue. We are confident that more temperate measures could in large part satisfy Ladue's stated regulatory needs without harm to the First Amendment rights of its citizens. As currently framed, however, the ordinance abridges those rights.

[Affirmed.]

Justice O'CONNOR, concurring.

It is unusual for us, when faced with a regulation that on its face draws content distinctions, to "assume, arguendo, the validity of the City's submission that the various exemptions are free of impermissible content or viewpoint discrimination." With rare exceptions, content discrimination in regulations of the speech of private citizens on private property or in a traditional public forum is presumptively impermissible, and this presumption is a very strong one. The normal inquiry that our doctrine dictates is, first, to determine whether a regulation is content-based or content-neutral, and then, based on the answer to that question, to apply the proper level of scrutiny. Over the years, some cogent criticisms have been leveled at our approach. And it is quite true that regulations are occasionally struck down because of their content-based nature, even though common sense may suggest that they are entirely reasonable. The content distinctions present in this ordinance may, to some, be a good example of this.

But though our rule has flaws, it has substantial merit as well. It is a rule, in an area where fairly precise rules are better than more discretionary and more subjective balancing tests. On a theoretical level, it reflects important insights into the meaning of the free speech principle—for instance, that content-based speech restrictions are especially likely to be improper attempts to value some forms of speech over others, or are particularly susceptible to being used by the government to distort public debate. On a practical level, it has in application generally led to seemingly sensible results. And, perhaps most importantly, no better alternative has yet come to light.

I would have preferred to apply our normal analytical structure in this case, which may well have required us to examine this law with the scrutiny appropriate to content-based regulations. Perhaps this would have forced us to confront some of the difficulties with the existing doctrine; perhaps it would have shown weaknesses in the rule, and led us to modify it to take into account the special factors this case presents. But such reexamination is part of the process by which our rules evolve and improve.

Nonetheless, I join the Court's opinion, because I agree with its conclusion in Part IV that even if the restriction were content-neutral, it would still be invalid, and because I do not think Part III casts any doubt on the propriety of our normal content discrimination inquiry.

12th ED., p. 1355; IND.RTS., p. 1026
Add after discussion of Tornillo:

ACCESS, CABLE TELEVISION, AND THE FIRST AMENDMENT

Red Lion Broadcasting upheld mandatory access and related restrictions on the editorial freedom of broadcasters, and Miami Herald v. Tornillo rejected arguably analogous requirements with respect to the print press. With the rise of cable television, a looming issue for some years has been the question of whether the Supreme Court would permit as many (or more) restrictions on the freedom of cable operators as it has permitted with respect to broadcasters, or instead treat cable operators as editors with the same First Amendment editorial freedom as was protected in Tornillo, or whether the unique characteristics of cable might warrant treatment different both from broadcast and from print. Although numerous lower court decisions had confronted various aspects of this issue over the past ten years, the Supreme Court repeatedly denied requests for certiorari, or dealt with cable television questions on other grounds.

Finally, the issue came before the Court, in a case that had most of the broadcast and cable industry actively involved as parties or amici. Although the broad question was the way in which the First Amendment would be applied to cable television, the specific issue before the Court was the constitutionality of the so-called "must carry" regulations. These regulations, part of the Cable Television Consumer Protection and

Competition Act of 1992, require operators of cable systems to carry local broadcast stations (both commercial and non-commercial) without charge to consumers. The number of broadcast signals that cable operators are required to carry under the regulations varies with the number of subscribers and cable channels, but can be up to as many as one third of the channels offered by the cable operator. The rationale for the must-carry regulations is an effort by Congress to preserve the competitive viability of broadcast stations, particularly local ones, in the face of a perceived competitive advantage by cable operators, most of whom have a monopoly in their markets. Moreover, Congress perceived that cable operators, in order to maximize their competitive advertising position, would have an incentive not to carry broadcast stations unless they were required by law to do so.

The cable operators challenged the must-carry regulations on First Amendment grounds, but in TURNER BROADCASTING SYSTEM, INC. v. FCC, 514 U.S. __ (1994), the Court did not make a final decision on the constitutionality of the must-carry rules. It did, however, go a long way toward establishing the constitutional framework within which many future regulations of the cable industry will be evaluated.

Justice KENNEDY wrote for the Court with respect to most of the issues dealt with in his opinion. He refused to re-evaluate the scarcity rationale of Red Lion, which he characterized as being based on the "unique physical limitations of the broadcast medium," but at the same time he also rejected the argument of the United States that the Red Lion approach ought to apply to cable as well. Although he recognized that there were similarities between cable and broadcast in market structure if not in physical characteristics, he rejected the argument that "dysfunction or failure in a speech market [is sufficient] to shield a speech regulation" from otherwise applicable First Amendment principles.

Turning then to general First Amendment principles, Justice Kennedy refused to characterize the must-carry regulations as content-based. "Although the provisions interfere with cable operators' editorial discretion by compelling them to offer carriage to a certain minimum number of broadcast stations, the extent of the interference does not depend upon the content of the cable operators' programming. [Nothing] in the Act imposes a restriction, penalty, or burden by reason of the views, programs, or stations the cable operator has selected or will select. [Moreover,] the privileges conferred by the must-carry provisions [on broadcasters] are also unrelated to content. The rules benefit all full-power broadcasters who request carriage—be they commercial or non-commercial, independent or network-affiliated, English or Spanish language, religious or secular. [Every] full power [broadcaster] is eligible, [provided] only that the broadcaster operates within the same television market as a cable system. [In] short, Congress' acknowledgment that broadcast television stations make a valuable contribution to the Nation's communications system does not render the must-carry scheme content-based."

Justice KENNEDY also rejected the cable operators' argument that strict scrutiny was required by Miami Herald v. Tornillo and Pacific Gas and Electric (immediately below), because cable operators operated as editors in the selection of material to appear on their systems. As a result, they argued, this "forced speech" could only be justified "if narrowly tailored to a compelling government interest." But this standard was inapplicable, Justice Kennedy concluded, because the access rules in those cases were content-based, and those involved here were content-neutral. The must-carry regulations "are not activated by any particular message spoken by cable operators and thus exact no content-based penalty." Two other features served for Justice Kennedy to distinguish Tornillo. "Given cable's long history of serving as a conduit for broadcast signals, there appears little risk that cable viewers would assume that the broadcast stations carried on a cable system convey ideas or messages endorsed by the cable operator. [In addition,] the asserted analogy to Tornillo ignores an important technological difference between newspapers and cable television. Although [both] may enjoy monopoly status in a given locale, the cable operator exercises far greater control over access to the relevant medium. A daily newspaper, no matter how secure its local monopoly, does not possess the power to obstruct readers' access to other competing publications—whether they be weekly local newspapers, or daily newspapers published in other cities. Thus, when a newspaper asserts exclusive control over its own news copy, it does not thereby prevent other newspapers from being distributed to willing recipients in the same locale. The same is not true of cable. [Simply] by virtue of its ownership of the essential pathway for cable speech, a cable operator can prevent its subscribers from obtaining access to programming it chooses to exclude."

After rejecting several other arguments for strict scrutiny, such as the argument that the must-carry regulations favored some speakers or some segments of the press over others, Justice Kennedy concluded that the appropriate analytical framework, established by United States v. O'Brien and Ward v. Rock Against Racism, was "the intermediate level of scrutiny applicable to content-neutral regulations that impose an incidental burden on speech." Applying this standard, he said the Court had "no difficulty" concluding that the government interest in promoting competition and preserving broadcasting were "important governmental interests." When he turned to the question whether the must-carry regulations would in fact advance those interests, however, Justice Kennedy found the record insufficient to make that determination. Writing now only for a plurality, he acknowledged the importance of respecting the predictive, factual, and economic judgments of Congress, but cautioned "that Congress' predictive judgments are entitled to substantial deference does not mean, however, that they are insulated from meaningful judicial review altogether. [The] obligation to exercise independent judgment [of the facts bearing on issues of constitutional law] when First Amendment rights are implicated is not a license to reweigh the evidence de novo, or to replace Congress' factual predictions with our own. Rather, it is to assure that, in formulating its judgments, Congress has drawn reasonable inferences based on substantial evidence." Applying this standard, Justice Kennedy found a "paucity of evidence indicating that broadcast television is in jeopardy," as well as no "findings concerning the actual effects of must-carry on the speech of cable operators and cable programmers." Because, he argued, these issues are central to the "narrow tailoring step of the O'Brien analysis," he concluded that it was "necessary to permit the parties to develop a more thorough factual record, and to allow the District Court to resolve any factual disputes remaining," and so a remand was necessary.

Justice BLACKMUN's brief concurrence emphasized the importance of deferring to congressional factual judgments, although he agreed with the remand. Justice STEVENS, concurring in part and concurring in the judgment, agreed with all of Justice Kennedy's opinion except Justice Kennedy's reasons for remand, for Justice Stevens believed the record sufficient to sustain the regulations. But he agreed to the remand nevertheless. "It is [my] view that we should affirm the judgment of the [three-judge] District Court. Were I to vote to affirm, however, no disposition of this appeal would command the support of a majority of this Court. An accommodation is therefore necessary. Accordingly, because I am in substantial agreement with Justice Kennedy's analysis of the case, I concur in the judgment vacating and remanding."

Justice O'CONNOR, joined by Justices Scalia and Ginsburg, and in part by Justice Thomas, concurred in part and dissented in part. "I cannot avoid the conclusion that [the Act's] preference for broadcasters over cable programmers is justified with reference to content. [Preferences] for diversity of viewpoint, for localism, for educational programming, and for news and public affairs all make reference to content. They may not reflect hostility to particular points of view, or a desire to suppress certain subjects because they are controversial or offensive. They may be quite benignly motivated. But benign motivation [is] not enough to avoid the need for strict scrutiny of content-based justifications. [My] conclusion that the must-carry rules are content-based leads me to conclude that they are an impermissible restraint on the cable operators' editorial discretion as well as on the cable programmers' speech." As a result, Justice O'Connor would have reversed the judgment below and held the must-carry regulations unconstitutional. Justice GINSBURG wrote a short separate opinion, joining those parts of the Court's opinion subjecting cable television to general First Amendment principles and not the broadcast-specific ones of Red Lion, but stressing that she saw this as a case of content-based regulation, as to which the government's justifications were insufficient.

12th ED., p. 1356; IND.RTS., p. 1027
Add after Pacific Gas and Electric:

HURLEY AND SOUTH BOSTON ALLIED WAR VETERANS COUNCIL v. IRISH–AMERICAN GAY, LESBIAN AND BISEXUAL GROUP OF BOSTON

518 U.S. ___, 115 S.Ct. ___, 132 L.Ed.2d ___ (1995).

Justice SOUTER delivered the opinion of the Court.

The issue in this case is whether Massachusetts may require private citizens who organize a parade to include among the marchers a group imparting a message the organizers do not wish to convey. We hold that such a mandate violates the First Amendment.

I. March 17 is set aside for two celebrations in South Boston. As early as 1737, some people in Boston observed the feast of the apostle to Ireland, and since 1776 the day has marked the evacuation of royal troops and Loyalists from the city, prompted by the guns captured at Ticonderoga and set up on Dorchester Heights under General Washington's command. [Although] the General Court [the legislature—ed.] of Massachusetts did not officially designate March 17 as Evacuation Day until 1938, the City Council of Boston had previously sponsored public celebrations of Evacuation Day, including notable commemorations on the centennial in 1876, and on the 125th anniversary in 1901, with its parade, salute, concert, and fireworks display.

The tradition of formal sponsorship by the city came to an end in 1947, however, when Mayor James Michael Curley himself granted authority to organize and conduct the St. Patrick's Day–Evacuation Day Parade to the petitioner South Boston Allied War Veterans Council, an unincorporated association of individuals elected from various South Boston veterans groups. Every year since that time, the Council has applied for and received a permit for the parade, which at times has included as many as 20,000 marchers and drawn up to 1 million watchers. No other applicant has ever applied for that permit. Through 1992, the city allowed the Council to use the city's official seal, and provided printing services as well as direct funding.

1992 was the year that a number of gay, lesbian, and bisexual descendants of the Irish immigrants joined together with other supporters to form the respondent organization, GLIB, to march in the parade as a way to express pride in their Irish heritage as openly gay, lesbian, and bisexual individuals, to demonstrate that there are such men and women among those so descended, and to express their solidarity with like individuals who sought to march in New York's St. Patrick's Day Parade. Although the Council denied GLIB's application to take part in the 1992 parade, GLIB obtained a state-court order to include its contingent, which marched "uneventfully" among that year's 10,000 participants and 750,000 spectators.

In 1993, after the Council had again refused to admit GLIB to the upcoming parade, the organization and some of its members filed this suit against the Council, the individual petitioner John J. "Wacko" Hurley, and the City of Boston, alleging violations of the State and Federal Constitutions and of the state public accommodations law, which prohibits "any distinction, discrimination or restriction on account of . . . sexual orientation . . . relative to the admission of any person to, or treatment in any place of public accommodation, resort or amusement." Mass.Gen.Laws § 272:98. After finding that "[f]or at least the past 47 years, the Parade has traveled the same basic route along the public streets of South Boston, providing entertainment, amusement, and recreation to participants and spectators alike," the state trial court ruled

that the parade fell within the statutory definition of a public accommodation, which includes "any place ... which is open to and accepts or
solicits the patronage of the general public and, without limiting the
generality of this definition, whether or not it be ... (6) a boardwalk or
other public highway [or] ... (8) a place of public amusement, recreation, sport, exercise or entertainment." The court found that the
Council had no written criteria and employed no particular procedures
for admission, voted on new applications in batches, had occasionally
admitted groups who simply showed up at the parade without having
submitted an application, and did "not generally inquire into the specific
messages or views of each applicant." The court consequently rejected
the Council's contention that the parade was "private" (in the sense of
being exclusive), holding instead that "the lack of genuine selectivity in
choosing participants and sponsors demonstrates that the Parade is a
public event." It found the parade to be "eclectic," containing a wide
variety of "patriotic, commercial, political, moral, artistic, religious,
athletic, public service, trade union, and eleemosynary themes," as well
as conflicting messages. While noting that the Council had indeed
excluded the Ku Klux Klan and ROAR (an antibusing group), it attributed little significance to these facts, concluding ultimately that "[t]he
only common theme among the participants and sponsors is their public
involvement in the Parade."

The court rejected the Council's assertion that the exclusion of
"groups with sexual themes merely formalized [the fact] that the Parade
expresses traditional religious and social values," and found the Council's "final position [to be] that GLIB would be excluded because of its
values and its message, i.e., its members' sexual orientation." This
position, in the court's view, was not only violative of the public
accommodations law but "paradoxical" as well, since "a proper celebration of St. Patrick's and Evacuation Day requires diversity and inclusiveness." The court rejected the notion that GLIB's admission would
trample on the Council's First Amendment rights since the court understood that constitutional protection of any interest in expressive association would "requir[e] focus on a specific message, theme, or group"
absent from the parade. "Given the [Council's] lack of selectivity in
choosing participants and failure to circumscribe the marchers' message," the court found it "impossible to discern any specific expressive
purpose entitling the Parade to protection under the First Amendment."
It concluded that the parade is "not an exercise of [the Council's]
constitutionally protected right of expressive association," but instead
"an open recreational event that is subject to the public accommodations
law." [Accordingly,] it ruled that "GLIB is entitled to participate in the
Parade on the same terms and conditions as other participants." The
Supreme Judicial Court of Massachusetts affirmed, seeing nothing clearly erroneous in the trial judge's findings that GLIB was excluded from
the parade based on the sexual orientation of its members, that it was
impossible to detect an expressive purpose in the parade, that there was
no state action, and that the parade was a public accommodation within
the meaning of § 272:92A. [We] granted certiorari to determine whether the requirement to admit a parade contingent expressing a message

not of the private organizers' own choosing violates the First Amendment. We hold that it does and reverse.

II. Given the scope of the issues as originally joined in this case, it is worth noting some that have fallen aside in the course of the litigation, before reaching us. Although the Council presents us with a First Amendment claim, respondents do not. Neither do they press a claim that the Council's action has denied them equal protection of the laws in violation of the Fourteenth Amendment. While the guarantees of free speech and equal protection guard only against encroachment by the government and "erec[t] no shield against merely private conduct" Shelley v. Kraemer [1948, above, 12th Ed., p. 899; Ind.Rts., p. 570], respondents originally argued that the Council's conduct was not purely private, but had the character of state action. The trial court's review of the city's involvement led it to find otherwise, however, and although the Supreme Judicial Court did not squarely address the issue, it appears to have affirmed the trial court's decision on that point as well as the others. In any event, respondents have not brought that question up either in a cross-petition for certiorari or in their briefs filed in this Court. When asked at oral argument whether they challenged the conclusion by the Massachusetts' courts that no state action is involved in the parade, respondents' counsel answered that they "do not press that issue here." In this Court, then, their claim for inclusion in the parade rests solely on the Massachusetts public accommodations law.

There is no corresponding concession from the other side, however, and certainly not to the state courts' characterization of the parade as lacking the element of expression for purposes of the First Amendment. Accordingly, our review of petitioners' claim that their activity is indeed in the nature of protected speech carries with it a constitutional duty to conduct an independent examination of the record as a whole, without deference to the trial court. Bose Corp. v. Consumers Union of United States, Inc., 466 U.S. 485 (1984). The "requirement of independent appellate review ... is a rule of federal constitutional law," which does not limit our deference to a trial court on matters of witness credibility, Harte–Hanks Communications, Inc. v. Connaughton, 491 U.S. 657 (1989), but which generally requires us to "review the finding of facts by a State court ... where a conclusion of law as to a Federal right and a finding of fact are so intermingled as to make it necessary, in order to pass upon the Federal question, to analyze the facts." Fiske v. Kansas, 274 U.S. 380 (1927). This obligation rests upon us simply because the reaches of the First Amendment are ultimately defined by the facts it is held to embrace, and we must thus decide for ourselves whether a given course of conduct falls on the near or far side of the line of constitutional protection. Even where a speech case has originally been tried in a federal court, subject to the provision of Federal Rule of Civil Procedure 52(a) that "[f]indings of fact ... shall not be set aside unless clearly erroneous," we are obliged to make a fresh examination of crucial facts. Hence, in this case, though we are confronted with the state courts' conclusion that the factual characteristics of petitioners' activity place it within the vast realm of non-expressive conduct, our obligation is to " 'make an independent examination of the whole record,' ... so as to assure ourselves that th[is] judgment does not constitute a forbidden intrusion on the field of free expression." New York Times v. Sullivan.

III. A. If there were no reason for a group of people to march from here to there except to reach a destination, they could make the trip without expressing any message beyond the fact of the march itself. Some people might call such a procession a parade, but it would not be much of one. Hence, we use the word "parade" to indicate marchers who are making some sort of collective point, not just to each other but to bystanders along the way. Indeed a parade's dependence on watchers is so extreme that nowadays, as with Bishop Berkeley's celebrated tree, "if a parade or demonstration receives no media coverage, it may as well not have happened." Parades are thus a form of expression, not just motion, and the inherent expressiveness of marching to make a point explains our cases involving protest marches.

The protected expression that inheres in a parade is not limited to its banners and songs, however, for the Constitution looks beyond written or spoken words as mediums of expression. Noting that "[s]ymbolism is a primitive but effective way of communicating ideas," West Virginia Bd. of Ed. v. Barnette, our cases have recognized that the First Amendment shields such acts as saluting a flag (and refusing to do so), wearing an arm band to protest a war, displaying a red flag, and even "[m]arching, walking or parading" in uniforms displaying the swastika. As some of these examples show, a narrow, succinctly articulable message is not a condition of constitutional protection, which if confined to expressions conveying a "particularized message," would never reach the unquestionably shielded painting of Jackson Pollock, music of Arnold Schonberg, or Jabberwocky verse of Lewis Carroll.

Not many marches, then, are beyond the realm of expressive parades, and the South Boston celebration is not one of them. Spectators line the streets; people march in costumes and uniforms, carrying flags and banners with all sorts of messages (e.g., "England get out of Ireland," "Say no to drugs"); marching bands and pipers play, floats are pulled along, and the whole show is broadcast over Boston television. To be sure, we agree with the state courts that in spite of excluding some applicants, the Council is rather lenient in admitting participants. But a private speaker does not forfeit constitutional protection simply by combining multifarious voices, or by failing to edit their themes to isolate an exact message as the exclusive subject matter of the speech. Nor, under our precedent, does First Amendment protection require a speaker to generate, as an original matter, each item featured in the communication. Cable operators, for example, are engaged in protected speech activities even when they only select programming originally produced by others. Turner Broadcasting. For that matter, the presentation of an edited compilation of speech generated by other persons is a staple of most newspapers' opinion pages, which, of course, fall squarely within the core of First Amendment security, Miami Herald v. Tornillo, as does even the simple selection of a paid noncommercial advertisement for inclusion in a daily paper. The selection of contingents to make a parade is entitled to similar protection.

Respondents' participation as a unit in the parade was equally expressive. GLIB was formed for the very purpose of marching in it, as the trial court found, in order to celebrate its members' identity as openly gay, lesbian, and bisexual descendants of the Irish immigrants, to show that there are such individuals in the community, and to support the like men and women who sought to march in the New York parade. The organization distributed a fact sheet describing the members' intentions, and the record otherwise corroborates the expressive nature of GLIB's participation. In 1993, members of GLIB marched behind a shamrock-strewn banner with the simple inscription "Irish American Gay, Lesbian and Bisexual Group of Boston." GLIB understandably seeks to communicate its ideas as part of the existing parade, rather than staging one of its own.

B. The Massachusetts public accommodations law [has] a venerable history. At common law, innkeepers, smiths, and others who "made profession of a public employment," were prohibited from refusing, without good reason, to serve a customer. As one of the 19th century English judges put it, the rule was that "[t]he innkeeper is not to select his guests[;] [h]e has no right to say to one, you shall come into my inn, and to another you shall not, as every one coming and conducting himself in a proper manner has a right to be received; and for this purpose innkeepers are a sort of public servants." Rex v. Ivens, 173 Eng.Rep. 94 (1835).

After the Civil War, [Massachusetts] was the first State to codify this principle to ensure access to public accommodations regardless of race. See Act Forbidding Unjust Discrimination on Account of Color or Race, 1865 Mass. Acts, ch. 277 (May 16, 1865). In prohibiting discrimination "in any licensed inn, in any public place of amusement, public conveyance or public meeting," the original statute already expanded upon the common law, which had not conferred any right of access to places of public amusement. As with many public accommodations statutes across the Nation, the legislature continued to broaden the scope of legislation, to the point that the law today prohibits discrimination on the basis of "race, color, religious creed, national origin, sex, sexual orientation ..., deafness, blindness or any physical or mental disability or ancestry" in "the admission of any person to, or treatment in any place of public accommodation, resort or amusement." Provisions like these are well within the State's usual power to enact when a legislature has reason to believe that a given group is the target of discrimination, and they do not, as a general matter, violate the First or Fourteenth Amendments. Roberts v. United States Jaycees [1984, below, 12th Ed., p. 1408; Ind.Rts., p. 1079.] Nor is this statute unusual in any obvious way, since it does not, on its face, target speech or discriminate on the basis of its content, the focal point of its prohibition being rather on the act of discriminating against individuals in the provision of publicly available goods, privileges, and services on the proscribed grounds.

C. In the case before us, however, the Massachusetts law has been applied in a peculiar way. Its enforcement does not address any dispute about the participation of openly gay, lesbian, or bisexual individuals in various units admitted to the parade. The petitioners disclaim any intent to exclude homosexuals as such, and no individual member of GLIB claims to have been excluded from parading as a member of any group that the Council has approved to march. Instead, the disagreement goes to the admission of GLIB as its own parade unit carrying its own banner. Since every participating unit affects the message conveyed by the private organizers, the state courts' application of the statute produced an order essentially requiring petitioners to alter the expressive content of their parade. Although the state courts spoke of the parade as a place of public accommodation, once the expressive character of both the parade and the marching GLIB contingent is understood, it becomes apparent that the state courts' application of the statute had the effect of declaring the sponsors' speech itself to be the public accommodation. Under this approach any contingent of protected individuals with a message would have the right to participate in petitioners' speech, so that the communication produced by the private organizers would be shaped by all those protected by the law who wished to join in with some expressive demonstration of their own. But this use of the State's power violates the fundamental rule of protection under the First Amendment, that a speaker has the autonomy to choose the content of his own message.

"Since all speech inherently involves choices of what to say and what to leave unsaid," Pacific Gas & Electric, one important manifestation of the principle of free speech is that one who chooses to speak may also decide "what not to say." [Outside the commercial advertising] context [the state] may not compel affirmance of a belief with which the speaker disagrees. Indeed this general rule, that the speaker has the right to tailor the speech, applies not only to expressions of value, opinion, or endorsement, but equally to statements of fact the speaker would rather avoid, subject, perhaps, to the permissive law of defamation. Nor is the rule's benefit restricted to the press, being enjoyed by business corporations generally and by ordinary people engaged in unsophisticated expression as well as by professional publishers. Its point is simply the point of all speech protection, which is to shield just those choices of content that in someone's eyes are misguided, or even hurtful. Petitioners' claim to the benefit of this principle of autonomy to control one's own speech is as sound as the South Boston parade is expressive. Rather like a composer, the Council selects the expressive units of the parade from potential participants, and though the score may not produce a particularized message, each contingent's expression in the Council's eyes comports with what merits celebration on that day. Even if this view gives the Council credit for a more considered judgment than it actively made, the Council clearly decided to exclude a message it did not like from the communication it chose to make, and that is enough to invoke its right as a private speaker to shape its expression by speaking on one subject while remaining silent on another. The message it disfavored is not difficult to identify. Although GLIB's point (like the Council's) is not wholly articulate, a contingent marching behind the organization's banner would at least bear witness to the fact that some Irish are gay, lesbian, or bisexual, and the presence of the organized marchers would suggest their view that people of their sexual orientations have as much claim to unqualified social acceptance as heterosexuals and indeed as members of parade units organized around other identifying characteristics. The parade's organizers may not believe these facts about Irish sexuality to be so, or they may object to unqualified social acceptance of gays and lesbians or have some other reason for wishing to keep GLIB's message out of the parade. But whatever the reason, it boils down to the choice of a speaker not to propound a particular point of view, [a choice] beyond the government's power to control.

Respondents argue that any tension between this rule and the Massachusetts law falls short of unconstitutionality, citing the most recent of our cases on the general subject of compelled access for expressive purposes, Turner Broadcasting. There we reviewed regulations requiring cable operators to set aside channels for designated broadcast signals, and applied only intermediate scrutiny. Respondents contend on this authority that admission of GLIB to the parade would not threaten the core principle of speaker's autonomy because the Council, like a cable operator, is merely "a conduit" for the speech of participants in the parade "rather than itself a speaker." But this metaphor is not apt here, because GLIB's participation would likely be perceived as having resulted from the Council's customary determination about a unit admitted to the parade, that its message was worthy of presentation and quite possibly of support as well. A newspaper, similarly, "is more than a passive receptacle or conduit for news, comment, and advertising," and we have held that "[t]he choice of material . . . and the decisions made as to limitations on the size and content . . . and treatment of public issues . . .—whether fair or unfair—constitute the exercise of editorial control and judgment" upon which the State can not intrude. Tornillo. [When] dissemination of a view contrary to one's own is forced upon a speaker intimately connected with the communication advanced, the speaker's right to autonomy over the message is compromised.

Parades and demonstrations, in contrast [to the offerings of cable television operators], are not understood to be so neutrally presented or selectively viewed. Unlike the programming offered on various channels by a cable network, the parade does not consist of individual, unrelated segments that happen to be transmitted together for individual selection by members of the audience. Although each parade unit generally identifies itself, each is understood to contribute something to a common theme, and accordingly there is no customary practice whereby private sponsors disavow "any identity of viewpoint" between themselves and the selected participants. Practice follows practicability here, for such disclaimers would be quite curious in a moving parade. Without deciding on the precise significance of the likelihood of misattribution, it nonetheless becomes clear that in the context of an expressive parade, as with a protest march, the parade's overall message is distilled from the individual presentations along the way, and each unit's expression is perceived by spectators as part of the whole.

[In] this case [there] is no [claim] that some speakers will be destroyed in the absence of the challenged law. True, the size and success of petitioners' parade makes it an enviable vehicle for the dissemination of GLIB's views, but that fact, without more, would fall far short of supporting a claim that petitioners enjoy an abiding monopoly of access to spectators. Considering that GLIB presumably would have had a fair shot (under neutral criteria developed by the city) at obtaining a parade permit of its own, respondents have not shown that petitioners enjoy the capacity to "silence the voice of competing speakers," as cable operators do with respect to program providers who wish to reach subscribers.

[The] statute is a piece of protective legislation that announces no purpose beyond the object both expressed and apparent in its provisions, which is to prevent any denial of access to (or discriminatory treatment in) public accommodations on proscribed grounds, including sexual orientation. On its face, the object of the law is to ensure by statute for gays and lesbians desiring to make use of public accommodations what the old common law promised to any member of the public wanting a meal at the inn, that accepting the usual terms of service, they will not be turned away merely on the proprietor's exercise of personal preference. When the law is applied to expressive activity in the way it was done here, its apparent object is simply to require speakers to modify the content of their expression to whatever extent beneficiaries of the law choose to alter it with messages of their own. But in the absence of some further, legitimate end, this object is merely to allow exactly what the general rule of speaker's autonomy forbids.

It might, of course, have been argued that a broader objective is apparent: that the ultimate point of forbidding acts of discrimination toward certain classes is to produce a society free of the corresponding biases. Requiring access to a speaker's message would thus be not an end in itself, but a means to produce speakers free of the biases, whose expressive conduct would be at least neutral toward the particular classes, obviating any future need for correction. But if this indeed is the point of applying the state law to expressive conduct, it is a decidedly fatal objective. Having availed itself of the public thoroughfares "for purposes of assembly [and] communicating thoughts between citizens," the Council is engaged in a use of the streets that has "from ancient times, been a part of the privileges, immunities, rights, and liberties of citizens." Hague v. CIO. Our tradition of free speech commands that a speaker who takes to the street corner to express his views in this way should be free from interference by the State based on the content of what he says. The very idea that a noncommercial speech restriction be used to produce thoughts and statements acceptable to some groups or, indeed, all people, grates on the First Amendment, for it amounts to nothing less than a proposal to limit speech in the service of orthodox expression. The Speech Clause has no more certain antithesis. While the law is free to promote all sorts of conduct in place of harmful behavior, it is not free to interfere with speech for no better reason than promoting an approved message or discouraging a disfavored one, however enlightened either purpose may strike the government.

New York State Club Association [1989, below, 12th Ed., p. 1409; Ind.Rts., p. 1080] is also instructive by the contrast it provides. There, we turned back a facial challenge to a state antidiscrimination statute on the assumption that the expressive associational character of a dining club with over 400 members could be sufficiently attenuated to permit application of the law even to such a private organization, but we also recognized that the State did not prohibit exclusion of those whose views were at odds with positions espoused by the general club memberships. In other words, although the association provided public benefits to which a State could ensure equal access, it was also engaged in expressive activity; compelled access to the benefit [did] not trespass on the organization's message itself. If we were to analyze this case strictly along those lines, GLIB would lose. Assuming the parade to be large enough and a source of benefits (apart from its expression) that would generally justify a mandated access provision, GLIB could nonetheless be refused admission as an expressive contingent with its own message just as readily as a private club could exclude an applicant whose manifest views were at odds with a position taken by the club's existing members.

IV. Our holding today rests not on any particular view about the Council's message but on the Nation's commitment to protect freedom of speech. Disapproval of a private speaker's statement does not legitimize use of the Commonwealth's power to compel the speaker to alter the message by including one more acceptable to others.

[Reversed.]

Chapter 13(8)

FREEDOM OF EXPRESSION IN SOME SPECIAL CONTEXTS

12th ED., p. 1367; IND. RTS., p. 1038

Add at end of footnote 2:

Campaign finance reform failed to pass in the 103rd Congress, but the 104th Congress has several proposals before it including constitutional amendment proposals S.J.Res. 18 and H.J.Res. 65. S.J.Res. 18 would grant Congress, state and local governments the power to set reasonable expenditure limits for elections. H.J.Res. 65 bundles together a term limits proposal with a campaign finance clause that would prohibit receiving contributions or making expenditures until 18 months before the end of the term being served, and gives Congress the power to limit contributions and expenditures. Other legislation affecting campaign finance includes H.R. 274, providing for free broadcast advertising, H.R. 732, a bill which focuses on House of Representatives campaign finance reform, H.R. 1837, a bill to establish a commission on Federal election reform, H.R. 1427, the Campaign Finance System Reform Act, and S. 10, the Comprehensive Congressional Reform Act of 1995. The chance of passage for all of these proposals is dim in a year before a Presidential election.

12th ED., p. 1374; IND. RTS., p. 1045

Add as new Notes after Note 4:

5. *Restrictions on polling place electioneering.* In BURSON v. FREEMAN, 504 U.S. 191 (1992), the Court confronted an issue mentioned but not decided in Mills v. Alabama (1966, noted above, 12th Ed., p. 1362; Ind.Rts., p. 1033): the extent to which a state could regulate electioneering and related conduct in the immediate vicinity of a polling place. At issue was a Tennessee law that created what was in effect "an election-day 'campaign-free zone.'" Within 100 feet of any polling place, there was to be no solicitation of votes, no distribution of campaign literature, and no display of campaign posters or signs. Although there was no opinion of the Court, a majority of the Supreme Court held that the law was constitutionally permissible.

Justice BLACKMUN's plurality opinion, joined by Chief Justice Rehnquist and Justices White and Kennedy, reiterated that the First Amendment's hostility to content regulation extended to regulations that excluded entire topics (as here) as well as regulations that excluded particular viewpoints. Thus he maintained that this statute must be subject to "exacting scrutiny" according to the standard formula (see Perry Education Association v. Perry Local Educators Ass'n, 1983, set out above, 12th Ed., p. 1317; Ind.Rts., p. 988) of requiring that a regulation be "necessary to serve a compelling interest and that it [be] narrowly drawn to achieve that end." Justice Blackmun first agreed that Tennessee's interest in election integrity and in protecting the right of citizens "to vote freely for the candidates of their choice" satisfied the compelling interest standard. And while acknowledging that laws rarely satisfied the requirement that they be "necessary" to serve compelling interests, he maintained that this was one of those laws. "Today, all 50 States limit access to the areas in or around polling places [in order to prevent] voter intimidation and election fraud. [The] link between ballot secrecy and some restricted zone surrounding the voting area is not merely timing, it is common sense. The only way to preserve the secrecy of the ballot is to limit access to the area around the voter. [The] real question then is *how large* a restricted zone is permissible or sufficiently tailored. [We] do not think that the minor geographic limitation of [this law] constitutes [a] significant impingement [on constitutionally protected rights]. [The State has] asserted that the exercise of free speech rights conflicts with another fundamental right, the right to cast a ballot in an election free from the taint of intimidation and fraud. A long history, a substantial consensus, and simple common sense show that some restricted zone around polling places is necessary to protect that fundamental right. Given the conflict between these two rights, we hold that requiring solicitors to stand 100 feet from the entrances to polling places does not constitute an unconstitutional compromise."

Justice KENNEDY, although joining the plurality opinion, also filed his own concurring opinion. Reiterating his concerns about the compelling interest standard as applied to content-based restrictions (see his opinion in Simon & Schuster, Inc. v. New York State Crime Victims Board, 1991, described below, addition to 12th Ed., p. 1499; Ind.Rts., p. 1170), Justice Kennedy maintained that the compelling interest standard may nevertheless "have a legitimate role [in] sorting out what is and what is not a content-based restriction. [Here] the compelling interest standard is adopted [not] to justify or condemn a category of suppression but to determine the accuracy of the justification the State gives for its law. The outcome of that analysis is that the justification for the speech restriction is to protect another constitutional right. [There] is a narrow area in which the First Amendment permits freedom of expression to yield to the extent necessary for the accommodation of another constitutional right. That principle can apply here[, for the State] acts to protect the integrity of the polling place where citizens exercise the [fundamental] right to vote."

Justice SCALIA concurred in the judgment. He maintained that the definition of a public forum must necessarily, in order to "be a tool of analysis rather than a conclusory label, [derive] its content from *tradition*. Because restrictions on speech around polling places on election day are as venerable a part of the American tradition as the secret ballot, [this law] does not restrict speech in a traditional public forum, and the 'exacting scrutiny' the Court purports to apply is inappropriate."

Justice STEVENS, joined by Justices O'Connor and Souter, dissented. Although he agreed with the use of the compelling interest standard, he disagreed that that standard was satisfied here. Because Mills v. Alabama precluded last-minute campaigning from being a compelling state interest, he argued, only laws whose interests were limited to securing orderly access to the polls could survive First Amendment scrutiny. "[T]he Tennessee statute does not merely regulate conduct that might inhibit voting; it bars the simple 'display of campaign materials.' Bumper stickers on parked cars and lapel buttons on pedestrians are taboo. The notion that such sweeping restrictions on speech are necessary to maintain the freedom to vote and the integrity of the ballot box borders on the absurd. [The plurality's] analysis is deeply flawed; it confuses history with necessity, and mistakes the traditional for the indispensable. The plurality's reasoning combines two logical errors: First, the plurality assumes that a practice's long life itself establishes its necessity; and, second, the plurality assumes that a practice that was once necessary remains necessary until it is ended. [Our] elections are far less corrupt, far more civil, and far more democratic today than 100 years ago. These salutary developments have substantially eliminated the need for what is [a] sweeping suppression of core political speech. [Tennessee's] content-based discrimination is particularly problematic because [it] will inevitably favor certain groups of candidates[, those which] rely heavily on last-minute campaigning. Candidates with fewer resources, candidates for lower visibility offices, and 'grassroots' candidates benefit disproportionately from last-minute campaigning near the polling place. [The] hubbub of campaign workers outside a polling place may be a nuisance, but it is also the sound of a vibrant democracy." *

6. *Issues of disclosure and identification.* Buckley upheld various disclosure requirements, and other campaign finance laws contain similar requirements. To what extent are disclosure requirements with respect to contributors and expenditures in tension with the constitutional right of anonymous political advocacy most recently reaffirmed in McIntyre v. Ohio Elections Commission, 517 U.S. ___ (1995), described at length above, addition to 12th Ed., p. 1270; Ind.Rts., p. 941? The Court in McIntyre took pains to distinguish Buckley, but the possibility remains that McIntyre opens the door to future challenges to various forms of compelled disclosure in the context of campaign contributions and expenditures.

12th ED., p. 1393; IND. RTS., p. 1064
Add as new Note after Note 3 on Landmark:

4. *Public statements by parties and attorneys.* Most cases involving speech allegedly harmful to the administration of justice involve speakers not themselves part of the proceedings, but in GENTILE v. STATE BAR OF NEVADA, 501 U.S. 1030 (1991), the Court confronted the extent to which the First Amendment circumscribed the power of courts to restrict the speech of litigants and attorneys. Gentile was the attorney for the defendant in a widely publicized criminal trial, and was reprimanded by the State Bar of Nevada for holding a press conference shortly after his client's indictment at which he made statements purportedly in violation of the Nevada Supreme Court rule modeled after ABA Model Rule of Professional Conduct 3.6, which prohibits public extrajudicial statements about pending litigation that a lawyer knows or should know would "have a substantial likelihood of materially prejudicing an adjudicative proceeding."

---

* Justice Thomas took no part in the decision of the case.

Writing for a majority on the issue of the standard to be applied in evaluating such a rule, Chief Justice REHNQUIST rejected both a "clear and present danger" or "imminent threat" standard, starting with the premise that extrajudicial comments by attorneys about facts or evidence to be presented "undermine" the "basic tenet" that "the outcome of a criminal trial is to be decided by impartial jurors." He also relied on the numerous restrictions imposed on "participants in the litigation" in the courtroom and in discovery (see Seattle Times Co. v. Rhinehart, 467 U.S. 20 (1984), upholding restrictions on public disclosure of information secured in the course of discovery), concluding that prior cases "rather plainly indicate that the speech of lawyers representing clients in pending cases may be regulated under a less demanding standard than that established for regulation of the press in Nebraska Press Association v. Stuart [1976; described below, 12th Ed., p. 1467; Ind. Rts., p. 1138], and the cases which preceded it." As a result, the majority specifically approved the "substantial likelihood of material prejudice" standard adopted by the majority of states, taking it to be an appropriate result of the "balance" between the interests protected by the First Amendment and a state's interests in protecting the "integrity and fairness" of its judicial system, and finding it to be appropriately narrowly tailored, viewpoint neutral, and in furtherance of a "substantial" state interest.

When it came to applying this principle to this case, however, the Chief Justice's opinion no longer represented the majority, for Justice O'CONNOR, who agreed with the Chief Justice on the general principles to be employed, thought that the Nevada rule in this case was unconstitutionally vague. She thus agreed as to outcome with the opinion of Justice KENNEDY, who announced the judgment of the Court, and who, joined by Justices Marshall, Blackmun, and Stevens, argued that this was a case of political speech (Gentile had argued that his client was a scapegoat for what was in fact a case of theft by the police) and could only be restricted, even in this context, when there was "imminent and substantial harm." Justice Kennedy went on to note that there was nothing special about the words "clear and present danger," and just as the words "serious and imminent threat" could represent the same idea and thus be constitutionally permissible, so too could a "substantial likelihood of material prejudice" standard differ from that only by "mere semantics." But that was not the case as the Rule had been interpreted in Nevada, however, and he thus found this rule as interpreted both excessively vague and insufficiently speech-protective. Moreover, there was nothing in the record indicating to him that the attorney here knew or could have known that his statements had a substantial likelihood of causing material prejudice.

12th ED., p. 1402; IND. RTS., p. 1073
Add at end of footnote 2 (on p. 1403 (1074)):

The Court continues to struggle with distinguishing between constitutionally permissible and constitutionally impermissible charges levied on members of public employee unions or their equivalents. In Lehnert v. Ferris Faculty Association, 500 U.S. 507 (1991), a remarkably complex alignment of opinions demonstrated the continuing intractability of the problem. Although Justice Scalia, joined by Justices O'Connor, Souter, and (in large part) Kennedy, maintained that the First Amendment precludes imposing on dissenters charges for any union activities not part of the union's *statutory* duties, Justice Blackmun's plurality opinion, joined by Chief Justice Rehnquist and Justices White and Stevens, adopted a narrower rule pursuant to which permissible charges were not limited to those part of the union's statutory mandate, but could include charges for "legislative lobbying or other union political activities" as long as, and only as long as, they were part of "the limited context of contract ratification and implementation." Even this rule, however, representing the minimum requirements for eight Justices (Justice Marshall dissented, except as to those charges upheld by the majority), makes clear that the principles of Abood continue to be applied with increasing stringency, and that most of the Court remains antagonistic towards mandatory charges for activities that can even remotely be characterized as political.

12th ED., p. 1434; IND. RTS., p. 1105
Add to footnote 2:

The long-awaited revision of the Hatch Act was finally passed in the 103rd Congress, and signed by President Clinton on October 6, 1994 (P.L. 103–94). The new law bars federal employees from engaging in political activity while on the job, including wearing campaign buttons, which had been allowed under the old Hatch Act. It allows much more extensive political activity by federal employees while they are not working, however, including public endorsement of candidates, holding office in political parties, participation in campaigns and political rallies, and raising political funds for agency political action committees. Under the new law, federal employees may still not run for partisan elective offices or solicit campaign funds from the general public. Certain federal employees in sensitive positions, such as members of the FBI, Federal Election Commission, Secret Service, and CIA and other investigative and intelligence agencies, remain subject to the original Hatch Act.

12th ED., p. 1434; IND. RTS., p. 1105
Add after Pickering:

c.   The scope and application of Pickering were central in UNITED STATES v. NATIONAL TREASURY EMPLOYEES UNION, 516 U.S. ___ (1995), in which the Court struck down a 1989 federal law prohibiting almost all federal employees from accepting compensation for making speeches or writing articles. The law was challenged by a group of federal employees whose compensated outside activities were largely unrelated to their governmental responsibilities, for example an aerospace engineer at the Goddard Space Flight Center who lectured on black history, and a Food and Drug Administration microbiologist who did written, radio, and television reviews of dance performances. Writing for the majority, Justice STEVENS held the restriction unconstitutional. Although he noted that the Court "normally accord[s] a stronger presumption of validity to a congressional judgment than to an individual executive's disciplinary action," he concluded that "[t]he widespread impact of the honoraria ban [gives] rise to far more serious concerns than could any single supervisory decision." Moreover, "[a]lthough [the ban] neither prohibits any speech nor discriminates among speakers based on the content of their messages, its prohibition on compensation unquestionably imposes a significant burden on expressive activity." In evaluating this burden, the Court drew a distinction between job-related speech (see Snepp v. United States, immediately below, and Connick v. Meyers, 1983, below, 12th Ed., p. 1439; Ind.Rts., p. 1110) and cases, like Pickering, in which an employee speaks out as a citizen upon a matter of public concern. Given this distinction, Justice Stevens concluded that this restriction constituted a large-scale version of the situation presented in Pickering. "Respondents' expressive activities in this case fall within the protected category of citizen comment on matters of public concern rather than employee comment on matters related to personal status in the workplace. The speeches and articles for which they received compensation in the past were addressed to a public audience, were made outside the workplace, and involved content largely unrelated to their government employment."

Concluding therefore that this restriction constituted a "burden" that "abridges speech," Justice Stevens turned to the government's purported justifications. "Because the vast majority of the speech at issue in this case does not involve the subject matter of government and takes place outside the workplace, the Government is unable to justify [the restriction] on the grounds of immediate workplace disruption asserted in Pickering. [Instead], the Government submits that the ban comports with the First Amendment because the prohibited honoraria 'were reasonably deemed by Congress to interfere with the efficiency of the public service.' United Public Workers v. Mitchell." But the Court found United Public Workers unavailing, concluding that the goal in that case of protecting employee morale and protecting employees from political pressure was inapplicable here. "The Government's underlying concern is that federal officers not misuse or appear to misuse power by accepting compensation for their unofficial and nonpolitical writing and speaking activities. This interest is undeniably powerful, but the Government cites no evidence of misconduct related to honoraria in the vast rank and file of federal employees below grade GS–16. [The] Government has based its defense of the ban on abuses of honoraria by Members of Congress. Congress could reasonably assume that payments of honoraria to judges or high-ranking officials in the Executive Branch might generate a similar appearance of improper influence. Congress could not, however, reasonably extend that assumption to [an] immense class of workers with negligible power to confer favors on those who might pay to hear them speak or to read their articles." Justice Stevens then noted that the alleged reasons for the restriction were also undercut by some of the exemptions (such as one for a series of articles related to the author's employment, although single articles unrelated to the author's employment were prohibited), and by the fact that the prohibition singled out expressive activity, and did not prohibit compensation for various other "off-duty" activities. "These anomalies [underscore] our conclusion: the speculative benefits the honoraria ban may provide [are] not sufficient to justify this crudely crafted burden on [expressive] activities."

Justice O'CONNOR concurred in the judgment in part and dissented in part. She relied more heavily than the majority on the balancing dimensions of Pickering, and placed particular weight on the way in which "[a]s the magnitude of the intrusion on employees' interests rises, so does the Government's burden of justification. [The] Government, when it acts as employer, possesses substantial leeway; in appropriate circumstances, it may restrain speech that the Constitution would otherwise protect. [In] this case, however, the Government has exceeded the limits of its latitude. The bare assertion of interest in a wide-ranging prophylactic ban here, without any showing that Congress considered empirical or anecdotal data pertaining to abuses by lower-level executive employees, cannot suffice to outweigh the substantial burden on the 1.7 million affected employees. I agree [the ban] is unconstitutional to the extent that it bars this class of employees from receiving honoraria for expressive activities that bear no nexus to government employment." This last qualification explained the dissenting part of Justice O'Connor's opinion, for unlike the majority she would not have struck down the entire ban, but only its application to activities unrelated to government employment.

Chief Justice REHNQUIST, joined by Justices Scalia and Thomas, dissented. "The Court's opinion [understates] the weight which should be accorded to the governmental justifications for the honoraria ban and overstates the amount of speech which actually will be deterred. [Its] discussion of the impact of the statute [is] carefully limited to only a handful of the most appealing individual situations, but when it deals with the remedy it suddenly shifts gears and strikes down the statute as applied to the entire class of Executive Branch employees below grade GS–16." [The] honoraria ban is neither content nor viewpoint based. As a result, the ban does not raise the specter of Government control over the marketplace of ideas. [Unlike] our prototypical application of Pickering which normally involves a response to the content of employee speech, the honoraria ban prohibits no speech and is unrelated to the message or the viewpoint expressed by the government employee. [Because] there is only a limited burden on respondents' First Amendment rights, Congress reasonably could have determined that its paramount interests in preventing impropriety and the appearance of impropriety in its work force justified the honoraria ban.

12th ED., p. 1437; IND. RTS., p. 1108
Add as new Note 4:

4. *First Amendment activity as criminal evidence.* Implicit in most of the freedom of association and employee qualification cases is the premise that the relevance of the information provided by knowledge of someone's association is sufficiently small that it is frequently outweighed by the inhibiting effects on constitutionally protected association of requiring the association to be disclosed. But as most of the cases make clear, there are likely to be associations that do have some bearing on the fitness to perform some task, and thus the doctrine has been concerned with narrowing the scope of permissible inquiry rather than holding categorically that one's constitutionally-protected associations may never be the basis for adverse governmental action. In this respect the issues are similar when prosecutors seek to use activities protected by the First Amendment as evidence in a criminal proceeding. Consider, for example, whether evidence about the books one owns or takes out of the library may be used as evidence in a trial in which one is charged with (and there is other evidence of) committing the kinds of crimes described in the books. If a defendant is charged with unlawful bombing of a public building, may the prosecution introduce evidence that the defendant's library contains books of instructions on the manu-

facture of explosives? See United States v. Giese, 597 F.2d 1170 (9th Cir.1979).

The issue has been before the Supreme Court several times. In United States v. Abel, 469 U.S. 45 (1984), for example, the Court held that the prosecution could use membership in an organization (the Aryan Brotherhood) whose members had sworn to lie for each other to impeach a defense witness at trial. More commonly the issue arises in the context of sentencing, where the question is whether one's First Amendment-protected activities can be taken into account either in sentencing generally or in the sentencing phase of a capital case. In the most recent of these cases, DAWSON v. DELAWARE, 503 U.S. 159 (1992), the Court, with Chief Justice REHNQUIST writing for an 8–1 majority, held that "the Constitution does not erect a per se barrier to the admission of evidence concerning one's beliefs and associations at sentencing simply because those beliefs and associations are protected by the First Amendment." The Chief Justice went on, however, to conclude that the use of such associations in this case was constitutionally impermissible. The defendant Dawson had also been a member of the Aryan Brotherhood, a white racist prison gang that started in California and which had "chapters" in many prisons throughout the country. His membership in the Aryan Brotherhood had been introduced by the prosecution at the sentencing phase of Dawson's murder trial, and Dawson had been sentenced to death. The Supreme Court, however, held that membership in this constitutionally protected association was "totally without relevance" to the specific crime with which Dawson had been charged, and thus its introduction violated the First Amendment. "Even if the [group] to which Dawson belongs is racist, those beliefs [had] no relevance to the sentencing proceeding in this case. For example, the Aryan Brotherhood evidence was not tied in any way to the murder of Dawson's victim. [Because] the prosecution did not prove that the Aryan Brotherhood had committed any unlawful or violent acts, or had even endorsed such acts, the Aryan Brotherhood evidence was also not relevant to help prove any aggravating circumstances. In many cases, for example, associational evidence might serve a legitimate purpose in showing that a defendant represents a future danger to society. A defendant's membership in an organization that endorses the killing of any identifiable group, for example, might be relevant to a jury's inquiry into whether the defendant will be dangerous in the future. Other evidence concerning a defendant's associations might be relevant in proving other aggravating circumstances. But the inference which the jury was invited to draw in this case tended to prove nothing more than the abstract beliefs of the Delaware chapter[, which] have no bearing on the issue being tried. [We] conclude that Dawson's First Amendment rights were violated [because] the evidence proved nothing more than Dawson's abstract beliefs."

Justice THOMAS was the only dissenter. He argued that Dawson himself had introduced evidence of his good character, including membership in various "respectable" organizations such as Alcoholics Anonymous. And with character at issue in sentencing, organizational membership that would show character of a different kind, Justice Thomas argued, was relevant as well. "The Court asserts that the gang membership evidence had no relevance because it did nothing more than indicate Dawson's 'abstract' racist 'beliefs.' The Court suggests that Dawson's membership in a prison gang would be relevant if the gang had endorsed or committed 'unlawful or violent acts' such as drug use, escape, or the murder of other inmates. Yet, because the State failed to prove the Aryan Brotherhood's activities, the Court reasons, the jury could do no more than infer that Dawson shared the gang's racist beliefs. I disagree. [A] jury reasonably could conclude from Dawson's membership in a prison gang that he had engaged in some sort of forbidden activities while in prison. The evidence also tended to establish future dangerousness and to rebut Dawson's attempt to show that he was kind to others. [Just] as defense counsel may assume when introducing mitigating evidence that a jury understands the nature of a church choir, a softball team, or the Boy Scouts, so too may a prosecutor assume when rebutting this evidence that a jury knows the nature of a prison gang."

The limited nature of the holding in Dawson was established a year later, however. In WISCONSIN v. MITCHELL, 506 U.S. ___ (1993), which is set out in full above, addition to 12th Ed., p. 1248; Ind.Rts., p. 919, Chief Justice REHNQUIST wrote for a unanimous Court in reversing the Wisconsin Supreme Court's conclusion that allowing evidence of a defendant's communicative or associational activities to be used as the basis for sentence-enhancement in subsequent criminal proceedings would have an undue "chilling effect" on protected speech.

12th ED., p. 1445; IND.RTS., p. 1116
Add after Rankin v. McPherson:

A NOTE ON FIRST AMENDMENT PROCEDURE

A peripheral but recurring theme in this and the previous two chapters has been the use of procedural rulings to safeguard the substantive protections of freedom of speech and freedom of the press. As noted briefly above (12th Ed., p. 1065; Ind.Rts., p. 736), cases like Bose Corp. v. Consumers Union, 466 U.S. 485 (1984), with respect to defamation, and Jacobellis v. Ohio, 378 U.S. 184 (1964), with respect to obscenity, establish the obligation of appellate courts to conduct independent factual scrutiny of materials found to be constitutionally unprotected, so as to prevent unreviewable determinations of non-protection based upon misapplication of the correct legal standard. At times (e.g., Speiser v. Randall, 357 U.S. 513 (1958), noted above, 12th Ed., p. 1206; Ind.Rts., p. 877; Philadelphia Newspapers, Inc. v. Hepps, 475 U.S. 767 (1986), discussed on this issue above, 12th Ed., p. 1089; Ind.Rts., p. 760), the Court has held that the burden of proof must be on the state or a defamation plaintiff to prove non-protection, rather than it being on the speaker to establish protection. New York Times v. Sullivan (1964; above, 12th Ed., p. 1078; Ind.Rts., p. 749) raises the plaintiff's burden of proof to one of "convincing clarity" in order to protect public criticism of officials. And Freedman v. Maryland (1965; described above, 12th Ed., p. 1206; Ind.Rts., p. 877) is among the most prominent of prior restraint cases making it clear that prior restraints will be permitted only under the tightest of procedural safeguards.

What all of these cases have in common is a concern that without appropriate procedures the substantive protections of the First Amendment will be excessively at risk. The Court, however, has never systematically dealt with the question of First Amendment procedure. At times it has, as the cases above show, imposed special procedural requirements to safeguard the substance of the First Amendment. And at times it has refused to do so, arguing that the appropriate degree of protection of First Amendment values is built into the substantive standard, such that adding special procedural protection in the service of an interest already used to design the substantive standard would be a form of "double counting." See Keeton v. Hustler Magazine, Inc., 465 U.S. 770 (1984), refusing to impose special rules of personal jurisdiction for interstate defamation cases.

Although the Supreme Court has yet to deal comprehensively with the issue, it was the highlight of the opinions of a divided Court in WATERS v. CHURCHILL, 509 U.S. ___ (1994). At issue was a claim by a public employee arising under the principles set forth in Connick v. Myers. Churchill was a nurse who was dismissed for having engaged in a conversation, during a dinner break at the public hospital at which she worked, in which she criticized her supervisors, the department in which she worked, and the policies of that department. These criticisms were made to another employee who was considering transferring to Churchill's department. Churchill claimed her firing violated the rules set forth in Connick, and the case came to the Supreme Court primarily on issues of First Amendment procedure. Justice O'CONNOR wrote for a plurality also including Chief Justice Rehnquist and Justices Souter and Ginsburg, and she noted that the "dispute is over how the factual basis for applying the [Connick] test—what the speech was, in what tone it was delivered, what the listener's reactions were—is to be determined. Should the court apply the Connick test to the speech as the government employer found it to be, or should it ask the jury to determine the facts for itself? [We] agree that it is important to ensure not only that the substantive First Amendment standards are sound, but also that they are applied through reliable procedures. That is why we have often held some procedures—a particular allocation of the burden of proof, a particular quantum of proof, a particular type of appellate review, and so on—to be constitutionally required in proceedings that may penalize protected speech. [Nonetheless,] not every procedure that may safeguard protected speech is constitutionally mandated. [Each] procedure involves a different mix of administrative burden, risk of erroneous punishment of protected speech, and risk of erroneous exculpation of unprotected speech. Though the First Amendment creates a strong presumption against punishing protected speech even inadvertently, the balance need not always be struck in that direction. We have never, for instance, required proof beyond a reasonable doubt in civil cases where First Amendment interests are at stake, though such a requirement would protect speech more than the alternative standards would. Likewise, the possibility that defamation liability would chill even true speech has not led us to require an actual malice standard in all libel cases. Nor has the possibility that overbroad regulations may chill commercial speech convinced us to extend the overbreadth doctrine into the commercial speech area. We have never set forth a general test to determine when a procedural safeguard is required by the First Amendment—just as we have never set forth a general test to determine what constitutes a compelling state interest, or what categories of speech are so lacking in value that they fall outside the protection of the First Amendment, or many other matters—and we do not purport to do so now. [None] of us has discovered a general principle to determine [which] procedural requirements are mandated by the First Amendment and [which] are not. [We] must therefore reconcile ourselves to answering the question on a case-by-case basis, at least until some general rule emerges. [The] propriety of a proposed procedure must turn on the particular context in which the question arises—on the cost of the procedure and the relative magnitude and constitutional significance of the risks it would decrease and increase."

Applying this approach here, the plurality focused on the special role of the government as employer, and the way in which this fact "gives it a freer hand in regulating the speech of its employees than it has in regulating the speech of the public at large. [For example,] though a private person is perfectly free to uninhibitedly and robustly criticize a state governor's legislative program, we have never suggested that the Constitution bars the governor from firing a high-ranking deputy for doing the same thing. Government employee speech must be treated differently with regard to procedural requirements as well. For example, speech restrictions must generally precisely define the speech they target. Yet surely a public employer may, consistently with the First Amendment, prohibit its employees from being 'rude to customers,' a standard almost certainly too vague when applied to the public at large. [The] key to First Amendment analysis of government employment decisions, then, is this: The government's interest in achieving its goals as effectively and efficiently as possible is elevated from a relatively subordinate interest when it acts as sovereign to a significant one when it acts as employer. The government cannot restrict the speech of the public at large just in the name of efficiency. But where the government is employing someone for the very purpose of achieving its goals, such restrictions may well be appropriate. [Thus, we] think employer decisionmaking will not be unduly burdened by having courts look to the facts as the employer *reasonably* found them to be. It may be unreasonable, for example, for the employer to come to a conclusion based on no evidence at all. [Yet we] have never held that it is a violation of the Constitution for a government employer to discharge an employee based on substantively incorrect information." Justice O'Connor then went on to say that application of this standard of reasonable apprehension of the facts would have justified the dismissal of Churchill for the statements the supervisor reasonably believed Churchill to have made, since even if the statements were on a matter of public concern (something the plurality did not decide), "the potential disruptiveness of the speech as reported [was] enough to outweigh whatever First Amendment value it might have had."

Justice SOUTER also wrote a separate concurring opinion to clarify his understanding of the plurality opinion. "[A] public employer who reasonably believes a third-party report that an employee engaged in constitutionally unprotected speech may punish the employee in reliance on that report, even if it turns out that the employee's actual remarks were constitutionally protected. I add these words to emphasize [that] the public employer must not only reasonably investigate the third-party report, but must actually believe it." Justice Souter also noted that the plurality opinion on the reasonableness test "is clearly the one that lower courts should apply[, since] a majority of the Court agrees that employers whose conduct survives the plurality's reasonableness test cannot be held constitutionally liable[; and] a majority (though a different one) is of the view that employers whose conduct fails the plurality's reasonableness test have violated the Free Speech Clause."

Justice Souter's final observations were prompted by the alignment of the other opinions. Justice SCALIA, joined by Justices Kennedy and Thomas, accused the plurality of unnecessarily expanding the protections of Connick, and of unwisely engrafting a separate procedural requirement onto Connick, the effect of which, he argued, would be to "expand[ ] the protection accorded a government employee's public-interest speech from (1) protection against retaliation, to (2) protection against retaliation and mistake." He thus objected to the reasonableness standard in its own right, and to the broader idea of creating separate procedural First Amendment rights in this area. "What [Justice O'Connor] proposes is, at bottom, not new protections for established First Amendment rights, but rather new First Amendment rights. [The] critical inquiry for the factfinder [is] whether the employment decision was [retaliatory for the exercise of the constitutional right of free speech.] A category of employee speech is certainly not being 'retaliated against' if it is no more and no less subject to being mistaken than is any other category of speech or conduct."

Justice STEVENS, on the other hand, joined by Justice Blackmun, objected to the plurality's reasonableness test as being insufficiently protective of speech. "The [constitutional] violation does not vanish merely because the firing was based upon a reasonable mistake about what the employee said. [There] is nothing unfair or onerous about putting the risk of error on the employer in these circumstances. [A] proper regard for [the principle of deliberation within the government, like deliberation about it,] requires that, before firing a public employee for her speech, management get its facts straight."

12th ED., p. 1446; IND. RTS., p. 1117

Add at end of footnote 1 (on p. 1447 (1118)):

For a subsequent application of TWR's distinction between permissible and impermissible forms of content regulation based on whether the regulation was aimed at the suppression of dangerous ideas, see Leathers v. Medlock, 499 U.S. 439 (1991), described at length below, addition to 12th Ed., p. 1499; Ind. Rts., p. 1170.

12th ED., p. 1447; IND. RTS., p. 1118
Add immediately after discussion of Regan v. Taxation With Representation:

RUST v. SULLIVAN

500 U.S. 173, 111 S.Ct. 1759, 114 L.Ed.2d 233 (1991).

[This case, conjoining due process questions about the current scope of abortion rights with First Amendment issues about restrictions imposed on grantees of government funds, is set out in full above, addition to 12th Ed., p. 553; Ind. Rts., p. 224.]

12th ED., p. 1470; IND. RTS., p. 1141
Add at end of footnote 5:

On the issue of restrictions on the out-of-court statements of attorneys involved in litigation, see Gentile v. State Bar of Nevada, 501 U.S. 1030 (1991), described at length above, addition to 12th Ed., p. 1393; Ind. Rts., p. 1064.

12th ED., p. 1499; IND. RTS., p. 1170
Add as new Notes after Note 4 (Arkansas Writers' Project):

5. LEATHERS v. MEDLOCK, 499 U.S. 439 (1991): This case addressed the question, left open by the majorities in Minneapolis Star and Arkansas Writers' Project, whether the First Amendment was violated by tax exemptions or similar programs available to some general classes of publications but not others. At issue was Arkansas' extension of its generally applicable sales tax on goods and services to cable television services while continuing to exempt newspapers, magazines, and satellite broadcast services. The cable services argued that this was an unconstitutional form of content discrimination, but the Court, with Justice O'CONNOR writing for the majority, rejected that contention and upheld the distinction. She stressed the similarity between Minneapolis Star and Arkansas Writers' Project, explaining that the tax in Minneapolis Star targeted a narrow group of large newspapers in much the same way that the tax exemption in Arkansas Writers' Project was available only for a comparatively small group of publications selected on the basis of content. "These cases demonstrate that differential taxation of First Amendment speakers is constitutionally suspect when it threatens to suppress the expression of particular ideas or viewpoints." But here, Justice O'Connor maintained, the tax was unlike the tax in Minneapolis Star because it was generally applicable, and unlike the exemption in Arkansas Writers' Project because by extending the tax to all cable operators there was none of the risk accompanying a tax whose incidence fell on only a small segment of the media. "The danger from a tax scheme that targets a small number of speakers is the danger of censorship; a tax on a small number of speakers runs the risk of affecting only a limited range of views. The risk is similar to that from content-based regulation: it will distort the market for ideas. [There] is no comparable danger from a tax on the services provided by a large number of cable operators offering a wide variety of programming throughout the State. [This] is not a tax structure that resembles a penalty for particular speakers or particular ideas. [There is] no evi-

dence [that] this material differs systematically in its message from that communicated by satellite broadcast programming, newspapers, or magazines.''

Justice O'Connor relied on Regan v. Taxation With Representation of Washington (1983, described above, 12th Ed., p. 1446; Ind. Rts., p. 1117) to dismiss the argument that distinctions among different media are themselves unconstitutional apart from issues of content discrimination. [Note the discussion of format discrimination above, 12th Ed., p. 1216; Ind. Rts., p. 887]. ''[Regan] stands for the proposition that a tax scheme that discriminates among speakers does not implicate the First Amendment unless it discriminates on the basis of ideas. [Differential] taxation of speakers, even members of the press, does not implicate the First Amendment unless the tax is directed at, or presents the danger of suppressing, particular ideas. That was the case in Grosjean, Minneapolis Star, and Arkansas' Writers, but it is not the case here.''

Justice MARSHALL, joined by Justice Blackmun, dissented, objecting to the majority's conclusion that a tax on the media was permissible or not depending on whether the size of the taxed class was small or large. In addition to worrying about the lack of any guidelines for determining when the taxed class was ''large'' enough or enough resembled a ''penalty'' to diminish concerns about the possibility of abuse, Justice Marshall disagreed with the conclusion that only intramedia discrimination held out the dangers of distortion of the marketplace of ideas. ''The majority's [analysis] calls into question whether any obligation to treat media actors even-handedly survives today's decision. [We] have previously recognized that differential taxation *within* an information medium distorts the marketplace of ideas by imposing on some speakers costs not borne by their competitors. Differential taxation *across* different media likewise [does the same] where, as here, the relevant media compete in the same information market.''

6. SIMON & SCHUSTER, INC. v. NEW YORK STATE CRIME VICTIMS BOARD, 502 U.S. 105 (1991). New York has had since 1977 a statute providing that any income that a person ''accused or convicted of a crime'' shall earn from books or other accounts of the crime shall be turned over to the Crime Victims Board, which holds the money in escrow to satisfy civil judgments secured by crime victims against the ''accused or convicted'' person. Called the ''Son of Sam'' law on account of the name of the book about serial murderer David Berkowitz, the statute had been used rarely since its enactment. It was used primarily against well-known defendants, all convicted, such as Jean Harris, the convicted killer of the ''Scarsdale Diet'' doctor, Mark Chapman, the killer of John Lennon, and R. Foster Winans, convicted of insider trading on the basis of disclosing in advance to a confederate the contents of the columns he wrote for the Wall Street Journal.

In 1986 the Crime Victims Board sought to take hold of the Henry Hill's share of the profits of a book, published by Simon & Schuster, entitled Wiseguy: Life in a Mafia Family. The co-author, Henry Hill, had admitted in the book and in court to planning the 1978–1979 Boston College basketball point shaving scandal, a six million dollar theft from

Lufthansa Airlines in 1978, and numerous other crimes. But when the Crime Victims Board attempted to secure from Simon & Schuster all moneys owing to Hill, Simon & Schuster challenged the law on First Amendment grounds. Although the statute was upheld by the District Court and Court of Appeals, the Second Circuit's judgment was reversed by a unanimous Supreme Court, with Justice O'CONNOR writing the opinion.

Justice O'Connor relied heavily on Arkansas Writer Project and Leathers v. Medlock, concluding that a "statute is presumptively inconsistent with the First Amendment if it imposes a financial burden on speakers because of the content of their speech. [The] Son of Sam law is such a content-based statute. It singles out income derived from expressive activity for a burden the state places on no other income, and it is directed only at works with a specified content. Whether the First Amendment 'speaker' is considered to be Henry Hill, whose income the statute places in escrow because of the story he told, or Simon & Schuster, which can publish books about crime with the assistance of only those criminals willing to forgo remuneration for at least five years, the statute plainly imposes a financial disincentive only on speech of a particular content."

Justice O'Connor's opinion acknowledged that the state had a "compelling interest" in ensuring compensation for crime victims, and in precluding criminals from profiting from their crimes. The state did not, however, have a compelling interest in proceeds from "storytelling" as distinct from any other method of profiting from a crime. "The distinction drawn by the Son of Sam law has nothing to do with the State's interest in transferring the proceeds of crime from criminals to their victims. [The] state has a compelling interest in compensating victims from the fruits of the crime, but little if any interest in limiting such compensation to the proceed's of the wrongdoer's speech about crime."

Because the content distinction was thus presumptively unconstitutional, Justice O'Connor went on to see if the statute was "narrowly tailored" to achieve the general and permissible interest in victim compensation. Here she relied significantly on the over-inclusiveness of the statute, noting not only that an accusation of crime was sufficient, but also that under the Board's rulings admissions of crimes in the book at issue could qualify the book. Under this interpretation, Justice O'Connor concluded, works such as The Autobiography of Malcolm X, Henry David Thoreau's Civil Disobedience, and the Confessions of Saint Augustine could all come within the reach of the law, thus making it clear that the law was hardly narrowly tailored to serve victim compensation interests, and thus could not survive the First Amendment Challenge.

Justice BLACKMUN concurred in the judgment, making indicating that a focus on the *under*-inclusiveness of this statute would provide guidance for the many other states with similar legislation on the books. Justice KENNEDY also concurred in the judgment, but his longer opinion was a direct attack on the majority's use of the "compelling interest" and "narrowly tailored" standards. "The [statute] imposes severe restrictions on authors and publishers, using as its sole criterion the content of what is written. The regulated content has the full protection of the First Amendment and this, I submit, is itself a full and sufficient reason for holding the statute unconstitutional. In my view it is both unnecessary and incorrect to ask whether the State can show that the statute 'is necessary to serve a compelling state interest and is narrowly drawn to achieve that end.' That test or formulation derives from our equal protection jurisprudence, and has no real or legitimate place when the Court considers the straightforward question whether the State may enact a burdensome restriction on speech based on content only, apart from any considerations of time, place, and manner or the use of public forums. Here a law is directed to speech alone where the speech in question is not obscene, not defamatory, not words tantamount to an act otherwise criminal, not an impairment of some other constitutional right, not an incitement to lawless action, and not calculated or likely to bring about imminent harm the State has the substantive power to prevent. No further inquiry is necessary to reject the State's argument. [Borrowing] the compelling interest and narrow tailoring analysis is ill-advised when all that is at issue is a content-based restriction, for resort to the test might be read as a concession that States may censor speech whenever they believe there is a compelling justification for doing so. [While] it cannot be said with certainty that [obscenity, defamation, and situations presenting some grave and imminent danger the government has the power to prevent] are or will remain the only ones that are without First Amendment protection, [the] use of these traditional legal categories is preferable to the sort of ad hoc balancing that the Court henceforth must perform in every case if the analysis here used becomes our standard test." *

7. COHEN v. COWLES MEDIA CO., 501 U.S. 663 (1991): Here the Minneapolis Star & Tribune was again one of the parties as the Court continued to hold the media fully bound by laws of general applicability not singling out the media for special attention or restriction. Cohen was a campaign worker in a gubernatorial campaign who had provided to reporters of the Minneapolis Star (and another newspaper) information about past criminal activities of a candidate for Lieutenant Governor in the same election, and had provided that information under an explicit promise of confidentiality. The information turned out to be technically accurate but its import substantially exaggerated (one of the "crimes" was participation in a political protest regarding hiring minority workers, and the charges were ultimately dismissed), and both papers then wrote stories identifying Cohen by name, who was then fired by his employer. He sued both papers under a promissory estoppel theory in the Minnesota state courts, and was awarded judgment in the amount of $200,000. In the Supreme Court, the newspapers argued that

---

* Shortly after the decision in Simon & Schuster, New York enacted new legislation (1992 N.Y. Laws 618) that was no longer speech- or publication-specific. The issues raised promise to persist, as Mary Jo Buat-tafuco, the victim in the "Amy Fisher case" in which a teenager was convicted of shooting her alleged lover's wife, has begun attempts to reach any funds that Fisher has earned as a result of the events.

the judgment was a penalty for the publication of accurate information, but Justice WHITE's majority opinion rejected that characterization. Instead he saw this case as merely one of application of generally applicable contract law principles to a promise that happened to have been made by a newspaper, with the result consequently controlled by Branzburg v. Hayes and all of the business regulation cases (noted in Minneapolis Star) holding the first amendment no bar to press responsibility for compliance with laws of general applicability. "[G]enerally applicable laws do not offend the First Amendment simply because their enforcement against the press has incidental effects on its ability to gather and report the news. [The] Minnesota doctrine of promissory estoppel is a law of general applicability," and thus the press is no more immune from it than they are from the antitrust laws, labor laws, copyright laws, laws against theft, and, as in Branzburg, laws requiring citizens to be subject to subpoena.

Justice BLACKMUN, joined by Justices Marshall and Souter, dissented, characterizing this case as one involving publication of the truthful information that Cohen had engaged in certain behavior in telling reporters what he told them, and thus the case was controlled by those cases (e.g., Smith v. Daily Mail Publishing Co., 443 U.S. 97 (1979), dealing with publication of officially available information regarding the name of a juvenile sex offense victim) recognizing the strength of the right of the press to publish truthful information. Justice SOUTER, joined by Justices Marshall, Blackmun, and O'Connor, also dissented, agreeing with Justice Blackmun that the case was best not characterized as one involving a law of general applicability, but arguing as well that even if that were the case it would still be necessary to balance the interests in each particular case and take account of the extent of the burden on constitutionally recognized interests. In this case, he argued, the balancing process must take account of the importance of the information published to voters in a current election, and thus he would not have allowed the damage judgment to stand.

Chapter 14(9)

THE CONSTITUTION AND RELIGION: "ESTABLISHMENT" AND "FREE EXERCISE"

12th ED., p. 1517; IND. RTS., p. 1188
Add after Grand Rapids case:

ZOBREST v. CATALINA FOOTHILLS SCHOOL DISTRICT, 510 U.S. ___ (1993), relied heavily on Mueller (and Witters, immediately below) in upholding against an establishment clause challenge the use of governmentally-funded sign-language interpreters for deaf students in parochial school classrooms. Under the Individuals with Disabilities Education Act, 20 U.S.C. 1400, and its Arizona counterpart, schools are required to have, inter alia, classroom sign-language interpreters for hearing-impaired students. James Zobrest, deaf since birth, had requested that the state provide him an interpreter to accompany him to classes at a Catholic high school, a request within the scope of the federal and state laws. The state maintained that interpreting the law to require a publicly-paid interpreter in parochial classrooms would violate the establishment clause, but Chief Justice REHNQUIST, writing for the majority disagreed. "[W]e have consistently held that government programs that neutrally provide benefits to a broad class of citizens defined without reference to religion are not readily subject to an Establishment Clause challenge just because sectarian institutions may also receive an attenuated financial benefit. [Because] the Individuals with Disabilities Education Act [does not distinguish between public and private or sectarian and nonsectarian schools and thus] creates no financial incentive for parents to choose a sectarian school, an interpreter's presence there cannot be attributed to state decisionmaking." Chief Justice Rehnquist went on to reject the argument that the physical presence of a state employee in the sectarian classroom made a difference. "[T]he Establishment Clause lays down no absolute bar to the placing of a public employee in a sectarian school. [Nothing] in this record suggests that a sign-language interpreter would do more than accurately interpret whatever material is presented to the class as a whole. [Because the] sign-language interpreter [will] neither add to nor subtract from [a pervasively sectarian environment freely chosen by the parents,] the provision of such assistance is not barred by the Establishment Clause."

Justice O'CONNOR, joined by Justice Stevens, dissented, maintaining that the case should be remanded for lower court consideration of the statutory issues before reaching the constitutional questions. Justice BLACKMUN, joined by Justice Souter, agreed with Justice O'Connor that the constitutional issues should not have been reached (and in this part of his opinion he was joined by Justices Stevens and O'Connor), but went on to disagree with the majority on the merits of the Establishment Clause issue. Stressing that the publicly-paid interpreter would incontestably be conveying religious messages and be operating as a conduit of overtly sectarian messages, he noted that "[u]ntil now, the Court never has authorized a public employee to participate directly in religious indoctrination. Yet that is the consequence of today's decision."

12th ED., p. 1520; IND.RTS., p. 1191

Add to Note on "Involvement of Religious Organizations" after Bowen v. Kendrick:

BOARD OF EDUCATION OF KIRYAS JOEL VILLAGE SCHOOL DISTRICT v. GRUMET, 515 U.S. ___ (1994), invalidated a special New York law that had allowed a particular community of highly religious Hasidic Jews to create its own school district in order to avoid having the community's special-needs children attend the local public schools. As described in the majority (on most of the issues) opinion of Justice SOUTER, "The Village of Kiryas Joel in Orange County, New York, is a religious enclave of Satmar Hasidim, practitioners of a strict form of Judaism. The village fell within the Monroe–Woodbury Central School District until a special state statute passed in 1989 carved out a separate district, following village lines, to serve this distinctive population. [The] residents of Kiryas Joel are vigorously religious people who make few concessions to the modern world and go to great lengths to avoid assimilation into it. They interpret the Torah strictly; separate the sexes outside the home; speak Yiddish as their primary language; eschew television, radio, and English-language publications, and dress in distinctive ways that include headcoverings and special garments for boys and modest dresses for girls. Children are educated in private religious schools, most boys at the United Talmudic Academy where they receive a thorough grounding in the Torah and limited exposure to secular subjects, and most girls at Bais Rochel, an affiliated school with a curriculum designed to prepare girls for their roles as wives and mothers."

Because these schools did not offer services to handicapped children, however, services to which children were entitled under both state and federal law, the local school district first offered these special services at an annex to one of the private religious schools. In response to the Grand Rapids and Aguilar cases (above, 12th Ed., p. 1516; Ind.Rts., p. 1187), however, this arrangement was ended, and the Kiryas Joel children with special needs were sent to the local public school. This was highly unsatisfactory to the parents of the children sent to the public school, largely because of the dramatically different environment the children confronted in the public schools. As a result, the New York legislature passed a statute constituting the Village of Kiryas Joel, by name, as a separate school district, with all of the powers of a separate school district. In fact, the district served only to operate a school for children with special needs, and all other children continued to attend the private schools located in Kiryas Joel.

Relying heavily on Larkin v. Grendel's Den, Justice Souter's opinion found that this plan, like that in Larkin, involved a violation of the principle that "a State may not delegate its civic authority to a group chosen according to a religious criterion. [That] individuals who happen to be religious may hold public office does not mean that a state may deliberately delegate discretionary power to an individual, institution, or community on the ground of religious identity. If New York were to delegate civic authority to 'the Grand Rebbe,' Larkin would obviously require invalidation (even though [the] Grand Rebbe may run for, and serve on his local school board), and the same is true if New York delegates political authority by reference to religious belief. Where 'fusion' is an issue, the difference lies in the distinction between a government's purposeful delegation on the basis of religion and a delegation on principles neutral to religion, to individuals whose religious identities are incidental to their receipt of civil authority." Justice Souter found in the design of this district, in the existence of the special law, and in the unquestioned legislative intent a purpose of designing the district for a particular religious group, too close a parallel to permit the law to stand.

Justice BLACKMUN wrote a brief concurring opinion to emphasize that Justice Souter's opinion should be seen as an application of Lemon v. Kurtzman and not a repudiation of it. Justice STEVENS, joined by Justices Blackmun and Ginsburg, also wrote a concurring opinion, focusing on the impermissibility of a state trying to foster religious segregation. "New York created a special school district for the members of the Satmar religious sect in response to parental concern that children suffered 'panic, fear and trauma' when 'leaving their own community and being with people who were so different.' To meet those concerns, the State could have taken steps to alleviate the children's fear by teaching their schoolmates to be tolerant and respectful of Satmar customs. [This] would raise no constitutional concerns and would further the strong public interest in promoting diversity and understanding in the public schools. Instead, the State responded with a solution that affirmatively supports a religious sect's interest in segregating itself and preventing its children from associating with their neighbors. The isolation of these children, while it may protect them from 'panic, fear and trauma,' also unquestionably increased the likelihood that they would remain within the fold, faithful adherents of their parents' religious faith. [Affirmative] state action in aid of segregation of this character is [fairly] characterized as establishing, rather than merely accommodating, religion."

Justice O'CONNOR concurred in part and concurred in the judgment. She made some general comments about the "slide away from" Lemon's unitary approach to problems that she felt could not be dealt with properly under one unitary test, but her opinion focused heavily on the issue of accommodation. "[W]hat makes accommodation permissible, even praiseworthy, is not that government is making life easier for some particular religious group as such. Rather, it is that the government is accommodating a deeply held belief. Accommodations may thus justify treating those who share this belief differently from those who do not; but they do not justify discriminations based on sect. A state law prohibiting the consumption of alcohol may exempt sacramental wines, but it may not exempt sacramental wine used by Catholics but not by Jews." As a result, Justice O'Connor focused on the lack of generality in the law that had created the Kiryas Joel school district. "There is nothing improper about a legislative intention to accommodate a religious group, so long as it is implemented through generally applicable legislation. [A] district created under a generally applicable scheme would be acceptable even though it coincides with a village which was consciously created by its voters as an enclave for their religious group." Justice KENNEDY, concurring in the judgment, also concentrated on accommodation, but was not troubled by the particularity of the law. For him, the fatal defect lay in the "religious gerrymandering," the way in which New York drew "political boundaries on the basis of religion." Justice SCALIA, joined by Chief Justice Rehnquist and Justice Thomas, dissented, opening with "The Court today finds that the Powers That Be, up in Albany, have conspired to effect an establishment of the Satmar Hasidim. I do not know who would be more surprised at this discovery: the Founders of our Nation or Grand Rebbe Joel Teitelbaum, founder of the Satmar. The Grand Rebbe would be astounded to learn that after escaping brutal persecution and coming to America with the modest hope of religious toleration for their ascetic form of Judaism, the Satmar have become so powerful, so closely allied with Mammon, as to have become an 'establishment' of the Empire State." Justice Scalia went on to note that this case was different from Larkin in that the power here was reposed in the community, in the electorate, and not by law in religious officials. Moreover, he argued, the accommodation here was primarily one of culture and not of religion, since it was cultural differences more than anything that had created the problem in the first instance, even though the cultural differences were associated with a particular religion. This, he argued, was especially important given that the law was facially non-religious, and "unelected judges" should not feel so free to impeach a facially neutral law. "[T]he Court sets aside, on the flimsiest of evidence, the strong presumption of validity that attaches to facially neutral laws, and invalidates the present accommodation because it does not trust New York to be as accommodating toward other religions (presumably less powerful than the Satmar Hasidim) in the future." *

12th ED., p. 1529; IND. RTS., p. 1200
Add at end of footnote 2:

In 1994, Senator Helms managed to attach an amendment to an education funding bill called the Goals 2000: Educate America Act (S. 1150), adding a provision denying funding to an educational institution which "effectively prevented" a student from engaging in voluntary, "constitutionally protected school prayer". The House adopted a similar amendment to its version of the bill, H.R. 6. When the conference committee considerably weakened the provision by providing that federal funds could not be used to deny students the right to pray voluntarily (H.R. 1804, see H.Rpt. 103–446), Senator Helms mounted an

---

* Four days after the Court's decision in Kiryas Joel, the New York legislature, relying explicitly on Justice O'Connor's opinion and the fact that it was necessary for the creation of a majority, passed a general law not limited to Kiryas Joel, but aiming to produce the same result as that produced by the invalidated specific law.

unsuccessful filibuster to stop passage of the legislation before an April 1 deadline. The bill was signed into law March 31, 1994 (P.L. 103–227). In the 104th Congress, school prayer has again become a hot issue. Constitutional amendment proposals include H.J. Res. 10 and 67 (voluntary prayer in public schools programs or activities is allowed and state prescription of content prohibited), H.J. Res. 16 and S.J. Res. 6 (individual or group prayer in public schools or public institutions allowed, state prescription of content prohibited, state requirement of participation in prayer prohibited), H.J. Res. 19 (individual or group prayer in public schools or public institutions allowed, state requirement of participation in prayer prohibited), S.J. Res. 7 (nothing in the Constitution or its amendments shall be construed to prohibit or require voluntary prayer in public schools or public school extracurricular activities). More general religious freedom amendment proposals include S.J. Res. 24 and S.J. Res. 33, which have identical first clauses: "The right of citizens of the United States to the free exercise of religion shall not be denied or abridged by the United States or by any State." S.J. Res. 33 adds another clause: "The Congress shall have the power to enforce, by appropriate legislation, the provisions of this article." Although the popular press has reported on another constitutional amendment proposal, the so-called Religious Equality Amendment, being supported by the Christian right, the text of the actual amendment was not yet finalized as of the closing date of this supplement.

The states have also begun to rely on the refusal of the Supreme Court to review the Fifth Circuit ruling in Jones v. Clear Creek Independent School Dist., 977 F.2d 963 (1992), cert. denied, 113 S.Ct. 2950 (1993), which allowed school prayer that was spontaneous, initiated and led by students, nonsectarian, and did not proselytize. Alabama, Arkansas, Georgia, Louisiana, Mississippi, New Mexico, Tennessee and Virginia have all recently enacted legislation which meets these standards. Bills are pending in Alabama, Delaware, Kansas, Kentucky, North Carolina, Pennsylvania, South Carolina, Texas and Utah.

12th ED., p. 1529; IND. RTS., p. 1200
Add at end of School Prayer materials:

LEE v. WEISMAN

504 U.S. ___, 112 S.Ct. 2649, 120 L.Ed.2d 467 (1992).

Justice KENNEDY delivered the opinion of the Court.

School principals in [Providence,] Rhode Island, are permitted to invite members of the clergy to offer invocation and benediction prayers as part of the formal graduation ceremonies for [public] middle schools and high schools. The question [is] whether including clerical members who offer prayers as part of the official school graduation ceremony is consistent with [the] First Amendment....

I.   A.   Deborah Weisman graduated from Nathan Bishop Middle School [at] a formal ceremony in June 1989. She was about 14 years old. For many years it has been the policy of the School Committee and the Superintendent of Schools to permit principals to invite members of the clergy to give invocations and benedictions at middle school and high school graduations. Many, but not all, of the principals elected to include prayers as part of the graduation ceremonies. Acting for himself and his daughter, Deborah's father, Daniel Weisman, objected to any prayers at Deborah's middle school graduation, but to no avail. The school principal, petitioner Robert E. Lee, invited a rabbi to deliver prayers at the graduation exercises for Deborah's class. Rabbi Leslie Gutterman, of the Temple Beth El in Providence, accepted. It has been the custom of Providence school officials to provide invited clergy with a pamphlet entitled "Guidelines for Civic Occasions," prepared by the

National Conference of Christians and Jews. The Guidelines recommend that public prayers at nonsectarian civic ceremonies be composed with "inclusiveness and sensitivity," though they acknowledge that "[p]rayer of any kind may be inappropriate on some civic occasions." The principal gave Rabbi Gutterman the pamphlet [and] advised him the invocation and benediction should be nonsectarian. Rabbi Gutterman's prayers were as follows:

"INVOCATION: God of the Free, Hope of the Brave: For the legacy of America where diversity is celebrated and the rights of minorities are protected, we thank You. May these young men and women grow up to enrich it. For the liberty of America, we thank You. May these new graduates grow up to guard it. For the political process of America in which all its citizens may participate, for its court system where all may seek justice we thank You. May those we honor this morning always turn to it in trust. For the destiny of America we thank You. May the graduates of Nathan Bishop Middle School so live that they might help to share it. May our aspirations for our country and for these young people, who are our hope for the future, be richly fulfilled. AMEN"

"BENEDICTION: O God, we are grateful to You for having endowed us with the capacity for learning which we have celebrated on this joyous commencement. Happy families give thanks for seeing their children achieve an important milestone. Send Your blessings upon the teachers and administrators who helped prepare them. The graduates now need strength and guidance for the future, help them to understand that we are not complete with academic knowledge alone. We must each strive to fulfill what You require of us all: To do justly, to love mercy, to walk humbly. We give thanks to You, Lord, for keeping us alive, sustaining us and allowing us to reach this special, happy occasion. AMEN".

The record in this case is sparse, [and] we are unfamiliar with any fixed custom or practice at middle school graduations. [We] are not so constrained with reference to high schools, however. High school graduations are such an integral part of American cultural life that we can with confidence describe their customary features, confirmed by [the] record and by the parties' representations. [In] the Providence school system, most high school graduation ceremonies are conducted away from the school, while most middle school ceremonies are held on school premises. Classical High School, which Deborah now attends, has conducted its graduation ceremonies on school premises. The parties stipulate that attendance at graduation ceremonies is voluntary. The graduating students enter as a group [and] sit together, apart from their families. We assume the clergy's participation in any high school graduation exercise would be about what it was at Deborah's middle school ceremony. There the students stood for the Pledge of Allegiance and remained standing during the Rabbi's prayers. Even on the assumption that there was a respectful moment of silence both before and after the prayers, the Rabbi's two presentations must not have extended much beyond a minute each, if that. We do not know whether he remained on stage during the whole ceremony, or whether the students received individual diplomas on stage, or if he helped to congratulate them.

The school board (and the United States, which supports it as amicus curiae) argued that [short] prayers [at] graduation exercises are of profound meaning to many students and parents throughout this country who consider that due respect and acknowledgement for divine guidance and for the deepest spiritual aspirations of our people ought to be expressed at an event as important in life as a graduation. We assume this to be so, [for] the significance of the prayers lies also at the heart of Daniel and Deborah Weisman's case.

B. Deborah's graduation was held on the premises of Nathan Bishop Middle School. Four days before the ceremony, Daniel Weisman, [as] a Providence taxpayer and as next friend of Deborah, sought a temporary restraining order in the United States District Court [to] prohibit school officials from including an invocation or benediction in the graduation ceremony. The court denied the motion for lack of adequate time to consider it. Deborah and her family attended the graduation, where the prayers were recited. Daniel Weisman [then] filed an amended complaint seeking a permanent injunction barring [officials] of the Providence public schools from inviting the clergy to deliver invocations and benedictions at future graduations. We find it unnecessary to address Daniel Weisman's taxpayer standing, for a live and justiciable controversy is before us. Deborah Weisman is enrolled as a student at Classical High School in Providence and from the record it appears likely [that] an invocation and benediction will be conducted at her high school graduation.

[The] District Court held that petitioners' practice of including invocations and benedictions in public school graduations violated the Establishment Clause, and it enjoined petitioners from continuing the practice. [The Court of Appeals] affirmed. We granted certiorari, and now affirm.

II. These dominant facts [control] the confines of our decision: State officials direct the performance of a formal religious exercise at promotional and graduation ceremonies for secondary schools. Even for those students who object to the religious exercise, their attendance and participation in the state-sponsored religious activity are in a fair and real sense obligatory, though the school district does not require attendance as a condition for receipt of the diploma.

This case does not require us to revisit the difficult [questions] of the definition and full scope of the principles governing the extent of permitted accommodation by the State for the religious beliefs and practices of many of its citizens. For without reference to those principles in other contexts, the controlling precedents as they relate to prayer and religious exercise in primary and secondary public schools compel the holding here that the policy of the city [is unconstitutional.] We can decide the case without reconsidering the general constitutional framework by which public schools' efforts to accommodate religion are measured. Thus we do not accept the invitation of petitioners and [the] United States to reconsider [Lemon.] The government involvement with religious activity in this case is pervasive, to the point of creating a state-sponsored and state-directed religious exercise in a public school. [That] involvement is as troubling as it is undenied. A school official, the principal, decided that an invocation and a benediction should be given; this is a choice attributable to the State, and from a constitutional perspective it is as if a state statute decreed that the prayers must occur. The principal chose the religious participant, here a rabbi, and that choice is also attributable to the State. [The] State's role did not end with the decision to include a prayer and with the choice of clergyman. Principal Lee provided Rabbi Gutterman with a copy of the "Guidelines for Civic Occasions," and advised him that his prayers should be nonsectarian. Through these means the principal directed and controlled the content of the prayer. Even if the only sanction for ignoring the instructions were that the rabbi would not be invited back, we think no religious representative who valued his or her continued reputation and effectiveness in the community would incur the State's displeasure in this regard. It is a cornerstone principle [that] "it is no part of the business of government to compose official prayers for any group of the American people to recite as a part of a religious program carried on by government," Engel, and that is what the school officials attempted to do.

Petitioners argue [that] the directions [were] a good-faith attempt by the school to ensure that the sectarianism which is so often the flashpoint for religious animosity be removed from the graduation ceremony. [The] school's explanation, however, does not resolve the dilemma caused by its participation. The question is not the good faith of the school in attempting to make the prayer acceptable to most persons, but the legitimacy of its undertaking that enterprise at all when the object is to produce a prayer to be used in a formal religious exercise which students, for all practical purposes, are obliged to attend.

We are asked to recognize the existence of a practice of nonsectarian prayer, prayer within the embrace of what is known as the Judeo–Christian tradition, prayer which is more acceptable than one which, for example, makes explicit references to the God of Israel, or to Jesus Christ, or to a patron saint. There may be some support [for the observation that] there has emerged in this country a civic religion, one which is tolerated when sectarian exercises are not. If common ground can be defined which permits once conflicting faiths to express the shared conviction that there is an ethic and a morality which transcend human invention, the sense of community and purpose sought by all decent societies might be advanced. But though the First Amendment does not allow the government to stifle prayers which aspire to these ends, neither does it permit the government to undertake that task for itself. [Though] the efforts of the school officials in this case to find common ground appear to have been a good-faith attempt to recognize the common aspects of religions and not the divisive ones, our precedents do not permit school officials to assist in composing prayers as an incident to a formal exercise for their students. And these same precedents caution us to measure the idea of a civic religion against the central meaning of the Religion Clauses, [which] is that all creeds must be tolerated and none favored. The suggestion that government may establish an official or civic religion as a means of avoiding the establishment of a religion with more specific creeds [is] a contradiction that cannot be accepted.

[We] turn our attention now to [the] position of the students, both those who desired the prayer and those who did not. To endure the speech of false ideas or offensive content and then to counter it is part of learning how to live in a pluralistic society, a society which insists upon open discourse towards the end of a tolerant citizenry. And tolerance presupposes some mutuality of obligation. It is argued that our constitutional vision of a free society requires confidence in our own ability to accept or reject ideas of which we do not approve, and that prayer at a high school graduation does nothing more than offer a choice. By the time they are seniors, high school students no doubt have been required to attend classes and assemblies and to complete assignments exposing them to ideas they find distasteful or immoral or absurd or all of these. Against this background, students may consider it an odd measure of justice to be subjected during the course of their educations to ideas deemed offensive and irreligious, but to be denied a brief, formal prayer ceremony that the school offers in return. This argument[, however, overlooks] a fundamental dynamic of the Constitution. The First Amendment protects speech and religion by quite different mechanisms. Speech is protected by insuring its full expression even when the government participates, for the very object of some of our most important speech is to persuade the government to adopt an idea as its own. The method for protecting freedom of worship and [conscience] in religious matters is quite the reverse. In religious debate or expression the government is not a prime participant, for the Framers deemed religious establishment antithetical to the freedom of all. The Free Exercise Clause embraces a freedom [that] has close parallels in the speech provisions of the First Amendment, but the Establishment Clause is a specific prohibition on forms of state intervention in religious affairs with no precise counterpart. [The] explanation lies in the lesson of history that [in] the hands of government what might begin as a tolerant expression of religious views may end in a policy to indoctrinate and coerce.

[As] we have observed before, there are heightened concerns with protecting freedom of conscience from subtle coercive pressure in the elementary and secondary public schools. Our decisions [recognize] that prayer exercises in public schools carry a particular risk of indirect coercion. The concern may not be limited to the context of schools, but it is most pronounced there. What to most believers may seem nothing more than a reasonable request that the nonbeliever respect their religious practices, in a school context may appear to the nonbeliever or dissenter to be an attempt to employ the machinery of the State to enforce a religious orthodoxy. We need not look beyond the circumstances of this case to see the phenomenon at work. The [school's] supervision and control of a high school graduation ceremony places public pressure, as well as peer pressure, on attending students to stand as a group or, at least, maintain respectful silence during the Invocation and Benediction. This pressure, though subtle and indirect, can be as real as any overt compulsion. Of course, in our culture standing or remaining silent can signify adherence to a view or simple respect for the views of others. And no doubt some persons who have no desire to join a prayer have little objection to standing as a sign of respect for those who do. But for the dissenter of high school age, who has a reasonable perception that she is being forced by the State to pray in a manner her conscience will not allow, the injury is no less real. [For] many, if not most, of the students at the graduation, the act of standing or remaining silent was an expression of participation in the Rabbi's prayer. That was the very point of the religious exercise. It is of little comfort to a dissenter, then, to be told that for her the act of standing or remaining in silence signifies mere respect, rather than participation. What matters is that, given our social conventions, a reasonable dissenter in this milieu could believe that the group exercise signified her own participation or approval of it. Finding no violation under these circumstances would place objectors in the dilemma of participating, with all that implies, or protesting. We do not address whether that choice is acceptable if the affected citizens are mature adults, but [the] State may not [place] primary and secondary school children in this position. Research in psychology supports the common assumption that adolescents are often susceptible to pressure from their peers towards conformity, and that the influence is strongest in matters of social convention. Brittain, Adolescent Choices and Parent–Peer Cross–Pressures, 28 Am. Soc.Rev. 385 (1963); Clasen & Brown, The Multidimensionality of Peer Pressure in Adolescence, 14 J.Youth & Adolescence 451 (1985); Brown, Clasen & Eicher, Perceptions of Peer Pressure, Peer Conformity Dispositions, and Self–Reported Behavior Among Adolescents, 22 Developmental Psych. 521 (1986). [The] government may no more use social pressure to enforce orthodoxy than it may use more direct means.

[There] was a stipulation [that] attendance at graduation [ceremonies] is voluntary. Petitioners and the United States [made] this a center point of the case, arguing that the option of not attending [excuses] any inducement or coercion in the ceremony itself. The argument lacks all persuasion. Law reaches past formalism. And to say a teenage student has a real choice not to attend her high school graduation is formalistic in the extreme. True, Deborah could elect not to attend commencement without renouncing her diploma; but we shall not allow the case to turn on this point. Everyone knows that in our society and in our culture high school graduation is one of life's most significant occasions. A school rule which excuses attendance is beside the point. Attendance may not be required by official decree, yet it is apparent that a student is not free to absent herself from the graduation exercise in any real sense of the term "voluntary," for absence would require forfeiture of those intangible benefits which have motivated the student through youth and all her high school years. Graduation is a time for family and those closest to the student to celebrate success and express mutual wishes of gratitude and respect, all to the end of impressing upon the young person the role that it is his or her right and duty to assume in the community and all of its diverse parts.

The importance of the event is the point the school district and the United States rely upon to argue that a formal prayer ought to be permitted, but it becomes one of the principal reasons why their argument must fail. Their contention, one of considerable force were it not for the constitutional constraints applied to state action, is that the prayers are an essential part of these ceremonies because for many persons an occasion of this significance lacks meaning if there is no recognition, however brief, that human achievements cannot be understood apart from their spiritual essence. We think the Government's position that this interest suffices to force students to choose between compliance or forfeiture demonstrates fundamental inconsistency in its argumentation. It fails to acknowledge that what for many of Deborah's classmates and their parents was a spiritual imperative was for Daniel and Deborah Weisman religious conformance compelled by the State.

[The] Government's argument gives insufficient recognition to the real conflict of conscience faced by the young student. The essence of the Government's position is that with regard to a civic, social occasion of this importance it is the objector, not the majority, who must take unilateral and private action to avoid compromising religious scruples. [This] turns conventional First Amendment analysis on its head. [The] State cannot require one of its citizens to forfeit his or her rights and benefits as the price of resisting conformance to state-sponsored religious practice. To say that a student must remain apart from the ceremony at the opening invocation and closing benediction is to risk compelling conformity in an environment analogous to the classroom setting, where we have said the risk of compulsion is especially high. Just as in [Engel and Abington] we found that [permitting] a student to be voluntarily excused from attendance or participation in the daily prayers did not shield those practices from invalidation, the fact that attendance at the graduation ceremonies is voluntary in a legal sense does not save the religious exercise.

Inherent differences between the public school system and a session of a State Legislature distinguish this case from Marsh v. Chambers [1983; below, 12th Ed., p. 1540; Ind.Rts., p. 1211.] [The] atmosphere at the opening of a session of a state legislature where adults are free to enter and leave with little comment and for any number of reasons cannot compare with the constraining potential of the one school event most important for the student to attend. [Engel and Abington] require us to distinguish the public school context. [We] recognize that, at graduation time and throughout the course of the educational process, there will be instances when religious values, religious practices, and religious persons will have some interaction with the public schools and their students. But these matters, often questions of accommodation of religion, are not before us. The sole question presented is whether a religious exercise may be conducted at a graduation ceremony in circumstances where [young] graduates who object are induced to conform. No holding by this Court suggests that a school can persuade or compel a student to participate in a religious exercise....

[Affirmed.]

Justice BLACKMUN, with whom Justice STEVENS and Justice O'CONNOR join, concurring.

Nearly half a century of review and refinement of Establishment Clause jurisprudence has distilled one clear understanding: Government may neither promote nor affiliate itself with any religious doctrine or organization, nor may it obtrude itself in the internal affairs of any religious institution. [There] can be "no doubt" that the "invocation of God's blessings" delivered at Nathan Bishop Middle School "is a religious activity." Engel. [The] question then is whether the government has "plac[ed] its official stamp of approval" on the prayer. As the Court ably demonstrates, when the government "compose[s] official prayers," selects the member of the clergy to deliver the prayer, has the prayer delivered at a public school event that is planned, supervised and given by school officials, and pressures students to attend and participate in the prayer, there can be no doubt that the government is advancing and promoting religion.[1] . . .

II. [The] Court holds that the graduation prayer is unconstitutional because the State "in effect required participation in a religious exercise." Although [proof] of government coercion is not necessary to prove an Establishment Clause violation, it is sufficient. [But] it is not enough that the government restrain from compelling religious practices: it must not engage in them either. The Court repeatedly has recognized that a violation of the Establishment Clause is not predicated on coercion. [The] mixing of government and religion can be a threat to free government, even if no one is forced to participate. When the government puts its imprimatur on a particular religion, it conveys a message of exclusion to all those who do not adhere to the favored beliefs. A government cannot be premised on the belief that all persons are created equal when it asserts that God prefers some. [Democratic] government will not last long when proclamation replaces persuasion as the medium of political exchange.

Likewise, we have recognized that "[r]eligion flourishes in greater purity, without than with the aid of Gov[ernment]." Memorial and Remonstrance. [The] favored religion may be compromised as political figures reshape the religion's beliefs for their own purposes; it may be reformed as government largesse brings government regulation. Keeping religion in the hands of private groups minimizes state intrusion on religious choice. . . .

Justice SOUTER, with whom Justice STEVENS and Justice O'CONNOR join, concurring.

I join the whole of the Court's opinion, and fully agree that prayers at public school graduation ceremonies indirectly coerce religious observance. I write separately nonetheless on two issues [that] underlie my independent resolution of this case: whether the Clause applies to governmental practices that do not favor one religion or denomination

---

1. In this case, the religious message it promotes is specifically Judeo–Christian. The phrase in the benediction: "We must each strive to fulfill what you require of us all, to do justly, to love mercy, to walk humbly" obviously was taken from the Book of the Prophet Micah, ch. 6, v. 8. [Footnote by Justice Blackmun.]

over others, and whether state coercion of religious conformity, over and above state endorsement of religious exercise or belief, is a necessary element of an Establishment Clause violation.

I. Forty-five years ago, this Court announced a basic principle [from] which it has not strayed: the Establishment Clause forbids not only state practices that "aid one religion ... or prefer one religion over another," but also those that "aid all religions." Everson. Today we reaffirm that [the] Establishment Clause forbids state-sponsored prayers in public school settings no matter how nondenominational the prayers may be. In barring the State from sponsoring generically Theistic prayers where it could not sponsor sectarian ones, we hold true to a line of precedent from which there is no adequate historical case to depart.

A. Since Everson, we have consistently held the Clause applicable no less to governmental acts favoring religion generally than to acts favoring one religion over others. [Such] is the settled law. Here, as elsewhere, we should stick to it absent some compelling reason to discard it.

B. Some have challenged this precedent by reading the Establishment Clause to permit "nonpreferential" state promotion of religion. The challengers argue that, as originally understood by the Framers, "[t]he Establishment Clause did not require government neutrality between religion and irreligion nor did it prohibit the Federal Government from providing nondiscriminatory aid to religion." Wallace v. Jaffree (Rehnquist, J., dissenting). While a case has been made for this position, it is not so convincing as to warrant reconsideration of our settled law; indeed, I find in the history of the Clause's textual development a more powerful argument supporting the Court's jurisprudence following Everson. When James Madison arrived at the First Congress with a series of proposals to amend the National Constitution, one of the provisions read that "[t]he civil rights of none shall be abridged on account of religious belief or worship, nor shall any national religion be established, nor shall the full and equal rights of conscience be in any manner, or on any pretext, infringed." Madison's language did not last long. [A] Select Committee of the House [changed] it to read that "no religion shall be established by law, nor shall the equal rights of conscience be infringed." Thence [the] Committee of the Whole [adopted] an alternative proposed by Samuel Livermore of New Hampshire: "Congress shall make no laws touching religion, or infringing the rights of conscience." Livermore's proposal would have forbidden laws having anything to do with religion and was thus not only far broader than Madison's version, but broader even than the scope of the Establishment Clause as we now understand it. The House rewrote the amendment once more before sending it to the Senate, this time adopting [language] derived from a proposal by Fisher Ames of Massachusetts: "Congress shall make no law establishing Religion, or prohibiting the free exercise thereof, nor shall the rights of conscience be infringed." Perhaps [the] Representatives had thought Livermore's proposal too expansive, or perhaps [they] had simply worried that his language would not "satisfy the demands of those who wanted something said specifically against establishments of religion." L. Levy, The Establishment

Clause (1986). We do not know; what we do know is that the House rejected the Select Committee's version, which arguably ensured only that "no religion" enjoyed an official preference over others, and deliberately chose instead a prohibition extending to laws establishing "religion" in general.

[This] sequence [confirms] that the Framers meant the Establishment Clause's prohibition to encompass nonpreferential aid to religion. In September 1789, the Senate considered a number of provisions that would have permitted such aid, and ultimately it adopted one of them. First, it briefly entertained this language: "Congress shall make no law establishing One Religious Sect or Society in preference to others, nor shall the rights of conscience be infringed." After rejecting two minor amendments to that proposal, the Senate dropped it altogether and chose a provision identical to the House's proposal, but without the clause protecting the "rights of conscience." With no record of the Senate debates, we cannot know what prompted these changes, but the record does tell us that, six days later, the Senate went half circle and adopted its narrowest language yet: "Congress shall make no law establishing articles of faith or a mode of worship, or prohibiting the free exercise of religion." The Senate sent this proposal to the House. [Though] it accepted much of the Senate's work on the Bill of Rights, the House rejected the Senate's version of the Establishment Clause and called for a joint conference committee, to which the Senate agreed. The House conferees ultimately [persuaded] the Senate to accept [as] the final text of the Religion Clauses: "Congress shall make no law respecting an establishment of religion, or prohibiting the free exercise thereof." What is remarkable is that, unlike the earliest House drafts or the final Senate proposal, the prevailing language is not limited to laws respecting an establishment of "a religion," "a national religion," "one religious sect," or specific "articles of faith." The Framers repeatedly considered and deliberately rejected such narrow language and instead extended their prohibition to state support for "religion" in general.

[What] we thus know of the Framers' experience underscores the observation of one prominent commentator, that confining the Establishment Clause to a prohibition on preferential aid "requires a premise that the Framers were extraordinarily bad drafters—that they believed one thing but adopted language that said something substantially different, and that they did so after repeatedly attending to the choice of language." [1] Laycock [citation in footnote 1.] We must presume, since there is no conclusive evidence to the contrary, that the Framers

---

1. Some commentators have suggested that by targeting laws respecting "an" establishment of religion, the Framers adopted the very nonpreferentialist position whose much clearer articulation they repeatedly rejected. R. Cord, Separation of Church and State: Historical Fact and Current Fiction (1988). Yet the indefinite article before the word "establishment" is better seen as evidence that the Clause forbids any kind of establishment, including a nonpreferential one. If the Framers had wished, for some reason, to use the indefinite term to achieve a narrow meaning for the Clause, they could far more aptly have placed it before the word "religion." Laycock, "Nonpreferential" Aid to Religion: A False Claim About Original Intent, 27 Wm. & Mary L.Rev. 875 (1986). [Footnote by Justice Souter.]

embraced the significance of their textual judgment.[2] Thus, on balance, history neither contradicts nor warrants reconsideration of the settled principle that the Establishment Clause forbids support for religion in general no less than support for one religion or some.

C. While these considerations are, for me, sufficient to reject the nonpreferentialist position, one further concern animates my judgment. In many contexts, including this one, nonpreferentialism requires some distinction between "sectarian" religious practices and those that would be, by some measure, ecumenical enough to pass Establishment Clause muster. Simply by requiring the enquiry, nonpreferentialists invite the courts to engage in comparative theology. I can hardly imagine a subject less amenable to the competence of the federal judiciary, or more deliberately to be avoided where possible. This case is nicely in point. Since the nonpreferentiality of a prayer must be judged by its text, Justice Blackmun pertinently observes that Rabbi Gutterman drew his exhortation "[t]o do justly, to love mercy, to walk humbly" straight from the King James version of Micah, ch. 6, v. 8. At some undefinable point, the similarities between a state-sponsored prayer and the sacred text of a specific religion would so closely identify the former with the latter that even a nonpreferentialist would have to concede a breach of the Establishment Clause. And even if Micah's thought is sufficiently generic for most believers, it still embodies a straightforwardly Theistic premise, and so does the Rabbi's prayer. Many Americans who consider themselves religious are not Theistic; some, like several of the Framers, are Deists who would question Rabbi Gutterman's plea for divine advancement of the country's political and moral good. Thus, a nonpreferentialist who would condemn subjecting public school graduates to, say, the Anglican liturgy would still need to explain why the government's preference for Theistic over non-Theistic religion is constitutional. Nor does it solve the problem to say that the State should promote a "diversity" of religious views; that position would necessarily compel the government and, inevitably, the courts to make wholly inappropriate judgments about the number of religions the State should sponsor and the relative frequency with which it should sponsor each....

II. Petitioners rest most of their argument on a theory that [the] Establishment Clause [does] not forbid the state to sponsor affirmations of religious belief that coerce neither support for religion nor participation in religious observance. I appreciate the force of some of the arguments supporting a "coercion" analysis of the Clause. But we could

2. In his dissent in Wallace v. Jaffree, the Chief Justice rested his nonpreferentialist interpretation partly on the post-ratification actions of the early national government. Aside from the willingness of some (but not all) early Presidents to issue ceremonial religious proclamations, which were at worst trivial breaches of the Establishment Clause, he cited such seemingly preferential aid as a treaty provision, signed by Jefferson, authorizing federal subsidization of a Roman Catholic priest and church for the Kaskaskia Indians. But this proves too much, for if the Establishment Clause permits a special appropriation of tax money for the religious activities of a particular sect, it forbids virtually nothing. Although evidence of historical practice can indeed furnish valuable aid in the interpretation of contemporary language, acts like the one in question prove only that public officials, no matter when they serve, can turn a blind eye to constitutional principle. [Footnote by Justice Souter.]

not adopt that reading without abandoning our settled law, a course that [the] text of the Clause would not readily permit. Nor does the extratextual evidence of original meaning stand so unequivocally at odds with the textual premise inherent in existing precedent that we should fundamentally reconsider our course.

A. Over the years, this Court has declared the invalidity of many noncoercive state laws and practices conveying a message of religious endorsement. [Our] precedents may not always have drawn perfectly straight lines. They simply cannot, however, support the position that a showing of coercion is necessary to a successful Establishment Clause claim.

B. Like the provisions about "due" process and "unreasonable" searches and seizures, the constitutional language forbidding laws "respecting an establishment of religion" is not pellucid. But virtually everyone acknowledges that the Clause bans more than formal establishments of religion in the traditional sense, that is, massive state support for religion through, among other means, comprehensive schemes of taxation. This much follows from the Framers' explicit rejection of simpler provisions prohibiting either the establishment of a religion or laws "establishing religion" in favor of the broader ban on laws "respecting an establishment of religion." [In] Madison's words, the Clause in its final form forbids "everything like" a national religious establishment, and, after incorporation, it forbids "everything like" a State religious establishment. The sweep is broad enough that Madison himself characterized congressional provisions for legislative and military chaplains as unconstitutional "establishments." While petitioners insist that the prohibition extends only to the "coercive" features and incidents of establishment, they cannot easily square that claim with the constitutional text. The First Amendment forbids not just laws "respecting an establishment of religion," but also those "prohibiting the free exercise thereof." Yet laws that coerce nonadherents [would] virtually by definition violate their right to religious free exercise. Thus, a literal application of the coercion test would render the Establishment Clause a virtual nullity....

C. Petitioners argue from the political setting in which the Establishment Clause was framed, and from the Framers' own political practices following ratification, that government may constitutionally endorse religion so long as it does not coerce religious conformity. The setting and the practices warrant canvassing, but while they yield some evidence for petitioners' argument, they do not reveal the degree of consensus in early constitutional thought that would raise a threat to stare decisis by challenging the presumption that the Establishment Clause adds something to the Free Exercise Clause that follows it. The Framers adopted the Religion Clauses in response to a long tradition of coercive state support for religion, particularly in the form of tax assessments, but their special antipathy to religious coercion did not exhaust their hostility to the features and incidents of establishment.

[Petitioners] contend that because the early Presidents included religious messages in their inaugural and Thanksgiving Day addresses, the Framers could not have meant the Establishment Clause to forbid noncoercive state endorsement of religion. The argument ignores the fact, however, that Americans today find such proclamations less controversial than did the founding generation, whose published thoughts on the matter belie petitioners' claim. President Jefferson, for example, steadfastly refused to issue Thanksgiving proclamations of any kind, in part because he thought they violated the Religion Clauses. [During] his first three years in office, James Madison also refused to call for days of thanksgiving and prayer, though later, amid the political turmoil of the War of 1812, he did so on four separate occasions. [Madison's] failure to keep pace with his principles in the face of congressional pressure cannot erase the principles. He admitted to backsliding, and explained that he had made the content of his wartime proclamations inconsequential enough to mitigate much of their impropriety. While his writings suggest mild variations in his interpretation of the Establishment Clause, Madison was no different in that respect from the rest of his political generation. That he expressed so much doubt about the constitutionality of religious proclamations, however, suggests a brand of separationism stronger even than that embodied in our traditional jurisprudence. So too does his characterization of public subsidies for legislative and military chaplains as unconstitutional "establishments." [To] be sure, the leaders of the young Republic engaged in some of the practices that separationists like Jefferson and Madison criticized. The First Congress did hire institutional chaplains, and Presidents Washington and Adams unapologetically marked days of "public thanksgiving and prayer." Yet in the face of the separationist dissent, those practices prove, at best, that the Framers simply did not share a common understanding of the Establishment Clause, and, at worst, that they, like other politicians, could raise constitutional ideals one day and turn their backs on them the next....

III. While the Establishment Clause's concept of neutrality is not self-revealing, our recent cases have invested it with specific content: the state may not favor or endorse either religion generally over nonreligion or one religion over others....

A. That government must remain neutral in matters of religion does not foreclose it from ever taking religion into account. The State may "accommodate" the free exercise of religion by relieving people from generally applicable rules that interfere with their religious callings. [Such] accommodation does not necessarily signify an official endorsement of religious observance over disbelief. In everyday life, we routinely accommodate religious beliefs that we do not share. A Christian inviting an Orthodox Jew to lunch might take pains to choose a kosher restaurant; an atheist in a hurry might yield the right of way to an Amish man steering a horse-drawn carriage. In so acting, we express respect for, but not endorsement of, the fundamental values of others. We act without expressing a position on the theological merit of those values or of religious belief in general, and no one perceives us to have taken such a position.

The government may act likewise. Most religions encourage devotional practices that are at once crucial to the lives of believers and idiosyncratic in the eyes of nonadherents. By definition, secular rules of general application are drawn from the nonadherent's vantage and, consequently, fail to take such practices into account. Yet when enforcement of such rules cuts across religious sensibilities, as it often does, it puts those affected to the choice of taking sides between God and government. In such circumstances, accommodating religion reveals nothing beyond a recognition that general rules can unnecessarily offend the religious conscience when they offend the conscience of secular society not at all. Thus, in freeing the Native American Church from federal laws forbidding peyote use, Drug Enforcement Administration Miscellaneous Exemptions, 21 C.F.R. 1307.31, the government conveys no endorsement of peyote rituals, the Church, or religion as such; it simply respects the centrality of peyote to the lives of certain Americans.

B. Whatever else may define the scope of accommodation permissible under the Establishment Clause, one requirement is clear: accommodation must lift a discernible burden on the free exercise of religion. Concern for the position of religious individuals in the modern regulatory state cannot justify official solicitude for a religious practice unburdened by general rules; such gratuitous largesse would effectively favor religion over disbelief. By these lights one easily sees that, in sponsoring the graduation prayers at issue here, the State has crossed the line from permissible accommodation to unconstitutional establishment.

Religious students cannot complain that omitting prayers from their graduation ceremony would, in any realistic sense, "burden" their spiritual callings. To be sure, many of them invest this rite of passage with spiritual significance, but they may express their religious feelings about it before and after the ceremony. They may even organize a privately sponsored baccalaureate if they desire the company of like-minded students. Because they accordingly have no need for the machinery of the State to affirm their beliefs, the government's sponsorship of prayer at the graduation ceremony is most reasonably understood as an official endorsement of religion and, in this instance, of Theistic religion. One may fairly say, as one commentator has suggested, that the government brought prayer into the ceremony "precisely because some people want a symbolic affirmation that government approves and endorses their religion, and because many of the people who want this affirmation place little or no value on the costs to religious minorities." Laycock, *Summary and Synthesis: The Crisis in Religious Liberty,* 60 Geo.Wash.L.Rev. 841 (1992).[3] ...

Justice SCALIA, with whom the Chief Justice [REHNQUIST], Justice WHITE, and Justice THOMAS join, dissenting.

---

3. If the State had chosen its graduation day speakers according to wholly secular criteria, and if one of those speakers (not a state actor) had individually chosen to deliver a religious message, it would have been harder to attribute an endorsement of religion to the State. But that is not our case. Nor is this a case where the State has, without singling out religious groups or individuals, extended benefits to them as members of a broad class of beneficiaries defined by clearly secular criteria. Finally, this is not a case like Marsh v. Chambers, in which government officials invoke spiritual inspiration entirely for their own benefit without directing any religious message at the citizens they lead. [Footnote by Justice Souter.]

[In] holding that the Establishment Clause prohibits invocations and benedictions at public-school graduation ceremonies, the Court—with nary a mention that it is doing so—lays waste a tradition that is as old as public-school graduation ceremonies themselves, and that is a component of an even more longstanding American tradition of nonsectarian prayer to God at public celebrations generally. As its instrument of destruction, the bulldozer of its social engineering, the Court invents a boundless, and boundlessly manipulable, test of psychological coercion. [Today's] opinion shows [why that] fortress which is our Constitution cannot possibly rest upon the changeable philosophical predilections of the Justices of this Court, but must have deep foundations in the historic practices of our people.

I. [The] history and tradition of our Nation are replete with public ceremonies featuring prayers of thanksgiving and petition. Illustrations of this point have been amply provided in our prior opinions, but since the Court is so oblivious to our history as to suggest that the Constitution restricts "preservation and transmission of religious beliefs ... to the private sphere," it appears necessary to provide another brief account.

From our Nation's origin, prayer has been a prominent part of governmental ceremonies and proclamations. The Declaration of Independence ["appeal[ed]] to the Supreme Judge of the world for the rectitude of our intentions" and avowed "a firm reliance on the protection of divine Providence." In his first inaugural address, after swearing his oath of office on a Bible, George Washington deliberately made a prayer a part of his first official act as President. [Such] supplications have been a characteristic feature of inaugural addresses ever since. Thomas Jefferson [prayed] in his first inaugural address. [In] his second inaugural address, Jefferson acknowledged his need for divine guidance and invited his audience to join his prayer. [Similarly,] James Madison, in his first inaugural address, placed his confidence "in the guardianship and guidance of that Almighty Being whose power regulates the destiny of nations, whose blessings have been so conspicuously dispensed to this rising Republic, and to whom we are bound to address our devout gratitude for the past, as well as our fervent supplications and best hopes for the future." Most recently, President Bush [asked] those attending his inauguration to bow their heads, and made a prayer his first official act as President.

Our national celebration of Thanksgiving likewise dates back to President Washington[, who] proclaimed November 26, 1789, a day of thanksgiving to 'offe[r] our prayers and supplications to the Great Lord and Ruler of Nations, and beseech him to pardon our national and other transgressions ..." This tradition of Thanksgiving Proclamations— with their religious theme of prayerful gratitude to God—has been adhered to by almost every President. The other two branches of the Federal Government also have a long-established practice of prayer at public events. [Congressional] sessions have opened with a chaplain's prayer ever since the First Congress. And this Court's own sessions have opened with the invocation "God save the United States and this Honorable Court" since the days of Chief Justice Marshall....

II.   The Court presumably would separate graduation invocations and benedictions from other instances of public "preservation and transmission of religious beliefs" on the ground that they involve "psychological coercion."   I find it a sufficient embarrassment that our Establishment Clause jurisprudence regarding holiday displays [has] come to "requir[e] scrutiny more commonly associated with interior decorators than with the judiciary."   American Jewish Congress v. Chicago, 827 F.2d 120 (Easterbrook, J., dissenting).   But interior decorating is a rock-hard science compared to psychology practiced by amateurs.   A few citations of "[r]esearch in psychology," that have no particular bearing upon the precise issue here, cannot disguise the fact that the Court has gone beyond the realm where judges know what they are doing.   The Court's argument that state officials have "coerced" students to take part in the invocation and benediction at graduation ceremonies is, not to put too fine a point on it, incoherent. . . .

A.   The Court declares that students' "attendance and participation in the [invocation and benediction] are in a fair and real sense obligatory."   But what exactly is this "fair and real sense"?   According to the Court, students at graduation who want "to avoid the fact or appearance of participation," in the invocation and benediction are psychologically obligated by "public pressure, as well as peer pressure, . . . to stand as a group or, at least, maintain respectful silence" during those prayers. This assertion—the very linchpin of the Court's opinion—is almost as intriguing for what it does not say as for what it says.   It does not say, for example, that students are psychologically coerced to bow their heads, place their hands in a Dürer-like prayer position, pay attention to the prayers, utter "Amen," or in fact pray.   (Perhaps further intensive psychological research remains to be done on these matters.)   It claims only that students are psychologically coerced "to stand . . . or, at least, maintain respectful silence."   Both halves of this disjunctive (both of which must amount to the fact or appearance of participation in prayer if the Court's analysis is to survive on its own terms) merit particular attention.   To begin with the latter: The Court's notion that a student who simply sits in "respectful silence" during the invocation and benediction (when all others are standing) has somehow joined—or would somehow be perceived as having joined—in the prayers is nothing short of ludicrous.   We indeed live in a vulgar age.   But surely "our social conventions" have not coarsened to the point that anyone who does not stand on his chair and shout obscenities can reasonably be deemed to have assented to everything said in his presence.   Since the Court does not dispute that students exposed to prayer at graduation ceremonies retain (despite "subtle coercive pressures") the free will to sit, there is absolutely no basis for the Court's decision.   It is fanciful enough to say that "a reasonable dissenter," standing head erect in a class of bowed heads, "could believe that the group exercise signified her own participation or approval of it."   It is beyond the absurd to say that she could entertain such a belief while pointedly declining to rise.

But let us assume the very worst, that the nonparticipating graduate is "subtly coerced" . . . to stand!   Even that half of the disjunctive does not remotely establish a "participation" (or an "appearance of participation'') in a religious exercise. The Court acknowledges that "in our culture standing ... can signify adherence to a view or simple respect for the views of others." (Much more often the latter than the former, I think, except perhaps in the proverbial town meeting, where one votes by standing.) But if it is a permissible inference that one who is standing is doing so simply out of respect for the prayers of others that are in progress, then how can it possibly be said that a "reasonable dissenter ... could believe that the group exercise signified her own participation or approval"? Quite obviously, it cannot.

[I] also find it odd that the Court concludes that high school graduates may not be subjected to this supposed psychological coercion, yet refrains from addressing whether "mature adults" may. I had thought that the reason graduation from high school is regarded as so significant an event is that it is generally associated with transition from adolescence to young adulthood. Many graduating seniors, of course, are old enough to vote. Why, then, does the Court treat them as though they were first-graders? Will we soon have a jurisprudence that distinguishes between mature and immature adults?

B. The other "dominant fac[t]" identified by the Court is that "[s]tate officials direct the performance of a formal religious exercise" at school graduation ceremonies. "Direct[ing] the performance of a formal religious exercise" has a sound of liturgy to it, summoning up images of the principal directing acolytes where to carry the cross, or showing the rabbi where to unroll the Torah. A Court professing to be engaged in a "delicate and fact-sensitive" line-drawing would better describe what it means as "prescribing the content of an invocation and benediction." But even that would be false. All the record shows is that principals of the Providence public schools [have] invited clergy to deliver invocations and benedictions at graduations; and that Principal Lee invited Rabbi Gutterman, provided him a two-page flyer [giving] general advice on inclusive prayer for civic occasions, and advised him that his prayers at graduation should be nonsectarian. How these facts can fairly be transformed into the charges that Principal Lee "directed and controlled the content of [Rabbi Gutterman's] prayer," that school officials "monitor prayer," and attempted to "compose official prayers," and that the "government involvement with religious activity in this case is pervasive," is difficult to fathom. The Court identifies nothing in the record remotely suggesting that school officials have ever drafted, edited, screened or censored graduation prayers, or that Rabbi Gutterman was a mouthpiece of the school officials....

III. The deeper flaw in the Court's opinion does not lie in its wrong answer to the question whether there was state-induced "peer-pressure" coercion; it lies, rather, in the Court's making violation of the Establishment Clause hinge on such a precious question. The coercion that was a hallmark of historical establishments of religion was coercion of religious orthodoxy and of financial support by force of law and threat of penalty. [Thus,] while I have no quarrel with the Court's general proposition that the Establishment Clause "guarantees that government may not coerce anyone to support or participate in religion or its exercise," I see no warrant for expanding the concept of coercion beyond acts backed by threat of penalty—a brand of coercion that, happily, is readily discernible to those of us who have made a career of reading the disciples of Blackstone rather than of Freud. The Framers were indeed opposed to coercion of religious worship by the National Government; but, as their own sponsorship of nonsectarian prayer in public events demonstrates, they understood that "[s]peech is not coercive; the listener may do as he likes." American Jewish Congress v. Chicago, 827 F.2d at 132 (Easter-brook, J., dissenting).

This historical discussion places in revealing perspective the Court's extravagant claim that the State has "for all practical purposes," and "in every practical sense," compelled students to participate in prayers at graduation. Beyond the fact [that] attendance at graduation is voluntary, there is nothing in the record to indicate that failure of attending students to take part in the invocation or benediction was subject to any penalty or discipline. Contrast this with, for example, the facts of Barnette: Schoolchildren were required by law to recite the Pledge of Allegiance; failure to do so resulted in expulsion, threatened the expelled child with the prospect of being sent to a reformatory for criminally inclined juveniles, and subjected his parents to prosecution (and incarceration) for causing delinquency. To characterize the "subtle coercive pressures," allegedly present here as the "practical" equivalent of the legal sanctions in Barnette is ... well, let me just say it is not a "delicate and fact-sensitive" analysis.

The Court relies on our "school prayer" cases. But whatever the merit of those cases, they do not support, much less compel, the Court's psycho-journey. In the first place, Engel and Abington do not constitute an exception to the rule, distilled from historical practice, that public ceremonies may include prayer; rather, they simply do not fall within the scope of the rule (for the obvious reason that school instruction is not a public ceremony). Second, we have made clear our understanding that school prayer occurs within a framework in which legal coercion to attend school (i.e., coercion under threat of penalty) provides the ulti-mate backdrop....

IV. Our religion-clause jurisprudence has become bedeviled (so to speak) by reliance on formulaic abstractions that are not derived from, but positively conflict with, our long-accepted constitutional traditions. Foremost among these has been the so-called Lemon test, which has received well-earned criticism from many members of this Court. The Court today demonstrates the irrelevance of Lemon by essentially ignor-ing it, and the interment of that case may be the one happy byproduct of the Court's otherwise lamentable decision. Unfortunately, however, the Court has replaced Lemon with its psycho-coercion test, which suffers the double disability of having no roots whatever in our people's historic practice, and being as infinitely expandable as the reasons for psycho-therapy itself.

Another happy aspect of the case is that it is only a jurisprudential disaster and not a practical one. Given the odd basis for the Court's decision, invocations and benedictions will be able to be given at public-school graduations next June, as they have for the past century and a half, so long as school authorities make clear that anyone who abstains from screaming in protest does not necessarily participate in the prayers. All that is seemingly needed is an announcement, or perhaps a written insertion at the beginning of the graduation Program, to the effect that, while all are asked to rise for the invocation and benediction, none is compelled to join in them, nor will be assumed, by rising, to have done so. That obvious fact recited, the graduates and their parents may proceed to thank God, as Americans have always done, for the blessings He has generously bestowed on them and on their country....

The reader has been told much in this case about the personal interest of Mr. Weisman and his daughter, and very little about the personal interests on the other side. They are not inconsequential. Church and state would not be such a difficult subject if religion were, as the Court apparently thinks it to be, some purely personal avocation that can be indulged entirely in secret, like pornography, in the privacy of one's room. For most believers it is not that, and has never been. Religious men and women of almost all denominations have felt it necessary to acknowledge and beseech the blessing of God as a people, and not just as individuals, because they believe in the "protection of divine Providence," as the Declaration of Independence put it, not just for individuals but for societies; because they believe God to be, as Washington's first Thanksgiving Proclamation put it, the "Great Lord and Ruler of Nations." One can believe in the effectiveness of such public worship, or one can deprecate and deride it. But the longstanding American tradition of prayer at official ceremonies displays with unmistakable clarity that the Establishment Clause does not forbid the government to accommodate it.

[For] the foregoing reasons, I dissent.

12th ED., p. 1531; IND. RTS., p. 1202

Add at end of Note 2 (after discussion of Mergens):

In LAMB'S CHAPEL v. CENTER MORICHES UNION FREE SCHOOL DISTRICT, 509 U.S. ___ (1993), the Court overturned on free speech grounds a school district's prohibition on the after-hours use of school facilities by religious groups or for religious purposes. The facts and free speech aspects of the case are described above, addition to 12th Ed., p. 1316; Ind.Rts., p. 1287. But as in Widmar, the Court rejected the argument that the exclusion was a permissible content-based restriction on speech because the restriction was mandated by the establishment clause. Justice WHITE's opinion for the Court found the school district's fears of a possible establishment clause violation "unfounded." "The showing of this film would not have been during school hours, would not have been sponsored by the school, and would have been open to the public, not just to church members. [Under] these circumstances, as in Widmar, there would have been no realistic danger that the community would think that the District was endorsing religion or any particular creed, and any benefit to religion or to the Church would have been no more than beneficial. As in Widmar, permitting District property to be used to exhibit the film involved in this case would not have been an establishment of religion under the three-part test articulated in Lemon v. Kurtzman."

Justice SCALIA, joined by Justice Thomas, concurred in the judgment, writing separately to castigate the majority for continuing to rely on the Lemon test. "Like some ghoul in a late-night horror movie that repeatedly sits up in its grave and shuffles abroad, Lemon stalks our Establishment Clause jurisprudence once again, frightening [ ] little children and school attorneys." Justice Scalia noted that a majority of the now-sitting Justices had repudiated the test, but that the Court continued to recognize it. "The secret of the Lemon test's survival, I think, is that it is so easy to kill. It is there to scare us (and our audience) when we wish it to do so, but we can command it to return to the tomb at will. When we wish to strike down a practice it forbids, we invoke it; when we wish to uphold a practice it forbids, we ignore it entirely. Sometimes, we take a middle course, calling its three prongs 'no more than helpful signposts.' Such a docile and useful monster is worth keeping around, at least in a somnolent state; one never knows when one might need him." [4]

Justice Scalia also objected to the majority's reliance on the "endorsement" concept, and this was the theme of Justice KENNEDY's separate opinion, concurring in part and concurring in the judgment. Justice Kennedy agreed with Justice Scalia's criticism of the majority's invocation of Lemon, and went on to note that "use of the phrase 'endorsing religion' [cannot] suffice as a rule of decision consistent with our precedents and our traditions in this part of our jurisprudence."

As noted above, addition to 12th Ed., p. 1316, Ind.Rts., p. 987, the Court in ROSENBERGER v. UNIVERSITY OF VIRGINIA, 519 U.S. ___ (1995), struck down on free speech grounds the University of Virginia's exclusion of religious activities from its program of paying the expenses of various student organizations and publications. Although the University did not press the claim that the exclusion was required by the Establishment Clause, it had raised the issue below, and it had been included in the grant of certiorari. Consequently, Justice KENNEDY's majority opinion devoted considerable attention to rejecting the claim that the exclusion was required in order to avoid what would otherwise have been an unconstitutional state financial support of religious activities.

Making no use of the Lemon test, Justice Kennedy relied heavily on the fact that the program was "neutral toward religion," and thus different "from a tax levied for the direct support of a church or group of churches. [The] disbursements from the [Student Activities Fund] go to private contractors for the cost of printing that which is protected under the Speech Clause of the First Amendment. That is a far cry from a general public assessment designed and effected to provide financial

---

4. In a footnote, Justice White showed himself to be unamused by the language employed in Justice Scalia's opinion. "While we are somewhat diverted by Justice Scalia's evening at the cinema, we return to the reality that there is a proper way to inter an established decision and Lemon, however frightening it might be to some, has not been overruled."

support for a church. [It] does not violate the Establishment Clause for a public university to grant access to its facilities on a religion neutral basis to a wide spectrum of student groups, including some groups which use meeting rooms for sectarian activities, accompanied by some devotional exercises. Widmar; Mergens. This is so even where the upkeep, maintenance, and repair of the facilities attributed to those uses is paid from a student activities fund to which students are required to contribute. Widmar. [It follows that] public university may maintain its own computer facility and give student groups access to that facility, including the use of printers, on a religion neutral, say first-come-first-served basis. If a religious student organization obtained access on that religion-neutral basis and used a computer to compose or a printer or copy machine to print speech with a religious content or viewpoint, the State's action in providing the group with access would no more violate the Establishment Clause than would giving those groups access to an assembly hall. There is no difference in logic or principle [between] a school using its funds to operate a facility to which students have access, and a school paying a third-party contractor to provide the facility on its behalf."

Justice O'CONNOR joined the majority opinion, and in addition issued a concurring opinion, in which she focused on the specific situation presented in this case, and concluded that in this "context [it is] improbable [that there will be] any perception of government endorsing of the religious message. [The] widely divergent viewpoints of [the] many purveyors of opinion [who are] supported on an equal basis by the University [significantly] diminishes the danger that the message of any one publication is perceived as endorsed by the University. [Particular] features of the University's program—such as explicit disclaimer, the disbursements of funds directly to third-party vendors, the vigorous nature of the forum at issue, and the possibility for objecting students to opt out—convince me that providing such assistance in this case would not carry the danger of impermissible use of public funds to endorse Wide Awake's religious message." Justice THOMAS also accompanied his agreement with the majority opinion with a separate concurrence, mainly devoted to challenging the dissent's analysis of the history of the creation of the Establishment Clause. According to Justice Thomas, Madison did not "embrace the argument [that] monetary subsidies are constitutionally different from other neutral benefits programs. [I] find much to commend [the] view [that] the experience in Virginia is consistent with the view that the Framers saw the Establishment Clause simply as a prohibition on governmental preferences for some religious faiths over others. [Moreover,] the historical evidence of government support for religious entities through property tax exemptions is overwhelming. [A] tax exemption in many cases is economically and functionally indistinguishable from a direct monetary subsidy. In one instance, the government relieves religious entities (along with others) of a generally applicable tax; in the other, it relieves religious entities (along with others) of some or all of the burden of that tax by returning it in the form of a cash subsidy. Whether the benefit is provided at the front or back end of the taxation process, the financial aid to religious groups is undeniable. The analysis under the Establishment Clause must also be the same."

Justice SOUTER, joined by Justices Stevens, Ginsburg, and Breyer, dissented, in part on the grounds that Wide Awake's free speech rights had not been violated, but mainly on the grounds that this subsidy violated the Establishment Clause, because it was an example of "using public funds for the direct subsidization of preaching the word. [If] the Clause was meant to accomplish nothing else, it was meant to bar this use of public money." Relying heavily on historical sources from the founding period, Justice Souter concluded that the original intentions, supported by subsequent case law, were plainly to prohibit state financial subsidy for religious preaching. "Why does the Court not apply this clear law to these clear facts and conclude, as I do, that the funding scheme here is a clear constitutional violation? The answer must be in part that the Court fails to confront the evidence [of the] patently and frankly evangelistic character of [this] magazine." And Justice Souter also argued that even the neutrality that was central for the majority could not save a plan that provided direct financial assistance for religious proselytization. "Evenhandedness as one element of a permissibly attenuated benefit is [a] far cry from evenhandedness as a sufficient condition for direct financial support of religious proselytization, and our cases have unsurprisingly repudiated any such attempt to cut the Establishment Clause down to a mere prohibition against unequal direct aid. [The] Court is ordering an instrumentality of the State to support religious evangelism with direct funding. That is a flat violation of the Establishment Clause."

In CAPITOL SQUARE REVIEW AND ADVISORY BOARD v. PINETTE, 519 U.S. ___ (1995), the Court dealt with the same question of whether a content-based limitation on speech was required (or permitted) by the Establishment Clause. Here the question arose in a quite different context from that in Rosenberger, and here the case generated a more divided set of opinions.

The question presented in the case was whether Columbus, Ohio, could exclude from Capitol Square, a ten-acre state-owned plaza surrounding the Ohio statehouse and generally open for "free discussion of public questions or for activities of a broad public purpose," a large cross proposed to be erected by the Ku Klux Klan. Although the Justices plainly suspected that the exclusion was based on state disagreement with the Klan's message, the free speech issue was not before the Court, which was limited to considering whether exclusion of the cross was required by the Establishment Clause.

Justice SCALIA announced the judgment of the Court and issued an opinion that was partly the court and partly an opinion joined by Chief Justice Rehnquist and Justices Kennedy and Thomas. Ohio conceded the content-based exclusion, and conceded that it would otherwise violate the Free Speech Clause of the First Amendment, but claimed that what was otherwise impermissible was commanded by the dictates of the Establishment Clause. Writing for the Court, Justice Scalia relied on Lamb's Chapel, noting that the public forum at issue here presented even a stronger case for inclusion than the school facilities at issue in Lamb's Chapel. But writing in response to the State's argument that permitting the cross on this particular piece of property "may produce the perception that the Cross bears the State's approval," Justice Scalia wrote only for the above-mentioned plurality. Here he argued that the determinative factor in judging whether endorsement was the relevant inquiry was "the difference between government speech and private speech." He went on to say that "Petitioners assert, in effect, that that distinction disappears when the private speech is conducted too close to the symbols of government. But that, of course, must be merely a subpart of a more general principle: that the distinction disappears whenever private speech can be mistaken for government speech. That proposition cannot be accepted, at least where, as here, the government has not fostered or encouraged the mistake. [But given] an open forum and private sponsorship, erroneous conclusions do not count. [Capitol] Square is a genuinely public forum, is known to be a public forum, and has been widely used as a public forum for many, many years. Private religious speech cannot be subject to veto by those who see favoritism where there is none. [If] Ohio is concerned about misperceptions, nothing prevents it from requiring all private displays in the Square to be identified as such."

Justice THOMAS also issued a separate concurrence, in which he questioned the posture in which the Court found itself. "The fact that the legal issue before us involves the Establishment Clause should not lead anyone to think that a cross erected by the Ku Klux Klan is a purely religious symbol. The erection of such a cross is a political act, not a Christian one. There is little doubt that the Klan's main objective is to establish a racist white government in the United States. In Klan ceremony, the cross is a symbol of white supremacy and a tool for the intimidation and harassment of racial minorities, Catholics, Jews, Communists, and any other groups hated by the Klan. The cross is associated with the Klan not because of religious worship, but because of the Klan's practice of cross-burning. [The] Klan simply has appropriated one of the most sacred of religious symbols as a symbol of hate. In my mind, this suggests that this case may not have truly involved the Establishment Clause, although I agree with the Court's disposition because of the manner in which the case has come before us. In the end, there may be much less to this case than meets the eye."

Justice O'CONNOR, joined by Justices Souter and Breyer, concurred in part and concurred in the judgment. Focusing primarily on the endorsement question, she parted company with the plurality on the question whether and when non-governmental speech could create the impression of government endorsement. "I believe that an impermissible message of endorsement can be sent in a variety of contexts, not all of which involve direct government speech or outright favoritism. [This] is [not] to suggest that I would be likely to come to a different result from the plurality where truly private speech is allowed on equal terms in a vigorous public forum that the government has administered properly. [In other cases to] the plurality's consideration of the open nature of the forum and the private ownership of the display, [I] would add the presence of a sign disclaiming government sponsorship or endorsement on the Klan cross, which would make the State's role clear to the community." More fundamentally, however, Justice O'Connor made it clear that she "part[ed] company with the plurality on a fundamental point: I disagree that '[i]t has radical implications for our public policy to suggest that neutral laws are invalid whenever hypothetical observers may—even reasonably—confuse an incidental benefit to religion with State endorsement.' On the contrary, when the reasonable observer would view a government practice as endorsing religion, [the] practice [is] invalid. [The] Establishment Clause imposes affirmative obligations that may require a State, in some situations, to take steps to avoid being perceived as supporting or endorsing a private religious message. [Where] the government's operation of a public forum has the effect of endorsing religion, even if the governmental actor neither intends nor actively encourages that result, the Establishment Clause is violated." Objecting to what she saw as the plurality's "per se rule" about government speech and private speech, Justice O'Connor concluded that Establishment Clause inquiries "should remain flexible," and that "the endorsement test supplies an appropriate standard for [our] inquiry." And in applying that test, she urged that it be considered in light not of "the actual perception of individual observers, who naturally have differing degrees of knowledge," but of " 'the "objective" meaning of the [government's] statement in the community' Lynch," [which is] similar to the 'reasonable person' in tort law."

Justice SOUTER, joined by Justices O'Connor and Breyer, also concurred in part and concurred in the judgment. "I vote to affirm in large part because of the possibility of affixing a sign to the cross adequately disclaiming any government sponsorship or endorsement of it." Like Justice O'Connor's, Justice Souter's opinion disagreed sharply with the plurality's "per se rule," and noted that the possibility of reasonable misperception could have existed even in this case. "Given the domination of the square by the government's own displays, one would not be a dimwit as a matter of law to think that an unattended religious display there was endorsed by the government. [I would apply] the endorsement test to private speech in public forums, [and the plurality's view] creates a serious loophole in the protection provided by the endorsement test. [By] allowing government to encourage what it cannot do on its own, the proposed per se rule would tempt a public body to contract out of its establishment of religion, by encouraging the private enterprise of the religious to exhibit what the government could not exhibit itself."

Justice STEVENS dissented, arguing that there should be "a strong presumption against the installation of unattended religious symbols on public property." Justice GINSBURG also dissented, finding the possibility of a disclaimer insufficient. Without an actual and "sturdy" disclaimer, she found the unattended display of the cross to violate the Establishment Clause.

12th ED.; p. 1584; IND. RTS., p. 1255:
Add as new footnote following "[I] dissent.":

The 103rd Congress reversed the result of Employment Division, Oregon Dept. of Human Resources v. Smith by passing the American Indian Religious Freedom Act (P.L.

103–344) on October 6, 1994. The act specifically protects the rights of Native Americans to ingest peyote during religious ceremonies and prohibits states from discriminating against those who use the hallucinogen as part of Indian religious ceremonies.

12th ED., p. 1585; IND.RTS., p. 1256
Add at end of footnote 1:

The Religious Freedom Restoration Act of 1993 was signed into law on November 16, 1993 (P.L. 103–141). The Act mandates that "Government shall not substantially burden a person's exercise of religion even if the burden results from a rule of general applicability." The congressional findings include an express disavowal of Employment Division v. Smith, and an intention to return to the compelling interest standard in Sherbert and Yoder. The Act codifies the "least restrictive means" and "compelling interest" tests, although section 7 says that the statute does not affect the Establishment Clause itself.

12th ED., p. 1586; IND. RTS., p. 1257
Add after Smith and subsequent Note:

CHURCH OF THE LUKUMI BABALU AYE, INC. v. CITY OF HIALEAH

509 U.S. ___, 113 S.Ct. 2217, 124 L.Ed.2d 472 (1993).

JUSTICE KENNEDY delivered the opinion of the Court, except as to Part II–A–2.*

The principle that government may not enact laws that suppress religious belief or practice is so well understood that few violations are recorded in our opinions. Concerned that this fundamental nonpersecution principle of the First Amendment was implicated here, however, we granted certiorari. Our review confirms that the laws in question were enacted by officials who did not understand, failed to perceive, or chose to ignore the fact that their official actions violated the Nation's essential commitment to religious freedom....

I.A. This case involves practices of the Santeria religion, which originated in the nineteenth century. When hundreds of thousands of members of the Yoruba people were brought as slaves from eastern Africa to Cuba, their traditional African religion absorbed significant elements of Roman Catholicism. The resulting syncretion, or fusion, is Santeria, "the way of the saints." The Cuban Yoruba express their devotion to spirits, called orishas, through the iconography of Catholic saints, Catholic symbols are often present at Santeria rites, and Santeria devotees attend the Catholic sacraments. The Santeria faith teaches that every individual has a destiny from God, a destiny fulfilled with the aid and energy of the orishas. The basis of the Santeria religion is the nurture of a personal relation with the orishas, and one of the principal forms of devotion is an animal sacrifice.

The sacrifice of animals as part of religious rituals has ancient roots. Animal sacrifice is mentioned throughout the Old Testament, and it played an important role in the practice of Judaism before destruction of

* The Chief Justice, Justice Scalia and Justice Thomas join all but Part II–A–2 of this opinion. Justice White joins all but Part II–A of this opinion. Justice Souter joins only Parts I, III, and IV of this opinion ... [Footnote by Justice Kennedy.]

the second Temple in Jerusalem. In modern Islam, there is an annual sacrifice commemorating Abraham's sacrifice of a ram in the stead of his son. According to Santeria teaching, the orishas [depend] for survival on the sacrifice. Sacrifices are performed at birth, marriage, and death rites, for the cure of the sick, for the initiation of new members and priests, and during an annual celebration. Animals sacrificed [include] chickens, pigeons, doves, ducks, guinea pigs, goats, sheep, and turtles. The animals are killed by the cutting of the carotid arteries in the neck. The sacrificed animal is cooked and eaten, except after healing and death rituals.

Santeria adherents faced widespread persecution in Cuba, so the religion and its rituals were practiced in secret. [The] religion was brought to this Nation most often by exiles from the Cuban revolution. The District Court estimated that there are at least 50,000 practitioners in South Florida today.

B. Petitioner Church of the Lukumi Babalu Aye, Inc. (Church) [and] its congregants practice the Santeria religion. [In] April 1987, the Church leased land in the city of Hialeah, Florida, and announced plans to establish a house of worship as well as a school, cultural center, and museum. [The] prospect of a Santeria church in their midst was distressing to many members of the Hialeah community, and [prompted] the city council to hold an emergency public session on June 9, 1987. [At] the [meeting] the city council adopted Resolution 87–66, which noted the "concern" ["that] certain religions may propose to engage in practices which are inconsistent with public morals, peace or safety," and declared that "[t]he City reiterates its commitment to a prohibition against any and all acts of any and all religious groups which are inconsistent with public morals, peace or safety." Next, the council approved [Ordinance] 87–40, that incorporated [Florida's] animal cruelty laws. Among other things, the incorporated [Fla.Stat. 828.12] subjected to criminal punishment "[w]hoever ... unnecessarily or cruelly ... kills any animal." The city council desired to undertake further legislative action, [and] Hialeah's city attorney requested an opinion from the attorney general of Florida as to whether § 828.12 prohibited "a religious group from sacrificing an animal in a religious ritual or practice" and whether the city could enact ordinances "making religious animal sacrifice unlawful." The attorney general responded [that] the "ritual sacrifice of animals for purposes other than food consumption" was not a "necessary" killing and so was prohibited by § 828.12. [He] advised that religious animal sacrifice was against state law [and could also be prohibited by city ordinance.]

The city council responded first with [a Resolution noting] its residents' "great concern regarding the possibility of public ritualistic animal sacrifices." [The] resolution declared the city policy "to oppose the ritual sacrifices of animals" within Hialeah and announced that any person or organization practicing animal sacrifice "will be prosecuted." In September 1987, the city council adopted three substantive ordinances addressing the issue of religious animal sacrifice. Ordinance 87–52 defined "sacrifice" as "to unnecessarily kill, torment, torture, or mutilate an animal in a public or private ritual or ceremony not for the primary purpose of food consumption," and prohibited owning or possessing an animal "intending to use such animal for food purposes." It restricted application of this prohibition, however, to any individual or group that "kills, slaughters or sacrifices animals for any type of ritual, regardless of whether or not the flesh or blood of the animal is to be consumed." The ordinance contained an exemption for slaughtering by "licensed establishment[s]" of animals "specifically raised for food purposes." Declaring, moreover, that the city council "has determined that the sacrificing of animals within the city limits is contrary to the public health, safety, welfare and morals of the community," the city council adopted Ordinance 87–71. That ordinance defined sacrifice as had Ordinance 87–52, and then provided that "[i]t shall be unlawful for any person, persons, corporations or associations to sacrifice any animal within the corporate limits of the City of Hialeah, Florida." The final Ordinance, 87–72, defined "slaughter" as "the killing of animals for food" and prohibited slaughter outside of areas zoned for slaughterhouse use. The ordinance provided an exemption, however, for the slaughter or processing for sale of "small numbers of hogs and/or cattle per week in accordance with an exemption provided by state law." All ordinances and resolutions passed the city council by unanimous vote. Violations [were] punishable by fines not exceeding $500 or imprisonment not exceeding 60 days, or both.

Following enactment of these ordinances, the Church [filed] this action [in] the United States District Court for the Southern District of Florida. [After] a 9–day bench trial, [the] District Court ruled for the city, finding no violation of [the] Free Exercise Clause. [The] Court of Appeals for the Eleventh Circuit affirmed. . . .

II. [The] city does not argue that Santeria is not a "religion" within the meaning of the First Amendment. Nor could it. Although [animal] sacrifice may seem abhorrent to some, "religious beliefs need not be acceptable, logical, consistent, or comprehensible to others in order to merit First Amendment protection." Thomas v. Review Bd. Given the historical association between animal sacrifice and religious worship, petitioners' assertion that animal sacrifice is an integral part of their religion "cannot be deemed bizarre or incredible." Frazee v. Illinois Dept. of Employment Security, 489 U.S. 829 (1989). Neither the city nor the courts below have questioned the sincerity of petitioners' professed desire to conduct animal sacrifices for religious reasons.

[Our free exercise] cases establish [that] a law that is neutral and of general applicability need not be justified by a compelling governmental interest even if the law has the incidental effect of burdening a particular religious practice. Smith. Neutrality and general applicability are interrelated, and [failure] to satisfy one is a likely indication that the other has not been satisfied. A law failing to satisfy these requirements must be justified by a compelling governmental interest and must be narrowly tailored to advance that interest. . . .

A. [At] a minimum, [the] Free Exercise Clause pertains if the law at issue discriminates against some or all religious beliefs or regulates or prohibits conduct because it is undertaken for religious reasons. [These] principles, though not often at issue in our cases, have played a role in some. In McDaniel v. Paty, 435 U.S. 618 (1978), for example, we invalidated a State law that disqualified members of the clergy from holding certain public offices, because it "impose[d] special disabilities on the basis of ... religious status." Smith....

1. Although a law targeting religious beliefs as such is never permissible, if the object of a law is to infringe upon or restrict practices because of their religious motivation, the law is not neutral; and it is invalid unless it is justified by a compelling interest and is narrowly tailored to advance that interest. There are, of course, many ways of demonstrating that the object or purpose of a law is the suppression of religion or religious conduct. [We] must begin with its text, for the minimum requirement of neutrality is that a law not discriminate on its face. A law lacks facial neutrality if it refers to a religious practice without a secular meaning discernable from the language or context. Petitioners contend that three of the ordinances fail this test of facial neutrality because they use the words "sacrifice" and "ritual," words with strong religious connotations. We agree that these words are consistent with the claim of facial discrimination, but the argument is not conclusive. The words "sacrifice" and "ritual" have a religious origin, but current use admits also of secular meanings.

[We] reject the contention advanced by the city that our inquiry must end with the text of the laws. [Facial] neutrality is not determinative, [and] official action that targets religious conduct for distinctive treatment cannot be shielded by mere compliance with the requirement of facial neutrality. The Free Exercise Clause protects against governmental hostility which is masked, as well as overt.

The record in this case compels the conclusion that suppression of the central element of the Santeria worship service was the object of the ordinances. [Resolution 87–66] recited that "residents and citizens of the City of Hialeah have expressed their concern that certain religions may propose to engage in practices which are inconsistent with public morals, peace or safety," and "reiterate[d]" the city's commitment to prohibit "any and all [such] acts of any and all religious groups." No one suggests, and on this record it cannot be maintained, that city officials had in mind a religion other than Santeria.

It becomes evident that these ordinances target Santeria sacrifice when the ordinances' operation is considered. Apart from the text, the effect of a law in its real operation is strong evidence of its object. To be sure, adverse impact will not always lead to a finding of impermissible targeting. For example, a social harm may have been a legitimate concern of government for reasons quite apart from discrimination. Reynolds. The subject at hand does implicate, of course, multiple concerns unrelated to religious animosity, for example, the suffering or mistreatment visited upon the sacrificed animals, and health hazards from improper disposal. But the ordinances when considered together disclose an object remote from these legitimate concerns[, an] impermissible attempt to target petitioners and their religious practices.

[Almost] the only conduct subject to [the ordinances] is the religious exercise of Santeria church members. [Ordinance] 87–71 [prohibits] the sacrifice of animals but defines sacrifice as "to unnecessarily kill ... an animal in a public or private ritual or ceremony not for the primary purpose of food consumption." The definition excludes almost all killings of animals except for religious sacrifice, and the primary purpose requirement narrows the proscribed category even further [by] exempting Kosher slaughter. We need not discuss whether this differential treatment of two religions is itself an independent constitutional violation. It suffices to recite this feature of the law as support for our conclusion that Santeria alone was the exclusive legislative concern. The net result of the gerrymander is that few if any killings of animals are prohibited other than Santeria sacrifice, which is proscribed because it occurs during a ritual or ceremony and its primary purpose is to make an offering to the orishas, not food consumption. Indeed, careful drafting ensured that, although Santeria sacrifice is prohibited, killings that are no more necessary or humane in almost all other circumstances are unpunished.

Operating in similar fashion is Ordinance 87–52, which prohibits the "possess[ion], sacrifice, or slaughter" of an animal with the "inten[t] to use such animal for food purposes." This prohibition [applies] if the animal is killed in "any type of ritual" and there is an intent to use the animal for food. [The] ordinance exempts, however, "any licensed [food] establishment" with regard to "any animals which are specifically raised for food purposes," if the activity is permitted by zoning and other laws. This exception, too, seems intended to cover Kosher slaughter. Again, the burden of the ordinance [falls] on Santeria adherents but almost no others.

[Ordinance] 87–40 incorporates the Florida animal cruelty statute. Its prohibition is broad on its face, punishing "[w]hoever ... unnecessarily ... kills any animal." The city claims that this ordinance is the epitome of a neutral prohibition. The problem, however, is the interpretation given to the ordinance by respondent and the Florida attorney general. Killings for religious reasons are deemed unnecessary, whereas most other killings fall outside the prohibition. The city [deems] hunting, slaughter of animals for food, eradication of insects and pests, and euthanasia as necessary. [Indeed,] one of the few reported Florida cases decided under § 828.12 concludes that the use of live rabbits to train greyhounds is not unnecessary.

[We] also find significant evidence of the ordinances' improper targeting of Santeria sacrifice in the fact that they proscribe more religious conduct than is necessary to achieve their stated ends. [Indeed,] counsel for the city conceded at oral argument that, under the ordinances, Santeria sacrifices would be illegal even if they occurred in licensed, inspected, and zoned slaughterhouses. [Under] similar analysis, narrower regulation would achieve the city's interest in preventing cruelty to animals. With regard to the city's interest in ensuring the adequate care of animals, regulation of conditions and treatment, regardless of why an animal is kept, is the logical response to the city's concern, not a prohibition on possession for the purpose of sacrifice.

The same is true for the city's interest in prohibiting cruel methods of killing. Under federal and Florida law and Ordinance 87–40, [killing] an animal by the "simultaneous and instantaneous severance of the carotid arteries with a sharp instrument"—the method used in Kosher slaughter—is approved as humane. The District Court found that, though Santeria sacrifice also results in severance of the carotid arteries, the method used during sacrifice is less reliable and therefore not humane. If the city has a real concern that other methods are less humane, however, the subject of the regulation should be the method of slaughter itself, not a religious classification that is said to bear some general relation to it. . . .

2. In determining if the object of a law is a neutral one, [we] can also find guidance in our equal protection cases. [Here,] as in equal protection cases, we may determine the city council's object from both direct and circumstantial evidence. Relevant evidence includes, among other things, the historical background of the decision under challenge, the specific series of events leading to the enactment or official policy in question, as well as the legislative or administrative history, including contemporaneous statements made by members of the decisionmaking body.

[The] minutes and taped excerpts of the June 9 session [evidence] significant hostility exhibited by residents, members of the city council, and other city officials toward the Santeria religion and its practice of animal sacrifice. The public crowd that attended the June 9 meetings interrupted statements by council members critical of Santeria with cheers. [When] Councilman Martinez, a supporter of the ordinances, stated that in prerevolution Cuba "people were put in jail for practicing this religion," the audience applauded. [Then] Councilman Martinez [questioned,] "if we could not practice this [religion] in our homeland [Cuba], why bring it to this country?" Councilman Cardoso said that Santeria devotees at the Church "are in violation of everything this country stands for." Councilman Mejides indicated that he was "totally against the sacrificing of animals" and distinguished Kosher slaughter because it had a "real purpose." The "Bible says we are allowed to sacrifice an animal for consumption," he continued, "but for any other purposes, I don't believe that the Bible allows that." The president of the city council [asked], "What can we do to prevent the Church from opening?" Various Hialeah city officials made comparable comments. The chaplain of the Hialeah Police Department told the city council that Santeria was a sin, "foolishness," "an abomination to the Lord," and the worship of "demons." He advised the city council that "We need to be helping people and sharing with them the truth that is found in Jesus Christ." He concluded: "I would exhort you . . . not to permit this Church to exist." . . .

3. In sum, the neutrality inquiry leads to one conclusion: The ordinances had as their object the suppression of religion. The pattern we have recited discloses animosity to Santeria adherents and their religious practices; the ordinances by their own terms target this religious exercise; the texts of the ordinances were gerrymandered with care to proscribe religious killings of animals but to exclude almost all

secular killings; and the ordinances suppress much more religious conduct than is necessary in order to achieve the legitimate ends asserted in their defense. These ordinances are not neutral, and the court below committed clear error in failing to reach this conclusion.

B. We turn next to a second requirement of the Free Exercise Clause, [that] laws burdening religious practice must be of general applicability. All laws are selective to some extent, but categories of selection are of paramount concern when a law has the incidental effect of burdening religious practice. [The] principle that government, in pursuit of legitimate interests, cannot in a selective manner impose burdens only on conduct motivated by religious belief is essential to [the] Free Exercise Clause. In this case we need not define with precision the standard used to evaluate whether a prohibition is of general application, for these ordinances fall well below the minimum standard necessary to protect First Amendment rights.

Respondent claims that [the] ordinances advance two interests: protecting the public health and preventing cruelty to animals. The ordinances are underinclusive for those ends, [failing] to prohibit non-religious conduct that endangers these interests in a similar or greater degree than Santeria sacrifice does. The underinclusion is substantial, not inconsequential. Despite the city's proffered interest in preventing cruelty to animals, the ordinances are drafted with care to forbid few killings but those occasioned by religious sacrifice. Many types of animal deaths or kills for nonreligious reasons are either not prohibited or approved by express provision. For example, fishing [is] legal. Extermination of mice and rats within a home is also permitted. Florida law incorporated by Ordinance 87–40 sanctions euthanasia of "stray, neglected, abandoned, or unwanted animals"; destruction of animals judicially removed from their owners "for humanitarian reasons" or when the animal "is of no commercial value"; the infliction of pain or suffering "in the interest of medical science"; the placing of poison in one's yard or enclosure; and the use of a live animal "to pursue or take wildlife or to participate in any hunting" and "to hunt wild hogs."

The city [asserts] that animal sacrifice is "different" from the animal killings that are permitted by law. According to the city, it is "self-evident" that killing animals for food is "important"; the eradication of insects and pests is "obviously justified"; and the euthanasia of excess animals "makes sense." These ipse dixits do not explain why religion alone must bear the burden, when many of these secular killings fall within the city's interest in preventing the cruel treatment of animals.

The ordinances are also underinclusive with regard to the city's interest in public health, which is threatened by the disposal of animal carcasses in open public places and the consumption of uninspected meat. Neither interest is pursued by respondent with regard to conduct that is not motivated by religious conviction. The health risks posed by the improper disposal of animal carcasses are the same whether Santeria sacrifice or some nonreligious killing preceded it. The city does not, however, prohibit hunters from bringing their kill to their houses, nor does it regulate disposal after their activity. Despite substantial testimony at trial that the same public health hazards result from improper disposal of garbage by restaurants, restaurants are outside the scope of the ordinances.

[The] ordinances are underinclusive as well with regard to the health risk posed by consumption of uninspected meat. Under the city's ordinances, hunters may eat their kill and fisherman may eat their catch without undergoing governmental inspection. Likewise, state law requires inspection of meat that is sold but exempts meat from animals raised for the use of the owner and "members of his household and nonpaying guests and employees." ...

III. A law burdening religious practice that is not neutral or not of general application must undergo the most rigorous of scrutiny. To satisfy [the] First Amendment, a law restrictive of religious practice must advance "interests of the highest order" and must be narrowly tailored in pursuit of those interests. Wisconsin v. Yoder. The compelling interest standard that we apply once a law fails to meet the Smith requirements is not "water[ed] ... down" but "really means what it says." A law that targets religious conduct for distinctive treatment or advances legitimate governmental interests only against conduct with a religious motivation will survive strict scrutiny only in rare cases. It follows [that] these ordinances cannot withstand this scrutiny.

First, even were the governmental interests compelling, the ordinances are not drawn in narrow terms to accomplish those interests. As we have discussed, all four ordinances are overbroad or underinclusive in substantial respects. [Respondent] has not demonstrated, moreover, [that] its governmental interests are compelling. Where government restricts only conduct protected by the First Amendment and fails to enact feasible measures to restrict other conduct producing substantial harm or alleged harm of the same sort, the interest given in justification of the restriction is not compelling. ...

IV. The Free Exercise Clause commits government itself to religious tolerance, and upon even slight suspicion that proposals for state intervention stem from animosity to religion or distrust of its practices, all officials must pause to remember their own high duty to the Constitution and to the rights it secures. Those in office must be resolute in resisting importunate demands and must ensure that the sole reasons for imposing the burdens of law and regulation are secular. Legislators may not devise mechanisms, overt or disguised, designed to persecute or oppress a religion or its practices. The laws here in question were enacted contrary to these constitutional principles, and they are void.

Reversed.

Justice SCALIA, with whom the Chief Justice [REHNQUIST] joins, concurring in part and concurring in the judgment.

The Court analyzes the "neutrality" and "general applicability" of the Hialeah ordinances in separate sections (Parts II–A and II–B, respectively), and allocates various invalidating factors to one or the other of those sections. If it were necessary to make a clear distinction between the two terms, I would draw a line somewhat different from the Court's. But I think it is not necessary, and would frankly acknowledge that the terms are not only "interrelated," but substantially overlap.

The terms "neutrality" and "general applicability" [are] used in Smith and earlier cases to describe those characteristics which cause a law that prohibits an activity a particular individual wishes to engage in for religious reasons nonetheless not to constitute a "law ... prohibiting the free exercise" of religion. [In] my view, the defect of lack of neutrality applies primarily to those laws that by their terms impose disabilities on the basis of religion (e.g., a law excluding members of a certain sect from public benefits); whereas the defect of lack of general applicability applies primarily to those laws which, though neutral in their terms, through their design, construction, or enforcement target the practices of a particular religion for discriminatory treatment. But certainly a law that is not of general applicability (in the sense I have described) can be considered "nonneutral"; and certainly no law that is nonneutral (in the relevant sense) can be thought to be of general applicability. Because I agree with most of the invalidating factors set forth in Part II of the Court's opinion, and because it seems to me a matter of no consequence under which rubric [each] invalidating factor is discussed, I join the judgment of the Court and all of its opinion except section 2 of Part II-A.

I do not join that section because it departs from the opinion's general focus on the object of the laws at issue to consider the subjective motivation of the lawmakers, i.e., whether the City Council actually intended to disfavor the religion of Santeria. [The] First Amendment does not refer to the purposes for which legislators enact laws, but to the effects of the laws enacted: "Congress shall make no law ... prohibiting the free exercise [of religion] ... ." This does not put us in the business of invalidating laws by reason of the evil motives of their authors. Had the City Council set out resolutely to suppress the practices of Santeria, but ineptly adopted ordinances that failed to do so, I do not see how those laws could be said to "prohibi[t] the free exercise" of religion. Nor, in my view, does it matter that a legislature consists entirely of the pure-hearted, if the law it enacts in fact singles out a religious practice for special burdens. Had the ordinances here been passed with no motive on the part of any councilman except the ardent desire to prevent cruelty to animals (as might in fact have been the case), they would nonetheless be invalid.

Justice SOUTER, concurring in part and concurring in the judgment.

This case turns on a principle about which there is no disagreement, that the Free Exercise Clause bars government action aimed at suppressing religious belief or practice. The Court holds that Hialeah's animal-sacrifice laws violate that principle, and I concur in that holding without reservation.

Because prohibiting religious exercise is the object of the laws at hand, this case does not present the more difficult issue addressed in Smith, which announced the rule that a "neutral, generally applicable" law does not run afoul of the Free Exercise Clause even when it prohibits religious exercise in effect. The Court today refers to that rule in dicta, and despite my general agreement with the Court's opinion I do not join Part II, [for] I have doubts about whether the Smith rule merits adherence. I write separately to explain why the Smith rule is not germane to this case and to express my view that, in a case presenting the issue, the Court should reexamine the rule Smith declared.

I. According to Smith, if prohibiting the exercise of religion results from enforcing a "neutral, generally applicable" law, the Free Exercise Clause has not been offended. I call this the Smith rule to distinguish it from the noncontroversial principle, also expressed in Smith though established long before, that the Free Exercise Clause is offended when prohibiting religious exercise results from a law that is not neutral or generally applicable. It is this noncontroversial principle [that] is at issue here. But before turning to [Smith,] it will help to get the terms in order, for the significance of the Smith rule is not only in its statement that the Free Exercise Clause requires no more than "neutrality" and "general applicability," but in its adoption of a particular, narrow conception of free-exercise neutrality.

That the Free Exercise Clause contains a "requirement for governmental neutrality," Yoder, is hardly a novel proposition; though the term does not appear in the First Amendment, our cases have used it as shorthand to describe [part of] what the Clause commands. Nor is there anything unusual about the notion that the Free Exercise Clause requires general applicability, though the Court, until today, has not used exactly that term in stating a reason for invalidation. While general applicability is, for the most part, self-explanatory, free-exercise neutrality is not self-revealing. A law that is religion neutral on its face or in its purpose may lack neutrality in its effect by forbidding something that religion requires or requiring something that religion forbids. A secular law, applicable to all, that prohibits consumption of alcohol, for example, will affect members of religions that require the use of wine differently from members of other religions and nonbelievers, disproportionately burdening the practice of, say, Catholicism or Judaism. Without an exemption for sacramental wine, Prohibition may fail the test of religion neutrality.

It does not necessarily follow, [of] course, that the First Amendment requires an exemption from Prohibition; that depends on the meaning of neutrality as the Free Exercise Clause embraces it. The point here is the unremarkable one that our common notion of neutrality is broad enough to cover not merely what might be called formal neutrality, which as a free-exercise requirement would only bar laws with an object to discriminate against religion, but also what might be called substantive neutrality, which, in addition to demanding a secular object, would generally require government to accommodate religious differences by exempting religious practices from formally neutral laws. If the Free Exercise Clause secures only protection against deliberate discrimination, a formal requirement will exhaust the Clause's neutrality command; if the Free Exercise Clause, rather, safeguards a right to engage in religious activity free from unnecessary governmental interference, the Clause requires substantive, as well as formal, neutrality.[1]

Though Smith used the term "neutrality" without a modifier, the rule it announced plainly assumes that free-exercise neutrality is of the formal sort. Distinguishing between laws whose "object" is to prohibit religious exercise and those that prohibit religious exercise as an "incidental effect," Smith placed only the former within the reaches of the Free Exercise Clause; the latter, laws that satisfy formal neutrality, Smith would subject to no free-exercise scrutiny at all, even when they prohibit religious exercise in application. The four Justices who rejected the Smith rule, by contrast, read the Free Exercise Clause as embracing what I have termed substantive neutrality.

[The] proposition for which the Smith rule stands, then, is that formal neutrality, along with general applicability, are sufficient conditions for constitutionality under the Free Exercise Clause. That proposition is not at issue in this case, however, for Hialeah's [ordinances] are not neutral under any definition, any more than they are generally applicable. This case, rather, involves the noncontroversial principle repeated in Smith, that formal neutrality and general applicability are necessary conditions for free-exercise constitutionality. [In] applying that principle the Court does not tread on troublesome ground.

[The] Court also rightly finds Hialeah's laws to fail the test of general applicability, and [the] Court [need] not discuss the rules that apply to prohibitions found to be generally applicable. The [Court's] suggestions on that score are dicta.

II. In being so readily susceptible to resolution by applying the Free Exercise Clause's "fundamental nonpersecution principle," this is far from a representative free-exercise case. While [Hialeah] has provided a rare example of a law actually aimed at suppressing religious exercise, Smith was typical of our free-exercise cases, involving as it did a formally neutral, generally applicable law. The rule Smith announced, however, was decidedly untypical of the cases involving the same type of law. Because Smith left those prior cases standing, we are left with a free-exercise jurisprudence in tension with itself, a tension that should be addressed [by] reexamining the Smith rule in the next case that would turn upon its application.

A. In developing standards to judge the enforceability of formally neutral, generally applicable laws, [the] Court has addressed the concepts of neutrality and general applicability by indicating, in language hard to read as not foreclosing the Smith rule, that the Free Exercise Clause embraces more than mere formal neutrality, and that formal neutrality and general applicability are not sufficient conditions for free-

---

1. One might further distinguish between formal neutrality and facial neutrality. While facial neutrality would permit discovery of a law's object or purpose only by analysis of the law's words, structure and operation, formal neutrality would permit enquiry also into the intentions of those who enacted the law. For present purposes, the distinction between formal and facial neutrality is less important than the distinction between those conceptions of neutrality and substantive neutrality. [Footnote by Justice Souter.]

exercise constitutionality: "In a variety of ways we have said that '[a] regulation neutral on its face may, in its application, nonetheless offend the constitutional requirement for governmental neutrality if it unduly burdens the free exercise of religion.'" Thomas, quoting Yoder. Not long before the Smith decision, indeed, the Court specifically rejected the argument that "neutral and uniform" requirements for governmental benefits need satisfy only a reasonableness standard, in part because "[s]uch a test has no basis in precedent." Hobbie v. Unemployment Appeals Comm'n. [Thus] we have applied the same rigorous scrutiny to burdens on religious exercise resulting from the enforcement of formally neutral, generally applicable laws as we have applied to burdens caused by laws that single out religious exercise.

[Though] Smith sought to distinguish the free-exercise cases in which the Court mandated exemptions from secular laws of general application, I am not persuaded. [Since] holding in 1940 that the Free Exercise Clause applies to the States, the Court repeatedly has stated that the Clause sets strict limits on the government's power to burden religious exercise, whether it is a law's object to do so or its unanticipated effect. Smith responded to these statements by suggesting that the Court did not really mean what it said, detecting in at least the most recent opinions a lack of commitment to the compelling-interest test in the context of formally neutral laws. But even if the Court's commitment were that pallid, it would argue only for moderating the language of the test, not for eliminating constitutional scrutiny altogether. In any event, I would have trouble concluding that the Court has not meant what it has said in more than a dozen cases over several decades, particularly when in the same period it repeatedly applied the compelling-interest test to require exemptions, even in a case [Frazee] decided the year before Smith. [Whatever] Smith's virtues, they do not include a comfortable fit with settled law.

B. The Smith rule, in my view, may be reexamined consistently with principles of stare decisis. To begin with, the Smith rule was not subject to "full-dress argument" prior to its announcement. Mapp v. Ohio, 367 U.S. 643 (1961) (Harlan, J., dissenting). The State of Oregon in Smith contended that its refusal to exempt religious peyote use survived the strict scrutiny required by "settled free exercise principles." [Respondents] joined issue on the outcome of strict scrutiny on the facts before the Court, and neither party squarely addressed the proposition the Court was to embrace, that the Free Exercise Clause was irrelevant to the dispute. Sound judicial decisionmaking requires "both a vigorous prosecution and a vigorous defense" of the issues in dispute, Christiansburg Garment Co. v. EEOC, 434 U.S. 412 (1978), and a constitutional rule announced sua sponte is entitled to less deference than one addressed on full briefing and argument.

The Smith rule's vitality as precedent is limited further by the seeming want of any need of it in resolving the question presented in that case. [The] majority never determined that the case could not be resolved on the narrower ground, going instead straight to the broader constitutional rule. But the Court's better practice, one supported by the same principles of restraint that underlie the rule of stare decisis, is not to "formulate a rule of constitutional law broader than is required by the precise facts to which it is to be applied." Ashwander v. TVA [1936; below, 12th Ed., p. 1640; Ind.Rts., p. 1311]. . . .

I do not, of course, mean to imply that a broad constitutional rule announced without full briefing and argument necessarily lacks precedential weight. Over time, such a decision may become "part of the tissue of the law," Radovich v. National Football League, 352 U.S. 445 (1957) (Frankfurter, J., dissenting), and may be subject to reliance in a way that new and unexpected decisions are not. Smith, however, is not such a case. By the same token, by pointing out Smith's recent vintage I do not mean to suggest that novelty alone is enough to justify reconsideration. "[S]tare decisis," as Justice Frankfurter wrote, "is a principle of policy and not a mechanical formula," Helvering v. Hallock, 309 U.S. 106 (1940), and the decision whether to adhere to a prior decision, particularly a constitutional decision, is a complex and difficult one that does not lend itself to resolution by application of simple, categorical rules, but that must account for a variety of often competing considerations.

The considerations of full-briefing, necessity, and novelty thus do not exhaust the legitimate reasons for reexamining prior decisions, or even for reexamining the Smith rule. One important further consideration warrants mention here, however, because it demands the reexamination I have in mind. Smith presents not the usual question of whether to follow a constitutional rule, but the question of which constitutional rule to follow, for Smith refrained from overruling prior free-exercise cases that contain a free-exercise rule fundamentally at odds with the rule Smith declared. [The] result is an intolerable tension in free-exercise law which may be resolved, consistently with principles of stare decisis, in a case in which the tension is presented and its resolution pivotal.

While the tension on which I rely exists within the body of our extant case law, a rereading of that case law will not, of course, mark the limits of any enquiry directed to reexamining the Smith rule, which should be reviewed in light not only of the precedent on which it was rested but also of the text of the Free Exercise Clause and its origins. As for text, [suffice] it to say that a respectable argument may be made that the pre-Smith law comes closer to fulfilling the language of the Free Exercise Clause than the rule Smith announced. The Clause draws no distinction between laws whose object is to prohibit religious exercise and laws with that effect, on its face seemingly applying to both.

Nor did Smith consider the original meaning of the Free Exercise Clause, though overlooking the opportunity was no unique transgression. Save in a handful of passing remarks, the Court has not explored the history of the Clause since its early attempts, [attempts] that recent scholarship makes clear were incomplete. McConnell, The Origins and Historical Understanding of Free Exercise of Religion, 103 Harv.L.Rev. 1409 (1990). The curious absence of history from our free-exercise decisions creates a stark contrast with our cases under the Establishment Clause, where historical analysis has been so prominent. This is not the place to explore the history that a century of free-exercise opinions have overlooked, and it is enough to note that, when the opportunity to reexamine Smith presents itself, we may consider recent scholarship raising serious questions about the Smith rule's consonance with the original understanding and purpose of the Free Exercise Clause. There appears to be a strong argument [that] the Clause was originally understood to preserve a right to engage in activities necessary to fulfill one's duty to one's God, unless those activities threatened the rights of others or the serious needs of the State. . . .

III.   The extent to which the Free Exercise Clause requires government to refrain from impeding religious exercise defines nothing less than the respective relationships in our constitutional democracy of the individual to government and to God. "Neutral, generally applicable" laws, drafted as they are from the perspective of the nonadherent, have the unavoidable potential of putting the believer to a choice between God and government. Our cases now present competing answers to the question when government, while pursuing secular ends, may compel disobedience to what one believes religion commands. The case before us is rightly decided without resolving the existing tension, which remains for another day when it may be squarely faced.

JUSTICE BLACKMUN, with whom JUSTICE O'CONNOR joins, concurring in the judgment.

The Court holds today that [Hialeah] violated the First and Fourteenth Amendments when it passed a set of restrictive ordinances explicitly directed at petitioners' religious practice. With this holding I agree. I write separately to emphasize that the First Amendment's protection of religion extends beyond those rare occasions on which the government explicitly targets religion (or a particular religion) for disfavored treatment, as is done in this case. In my view, a statute that burdens the free exercise of religion "may stand only if the law in general, and the State's refusal to allow a religious exemption in particular, are justified by a compelling interest that cannot be served by less restrictive means." Smith (dissenting opinion). The Court, however, [applies] the test announced in Smith, under which "a law that is neutral and of general applicability need not be justified by a compelling governmental interest even if the law has the incidental effect of burdening a particular religious practice." I continue to believe that Smith [wrongly] ignored the value of religious freedom as an affirmative individual liberty and treated the Free Exercise Clause as no more than an antidiscrimination principle. Thus, while I agree with the result the Court reaches in this case, I arrive at that result by a different route.

When the State enacts legislation that intentionally or unintentionally places a burden upon religiously motivated practice, it must justify that burden by "showing that it is the least restrictive means of achieving some compelling state interest." Thomas v. Review Bd. A State may no more create an underinclusive statute, one that fails truly to promote its purported compelling interest, than it may create an overinclusive statute, one that encompasses more protected conduct than necessary to achieve its goal. In the latter circumstance, the broad scope of the statute is unnecessary to serve the interest, and the statute fails for that reason. In the former situation, the fact that allegedly harmful conduct falls outside the statute's scope belies a governmental assertion that it has genuinely pursued an interest "of the highest order." If the State's goal is important enough to prohibit religiously motivated activity, it will not and must not stop at religiously motivated activity.

When a law discriminates against religion as such, as do the ordinances in this case, it automatically will fail strict scrutiny under Sherbert. This is because a law that targets religious practice for disfavored treatment both burdens the free exercise of religion and, by definition, is not precisely tailored to a compelling governmental interest. [In] my view, regulation that targets religion in this way, ipso facto, fails strict scrutiny.

[It] is only in the rare case that a state or local legislature will enact a law directly burdening religious practice as such. Because the respondent here does single out religion in this way, the present case is an easy one to decide. A harder case would be presented if petitioners were requesting an exemption from a generally applicable anticruelty law. The result in the case before the Court today, and the fact that every Member of the Court concurs in that result, does not necessarily reflect this Court's views of the strength of a State's interest in prohibiting cruelty to animals. This case does not present [the] question whether the Free Exercise Clause would require a religious exemption from a law that sincerely pursued the goal of protecting animals from cruel treatment. The number of organizations that have filed amicus briefs on behalf of this interest, however, demonstrates that it is not a concern to be treated lightly.

Chapter 15(10)

PROPER CONDITIONS FOR CONSTITUTIONAL ADJUDICATION: INTERESTED PARTIES; CONCRETE CONTROVERSIES; JUSTICIABLE ISSUES

12th ED., p. 1595; IND. RTS., p. 1266

Add at end of footnote 7:

Where a case is otherwise properly before a federal court, however, the ban on advisory opinions does not preclude a judicial decision on a particular matter within the case that is not contested between the parties, at least where the issue is jurisdictional or similarly fundamental. Thus, Justice Souter's opinion for a unanimous Court in United States National Bank of Oregon v. Independent Insurance Agents of America, Inc., 508 U.S. ___ (1993), held that neither Article III nor prudential concerns stood in the way of a decision about whether the statute that formed the basis of the real dispute between the parties was actually law, even though the parties did not disagree that it was. (At issue was the possibility that the statute had been inadvertently repealed, but the Supreme Court held that a scrivener's error in punctuation did not produce a repeal of the relevant 1918 statute).

The Court's insistence on judicial judgments not being subject to non-judicial review continues, and in the context of congressional as well as executive reopening of the judgments of federal courts. See Plaut v. Spendthrift Farm, Inc., 517 U.S. ___ (1995), described at length above, addition to 12th Ed. and Ind.Rts., p. 43.

12th ED., p. 1621; IND. RTS., p. 1292

Add to end of first paragraph of footnote 4:

Similarly, standing to challenge a procedural ruling (e.g., removal from state to federal court) is sufficient if the plaintiff has been procedurally injured by the procedural ruling, a determination independent of plaintiff's underlying standing on the merits. See International Primate Protection League v. Administrators of Tulane Educational Fund, 500 U.S. 72 (1991).

12th ED., p. 1621; IND. RTS., p. 1292

Add at end of Note 4:

The Hunt standard for associational standing was recently applied where a state rather than a private association or a state agency (as in Hunt itself) is the plaintiff. In Wyoming v. Oklahoma, 502 U.S. 437 (1992), like Hunt a dormant commerce clause case, the Court, with Justice White writing for the majority, explicitly recognized Wyoming's standing to sue in an original jurisdiction case both because Wyoming could represent those Wyoming mining concerns that would clearly have had standing in their own right, and because Wyoming's own interests in collecting severance taxes were implicated in the decision. Even though those tax interests were dependent on the revenues of the coal companies whose financial interests were directly implicated by an Oklahoma statute requiring that Oklahoma generating plants use 10% Oklahoma-mined coal, Wyoming's derivative interests were sufficiently concrete, when combined with its interests as representative of the coal companies, to permit standing. Justice Scalia, joined by Chief Justice Rehnquist and Justice Thomas, dissented from the majority's holding as to standing, arguing that standing must be evaluated in light of the rules governing the stage the litigation has reached. Where the case arose on the grant by a Special Master of the plaintiff's motion for summary judgment, Justice Scalia maintained, the facts showing standing to exist would have to be especially clear, a showing he claimed was not satisfied here. Moreover, he argued that the essential part of Hunt was in allowing an association to sue on behalf of its members, with the suggestion that the association could sue in its own right being mere dicta, and dicta that did not survive more recent cases, like Allen and Valley Forge, which tightened the standing requirements in the service of separation of powers and prudential considerations. Where, as here, the state did not fit within the zone of interests protected by the relevant legal principle, there was no cause to allow it to sue rather than those private companies directly injured by the Oklahoma requirement at issue, and directly within the zone of interests protected by the dormant commerce clause. Justice Thomas, joined by Chief Justice Rehnquist and Justice Scalia, wrote a separate dissent, emphasizing the novelty of allowing a state to claim standing where its injuries were restricted to loss of tax revenues, and arguing as well that standing requirements should be applied especially stringently in original jurisdiction cases to make sure that only in cases where the states *qua* states are the primary disputants should original jurisdiction be allowed.

12th ED., p. 1621; IND. RTS., p. 1292
Add new Note 5:

5. *The Continuing Importance of Concreteness.* In NORTHEASTERN FLORIDA CHAPTER, GENERAL CONTRACTORS OF AMERICA v. CITY OF JACKSONVILLE, 510 U.S. ___ (1993), the Court made it clear that the rigor with which Warth would be applied was largely a function of the degree of concreteness of the plaintiff's planned conduct. Jacksonville, Florida, had adopted a plan to give preferences in city construction contracting to minority-owned businesses (a plan not unlike the one at issue in Richmond v. J.A. Croson Co., 1989, set out above, 12th Ed., p. 791; Ind.Rts., p. 462), and non-minority contractors challenged the plan on equal protection grounds. The lower federal courts had dismissed the suit for lack of standing, holding that the plaintiffs had not pointed to any contracts they would have won in the absence of the plan. The Supreme Court, however, with Justice THOMAS writing for the 7–2 majority, reversed and held that the plaintiffs had sufficient standing to sue. Justice Thomas distinguished Warth partly because of the distinction between the substantive claims involved in the two cases, for here, unlike in Warth, the claim "involve[d] an allegation that some discriminatory classification prevented the plaintiff from competing on an equal footing in its quest for a benefit." But Justice Thomas did not press this distinction very hard, and relied mainly on the fact on the differences in the concreteness of the plans of the respective plaintiffs. "Unlike petitioner, which alleged that its members regularly bid on contracts in Jacksonville and would bid on those that the city's ordi-

nance makes unavailable to them, the construction association in Warth did not allege that 'any member had applied . . . for a building permit or a variance with respect to a current project.' " Having thus distinguished Warth, Justice Thomas found the case most similar to cases like Regents of University of California v. Bakke [1978, above, 12th Ed., p. 760; Ind.Rts., p. 431], in which an allegation of unconstitutional exclusion from an eligibility pool as sufficient to confer standing, even without a showing that the plaintiffs would necessarily have succeeded within the properly constituted eligibility pool.[5]

12th ED., p. 1623; IND. RTS., p. 1294
Add after Schweiker v. Chilicky citation in second paragraph of footnote 3:

On the Court's continuing inclination to interpret Bivens narrowly, see, most recently, Federal Deposit Insurance Corp. v. Meyer, 508 U.S. ___ (1994), refusing to allow a Bivens remedy directly against a federal *agency*. The Court's unanimous opinion was written by Justice Thomas, who explained the rationale as follows: "[T]he purpose of Bivens is to deter the *officer*. If we were to imply a damages action directly against federal agencies, thereby permitting claimants to bypass [the] qualified immunity [ordinarily available to individual officers], there would be no reason for aggrieved parties to bring damages actions against individual officers. [Thus,] the deterrent effects of the Bivens remedy would be lost."

12th ED., p. 1623; IND. RTS., p. 1294
Add to end of footnote 3:

In Franklin v. Gwinnett County Public Schools, 503 U.S. 60 (1992), however, the Court was unanimous in relying on Cannon and implying a private right of action on behalf of a student who had been sexually harassed against the school district that employed (but did not discipline) the offending teacher. And in McCarthy v. Madigan, 503 U.S. 140 (1992), the Court held that a prisoner bringing a Bivens action need not first exhaust administrative remedies available under the grievance procedure of the Federal Bureau of Prisons.

12th ED., p. 1623; IND. RTS., p. 1294
Add at end of text of Note 2:

The Court's increased reliance on the constitutional rather than prudential aspects of standing was apparent in LUJAN v. DEFENDERS OF WILDLIFE, 504 U.S. 555 (1992). The plaintiffs had challenged an interpretation by the Secretary of the Interior that held that the Endangered Species Act's requirement that all agencies ensure that any of their actions not jeopardize endangered species did not apply to actions taken by agencies outside of the United States or the high seas. The plaintiff organization maintained that some of its members were injured because they had specific plans to observe some of the affected species, and that it has suffered "procedural injury" because the Act's "citizen-suit" provision created a cause of action for all citizens for all violations of the Act's procedural requirements.

In rejecting plaintiff's standing claims, Justice SCALIA's majority opinion (on all but one issue) stressed the constitutional aspect of the Court's standing requirements, and focused here on the distinction between injuries caused directly by governmental action and injuries

---

5. Justice O'Connor, joined by Justice Blackmun, dissented on mootness grounds (see below, addition to 12th Ed., p. 1628; Ind.Rts., 1299), but did not reach the standing question.

requiring the intervention of another governmental entity, in this case the agencies relieved by the interpretation from some constraints of the Endangered Species Act. "When [a] plaintiff's asserted injury arises from the government's allegedly unlawful regulation (or lack of regulation of *someone else,* much more is needed. In that circumstance, causation and redressability ordinarily hinge on the response of the regulated (or regulable) third party to the government action or inaction—and perhaps on the response of others as well. [Then] it becomes the burden of the plaintiff to adduce facts showing that those choices have been or will be made in such manner as to produce causation and permit redressability of injury. Warth. Thus, when the plaintiff is not himself the object of the government action or inaction he challenges, standing is not precluded, but is ordinarily "substantially more difficult" to establish. Allen."[†]

In applying this standard, Justice Scalia held that the members' allegation that they had and would again travel to the habitats of the potentially affected species, for the purpose of observing and studying those species, was too remote. "Such 'some day' intentions—without any description of concrete plans, or indeed even any specification of *when* the some day will be—do not support a finding of the 'actual or imminent' injury that our cases require." And he rejected as well claims about various other connections between the plaintiffs and the potentially endangered animals. "Under these theories, anyone who goes to see Asian elephants in the Bronx Zoo, and anyone who is a keeper of Asian elephants in the Bronx Zoo, has standing to sue because the Director of AID did not consult with the Secretary regarding the AID-funded project in Sri Lanka. This is beyond all reason." And the Court also rejected the procedural injury claim, holding that it was in effect an otherwise-impermissible taxpayer suit, and that all of the Court's precedents regarding taxpayer suits to enforce provisions of the Constitution were equally applicable to suits to enforce Acts of Congress, even where, as here, certain citizen suits were specifically allowed by the statute. "The question presented here is whether the public interest in proper administration of the laws (specifically, in agencies' observance of a particular, statutorily prescribed procedure) can be converted into an individual right by a statute that denominates it as such, and that permits all

---

[†] On this dimension of Lujan, note also UNITED STATES v. HAYS, 519 U.S. ___ (1995), in which the Court, with Justice O'CONNOR writing for the majority, held that only residents of a legislative district suffered the "individualized harm" necessary to challenge the districting on equal protection grounds (see Shaw v. Reno, 1993, above, 12th Ed., p. 819; Ind.Rts., p. 490), and that the claims of residents of other congressional districts in the same state were too remote to allow them standing to challenge the constitutionality of the redistricting. "Where a plaintiff resides in a racially gerrymandered district, [the] plaintiff has been denied equal treatment because of the legislature's reliance on racial criteria, and therefore has standing to challenge the legislature's action. Voters in such districts may suffer the special representational harms racial classifications can cause in the voting context. On the other hand, where a plaintiff does not live in such a district, he or she does not suffer those special harms, and any inference that the plaintiff has personally been subjected to a racial classification would not be justified absent specific evidence tending to support that inference. [Otherwise,] that plaintiff would be asserting only a generalized grievance against government conduct of which he or she does not approve."

citizens (or, for that matter, a subclass of citizens who suffer no concrete harm) to sue. If the concrete-injury requirement has the separation-of-powers significance we have always said, the answer must be obvious: To permit Congress to convert the undifferentiated public interest in executive officers' compliance with the law into an 'individual right' vindicable in the courts is to permit Congress to transfer from the President to the courts the Chief Executive's most important constitutional duty, to 'take Care that the Laws be faithfully executed.' "

Writing on this issue only for a plurality, Justice Scalia also held that there was not sufficient redressability for standing to exist. "As in Simon, it is entirely conjectural whether the nonagency activity that affects respondents will be altered or affected by the agency activity they seek to achieve." Justice KENNEDY, joined by Justice Souter, had agreed with the balance of Justice Scalia's opinion, thus making it an opinion of the Court, but felt that the redressability issue need not be reached in this case. Justice STEVENS concurred in the judgment because of his reading of the substantive effect of the statute at issue, but disagreed with the Court's resolution of the standing issue, finding the members' allegations sufficiently concrete, their plans sufficiently imminent, and their claims sufficiently redressable. Justice BLACK-MUN, joined by Justice O'Connor, dissented, focusing his dissent on the majority's seemingly increased willingness to impose constitutional constraints even where it appears that Congress has affirmatively authorized something akin to citizen standing. "It is to be hoped that over time the Court will acknowledge that some classes of procedural duties are so enmeshed with the prevention of a substantive, concrete harm that an individual plaintiff may be able to demonstrate a sufficient likelihood of injury just through the breach of that procedural duty. [There] is no room for a per se rule or presumption excluding injuries labeled 'procedural' in nature. [I] cannot join the Court on what amounts to a slash-and-burn expedition through the law of environmental standing." *

12th ED., p. 1626; IND. RTS., p. 1297
Add at beginning of footnote 5:

The Court now routinely cites Singleton v. Wulff as the source of the standards for determining third party standing, the most recent example being its decision recognizing the standing of a white defendant to challenge the peremptory exclusion of black jurors by the prosecution. Powers v. Ohio, 499 U.S. 400 (1991), described above, addition to 12th Ed., p. 705; Ind. Rts., p. 376.

12th ED., p. 1628; IND. RTS., p. 1299
Add to footnote 10:

When a defendant voluntarily ceases the challenged conduct after the commencement of litigation, is the case moot? Not necessarily, the Court said in Mesquite v. Aladdin's Castle, Inc., 455 U.S. 283 (1982), because of the possibility that the defendant will again recommence the same course of conduct after the dismissal of the litigation. In Northeastern Florida Chapter, Associated General Contractors of America v. City of Jacksonville, 510

---

* Note also Justice Scalia's argument for rigorous enforcement of the causation and redressability requirements in Franklin v. Massachusetts, 505 U.S. ___ (1992), described below, addition to 12th Ed., p. 1671; Ind.Rts., p. 1342.

U.S. ___ (1993), the Court, with Justice Thomas writing for the majority, relied on the Mesquite case in refusing to find moot a challenge to an affirmative action program for minority contractors. Shortly after the Supreme Court granted certiorari to review the Court of Appeals' decision on standing, the defendant city substantially modified the program. The Court held, however, that the possibility of reverting, combined with the fact that the modified program was still subject to the same general variety of challenge, together precluded a finding of mootness. Justice O'Connor, joined by Justice Blackmun, dissented on the mootness issue, arguing that the modified program was sufficiently different that it was best dealt with in a new lawsuit. On the Court's resolution of the standing issue, see above, addition to 12th Ed., p. 1621; Ind.Rts., p. 1292.

12th ED., p. 1628; IND. RTS., p. 1299
Add to parenthetical in last sentence of footnote 12:

The Court's most recent mootness cases are Church of Scientology of California v. Zolin, 506 U.S. ___ (1992), holding that compliance with an unlawful seizure (by the Internal Revenue Service) did not render the controversy moot, since remedies were available to mitigate the effects of the unnecessary compliance; and U.S. Bancorp Mortgage Co. v. Bonner Mall Partnership, 515 U.S. ___ (1994), holding that although mootness represents an Article III barrier to further disposition on the merits, it does not bar the entry of rulings necessary to conclude a case under review.

12th ED., p. 1629; IND. RTS., p. 1300
Add after first sentence of second paragraph of footnote 14:

The general rule is that the mootness of the class representative's claim does not moot the claims of other members of an already-certified class. See Riverside County, California v. McLaughlin, 500 U.S. 44 (1991).

12th ED., p. 1634; IND. RTS., p. 1305
Add at end of footnote 7:

On the frequent appearance of ripeness issues in 'takings' cases generally, see especially, and most recently, Lucas v. South Carolina Coastal Council, 505 U.S. ___ (1992), set out above, addition to 12th Ed., p. 476; Rts., p. 147.

12th ED., p. 1635; IND. RTS., p. 1306
Add to footnote 9:

Indeed, Abbott Laboratories is but one of a large number of cases in which ripeness issues arise when administrative regulations are challenged immediately upon promulgation. The most recent of these cases, RENO v. CATHOLIC SOCIAL SERVICES, INC., 510 U.S. ___ (1993), dealt in an important way with ripeness issues presented in a context somewhat different from most of this considered in this section. Although the common issue arises in the context of a challenge to a *prohibition* not yet enforced against the challenger, Reno v. Catholic Social Services involved an immigration regulation controlling what the Court referred to as "access to a benefit." Thus the case resembled standing cases such as Warth and Northeastern Florida Contractors in raising justiciability questions about a potential applicant who not only had yet to apply for the benefit, but who, even if successful in the instant litigation, still might not receive the benefit upon application. Writing for the Court, Justice SOUTER reaffirmed that ripeness doctrine is drawn from both Article III and prudential concerns, and that in either case the courts could consider ripeness questions even if not raised by the parties. Turning to the issue itself, Justice Souter held the case not ripe for decision, saying that in access to benefit cases "a class member's claim would ripen only once he took the affirmative steps that he could take before the INS blocked his path by applying the regulation to him." Justice O'CONNOR, concurring in the judgment, agreed that the Court's "prior cases concerning anticipatory challenges to agency rules do not specify when an anticipatory suit may be brought against a benefit-conferring rule. [An] anticipatory suit by a would-be beneficiary, who has not yet applied for the benefit that the rule denies him, poses different ripeness problems than a pre-enforcement suit against a duty-creating rule. Even if he succeeds in his anticipatory action, the would-be beneficiary will not receive the benefit until he actually applies for it; and the agency might then deny him the benefit on grounds other than his ineligibility under the rule. By contrast, a successful suit against the duty-creating rule will relieve the plaintiff immediately of a burden that he otherwise would bear." Unlike the seemingly more strict rule set forth by the majority for such cases, however, Justice O'Connor argued that even in the benefit-conferring situation lack of ripeness should not be a bar when the court can make "a firm prediction that the plaintiff will apply for the benefit, and that the agency will deny the application by virtue of the rule." Justice STEVENS, joined by Justice Blackmun, dissented, also objecting to the majority's per se approach to ripeness in access to benefits cases, and noting the tension between the result here and that in Northeastern Florida Contractors. "[That is,] of course, an equal protection case, while respondents in this case are seeking a statutory benefit. If this distinction has any relevance to a ripeness analysis, then it should mitigate in favor of finding ripeness here; I assume we should be more reluctant to overcoming jurisdictional hurdles to decide constitutional issues than to effectuate statutory programs."

12th ED., p. 1640; IND. RTS., p. 1311
Add as new footnote at end of Note 2:

* On the seventh rule, the Court repeatedly refers to Edward J. DeBartolo Corp. v. Florida Gulf Coast Building & Construction Trades Council (1988, noted above, 12th Ed., p. 1399; Ind.Rts., p. 1070): "Where an otherwise acceptable construction of a statute would create serious constitutional problems, the Court will construe the statute to avoid such problems unless such construction is plainly contrary to the intent of Congress." For the most recent applications of this principle, see Concrete Pipe and Products of California, Inc. v. Construction Laborers Pension Trust for Southern California, 510 U.S. __ (1993); and United States v. X-Citement Video, Inc., 515 U.S. __ (1994), described above, addition to 12th Ed., p. 1125; Ind.Rts., p. 796. At times, however, the rule may conflict with the rule that the Supreme Court is reluctant to decide issues not pressed or decided below. On this basis, Chief Justice Rehnquist rejected the possibility of preferring the statutory ground to the constitutional one in Zobrest v. Catalina Foothills School District (1993, described above, addition to 12th Ed., p. 1517; Ind.Rts., p. 1188), over the objections of four dissenters who argued that in such a case the Court should remand for consideration of the statutory issues rather than proceeding directly to decide the constitutional ones.

12th ED., p. 1650; IND. RTS., p. 1321
Add at end of footnote 8:

The Court continued to stress the limits of Younger in Ankenbrandt v. Richards, 504 U.S. 689 (1992): "We have never applied the notions of comity so critical to [Younger] when no state proceeding was pending nor any assertion if important state interest made. [Absent] any *pending* proceedings in state tribunals, [application] by the lower courts of Younger abstention was clearly erroneous."

12th ED., p. 1657; IND. RTS., p. 1328
Add at end of footnote 6:

In New York v. United States, 505 U.S. 144 (1992), set out above, addition to 12th Ed., p. 175, Justice O'Connor's majority opinion gave strong signals that the Court would be willing to reconsider Luther v. Borden and the traditional assumption of Guarantee Clause non-justiciability. Indeed, by indicating directly what the Guarantee Clause result would have been had it been justiciable, Justice O'Connor seemed to provide a strong case against some of the bases for non-justiciability.

12th ED., p. 1671; IND. RTS., p. 1342
Add at end of Note 2a on Congressional Districting:

In U.S. DEPARTMENT OF COMMERCE v. MONTANA, 503 U.S. 442 (1992), the Court addressed the issue of apportionment of Representatives among rather than within the states. Article I, sec. 2, as amended by section 2 of the Fourteenth Amendment, requires that

"Representatives shall be apportioned among the several states according to their respective numbers, ..." It turns out, however, that any method for doing so, in light of the problem of fractions, and in light of the fact that state boundaries cannot be redrawn, will be in some way unequal. Treating fractions as non-seats tends, for complex mathematical reasons, to favor large states over small, and treating fractions as whole seats favors small over large. Other methods also produce paradoxical or unequal results under some circumstances. In 1911 Congress approved the current size of the House (435 members) and use of the "method of major fractions" for apportionment among the states. Under that method, first proposed by Daniel Webster and in force from 1842 until 1850, only fractional remainders greater than one-half would entitle a state to a seat on account of that fraction. Thereafter Congress authorized a committee of the National Academy of Sciences to come up with a method. It concluded that any of five methods (including Webster's) would be plausible, but that a complex formula called the "method of equal proportions" would be best among those because its preference for minimizing relative rather than absolute discrepancy in district size was thought to be the fairest.

Congress adopted this method in 1941, and it was challenged by Montana in 1990. Montana's interest was based on the fact that it would receive two Representatives rather than one under two of the five methods first endorsed by the committee, but that it received only one under the current method of equal proportions. It argued that the method of equal proportions constituted an unjustified deviation from the constitutional ideal of equal representation, and its argument was accepted by a majority of the three-judge District Court. On direct appeal to the Supreme Court, however, the Court reversed the three-judge court and rejected Montana's argument, with Justice STEVENS writing for a unanimous Court.

Relying heavily on Baker v. Carr and Wesberry v. Sanders, Justice Stevens rejected the federal government's argument that congressional selection among methods was a non-justiciable political question. "The case before us today is 'political' in the same sense that Baker v. Carr was a 'political case.' It raises an issue of great importance to the political branches. [But the] controversy between Montana and the Government turns on the proper interpretation of the relevant constitutional provisions. As our previous [decisions] make clear, the interpretation of the apportionment provisions of the Constitution is well within the competence of the Judiciary. [The] political question doctrine does not place this kind of constitutional interpretation outside the proper domain of the Judiciary."

Justice Stevens went on, however, to note that willingness to exercise judicial review and thus to decide the case does not preclude deciding the case with due regard for decisions made by other branches. Because "the constitutional guarantee of a minimum of one Representative for each State inexorably compels a significant departure from the [numerical] ideal," some degree of commonsense understanding and compromise was necessary. Without that requirement, he noted, the same standards applied within states could be applied to apportionment among states, but then neither Alaska, Vermont, nor Wyoming would have any Representatives at all. So the "constitutional framework that generated the need for compromise in the apportionment process must also delegate to Congress a measure of discretion that is broader than that accorded to the States in the much easier task of determining district sizes within State borders. [Congress'] apparently good-faith choice of a method of apportionment of Representatives among the several States 'according to their respective Numbers.' commands far more deference than a state districting decision that is capable of being reviewed under a relatively rigid mathematical standard. [The] decision to adopt the method of equal proportions was made by Congress after decades of experience, experimentation, and debate about the substance of the constitutional requirement. Independent scholars supported both the basic decision to adopt a regular procedure to be followed after each census, and the particular decision to use the method of equal proportions. For a half century the results of that method have been accepted by the States and the Nation. That history supports our conclusion that Congress had ample power to enact the statutory procedure in 1941 and to apply the method of equal proportions after the 1990 census."

Parallel deference was apparent in FRANKLIN v. MASSACHU-SETTS, 505 U.S. ___ (1992), in which Massachusetts claimed that it had been unconstitutionally deprived of one of its seats in Congress as a result of the decision by the Census Bureau to allocate overseas military personnel to states depending on their "home of record" (often selected for tax purposes) rather than their "real" residence overseas (or elsewhere). Justice O'CONNOR's opinion for the Court (in most respects) found that Massachusetts had standing to challenge the action, but that there was no conflict between the method of allocation employed and the Article I requirements that representatives be apportioned to the states "according to their respective numbers" and based on an "actual enumeration." Justice O'Connor reviewed the text and history of the relevant clauses and concluded that "the Secretary of Commerce made a judgment, consonant with, though not dictated by, the text and history of the Constitution, that many federal employees temporarily stationed overseas had retained their ties to the States and could be counted towards their States' representation in Congress. [Massachusetts has] not demonstrated that eliminating overseas employees entirely from the state counts will make representation in Congress more equal."

12th ED., p. 1672; IND. RTS., p. 1343
Add as new footnote at end of Note 2:

For a recent case applying the more deferential approach of Mahan v. Howell and Brown v. Thomson, and unanimously striking down a lower court ruling that total deviations of greater than 10% could never "be justified by a policy of preserving the boundaries of political subdivisions," see Voinovich v. Quilter, 507 U.S. ___ (1993).

12th ED., p. 1673; IND. RTS., p. 1344
Add at end of footnote 3:

For a recent case in which the claim was not that multi-member districts diluted minority voter power, but rather that certain single-member districts so concentrated minority voting power that they prevented minority influence in a larger number of districts, see Voinovich v. Quilter, 507 U.S. __ (1993). On the Court's reluctance to enter a particular apportionment dispute while a state is itself engaged in reapportioning itself, judicially or legislatively, see the unanimous decision in Growe v. Emison, 507 U.S. __ (1993).

12th ED., p. 1674; IND. RTS., p. 1345
Add after Davis v. Bandemer:

c. *Political gerrymandering on racial grounds.* When race matters in politics, the line between racial and political gerrymandering becomes contentious, especially in light of the special constitutional scrutiny applicable to race. These issues were central to the various opinions in SHAW v. RENO, 510 U.S. __ (1993), in which Justice O'CONNOR's opinion for the Court, over strong dissents, concluded that oddly shaped districts created for the sole purpose of ensuring minority representation presumptively violated the Equal Protection Clause. The case is set out above, addition to 12th Ed., p. 819; Ind. Rts., p. 490.

Appendix A

THE CONSTITUTION OF THE UNITED STATES OF AMERICA

12th ED. and IND. RTS., p. A–15

Add as new paragraph after Amendment XXVI [1971]:

AMENDMENT XXVII [1992].

No law varying the compensation for the services of the Senators and Representatives shall take effect until an election of Representatives shall have intervened.*

* The 27th amendment was proposed by James Madison in 1789 as part of the same package as the Bill of Rights. It was approved by the first Congress in the same year, and by 1792 six states had ratified it. A seventh joined in 1873, and then nothing happened until 1978, when the movement to add the amendment was reinvigorated. The eighth ratification occurred in 1978, and another 32 states joined as of May 12, 1992. Although a sufficient number of states had thus seemingly ratified the amendment, several members of Congress expressed concern about the non-contemporaneous nature of the ratification, citing Dillon v. Gloss (1921, above, 12th Ed., p. 1654; Ind.Rts., p. 1325) and Coleman v. Miller (1939, above, 12th Ed., p. 1653; Ind. Rts., p. 1324). Resolutions were proposed (S.Res. 295, S.Con.Res. 117 and 118; H.Con.Res. 194) to take on the issue of whether the amendment was to be considered part of the Constitution, and both the House and Senate Judiciary committees had scheduled hearings on the matter. On May 13, 1992, however, the Archivist of the United States, Don W. Wilson, announced that he would certify the adoption of the amendment. On May 14, 1992, House Speaker Thomas Foley backed away from an earlier challenge to the validity of the amendment, and agreed that it was now to be considered part of the Constitution. Many ascribed his decision to political considerations, claiming that Foley believed that the American electorate was unlikely to support an expensive constitutional challenge to preserve Congressional pay raises in a year which had already seen extensive scandals in the House bank and post office. Under current law, however, automatic cost of living adjustments (COLAs) for Congress are scheduled to take place in 1993, and challenges based on the lack of contemporaneous ratification are still possible.

Appendix B

TABLE OF JUSTICES

12th ED. and IND. RTS., p. B-6 (Appendix B)
Amend table of Justices as follows:

* (1) Burger, Warren E. (1907–1995). Rep. from Va. and Minn. (1969–1986). Resigned.[1]

(7) White, Byron R. (1917–___). Dem. from Colorado (1962–1993). Retired.[2]

(6) Marshall, Thurgood (1908–1993). Dem. from N.Y. (1967–1991). Retired.[3]

(3) Blackmun, Harry A. (1908–___). Rep. from Minn. (1970–1994). Retired.[4]

12th ED. and IND. RTS., p. B-7
Add after Souter, David H.

(6) Thomas, Clarence (1948–___). Rep. from Va. (1992–___).[5]

1. Former Chief Justice Warren Burger died of congestive heart failure on June 25, 1995. His casket was taken to the Supreme Court on June 28, 1995 where he was honored by fellow Justices and Supreme Court employees. He was buried in Arlington National Cemetery on June 29, 1995.

2. On March 19, 1993, Justice White informed President Clinton of his intention to retire at the completion of the Court's 1992 Term. His brief statement noted that "It has been an interesting and exciting experience to serve on the court," but now "someone else should be permitted to have a like experience."

3. On June 27, 1991, the last day of the 1990 Term, Justice Thurgood Marshall announced his retirement from the Court, effective upon the qualification of his successor. He offered age and health as the reasons for his retirement, which came less than a week before his eighty-third birthday. Justice Marshall died of heart failure in Bethesda Naval Hospital on January 23, 1993.

4. On April 6, 1994, Justice Blackmun's resignation from the Supreme Court was accepted by President Clinton. At the press conference announcing his retirement, Justice Blackmun noted, "It's not easy to step aside, but I know what the numbers are and it's time."

5. Justice Thomas, then Judge of the United States Court of Appeals for the District of Columbia, was nominated by President Bush on July 1, 1991, to succeed Justice Marshall. Throughout the summer of 1991, controversy about Justice Thomas's nomination increased, and there was considerable focus on what some opponents characterized as a lack of vigorous enforcement of the civil rights laws during Thomas's tenure as Chairman of the Equal Employment Opportunity Commission. Great attention was also paid to questions of constitutional interpretation, with a particular focus on Thomas's alleged attraction to "natural law." See above, addition to 12th Ed., p. 519; Ind.Rts., p. 180.

On August 28, 1991, the American Bar Association rated Thomas "qualified" to serve as a Member of the Supreme Court. Hearings before the Senate Judiciary Committee commenced on September 10, 1991, and, after extensive hearings on a wide range of questions of substantive law and

451

(7) Ginsburg, Ruth B. (1933–___). Dem. from District of Columbia (1993–___).[6]

(3) Breyer, Stephen G. (1938–___). Dem. from Mass. (1994–___).[7]

judicial philosophy, the Committee voted 7–7 on September 27. But although the split vote did not produce a favorable recommendation, the Committee voted 13–1 to send the nomination on to the full Senate. On October 5, however, two days before the full Senate was to vote, Professor Anita F. Hill of the University of Oklahoma School of Law came forward with allegations, made earlier to the Committee, that she had been sexually harassed by Thomas when she was an attorney at the EEOC. The Judiciary Committee reopened hearings, which were televised and widely discussed, and the date for the Senate vote was postponed. On October 15, 1991, the Senate voted 52–48 to approve the nomination, and Justice Thomas was sworn in as a Justice of the Supreme Court on October 18, 1991.

6. After publicly considering some number of possible successors for Justice White, President Clinton nominated Judge Ruth Bader Ginsburg of the United States Court of Appeals for the District of Columbia to replace Justice White. Prior to being appointed by President Carter to the bench in 1980, Judge Ginsburg had been a law professor at Rutgers and Columbia law schools with specializations in comparative law, civil procedure and sex discrimination, and had been a central figure in constitutional, judicial and legislative initiatives on gender-based discrimination. Hearings were held July 20–23, 1993, and after a unanimous recommendation by the Judiciary Committee, Judge Ginsburg's nomination was confirmed by the Senate on August 3, 1993, by a vote of 96–3. She was sworn in on August 10, 1993.

7. President Clinton nominated Stephen G. Breyer, Chief Judge of the U.S. Court of Appeals for the First Circuit to replace Justice Blackmun on May 13, 1994. Judge Breyer had been a Harvard law professor specializing in administrative law, antitrust and government regulation before his appointment to the bench. Hearings were held in the Senate from July 12–14, 1994 and his nomination was unanimously approved by the Judiciary Committee on July 19, 1994. Justice Breyer was sworn in twice, first by the Chief Justice in a private ceremony on August 4, 1994 at Justice Rehnquist's home in Vermont, and then by Justice Scalia in a public ceremony at the White House on August 12, 1994.

†